Historical Guide

to

Union County, Oregon

Roads

By

Dave & Trish Yerges

Front Cover

> Fall scene of Myers Road winding through Pumpkin Ridge territory north of Summerville, Oregon. Photo and page designed by Dave Yerges, fall 2019.

Back Cover

> Eighty-two photos of Union County, Oregon road signs, taken by Dave Yerges, 2021. Page designed by Dave Yerges, 2021.

Printed in the United States of America
First Edition 2022; Revision 2023

ISBN 978-0-9764384-9-6

To the memory of Oregon Trail pioneers John and Lucinda McDowell, whose wagon wheels were among the first to create roads in the Grande Ronde Valley; and to our children, Heather, Tess and Mark, and our sister, Terri

Introduction

Authors Dave and Trish Yerges are pleased to release "Historical Guide to Union County, Oregon Roads," a journey into the fascinating and sometimes never-before-told stories behind the names of Union County roads.

The Yerges team have been writing Union County history since 1999, starting with 20 of the Union County Century Farm and Ranch stories published in *The Valley News.* They also wrote the histories of local industry, inventors, one-room schools, county cemeteries, and residents of historical interest and achievements.

Their involvement in local history increased after August 2006, when Trish started working as a freelance correspondent for *The La Grande Observer.* In this capacity, she has written many features about people in Union County, who have ties to its settlement history starting in 1861.

She has also written about individuals associated with the Elgin Stampeders and those honored as Stampede Legends, queens or grand marshals, some of whom were charter members of the organization when it was founded in June 1946.

In addition to these histories, Dave has spent years developing his own collection of historic maps and photos, as well as a list of wagon trains and travelers who migrated to Oregon. He has been a photo contributor and editor of other local history books, including the four Hot Lake publications written by Richard Roth. He has also contributed research toward the history articles written by Dick Mason, long-time staff writer for *The La Grande Observer.*

As an avid reader and researcher of local history, Dave discovered a basic need for indexes to existing local history books. Consequently, he and Trish spent a winter creating *Index to An Illustrated History of Union and Wallowa Counties* and an index to Bernal D. Hug's *History of Union County* and its supplements.

Together they compiled and reprinted the newspaper columns written by Jesse L. Hindman, originally published in the *Elgin Recorder* called "Observations and Opinions," covering Union County history from 1939-1941.

Dave went on to write *The Inventors of Union County Oregon and Their Inventions.* Dave and Trish also wrote, *The History of Pondosa Pine Lumber Company* and the *Memorial History of Ross Paxton* of Elgin and Union, a young man who later became an award-winning illustrator in Manhattan, New York. Paxton's first computer-aided illustrations were drawn for Dave and Trish's first bilingual children's book, *The Adventures of Scooper the Beagle Dog.*

Dave also spent hours adding photos and maps and then reprinting *The La Grande School District No. 1 (1862-1937)* and Doran H. Stearns' *1882 Oregon Papers and Sketches in Union County,* both rich in local history and hand drawn illustrations.

The marketing of their new and reprinted history books and photographs was done primarily on

Facebook and at their former business, The Mitre's Touch Gallery in La Grande, which closed after the 2020 pandemic year. Dave continues to offer the same histories that were formerly available through the Mitre's Touch Gallery.

This publication seemed to us like the culmination of 24 years of historical work bound in one cover titled *Historical Guide to Union County, Oregon Roads*. The authors are finding that first-hand sources of history are dwindling because of age and time, and with them some histories are lost. It is with gratitude that the authors have been able to unearth some of these stories and solve a history mystery or two.

Researching for this book was challenging because as one earlier historian wrote: "True documentation is difficult to obtain since records were neither kept, photographs were rare, and the property history was sketchy. Many families lived in cabins, houses, etc., that were built, lived in and often abandoned, but never owned." *(Clayton Warnstaff of Fox Hill)*

Consequently, the authors relied on personal interviews they have conducted over the last 24 years, when people were still living to tell the story. They've also drawn from unpublished memoirs. The wealth of information gleaned from the 1897-1964 archives of *The La Grande (Evening) Observer* and other newspapers is frequently cited.

For all the criticisms that newspapers must take from their reading public, they are still among the best repositories of history you'll ever find, and for that they must be commended. The authors also used credible online and off-the-shelf resources, and have referenced them in *italics* for those who would like to read directly from the source.

The authors would like to acknowledge Hanley Jenkins III, retired from the Union County Planning Department and all those who were interviewed and who contributed to this book so enthusiastically. Also, a special thank you to Terri Landowski for her resource support; to Gerald Hopkins and Charlie Horn of the Elgin Museum and Historical Society, to the Union County Museum, as well as Mort Gordon and Bob Crouser of Elgin and George Neer of La Grande, our test readers of the first manuscript.

Lastly, we want to express our gratitude to past historians, who had the foresight to record the happenings of their day. No written history is ever perfect or all encompassing, but it still has great value when combined with already existing chronicles. This historical book attempts to do that, compiling from the many scattered archives and bringing in fresh testimonies or unpublished manuscripts written by people who had some details to offer.

We hope this book will not only enlighten and entertain readers, but also become an important resource book in home libraries and for future historians, who have the heart and courage to commit facts and testimonies to paper.

PREFACE

*"We wanted to honor the historical naming system that was out there
as much as we possibly could."*
— Hanley Jenkins III
Union County Planning Director
(1979-2016)

Before there were county roads, there were wagon tracks. One covered wagon after another rolled by the Grande Ronde Valley, their wheels pressing tall rye and bunch grasses beneath them as they joggled and waggled along. Those settlers were heading toward the Willamette Valley with promise of tillable land and fair weather.

On their way, some settlers stopped to rest and water their stock along the Grande Ronde River before continuing their journey west. One of those families was the Henry and Emily Leasy family with six children from Iowa, resting for two weeks in September 1861. Also, camping out in the area now known as Old Town La Grande were Stephen Coffin and four or five other men.

As the Leasys started to pull out from the Grande Ronde Valley to continue their journey over the Blue Mountains, three traders coming into the valley from Umatilla convinced the Leasys to turn around and stay because they were going to open a supply store and settlement. In October 1861, Benjamin Brown's family accompanied by a party of 12 men from the Umatilla country arrived with the intent of establishing a settlement.

The ensuing year brought additional settlers to this valley on the Nebraska Train, the Yount Train, the Hunter Train, the Manville Train, the Kenneday Train, the Bristle Train with the Iowa City Boys, the Wade Train, the Glenn Train, the Thomas Train, and the William Jack Train, to name a few—and that was just 1862.

By late September 1862, when pioneer settler James McClung rolled into La Grande, he said the settlement had five homes, a blacksmith shop and a store. *(James McClung pioneer diary, Powerful Rocky, Jack Evans, 1991, pg. 319)*

That year, the Samuel Harvey McAlister family arrived to the valley with the 42-wagon Yount Train, and 3-1/2 year-old Susan McAlister was with them. Years later she recounted her parents' homestead story.

"The homes of the settlers that first year (1862) were not much more than wind breaks. There was only time in which to build one room log huts with dirt floors, sod roofs, fire places for heat and tallowed paper for windows." — *Susan McAlister Williamson, pioneer*

Within a year or two, scattered homes quickly became communities, and the imprint of those wagon wheels started connecting those communities to one another. Among the first of those wagon roads in Union County was the one formed from La Grande to Forest Cove, later called "The Cove" and then simply Cove.

Other dirt roads developed as pioneers followed and improved the Native American trails long in use before settlers came, such as Blackhawk Trail, which led along the Grande Ronde River to good camping, water and harvesting grounds. With frequent use by horses, carriages and wagons, under wet weather conditions, these dirt roads quickly deteriorated into muddy, deeply rutted and unuseable pathways. The need for road construction projects became quite clear.

In the *La Grande Observer, Feb., 24, 1961, pg 25* there was an article that explained the role that Native American trails played in our present day county roads. It was titled, "Union County Indian Trails Led To First Start of Road Projects," and it read:

"Indians established perhaps the best routes in Union County by centuries of travel. Early explorers used Indian guides whenever possible and followed Indian trails.

Fur traders followed on their heels. In 1843, the Great Migration of emigrants to the Willamette Valley followed Indian trails, rolling down Ladd Canyon, skirting along the west edge of the valley, climbing over the hills west of where La Grande now stands, following the Indian route to the Starkey country, then hewing a road over to the present Umatilla County.

Travel continued over this Oregon Trail through the Grande Ronde Valley every year.

The first county road was constructed under the supervision of Judge Lichtenthaler and his court, due to the granting of Charles Goodnough's petition to build a road from Oro Dell east along the north side of the river to intersect the Walla Walla road.

In later years it was officially named the Black Hawk Trail in honor of a friendly Umatilla Indian who frequently visited homesteaders who lived there.

The county was divided into road districts early. Much of the county road building was financed by poll tax, which required each adult man to furnish two days of labor each year for road work.

The Walla Walla Trail was opened to wagon traffic and became known as the Lincton Road. Local roads and those over the mountains too numerous to mention were constructed as the years went on. As homesteaders moved farther out, individually or in cooperation with neighbors they built their own roads to the nearest town.

How wisely the Indians established their trails and how wise pioneers were in following them is conveyed by the fact that all the main old routes into the valley except for the Thomas and Ruckles route are now modern, paved highways.

On July 3, 1923, a great celebration was held atop the Blue Mountains at Meacham. The last link in the new Oregon Trail was being finished.

A graveled highway would now extend from Portland to the East Coast, crossing the Grande Ronde Valley." (End of article)

The Walla Walla Trail and others were heavily used during the 1862-1868 gold rush in Eastern

Oregon, which brought droves of miners and settlers to this area. The demand for good roads was a priority if mining supplies and food provisions were going to be transported routinely from the Umatilla Landing, across the Blue Mountains to Auburn in Baker County, Oregon and the mining district beyond.

La Grande played an important role in freighting over these trails, as the *La Grande Observer, June 17, 1916, pg 20* issue explained:

"With the discovery of gold and rapid increase in immigration, La Grande approached a boom stage. It was especially the headquarters for freighters, who were kept busy supplying the up-country mining camps as far south as Boise.

On account of the snow in the mountains, it was a practice to haul supplies over the hills from Umatilla in the summer season and store the goods at La Grande; and then during the large portion of the winter season and particularly while the mountain traveling was bad, the freight that had been stored could be taken to the mining camps.

La Grande became a re-distributing center and its streets frequently became the center of such scenes as are shown in the picture taken in 1868." (The photo was supposedly B Street near Mill Creek, a business thoroughfare in La Grande.) (End of article)

Historically, the Oregon Trail was traveled in 1843 by the exploring party of John Charles Fremont and the first, large immigration train of Marcus Whitman. Then there was the Birch Creek-Grande Ronde Military Road built in 1862. However, these roads did not hold up to the traffic of frequent freight wagons, so other roads were built like the Dealy Wagon Road in 1863-64, replaced by the Thomas and Ruckle Road built in 1865-66, and the latter replaced by the Meacham Toll Road built in 1867—to name a few.

Wagon road companies were contracted to build freighting roads across the Blue Mountains to eastern Oregon. Among them were the Blue Mountain Wagon Road Company and the Dealy Wagon Road Company. Until the railroad came through Union County in 1884 and captured a large part of the freighting market, good roads were imperative to the sustenance of eastern Oregon communities and the mining district.

Likewise, Union County road conditions, improvements, funding and new construction were very important issues for the local residents. Small groups of residents petitioned the county court for construction of roads, the first petition being submitted on March 9, 1865 for a road from Oro Dell to Walla Walla Road near the Big Lake. (This lake has since dried up and been farmed over.)

"At the regular meeting of the county court held in February 1865, the county was divided into eleven road districts, and for the sake of preserving the names of those who laid the foundation for the excellent roads of which Union Co-unty is now proud, we give the name of these first supervisors in the numerical order of their respective districts: Benjamin Brown, William Proebstel, E. C. Crane, James Rinehart, E.D. Sillsby, Jesse Owenby, Joseph Yout (Yount), A.R. Robinson, George Barlow, J. M. Garrettson, and William King." *(An Illustrated History of Union and Wallowa Counties, 1902, pg. 194)*

Later, road issues were addressed by community road committees and then by the county planning department and the county road department.

One such committee was the Commercial Club's Good Roads Committee captained by Dr. M. K. Hall, which circulated a petition asking for a special election in this county to vote on a $400,000 bond issue to obtain funds to build graveled roads that would create an 80-mile network of roads to connect communities. *(La Grande Observer, June 11, 1915, pg. 1)*

The article read, "The plan calls for a road from Cricket Flat through Elgin into La Grande via Imbler with roads branching off to Summerville. Another road will go to Cove via a line as yet undetermined by the committee, but from this cross-valley trunk the Godly lane will be graveled, in accordance with this plan to afford passage to Union. Hot Lake is to be connected up in a suitable way. The distribution of these 80 miles of road will therefore connect every town in the valley, one with the other. It will incidentally make passable about seven miles of bad road between Union and North Powder."

Today, Union County, Oregon, encompasses 2,038 square miles, and is home to several communities. There are 650 miles of county roads with 89 bridges linking these communities. *(2018 Union County stats)*

There has always been a strong community interest in maintaining the roads. In the *La Grande Observer of July 29, 1926, pg. 4,* an article was published praising the residents for their keen attention to their county roads.

The article read: "Union county has a right to be proud of her roads. No similar territory in the Northwest has better all-weather roads, considered from the standpoint of serving rural population on an economical basis. And gradually the gravel highways of the county are being extended."

There has also been a strong community interest in road naming. Even the Union County Historical Society promoted names they valued historically.

"County Judge C. K. McCormick and Charles H. Reynolds, eastern Oregon representative on the state good roads committee were the guest speakers at the Union County Historical society's booster meeting and quarterly banquet... The Historical society has been working for some time on the matter of naming the roads of the county as memorials to prominent pioneers and the two men were invited to discuss the project with the society and also the means to be used to reach that objective." *(Eastern Oregon Review, May 2, 1947, pg. 1)*

The historical society cast a unanimous vote to pursue the memorial road naming project and on the local committee to do so were J.D. Woodell, chairman, Mrs. Kate R. Hanley and Mrs. Carrie H. Spencer. They selected 25 roads in Union County to start with and the remaining roads would be classified later, the aforementioned newspaper article read.

Up until this time, roads were named informally by those residing on them. Some were named after their earliest settler, others by a geographic feature, and still others by descriptive names of plants or wildlife commonly seen there.

As a result, there existed duplicate or triplicate road names, such as Foothill Road south of La Grande and a couple of Foothill Roads around Elgin on the north end of the county and near Hot Lake. There were also sound-alike road names, such as Five Point Creek Road and Phys Point Road out by Cove. At times, roads were given hyphenated two family names like the "Parsons-Hug" Road, indicating a resident living on each end of the road.

These varying circumstances grew to be a confusing problem for mail delivery, freight delivery and for emergency responders, so that by 1988 county officials across the state of Oregon felt compelled to create a uniform road naming system.

Confronting the issue in Union County was Hanley Jenkins III, who served as Union County Planning Director for 36 years from 1979 to 2016. He was instrumental in drafting the procedures for road naming, renaming and the assignment of rural addresses for Union County.
Jenkins explained how this all transpired in a 2010 interview with the authors.

"We had to have a uniform road naming system," Jenkins said. "You can't have duplicate or sound-alike names in order to make it work, so we have a road naming ordinance (#1988-3) that we had to adopt as a part of this."

Jenkins said that in 1988, he knew the county had to come up with a uniform road naming system, but he wasn't sure exactly how to accomplish this. Consequently, he went around and met with a number of other counties, four of whom had systems that were similar to what Union County was contemplating for itself.

"So I visited those counties when I was out for other meetings," Jenkins said, "and at the time, the GPS technology wasn't as advanced as it is now, so what we came up with was a system that is based on the Oregon State Plane Coordinate System."

This system originates with a point on the southwest Oregon Coast, an x-axis that runs along the south boundary of the State of Oregon and a y-axis that runs along the north, which is just off the coast of the State, Jenkins explained.

"In that grid, you pick any point and there is an x and y axis number for that point," he said. "That's the 5-digit (addressing) number which is based on whether or not you're on a road that runs predominately north-south or east-west."

If someone calls 9-1-1 and gives the dispatcher an address real quickly, the emergency responder can send the volunteers out west of La Grande or east of La Grande depending on what he understood, Jenkins explained.

"So we adopted our road naming ordinance with no duplicate or sound-alike names," he said, "yet we wanted to honor the historical naming system that was out there as much as we possibly could."

A lot of the road names changed because of the uniform rural addressing systems, and some residents liked the changes while others did not.

According to the Road Naming and Rural Addressing Ordinance #1988-3, "Roads running generally north-south shall be known as "roads"; roads running generally east-west shall be known as "lanes"; roads dead-ending 1000 feet or less from their beginning point shall be known as "drive"; and roads whose beginning and ending points intersect on a common road shall be known as "loops."

Furthermore, "Road names were limited to a maximum of twelve letters and two words, excluding the suffix directional indicator, such as road, lane or loop." As a result, roads named with dual surnames (Parsons-Hug) were changed to just one of those names. In this case, Parsons Lane was the new name of the road.

The ordinance prohibited duplications with other existing roads, and no similar sounding or confusing names were allowed.

Under the ordinance, residents may file an application to name or rename a road. It could be submitted to the Union County Planning Department for consideration, and it had to include a reason for the request.

Since this was possible, some residents started to name their short rural access roads by a relative's name. Some combined the names of husband and wife, such as Phil and Lynda which made the hybrid Philynda Loop.

This was allowed by the ordinance as follows: "Any private road that provides access to three or more buildings requires a name in order to promote the health, safety and welfare of the public."

This is the case for Frances Lane, Ernest Road, Craddock Road, Happy Walrus Road and many others.

Some residents objected to the ordinance because they felt it allowed a proliferation of new names for roads they consider personal driveways to three or four houses. However, as it stands today, if ordinance conditions are met, this is permitted.

The uniform road naming system impacts about 15 different entities, including county agencies, institutions and critical public services. One public service that has clearly been impacted by the 1988-3 ordinance on road naming and rural addressing is the U.S. postal service and its rural route carriers. Morton Gordon of Elgin, who worked as a rural route carrier for 28 years (1966-1995) was very familiar with the evolution of road names in north Union County.

"I started in July 1966 and technically there was only one route here then about 75 miles long," Gordon said. "Within about ten or twelve years, it was 132 miles long and between 300 and 350 customers."

He explained that the rural mail deliveries grew into three routes: the Cricket Flat area east of the Grande Ronde River was Route #1; and the area west of the river was Route #2; and the Indian Creek---Clark Creek route which was Route #3.

He recalled that the roads had dual names when the grid system came into effect in 1988. "The earliest (settler) residents on that road got their names on the road sign," he said.

Occasionally, he saw mail addressed to residents with the dual-name road address written on the envelope, but technically, an address consisted of a rural route number and a box number. Later that was replaced by a house number and road name.

When things changed over to the five-digit residential address numbering system, "it took years for people to drop the route number on their addressed envelopes," Gordon said.

He also noted that on these county roads, it was common for the mail boxes to be drifted in after snow storms or buried by the snow plows themselves. This made it very challenging for him as a mail carrier to put mail in the boxes along these roads.

"So I took the option of putting the mail boxes on the upwind side of the road and let the snow plow put the snow on the downwind side of the road. It just helped a lot," Gordon said.

The mail boxes weren't necessarily in numerical sequence, Gordon said, "so going to the grid system, although it was opposed by a lot by the residents, was a good thing." *(Morton Gordon interview, April 14, 2018)*

This alphabetical listing of roads in this book is based on a county register of road names and names found on older and current maps. Please forgive any omission you find as we relied on the county records for the foregoing enumeration. It may not be a perfect listing.

In working through the list of roads, we were surprised that there are no roads named after Benjamin Brown or Leasy on the county list, so we spent some time talking about them in the Marks Road entry.

This history was a labor of love on the authors' part, and we hope you'll enjoy reading it as much as we enjoyed writing and compiling it.

Historical Guide to Union County, Oregon
Roads

Airport Lane - This lane is on the south side of the La Grande-Union Airport (KLGD). It runs along the south border of the airport grounds, close enough to watch planes fly in and out. This road #29 is 2.9 miles long and located in Township 3S R38E Section 24.

According to the *La Grande Observer, Aug. 31, 1927, pages 1-2,* there was an air strip in existence. "The government officials have hinted broadly that the time is not far distant when La Grande and other larger cities in eastern Oregon will have their own air depots.

Government officials, connected with the airways division of the bureau of light houses, department of commerce, have been conducting surveys in this territory all summer and early this month, officially announced that a large emergency landing field, on the J. F. Phy property along the Old Oregon Trail highway, would be ready for use this fall. It will be surrounded by border beacon lights placed at 200 foot intervals and all obstructions to approach for take off will be mounted with red lights.

In local circles, remembering hints of a future local service, it is predicted that this is the first step toward the eventual opening of a permanent airport, which will not only take and give United States mail, but will also serve passengers." (End of article excerpt)

In 1928, the local newspaper started printing a column called "La Grande Air Field Personals" in which it stated on March 7, 1928, page 3 as follows:

"As Leon Cuddehack, chief pilot for the Varney air mail line with headquarters in Boise, Idaho, was passing through on his way home from a trip to Pendleton, he stopped at the field for a few minutes Sunday. He was making the trip by car.

Ralph Fifer, mechanic for the Varney Company and in charge of the mail hanger and the emergency field at the airport here, left Friday for Boise where he was summoned to resume his duties in the air service there. He was accompanied by his wife.

E. E. Bert, of La Grande, who has been employed by the air mail company ever since its establishment here in January, has been assigned to take Mr. Fifer's place in the way of looking after the hanger and the ships as they pass through. Mr. Bert was formerly a state traffic officer in La Grande and worked in that capacity for two years.

"Hap" Roundtree, pilot-instructor for the flying school here, was busy all day Sunday taking passengers for air rides in the plane owned by the school. The ship was operated during the day from the Gekeler field just east of La Grande on the Oregon Trail highway." (End of article)

In 1929, the flying school presented a plan to the city of La Grande trying to interest them in leasing the government airport, thus converting it into a municipal field. *(La Grande Observer, March 21, 1929, pg. 1, 5)*

The city of La Grande signed a lease, taking over all of the government equipment on September 13, 1932. In October 1932, the airport was dedicated as Rankin Field and several thousand spectators witnessed the dedication of the field and paid tribute to Dudley Rankin, La Grande aviator who died from injuries sustained while working on his plane in Walla Walla, and for whom the field is named.

"Mr. Rankin, the former local aviator, was prominent in aviation circles in the state and was indefatigable in his efforts to promote flying in Eastern Oregon. It also was through his efforts and those of other air enthusiasts in this vicinity that the La Grande Aeronautical Association was formed and Rankin Field established." *(La Grande Observer, Oct. 10, 1932, pg. 1, 3)*

It was seven and one half years later when the city of La Grande purchased the ground on which the airport was located. Over the next four years, the city improved the new airport by building runways, installing lights and other equipment.

The La Grande-Union Airport dedication ceremony was held on October 11, 1942 with master of ceremonies Fred E. Kiddle. Dr. C. L. Gilstrap, chairman of the aviation committee for the La Grande Chamber of Commerce, announced the dedication ceremony in advance in the *La Grande Observer, Mon., Sept. 28, 1942 page 1.*

The KLGD airport is used heavily by the Blue Mountain chapter of the Experimental Aviation Association, which holds meetings there and flies in and out of Union County. The club was founded in 2014, and they have about 20 members, who all fly single engine land planes. The president of the club is Jim Holloway of La Grande. He welcomes all Union County residents, "Come and see your airport."

Alicel Lane - This 3.79-mile lane intersects with Highway 82 north of La Grande, and heading east, it eventually joins to Gray's Corner Road that travels north and south along the base of Mt. Harris on the east side of the Grande Ronde Valley. It is located in the La Grande district in Township 2S R39E Section 10, designated road #130A.

In its early history, Alicel Lane led through a rural community also called Alicel, which had a one-room schoolhouse to educate the children who resided in this area. Alicel was also the name of a station on the Joseph Branch of the Union Pacific Railroad. *(Oregon Geographic Names (1982).*

Alicel was platted on March 17, 1890 and was comprised of First through Seventh Streets, Main Street and Railroad Street. On the plat map of Alicel, J.K. Romig was listed as the "trustee." By September 1915, Romig had sold 15 lots in Alicel to G. B. Courtright.

How was Alicel really named? There are conflicting stories out there, but the following is the earliest newspaper article and the most credible account of the naming of Alicel. Other later newspaper articles explained it differently, but usually the earliest record is the most correct, therefore, it earned its place in this book.

According to the *September 20, 1915 La Grande Observer,* Alicel was named this way:

"J. K. Romig bought a quarter section tract along the newly constructed branch road for the purpose of platting a town site. The land was purchased from Mrs. Alice Ladd. When the grantor signed her name to the deed, the purchaser took the cue for the name of the proposed town. It was by adding the initial letter of Ladd to the given name, Alice, and thus it became Alicel."

Who was James Kincaid Romig?   He was a business man, a member of the Masons, a mine superintendent and a merchant in Baker City. He was described as one of the leading mining men in Eastern Oregon, *(La Grande Observer, Dec. 2, 1902)*. He was the manager of the Sanger mine in Baker County, *(La Grande Observer, Jan. 6, 1902)*, and president of the Virtue mine in the same county. He purchased and sold real estate in La Grande, Alicel and Elgin. There is a Romig Addition on the plat map of La Grande. He died October 16, 1927 in Baker City.

Mrs. Alice Ladd and her husband Charles W. Ladd were well known in Union County. They had one daughter, Florence Ladd Winans of Seattle, Washington. Florence was born and raised in La Grande and left the area about 1903. She married Earl Winans of Seattle.

Charles Ladd was Alice's first husband, according to her obituary in 1919, which states that she was then married to George Tucker of Seattle. She died in Seattle on March 27, 1919, a victim of the pandemic influenza of that time.

Historically and more correctly renamed the "1918 Influenza," which was also called in its day "La Grippe," was in fact the influenza A virus. It struck in three waves, the spring and fall of 1918, and again in the spring of 1919. By November 1919 the influenza stopped because it ran out of people who were susceptible and the survivors had immunity.

In the first 10 months, it killed 550,000 Americans. It was unlike any other influenza experienced before, and it put the patient in bed with pneumonia. The patients all followed a similar disease progression. They turned blue, hemorrhaged, lungs swelled with fluids and the patients died, sometimes all within 24 hours. Live patients taken ill and transported by ambulances had toe tags placed on them even before they died, as death was anticipated in most cases. *(Influenza 1918, American Experience on OPB)*

The "1918 Influenza" pandemic came to an end in the summer of 1919, but not before it claimed Alice's life. Her husband, George Tucker, and daughter Florence Ladd Winans survived her, according to the obituary. *(La Grande Observer, Mar. 30, 1919, pg. 5)*

Also surviving Alice's death was her first husband, Charles W. Ladd. He died on July 16, 1932 at age 69 in Portland, where his sister, Mrs. Eva Andross, lived. His daughter, Florence Ladd Winans, was mentioned in the obituary.

Charles was born at the Ladd family home at Ladd Hill in 1863. He was reportedly one of the first white children born in the Grande Ronde Valley and a member of the family after whom Ladd Hill and Ladd Canyon were named.   At one time his parents, John R. and Rachel Ladd conducted a restaurant and hotel on the Old Trail road to serve settlers passing through. *(La Grande Observer, July 26, 1932, pg. 1; Oregon Geographic Names, 1982)*

Anson Road - This road #27A is 1.54 miles long in the La Grande district in Township 3S R38E Section 12.

It was named after the English silversmith, Joseph Anson, who was born in Wolverhampton, Staffordshire, England on August 15, 1837. He was one of 18 children born to George Joseph and Margaret (Dinning) Anson.

Ten-year-old Joseph Anson came with his parents by ship to the United States in 1847. He married Amelia B. Newell in Iowa on Nov. 30, 1865, and they came to the Grande Ronde Valley over the Oregon Trail to homestead 240 acres 1-1/2 miles southeast of Island City, Oregon.

Joseph became engaged in raising horses. "Everyone put their horses on the range to graze. It was all open land then. Not much of it was claimed yet for homesteads," Claude Anson said. *(Claude Anson interview, November 2000)*

At one time, Joseph Anson, also known as Jody Anson by his neighbors, had 1,500 horses, and he owned 800 acres on what became known, since 1872, as Whiskey Creek up the Grande Ronde River in Wallowa County.

Joseph and Amelia had five children: Minnie (1866), Newell (1868), Nellie (1869), J. Orlin (1872) and James (1874). Amelia died a week after baby James was born on February 23, 1874, so Minnie, 7, was immediately thrust into the role of mother to the younger children.

Orlin Anson often helped his father Joseph by riding range for him, and during that time, Orlin became familiar with members of the Umatilla tribe.

"Our horses would go over on the Umatilla side," Orlin said, "and we had to gather them up. I became well acquainted with an old Indian woman, who we called 'Old Lady Long Hair' because she wore her hair in long braids that reached nearly to her knees. Her cabin was south of Deadman's Pass, down in the deep canyon. I used to visit her at her cabin, and stay over night at her place."

The Umatilla woman and her riders developed a trusting relationship with Orlin Anson and his herdsmen.

"One year," Orlin said, "we had about 40 of her horses in our band when we brought them in to feed. We sent word that we had them and for her not to worry about them as we had plenty of feed and were taking care of them. That was the last time we had to do much riding on the Umatilla side. She always had her riders bring our horses in and would keep them for us. She kept us informed as to where they were. She died before many years."

This experienced horsewoman was known by her own people as Lucy Long Braids, and she was the ancestress of one of the accomplished musicians who appeared on an Indian Festival of Arts program in La Grande.

Joseph Anson did some trading with the Umatilla Indians and became friends with the chiefs. Occasionally, they would travel to his home to visit with him.

"Umatilla Indians would come to talk with Grandpa," Claude Anson said. "I was so little then that when I saw them coming, I'd run and hide."

When Orlin was a boy, the Joseph Anson farm was the largest horse breeding operation in the area. It was not surprising that Orlin was raised in a saddle and became a true cattleman and horseman. After finishing elementary school, he went to the Snake River country for nine years with his family and helped pasture Anson horses in that area. During those years, Orlin became acquainted with a Umatilla Indian girl, who also herded horses on adjoining land.

"In 1886, when I was 14 years old, I went to the Snake River country for several years and pastured our horses on the hills there," Orlin said. "While there I rode range for over a year on one side of the canyon, and a girl about my age rode on the other side of the canyon. We ate our lunch across from each other, but never spoke to each other. It was one and a half miles to where she was. Her father was crippled and could not ride well. He would sit out on a point with a big spyglass and watch her and the stock."

One time Orlin shot a deer that he wanted to share with this girl's family. "I waved to her to come over," Orlin said. She had to ride seven miles to get across to where I was. Her father came with her, and we visited all night. I offered them some meat. They did not want to take half of it, but I told them that they could throw it away as I could not use all of it. Her father said they would take it and not throw it away, as he would salt it down."

Orlin Anson never forgot their cross-canyon friendship during those years. "She was a pretty woman," Orlin said, "and she seemed like a wonderful person. It was 30 years before I ever talked to her again. She was in Baker, and that was the last time I ever saw her."

Orlin married Miss Mabel McMurry on November 28, 1901. He tried to operate a livery stable but that was short lived because the trains came in and took over the horse freighting business and later cars replaced horses.

The Anson farm saw so many changes after that. Orlin bought a tractor, and Mabel got her first hand-operated agitating washing machine from her father-in-law Joseph. Joseph died in 1933 and his estate was divided among his heirs. Orlin bought out most of the heirs and operated the farm until his own death on October 14, 1963.

Then Orlin's son Claude took over the farm with his wife Leola Dot Latham. They did general farming and Claude also operated a ski shop in the commercial district of La Grande for about 30 years. It was called "Little Alps Ski Shop" and later the "Anson Ski Shop."

He was a highly skilled skier, and by the time he was 88, he had skied two million vertical feet. He was a charter member of the Anthony Lakes Ski Patrol when it was founded in 1963, but when he was 80, he left the patrol and at 88, he hung up his skis for good.

Claude passed the farm along in trust to his daughter Dot Ann Ricker, and now her son, Curt Ricker and his wife Tatiana live on the farm and operate it.

"We've gone from general farming and herding horses to breeding work horses and raising cattle to dryland farming and now to specialized farming," Claude said in summary.

The Anson's story is a true Western in every sense, and their farm was designated a Century Farm with the Oregon State Historical Society in 1965, having been operated continuously by family relatives: Joseph Anson, then Orlin Anson, then Claude Anson and later Claude's grandson, Curt Ricker. *(Claude Anson and Curt Ricker interview, November 2000; Wilbur Anson's written family history; and excerpts from the La Grande Observer, La Grande, Oregon)*

Antelope Peak Road - This road is southwest of North Powder and leaves Anthony Lakes Road, traveling through thick forest land and crossing numerous streams that empty into the North Powder River. It also crosses Dutch Flat Creek and meanders over Bulger Ditch until it connects with Bulger Flat Lane. This road is located in the majestic Elkhorn Mountains, a hospitable habitat for antelope, but there are no residents living on the road.

Anthony Lake Road - Described as a well maintained, all-weather road, it turns into U.S. Forest Service Road 73 and winds 16 miles into the gorgeous Elkhorn Mountains where travelers and winter sports enthusiasts will enjoy Anthony Lakes ski resort and plenty of powdery snow.

The name Anthony was derived from William "Doc" Anthony, "who came to Baker County in 1864 and settled along the lake's banks. Anthony, who was listed in the 1880 census as both a farmer and a doctor, ranched on this property and for a time collected toll for the Dealy Wagon Road (See Starkey Road entry). His farm was about a mile north of the mouth of Anthony Creek. Anthony died in October 1914 at age 85. In the 1930s, skiers began to utilize the slopes above Anthony Lakes, and after World War II, a major ski area was developed." *(Oregon Geographic Names, 7th Edition, pg. 27-28)*

The route of the Dealy Wagon Road went up the North Powder River to the mouth of Anthony Creek. "The starting point (of the Dealy Wagon Road) on the Powder River Valley side was at the old Doc Anthony homestead, later owned by B. F. Sorenson, where the toll gate was located. Doc Anthony was in charge of the gate." *(W. E. Barnett's Historical Data on the Daley Road)*

Antles Lane - This .94 mile long road is in the Union district, designated as road #123 and located in Township 3S R40E Section 14. It was named after Averill A. Antles, who was a resident of Cove in 1900.

Antles was born in Mount Pleasant, Iowa, on May 6, 1857. He moved from there to Stanton, Nebraska, where he attended school, afterward going to Western Normal at Lincoln, Nebraska and then to Normal at Warrensburg, Missouri for one year.

He was superintendent of schools at Carterville, Missouri, for several years. He married Lulu May McCallister (1867-1950) on November 29, 1889, and they had five children, all of whom survived him: Harry Antles, Mrs. Clifford Kail, Floyd Antles, Mrs. Thomas R. Conklin and Archer Antles.

In 1912, he was head of the fruit union in the cherry district. *(La Grande Observer, Jan. 25, 1912, pg. 8)* In 1915, he and F. E. Roberts shipped a car of apples. He was also a Cove District 15 school director from 1913-1927. *(La Grande Observer, June 27, 1927, pg. 6)*

Averill A. Antles, 71, died in January 1939 with a burial at the Cove Cemetery. *(La Grande Observer, Jan. 26, 1939, pg. 7)*

Asla Lane - This public unmaintained road is short, only .11 miles in length and is located in the La Grande district in Township 2S R38E Section 33. It is named after Felix Asla Sr. (1879-1960) and Grace Vincento (Unamuno) Asla (1892-1969).

According to one family tree, their ten children were: Pedro (1909-1910), Felicia (1911-1950), Francessa "Frances" (1912-1976), Marian Aurora (1913-1985), Eudora (1914-), Amelia (1915-2000), Ralph Cedric (1917-1998), Mitchell (1920-1993), Felix Jr. (1924-1952) and Josephine (1925-1999). The family was of Spanish Basque heritage.

Felix Asla Sr. died on March 12, 1960 in Union County; and his wife Grace died on January 1, 1969 in Baker County. Both were buried in Hillcrest Cemetery, La Grande. Their son Felix Asla Jr. was born February 9, 1924 in Oregon and died on August 1, 1952 in North Korea.

Aspen Road - This private road is located in Township 3S R38E Section 16, diverting off of Igo Lane in the La Grande maintenance district, where native Aspen trees are plentiful and their fall colors are stunning.

Badger Flat Lane - This 1/2-mile long lane leaves Medical Springs Highway 203 just west of Catherine Creek State Park. It is located in Township 5S R40E Section 1, designated road #145, south east of Union.

Badger Flat is just one of about 29 different flats in Union County. It had pasture for sheep and cattle, and it also had a cabin on it for cattlemen or loggers, which was the reason it was called Badger Flat camp.

"A cabin on Badger Flat owned by Mrs. Iva Mulvehill was destroyed by dynamite recently, the work of person or persons unknown. Mrs. Mulvehill said the cabin was usually left unlocked for the benefit of woodsmen and cattlemen in the area, and that she usually spent a few days there with friends each summer." *(La Grande Observer, June 16, 1955, pg. 4)*

As far as the county road was concerned, the *La Grande Observer of March 28, 1941,* stated a portion of it was being fenced and graveled, a great improvement for the road as it was almost impassable in winter.

Where Badger Flat Lane ends, it forks off into logging roads. In March 1915, a man named Don Vandervanter started a sawmill on Badger Flat. Badger Flat was also home to the Jacobs and Hess Lumber Company sawmill.

"By all reports there is a good size crew of men at the Jacobs and Hess sawmill and logging outfit at the Badger Flat plant this winter." *(La Grande Observer, Jan. 28, 1924, pg. 7)* This mill produced lumber and boxes, but its prosperity didn't last long.

"The Jacobs brothers were called to Union Friday by a fire that caused $2,000 loss to their mill at Badger Flat." *(La Grande Observer, June 10, 1925, pg. 7)*

Looking back, it almost appears this flat was more than once troubled by a mysterious arsonist of its own.

This road name is a combination of family name, geography and wildlife. It was rich in wildlife, and it was being line trapped in 1923. It's possible that some badgers inhabited this flat, but more likely the road received its name from an early settler.

His name was Francis Marion Badger, who came to Union County in the 1890s and homesteaded in Section 19 of Township 5 S, R41 E, purchasing that land on September 19, 1898.

Francis Marion Badger was born in October 1845 in Indiana, the son of Ebenezer Badger (1812-1880) and Margaret Wyant (1818-1896). Francis had six brothers and four sisters. The family's migration history starts in Waltz, Wabash County, Indiana *(1850 Federal Census)*, and then the family moved to Chariton, Lucas County, Iowa *(1856 Iowa Census and 1860 Federal Census)*.

On May 26, 1871 in Pottawattamie, Iowa, he married Cecelia "Celia" Clark. Celia was born in Iowa on December 19, 1854. Francis and Celia initially lived in Lincoln, Adams County, Iowa *(1880 Federal Census)*. They had three children, Maude (1874-1875) born in Chariton, Iowa; Ross "Jinks" (1876-1960) born in Iowa, and Bessie Thelma (1887-1982), born in Nebraska. *(1900 Federal Census)*

About 1890, they moved west to Oregon, and the Badger family was noted on the *1900 Federal Census* as residents of the city of Union, Oregon. Celia and the two children lived on College Avenue, and Francis lived alone on Madison Street.

Francis' work was apparently seasonal as he revealed that he had not worked for four months in the last year. (*1900 Federal Census*) Then after 1900, he could no longer be located in Union County, Oregon. The city directories of 1903 and 1910 list Celia Badger as a widow of Francis Badger, but no grave or obituary could be found for him.

Celia Badger died in Union, Oregon on September 21, 1920 at 65 years of age and is buried at the Union Cemetery. There is no record of her husband being buried in that cemetery, and her obituary never mentions her husband.

The Badger story continues with their son, Ross "Jinks" Badger, who grew up to be a fruit farmer in the Meadow Lawn subdivision in the Union district of Oregon. He met Erma Webb, a native of Utah, who came with her family to Union County in 1901. They were married on April 17, 1906 in Union where they made their home and raised a family.

Ross Badger's obituary went on to tell a little more of his history. Ross, 83, a retired farmer of Union died at his home Sunday, April 17, 1960. He was born at Council Bluffs, Iowa, on October 2, 1876 and came to Union County with his parents when he was 13 years old. Surviving him were his widow, Erma of Union, a son, Lt. Col. Ralph Badger, Alexandria, Virginia; a daughter, Mrs. Clarice Koehler of Union; a sister, Mrs. Bessie Jones of Union and seven grandchildren and four great grandchildren.

Ross was buried at the Union Cemetery, and three years later his wife, Erma (1878-1963) was laid beside him.

One interesting experience that Ross had in his lifetime happened when he was hunting for grouse in August 1905. He found a human skull about 30 feet from Catherine Creek on the right bank. There was a lot of speculation as to whose remains it was. Some thought it might be the skull of an old man, a recluse named M. Hill, who in February 1901, went missing from his cabin which was three-quarters of a mile from where the skull was found. Others thought, since M. Hill had a large head, that this skull was too small to be his. In any case, a searching party was likely going to look for other skeletal remains to see if they could solve the mystery, and if not, it will just join the long list of those "lost in the great west." *(La Grande Observer, Aug. 26, 1905, pg. 3)*

Bagwell Road - This road #73 is 1.25 miles long and starts off of Olsen Road and travels south blending into North Powder-Ladd Canyon Road, which then enters the city of North Powder on its north side. There are currently two landowners noted on this road. It's location is in Township 5S R39E Sections 15-16-33 in the North Powder district.

Historically, this road is named after Joseph Arthur Bagwell, who was born October 31, 1872 in Dunns Rock, Transylvania, North Carolina. His parents were John Christopher Bagwell (1849-1930) and Mary Adeline Cison Bagwell (1849-1901). Joseph Bagwell died at age 81 on September 1, 1954 in Los Angeles, California, and he was buried in Inglewood Park Cemetery, Inglewood, California.

According to Joseph's paper trail, he considered Brevard, North Carolina his home town. From there he engaged in farming in Kansas for a few years, and then he moved west to Umatilla County, Oregon. He farmed land in the La Grande territory as well as in the Pendleton-Myrick-Helix-Adams country.

In Umatilla County, he acquired a homestead patent on land in 1904, and made Adams, Oregon his headquarters for his wheat farming operation. He was a successful buyer and seller of real estate, continually adding on acreage to his operation.

Friends and family back in Brevard were curious about his life in Umatilla County, so he wrote a letter that was published in the *Brevard News, Aug. 26, 1904* paper in Brevard, Transylvania, North Carolina. His letter is like a time capsule and worth including in this entry.

He prefaced his letter by saying that any description of Umatilla County would fail to give one even a fair idea of the country or its resources, but he would try.

"It is not a country where one can gather wealth off hand. To make money here now one must have some capital to commence business with. The time was when vacant government land could be had for the settling, but that time has long gone by. The lands are worth now from $20 to $300 per acre and more on the market.

Wheat land in this vicinity runs about $60 per acre without improvements and is yielding this year an average of about 40 bushels of No. 1 wheat, with at this time 65 cents per bushel, thus giving an income of $26 per acre. This represents two years labor as the ground only produces a crop every two years, laying fallow every other year.

This (Umatilla County) is a mountain valley flanked on the east, north and south by the Blue Mountains and on the west by the Columbia river. The lands along the Columbia river are, for the most part, a barren waste of sand, running from 3 to 10 miles in width. Then the grain lands begin, rather poor at first but increasing in fertility as one gets nearer the mountains, the best land being on the low lying foothills.

On the latter class of land all kinds of fruit, berries and vegetables, such as are adapted to the north temperate zone, grow to perfection. As an example, one man near Milton in this valley harvested one and one half acres of strawberries this season for which he received $900. The land is gently rolling, there being comparatively none that could be classed as "level."

The country is fast assuming all the airs of civilization. In this county, with a voting population of a little over 4,300, we have 14 towns and villages running from 8,000 population in Pendleton, the county seat, to 50 in Umatilla, a railroad town on the Columbia. The best of schools public and private, churches, saloons, stores etc. are to be found everywhere.

The idea that because we are farther west than Chicago that consequently we are beyond the pale of civilization, is entirely false. Once in a while an "old resident" Indian scout, Hudson Bay trapper or some of those well known pioneers of the northwest are met with, but they are so few nowadays as to be almost as much of a curiosity as if met with in Brevard.

The question about wages can be answered in a few words. Ordinary farm wages run about $30 per month and found, while during the harvest season they run from $1.50 per day to as high as $6.00 and $8.00, according to the class of work. The latter wages being paid to skilled machine men handling large combined harvester, etc.

Living costs here about the same as it does there compared with the wages paid. I would hesitate to advise anyone to come "west" who expected to work for a living as there is only about nine months work in the year for everybody, some few men only being employed the year round on the big ranches.

In regard to the political situation, I will only add that since coming west, I have often regretted that we could not have old Transylvania county transplanted here in a bulk as it might change the political aspect. As it is, I have almost ceased to vote, being in the helpless minority." Letter signed Joseph A. Bagwell, Pendleton, Oregon.

Not long after this letter, his words were put to the test when it came to how Umatilla County, Oregon was equipped to treat a serious disease that he caught.

In the *Athena Press of June 27, 1905*, it read: "Joe Bagwell, who has been making this place (Adams) his headquarters for some time, was taken to the hospital Saturday. His case was diagnosed as typhoid."

Typhoid is caused by water or food contaminated with salmonella bacterium, and it can produce a fever, painful organ failure and sepsis. This illness is very preventable, and it's transmission follows a fecal-mouth route. The first vaccine created for typhoid was in 1909. Yet without that advantage in 1905, Bagwell surprisingly pulled through it.

During his life, Joseph Bagwell appears to have married three times and had a child by each wife. The first wife is unknown, but she resided with him at his home in Myrick, Oregon, between Pendleton and Helix, Oregon. During the week of Nov. 8, she gave birth to a son.

"J. A. Bagwell was in town (Pendleton) from Myrick today, singing praises of a little son who arrived at his home last week." *(East Oregonian, Nov. 16, 1908, pg. 5)* Their paper trail ends there.

On December 3, 1908, Bagwell traveled back to Anderson, South Carolina where he was going to visit his old home during the winter. *(East Oregonian, Dec. 4, 1908, pg. 5)* He was back in Umatilla County on business about nine days later.

"J. A. Bagwell of Adams, Umatilla county, was in the valley last week buying horses to take the place of mules on his 1,200-acre wheat ranch. He bought 11 in the vicinity of Enterprise and a number down about Wallowa.

Mr. Bagwell is a former Kansan but has been in the wheat raising business in Umatilla for several years. He rents two sections in the very heart of the best wheat district. He says quarter sections of wheat land over there are held at from $10,000 to $12,000. The land is farmed season after season to wheat with summer fallowing years between. The average crop in the best wheat district is 35 bushel to the acre, every two years. The land does not pay over 6 percent gross on that basis.

Mr. Bagwell is wonderfully taken with this county and predicts a big wheat production in the hill lands in a few years." *(The Enterprise News-Record, Dec. 12, 1908 pg. 1)*

Shortly after this article was written, Bagwell made a substantial purchase to help with the field work.

"J. A. Bagwell of Adams, came in last evening from Kansas City, Missouri, with a car load of 22 big and handsome Missouri mules, which he expects to use in Umatilla county wheat farms. Mr. Bagwell is quite confident that the mule is the proper animal to do the work and has brought along some handsome specimens." *(East Oregonian, Jan. 4, 1909, pg. 5)*

He married again on May 12, 1909 in Kansas to Mabel Neff of Perth, Sumner County, Kansas (1880-1920). "J. A. Bagwell of Adams, Ore., and Mabel Neff of Perth, Kansas, have secured a marriage license today." *(Wellington Daily News, Sumner County, Kansas, May 10, 1909)* Following their wedding, they made their home at Bagwell's wheat farm residence in Umatilla County, Oregon.

In 1910, they lived in Helix, Umatilla County, Oregon. Mabel gave birth to their daughter, Thelma Josephine (1915-1979). In 1918, the family moved to a new residence in Alhambra, Los Angeles County, California. Thelma was 4 years and 9 months old at the time of the *1920 Federal Census* there.

Joseph Bagwell prospered and bought and sold land frequently. He had a home and property interests in Union County, but he also had a homestead patent since 1904 on land near Helix, Umatilla County, Oregon and a home and properties in Los Angeles County, California. To care for their interests in all these places, they traveled back and forth as noted in the following social briefs in the *Eastern Oregonian* newspaper of Pendleton, Oregon.

"Mr. and Mrs. Bagwell just returned from southern California." *(East Oregonian, March 9, 1918 pg. 2)* "Mr. and Mrs. Bagwell have gone to La Grande." *(East Oregonian, July 22, 1918, pg. 8)* "Mr. and Mrs. Bagwell are going to Long Beach, California for the winter after harvesting crops near Helix and La Grande." *(East Oregonian, Aug. 5, 1918, pg. 8)*

In mid-September 1918, the deadly influenza had made its first appearance in southern California via infected navy men. By October, the mayor of Los Angeles had declared a state of public emergency, and the health commissioner issued a closure of all schools, and banned all public gatherings, including public funerals, movie houses, theaters, pool rooms and other public entertainments like parades.

It was the worst of times to travel there, a decision that Bagwell later came to regret.

"J. A. Bagwell has arrived in Los Angeles, having left Pendleton for that place by auto about two weeks ago. He reports a splendid trip over fine roads, but on arriving to Los Angeles, he found everything closed on account of the flu epidemic. Business houses are fumigated every morning, and the board of health advises against traveling. These conditions make the city very quiet." *(East Oregonian, Oct. 22, 1918, pg 3)*

The flu came in three waves: fall 1918, spring 1919 and fall 1919. Cases in the Los Angeles area peaked in April 1919, and the city was battling it with school closures, bans on social venues and enforced home quarantines. Those measures were working, so by 1920, cases were waning, and the bans on social gatherings were being lifted. The disease progression was rapid, sometimes leading to suffocating pneumonia only a few hours after onset.

On January 12, 1920, the census was taken there, and the Bagwell family were renting a place in South Chapel of the township of San Gabriel in the city of Alhambra, California. The enumerator listed Joseph, 45, born in North Carolina, Mabel, 39, born in Kansas, and Thelma, 4 years 9 months, born in Oregon.

There, Mabel (Neff) Bagwell contracted the influenza and died of pneumonia on February 20, 1920. *(East Oregonian, Feb. 21, 1920, pg. 1)* She died at age 39 years, 10 months and 29 days, and her husband and daughter, Thelma, accompanied the body to Perth, Kansas, where her parents were living. Interment occurred at Bethany Cemetery in Perth. *(The Wellington Daily News, Feb. 26, 1920, pg. 2)*

Her death certificate stated that the primary cause of death was a cerebral hemorrhage and the contributing cause was capillary bronchitis. The duration of her illness was only 1 day, the certificate read. *(Ancestry.com)*

"The funeral service for Mrs. Mabel Bagwell, who died on February 20, 1920, at Alhambra,

California, will be held at the Presbyterian church in Perth on Thursday morning at eleven o'clock. The body will arrive there Wednesday morning and be taken to the home of her parents, Mr. and Mrs. A. L. Neff, who live northwest of Perth. Burial will be in the Perth cemetery. *(The Wellington Daily News, Wellington, Kansas, Feb. 25, 1920, pg 1)*

About two years later, Bagwell's life took a marked turn for the better. His properties in Long Beach held a hidden treasure.

"Word has been received from J. A. Bagwell that a 1,500 barrel oil well was struck on his property in Long Beach, California, August 7, 1922. The oil is flowing and is free of water and sand, according to the information received. Mr. Bagwell, who formerly resided in Pendleton, states that five other wells are being drilled on his property." *(East Oregonian, Aug. 31, 1922, pg. 3)* His family said that after he struck oil, he was worth 15 to 20 million dollars. *(My Family Tree, Rootsweb)*

Five days after he struck oil, he also married his third wife, Bertha Louise Palmer from Los Angeles. His marriage was announced in the *East Oregonian, Aug. 12, 1922 on pg. 6.* If that wasn't enough good news, in 1924, Joseph and Bertha had a son, George Joseph Bagwell (1924-1972). Joseph shared 32 years together with Bertha, and he died on September 1, 1954 at the age of 81 in Los Angeles, California.

He was survived by his wife, Bertha Bagwell; daughter Mrs. Thelma J. (Bagwell) Collins; and son, George Joseph Bagwell. Joseph Bagwell was buried in Inglewood Park Cemetery, Inglewood, California.

The son, George Joseph Bagwell, 47, died on May 19, 1972 in Los Angeles County, California. Daughter Thelma (Bagwell) Collins died November 4, 1979 in Westminster, Orange County, California.

Bald Mountain Loop - This loop is located in northwest Union County. It is named after the mountain of the same name about two miles to the west. It has a bald ridge about 1- ½ miles long leading south up to the top of the 5,246 foot open summit. This loop is not listed on the official list of county roads, but it does appear on maps, so it has been included.

Baseline Lane - Formerly called Baseline Road, this 3.75-mile long road runs east-west north of Starkey, branching off of McIntyre Road, and it turns into Starkey Cow Camp Road. It used to be a county road before it was named Baseline Lane in the early 1970s. *(Gregory Tsiatos, 86, interview October 30, 2018)*

It is located in Township 3S R35E Section 34 in the La Grande maintenance district and is designated road #127 on the official county road listing.

Bates Lane - This 1.95-mile long road #110 was once part of rural mail route 2 La Grande in the Union district. It's location is in Township 4S R40E Section 14.

Bates Lane was named after Thomas William Bates (1879-1951), who came to the Grande Ronde Valley in 1891. He was born on November 14, 1879 to Lucius Chester Bates and Carrie Clerk in

Stillwater, Washington County, Minnesota. He married Laura Edna Elmer (1896-1971), whose mother was Doris Elmer, and two brothers were Harvey and Frank Elmer of Lower Cove.

In Bates' 1918 draft registration, he described himself as a farmer in Hot Lake, being 39 years of age with blue eyes, brown hair, medium height and a stout build. *(ancestry.com)*

Thomas Bates was said "to have come from the famous theatrical family of the same name." (*La Grande Observer, Sept. 25, 1904, pg 3)* He was inducted into the Elks Club in 1917, and he and his wife were socially active at the Blue Mountain Grange Hall.

He and his wife, Laura E. had seven children: Mable, Joe, Keith, Elmer, Edward, Ehrman, and Anna. Bates died on June 2, 1951 at the age of 71 years in the Grande Ronde Hospital after a long illness, and he was buried in the family plot in Grandview Cemetery. (*Findagrave.com)*

Bean-Coffin Lane - More accurately Beem-Coffin Lane. This 1.45-mile long lane is located in the Pumpkin Ridge territory north of Summerville, winding through beautiful foothill country and farmland. It's location is in Township 1N R39E Section 19 and is designated as road #136.

The name of this lane has been misspelled. An old-timer from Summerville, named Leland Everett "Pete" Von Der Ahe (1918-2004) claimed that it should be BEEM-Coffin Lane. *(Marvel Powelson interview, January 23, 2019)*

It appears that Leland was right because the *1935 Metsker Map* lists a landowner as John A. Logan Beem (1870-1946). John Beem was born on May 3, 1870 in the unincorporated town of Polk, Polk County, Missouri. His father, Thomas, 41, and his mother Elizabeth Baker Beem, 40, were farmers and had nine children including John.

The family was listed in the *1870 Federal Census* as residents of Grant Township, Missouri. (Some family genealogists spell the family name as Beam, which more closely resembles its mistaken spelling of Bean.)

Thomas Beem moved his family to the Indian Valley in Union County, Oregon on the outskirts of Elgin between 1876 and 1880 because they were listed in the *1880 Federal Census* when John was just 10 years old. Sadly, Thomas' wife Elizabeth died on May 27, 1883 in Elgin at the age of 51. Thomas continued to work hard on his property, and he earned his land patent in 1885 at that location.

John grew to manhood, and he bought land on what became Bean-Coffin Lane, land that John Gawith had proved up in 1888. Two years later in 1890, John's father passed away at the age of 61 years.

Thomas and wife Elizabeth are both buried in the Highland Cemetery on Good Road. There are other Beem burials there too, including: Cordelia Bell Beem (d. Oct. 31, 1948), George Harvey Beem (b. Mar. 23, 1885, d. Jan. 21, 1963), Warner Beem (1867-1942). *(Highland Cemetery Records)*

Thomas' son John Beem married Delilah Ellen Troy on November 13, 1891 in Elgin, and they farmed. During a period of 21 years, they had eight children: Amy Ellen (1892-1918), Verdie (1894-1969), Randall David (1897-1947), Dorothy Elizabeth (1900-1987), Docia (1907- ?), Edwin Lester (1909-1996), Delphia Delia (1913-1997) and the youngest (name unknown).

John Beem died on September 30, 1946 in La Grande, Oregon at the age of 76. He is buried at the Summerville Cemetery in Summerville, Union County, Oregon.

His wife, Delilah Beem, passed away at the Wallowa County Hospital on February 29, 1948. Her obituary stated that she was the daughter of David and Ellen Troy and was born at Elgin, Oregon on July 4, 1873. Of her eight children, four preceded her in death.

"Mrs. Beem spent her early childhood in and near Elgin and grew to young womanhood there. When she married, she moved with Mr. Beem to his homestead on Trout Creek near Enterprise where they lived for 11 years and where four of their children were born. Because of her physical condition she spent the last several years of her life with her youngest son." *(Obituary, Wallowa County Chieftain, March 4, 1948, pg. 1)*

The following children survived her: Verdi Hug of Summerville; Dorothy Holmsback of Toledo, Oregon; Edwin L. Beam of Enterprise, Oregon, and Delphia Hunt of Portland, Oregon.

Bean-Coffin Lane is also named after Edgar Coffin, son of Peter M. and Sarah "Frances" Coffin. Peter M. Coffin (1824-1906) was born in Nantucket, Rhode Island to Peter and Charlotte (Moores) Coffin. He was an adventurous fellow, having come to San Francisco by boat in 1849, and after a couple of business ventures, he came to the Grande Ronde Valley in 1862.

He took up farming, and with good business sense, he acquired several thousand acres of good land. He made and kept influential business contacts and was successful in his dealings.

He has the distinction of bringing the first kittens to the county from Walla Walla, and he was offered $25 for one of them. In 1889, he retired from many activities and lived in Union. In his older years he became blind in both eyes.

Peter married Mrs. Sarah Frances Purciel (1840-1907) on March 12, 1874. Some family trees say her last name was Purcell. She was born in Kentucky and raised in Illinois. She came to this county in 1871, and she had a daughter from her first husband. Peter died on March 8, 1906, and he was buried in the Elgin Cemetery. His stone epitaph reads: "He sleeps peacefully waiting for the great Life-giver."

Peter and Sarah had raised four children: Sarah's daughter, B.G., (b. 1870) from a previous marriage; Albert (b.1871), Nora (b.1873) and Edgar Coffin (b. 1875). Albert married Katie J. Schraff in Billings, Montana and lived there, but Edgar farmed on what became Bean-Coffin Lane. *(Peter Coffin, An Illustrated History of Union and Wallowa counties, 1902, pg. 268; Findagrave.com; ancestry.com)*

Sometimes this road was considered a precinct of Elgin, Imbler or Summerville, or it was called

Pumpkin Ridge, depending on what directory, newspaper clipping or census you looked at. In any case, it was home to the Edgar R. and Zada Coffin family.

Edgar Rely Coffin (1875-1955) and his wife Zada Ordell Gordon (1879-1938) had the following children: Grace Frances (1904-2000), Lovene Burniece (1907-1995), Lois Maxine (1910-1994), Dorothy Winifred Fowler (1912-2003), Hugh Gordon (1914-2003), Neva Priscilla (1917-1917), Marie Katherine (1918-1975), Marjorie May Round (1922-?) and Albert "Bud" Walter (1923-2003).

Zada Coffin died the morning of January 2, 1938 at home, four miles north of Summerville (Bean-Coffin Lane) after a long illness. Morticians Snodgrass and Zimmerman handled the funeral arrangements.

She was a native of Elgin, born January 26, 1879 and was just 58 years, 11 months and seven days of age when she died. Her husband and all of her children (except Neva) survived her. *(La Grande Observer, Jan. 3, 1938, pg. 6, obit.)*

Edgar Coffin died April 7, 1955, and his obituary from the *La Grande Observer, April 8, 1955, pg. 1* read in part:

"Edgar Coffin, 80-year-old life-long resident of Union County, died in a local hospital yesterday after a short illness. Mr. Coffin was a retired farmer living in the Summerville area. Mr. Coffin was born at Union on January 10, 1876. Survivors include sons, Hugh of La Grande; Albert of Tustin, Calif., and six daughters: Mrs. Grace Masterton, Mrs. Marie Spears, La Grande; Mrs. Louene Dailey, Wallowa, Ore.; Mrs. Lois Barton, Summerville and Mrs. Dorothy Fowler of Perry. Twenty-eight grandchildren and 11 great grandchildren survive. Edgar Coffin as interred at the Elgin Cemetery." [end of obit]

Behrens Lane - Formerly named the Lewis-Burns Corner Road on the *1935 Metsker Map*. This road #18 was designated as route #1 for mail delivery purposes, and it runs 2.42 miles in length in Township 1S R38E Sections 2-3 in the Imbler maintenance district.

The Lewis part of the lane name was derived from the family of John L. (1847-1924) and Sarah Chaplow Lewis; and the Behrens part of the lane name was derived from August (1862-1941) and Margaret Klein Behrens and sons Arthur (wife Audry Literal) and Fred O. (wife Veta Lee) Behrens; daughters Ruth, Nellie and others. *(1861 Canada Census, Chaplow family)*

John L. Lewis was a well-known carpenter in the Summerville area. He had an active part in building many Summerville area residences as well as the Pleasant Grove one-room schoolhouse on Hunter Road and the one-room Dry Creek schoolhouse on Summerville Road.

The Behrens name is often pronounced by locals as "Burns" and that phonetic spelling found its way onto the *1935 Metsker Map*. Later the words Lewis and Corner were dropped as the lane name, and it was refashioned as Behrens Lane after August Behrens' son, Frederick (1902-1993).

In 2019, the Behrens' two homes on the corner were occupied by descendants. The Behrens family came to this area in 1907, and they won out as the final name of this lane. *(One Room School, pg.*

This road history cannot be complete without mentioning another noteworthy resident on the "S" bend of the corner of Summerville Road and Behrens Lane, Emery Oliver (1912-2005) and his wife Thelma (Kennedy) Oliver (1926-2015).

During bad winter nights, this "S" section of the road was almost always impassable, so the Olivers kept their porch light on to let snow-stranded motorists see their way to their house for refuge, and an old rotary phone was left on the front porch for people to use to call for help if the Olivers were asleep.

Strangers and neighbors knocked on the Oliver's porch door late into the night, came in to warm up, drink something hot, and spend the night if needed, until plows could clear the road enough for them to resume their travels. *(Thelma Oliver interview, January 2008)*

After WWII, Emery Oliver was instrumental in getting the phone line to Summerville from Imbler. He helped to set up the posts and hang the wire. Emery had the distinction of being the (unofficial) mayor of Summerville, said informant Bill Howell of Imbler. *(Bill Howell interview, May 20, 2018)*

On the side of Emery's truck, it read, "Meanest Man in Summerville." Of course, nothing could have been farther from the truth, but Emery did enjoy a good joke and the distinctive title.

Thelma's father and mother brought the family to Elgin, Oregon from Pennyslvania. In Elgin, he made a living as a carpenter until his own death on February 18, 1955 at the age of 68 years. *(La Grande Observer, Feb. 19, 1955, pg. 1, obituary)*

Thelma went to school in Elgin and after WWII, she married Emery Oliver on March 23, 1947. They spent their wedding night and many days to follow reconstructing the burial records of the Summerville Cemetery. The mice had gotten at the old records and chewed up the pages, so the Olivers made it their joint project to recreate a comprehensive book of burials. No surprise then, that Emery became the historian of the Summerville Cemetery for decades to come.

After the passing of Emery on September 27, 2005 and Thelma Oliver on December 9, 2015, their farm home and land was sold to Sam Bussard, a farmer on Myers Road in Summerville, and it serves as a rental property. *(Carol Oliver interview, May 23, 2018)* The neighborhood doesn't seem the same without them.

Travelers still get stuck on the "S" curve near the old Oliver place, but the days of wintry mid-night hospitality, the porch light and telephone service passed away with the Olivers and cell phones. It is most appropriate then, to recognize the Olivers as part of Behrens Lane history.

Bennett Lane - This lane is located off Medical Springs Highway (State Highway 203) and part of the sub-division of Pondosa in Union County. It is located about 21 miles southeast of the city of Union and about 24 miles northeast of Baker City.

The property on this lane was sub-divided by Robert Leland Bennett and his wife Betty Jean (Gaddy)

Bennett. Nearby was the town site of Pondosa, which was home to sawmills owned in succession by the Stoddard Lumber Company (1926), the Collins-Pondosa Lumber Company (1931), and Mt. Emily Lumber Company (1958). The last mill and the town were put up for auction on May 5, 1959.

On June 20, 1959 a fire destroyed the mill, dry kiln, shop and 20 vacant homes. In 1966, Lester Neil Gaddy (b. 1924) purchased the town of Pondosa. He used some rentals as a down payment and with his GI Bill, he financed the rest. He operated the store, selling saw dust from the piles as mulch for plants and gardens. He died on March 10, 1983.

Lester Gaddy had an older sister named Betty "Jean" Gaddy. At age 20, Jean married Robert "Bob" Bennett, 19, on December 21, 1942 in Vancouver, Washington. Witnesses to the event were Robert's father Frank Ordway Bennett and Virginia M. Bennett. *(Ancestry.com)*

At the time of their marriage, Robert was a longshoreman and Betty was a defense worker, both residing in Portland. Forty years into their marriage, Jean and Bob Bennett purchased the Pondosa Store in 1983, when Jean's brother Lester Gaddy passed away.

The couple were featured in a story called "The Mill Town That Was" published in the *La Grande Observer's August 9, 2003* issue by writer Lisa Britton Jacoby.

In its heyday, Pondosa had 500 residents, but by 2003, its population was about 12, said Jean Bennett, then 81 years old. Pondosa used to be on the map, she said, but she didn't know what happened.

Jean and her husband, Bob, 80, owned and operated the Pondosa Store for 20 years. They moved in long after the town had begun to shrink. They still have stories, gleaned from the visitors who made a point to stop at the store for a soda, and maybe a bag of popcorn, wrote Britton.

The Bennetts kept a notebook handy at the store, something that visitors could write in. Many of those visitors had a connection to Pondosa, either they or their families used to live there. In that notebook, they would write their stories from the good old days in Pondosa.

"We have so many of the old-timers come in, and I've picked up a lot of stories from the people who used to live here," said Jean in that article. It became such a regular occurrence that she thought she better get a notebook and start recording these stories. She had at least two volumes of notebooks by the time she closed up shop there.

"The Bennett's store is on the ground floor of the old Pondosa Hotel, a boarding house that slept 24 men, two to a room. Metal numbers still adorn the doors to the second-story rooms. The wooden floors are pitted, marred by years of workers coming home in their hob-nailed boots. The Bennetts have restored seven of the 12 rooms, repairing the water stains and peeling plaster," wrote Britton.

Jean and Bob Bennett made this their home, and they did the best they could with it. They tried to offer a place for former Pondosa residents to sit and reminisce about the once booming sawmill town that they or their loved ones called home.

"We all have our beginnings," said Jean. "It was a booming place and everyone who lived here loved it. This is where their memories are." [end of article]

Benson Road - This road was once a county road that became annexed into the city of Union. Due to its past county road status, the authors wanted to include it in this book.

It was named after Union pioneer John A. "Dick" Benson who lived to the ripe old age of 95, being the second oldest living resident in Union County in 1962.

He was a retired cattle rancher and lived all his life in Union, where he was born on December 25, 1866, just one year after the Civil War drew to a close. His parents, natives of Virginia, migrated to Oregon from Missouri by covered wagon.

Benson grew up with a passion for horses from his father, who was a supplier of mounts for the U.S. Cavalry. As a young lad, he helped break and train animals for the family business. At the age of 16 and after his father died, Benson worked for the Shirley and Stewart livestock farm and rode with them on their cattle drives across the grasslands of Montana to the interior of Alberta, Canada and from the Grande Ronde Valley through southern Oregon.

Later, with the freight train coming into more general use, Benson had charge of train loads of horses which rolled from Eastern Oregon to the Midwest.

On July 14, 1904, he married Minnie Dougherty of Wallowa County. She was born in Pleasant Hill, Cass County, Missouri on October 13, 1877. Dick and Minnie celebrated their 50th wedding anniversary before her death on December 31, 1954, following a long illness. During their marriage they lived in Union. It doesn't appear that they had any children of their own. Dick worked at the retail butcher business and at large scale horse trading until 1915.

In that year, Benson and two brothers bought a cattle spread on Catherine Creek. They stocked the spread with cattle and operated under the ranch name of Benson Brothers, using the "Y L" and "61" irons. The Benson Brothers were also able bankers, and their Union bank was believed to be one of two banks in Oregon that did not close during the Great Depression.

Dick Benson retired as an active cattleman in 1930 at the age of 64. He continued buying, training and selling horses until the age of 90 when he was forced indoors due to failing health.

Dick Benson died January 16, 1962 at the Grande Ronde Hospital. Burial took place next to his wife, Minnie, at Union Victorian Cemetery in the city of Union, Oregon. Surviving him were three nephews: Alton Davis, Charles Davis and Richard Davis, nieces and other relatives. *(La Grande Observer, Jan. 17, 1962, pg. 1)*

Bidwell Road - Only a very short length of this road lies in Union County, and it is located in Township 6S R39E Section 22, designated road #108 in the North Powder maintenance district. It includes one business property owner at 150 Bidwell Road.

Bidwell Road begins at C. J.'s Country Store on the southeast edge of North Powder and leaves town to the southeast direction. The entire road is quite lengthy, and the majority of it lies in Baker County, but a history was available, so it follows.

The Bidwells were very well known horse breeders and ranchers in the Union-North Powder districts. The Bidwell history starts with patriarch, Charles Calvin Bidwell (1828-1915) and his wife Mary Ann (Gilbert) Bidwell (1839-1921), who brought their family to Union County in 1884. Charles became involved with the livery business.

According to *An Illustrated History of Union and Wallowa Counties, 1902, pg. 386* and his obituary on *accessgenealogy.com*, the following biographical information was published about the Bidwell family.

The patriarch, Charles Calvin Bidwell, was born in Verona, New York on February 20, 1827 (1828), and he migrated west toward Illinois and then to Fond du Lac, Wisconsin, where he met and married Mary A. Gilbert on September 5, 1858.

He then got a homestead in Minnesota. After the war, he moved to Missouri and then came to Union, Oregon, in 1887 (alternate 1884). He and his wife had five children: three boys and two girls. The oldest, Genevieve, died at four years of age. The others lived into adulthood: Frank, Chester, Homer and Emma.

Charles C. Bidwell died in Union, Oregon, November 25, 1915 at the age of 89 years, 9 months and 5 days. He was survived by his wife and four children: Frank Bidwell of Union, Chester Bidwell of Island City; Homer Bidwell of North Powder, and Mrs. Emma Clark of Union. His wife, Mary (Gilbert) died nearly six years later in North Powder on Tuesday, August 30, 1921 at the age of 82 years and 5 months.

Mary Ann Gilbert was born March 31, 1839, at Spencer, New York, and relocated with her parents to Fond du Lac, Wisconsin, where she reached womanhood and met Charles C. Bidwell. On September 5, 1859, she married him. Four of their children survived her: Chester, of Island City; Frank A., Homer C., and Mrs. Emma Clark, of North Powder, Oregon.

The family moved to Missouri and after several years residence there, they came to Union, Oregon. She resided in Union until June 1921 when she and her daughter moved to North Powder to live nearer to her sons. She was a kind and devoted mother, a good friend and neighbor. Many friends extend sincere sympathy to the bereaved family. [end of obituary info]

The Bidwell family's residential and migration history includes relocations to Virginia, then to the vicinity of St. Joseph, Missouri, and from there to Orleans, Nebraska and finally to Northeast Oregon.

Now our focus turns to the son, Homer C. Bidwell, who was born in Galesburg, Wisconsin on January 25, 1871. He migrated with his family to Union County in 1884, and after some time, Homer entered upon an apprenticeship to the miller's trade, which he learned and followed for five years. After this period, he took up farming and stock raising on his farm north of Union.

Homer also bought stock for Kiddle Brothers for two years, and then in 1898, he purchased the lot and stable where his business was transacted in 1902. The place was conveniently located and the buildings were comfortable and well arranged. In his stock Mr. Bidwell had the best that could be secured, and his business was conducted with care and wisdom. In addition to the livery business, he also had a feed business and also bought and sold horses. He had also engaged in the transportation line business and in stables.

He married Miss Rachel M. Brooks on May 3, 1898, the daughter of Samuel and Mary (Wade) Brooks, who came to Union County from Iowa in 1873, settling and farming immediately north of Imbler. (See Brooks Road entry)

Homer and Rachel had a son, Frank Deane Bidwell, born September 23, 1900. Homer was a member of several fraternity organizations and served as city councilman for two years.   *(An Illustrated History of Union and Wallowa counties, 1902, pg. 386)* Homer died when he was 60 years of age on June 24, 1931.

Nine years after Homer's death, his widow, Rachel Bidwell, 68, was noted in the *1940 Federal Census*, still residing and working in Union. Rachel had two years of college education and worked at a government job "assessing." She died on September 28, 1945 and was buried in the Union Victorian Cemetery in the city of Union, Oregon.

Homer and Rachel's son, Frank Deane Bidwell (1900-1973) lived in the North Powder and Haines area, and on September 3, 1925 in Baker County, he married Edith Doris Jacobson (1901-1977), both age 24. It was a first marriage for both of them, and Frank worked as a mechanic. When they lived in Haines, he was employed as a fireguard with the Forestry Service. It doesn't appear that they had children.

Frank Deane Bidwell died April 29, 1973 and was buried in the North Powder Cemetery, where Edith was interred following her death on November 16, 1977. *(Findagrave.com)*

Big Creek Road - This road #71 runs 1.96 miles and is located in southern Union County and runs south from Medical Springs along a creek of the same name. This creek starts near Flagstaff Butte and winds its way southwest until it joins the Powder River. The road is located in Township 6S R41E, Section 25 in the North Powder district.

Bird Lane - This private lane is located in Township 2S R38E Section 33. The road parallels Fruitdale Lane and is one of the five bird-named lanes in a mobile home park in the La Grande maintenance district.

Blackhawk Trail Lane - This road #7B is 2.19 miles long in the La Grande district, located in Township 2S R38E Section 31. It was named after Chief Blackhawk of the Umatilla tribe.

In 1862, the lane was simply called Indian Trail because it was used as a route for Native Americans who were passing through. It became a favorite route for travelers because of the well near the Joseph Anson Century Farm (located along Highway 237), where people could drink and rest from their journeys.

At times, the Native Americans who camped to rest on the Joseph Anson farm would approach his home and try to trade their beaded crafts for foods. As the story goes, this made Mrs. Anson quite apprehensive since she was sometimes at the house alone while her husband was away working. *(Claude Anson interview, November 2000)*

The Native American trails led to the start of Union County road projects, and in this regard Blackhawk Trail Lane has an early ranking in county road history.

"The first county road was constructed under the supervision of Judge Lichtenthaler and his court, due to the granting of Charles Goodnough's petition to build a road from Oro Dell east along the north side of the river to intersect the Walla Walla road. In later years, it was officially named the Black Hawk Trail in honor of a friendly Umatilla Indian who frequently visited homesteaders who lived there." (Excerpt of article ended) *(La Grande Observer, Feb. 24, 1961, pg. 25)*

The Blackhawk Trail passed near Riverside Park, where many travelers camped temporarily to rest. Riverside Park was officially established by the city of La Grande in 1909.

Blue Sky Drive - This drive is located by the airport, and is thought to have been given an aeronautic name descriptive of good flying weather.

Blue Spring Road - This road is located in the National Forest lands in northern Union County. There are seven cabins on this road leased from the Forest Service. Most of them were built in the 1960s or later. Two were built in the 1930s. This road is named after "Blue Spring" which is located in this area, and likely derived from the fact it is in the Blue Mountains.

Bodie Road - According to *Bernal D. Hug's 1961 Supplement of History of Union County, Oregon, page 170*, "Body (Bodie) was a passing track two miles east of Kamela named for an Indian."

This short road starts at the tiny community of Bodie and Bodie Siding and heads south and dead ends into timber land. Bodie Siding was the halfway point on the railroad section between Kamela to the north and Motanic to the south. Bodie community was located in Township 2S R36 E, Section 7. *(1935 Metsker Map)*

In 1943, the Union Pacific (UP) Railroad inventory showed Bodie Siding, and it had an operational station there at that time. But by 1946, it doesn't show it listed, so some time between 1943 and 1946, UP deactivated Bodie Siding. The UP Historical Society had no information about the origin of the name Bodie because their archives only went back as far as 1943. *(Union Pacific Historical Society, Wyoming, interview Nov. 27, 2018)*

To the best of our research, it appears that Bodie Siding became the new name in the mid-1930s when UP formally absorbed its subsidiary, the Oregon-Washington Railroad and Navigation Company's line through northeastern Oregon.

Furthermore, the name Bodie does not appear to have any ties to any Union County resident. It may have been the name of a UP employee, which wasn't an uncommon practice.

Bodie was home to a few residents including retired Union Pacific Railroad employee, John T. Campbell, who lived in Bodie for 35 years, starting in 1928, according to his obituary. (*La Grande Observer, Jan. 18, 1963, pg. 8*) Campbell also purchased lots 2 and 3 in Bodie from Mr. Charles E. Watkins in 1944. Watkins, 25, came to work as a saw mill laborer in 1910 and likely worked in the timber land in that section. Other residents who lived at Bodie included Elsie Harvey, Phyllis Shaw and Lena Gebber.

Today, there were six addresses on Bodie Road, and the oldest residence listed was built in 1930, while the other five were built in the 1970s and 1980s. There is a cabin near the tracks that is dilapidated from the weather and years of disuse.

One event that happened at Bodie Siding took place in 1947, when there was a derailment of four cars. There were no injuries, and a railroad wrecker came to clear the scene. (*La Grande Observer, Dec. 4, 1947, pg. 1*) Besides this account, very little was printed about Bodie. However, a much more interesting story of this site involves its earlier history when it was known as Casey Siding (1890s to 1936), named after landowner John Daniel Casey, a prominent lumberman, mercantile owner and Hilgard's mayor. (*1935 Metsker Map*)

J. D. Casey was born May 8, 1860 in Derryfinnan, Cork County, Ireland and came to Eastern Oregon in 1880. (*1900 Federal Census*) Called "the lumberman of Hilgard," he founded Casey Lumber Mill and interests in Meacham. (*La Grande Observer, Dec. 19, 1911, pg. 5*) Of course, he owned timber land in Section 7 where Bodie community was established.

An *1895 Oregon survey map* of Section 7 indicated there was a "house" located about a quarter mile from the Casey Siding, which may have been the railroad station house.

"That house was probably the telegrapher's house," said retired railroader Carroll Lester. "They had the pole line along the track, and that was your phone line, and you did your telegrapher work."

In time that was phased out. "It is understood that the OR&N will discontinue the use of telephone operators at Casey Siding." (*La Grande Observer, Jan. 21, 1919, pg. 6*) In 1900, Casey became the General Manager of the new 45-mile stretch on the Oregon-Washington Railroad and Navigation Company's line between Hilgard and Granite. (*Railroad Gazette, Feb. 9, 1900, pg. 111*)

Casey's business continued to expand in 1904 as mentioned in the article below:

"J.D. Casey, mayor of Hilgard, was a business visitor today. He has partially completed arrangements to start a lumber yard at Adams. He is operating two of the largest sawmills in the Blue mountains aside from the Perry mills. He owns a large tract of timber land near Meacham, which will be sawed next year, if his plans are carried out." (*East Oregonian, Dec. 3, 1904, pg. 7*)

Two years later he relocated his family to Pendleton "for the purpose of taking advantage of Pendleton's excellent schools." *(East Oregonian, Sept. 22, 1906, pg. 10)* He also wanted to take advantage of hauling his own timber from Hilgard, as the following newspaper announcement demonstrates.

"Colonel J.D. Casey of Hilgard was a business visitor in the city (La Grande) last night. Mr. Casey has built up an extensive lumber business and was here in the interest of that business. He will purchase a new engine here that is 120 horse-power that is guaranteed to haul 20,000 feet of logs at the rate of three miles an hour over a grade of five percent. This new traction will facilitate his large enterprise immensely." *(La Grande Observer, April 14, 1906, pg. 7)*

One year later, another article wrote of his continued success as a lumberman.

"J.D. Casey, of Hilgard, who handles about one-half of the wood output from the (Blue) mountains, received yesterday an order from a Walla Walla brick yard for 200 cords at $5 per cord. This was evidently considered a liberal offer and would have been a couple of months ago. There is no wood in the mountains that can now be had at any price, with the single exception of white fir, which is considered the most inferior of all woods. But even the white fir is taken when no other kind is available. *(La Grande Star, East Oregonian, Aug. 14, 1907, pg 7)* Casey was described in 1912 as "mayor, mill owner and principal citizen of Hilgard..." *(La Grande Observer, March 2, 1912, pg. 9)*

The year 1912 was pivotal as Casey and two lumbermen were approached by August J. Stange, native of Merrill, Wisconsin. Stange and other Midwestern lumbermen just incorporated Mt. Emily Timber Company in May 1912, and they were looking for timber land to buy. They made a great offer for Casey's timber land holdings.

"J. D. McKennon, of La Grande, J.D. Casey of Hilgard and the Rugg brothers of Pendleton are the principal individuals who disposed of their holdings. Stange has already bought up large areas of timber and the erection of a sawmill near or in La Grande is the supposed consequence of the extensive timber purchases. The precise figures are not given, but are estimated to be about $250,000. The deal is one of the very biggest ever recorded in this county." *(East Oregonian, Jan. 5, 1912, pg. 5)*

In his personal life, John D. Casey married Jennie Ama Scott on June 20, 1889, and they had five children, all born in Hilgard: Nora Estelle Hawes (1890-1985), Edgar Casey (1891-1896), Jennie L. (1893-1919, Influenza), John "Jack" Michael Casey (1896-1930), May Helen Robnett (1901-1960). *(ancestry.com, Thompson Tree)*

John D. Casey lost his wife Jennie Scott Casey in death on September 18, 1930 and ten days later, he lost his only living son, John Michael Casey, on September 28, 1930 to typhoid pneumonia. John Michael Casey had been working with his father in the lumber business in Meacham.

John D. Casey died on July 20, 1936 at age 76 years, 2 months and 10 days at St. Anthony's Hospital in Pendleton and was buried at Hilgard Cemetery in the family plot with his wife, Jennie and children: Edgar and John Michael. Little daughter Jennie L. Casey died in Portland on December 1, 1919 of the Spanish Influenza. It is presumed she received a burial there as she is not found on any online list of burials in Union or Umatilla county cemeteries. (ancestry.com)

Two children survived him: Mrs. (Nora) Roy Hawes of Meacham and Mrs. (May) Elmo Eugene Robnett of Bonneville along with 15 grandchildren. *(La Grande Observer, July 20, 1936, pg. 6)* His daughter, May Robnett, was later interred at the family plot at Hilgard Cemetery.

Bond Lane - This road #124A is 2.85 miles long in Township 3S R38E Section 22 of the La Grande District. It exits Highway 30, intersects Pierce Road and ends at Wright Road in rural Island City in the Hot Lake territory.

According to Cecil DeLong, 80, who was born on this road and lived on this road all his life, the road has always been called "Bond" after a farmer and his wife by that name, who lived on the far east end of the road. The Bond house was still there in 2018, but quite dilapidated. *(Cecil DeLong interview, April 18, 2018)*

Research in the *La Grande Observer* shows evidence that an Island City farmer by the name of Charles Wesley Bond lived there.

Confirming this is one article in the *Tuesday, February 15, 1917 issue of the La Grande Observer, pg. 4,* which stated: "Charles W. Bond Buys 640 Acres for $40,000." It continued, "One of the large deals of the season was consummated last week when the Eastern Oregon Realty Company sold 640 acres near Hot Lake to Charles W. Bond of La Grande for $40,000. The farm property is described in the deed as follows: East half of section 20 and west half of section 21, township 3 south, range 39 east." (End of article)

Charles Wesley Bond was born in Lawrenceburg, Anderson County, Kentucky on September 10, 1869, and he had been a resident of Union and Baker counties for 38 years combined.

During his marriage to Martha Elizabeth Herndon, they became parents to nine children: Lester, Elizabeth, Christine, Charles, Alvin, Dudley, Vergella, Champ and Turner. Of the nine, six were born in Anderson County, Kentucky, and the last three were born in the state of Oregon. The youngest, Turner, was the only child born in La Grande, Oregon (March 11, 1914).

Charles Wesley was known primarily as a farmer in Union County, and he died at the age of 77 on Sunday, December 1, 1946, after hospitalization and a three day illness. Services were held at Snodgrass funeral home and burial took place in Baker.

He was survived by his wife, Martha Elizabeth (Herndon) Bond, and seven children: Lester H. Bond and Mrs. Elizabeth Badsky, Haines; Mrs. S.O. Ledridge, Island City; Wesley Bond, La Grande; Mrs.

Kenneth Boyer and Champ Bond, Haines, and Turner Bond, Toledo, Oregon. He had 22 grandchildren and 1 great grandchild at the time of his death. *(La Grande Observer, Dec. 2, 1946, pg. 5)*

Booth Lane - Originally spelled Boothe, this road #126 was most often called Sam Boothe Lane and sometimes Boothe's Lane. It runs east and west 12.18 miles across the Grande Ronde Valley about a mile north of Island City. It is located in Township 2S R38E Section 28 in the La Grande and Union maintenance districts. (See also Couch Lane entry)

Booth Lane was named after Samuel Smith Boothe (1846-1921), born in Elm, Putnam County, Missouri, the son of Luther Jackson Boothe (b. 5/05/1819; d.11/02/1892) and Mary Ann Boothe (b. 3/08/1820; d.12/28/1899). The parents are buried in Ackles Cemetery on Mt. Glen Road north of La Grande.

Sam was a well-known pioneer and homesteader who farmed and resided on this road. He was married twice while he lived in this valley, first in 1869 to Nancy Eveline Wyatt in the city of Union; and in 1886 to Cora Gaines Dunnington in the city of Union, Oregon.

The *October 2, 1903 La Grande Observer, pg 4* stated: "Sam Boothe, the gentleman after whom the famous Boothe Lane received its name, was in the city yesterday. Mr. Boothe now resides near Union, having purchased a small place there. He says he has plenty of hogs, turkeys and good drinking water and is living a happy, easy life."

Boothe Lane had a road reputation which was described in the *February 4, 1904 La Grande Observer* as follows: "The indications now are that we are going to have a thaw, in which event there will be mud and the annual wail about Boothe's Lane."

But Boothe Lane became famous for another reason too. Samuel Booth sold his farm on Booth Lane to Walter M. Pierce (1861-1954), an enterprising wheat farmer, who became the 17th Governor of Oregon (1923-1927) and a congressman beginning in 1932. *(The Oregon History Project of the Oregon Historical Society)*

The Walter Pierce home, a white, boxy, two story structure was built in the 1890s and is located about a quarter mile west of Highway 82 on Booth Lane looking south.

Walter Pierce is likely the most famous person who ever resided on Booth Lane. In 1930, the Pierce home library held 4,000 books because the ex-governor was a ravenous reader, taking a few books in his briefcase everywhere he traveled.

He retired from politics in 1942 and wrote his memoirs, covering sixty years in public life. He returned to ranch life in Umatilla County. Walter Pierce died in 1954 at age 92.

The house on Booth Lane was vacated sometime in the 1990s and is currently owned by Allen Case, who lives next door to the home. Its past grandeur is still evident today, but in its long disuse, it has fallen into neglect. Allen Case has been residing on Booth Lane since 1950, and is the son of Elmer Case of the historic Case Brothers of Union County, including brothers Homer, Elmer, John and Wren Case, century farmers. *(Allen Case interview, 2017)*

One interesting post script about Booth Lane was that in 1865 a petition to the county court was drafted by farmer Frederick Proebstel's attorneys, complaining that the "road from Oro Dell to Walla Walla Road" (Booth Lane) was going through the improved part of his property, and he wanted compensation in the amount of $1,200.

On the east end of Booth Lane was another noteworthy residence, the Merrell C. Jasper Century Farm. After 16 years in the Willamette Valley, Missouri pioneers, Merrell C. Jasper and his wife Nancy J. (Means) Jasper, along with their eight children, retraced their wagon tracks across the Cascades and through the gritty, dusty Columbia Plateau to the rugged Blue Mountains to Union County, Oregon.

With full wagons and cattle following behind, herded by eleven-year-old William Robert Jasper, the family arrived in the Grande Ronde Valley and filed their homestead claim for 160 acres near Cove. Since then five generations have worked the soil of that farm, and at the 1985 Union County Fair, John T. "Bud" and Edna (Jasper) Jones received their well-earned century farm certificate registered with the Oregon State Century Farm and Ranch Program in Salem.

Merrell C. Jasper was born December 5, 1827 in Pulaski County, Kentucky, and later he migrated to Missouri. At age 25, Merrell and his brother Andrew and possibly other relatives, migrated across the Oregon Trail to western Oregon, passing by the uninhabited, grassy Grande Ronde Valley for the more acclaimed Willamette Valley.

There in Benton County, he married sixteen-year-old Nancy Jane Means on July 24, 1853. During their marriage, Nancy gave birth to eight children: James, Sylvina, William Robert, Susan Elvira, twins Nancy Catherine and Martha Emaline, Rhoda J., and George M. Jasper, born in 1865.

He and Nancy decided to pull up stakes there and go back to the Grande Ronde Valley, where Merrell Jasper commenced general farming near Cove. He pastured cattle, and they were content with their lives. However, just two years later on June 2, 1870, his wife Nancy died. She left in Merrell's charge seven of their eight children, four of whom were under the age of ten years. His eldest, Sylvina, married George G. Gray on February 22, 1874. She agreed to Gray's proposal under the stipulation that she could bring with her into the marriage, her little brother George, age 9, to raise. To this George Gray agreed.

Merrell remarried shortly thereafter to a widow with nine children of her own. Her name was Emily Jane (Rinehart) Morton, born in September 1834. They had two children of their own together, Frank and Willard, making Emily the mother of eleven children.

During his farming career, Merrell kept good records on every aspect of his farm operation. His assets were generous, and he died on April 9, 1885, at the age of 57 years and 4 months.

Five years earlier his son William "Bill" Robert Jasper married Susan "Clara" Kendall, and they had two children, Franklin Merrell and Edward Doak.

The day came when their son Edward took over the farming operation. He was a 1906 graduate of University of Oregon Eugene with a bachelor of arts degree. He wanted to continue his study in law, but he was called home to help on the farm because his father's arthritis was preventing him for doing all the work himself.

On the farm, Bill and Ed raised grains, alfalfa hay and had pasture for their cattle. Life went on for the Jasper family, and Ed gradually took on a prominent role in running the place. Bill and Clara retired from the farm in 1921, and they moved to Island City. Clara died of small pox at the age of 71 years on July 10, 1931. Bill survived her by just over a year. He died at the age of 75 on September 19, 1932.

In 1917, Ed married Florence McDonald, and they had four children: Donald, Margaret Edna (Jones), Rhoda J. Dawson and Mary Alice Johnson.

Ed was way ahead of his time with some of his ideas on products that could be made from wheat. In 1925, Ed Jasper created "health nuggets"—good idea, but in 1925 people weren't drawn to the word health, so he changed the name to wheat nuggets. He made his own wheat flour called Jasper's Granulated Graham, available in five pound bags for every housewife to take home and place in her kitchen stores. *(La Grande Observer, Nov. 16, 1927)*

The product grew in popularity and a lot of planning went into its distribution. The business was growing, and then everything came to a sudden halt on December 4, 1935, when Ed Jasper died of pneumonia. He had been standing outside the house in the rain talking to a business colleague too long, and he came inside soaking wet and chilled to the bone. Soon afterward he developed pneumonia and it overtook him. He was just 53 years old, and without him to handle the business affairs, his widow was quite lost as to what to do, so she sold the Jasper mill to C. W. Bond, but he wasn't able to keep it going.

Ed Jasper's death was a great loss to the family and to the agricultural industry of Union County. He was such an enterprising man with a futuristic mind, cut down in the prime of his life. It would be many decades later before any company came up with granola bars or breakfast bars.

Ed Jasper's daughter Edna (Jasper) Jones took over the farm in 1946 after she married John T. "Bud" Jones on November 6, 1943 in New Orleans. Bud was a dedicated farmer with a focus on soil conservation, something he was recognized for in 1991 and 1999. He also had a lot to do with getting the Ag Center built in Island City, Edna said in a 2002 interview.

Bud and Edna loved farming and lived a full life. They left an imprint on this earth that anyone traveling east on Booth Lane can see. It's a wind break, a long row of trees and shrubs planted with meaningful design. They flank the road almost regally, leading to their residence. This serves as a reminder to us all that we need to care for this earth, conserve its resources and show appreciation for the gift of wealth it imparts to us.

Bowman Loop - Formerly Steers-Bowman Road #83 in 1945. This is a 5.03-mile loop located in Township 3N R39E Section 25 in the Elgin maintenance district. It is located at the end of Palmer Junction Road, and both ends of the loop connect with Moses Creek Lane.

On one end of Bowman Loop was the residence of Sarah "Sadie" Ellen (Althiser) Steers, mentioned in the *1930 Federal Census*. At that time, she was operating a rooming house from her residence on this loop.

She was born on August 8, 1869 in Brown County, Illinois, and moved with her parents and siblings to Calwood, Callaway County, Missouri, where she met William Andrew Schaffer.

Sadie married William Schaffer on October 3, 1888 in Callaway County, Missouri. During their marriage they had four children: Ada (1889-1932), Opal (1891-1988), Harry Marvin (1894-1969), and Julia Inice (1899-1990).

She then relocated to Union County, Oregon, and on April 13, 1908 in La Grande, Oregon, she married Leroy Nelson Steers (1872-1948). They were listed on the *1910 Federal Census* as living on North Fourth Street in La Grande with three of her children, Ada, Harry and Julia Schaffer.

However, in a *1917 City Directory of Union County*, Sadie Steers was listed as a farmer out on Palmer Junction. She lived in a log cabin on her property. She was a member of the Rockwall Grange in rural Elgin. She might have been married to George D. Holland in 1929 briefly. When Sadie lived on Steers-Bowman Loop, she was remembered for the sun bonnets that she used to wear when she was outdoors.

After 1946, it appears that she began to sell off her farm land. Sometime after 1953, she moved to her last residence in La Grande at 1325 T Avenue, the home of her daughter, Mrs. Opal Miller, her caregiver.

She died July 1, 1958 at age 88 in the Grande Ronde Hospital after an extended illness. She had been a resident of Union County for about 50 years. *(Obit., La Grande Observer, July 2, 1958, pg. 8)* Following her death, she was buried in Summerville Cemetery. *(Findagrave.com; Maxine Bowman Hopkins interview, June 10, 2019)*

When the county roads were renamed in 1988, the Steers part of the road name was dropped, leaving only Bowman Loop as the name. However, historically, Sadie Steers lived on this road about 30 years longer than the Bowman family.

Bowman Loop was named after a cattle man named Cecil Conrad Bowman, who came to the Elgin district from Umapine, Oregon by 1940. He was born on March 11, 1894 in Stateline, Oregon, and he died on January 23, 1957 in Pendleton. He was buried at the I.O.O.F. Cemetery in Milton-Freewater, Oregon.

He married Alice Sarah Rambo (1894-1987) in Umapine, Oregon on January 1, 1912. They had a marriage license announcement printed in the *East Oregonian, Dec. 22, 1911, pg. 10.* During their marriage, they had 10 children: Leonard, B. Vernice, Mildred, Iva, Ina, Alvin, Deliah, Virgil, Lorraine and Velma. The family moved around a bit from Umapine to Weiser, Idaho, to Milton, Oregon, and then to Mann Creek, Idaho.

Then in 1935, Cecil Bowman moved to a ranch in rural Elgin on what became Bowman Loop, with his wife Sarah and some of their children, including Virgil, their youngest son. The family was noted on the *1940 Federal Census*.

Their son, Alvin Cecil Bowman was born September 22, 1919 in Milton, Umatilla County, Oregon, the sixth child in the family. When he was 18, Alvin Bowman married Beverly Jean Grimes, 16, (1923-2010) on February 23, 1938, in Walla Walla, Washington. That June, they had a baby girl named Beverly "Maxine" Bowman, and after her birth they were blessed with four more girls: Darleen, Kathleen, Debra and Denise.

By 1940, Alvin, Beverly and Maxine, 2, were living in the city of Pendleton where Alvin worked as a laborer for the Van Patten Lumber Company. They came to Elgin about 1944, and Alvin took over the operation of his father's ranch there. His father, Cecil, returned to Pendleton, where he lived the remainder of his life.

Maxine Bowman recalled her early life in Elgin. She attended first grade through third grade at a country school called Palmer Valley School. She remembered picking wild flowers with Mrs. Steers, she said.

The Bowman family then moved into town, where Maxine attended Stella Mayfield School for her fourth grade. Her fourth grade teacher was Miss Snorr, who was most attentive to Maxine's education and helped her to catch up academically with her other classmates.

The Alvin Bowman family left Elgin permanently about 1951 in Maxine's eighth grade. The family moved four more times to Coeur d'Alene, Idaho, Harrison and Post Falls, Idaho and ultimately to Jacksonville, Oregon where Maxine graduated in 1956. She got married the next year to a man she knew for 12 days, and they had 60 happy years together. "I've had the most wonderful life," she laughed.

Maxine mentioned that the Bowman family are not related to Bowman Trucking or to the Bowman-Hicks Lumber Company. *(Maxine Bowman Hopkins interview, June 9, 2019)*

Brooks Road - Formerly Ruckman-Imbler-Brooks Lane, as far back as 1945, this road #35 runs a length of 2.06 miles and is located in Township 1S R39E Section 8 in the Imbler maintenance district.

This road begins at the north city limits of Imbler going due north and terminating near the J. W. Tuttle property as it reaches Courtney Lane. The name Ruckman and Imbler were dropped, and Brooks remained the most appropriate historical name for this road.

Brooks Road is named after early pioneers to this valley, Samuel Leonard Brooks (1846-1931) and his wife Mary (Wade) Brooks (1845-1927), who migrated to the Grande Ronde Valley in 1873 from Iowa, starting out by train and finishing the last leg of the journey by wagon.

Samuel Brooks was born March 19, 1846 near Columbus, Ohio, to John Henry and Hannah (Rockwell) Brooks, natives of Vermont and Ohio respectively. The Brooks family moved in 1857 to Seymour, Wayne County, Iowa, where their son Samuel met and married Miss Mary Jane Wade on December 10, 1868.

Miss Wade was born on Oct. 29, 1845 in Monongalia County, West Virginia, the sixth of twelve children born to George Irvin Wade (1815-1896) and Ann Eakin, originally of Ohio and Pennsylvania. She moved with her parents to Seymour, Iowa, where she met Samuel Brooks. The newlyweds lived there for the next four years before migrating to Northeast Oregon.

Their migration started by train to Kelton, Utah, and then by wagon to the Grande Ronde Valley, where the Brooks eventually settled on and worked part of the Thomas Courtney land one and a half miles north of Imbler.

By 1912, Brooks had acquired 1,500 acres of prime farm land, 500 of it of it was sown in wheat, oats and barley. In those years, the land reportedly required no irrigation, holding ample ground moisture. On summer fallow land, he was able to raise 40 to 50 bushels of grain per acre. The rest of his land was in pasture. Samuel Brooks engaged in raising registered heavy draft horses, particularly Clydesdales.

On his property (Brooks Road) in 1896, construction commenced on their majestic, three story Victorian home with its ten rooms and their barn. The construction of the house was personally supervised by Mary Jane Brooks so that all details were to her liking. The house still stands in 2021, albeit badly neglected. The barn was in bad shape and lit afire by an arsonist.

Five Brooks children were raised in this home: Ida May (Mrs. W. H. Hawley) of McEwen, Baker County; Rachel (Mrs. H. C. Bidwell) of North Powder; Anna (Mrs. Michael Royes) of Summerville; Stella (Mrs. H. H. Huron) of Imbler; and Wade Brooks.

Samuel Brooks was an active member of the Farmers' Union, and was one of the most successful men of his community. He was regarded as a good citizen and gained the respect of a large number of close friends. *(Oregon Pictorial and Biographical Deluxe Supplement, 1912)*

Samuel Brooks died at nearly 85 years of age and Mary (Wade) Brooks at 81 years of age. They are both interred in the Summerville Cemetery, along with John Brooks (1879-1893) and Enid Brooks (1892-1894), possible victims of a diphtheria epidemic that claimed many young lives in Union County in the 1890s.

The descendants of Stella (Brooks) Huron are today's operators of the farm, and it is registered as a Century Farm with the Oregon Historical Society.

Brush Creek Road - This road is a descriptive name after Brush Creek in the Ladd Canyon area.

Buchanan Lane - This lane is located in Township 3S R38E Section 4, designated road #117 in the La Grande maintenance district, and it runs 1.59 miles.

It was named after William Dixon Buchanan (1829-1906) and his wife, Ellen Jane (Cullen) Buchanan (1829-1913), who left Tama of Tama County, Iowa, in April 1865 as part of a 75-wagon train.

William's original migration destination was California, but after five dusty months on the Oregon Trail, by the time his family reached the Grande Ronde Valley, it was already September and the cold, rainy season began, so they settled there.

The Buchanans had two wagons equipped for the journey west. William, Ellen and five of their children: Josephine, 12, William, 10, Harriet, 8, Joe, 5, and Amanda, 1 year, all rode in the same wagon pulled by oxen. The other wagon was also pulled by oxen, but it was driven by the two oldest boys, James Andrew, nearly grown, and David Monroe, 15. Three milking cows were tied to the rear of the wagons.

Coming across the trail, they did not encounter any harassment from the Indians, but the smaller train behind them had 63 head of cattle driven off and stolen by Indians. That train's captain thought the risk was too high to chase after the band of thieves. Instead, he sent a scout ahead to the Buchanan's train, asking for any extra cattle they could spare to help them pull their wagons. William Buchanan sold two of his oxen and replaced them with his two milk cows under the yoke. The third cow he sold because its feet had become so sore.

The attack on the train behind them only emphasized the need to take precautions. They camped in a circle and had a guard on watch at all times. For the most part, camp life was a time for women to wash clothes, bake loaves of bread and cook other foods. To relax, the travelers played music and the young ones danced. William played his violin, accompanied by players on guitar, banjo, the Jew's harp and harmonica.

As they continued their journey, one party after another bid their farewells and departed from the train as they reached their planned destination. Finally, at Pike's Peak, Colorado, the last party left the train, leaving only the Buchanans to continue to Boise.

For the next week, they traveled alone, until they saw in the distance another small train with two wagons carrying Mr. and Mrs. B. H. Lewis and family, and their son-in-law and daughter, Mr. and Mrs. Brooks Campbell, who were just married. They were headed for the Grande Ronde Valley, so they traveled together to Boise, where they rested their cattle and replenished their supplies.

When they arrived to the Grande Ronde Valley in September, the Buchanans decided to remain there to farm and raise stock. William established a farm east of Island City in the grange hall district, and they farmed there for 20 years before they moved to Harney County, Oregon. *(La Grande Observer, May 14, 1934, pg. 3; and July 12, 1938 pg. 4 and March 1, 1932, pg. 2)*

William D. Buchanan was born Oct. 9, 1829 in Howland Township, Trumbull County, Ohio. He had an older brother named Johnson Buchanan (1818-1849), and after that brother died prematurely in 1849, William married his widow, Ellen Cullen Buchanan, on March 21, 1850, and he raised his brother's son as his own. *(Marriage Registry of the Wabash Circuit Court of Indiana)*

The child's name was James Andrew Buchanan, born July 2, 1848 in Ohio, named after his grandfather, James Monroe Buchanan (1783-1864).
His mother Ellen (Cullen) Buchanan was born April 23, 1829, a native of Erie County, Pennsylvania. William and Ellen raised ten children: James Andrew Buchanan (1848-1911, son of Johnson Buchanan and Ellen Cullen); David Monroe Buchanan (1850-1894), Mary Josephine Spencer (1853-1936), William Thomas Buchanan Jr. (1855-1923), Harriet Jane Harrison (1857-1935)), Joseph Warren Buchanan (1860-1939), Albert Buchanan (1862-1863), Amanda Ellen Martin (1864-1936), Eliza Etta Martin (1866-1941), George Lemon Buchanan (1870-1925).

William Dixon Buchanan died April 29, 1906 in Harney County, Oregon, the address of his last residence. Ellen Buchanan died January 5, 1913 in Island City, Oregon. Both are interred at the Island City Cemetery.

Three children had predeceased Ellen, (Albert-1863; David Monroe-1894; and James A.-1911) and the others were at her bedside when the end came. *(La Grande Observer, Jan. 7, 1913, pg. 3)*

Bushnell Road - This road #11 comes off the south end of Twelfth Street in La Grande. It is located in Township 3S R38E Section 8 and runs 5.75 miles in length. It is named after Elmer Nathan Bushnell, a resident of the La Grande area since 1907.

When he first came to La Grande, he was a farmer, but then as the years passed he phased out of stock raising and farming and got into the auto wrecking business, which he handed down to his son Alfred.

Bushnell was born October 26, 1869 in Sprague, New London, Connecticut to John Fuller and Anna

(McGrannell) Bushnell.   He had been a resident of Union county for 36 years until his death on Tuesday, May 18, 1943 at the age of 73 years. His death was the result of a long illness. Burial took place at the Summerville Cemetery. Surviving him were his wife Elizabeth at their home 505 C Avenue, La Grande; one daughter, Winnie Bushnell of Seattle, Washington; a son Alfred of La Grande and one brother Herman J. Bushnell of St. Joe, Missouri. *(La Grande Observer, May 19, 1943, pg. 5)*

Bushnell's mother was foreign born in Ireland/Scotland, and she came to America in 1872. *(1910 Federal Census)* On his father's side of the family, the Bushnells, Elmer represents the eighth generation born in America. Elmer could boast that his relatives arrived in America in April 1635 from England, settling in Guilford, Connecticut. The first Bushnell to be born on American soil was his fifth great-grandfather, Joseph Bushnell, born 1651 in Connecticut.

The Bushnell family can trace their lineage back to William E. Bushnell (1524-1564) in England. Counting William, they can account for five generations who lived in England and eight generations after that to Elmer Bushnell (1869-1943), who were born in Connecticut.

In this book, the Bushnells rival the Owsleys, also from England, in their early settlement in America and recounting of more than a dozen generations in their family history. Not a lot of families can say this about their genealogy searches.

Our subject Elmer Bushnell was married to Elizabeth "Lizzie" Freel, and some records say they married in 1904 *(1910 Federal Census)*. They had four children: Elmer G., Winnie, Alfred, and Lillie. It appears that Elmer died in childhood.

The *1910 Federal Census* is the only source that name Winnie and Alfred as adopted children. Winnie was born in Oregon in 1901 and Alfred in Helena, Montana in 1904. *(Certificate of Delayed Birth Registration for Alfred, 1942)* Lillie was born in Idaho in 1911 and is noted on the *1920 Federal Census* as being 9 years old, but she doesn't show up ten years later in the 1930 census.

The family settled in La Grande, Oregon and started out as farmers. In a *1914 City Directory of Union County*, Elmer and Lizzie are listed as farmers with a residence at 201 Benton Avenue. They started to build up their acreage and raise stock.

In 1915, Elmer bought the O. W. Moon 160-acre farm four miles from La Grande, giving him a combined 480 acres that he used for stock raising. In 1919, he advertised 640 acres for rent or sale. In 1920, he advertised he would do plowing for others.

There were other mentions of Elmer Bushnell in the *La Grande Observer* as follows: In December 1920, he had a five-room house on four lots for rent in La Grande. In 1933, road work was scheduled to be done on Bushnell Lane. Then in 1936, Bushnell bought stock of Thompson's used auto parts and moved them to Bushnell's Wrecking House on W. Division Street in La Grande.

The *1940 Federal Census* indicated that Elmer, 71, worked as a janitor at a department store in La Grande. After Bushnell's death in 1948, his son, Alfred took over the business.

Alfred was born March 20, 1904 in Helena, Montana. Some records say his middle name was Jay, others say Jerry. He married Mrs. Nettie Loie (Greer) Finley, a widow.

He died prematurely at age 48 on March 8, 1953 at home following a heart attack and was interred at the Summerville Cemetery. His widow applied for and received an upright marble headstone for him due to his military service. His parents, who are buried nearby have no headstones. *(Summerville Cemetery records)*

Alfred's widow, Nettie Loie (Greer) Bushnell (1898-1999) was living on Division Street in La Grande at the time. Alfred's obituary stated he was born at New Castle, Wyoming, and that he came to La Grande in 1909. Alfred was a member of La Grande Aerie 259, Fraternal Order of Eagles. Surviving him were his wife, Nettie; a son Elwyn, Pendleton; a daughter, Donna, Aurora and a sister, Miss Winnie Bushnell, San Francisco.

Nettie Bushnell died in 1999 and was interred at the Hillcrest Cemetery in La Grande.

There are seven land owners on Bushnell Road today. Only one home on the road dates back to 1910 and a barn built in 1900.

Campbell Drive - This very short, public unmaintained drive is located off Highway 237 (Jasper Street) near Cove in Township 3S R40E Section 16. It is named after Larry L. and Karen J. Campbell, co-owners of the property when it was subdivided in 2004. *(Union County records)*

Canyon View Lane - This lane is west of Spout Springs on National Forest land. Some of the homes overlook the canyons of Woodward Creek or the North Fork of the Umatilla River, thus its name.

Carroll Lane - This private lane located Township 3S R39E Section 4 was named after J. Frank Carroll, who lived there and had an orchard. He was born August 14, 1899 and died on March 24, 1956.

His parents, Michael Stephen (1863-1924) and Alma J. were early settlers (1888). Michael is listed in a 1905 business directory as a fruit grower in May Park, and his son, Frank, eventually inherited the orchard.

According to long-time resident, Linda Peterson, Carroll was the name chosen by a majority of the then residents on the road because of the Carroll family history in the area. A well that used to water the orchard is still on the Coleman property. *(Linda Peterson interview, May 1, 2018)*

Carter Road - This road #33 is located off Booth Lane, and it was called Carter Road by at least April 13, 1916. It is located in Township 2S R39E Section 27, a 2.25 mile long county road in the Union district.

It is named after Marion Leslie (M. L.) Carter (1858-1935). He was born December 27, 1858 in Maryland, the son of Daniel and Martha E. (Hanna) Carter. Daniel Carter died in 1865, and Martha moved to Union County in 1876.

Marion Carter married Elma "Dora" Couch on March 15, 1882. They had five children, one died in infancy and a daughter died 1918. Dora Carter died May 8, 1927, and was buried in the Island City Cemetery.

Marion was a farmer on the Sand Ridge, but was also noted for his poetry. He died December 8, 1935 just as a book of his poetry was being readied for publishing at Metropolitan Publishing in Portland, Oregon. His son, Clarence, finished getting the book ready for publication.

Marion's story of the "Red Pepper" School is told in the *La Grande Observer, August 2, 1927*. His interest in roads was shown by an article in the *La Grande Observer of March 27, 1916*.

Case Road - Formerly Case Lane according to the *1935 Metsker Map of Union County*. This road #79 runs 1.50 miles in Township 2S R39E Section 8 in the La Grande maintenance district. It is named after century farmers William Jasper Case and his son, John Case.

William was born September 13, 1868 in Boone County, Arkansas, and he came to Union County, Oregon in 1898. Before he farmed, he was a teacher at Dry Creek School on Summerville Road north of Summerville, Alicel School and other one-room schoolhouses in the area.
He married Miss Ella Van Blokland, 24, on September 11, 1901. Her father, John Van Blokland, helped the couple purchase 160 acres from Mr. and Mrs. J. H. Hughes. A two story, four bedroom house was on the property already, adequate for their immediate needs. This became known later as the Case Century Farm on Case Road.

In January 1903, W. J. and Ella bought out her father's half interest in the property, and they became the sole owners of their farm. That same year Ella had their first child, John Henry. After him she had three more children: Elmer (1907), Vera Jane (1909) and Hugh (1911).

A period of expansion occurred, including farm buildings, a smokehouse, a blacksmith shop and a tank house. In 1914, they finished building their larger new home. Sadly, though, during its construction, their toddler, Hugh, had an accident that took his precious life. Hugh died on June 7, 1913.

The house was grand, having five bedrooms upstairs and five downstairs, creating 2800 square feet of living space. Coincidentally, in 1913, electrical power was brought through the Alicel area. This welcome amenity, along with indoor plumbing, made the house notably modern.

After this W. J. built a horse barn and machine shed. This horse barn was built over the course of a year (1914-1915) and it was so well built with mortise and peg construction that it's still standing today, over a century later.

In 1917, the Case family welcomed their last child into the family, William "Wren" Case. With a full house, the Case family worked hard to make their farm grow and prosper, and once again new construction was planned. This time they built a wood shed and an ice house in 1920, followed by a garage during the years 1926 and 1927.

The thirties brought the Great Depression, but the Cases managed to hold onto their property while others were being foreclosed due to a lack of money to pay the monthly mortgage. The Cases put most of their fields into alfalfa for hay and they increased their dairy herd for the production and sale of milk and other dairy products. Excess hay was sold and delivered for $8 a ton. Surely, adapting to the times helped them survive. They still owned the farm, although it was heavily mortgaged.

On May 17, 1931, Ella Case died and her sons Homer and Wren stayed on the farm, forming a partnership with their father, W. J. Case. It was called W. J. Case & Sons. Later another son Elmer returned to the farm and joined the business, and finally John Case did the same. The sons eventually bought out their father's interest in the farm, and together they built a family farming business called "Case Brothers."

Son John purchased his father's original acreage as part of the cooperative effort of Case Brothers. John retired from farming in 1975, and rented the original 160 acre W. J. Case farm to his nephew, Rodney R. Case, Homer and Lola Case's son.

The W. J. and Ella Case property was established in 1901 and recognized as a Century Farm through the efforts of grandson Rodney and Wendy Case, who still reside on the original farm acres. The couple have ceased working the land and leased it out to other farmers, but they reside in the historic Case home.

The widow Lola Case, 93, whose home was on the south end of Case Road, died September 12, 2014. Her home was rented out. *(Allen Case interview, May 22, 2018; Rodney/Wendy Case and Lola Case interviews, August 2001)*

Catherine Creek Lane - This road #141 is only .71 miles long and located in Township 5S R41E Section 21 in the Union maintenance district.

The creek itself was first named by the Native Americans as **Sac sac' hin ma**, meaning canyon of the fish hawk. However in 1861 or 1862, the very first European settlers to this valley named the creek Catherine as noted on a 1863 map of Union County.

Those first settlers along or near the creek were enumerated in an article called "Reminisces—A Talk about the Early Days of Union" in the *Oregon Scout, April 3, 1890 on page 1* written by C. F. Hinckley. They were Conrad Miller, Peter Coffin, Jabez S. Hinckley, Elisha Hiram Lewis, Mendel Crocker Israel, Frederick Nodine, John Andrew Jackson Chapman and D. S. Henry.

The article follows: "Mr. Peter Coffin and my father in the fall of 1862 located on Catherine Creek 320 acres of land on what is known as the Coffin Farm. Then, this was a wild Indian country, no settlement near, Powder River diggings (old Auburn) and Walla Walla being the nearest. There were only four settlers on Catherine Creek at that time, Mr. Conrad Miller, who settled on the Miller farm where the flouring mill now stands; Mr. E. H. Lewis, who still holds the fort on his original location, and is a hale and hearty old gentleman yet; Mr. M. C. Israel, who settled on the farm now owned by Mr. George Ames; and Mr. Fred Nodine, who located on the farm now known as the Swackhamer place in North Union. In the late fall of 1862, John Andrew Jackson Chapman and Mr. Henry located 320 acres of land this side of Catherine Creek, where the business part of Union is now located."

County historian Bernal D. Hug also listed the first six settlers along or near Catherine Creek. On the south side of the creek lived John Andrew Jackson Chapman and D. S. Henry. On the north side of Catherine Creek were Frederick Nodine and E. H. Lewis. Conrad Miller's place was west of E. H. Lewis and A. Busick's place was east of Frederick Nodine's place. *(History of Union County, Oregon, pg. 243-244)*

Any one of these men could have named Catherine Creek, especially someone like John Andrew Jackson Chapman, who reportedly named the town of Union.

"In the year 1862, a man by the name of John Chapman located a quarter section of land where the city of Union, Oregon now stands, says *the Republican*, and in the following year (1863), he employed Dave Thompson, now the Portland banker, but then a surveyor, to lay it out in town lots. It began at that period in the history of our country in which those questions which led up to the Civil War were being warmly discussed, Mr. Chapman, in deference to his patriotism and loyalty to his country, named his new town Union." *(Corvallis Gazette, Aug. 15, 1895, pg. 1)*

"Mr. J. A. J. Chapman understood surveying, so he helped everyone locate their claims in 1862, and when government surveyors came in the fall of 1863, they changed very few lines that Chapman had established." *(One Way Journey, by G. Walter Blacker, 1970, pg. 20)*

"David Thompson and his party of assistants, employed by the government, surveyed the Grande Ronde Valley in August, September and October of 1863, which was a very important step in the development of this new country, as up to this time there had always been the risk of losing your land to the squatters." *(One Way Journey, by G. Walter Blacker, 1970, pg. 22)*

It has always been held that Catherine Creek and the smaller tributary, Juliana Creek, were named after sisters from the same family; however, Juliana Creek has, at different times, been shown on road petition maps and county maps by other names. The county surveyor on all these road petitions was consistently Mr. Willis Skiff, but the road viewers were different people, which may account for the different creek names given at various times.

The following road petitions show the Juliana Creek with different names. Road petition #36 in April 1871 called it Elizabeth Creek. The various documents making up road petition #75 in February 20, 1876 refers to the same creek by three different names: Little Creek and July Ann Creek and Julia Ann Creek. Road petition #77 in March 7, 1876 called the creek again by the name Elizabeth Creek, and the documents making up road petition #81 in April 4, 1876 called the creek Little Creek and Juliana Creek.

All of the aforementioned petitions, except for #36, have the same legal description of starting and ending points of the road, so there is no doubt they are also talking about the same creek. In an September 19, 1885 issue of the *Oregon Scout*, it referred to this creek as Elizabeth Creek where supposedly some hogs died. Whoever named this creek was among the first settlers in this area. That may have been Frederick Nodine, who arrived in the valley on June 11, 1862. *(One Way Journal, G. Walter Blacker, pg. 13)* It was by late fall 1862 that he secured his own claim along Catherine creek and this smaller creek.

It is interesting that Catherine Creek bordered his land and the smaller creek ran right through it. That smaller creek, which some early records call Elizabeth Creek sounds very much like his wife's name Eliza Nodine.

One possible family that had female members named Catherine and Elizabeth was the James Hendershott family, who arrived to the valley in late fall of 1862. James had a mother named Catherine and two sisters named Catherine and Elizabeth. *(Goduck50 tree, ancestry.com)* It's possible that he named the larger creek Catherine and the smaller creek as Elizabeth after his own family members.

It's also possible that the creeks were named after French Canadian pioneer women, as the French settlement along Catherine Creek was there very early on in 1862, but the settlement didn't endure there. *(1867 Road Petition, Rd#16; See also Moses Creek Lane)*
The authors do not have solid evidence to nail down the namesake for Catherine or Juliana (Elizabeth) creeks, but they present reasonable possibilities. One thing is certain, however, the classic story that the creeks were named after sisters Catherine and Juliana Godley is not possible.

The reasoning for discrediting this classic story is based on the fact that the Godley family were not here in 1861-62 when Catherine Creek was named. Also, Thomas and M. E. Godley never had daughters named Catherine or Juliana, as the legend goes. (See Godley Road entry)

Perhaps this is why Mr. Dunham Wright did not go out on a limb to repeat this old story in the newspaper, but simply stated that Catherine creek was named after a pioneer woman. He played it safe.

Catherine Creek is 32.4 miles long and a tributary of the Grande Ronde River. It is the second-longest stream in the Grande Ronde Valley. Originating in the foothills of the Wallowa Mountains, it flows generally northwest through Catherine Creek State Park and the city of Union before joining the Grande Ronde River. *(Wikipedia; Oregon Geographical Names, pg. 138)*

The following article was written in the *La Grande Observer, Sept. 3, 1910, pg. 1,* titled "The Catherine Creek Road" which indicated the road was constructed before winter of 1910.

"W. O. Wigglesworth, who has the work of constructing the Catherine Creek road has had much experience along that line," says the *Union Scout*. "There are several hills to make, a lot of false rock work and the channel of Catherine Creek to change for almost a quarter of a mile.

At least two temporary crossings must be constructed all of which take time. When the road is completed it will be one of the finest drives on the coast and will be traveled by many people. It will also represent considerable engineering ability and good careful work.

It will shorten the distance from Union to the Catherine Creek regions by about a mile and a half. This road has been a long time coming but is now about here. Before the winter sets in, teams will be passing over this cutoff and everyone will be glad for the new road. So far the road has been built at a very small expense and the county will profit largely by the outlay. The *Scout* is in a position to know that the people are considerably indebted to the mayor, L. A. Wright, for this road. They are also indebted to Judge Henry, who has been a staunch friend and supporter of the road from the very start." [end of article]

Catherine Creek was more than just a creek in Union County, it was the site of an active sawmill that produced the lumber for these settlers' homes. "It is said that they used mostly cottonwood logs which were close at hand along the creek. They worked as a group and all helped on building each individual cabin. It was well into the winter (1862-63) before all were built," wrote historian Bernal D. Hug in *History of Union County, page 243*. In the early days, Catherine Creek was treated like a community, a place you could address on an envelope.

"Letters came to Union in early days directed to 'Catherine Creek, Grande Ronde Valley, Oregon, in care of C. Jacobs & Company, Walla Walla, W. T.' The mail was brought over on horseback, the carrier charging 75 cents for this trouble. It was three months before you could send a letter and receive an answer from the east. Mail went to Portland and then by steamer by the way of the Isthmus of Panama." *(Reminisces—A Talk about the Early Days of Union, Oregon Scout, April 3, 1890, pg. 1, by C. F. Hinckley)*

The research on Catherine Creek Lane, Catherine Creek, and Little Creek has been thorough; however, in spite of the effort, the namesake for Catherine Creek remains a history mystery.

Chadwick Lane - This public unmaintained road is located off Cove Highway 237 and provides access to 12 residences. It is located in Township 3S R40E Section 16 in the Union district, and it is only .30 miles long.

This lane is named after George Chadwick Sr. (1859-1924) and his wife, Alice Marie Smith (1856-1915).

George Chadwick was born on September 17, 1859 in Medina, Dane County, Wisconsin, the son of Rebecca Lesure (Lashur?), who was born in Pennsylvania, and Samuel Chadwick, who was born in England.

George's residential history shows that he lived in Medina at least through 1890. By 1900, the family had moved to Cove, Oregon. The *1910 Federal Census* lists George as a farmer and employer, owning his home free and clear.

He and Alice were married on March 19, 1884 in Dane County, Wisconsin, and during their marriage, they raised four children: Georgia Rebecca Kight (1889-1958), Hazel A. Borkgren (1891-1950), Lynn James Chadwick (1894-1962), and June Ella Richardson (1898-1996).

George Chadwick died on October 21, 1924 in Cove, and his burial took place in the city cemetery. *(ancestry.com)*

Chandler Loop - This road #13A is .42 miles in length and departs from and reconnects to Fruitdale Lane on the edge of La Grande. It is located in Township 2S R38E Section 33.

It is named after John Samuel Chandler of Wayne, Michigan. For many decades, this loop was simply referred to as Fruitdale and Route 1.

John S. Chandler was born February 5, 1838 in Wayne, Michigan, the son of Samuel (1813-1845) and Esther Hunt (1818-1884). John married Louisa Melinda Cooper in Flint, Michigan on February 8, 1864. She was born May 25, 1838 and died May 25, 1921. Both are interred at Island City Cemetery.

Their residence history shows that they lived in Michigan where the first two children were born, and then they moved to Denver, Nebraska, where the last three of their children were born.

His obituary printed in the *La Grande Observer, April 4, 1929, pg. 1*, stated that he had been a resident of the Grande Ronde valley for the last 27 years (since 1902). The *1910 Federal Census* confirmed that he and his family lived in La Grande as farmers.

They had five children as follows in order of birth: Esther Melinda (1865-1866), Harriet "Hattie" Louisa Stillwell (1866-1958), John Alden (1868-1959), Lester Samuel (1873-1889) and Zachariah (1879-1967). *(ancestry.com)*

Hattie, John and Zachariah survived to adulthood and were all living in La Grande at the time of their father's death on April 3, 1929 in La Grande, according to the obituary.

John Samuel Chandler died at the home of his youngest son, Zachariah, who was executor of his estate. His older son, John Alden (b. 1868; d. June 16, 1959) was operating the family farm. In 1937, John Alden Chandler raised and sold weiner pigs and sows. *(La Grande Observer, Oct. 19, 1937)* In 1938, he advertised the sale of Guernsey bulls, well marked and at an attractive price.

At that time, he listed Route 1 as his road address. *(La Grande Observer, June 22, 1938)*

John Alden Chandler had a son named Grant Gilbert, who was born March 26, 1905 and died on November 20, 1980. Grant's son, Dale Grant, is currently living on part of the property. *(Dale G. Chandler interview, May 8, 2018)*

Cherrywood Road - This private road is named for the cherry orchards located on the west end of Standley Lane in Township 2S R38E Section 9. The authors bought some of those cherries, and they made a great pie.

Choke Cherry Road - This private road was named for the choke cherry tree, and it comes off Wade Lane near the city of Cove.

Christensen Road - This short, public unmaintained road (.17 miles) is located in Township 2N R39E Section 26 off Palmer Junction Road that dead ends at the Christensen residence. It's been called by this name for as long as the old-timers can recall. *(Bob Crouser interview, April 16, 2018)*

Through research in the *La Grande Observer*, it appears this road was named after J. C. Christensen described as "a Union County farmer, who resides near Elgin." *(La Grande Observer, 5/16/1902)*

Although the newspaper uses a variety of spellings for this man, including Christenson, Christianson and Christiansen, the 1914 Polk's Union County Tax List writes it as Christensen. That's how it is also listed in the current Union County Tax Assessor's website.

James C. Christensen went down in Union County history as one of the 12 jurors, who convicted Pine Valley farmer Kelsey Porter in the State vs. Kelsey Porter case, a trial which commenced on February 12, 1896.

Christensen was a civic-minded man and a candidate for county commissioner in 1898, but lost. However, Christensen, who worked as a night policeman in 1917, became La Grande's Chief of Police by 1919. *(La Grande Observer, 11/16/1919, pg. 3)*

After arresting an unwanted person in La Grande, Chief of Police Christensen was commended for his speedy and efficient manner. *(La Grande Observer, July 23, 1920, pg. 1)*

"J. C. Christenson was born 30 years ago in Idaho. In 1860, he moved to this valley (Grande Ronde), locating near Summerville. Seven years later, he moved to his present home near Elgin." *(La Grande Observer, 5/19/1898, pg. 3)*

The article continued, "He imported the first blooded Jersey animal, the first blooded horses, same of hogs and chickens in his neighborhood. Ever since reaching maturity, he has continuously served as school director in his district. He also served as road supervisor one term."

J. C. Christiansen married Edith Unita Parker on January 1, 1880 in Union of Union County, Oregon. They made their home in Elgin. Edith was born December 9, 1885 on board the Brig Unity on the Atlantic Ocean while immigrating to the United States with her parents.

In the *1900 and 1910 Federal Censuses*, J. C. Christiansen and his wife Edith lived in Elgin, where he worked as a dray man. In the *1920 Federal Census*, J. C. Christiansen and wife Edith were living in La Grande, and he was working as a policeman; but in the *1930 Federal Census*, they were living in Seattle, Washington, where he worked as a night watchman at the iron works.

During their lives, J. C. Christiansen and Edith had five children: Mary Ellen (1880-1913), William Franklin (1882-1961), George Elmer (1885-1954), Marguerite Olive "Maggie" (1888-1971), Anna Belle (1891-1945).

James C. Christiansen was born February 24, 1860 in Fountain Green, Utah; and he died on February 15, 1939 in Seattle, Washington. Edith died June 12, 1935 in Seattle, Washington.

Chukar Road - This private road is located in Township 2S R38E Section 33 in the La Grande district and was named after the chukar partridge, a beautifully marked gaming bird that was replenished in Union County, Oregon in 1954. The gaming commission agents around the state of Oregon released 10,000 chukar partridges in April 1952 to replenish their colonies.

The commission wanted to release another 10,000 in 1953, including areas in Eastern Oregon where conditions are most suited for the survival of the species. *(La Grande Observer, April 13, 1953, pg. 5)* The first release of chukar partridges in Union County was made in 1954. A total of 560 of these birds were released in the foothills surrounding the valley during the summer. *(La Grande Observer, Dec. 31, 1954, pg. 4)*

Chumos Road - Formerly Crum-Hardy Road, this county road #60 runs 2.21 miles in Township 1S R40E Section 28 in the Elgin maintenance district. It is located on Cricket Flat 10 miles east of Elgin, and it is accessible off Hindman Road.

On the *1935 Metsker Map*, it is labeled Crum-Hardy Road after Elgin Mayor Jesse W. Crum and William H. Hardy.

Jesse Crum was an attorney at law with an office in the city of Elgin, and he became mayor of Elgin in 1937. He owned land on this road and raised cattle. *The Elgin Recorder of Oct. 31, 1946* printed his obituary, below in part:

"Jesse Crum, prominent in Union County political and civic affairs for many years through his practice as a lawyer, died Wednesday morning, October 30, 1946 at his home in Elgin following a long illness. He had been ill since April of this year, and had apparently rallied a time or two so that there was hope he would recover.

He first came to Elgin some 36 years ago (about 1910) as a bookkeeper, but shortly after his arrival, he ran for city recorder and won. At night he studied law by correspondence and was eventually admitted to the bar.

Mr. Crum was also noted in Elgin as city attorney and as a banker. He just recently assisted in the reorganization of the First State Bank of Elgin. He owned extensive property in the county and for many years was a producer of fine grade cattle." (End of obituary)

Crum was survived by his wife, Nellie Louisa (Hoge) Crum (1885-1963), one daughter, Genevieve LaRose Crum McCall (1912-1960); two brothers, George and McKinley, one sister, Ora Cimmiyotti. His father, Jeremiah Crum and three of his brothers, Willard E., Eugene, and Frank, all died within a month's period of time September through October 1898 of typhoid.

The East Oregonian newspaper wrote:

"Jeremiah A. Crum, an old resident of Olex, Ore., and a man well known throughout Gilliam county, died at his home, on Rock creek, October 8, of typhoid fever. The deceased was aged about 55 years, and had been a resident of Gilliam county for 15 years. He was married in Grand Ronde valley about 25 years ago to Miss Sarah Rinehart, a sister of G. W. Rinehart, of Condon. This is the fourth death recorded in Mr. Crum's family within the last month, three of his grown sons having died of typhoid." *(East Oregonian, Oct. 15, 1898, pg. 6)*

Jesse Crum's obituary stated that he was of the second generation descendant of Lewis Ludwig Rinehart Sr. (1801-1881) and his wife Elizabeth Ellis Rinehart (1808-1903). The Rineharts married in Tennessee in 1853, moved to Iowa quickly thereafter and then migrated to Lane County, Oregon. Their youngest daughter, Sarah Elizabeth Rinehart, married Jeremiah A. Crum, parents of our subject Jesse Crum. *(Findagrave.com)*

According to the *An Illustrated History of Union and Wallowa Counties, 1902, pg. 338* and the *Lewis Rinehart Family History*, the Rineharts left Iowa, arriving and settling ten miles south of Eugene on Camas Swale in 1853 (alt. September 12, 1854). Then in 1862, son Lewis Bird Rinehart and two older brothers returned to La Grande with cattle, built a house and then returned to the Willamette Valley. In the spring of 1863, they came back. "In the spring of 1870, Lewis rented out the old home (in Eugene) and moved to the Grande Ronde Valley because the boys had gone there with cattle several springs before and were doing well," stated the *Rinehart Family History*. Lewis settled in Summerville to pursue commercial businesses. This is the proud family heritage alluded to in the obituary of Jesse Crum.

As for the "Hardy" part of the original road name, it was taken from William Harrison Hardy and his wife, Mary Elizabeth Woodring. William was born April 20, 1863 at South Bend, Indiana, where he lived until the age of 15, when he and his parents, Emsley H. Hardy (1842-1926) and Elizabeth Line Hardy (1842-1927) moved to Kansas.

William lived there until the age of 21, when he married Mary Elizabeth Woodring at Coffeville, Kansas, on February 2, 1884. There they resided for about six years. Then they moved to Chandler, Oklahoma. After two years, they moved to Noel, Missouri and resided there for four years before returning to Kansas for two years.

Finally, in 1901, they moved to Elgin, making their home near there. William was a farmer, spending most of his life on a farm. He supported his wife and their six children: Royal (1885-1971), Harley Monroe (1887-1960), Olive Belle Watkins (1889-1966), Henry Hamilton (1893-1957) and Hazel Agnes Seward (1896-1975). One additional child died at the age of six years.

What is surprising about this county road name today is that neither the name Crum nor Hardy survived the 1988 road renaming process. In the final analysis, the road was renamed after another interesting fellow, Dr. James G. Chumos and his wife, Dr. Abigail Fowler-Chumos. James G. Chumos was born about 1871 in Sparta, Greece, and he married Mrs. Abigail Fowler in 1900.

Abigail Ayers Doe Fowler-Chumos had been the third wife of America's "great gun of phrenology" Orson Squire Fowler of New York. She was a practitioner, naturopath and a phrenologist as well. She gained national recognition as an orator and logician, and along with her husband, James Chumos, they often spent their winters on lecturing tours throughout Oregon and California. They had a residence in Seattle.

Abigail Fowler-Chumos often used her last two married surnames to market her lecturing tours and classes, bringing recognition to the literary work of her late husband, Professor Fowler and elevating her own reputation as well.

As an orator, Abigail often gave free lectures on topics like "Life's Deepest Laws" as related to the brain and nervous system; and "The Attributes of God in Man". For two weeks in January 1912, she offered health consultations daily from 9 a.m. to 9 p.m. at the Sommer Hotel in Elgin. She also taught classes about a new system of applying electricity to cure diseases of all kinds.

In 1903, Mrs. Abigail Fowler-Chumos wanted a summer home, so she purchased the ranch residence on what became Chumos Road. Her holdings included 1,440 acres of prime timber (about six million board feet) plus some grazing land.

From the *memoirs of Mary Edith Kellogg Neal of Elgin*, who at one time lived in the Chumos house, the following additional information was revealed about Mrs. Chumos.

"Mrs. Chumos was a lecturer. She traveled all over the country to San Francisco," wrote Mary Neal. "She was there when they had the big earthquake and fire in 1906. She had been married three times. The first husband was Fowler. When he died, she married a man by the name of Dough. Her last husband was named Chumos, and he was a composer. She never had any children, but was always doing for other people."

Neal's memoirs continued, "About half way between Elgin and where we lived in the mountains, she had a ranch and a log house. A family by the name of Frank Stewart lived there. They had some boys. Mrs. Stewart and my mother were good friends. We stayed there one night when my younger brother was born. Mrs. Chumos had skeletons in the closets upstairs. We were playing upstairs and opened the closet door, and we were frightened. Perhaps the skeletons were part of Dr. Chumos' lecturing? The Tuckers lived in the Chumos place in 1909." (End of excerpt, as published by the *Elgin Museum and Historical Society's newsletter, May 21, 2021, pg. 1)*

James Chumos, a teacher and theologian, started teaching Sunday school immediately, and in June 1903, the Chumos School District was formed. To encourage settlement in the Chumos District, James Chumos and his wife built a health resort. *(History of Elgin, Oregon, pg. 257)*

The Chumos one-room schoolhouse was built on the edge of the Chumos' meadow. On the other side of the meadow was their personal residence, a large, beautiful home on 15 or 20 acres that they cleared and fenced with rails. Also on the property was a hewed log barn for their herd of dairy cattle.

James Chumos authored songs and poems, the latter of which won favorable comment from President Woodrow Wilson, Col. Theodore Roosevelt and other prominent American leaders. *(La Grande Observer, June 22, 1917)*

Among his poems were "Seattle is Here to Stay", "Free America" and "The Blessed Old Bible". James and Abigail had also written a book together, according to Edna Teter Rush, author of *The One Room School, 1981.*

The Chumoses were only summer residents of Elgin, living most of the year in Seattle. It is noteworthy to add that while included in the *1920 King County, Washington census*, the Chumos name was transcribed "Chaconas".

In 1916, they arranged to sell their Chumos Road residence to two buyers in partnership from Seattle named Brown and Clark. In June 1917, the timberland was advertised for sale in the La Grande Observer. The Chumos name endures as a part of Union County's school history and still marks this beautiful country road, honoring an accomplished couple.

Clark Creek Road - This road #56 runs 6.52 miles in Township 1N R39E Section 14 in the Elgin district and travels along Clark Creek, which is a tributary of the Grande Ronde River. This gravel road makes for a very scenic Sunday drive, but it is best driven in a pickup.

To understand this road name, one has to know the origin of the creek's name. For this the *Oregon*

Geographic Names book, pg. 157 has very little to say. However, it does say the creek name is not Clarks Creek in the plural nor is it Clark's Creek in the possessive. The book states bluntly that those names should be discarded. Furthermore this reference book states the creek was never owned by anyone named Clark. That may be true, but the creek did run through one property owned by someone with a strong Clark ancestry.

The history detectives and authors of this book have discovered a viable namesake for Clark Creek. That person is William Clark Endicott, who may have named the creek in memory of his beloved mother, Lydia Clark.

William Clark Endicott along with his wife, Mary Jane (Bass) Endicott and their children left Grant, Dallas County, Missouri to establish a homestead outside of Elgin. On his homesteaded property in the Indian Creek territory flowed a creek, later called Clark Creek.

We learned about the Endicott family from Mary Jane Endicott's obituary published in the *Enterprise Record Chieftain, of Wallowa County, dated Thursday, Feb. 1, 1923.*

About Mary Jane (Bass) Endicott, it reads: "She was born in Illinois on December 15, 1850. When a child she moved to Buffalo, Missouri, where on September 17, 1867, she was united in marriage to W.C. Endicott.

In 1878 (alt. 1877) the Endicotts came with their family of little ones to the far west, arriving in Union County the fall of that year. There they made their home until 1892 when they came to Lostine, Wallowa County.

Mrs. Endicott was the mother of twelve children, eleven of whom survive her. One son died in 1900." *[Excerpt of obituary]*

William Endicott, his widowed father, his wife and kids came over the Oregon Trail in the "Endicott Train". It was the second of three trains that came over about the same time. The first train and the third train had some trouble with the Indians, but not the Endicott train. *(Bernal Hug's History of Union County, 1961 Supplement, pgs. 54-55)*

Another account of the Endicott's arrival to the Indian Creek territory was told by Mrs. Endicott's granddaughter, Mickey (Endicott) Blumenstein, the daughter of Ulric Ernest Endicott. It is recorded on pages 54-55 of *Bernal Hug's 1961 Supplement of the History of Union County, Oregon.*

"My people came by wagon train and homesteaded on Indian Creek in 1877. Great-grandfather (Joseph) Endicott is buried some place on Indian Creek. To date I have not been able to locate the exact spot.

William Clark Endicott's middle name is a memorial to his mother's side of the family. His mother died young and was laid to rest after which the family moved west. It was more than apparent that the Clark side of his family meant a great deal to him, and he missed his mother because he named one of his sons, Ira *Clark* Endicott and one of his daughters *Lydia* Ann Endicott.

All things considered, it is our best researched conclusion that both Clark Creek and subsequently

Clark Creek Road were named after pioneer settler William Clark Endicott who named the creek in memory of his beloved mother Lydia Clark.

William Clark Endicott died on July 1, 1922 in Newberg, Oregon where he and his wife had the custom of wintering in their final years of life. They had three daughters who lived there. *(La Grande Observer, Oct. 15, 1914, Thursday, pg. 5)* William Clark Endicott was laid to rest at the Joseph Cemetery in Wallowa County.

Clearwater Road - This private road is located off Fruitdale Lane in La Grande, and it is named after a Clearwater Pond in this vicinity. It is located in Township 2S R38E Section 34.

Commerce Road - This road #153 is located off Industrial Lane by the trailer factory, thus given the business style name. It is only .19 miles in length and provides access to this business in Township 2S R38E Section 35.

Common Lane - This is a private lane off of Conklin Road near Cove. It's located in Township 3S R40E Section 15 in the La Grande maintenance district.

Comstock Road - This road #84 departs off Mill Creek Lane in Cove, running south for .71 miles in length and located in Township 3S R40E Section 26 in the Union maintenance district.

The road is named after Ralph Seldon and Emma (Walsh) Comstock, the grandparents of Nancy Comstock, currently of Cove. Ralph was born June 8, 1882 in Kiowa, Thayer County, Nebraska, the son of John Erastus Comstock (1857-1942) and Alpharetta Elizabeth Lemmon (1859-1945).

He married Emma E. Walsh (1879-1958) in Waldo, Sheboygan County, Wisconsin on October 17, 1909, and they moved to South Dakota where they were noted on the *1910 Federal Census*, living in Dewitt, Perkins County, South Dakota, where on September 11, 1911, their first child, Ruth, was born.

After Ruth's birth, they moved to Cove, Oregon, where the rest of the children were born. They had six children: Ruth M., John S., Frances Mary, Harold R., Kathleen Mary Reta and Roy David Comstock (1922-2009).

Of those children, John S., 29, died at home from illness on January 14, 1942. His brothers, Harold and Roy, stayed in the Cove area to farm. Harold R. remained a bachelor and farmed with his parents. He died in 1979. Roy D. Comstock married and farmed in the area until his death on July 17, 2009. The other three siblings, Ruth, Frances and Kathleen, married and moved away.

"My grandparents Ralph and Emma came here in 1911 from Lemmon, South Dakota. Lemmon was named after Ralph's grandmother's side of the family. My grandfather's dad was John Erastus Comstock, and he married Alpharetta Elizabeth Lemmon, and the town of Lemmon, South Dakota was named after her brother George Edward Lemmon."

"My grandfather, Ralph Comstock, died March 22, 1963 in Union County," said Nancy Comstock. *(Interview May 30, 2019)*

Ralph Comstock lived the life of a busy farmer and endured his share of hardships, some from dangers common to farmers, but he demonstrated resilience and kept going, a fine example for us all to follow. The *La Grande Observer of April 23, 1932, pg. 6* had the following news clip about him:

"Not Working Yet — Ralph Comstock, prominent farmer up the Mill Creek canyon, was the victim of one of those unfortunate accidents last week and while he is still confined to the house, he is up and around and steadily improving. While harrowing in the field one day, the team which Mr. Comstock was driving became frightened and ran away. Mr. Comstock's injuries were confined to bad bruises and a severe shake-up, we are told."

His prominence in the community was made quite clear in the following report in the newspaper when he fell ill at age 55.

"Prominent Farmer Ill — Ralph Comstock, of Mill Creek canyon, above Cove, was stricken with a severe heart attack while preparing for dinner on Sunday. Dr. Haun was called, but was unable to get over to Cove on account of drifted roads. Mr. Comstock is a prominent cherry grower and dairyman of Cove and is master of Mt. Fanny grange; he also holds a high position in the Pomona grange." *(La Grande Observer, Feb. 4, 1937, pg. 5)*

Much to the relief of his family, Comstock recovered from that serious health emergency. In 1941, Ralph, 59, filled out a draft registration card required by law at that time. He said on the paperwork that he lived in Cove and that his phone number was Cove 174.

Ralph lived to see 80 years of life, which far exceeded the 66-1/2 years life expectancy of men in 1963. His death notice stated the following, in part:

"Ralph S. Comstock, 80, retired farmer of Cove, died Thursday, March 21, 1963 at a local hospital following a period of extended illness. Born in Nebraska, Mr. Comstock had lived in Cove for 51 years (since 1911). He is survived by two sons, Harold and Roy Comstock, both of Cove; three daughters, Mrs. Ruth Brounstein (Brownstein) and Frances Peterman of Portland and Mrs. Kathleen Dolan, San Jose, Calif.

Also surviving him are three brothers, E. C. and B. H. Comstock, both of Nampa, Ida., and R. W. Comstock, Baker; three sisters, Mrs. Edna McKee and Mrs. Lucy Robbins, both of Portland, and Mrs. Marguerite Dalton, Amita, La., and 11 grandchildren." *[end of obituary]* Though the obit did not mention this, he was predeceased by his wife, Emma, on November 3, 1958. *(Ancestry.com, Richard Brounstein tree)*

Cone Drive - This private drive is a curvy drive. It's located in Township 2N R39E Section 26 in the Elgin district. On one end it connects with Palmer Junction Road and on the other end, it connects with Cabin Creek Road. This road travels through a beautiful forest of cone-producing pine trees, thus its name. *(Russell Lawson interview, Aug. 22, 2018)*

Conklin Lane - This road #512 was once included in the county road registry, but it was annexed by the city of Cove, and for that reason is no longer considered a county road. It is located east of Cove, intersecting with Haefer Lane and Antles Road with several offshoots. Conklin Lane is the address for 41 property owners.

The lane is named after Albert George Conklin, who according to his death certificate #42, was born November 28, 1846 in Oneida County, New York, the youngest of 12 children born in his family. In 1893, he married Miss Fannie Carter of Grand Island, Nebraska.

Findagrave.com had a bio written on Mr. Conklin, which has been included in this entry. Please note that his birth year in this biography is different from what is on his death certificate and his gravestone.

"One of the successful fruit growers of Union county, residing near Cove, is Albert G. Conklin, owning a farm of one hundred and sixty acres. He is raising large quantities of prunes and apples and has a fine young pear orchard.

He was born in Oneida county, New York, in November, 1848, a son of Nathaniel and Clarinda (Hunt) Conklin, both of whom were born near Albany, New York. His father removed to Oneida county, New York, in 1830, where he followed general farming, fruit-raising and canning, and was a producer of garden seeds, becoming very prosperous.

[Albert] received a good common-school education, remaining with his parents until 1875, when he removed to Iowa and settled in O'Brien county. His farm, which was situated in one of the best sections of that state, produced liberally and after remaining on it for twelve years he sold out and came to Oregon. He stopped at Cove, arriving there in the evening, and on the following morning bought a farm of one hundred and sixty acres lying adjacent to the mountains.

Mr. Conklin has been twice married, his first union being with Miss Quackenbush, who died in Iowa. To that union one daughter, Bessie, was born, who is the wife of Roy Lay, of Cove. For his second wife Mr. Conklin chose Miss Fannie Conley, a daughter of B. F. Conley, of Brighton, Michigan. To this union three children were born, Albert, Phillip and Thomas, all attending school.

Mr. Conklin, who is a highly honored man in his community, has been a member of the school board for twenty years… He is greatly respected in the community and has long been regarded as one of its leading citizens. *(Centennial History of Oregon 1811-1912, pg. 1055)*

Albert George Conklin died at his home in Cove on March 22, 1921 and was buried in Cove Cemetery.

Conley Road - This county road #128B is 3.82 miles in length and travels through Township 2S R39-40E Sections 5 and 4 in the Union maintenance district.

Named after the Scotch-Irish settler named Archibald Colbert Conley (1837-1925). He was sometimes called "Archie Bird," or "Bird," or just "A.B." Conley. He and his wife, Josia Hopper, established a Century Farm on this road in 1891 about 3 miles northwest of Cove on the Sandridge.

A.B. Conley was born January 11, 1837 in the area west of Nashville, Tennessee. On January 4, 1858, he married Josia Hopper in Mt. Vernon, Illinois, where they made their home for the next 15 years. In 1873, they moved their family to Kansas, where they heard of the homesteading deals in Oregon.

Eagerly, they equipped four wagons with supplies and joined a fifth wagon belonging to another family, and they left Fort Scott, Kansas for Northeast Oregon on May 6, 1874. While en route, their son, Jo Frank, 9, lost one of his ponies in a buffalo stampede and never saw it again.

The Conley Train endured through hard rains and wind storms, and along the way, they gained a young scout, George Miller, who had his eye on more than the trail ahead. He fell in love with the lovely Matilda Conley, and they were married on January 1, 1875 in the Grande Ronde Valley. Thereafter, Miller worked as a farm laborer for his father-in-law.

A.B. Conley was Union County Sheriff for a while and a freight forwarder, but he was better remembered as a prominent grain grower. By 1893, Conley owned in one body 8,000 acres valued at $30 per acre and stretching 7-1/2 miles along Conley Road in front of his house. He was known in this region as "the Wheat King" and was one of the largest employers of farm laborers and hoboes in Northeast Oregon.

During A.B.'s life, he was never in partnership with any other man and never had a dispute he couldn't settle outside of court. He lived by two rules: never burn any bridges and keep setting goals. He was never afraid of being in continuous debt because it gave him goals to reach and a reason to keep working. He kept a positive outlook on life and business.

Conley Farms, as it is known today, was handed down from A.B. Conley to Jo Frank Conley to Merrell Conley, then to Mary Jane Conley and her husband "Sonny" Johnson.

For the most part, Mary Jane and Sonny have retired from the operation of Conley Farms. They have two children Darcy and Colby. Darcy and her husband have their own respective occupations outside the farm, but they still raise a few head of cattle on the farm. As far as the day-to-day operations, Colby is the one who primarily manages that with his father's consulting help on the side. *(Sonny and Mary Jane Conley Johnson interview, Jan. 2001 and Feb. 2019)* Colby's young son, Baylen, is taking a strong interest in the Century Farm, and so it appears the farm will not be short of a family operator in the future. *(Colby Johnson interview, Feb. 2019)*

Coombs Loop - This private loop runs off Grande Ronde River Road and loops around the Starkey Store and turns into Park Road which also connects to the Grande Ronde River Road. It is located in Township 3S R35E Section 36 in the La Grande maintenance district.

Starkey is an unincorporated community about 26 miles southwest of La Grande. It is about two miles south of Ukiah-Hilgard Highway 244 in the Blue Mountains.

The Starkey post office was established in 1879 and named after the first postmaster, John Starkey, who settled in the area in the 1870s. The originally proposed name of this community was Daleyville, but it was rejected by the U.S. Post Office. The post office closed in 1935, when Mount Emily Lumber Company took over the post office, the Starkey Store and the gas station. *(Greg Tsiatos interview, Oct. 30, 2018; Oregon Geographic Names, 1982, pg. 697)*

The lumber industry was largely responsible for the population increase and decrease in the Starkey district. In 1919, the population was 50; in 1931, it was up to 75. During the 1940s, the population grew again on account of a portable logging operation there, but after the Valsetz Lumber Company liquidated the town site in 1955, the population decreased.

Today, Starkey Store, owned by Greg Tsiatos, is the hub of the community, where people can buy food products and supplies. The community also has a cemetery.

Coombs Loop was named in honor of Edward Merritt Coombs (1842-1927) and his wife Mary E. Coombs (1847-1929). The name Coombs is traced back to the Anglo-Saxon tribes of Britain, and it means "short, straight valley."

Edward M. Coombs was born in Hudson, Maine, on August 20, 1842. A public family tree states he was born in Crawford, Washington County, Maine, but it doesn't offer a corroborating citation. Edward's father was George W. Coombs, and his mother was Rebecca Seavey Perkins. (*La Grande Observer of Feb. 4, 1927, pg. 1, obituary; ancestry.com*)

He was apparently named after his grandfather Edward C. Coombs, who according to the *1860 Federal Census*, was born in 1779 in New Brunswick, Canada, the territory north of Maine. It appears that the Coombs ancestors immigrated from Britain to New Brunswick, Canada, and from there into the U.S.

Edward's bride to be, Mary Elizabeth Hibbard, was born on May 4, 1847 in Saint George, New Brunswick, Canada. In the *1850 U.S. Federal Census*, Edward, 7, was living in the household of his father in Annsburg, Washington County, Maine.

When Edward reached 24 years of age, he married Mary Hibbard, 19, in Saint George on October 8, 1866.

The wedding record read that Edward Merritt Coombs of Saint George, County of Charlotte, (New Brunswick) and Mary Hibbard of the same place were married by license on the 8th day of October, 1866 by George D. Sodsor. It was signed on October 8, 1866.

Thereafter, the young couple made their home in Saint George and were listed together in the *1871 Canadian Census*. However, they immigrated to the U.S., and in the *1875 New York State Census*, they were living in Lionsdale, Lewis County, New York. Their migration westward was evident in the *1880 Federal Census*, as they were residing in Oconto, Wisconsin, where Edward worked in a saw mill.

In the *1900 and 1910 Federal Censuses*, the Coombs family were living in Starkey, Union County, Oregon. Together they came to the Grande Ronde Valley in 1889 and settled in the Starkey district. They built a log house, and they named their property "Mountain View Ranch." On February 6, 1899, Coombs purchased land in Union County, and he occupied himself in logging as well as breeding and selling horses. (*ancestry.com*)

Some of his contemporaries living in the Starkey district in 1904 were Harvey F. Briggs, Winfield S. McMillan and Henry Hagey.

On June 18, 1913, while living on the Mountain View Ranch near Starkey, the Coombs family endured one of the worst hail storms recorded there to that date. The hail measured one inch in diameter and covered the ground like snow. The storm effectively damaged the timothy hay crop and the fall wheat crop, but the community of Starkey itself was not impacted. *(La Grande Observer, June 25, 1913, pg. 2)*

After about 27 years of ranching in the Starkey district, Coombs and his wife retired from ranching and moved to May Park in La Grande in September 1916. There he took up fruit farming according to the *1920 Federal Census*. Coombs lived at this residence until his death on February 3, 1927. Mary Coombs died December 2, 1929 in La Grande.

Edward and Mary had 6 children during their marriage: Albina Roxana "Allie" (1871-1920), Polemna "Lem" Y. (1873-1947); Merritt Oscar (1874-1944); Robert I. (1885-1900); and Urania Pamela (1887-1981).

Three of the children survived their parents: two daughters, Mrs. Polemna Y. (Coombs) Young of Hilgard, who married Joseph Henry Young; and Urania Pamela (Coombs) Able of Echo, who married Thomas M. Able; and one son, Merritt Oscar Coombs of La Grande.

Edward M. and Mary E. Coombs were interred at the Grandview Cemetery in La Grande. According to a Coombs Loop resident, Gregory Tsiatos, 86, Coombs' nephew Pete Able inherited the Coombs estate. *(Tsiatos interview, Oct. 30, 2018)*

Cottonwood Road - This gravel road #203A is located off May Lane in La Grande and runs about one quarter mile in length near the Grande Ronde River in Township 3S R38E Section 5 in the La Grande maintenance district.

It is descriptive of the cottonwood trees that grow so plentifully along the river and cause so many people allergies in Union County.

Interestingly, the area where La Grande is now was an important Native American fishing village with a large fish weir trap. It was also important for hunting and camas gathering. The fishing village was located in a large meadow with luxuriant grass for horses. The Cayuse and Nez Perce word for the area was Qapqápa, meaning 'at cottonwood.' The Grande Ronde River was called Qapqápnim Wéele, meaning 'cottonwood stream.' *(They are Not Forgotten, 2015, pg. 168)*

Couch Lane - This road might be considered the west end of Booth Lane as it begins at Hunter Road and runs west for one mile, ending at the stop sign intersection of Mt. Glen Road. It runs through Township 2S R38E in Sections 27-28 in the La Grande maintenance district.

The authors found the road name on the *1980 Geologic Map of the La Grande SE Quadrangle Oregon*. This section of road has been annexed into Booth Lane, road #126. (See Booth Lane) Couch Lane is named after the family of Reuben Thomas Couch (1833-1888) and his wife, Amelia Anne Walker (1838-1920), who came to Union County in 1876.

Reuben T. Couch was born on September 22, 1833 in Bedford County, Tennessee, and Amelia Anne Walker was born November 25, 1838 also in Bedford County, Tennessee.

They married on January 16, 1860 in Linn County, Missouri, and made their home there for the next 16 years, during which time, Reuben engaged in farming. They had five children: Willard F. (1860), Elma "Dora" (1862), Ulysses G. (1864), Leonard (1867) and William R. (1874).

Then they moved to Union County where the following described their early history in the county. "Mr. and Mrs. Couch rented land for a time and then purchased their present home of 80 acres which is situated immediately northwest of Island City." *(An Illustrated History of Union and Wallowa counties, 1902, pg. 303)*

There Reuben resumed farming, and he and his wife had three more children: Belle (1877), John (1879), and Ethel (1883).

Reuben died young and an excerpt of his obituary follows:

"Couch—At his residence near Island City, on September 7, 1888, between 5 and 6 o'clock a.m. of paralysis, Reuben T. Couch, age 54 years, 11 months and 15 days.

Mr. Couch was born in Bedford County, Tennessee, September 22, 1833, and with his father's family moved to Linn County, Missouri in 1839, where he lived til 1876, when he moved to Oregon and has since resided in Union County; was married to Amelia A. Walker January 16, 1860.

He leaves a wife, eight children and two grandchildren to mourn his loss. Mr. Couch was a man of many sterling qualities, and his loss is not only a calamity to wife and children, but is keenly felt in the community. He was preparing to take a trip back to his old home in Linn County." *(The Oregon Scout, Sept. 14, 1888, pg. 5)*

Following his death, Amelia stayed on the farm with some of her children, and in 1890, she built a fine large house, and she had good barns and substantial outbuildings. The farm was in good shape. *(An Illustrated History of Union and Wallowa counties, 1902, pg. 303)*

Her sons grew up to be responsible men with their own accomplishments. Willard Couch, had a farm on Foothill Road. Ulysses Couch was a grain buyer, but then he became a county assessor and then county judge. Leonard Couch was a very accomplished newspaper man.

"The Wallowa News was founded by C. T. McDaniel and Leonard Couch in 1899 in response to a demand for a local newspaper made by a growing, thriving town. The first number appeared March 3, as a seven-column folio, in which it has since been issued. After three months connection with the enterprise, Mr. McDaniel retired and Leonard Couch assumed both the proprietorship and editorship, continuing to guide his journal over the shoals and through the torturous channels, which beset a newspaper's course until November 15, 1901, when he established the Wallowa Academy. Then E. F. Wood and S. W. Wood became proprietors." *(An Illustrated History of Union and Wallowa counties, 1902, pg. 665)*

Leonard continued in the newspaper business as evidenced below:

"The first issue of the Elgin Recorder is dated February 20, 1891. It was established and edited by

A. R. Tuttle, who, on account of ill health, sold it in 1901 to L. Couch, who is now its publisher and editor. It is well supported and devotes its best energies to the interests to Elgin and vicinity. It has always held rank among the best newspaper of the county." *(An Illustrated History of Union and Wallowa counties, 1902, pg. 235)*

Other news clippings about the Couch children show their activities. "Willard Couch, the Ladd Creek farmer brought in a four horse load of choice apples Tuesday." *(La Grande Observer, December 15, 1897, pg. 3)*

"William Couch of Island City, went through town this morning en route to Ladd Canyon to bring back some cattle." *(La Grande Observer, Dec. 16, 1897, pg. 3)*

"Mr. U. G. Couch of Island City, agent for the Pacific Coast Elevator Company, bought two large lots of wheat Saturday. The two lots amounted to 21,000 bushels, the larger portion of which had been stored at the Conley siding." *(La Grande Observer, Jan. 24, 1898, pg. 3)*

Their mother Amelia Couch, at some point, moved to Portland close to her youngest daughter, Ethel Robertson. Amelia died July 27, 1920 in Portland. Her body was brought back for burial in Ackles Cemetery where her husband Reuben and daughter Belle were already laid to rest.

Coughanour Lane - This lane runs west of North Powder for about nine miles from Highway 84 near North Powder Café to where Nice and Ellis Roads intersect. Coughanour Lane actually becomes Ellis Road at that nine-mile point.

This lane is designated road #103A and runs 4.28 miles in length. It is located in Township 6S R39E Section 22 in the North Powder maintenance district.

This lane is named after former Idaho State Senator William Albert Coughanour and his son, William "Will" M. Coughanour. The following information comes from a narrative written in the *History of Idaho: The Gem of the Mountains, Volume 3 by James H. Hawley, 1920, page 402-406.*

William Albert Coughanour was born on March 12, 1851, the son of Henry Snyder Coughanour (1817-1900) and Caroline Conkle Coughanour (1830-1898), in Belle Vernon, Fayette County, Pennsylvania. After attending schools there, he began to teach for two terms.

In March 1870, at age 20, he moved to Quartzburg, Idaho, where he became a partner with his uncle David E. Coughanour at the Gold Hill mine, which was profitable. On March 8, 1874, he married Galena Bunting (1847-1927). They "came directly to Quartzburg, Idaho, where he had made his home a few years before." *(Biennial Report by Idaho State Historical Society, pg. 87)*

After William A. Coughanour sold out his interests in the mine, he moved his family to Boise in 1886, and a year later, he moved them to his permanent home in Payette, Idaho, where he engaged in a variety of business ventures, including managing a lumber mill for 12 years, fruit (peach) growing and stock raising.

It was his profitable milling operations that allowed him to accumulate considerable farm lands for his stock raising ventures. He had 1,447 acres in the North Powder River territory, of which 1,200 were under cultivation and the rest in pasture for his cattle. Mr. Coughanour raised the largest recorded range steer in the world at that time, the narrative read. It was hay and grass fed, weighing 3,230 pounds.

William A. Coughanour also owned ranches comprising 1,200 acres or more in the Payette area, where he raised 100 head each of mules, horses, and cattle. He also raised Shetland ponies and had them advertised for sale in eastern Oregon as well as Idaho.

On November 7, 1927 in Payette, Galena died. William enjoyed a few additional years of life, but in early January 1936, he summoned his son, Will, to his bedside to say his goodbyes. William died on Saturday, January 4, 1936 at the age of 84 years, 298 days. He was interred at Riverside Cemetery, Payette, Idaho, in the family plot with his parents, two sisters and wife.
After his death, his son Will inherited all of his father's land in the North Powder country, and he continued in the stock raising business.

William "Will" Mootry Coughanour was born October 21, 1877 in the Idaho Territory. *(World War I Draft Registration card)* In the *1880 Federal Census*, when he was age two, he was living with his parents and older sister, Emma L., in Boise County, Idaho.

In 1887, his father moved the family to Payette, Idaho, where on July 31, 1888, the family house was struck with lightening and consumed by fire. The entire family escaped the house unharmed. Will grew to manhood, and at the age of 22, he was engaged as a salesman for his father's lumber business.

By 1900, it appears that his father started purchasing ranch land in North Powder, expanding his stock raising business, and Will was managing it long distance from Payette.

On January 5, 1902, Will Coughanour married Susan "Alta" Capitola Stroup (1880-1956) in Canyon, Idaho, and several years later they made their home in North Powder.

The business grew into one called Coughanour & Son, and they ambitiously maintained business connections with a market in Portland to buy their cattle and hogs. Consequently, in December 1916, Will shipped one car of cattle and one car of hogs to Portland. *(La Grande Observer, Dec. 13, 1916, pg. 6)* They routinely traveled to Portland to take care of business interests.

In May 1916, Will began to serve as Union County Commissioner. *(La Grande Observer, May 24, 1916, pg. 8)* Will and Alta spent the winter of 1917 in Los Angeles, California. *(La Grande Observer, Jan. 24, 1917, pg 3)*

Although they were residents of North Powder as early as 1913, as noted in the La Grande Observer, it appears that they maintained a residence in Payette, Idaho because in the January *1920 Federal Census*, Will and Alta were counted as residents living at 214 S. Ninth Street in Payette.

Later, in the *1930 Federal Census,* they were listed as residents on Second Street in North Powder with a roomer, John T. Peterson of Wisconsin, 22, a public school teacher. Will was described as a self-employed cattle stockman in that year according to the census. Some time after the 1930 census, Alta moved to Payette to live with her niece, according to the *1940 Federal Census.*

On January 6, 1937, Will, 59, married a 27-year-old widow named Mrs. Nina Bias Young. (ancestry.com)   She brought along her daughter, Barbara Ann Young, 9, from her previous marriage.

After their marriage, Will kept actively engaged in the stock raising business right up until his premature death on January 19, 1940 at the age of 62 years. *(Oregon Death Index; La Grande Observer articles show him doing business in late December 1939)*

After his death, his second wife of two years became the administrator of the estate. She rented out the ranch, and in 1942, the estate was finally settled. In 1943, she added to the Coughanour estate by purchasing the 412-acre Cal Wright ranch on Wolf Creek. Then on February 19, 1944, she married Emery Frank Pearson and moved away, thus apparently ending the history of the Coughanours in Union County, Oregon.

Courtney Lane - This lane is named for pioneer settler Thomas Benton Courtney of Morgantown, West Virginia. *(Ancestry.com)*

On the *1935 Metsker Map*, this lane was first called the Parks-Rinehart Road #135, and it was 4.17 miles in length in Township 1S R38E Section 12 in the Imbler maintenance district. The map has the name misspelled as Parks with an "s". It should be Park without an "s". That's the way the family spelled it and how it's spelled on the gravestones in Summerville Cemetery.

This road starts at the northeast limits of Summerville, running east past the Rinehart Station and terminating at the J. J. Hawks property. *(La Grande Observer, Oct. 1, 1945)* Today, it intersects with Highway 82 on the east end and Summerville Road on its west end. Along the drive, it intersects with Hug Road and Brooks Road.

Locals will tell you that Courtney Lane is frequently crossed by migrating herds of elk in the winter and sometimes a stray Angus cow. There's also an osprey nest atop an electrical pole at the intersection of Brooks and Courtney. Please don't disturb them. They nest every year and produce young.

The Park-Rinehart Road name came into use due to property holders at either end of the road. This included Wayne Park (1892-1985) and his wife Anna Rachel (Sanderson) Park (1895-1977) on the west end of the road and after the Henry Rinehart residence which was located at the east end of the road where it intersects with Highway 82. *(Morton Gordon interview, April 14, 2018)* The home is still standing and occupied in 2021.

Just one-quarter mile north of that residence on the east side of Highway 82 is Rinehart Lane where the Rinehart Station or train stop on the Union Pacific Railroad was once located. This is named after Henry Rinehart also. (See Rinehart Lane entry)

For the Park part of the old road name, it originated with Wayne Darr Park's father and mother, William Nephi Park (b.1854 UT) and Mary Elizabeth (Hill) Park (b.1863 UT), who were the oldest residents on this road.

The *1910 Federal Census of Summerville* enumerated the household this way: William N. Park, 56, was head of the house, wife Mary E, 49, son Hugh W. Park, 28, son Earl E., 26, daughter Pearl P, 25 and son Wayne D., 18.

Just ten years later the household profile changed to the following: Wayne D. Park, 27, head of house; Anna R., 24, his wife; William N., 66, father to Wayne; and Hugh W., 37, brother to Wayne. *(1920 Federal Census, Summerville, Oregon)*

Wayne appears to have taken over his father's farm and his brother Hugh helped him. Wayne Darr Park was born in Summerville on April 14, 1892, and he died in 1985 at 93 years of age. Wayne Park married Annie Rachel Sanderson (1895-1977). It doesn't appear as though they had any heirs.

The historic name Park-Rinehart Road was replaced with the name "Courtney Lane" after Thomas Benton Courtney, who settled there in 1868.

He married Annie Imbler, the sister of Jessie J. Imbler, on March 31, 1880, after whom the city of Imbler was named. The family stayed in the valley until about 1890. In 1931 in Walla Walla, Washington, Thomas Benton Courtney passed away. He was laid to rest there.

After Thomas Courtney and Annie Imbler died, the following relatives operated the farm: Samuel Brooks and Mary Jane Wade; Hugh Huron and Stella Brooks; George Royes Sr. and Mary Elizabeth Huron; George "G" Royes Jr. and his wife Valerie Eisiminger; and currently their son Sam Royes and family.

George and Valerie Royes and their son, Sam, operate the Thomas B. Courtney Century Farm today (Royes Farms) and produce wheat, grass seed and mint. *(Thelma Oliver interview, early Summerville resident and historian)* In 1963, George Royes was honored as Conservation Man of the Year by the Union County Wheat Growers Association.

About 1968, George Royes Sr. entered a partnership with Creston Shaw, a grass seed farmer of Alicel. Shaw started his farming in 1950 by renting 17 acres of land from his step-father, Mr. William "Will" Bull. Creston cleared it of weeds first and planted it with grass. "Then one day, two German bachelors, who farmed in the area, asked me if I would buy their 100-acre farm," Shaw said. "I told them I didn't have the money but I would rent it from them. That's how I got started with 100 acres."

From those small beginnings a partnership developed between the two grass seed growers, Royes and Shaw. In those years most growers were raising fescue crops, as did Shaw. But Shaw also developed his own private cleaning operation in Alicel and built business relationships and made contracts with three or four big buyers, including Scotts.

"When I came into the partnership, George Royes Sr. was a very successful grass seed grower and operator, but he hadn't gotten into contracts yet. I brought those companies into the partnership," Shaw said.

Even into his nineties, Shaw stayed engaged in the business operations by stopping by the seed plants and talking to employees.

In 2018, the Royes family and partner, Creston Jay Shaw and family, celebrated their 50th anniversary in business as Blue Mountain Seeds. They have a seed processing plant in the city of Imbler, and they bought the former Barenbrug plant in Alicel in September 2015. They hire about 22 people during their busy season. *(Creston Shaw interview, 2018; Thomas Courtney Century Farm story by Trish Yerges; Blue Mountain Seeds in Imbler Celebrates 50th anniversary by Trish Yerges, May 2018, La Grande Observer)*

Craddock Road - This gravel road departs from Standley Lane and accesses two residences, one of which was built in 1971 and is owned by Teddy J. Craddock. The road is short and dead ends at the second residence. *(Carrol L. Lester interview, neighbor, May, 2018)*

Craig Loop - Formerly Starns-Craig Road #21, it diverts off of Dry Creek Lane, making a large, winding loop 3.29 miles in total length until it reconnects with Dry Creek at the end of Hunter Road. It's located in Township 1N R38E Section 35 of the Imbler maintenance district. The name Starns was later dropped off the road sign, leaving it as Craig Loop.

The Starns part of the road name came from Benjamin Oakes Bradford Starns, who was born in 1868 in Kansas. He died in 1952 and was buried in Summerville Cemetery. He married Myrtle Estella Webb on July 3, 1891 in Oregon. She was born 1874 in Sandusky, Wisconsin and died in La Grande. She was buried in Summerville in 1943.

The Starns couple settled in rural Summerville in 1911, and they became parents to Herbert Sina, Hiram Oakes, Thomas Chauncy, Birdie, Hannah, and Linette.

In October of 1920, Benjamin "Oakes" transferred some land to his three sons. *(La Grande Observer, October 2, 1920, pg. 4)* It appears that Herbert and Hiram had been in school in Kansas City in 1929. *(La Grande Observer, December 29, 1921, pg. 8)*

Herbert was in Canyon County, Idaho for the *1930 Federal Census*, but in 1940, he was in the Summerville census.

In 1944, Benjamin Oakes Starns had a 30-acre dairy ranch for sale in rural Summerville. *(La Grande Observer, May 3, 1944, pg. 5)* Sadly, in 1952, Benjamin, 83, died. *(La Grande Observer, April 23, 1952, pg. 1)*

The road history continues with his son Herbert, who was born in 1892 in Moro, Oregon, and who remained single his entire life. The *1935 Metsker Map* shows his name as the only Starns landowner on that road. He died on May 17, 1974 in La Grande and was buried at Summerville Cemetery.

The second part of the early road name, Craig, was named after George Austin Craig (1883-1979) and wife, Dorothy (Buchanan) Craig (1889-1974).

At one time, two Craig households lived on this road. *(Thelma Oliver interview, early resident)* Historical research indicates those households included Mr. and Mrs. Daniel C. Craig and the George Craig family. George Craig had a son, Tom Chester Craig and his wife was Dorothy (1920-2004). Tom lived on Summerville Road. All of those Craigs are deceased or have moved away from Craig Loop.

There is some historical mention of George Craig's father Daniel C. Craig (1859-1946), who also lived on Craig Loop for a time.

"Mr and Mrs. George Craig were married Dec. 25, 1905 (in Puyallup, Washington) at the home of her (Dorothy's) parents, Mr. and Mrs. T. J. Buchanan at 10 o'clock on their 40th wedding anniversary. During February 1906, the (newlywed) couple moved to the Summerville area where he has been engaged in farming and logging. They have lived in their present house for the past 36 years. They had seven children." *(La Grande Observer, Dec 20, 1955 pg. 3)*

Crampton Road - This road exits the Robbs Hill Road--Fox Hill Road junction and on the north end connects with Mt. Emily Road. It brings access to four properties, the oldest two structures were built in 1930.

Clayton Warnstaff, a former resident of the "hill neighborhood" wrote about the Crampton family in his memoirs. He wrote that there was a homestead with a red house and outbuildings owned by Rufus Clay (1838-1889). Some of the original lumber from this red house was used later by property buyers Ted and Ralph Crampton to build their hunting cabin. Warnstaff said in his memoirs that the cabin burned down in 1993.

Ted and Ralph Crampton were the sons of Lewis and Birdie I. (Devlin) Crampton, who came to Union County in 1909 from Kansas. Lewis spent the next 40 years in Union County before his death on June 20, 1949 at the age of 72 years.

Afterward, his widow, Birdie, relocated to Hillsboro, Oregon to live near her daughter Edna Mercer. The surviving sons, Harold, Floyd "Ted" and Ralph were living in La Grande at the time of their father's death.

Ted Crampton was born Floyd Rogers Crampton on April 20, 1907 in Kansas. At the age of 2 years, he came with his family to Union County. He grew up there and married Mabel C. (1911-2006), and they raised a family.

In 1948, Ted and his brother, Ralph Crampton, built and co-owned the hunting cabin on Fox Hill, later named Crampton Road. In 1963, when Ralph and his family moved to Sisley Creek outside of Durkee, Ralph signed the cabin over to his brother Ted Crampton. At one time, Cramptons owned property on the right and left side of the road. *(Sharon Crampton interview, October 29, 2021)*

Ted died on July 4, 1975 and was buried in Grandview Cemetery in La Grande. His widow died October 8, 2006 at 95 years of age. *(La Grande Observer, Friday, November 4, 2011, obit)*

Ralph Crampton was 17 years younger than his brother Ted. He was born December 4, 1924 in La Grande, and on November 3, 1943, he married Irene Crist in La Grande. Ralph worked for the Union Pacific Railroad, and in 1963, the family moved to Sisley Creek outside of Durkee. In addition to working for the railroad, Ralph and Irene had a peach orchard for many years.

During their marriage, Ralph and Irene had three sons: Wayne (Carlene) of Island City; Fred (Sharon) of La Grande; and Jim of Gresham; and one daughter Ann Leach of McCall, Idaho.

Ralph died on January 10, 2009 at 84 years of age in Baker City, Baker County, Oregon. He was buried in Summerville Cemetery, one mile south of Summerville, Union County, Oregon. He was preceded in death by their baby sons, John Franklin Crampton, d. 1947 at 2 months old; and Don Howard Crampton, d.1949 at 12 hours old; one sister Edna, and two brothers, Harold, died 1943; and Ted Crampton, died 2006. *(La Grande Observer, January 15, 2009 obit)*

Today, there are no Crampton family members living on Crampton Road, and their hunters' cabin no longer exists, but historian Clayton Warnstaff wrote that he wanted the history of the people of the hill neighborhood to be remembered, and the authors have honored his request in this book. Best of all, the county has marked that land with a Crampton Road sign.

Crescent Road - This road #150 runs .32 miles north and south off Summerville Road on the northwest side of Imbler in Township 2S R38E Section 20 in the Imbler maintenance district.

The south half of this road that runs alongside the football field at the Imbler High School property has been called "lovers' lane" by some alumni. Of course, none of them will own up to knowing this personally, but it's been reported that "after football games, some kids climbed over the high board fence onto this dirt road to smoke cigarettes and smooch in secret," said our smiling informants. *(Bill and Florence Howell interview, May 20, 2018)*

Crisstad Road - This private road is located in Township 2S R38E off McAlister Road between I-84 and Hwy 30. It provides access to two businesses.

Crooked Creek Road - This road is a public unmaintained road that is .16 miles in length and located in Township 3S R38E Section 4 in the La Grande maintenance district. There are at least three other Crooked Creeks in Oregon, but the one in Union County is located off Buchanan Lane. It crosses Crooked Creek and brings access to four residences. It's named for its characteristics.

Curtis Road - Formerly the Hot Lake-Union Road, this road #12B is located off Highway 203 by Hot Lake and provides access to three residences. This gravel road is 2.65 miles long and located in Township 4S R39E Section 5 in the Union maintenance district.

In 1988, when the road names were changed, the part of the road from Hot Lake to Union Junction was changed to Curtis Road, and the part from Union Junction toward the city of Union was changed to Union Junction Lane.

This road is named after John Arthur Curtis, born March 18, 1928 in Harrisburg, Linn County, Oregon to Chester Arthur Curtis (1886-1948) and Della May (Tandy) Curtis (1891-1966).

John's siblings were Vella C. Curtis (1913 -), Alice C. (1916 -), Delta L. Powell (1918-1999), Charles Curtis (1921-), Dean Lee Curtis (1922-2005), Anna L. (1924 -) and Elnora Mae Malpass (1925-2016). *(Findagrave.com, 1930 and 1940 Federal Censuses)*

At age 18, John was working at his father's farm in Harrisburg, Linn County in Oregon. He was described as having a ruddy complexion, black hair, brown eyes, 6 foot 1 inch tall and 205 pounds. *(1946 Draft Registration)*

He married Dolores Grace Peterson on June 10, 1949 in Junction City, Lane County, Oregon. They initially made their home on the Curtis farm in Harrisburg. However, in the 1960s, they purchased a residence and farm in Union County on what became Curtis Road. The address was 56903 Curtis Road, according to the *U.S. Public Records Index, Volume 1*.

Their son Randall C. Curtis attended Eastern Oregon College in 1974 at which time the parents were living on Curtis Road, and according to public records, John and Dolores Curtis were still living in Union in 1996. However, at some point before 2012, they returned to Harrisburg, Linn County, Oregon.

The *Eugene Register-Guard of Lane County, Oregon, Sunday, June 3, 2012* issue printed the following obituary:

"Harrisburg— John Arthur Curtis of Harrisburg died June 1, 2012 of complications from kidney failure. He was 84. He was born March 18, 1928, in Harrisburg, to Chester and Della Tandy Curtis. He married Dolores Peterson on June 10, 1949 in Junction City. He was a CAT operator, heavy construction worker, farmer and rancher.

Survivors include his wife; two sons, Jack of Troutdale, and David of Harrisburg; a daughter, Laurie Gay Seale of Union; a brother, Charles of Harrisburg; a sister, Elnora Malpass of Eugene; four grandchildren and three great-grandchildren. He was preceded in death by his son Randal Christian Curtis in December 1992.

Private burial will be held at Alford Cemetery, Harrisburg. Arrangements by Murphy-Musgrove Funeral Home in Junction City. Remembrances to Cascade Hospice or Harrisburg Odd Fellows Lodge." [end of obituary]

Dark Canyon Road - This road exits NF-400 road and NF-21. The road forks off at one point and that fork dead ends. Both the fork road and the main road are called Dark Canyon Road, which makes this mountain road different from most other roads. According to Greg Tsiatos, "If you follow Meadow Creek about one and a half miles, you'll come to Dark Canyon. There used to be a dam up Dark Canyon." *(Greg Tsiatos interview, Oct. 30, 2018)*

Darr Road - Formerly Elgin-Darr Road, this road #78 runs 4.45 miles in Township 2N R39E Section 33 in the Elgin maintenance district. Part of the road is county maintained and the other part is public and unmaintained. The Elgin part of the road name was dropped, and today it is simply Darr Road.

It's named after early pioneers Jesse Sargent Darr and his wife Catherine Eve (Knifong) Darr. Jesse was born June 30, 1834 in Lebanon, Russell County, Virginia. He died at his home in Elgin on December 25, 1930 at age 96 years, 5 months and 26 days. His son, John Marcus and wife, Margaret and family were living with the 85-year-old widower Jesse Darr in 1920. *(La Grande Evening Observer, Dec. 26, 1930, pg 1; 1920 Federal Census)*

He married Catherine Eve Knifong on February 8, 1857 in Sullivan, Missouri. During his life, Jesse engaged in farming and stock raising in Elgin for 45 years, coming to this area on the Darr Train over the Oregon Trail in 1884 (alternate 1881 or 1882. (*An Illustrated History of Union and*

Accompanying him were his wife and ten children: Luella Jane (1857-1942), John Marcus (1859-1945), Samuel (1861-1938), George O. (1863-1864), Charles (1865-1931), Martha (1867-1962), Hester Emma Patten (1870-1954), Alta B. (1872-1951), William (1874-1940) and Joseph (1877-1934).

Catherine Eve (Knifong) Darr was born March 3, 1836 in Virginia, the daughter of John Jesse Knifong (1806-1864) and Anna Rogers (Lambert) Knifong (1810-1882). She died at her Elgin home on Sunday, March 25, 1905 at the age of 69 years. She had been in ill health for several months prior. Both she and Jesse were interred in the Elgin Cemetery.

Jeff Davis of Elgin can trace his lineage back to his great-great-grandfather Jesse Sargent Darr. Jeff's father was Charles Davis, grandmother was Verna Darr, great grandfather was William Darr and his great-great-grandfather was Jesse Sargent Darr.

Deal Canyon Lane - This partially paved lane is located west of La Grande and is named after Robert Deal (1840-1936). The road #119 is 1.50 miles long and is located in Township 3S R38E Section 7 in the La Grande maintenance district.

Robert Deal was born September 16, 1840 in Ohio, growing up on his father's farm near Barnesville. When he was 23 years of age, he started out with a team of oxen across the Plains to Oregon, arriving in La Grande on September 12, 1864.

He and his brother were engaged in the freighting business for many years, hauling from Umatilla Landing to Boise and Silver City, Idaho.

"Mr. Deal, when freighting in 1868 brought the first printing press into La Grande and two young men started a newspaper that year, to which Mr. Deal subscribed. Since then, except for a few years, when no newspaper was printed here, he has subscribed continuously to a home town paper, taking the Observer also ever since its origin. In other words, Mr. Deal has taken a La Grande paper since the first printing press rolled off a newspaper in this city." *(La Grande Observer, April 8, 1933, pg. 1)*

Deal returned to Ohio in the fall of 1868 by way of Portland, San Francisco, the Isthmus of Panama and then to New York aboard the steamer "Arizona" to marry Margaret Ball. After their wedding, he returned with her to La Grande in the spring of 1869 to resume freighting, farming and stock raising. In 1884, the railroad came through the Grande Ronde Valley, ending the horse-drawn freighting business as many knew it.

He was well liked by the community, and his friends and neighbors best remembered him riding his black horse, something he did up to age 93. He died January 29, 1936 at age 94 years. He is interred in Grandview Cemetery in La Grande.

His wife, Margaret E. Ball, was born February 26, 1844 in Kirkwood, Belmont County, Ohio, the daughter of Joseph P. Ball and Margaret Groves. She died June 9, 1913 in Union, Union County, Oregon.

During their marriage, Robert and Margaret Deal had six children: Della B. Mahaffey (1869-1946), William (1872-1940), May Ella (1873-1941), Mary E. (1876-before 1936), Robert Lee (1884-1970) and Daisy (1886-1887).

In the *1900 Federal Census*, the Deal family was listed at their residence on M Street in La Grande, including parents, two sons William and Robert Lee; and a daughter May. *(La Grande Evening Observer, April 8, 1933, pg. 1)*

Dean Road - This is a private road off of Lantz Lane near Cove in Township 3S R40E Section 10. There was a road petition #145 on file with the county dated September 1880 that mentioned Dean Road. These roads may not be the same road, but it shows that there has been a Dean family in the county for many years.

Dear Drive - This is a private drive off of Stackland Road near Cove in Township 3S R40E Section 14 in the Union maintenance district.

Delong Road - This private road is located in Township 3S R38E Section 23 in the La Grande maintenance district. In practical terms, it is off of Bond Lane and east of the truck stop on Highway 203 (US Highway 30).

This road is named after Jacob Pace Delong, born June 27, 1841 in Ohio. He married Savilla Anettie Horner in Perry, Ohio on May 5, 1864. *(Ohio marriage records)* They had eleven children, but not all of them lived to adulthood.

The parents came to Union County in 1888. From the *La Grande Observer of January 28, 1952*, it noted that "Fifty-five years ago, J. P. Delong walked to La Grande because the roads were too muddy." Jacob and Savilla Delong were both buried in the Summerville Cemetery in Union County.

Their eighth child was Ernest Homer Delong, born October 21, 1876. On September 16, 1900, Ernest married Fannie Alice Gekeler, daughter of George and Catherine Gekeler. Ernest and Fannie had eight children over the years, and this record will focus on the fourth child, Vernon Ernest Delong, born June 27, 1910. On December 11, 1932, he married Lois Jeanne Conley, daughter of A. B. and Vernetta (Golden) Conley.

Ernest, Fannie, Vernon and Lois are all interred in the Hillcrest Cemetery in La Grande.

Vernon and Lois had three children, including Phyllis Jean, Dale and Cecil G. Delong. Dale said that the road was put in around 1969 or 1970, so they could subdivide the land over the next few years. Today, both Cecil and Scott Delong own property on this road. *(Dale Delong interview, 2021)*

Depot Drive - This is a public unmaintained drive that runs .04 miles in length and is located in Township 2S R39E Section 7 in Alicel. There was once a depot in Alicel when it was platted.

Dial Lane - This lane designated road #19 in the Imbler maintenance district runs 1.08 miles in Township 1S R38E Sections 4-9. This road leaves Hunter Road and travels west in the rural Summerville area.

This lane is named after William Edward Dial, born November 4, 1898 in Salt Creek, Iowa, to Edward D. Dial and Lydia (Christie) Dial. The Edward Dial family was there for the *1900 Federal Census*, but in 1902, they came Union County, Oregon, where Edward lived for the next 41 years. *(La Grande Observer, July 26, 1943, pg. 3)*

In La Grande, Oregon, Lydia gave birth to her last child, Charles Earl Dial, on July 8, 1903. Sadly, Lydia Dial died of stomach cancer on September 4, 1903. She was 28 years old and left five children, including the youngest being just two months old at that time. She was buried in Hillcrest Cemetery in La Grande. *(La Grande Observer, Sept. 5, 1903, pg. 4)*

Baby Charles E. Dial was given into the care of Edward's sister Ella (Dial) Anson and her husband William Anson. *(Ancestry.com Rochell Brown family tree)*

Edward married Mary A. Schmitz on January 10, 1906 in Union County, Oregon, where he engaged in general farming. He farmed originally in the Owsley Canyon area in 1908 and later moved from there to the Fruitdale area. He and Mary had a son Raymond and daughter Florence together. Mary Dial died January 26, 1928 and was interred in the Grande View Cemetery in La Grande.

Edward died July 25, 1943 in La Grande at the Grande Ronde Hospital. He was also buried in the Grande View Cemetery next to his wife Mary.

Surviving him were five children: Porter, William E., Earl, Raymond, Joe, Mrs. Florence Beck; three sisters Mrs. William (Ella) Anson of La Grande, Mrs. Ruth Burton and Miss Rhoda Dial, both of Eldon, Iowa; two brothers, Harry and Tom Dial of Iowa.

Edward's son, William Earl Dial was married to Fanchon Eleanor Elliott on September 12, 1932 in Pendleton, Umatilla County, Oregon. They resided on Dial Lane before 1935. They were included on a *1940 Federal Census* in the Summerville district.

They had two children: William Earl Dial, Jr. born January 22, 1936 and Margaret E. born November 7, 1937. *(La Grande Observer, Nov. 9, 1937, pg. 6; La Grande Observer, Sept. 14, 1932, pg. 4)*

They moved to Milton-Freewater before 1965, where William Dial Sr. died on August 13, 1993.

Dorthy M Road - This road is located behind the large grainery bins in Alicel. On this road is property owned by Blue Mountain Seeds and United Grain Corporation of Oregon. This road is named after Dorthy M. Peacock. Her name is spelled correctly in this book entry.

Dorthy May (Nelson) Peacock, 86, died December 18, 2005 at her home in Alicel. She was buried next to her husband, William Asa Peacock (1910-1978) in the Summerville Cemetery. *(ancestry.com)*

She was born April 29, 1919, to Ole and Mabel M. Nelson in Minneapolis, Minnesota. In 1927, she traveled with her mother and stepfather, Charles Buckmaster, to Brooks, Oregon, in a Model T Ford. She married William Asa Peacock in Albany, Oregon on November 9, 1935. The couple spent 12 years in Alaska trapping and working with the Civil Aviation Administration.

In 1947, the family moved to western Oregon and began logging and operating portable sawmills. They moved to Northeast Oregon in 1956 and set up a sawmill on the face of Mount Harris. Within a few years the sawmill was moved down to Alicel on the valley floor, where it operated until 1995.

Following her husband's accidental death in 1978, she became involved in the family sawmill and involved herself in many civic groups.

She enjoyed camping, hunting, fishing, being at the deer camp on Mount Harris and keeping things in order, traveling, flower gardening, watching birds, reading, dancing and laughing at a good story. Nothing was more important to her than family and friends.

Survivors include her sons and their wives, Bill and Jane Peacock, Bob and Dorothy Peacock and Rick and Bobbi Peacock; seven grandchildren; five great-grandchildren and other relatives. *(Findagrave.com obituary)*

Dove Road - This private road is off Fruitdale Lane in La Grande, and it is one in a series of five roads named after birds. There is a mobile home park located here in Township 2S R38E Section 33 in the La Grande maintenance district.

Downs Road - This road #154 comes off Airport Lane and runs .24 miles into Smith Loop. It runs through an industrial area located in Township 3S R38E Section 24 in the La Grande maintenance district.

Draper Road - Formerly Curtis-Draper Road, this road #68 runs 1.65 miles off Bates Lane. It's located in Township 4S R40E Section 14 in the Union maintenance district.

It was called the Curtis-Draper Road early on, after farmers Benjamin F. Curtis and Elverdo Draper, but the Curtis name was dropped, leaving Draper as its official name. Both men have graves in the Union Cemetery.

Addressing the Curtis part of the road, it was named after Benjamin Franklin Curtis Sr. (1894-1977) and his wife, Emily Doblestine (1890-1979). They married on December 9, 1916 in Kuna, Idaho. They arrived to Union County sometime between 1924-1930 on Hickory Street in the city of Union before moving out to Little Creek Road where they were during the *1940 Federal Census*.

They had two children: Lenore Mabel (b.1917) and Benjamin Franklin Jr. (b.1918), both born in Kuna, Idaho. It seemed that in 1917, Benjamin lived in Lincoln, Nebraska, but he also had property in Wallowa County that he checked on that year. *(La Grande Observer, November 21, 1917, pg. 6)*

The son had moved to Grant County by 1940. Benjamin Sr. and Emily were still in Union County in 1944, but after March 1953 his business ads ceased to be published and by March 1955, they were living on the Oregon Coast. Then in 1960, their daughter visited them in Depot Bay, Oregon. Curtis died in 1977 and Emily died in 1979. They are both interred at Union Cemetery in Union, Oregon. The small headstone reads Ben F. Curtis 1894-1977.

The Draper part of this road name originates with the Draper patriarch Elverdo Draper. He was born August 28, 1848 in Green River, Columbia County, New York, the son of Henry and Emily (Palmer)

Draper. Ten years later, his family moved to Scott County, Iowa.

Census records show the following migration pattern for the Elverdo Draper family, starting in Le Claire, Scott County, Iowa in 1860. The household included Elverdo's parents: Henry Draper, 50 and Julia G., 47, and siblings William H., 19, John P., 18; Oscar, 17, Luda A., 15, Ann E., 13, Elverdo, 11, Leoline, 10, and Sarah Draper, 6.

Elverdo, 20, married 24-year-old Adeline Pelham (1844-1897) on November 26, 1868. In the *1870 Federal Census*, he and Adeline were living in Eden, Clinton County, Iowa. Their household included Elverdo, 22, Adeline, 25, and daughter Maryette Eunice, 7 months. Also living with them were Elverdo's brothers Leoline Draper, 20, and Martin Draper, 17, both farm laborers.

For two years following his marriage, he worked as a farm laborer for his father-in-law, until 1871, when he and Adeline moved to Union, Oregon, first by rail and then by horse team, arriving here on Oct. 26, 1871. *(Lulu Cockrell obituary)*

At first he worked for a Mr. Ames, who ran a dairy, but then he bought a place eight miles from Union on the Cove and Big Creek Road. He added to his property until he owned 1,480 acres all contiguously joined. He ran a dairy for three years, then switched to raising sheep. "He shipped his butter and other products to the mining centers and received his groceries from Umatilla Landing." *(An Illustrated History of Union and Wallowa Counties, 1902, pg. 308-9)*

In the *1880 Federal Census*, Elverdo, 33, and Adeline, 34, were living in the city of Union, Union County, Oregon. Their children were with them: Mary E., 11, Lulu Queva, 9, and Maude Ethel, 2. Also living with them was Merritt Marshall, 19, a servant.

In August 9, 1884, Elverdo Draper was assigned a tract of land from the United States government. This tract of land had originally been a bounty land grant to William Stafford. Elverdo did homestead other parcels of land in addition to this.

Adeline died on October 13, 1897 at age 53. They had been married 28 years. On April 12, 1898, Elverdo married Mary A. Kneeland. The next year (1899), he sold his flocks and bought cattle. He also raised between 150 to 300 tons of grass hay annually.

The *1900 Federal Census* showed that they lived in Union and their household included: Elverdo, 51, Mary (Kneeland), 50, son Dick Draper, 12, and a servant named Carrie Chandler, 19.

Elverdo's wife Mary Kneeland died July 11, 1900 after a long and painful illness, and on March 10, 1901, Elverdo married Miss Rosanna E. Doyles, the last of his three wives. Rosa gave birth to a son, Oscar H., born September 27, 1903 in Union.

The 1910 Federal Census showed that the family still lived in the city of Union, Oregon. In the house lived Elverdo and his wife Rosie, and sons Richard "Dick" Draper and Oscar Draper, 7. Finally, the 1920 Federal Census showed they were living in the city of Union, Oregon and the household included: Elverdo, 71, Rosa, 41, and children Oscar, 16, and Emily, 7.

Elverdo Draper died August 24, 1939 at age 90 in Union, Oregon and was buried in the family plot at the Union Cemetery.

His family's birth-death dates are as follows: his parents, Henry Draper (1810-1877), Emily Palmer Draper (1812-1861); his spouses were Adeline Pelham Draper (1844-1897), married 1868; Mary A. Draper (1839-1900), married 1899; Rosanna Eliza Doyle Draper (1878-1949), married 1901.

Elverdo's siblings were: William Henry Harrison Draper (1840-1909), John P. Draper (1842-1912), Oscar Draper (1843-1920), Rhoda A. Draper Smith (1845-1921), Leoline, Draper (1850-1887).

His children were: Maryette Eunice Draper Johnson (1869-1903), Lulu Cueva Draper Cockrell (1871-1938), Maude Ethel Draper Logan (1878-1943), and Dick Draper (1888-1951). *(Findagrave.com)*

Dry Creek Lane - Formerly Woodell-Gressman Lane, this road #20 runs 1.73 miles in Township 1N R38E Section 35 in the Imbler maintenance district. It intersects Summerville Road and has significant history attached to its name.

Early maps showed the original road name as Woodell-Gresham, but the authors learned that second name, Gresham, was a wrong spelling. The correct spelling was found in a *1900 Federal Census*—Henry Gressman, not Gresham. He was a farmer and neighbor of Joseph Thomas Woodell, thus the hyphenated road name Woodell-Gressman.

Further proof of the Gressman name is found in Union County road petition #231 dated May 1885 wherein it gives the legal description of what is now called Dry Creek Road. Two of the signers on the petition were William and son Henry Gressman. They would have been residents that lived along the proposed road site and signing in support of this proposed road construction. With the Gressman name clarified, the authors were able to find biographical information to share herein.

In 1880, Carl "Henry" Gressman lived next door to the Levi and Elizabeth Jane (East) Stewart family in Culbertson precinct in Hitchcock County, Nebraska, where Henry set his eyes upon their pretty daughter Mary Ellen Stewart. It would appear that after the 1880 census, the Gressman and Stewart families traveled together over the Oregon Trail, heading for Northeast Oregon.

By 1881, the Stewart family had made it as far as Silver City, Idaho, which branches off the traditional Oregon Trail. There, on May 22, 1881 Henry Gressman married Mary Ellen Stewart, who was born May 8, 1862. Shortly after their marriage, it appears that the Gressmans and Stewarts pulled up stakes and continued their journey to Union County, Oregon, where they arrived on November 27, 1881. *(Levi Stewart's obituary, 1924)*

By December of 1883, Mary E. (Stewart) Gressman gave birth to their first child, William Albert, in Summerville, Union County, Oregon. In 1885, Mary's mother, Elizabeth Jane (East) Stewart died in Summerville. Levi Stewart died October 6, 1924 in Multnomah County.

Henry and Mary Gressman had the following children during their marriage: William A. (1883), Olive "Anna" (1886), and Ellene (1890-1895). Only William A. and Olive lived to adulthood.

Henry proved up his homestead on May 16, 1888. The legal description was in Section 34,

Township 1N R38E, the west half of the southeast quarter. This parcel of land, approximately 80 acres, was located on the south side of Dry Creek Road.

During the *1900 Federal Census*, the Henry Gressman household included Henry, 42, a farmer; wife Mary E., 38; and children: William, 16, and Olive, 13. Also living with them was Henry's widowed mother Anna Gressman, 70, German born. Henry and Mary were natives of the Midwest and all their children were born in Oregon.

Henry's father William Henry Gressman (1819-1896) and mother Anna Magdalena (Dose) Gressman (1829-1901) both rest in peace in the Summerville Cemetery. They were married on April 2, 1857 in St. Louis, Missouri. *(Missouri, U.S. Marriage Records)*

On March 1, 1905 in Elgin, Henry's only living daughter, Olive Anna Gressman married the neighbor's son, Thomas McKinnis. Thomas was the son of John Livingood McKinnis and Rachel Harris. Olive was born December 12, 1886 and died August 4, 1956 in Washington state.

In 1906, Henry and Mary were still farming in Summerville, but then in 1909, they moved to Pleasant Hill, Lane County, Oregon. The *1910 and 1920 Federal Censuses* of this place showed that Henry and Mary engaged in farming there too.

Their son, William Albert (1883-1925), had attended college there, and he married a teacher named Bess Beulah Nagle on June 20, 1911. He continued his education and became an attorney. They had one son, Eugene E. Gressman (1917-2010) and they lived in Springfield, as did Henry and Mary and Thomas and Olive McKinnis.

Mary Gressman died June 3, 1922, at Mercy Hospital in Eugene, Oregon; Henry died November 4, 1930 at the home of his daughter near Ashland, Oregon. Both Mary and Henry were buried in Laurel Hill Cemetery in Springfield, Oregon.

Sadly, their son William A. Gressman died prematurely on October 18, 1925 in Springfield, Lane County, Oregon. His obituary shed some light on the Gressman family at that location. It read in part: "W. A. Gressman of Springfield Dies — William Albert Gressman, Springfield attorney, died last night at the home of his father in Springfield. Mr. Gressman was born December 9, 1883. He was survived by his wife, Bess B. Gressman and one son, Eugene E. Gressman and a sister, Mrs. Thomas McKinnis, all of Springfield. Interment will be at the Laurel Hill cemetery.

The attorney and his family moved to Springfield nearly two years ago, Mr. Gressman, taking offices in the Commercial State bank building, but being forced to give up his work because of ill health. Heart failure is given as the cause of his death." *(End of obit, The Eugene Guard, Mon., Oct. 19, 1925, pg. 8)*

Whatever William A. Gressman failed at achieving in his law career due to a short life, his son, Eugene "Gene" Gressman made up for. Gene lived a full 92 years of life, having been a University of North Carolina Law School Emeritus Professor, teaching law for many years. He was an expert on practice before the U.S. Supreme Court, having clerked for five years for Justice Frank Murphy in the 1940s and then he co-authored, over the ensuing years, nine editions of his authoritative book *Supreme Court Practice,* along with other law books, law review articles and hundreds of appellate briefs. His artist wife Nan died in 2004, the obituary read. *(Obit info, The News and Observer of Raleigh, North Carolina, Sun., April 11, 2010, pg. 26)*

As for the Gressman homestead back in Summerville, Oregon, the *1935 Metsker Map* shows Mike Royes as the new owner of the Henry Gressman farm on the Woodell-Gressman Lane.

The Woodell part of this road was named after Joseph Thomas Woodell, who came across the Oregon Trail with his father and some siblings, starting their journey from Bladensburg, Wapello County, Iowa. They joined six or seven wagons at Council Bluffs, Pottawattamie County on the western border of Iowa.

Their train was called the Manville Train after its Captain Manville. The train left Council Bluffs on April 9, 1862, and they met up with 30 to 35 more wagons in eastern Utah on the trail to Oregon. *(History of Union County, Bernal D. Hug, pg. 46)*

The Woodell party included the father, James Erwin Woodell, a widower with his sons: William "Bill" age 21, Joseph Thomas, 19, James Lorenzo, 13, Junius "Doon", 9, and a married daughter Eliza (Woodell) Wallsinger and her husband John Wallsinger and their two daughters, Maggie, 4, and Sallie, 3 weeks. With them were the Hasty family, a blind lad named Ephraim, 12, and Mrs. McCormick, who nursed others through sickness on the train.

After five months on the Oregon Trail, the Woodells and Wallsingers arrived in Union County, Oregon in September 1862 without a loss of life. How happy they were to see such an oasis as the Grande Ronde Valley.

James Erwin Woodell and his sons James Lorenzo, Junius "Doon" and William all took homesteads in the vicinity southwest of Imbler on what is now Woodell Lane. (See Woodell Lane entry)

However, this history focuses on another son, Joseph Thomas Woodell (1844-1915), who eventually took land about three miles northwest of Summerville, about six miles distance from his father and brothers' claims. On April 4, 1875 Joseph married Clara Alice Neville. At first, the newlyweds lived with her parents, the George Neville household, as noted in the *1880 Federal Census,* and they already had four children.

In need of their own home, Joseph T. Woodell proved up his homestead on February 1, 1882. In the *1900 Federal Census* Joseph and Clara's family grew to nine children: Simon T., Miles M., Walter A., Guy R., James A., Nettie, Ettie, May B., and Minnie B. Joseph farmed with the help of his oldest son Simon T.

It was apparent that Joseph T. Woodell valued education, so at the age of 32, he became involved with the Dry Creek School District #17.

"According to the minutes of the first school board meeting on record on April 3, 1876, Samuel Rutledge was elected clerk but soon moved away and J. T. Woodell was then appointed clerk. On May 29, 1885, the board of directors decided it was time to build a new school house, so in July they contracted with J. T. Woodell to build and finish a new school house." *(School Districts of Union County, Oregon, Stella M. Edvalson, 1965, pg. 70, 71)* More about the one-room rural school can be found under the Summerville Road entry.

The new Dry Creek School house was completed in July 1885. Woodell received $312.00 for his part of the construction, but the "total cost of the school house, fence, toilets, walks and ground was $1,052.69," stated Edna Teter Rush, author of *The One Room School.*

On February 7, 1903, Joseph's wife, Clara A. Woodell, died at her Summerville home from pneumonia. She rallied for a time, and they thought she was going to get well, but then she died. The funeral was held at the residence on February 9 at 11 o'clock. Burial took place at Summerville Cemetery.

After her death, Joseph retired from farming, and moved to Asotin, Washington. On October 21, 1909 in Kootenai, Idaho, Joseph married Mrs. Anna W. Wright. She was born March 12, 1869 in Providence, Utah, and died November 26, 1917. They made their home at Joseph's residence in Asotin, Washington, where he lived the remainder of his life.

Joseph Thomas Woodell died at his home on October 2, 1915 in Asotin, Asotin County, Washington. The obituary written in that area read:

"After an illness of only 3 days, J. T. Woodell passed away early last Sunday morning at his home in the east part of town, congestion of the lungs being the cause of death. Only a few people knew that Mr. Woodell was sick, and the announcement of his death came as a shock to his many friends. The remains were embalmed by Undertaker Merchant and shipped Monday morning to La Grande, Oregon, where funeral services were held Tuesday, and the body was interred at Summerville. The remains were accompanied by his widow and a brother, James L. Woodell, who had been there for a few days on a visit.

Mr. Woodell was born in Missouri 71 years ago, and when still a mere lad moved with his parents to Iowa. In 1862, he came to what is known as the Grande Ronde Valley, in Union County, Oregon, and there made his residence up to about eight years ago, when he moved to Asotin, where he resided up to the time of his death. In 1875, he was united in marriage to Miss Clara Alice Neville, and to this union twelve children were given, ten of whom survive their father—five sons and five daughters. His wife died in 1903, and in 1907, he was again married, this time to Mrs. A. W. Wright, who with his children mourn his passing.

Mr. Woodell was one of those big hearted pioneer characters whose life was crowded full of honorable deeds. Not withstanding, he had passed a three-score and ten in point of years, he did not look it and was an exceptionally active and energetic man, pursuing his daily labors in a manner similar to men much younger in years. During his years in Asotin, he built up a close friendship with all people, and general regret is felt at his being taken away." (End of obit) Joseph T. Woodell's son Miles M. Woodell took occupancy of the homestead when Joseph retired from farming it.

Miles Manly Woodell was born November 16, 1881 in Summerville, the second child of twelve born to Joseph Thomas Woodell and Clara Alice Neville. He grew up on the farm, helping his father and older brother, Simon, with farm chores.

Miles was married on July 30, 1905 to Katie Melissa Enola Baker in Summerville. They made their home on Woodell-Gressman Road, where they raised a family of four known children: Inez L. (Woodell) Fries, Lloyd A., Ava E. (Woodell) Paul, and Marjorie Lola (Woodell) Jarvis.

Fast forward to the summer of 2000, Inez (Woodell) Fries, 94, was in attendance at the ninth annual reunion of Dry Creek School District #17, a gathering held at the I.O.O.F. building in Summerville. Thirty-nine of the forty-three in attendance that day were alumni from Dry Creek School.

The authors interviewed Inez (Woodell) Fries at that reunion. "I taught at Dry Creek for four years from 1930 to 1934," she explained.

Fries was the 31st Dry Creek School teacher registered in the *Register of Teachers Employed*, a list of teachers dating back to 1899. From its first entry to its last entry in 1945, there were 37 teachers on record at Dry Creek, each instructor having completed the two-year Teacher's College Training course.

Fries' school year term started September 1, 1930 and went thirty-six weeks. She remembered her initial wages were $95 a month for the first three years; however in 1933 due to the Great Depression, her wages dropped by necessity to $70 a month. After four years of teaching, she earned her Teacher's Lifetime Certificate, and she retired to devote herself to raising and teaching her own children.

Her father, Miles Woodell, died on April 17, 1950 in St. Joseph Hospital in La Grande from coronary occlusion. His son-in-law, Henry Fries, was the informant for his death certificate information. The obituary states, in part, the following about his life.

"Miles M. Woodell, Retired Farmer Succumbs Today—Funeral services are being arranged for Miles M. Woodell, 68, Summerville, retired farmer and rural mail carrier, who died in a La Grande hospital today after a long illness.

Born in Summerville, he was a life-long resident and was a member of the Pleasant Grove Grange. Snodgrass Funeral Home will announce funeral arrangements later. Woodell served as a rural mail carrier for 37 years in the Summerville area. His widow Katie, son Lloyd of Portland, daughters Inez Fries of Summerville, Mrs. Byron Paul of Portland, and Mrs. J. W. Jarvis of Omaha, Nebraska survive him." He also had five sisters and two brothers who survived him. There were no surviving brothers living in Union County at the time of his death. (End of obit information from *La Grande Observer, April 17, 1950, pg. 1*)

Miles' wife, Mrs. Katie Woodell, 78, died April 3, 1961 at a La Grande hospital, after an extended illness. A Summerville resident for 75 years, Mrs. Woodell was born in La Grande on September 15, 1882. All four of her children survived her. *(La Grande Observer, April 4, 1961, pg. 7)*

Since the Woodell and Gressman families both moved off of the road, the combination road name was replaced with Dry Creek Lane, named for Dry Creek. This creek is fed each spring by melting snowpack from the Blue Mountain range. Though it usually runs dry by early June each year, the memories of Dry Creek, its road, school and the Woodells and Gressmans will not be forgotten while their histories are in writing.

The John Livingood McKinnis Century Farm was another noteworthy residence on this road. McKinnis bought this property in 1885, and his son, Clement, built the Victorian home on it in 1903. It was built from lumber milled from Clement's saw mill on Ruckle Road, and it was built from plans that his wife, Nettie, ordered from back East.

After Clement died in January 1953 at the age of 85 years, the home was passed to his daughter, Fern Westenskow, who was childless. She passed the home to her nephew, who was Clement's grandson, Charles Rhoads.

The property transferred to Charles' widow, Doris Rhoads, before it was sold to Dan and Nancy (Royes) McDonald in 2004. The tillable land was farmed first by George Royes Sr. and then Nancy's father, George Royes Jr. "G" during Doris' residency on Dry Creek Road. The McDonalds remodeled the Century Farm home in 2005 and added structures to the property since then.

John Livingood McKinnis was the eldest of nine children, being born July 5, 1843 in Jackson County, Ohio to Craner (1817-1897) and Catherine (Truseler) McKinnis.

John's residence in 1860 was in Knoxville, Marion County, Iowa. As a 20-year-old man, he bid farewell to his parents and joined up as a driver with the 40-wagon "Oliver Train" which left Iowa on May 10, 1864 destined for Oregon.

The journey was marked by some trouble with the Indians on the Upper Platt River, when the train was attacked and the Indians confiscated a significant number of their stock.

However, despite this loss, the train made it to the Grande Ronde Valley on October 10, 1864. Other immigrants with them included: H.W. Oliver and parents, John Van Blokland and family, Mr. Taal, and Gerrit Rysdam and family.

McKinnis engaged in a succession of occupations in his lifetime, including teaching in one-room schools, becoming county school superintendent in 1872, saw milling from 1890-96, building, and farming.

While working for the Oliver Saw Mill in rural Summerville, he met his future wife and the cook there, Miss Rachel Catherine Harris. She must have reached his heart through his stomach because they were married on March 3, 1867. Rachel was a native of Missouri, who with her parents, left Sullivan County, Missouri and came to Oregon in 1865 on the "Joe Knight Train." She is the daughter of Joseph and Mary Ann Harris, after whom Mount Harris was named.

During her marriage to John McKinnis, she became mother to eleven children, all born in Summerville, Oregon: Clement L., Beatrice T. (Hug), Herschel, Ina May (Bingaman), Frank, Hannah (Davidhizar); Thomas, who married the neighbor's daughter Olive Gressman; Rosa B. (Bade), James, Charles and Stella A. (Lee).

John L. McKinnis' life was characterized as ambitious and his efforts well directed. He died on February 14, 1925 and Rachel died July 30, 1914. A large monument marks their graves at the Summerville Cemetery. *(Union County Oregon Biographies; Doris Rhoads interview, Feb. 2001)*

Duck Road - This private road is located in Township 2S R38E Section 33 in La Grande, and it is one in a series of five roads named after birds. These five roads are part of a mobile home park on Fruitdale Lane.

Dutton Road - This road #55 runs 1.24 miles and connects Indian Creek Road to Clark Creek Road east of Elgin. It is located in Township 1N R40E Section 30 in the Elgin maintenance district.

On this road there were property owners named Gains "Gaius" L. and Virginia Jane Dutton. *(1935 Metsker Map)* Gains L. Dutton was born in Faribault, Rice County, Minnesota on May 9, 1882 to his parents Robert Dutton (1847-1920) age 35, and Evalyn Lavina Lorince Youmans, age 24. In the *1895 Minnesota census*, Robert Dutton, 47, was listed as a junk dealer and Gains was but 16 years old.

His marriage was announced in the *La Grande Observer, Sept. 25, 1917, pg. 5* as follows in part: Married this Afternoon—Mr. Gaius Dutton, a prominent stockman of Cove, and Miss Virginia Setterdahl, of Elgin, were married. Mr. and Mrs. Roy Fisher of Elgin, (Virginia's nephew), were present at the ceremony.

Virginia was born April 14, 1880 in West Virginia and died February 17, 1953 in La Grande at age 72. She was interred in Olney Cemetery in Pendleton, according to her obituary in the *La Grande Observer, Feb. 18, 1953 pg. 4.*

During their marriage, Gains engaged in general farming and stock raising. He and Virginia did not have children.

They resided in Elgin after their marriage and are noted there in the *1920 and 1930 Federal Censuses.* His obituary in the *La Grande Observer, Feb. 6, 1933 pg. 1* stated that he died at the Grande Ronde Hospital on February 4, 1933 (Saturday night) after a lingering illness. He was 50 years, 8 months and 26 days old at the time of his death. He was survived by his widow, Virginia; a sister Beatrice McCardle of Phoenix, Arizona; and a brother, Frank B. Dutton of Medford, Oregon.

Burial took place at the Elgin Cemetery. His memorial stone has the dates (1883-1933) which slightly differ from his obituary dates.

Eagle Creek Lane - This popularly named lane can be found near Pondosa and Medical Springs. It is located in Township 3S R38E Section 3 in the La Grande maintenance district.

It is named after Eagle Creek, which got its name from an incident involving two men, Knight and Abbott. They were herding cattle in the Powder River valley in 1861, when they came to a big creek and shot an eagle there. *(Thirty-one Years in Baker County, pg. 15)*

Eagle Drive - This public unmaintained road is off Buchanan Lane, south of Island City in Township 3S R38E Section 3.

East Lane - This is private lane off of Riddle Road in Township 3S R38E Section 4 in the La Grande district.

Eastern Oregon Court - This road #155A is only .15 miles in length in Township 3S R38E Section 24, constituting a court. It comes off Airport Lane and is used for commercial purposes.

Eighteenth Street - (See Grandview entry) Township 3S R38E Section 17.

Elgin Cemetery Road - This gravel road #77 intersects with Clark Creek Road southeast of Elgin, beginning at the small bridge that crosses Clark Creek. The Elgin Cemetery Road runs 1.25 miles in Township 1N R39E Section 26 south to Indian Creek Road. There are two property owners on this road and the large, gated Elgin Cemetery.

In this cemetery rests many pioneers whose stories will be told in this book, but it also includes a lesser known story of someone equally as interesting. In fact, this person is one of Union County's most successful career stories, Ross Elwyn Paxton (1931-2003).

Paxton was born on a farm in Elgin and educated by the well-known teacher Stella Mayfield, who later became the principal and namesake of Elgin's Elementary School. Paxton's family relocated to Union when he was a sophomore in high school. In his senior year, he was the editor and designer of "The 1949 Bobcat" yearbook that won second place in a national competition for its page layout and art.

Following his graduation from Union High School in 1949, he graduated in 1951 from the Burnley School of Professional Art in Seattle, Washington. On February 4, 1954, he traveled to Manhattan on a shoestring budget to pursue his art career.

There Paxton worked as a freelance illustrator at Hockaday Associates Ad agency. Two of his colleagues there were Andy Warhol (1926-1987), before he became the famous American pop artist; and Cynthia Rathbone (1939-1969), the adopted daughter of movie actor Basil Rathbone, who played Sherlock Holmes in 14 Hollywood films from 1939 to 1946.

Paxton recalled sharing a few lunches with Andy Warhol at the Serendipity restaurant on East 64th Street, and once at Andy's apartment. Paxton said that he thought he was one of a rare few to ever eat at Warhol's apartment on Lexington and 37th Street.

Andy's mother, Julia Warhol, who lived with Andy since 1951, made them a Czech stew that day. Paxton saw only the arms of this lady as she handed the bowls of stew to Andy through a curtain that closed off the kitchen from the dining room. Andy never introduced Paxton to his mother as she remained hidden in the kitchen.

When Andy's career took off, and he became the famous pop artist of that time, he stopped associating with Paxton. Andy became more flamboyant in his dress and was constantly surrounded by an entourage of admirers. He had no time for his former humble work associate, Paxton said.

In 1967, Paxton began a 27-year-long career working for AC&R Advertising in mid-town Manhattan, New York, illustrating for a number of prestigious clients. Estee Lauder was one of his main accounts for years. One of his co-workers was Judi DeSouter of Bronx, New York, who wrote the following about him.

"Ross was an extraordinary man with numerous talents and interest that made him unique and special," she wrote. "He was a kind, loving and generous man who made a difference in the lives of many people. His greatness is too vast to measure in words, but his life will continue to be celebrated by all of us who were lucky enough to call him our friend."

In late 2002, during his retirement, Paxton illustrated one last time. He did it as a favor for Trish and Dave Yerges of Summerville, Oregon, who wrote a bilingual children's book called "The Adventures of Scooper the Beagle Dog" published in 2004.

It was a first for Paxton—illustrating a children's book and by computer— and the first time since his retirement in 1991 that he illustrated anything, he said. When he did, he used retro style images from the 1940s, depicting scenes and things he remembered from his youth, growing up in Union County. He created these images with the help of computer-aided technology, another first for him.

A subsequent market testing of the book was done with elementary school children. We wanted to see if they liked the retro images in this book and if they understood his drawings, which they did.

Paxton lived his retirement years at his home in Edgewater, New Jersey, but in 2003, he decided to sell his home and relocate to Palm Springs, California, where, he said, "I hope to spend the last ten years of my life."

Sadly, that didn't happen. He died in his sleep at home on Tuesday, June 3, 2003 at the age of 72. De Souter and another friend found him resting in peace.

"I am grateful that Ross got to leave us while he slept," De Souter said. "I can't think of a better way to go, and I surely can't think of a person who deserved such a peaceful departure."

His cremains were sent home to his surviving brother, Bill Paxton of Union, and burial took place in the Paxton family plot on Cemetery Road outside of Elgin. Ross Paxton was remembered as a gentle soul, generous in word and deed. He was loved and missed by many. But in retrospect, he had this humorous comment to make about his life—"I may not have become as famous as Andy Warhol, but at least I outlived him. Ha!" *(2001-2003 emails with Ross Paxton)*

Elkanah Road - This road diverts off of Ukiah-Hilgard Highway 244 and is an access road for five recreational cabins.

The land is part of Camp Elkanah, established in 1956 and which straddles the highway, 90 acres on either side. Its richer history, however, begins in the 1920s when it was called Mount Emily Camp.

According to Greg Tsiatsos, who lived his entire life in the Starkey district, Mount Emily Camp was built about 1928, encompassing 240 acres for the purpose of housing Mt. Emily Timber Company employees and their families.

Mt. Emily Timber Company (later called Mt. Emily Lumber Company) was incorporated in May 1912 and operated until 1955. The following lumber men were its first officers: A.H. Stange, Merrill, Wisconsin, president; A. J. Stange of La Grande, vice-president; Charles J. Kinzel, Merrill, Wisconsin, secretary-treasurer.

Later, another set of officers living in La Grande managed the business operations. They were August John Stange (president), Lesley Kenneth Kinzel (general manager) and Fred Emil Lanzer (sales manager). August John Stange, of Merrill, Wisconsin, brought his wife, Priscilla, and two daughters, Jane and Ann, to La Grande as early as 1912 to start buying timberland. Stange eventually hired contractors to build the iconic Stange Manor in La Grande. *(ancestry.com)*

August Stange's son-in-law George William Decker of California was married to his daughter, Ann Stange. George Decker also became involved in the Mt. Emily Timber Company.

As a side note about the Stange Manor---A.H. Stange came to La Grande in 1924 to see his son August build his new house on Spring Street. Upon seeing its frame, he reportedly said to August, "What are you building, a chicken house with all these windows?" Though he apparently did not appreciate the new home's floor plan then, it was always considered an elegant residential icon in La Grande. *(Greg Tsiatsos interview, Oct. 30, 2018)*

A full article about the Stange family and their timber businesses, including Mt. Emily Timber Company, is found on page 7 of the *La Grande Observer, Jan. 12, 1924.*

The Mt. Emily Camp offered residential cabins for the mill families and a school for their children and those living in the Starkey area. The school was comprised of two pink boxcars placed next to each other. One box car housed first through fourth grade students and the other box car housed fifth through eighth grade students. This school was in the Starkey School District #51, according to Greg Tsiatsos of Starkey, who said he received his entire elementary education there.

In 1955, Mt. Emily Lumber Company was sold to Valsetz Lumber Company, and in November 1956, Valsetz donated Mount Emily Camp and 12 acres of surrounding forest land to the Blue Mountain Conservative Baptist Association of Eastern Oregon. *(Wikipedia, Mt. Emily Lumber Co.)*

In 1956, Mt. Emily Camp was renamed Camp Elkanah, a year-round facility offering summer camps, hosting events, and renting the facilities to other groups.

Ellis Road - This road #103 leaves Coughanour Lane in the North Powder district and runs 3.29 miles in Township 6S R39E Section 31, connecting to Anthony Lakes Highway in Baker County. It allows access to 12 properties.

This is cattle country, and there was a W. W. Ellis residing in the North Powder area, who was a farmer and stock raiser. He was born about 1840 in Indiana, although the *1910 Federal Census* states he was born in 1836. Both his mother and father were natives of Kentucky, the *1880 Federal Census* stated.

He married Mrs. Jane Johnson of Baker County on January 2, 1876. In the *1910 Federal Census* at age 74, he was living as a boarder in Island City. There were some Ellis men living in Baker County, but W. W. Ellis seems to be the only one in North Powder.

End Road - This road #17 runs 1.85 miles in Township 1S R38E Section 22 in the Imbler maintenance district. It's named after early residents of Union County, Jacob End (1850-1913) and his wife Samantha A. Smith (1863-1944). The *1935 Metsker Map* shows Samantha End as a property holder on this road.

Jacob "Jake" End was born April 8, 1850 in Bavaria, Germany, and he immigrated to America in either 1860 or 1867 depending on what source you read. On the censuses, he declared that he spoke and wrote English and was occupied as a farmer. In 1870, at age 28, he was living in a boarding house with other men, likely laborers, in Silver, Montana. The post office for that area was Helena.

On November 5, 1881, he married Samantha A. Smith, the daughter of James Smith. *(Ancestry.com)* Samantha was born October 12, 1863 in Iowa. She became mother to sons Percy (b.1882), Antone (b.1884), Cecil (b.1886) and lost two children in infancy, Joseph (1888, 8 mos.) and Katie (1892, 1 year). The babies were buried at Summerville Cemetery.

In those early years of marriage, sometimes the father-in-law made a visit. "James Smith, an old time resident of this place, who has been spending the winter with his son-in-law, Jacob End, and other old time friends, will take his departure on Tuesday evening's train for his home near Delight, Washington." *(La Grande Observer, Thursday, March 10, 1898, pg. 2)*

Life on the snowbound End Road of rural Summerville (Pleasant Grove) can be isolating but having guests stay the winter surely helps pass the time. However mail delivery can be lacking. One briefly in *the La Grande Observer of May 13, 1903, pg. 4* stated: "Jake End was in town from his home at the foot of Mt. Emily. He complains about not getting his mail."

"Old Jake" as some called him, died on July 27, 1913 and was buried at the Summerville Cemetery with his two baby children. His death notice was a bare bones statement: "Aged Summerville Man Dies — Jacob End, an aged resident of Summerville, died this morning at his residence there. No funeral arrangements have been made but the funeral will probably be held on Wednesday or Thursday of this week." *(La Grande Observer, Monday, July 28, 1913, pg. 8)*

After Jake's death, it appears that Samantha's second oldest son, "Tony" (Antone) and his wife may have lived with her at the homestead on End Road. One briefly from *the La Grande Observer of Sat. Nov. 12, 1932 pg. 3* stated: "Portland Visitor — Mrs. Samantha End and Mr. and Mrs. Tony End of Pleasant Grove, have been having as their guest their son and brother, Percy End, whose home is in Portland."

Percy M. End (1882-1947) was the eldest child of Jake and Samantha End, and about two years older than his brother Tony End (1884-1965). Percy's obituary can be found at *La Grande Observer, Monday, December 15, 1947 on page 1.*

Their mother Samantha A. (Smith) End died April 28, 1944 following a long illness, her obituary stated. She was buried alongside her husband at Summerville Cemetery.

In 2021, this gravel road remains the most densely populated road in the Pleasant Grove district with about 40 residences. The road is pretty straight and runs through the shady forest of tall pines, Douglas firs and Tamaracks. When driving this road, roll your windows down and take some deep breaths of pine tree fragrance.

Ernest Road - A private drive off Palmer Junction Road, named after Ernest "Ernie" Edgar Adams of Elgin, a laborer at Pondosa Pine Lumber Company, then a logger by trade and owner of Adams Supply Company in Elgin in the 1950s.

Ernie was born April 12, 1913 in Elgin, Oregon to J. W. Adams and Emily Jane Law. Ernie married twice, first to Frances Gilkison in 1933. She died in 2004. Ernie then married Laurose Mae (Harris) Hibberd in 2005. He died June 9, 2006 and was buried in the Elgin Cemetery with his wife Frances and other relatives. *(Findagrave.com; ancestry.com)*

Ernie was employed on the rip saw at Bill Moore's Pondosa Pine Lumber Company in Elgin, and in those Depression years being employed offered unusual security. If a man gave up his job at the plant, there was easily another to take his place, so Ernie was dedicated to his job and didn't want to lose it.

One frigid wintry day in 1934, the plant temperature fell to 30 degrees below zero and the grease in the machines stiffened up so that nothing worked. Moore sent Ernie and the other men home until it warmed up. Well, Ernie and the other men were so desperate to get back to work and earn money that as soon as the thermometer rose to 20 degrees below zero they all went back to work.

Ernie got the news late and quickly started out for the plant. While en route, Moore sent his wife, Lucille, to get him in a taxi. She knocked at his residence door but soon learned he had already left for the plant on foot. Ernie was certainly dedicated to his family's support and to Bill Moore, who was known to be a tough task master.

Ernie said, "Bill Moore was determined. He kept the mill going when other people wouldn't have." *(The History of Pondosa Pine Lumber Company, Dave & Trish Yerges, 2003)*

Ernie was still working at Pondosa Pine Lumber Company when he registered for the WWII draft on October 16, 1940. Moore succeeded in getting the lumber company designated as a defense plant so that he could keep all his men on payroll during the war and so he could have access to raw wood.

Due to poor health, Moore sold the mill in 1943, and its new owner wasn't interested in buying the Moore Field baseball park, which Bill Moore founded to bring semi-professional teams to Elgin. At the time, it was one of the most modern fields around, including lights for night games. After Moore's death, however, the Elgin Chamber of Commerce hired Ernie to take down the grandstands at the ball field and relocate them to the Elgin High School football field and the Elgin Stampede grounds.

In 1955, Ernie Adams became the president of the Elgin Rod and Gun Club. *(La Grande Observer, May 26, 1955, pg. 6)* In 1961, he was president of the Elgin High School Alumni Association. *(La Grande Observer, May 25, 1961, pg. 1)*

Also in January 1961, Ernie Adams was elected president of the Elgin Stampeders, an organization that was founded in June 1946 as a riding club and eventually turned into a rodeo organization, which hosts the Elgin Stampede Rodeo annually in July.

Ernie Adams was well liked, and he contributed richly to the community of Elgin during his long life.

Evergreen Road - This private road is located in Township 2S R38E in Section 33 in the La Grande maintenance district.

The name is rather misleading as there are not many evergreen trees along this road. It seems to run north-south and it is flanked by cultivated fields. It serves 17 residences, according to *Union County Tax Assessor* records. It appears that Mark H. Anderson owns the oldest house and barn on this road, both built in 1910.

Evers Canyon Road - This private road is located in Township 2N R39E in Section 36 in the Elgin maintenance district.

This road is named after Charles "Orris" Evers, born March 21, 1896 in Isle LaMotte, Grande Isle County, Vermont, to parents John and Marcia (Doolin) Evers. His father remarried Eva Leota Phillips Green. Then John Evers died. His son, Orris lived with his step-mother Eva, and then she married Johnathan Green. The *1920 Federal Census* shows the Green family living in Elgin on a farm.

Orris Evers married Pearl Estella Blanchard on February 22, 1921, and they made their home in Elgin, where they raised three daughters and one son. One of their daughters, Eloine Leota, born October 22, 1923, married Albertus Hardy (1914-1988) on November 1, 1946. They had five children: Don, David, Jeff, Steven, and Alice.

During his life, Orris was paid for general road labor. On one occasion, it was published that he was paid $18.96 for this work. *(La Grande Observer, Dec. 31, 1942, pg. 4)*

Orris Evers died January 20, 1963 at his home in Elgin at the age of 66 years. He was buried in the Elgin Cemetery. His wife, Pearl Evers, died in 1993. Daughter Alice said the road had no name until 1988 when the county road naming system was instituted. *(Alice Hardy interview, Dec. 3, 2019)*

Finley Creek Lane - (Findley Creek Lane) This private lane runs off Ruckle Road and dead ends in Township 1N R38E Section 28 in the Imbler maintenance district.

This name is a geographic road name after Finley Creek, which flows in the Blue Mountains northwest of Summerville, and it appears to be a tributary of Willow Creek.

Several ranchers of the Summerville district conducted their annual fall roundup of summer range stock in the Finley Creek area, and they bunked in a cow camp there. You can see a "Finley Camp" noted on the *1935 Metsker Map* of Township 1N R38E Section 6. Cattle which were turned out earlier in the year on national forest lands were gathered together, with their progeny, and herded to their winter safety and plenty of the various home ranches.

Alex McKenzie, county commissioner (1938-1942), Dillard Choate, Arthur Behrens, Bert Oliver, Frank Oliver, Frank Woodell, Clyde Myers, Hugh Parks and Earl Parks are the cattlemen who conducted the roundup. All together, an estimated seven or eight hundred head of stock will be involved in the roundup. Each of the ranchers have claim to some of the cattle. *(La Grande Observer, Oct. 15, 1942, pg. 1)*

In the search for the elusive man behind the name of Finley Camp, Finley Creek and by extension Finley Creek Road, the authors had to consider possible variations of the name Finley, and that's how they found him.

Living in the Summerville area was Alexander Blakey Findley and his wife Sarah Jane (Reeves) Findley, who were on the *Summerville 1870 Federal Census*. As is common, census documents sometimes wrote surnames differently, such as Finley, Findley or even Findlay, so it's understandable how geographic names get mixed up.

Alexander Blakey Findley made quite a name for himself in the State of Oregon, being affiliated with the state grange and the State Pioneer Association. It was said that he was personally acquainted with the late Dr. McLoughlin, the Hudson Bay factor.

His obituary states that he was born January 15, 1838 in Indiana. His gravestone says September 3, 1838 and state archives say September 15, 1838. In any case, in 1847 at the age of nine he accompanied his parents to Vancouver, Washington, arriving there in the fall of that year. Then by 1852, he was living in Oregon City, his obituary stated.

On February 14, 1859 in Marion County, Oregon, he married Sarah Jane Reeves, a native of Benton County, Missouri. She was born there on October 25, 1842, the daughter of Lenoir Reeves and Mourning Walker. She died August 10, 1922 in Cedar Mill, Washington County, Oregon. *(State Archives)*

Alexander Findley preceded her in death at the age of 73 on March 8, 1912 in Hillsboro, Oregon. He was touted as a Pioneer of Oregon and as "the man who crossed the Plains in 1847." He eventually moved to Union County, Oregon in 1863.

On that *1870 Federal Census of Summerville*, the Findley household consisted of six members: A. B. Findley, 32, Sarah Jane, 28 and four children ages 9 to 2.

The records of *Findagrave.com* give a more complete profile of the children: Florence Mary Findley Johnson (1860-1930), Everett E. Findley (1862-1878), Bertha Edyth Findley (1864-1870), George Madison Findley (1868-1878), John F. (1871-1878), Levi S. Findley (1873-1878), Emma D. Findley (1873-1878), Lora E. Findley (1877-1878), and Henry Ross Findley (1879-1963).

The Findley family were living in Summerville at least by 1868 because George Madison Findley was born there, and his sister Bertha Edyth died there on November 8, 1870. She was buried in the Summerville Cemetery, which the Findley memoirs described as a rather new cemetery on a hill between Willow Creek and the Sand Ridge.

Summerville Cemetery fits that geographic description, and in fact, it was newly established in 1866 with its first burial. Records of the Findley girl's burial seems to be missing from the ledger, but when one takes into consideration that the early Summerville Cemetery record book was chewed apart by mice and was painstakingly reconstructed by caretaker Emery Oliver and his new bride

Thelma Oliver to the best of their ability, you can understand how some names were eaten and carried away inside the bellies of mice. *(Emery Oliver Interview, 2000)*

By 1876, the Findley family lived in the Lostine area of Wallowa County. They were noted in historical publications as the first white family to settle in that area. Findley also went down in history as almost causing a tragic war in Northeast Oregon between all the European settlers and the Nez Perce, who have lived there for longer than anyone can remember. *(An Illustrated History of Union and Wallowa Counties, Oregon, 1902, pg. 481-482)*

In 1878, two years after this upheaval, the Findleys faced an unthinkable loss of life from a diphtheria epidemic that raged through what we know today as Wallowa, Union and Baker counties.

According to the written memoirs of Alexander B. and Sarah Jane Findley, six of their children died of diphtheria within a period of 18 days. The plague in their home began on July 15, 1878 when George and Levi "Sammy" died and continued as follows: on July 19, John F. died; on July 21, Everett E. died; on July 28, Emma died; and on August 1, their infant Lora E. Findley died. All six children were buried in the West Side Cemetery in Lostine, Wallowa County, Oregon.

One can only imagine the wrenching sorrow in the hearts of the Findley parents and their surviving daughter Florence. The last child Henry wasn't born until the following year in 1879.

In 1885, *Postmaster Records for Union County* listed A. B. Findley as the postmaster of Imnaha. It was in this territory that in February 1884 his eldest child, Florence Mary Findley married John William "Jack" Johnson (1850-1931), a native of England, and a cattleman of Wallowa County.

Florence died in Imnaha in 1930 and is buried there. She was mother to four children.

In 1898, A. B. Findley sold out his interests in Wallowa County and moved to Cedar Mill in Washington County, Oregon, a suburb of metropolitan Portland. It appears he and his wife lived the remainder of their lives in the Willamette Valley.

Alexander Findley was a farmer/rancher wherever he settled, and he lived in the Summerville area after which a creek, camp and road were named for him. There was no other Findley character as prominent in history as he was that would be the namesake for Finley Creek Lane.

Fish Trap Road - This private gravel road leaves Highway 82 running east, a short distance, allowing access to four residences.

Some well known residents on this road include long-time Elgin grocer Scott Ludwig and his wife Katie Ludwig, Grande Ronde Hospital imaging technician; and their neighbors, retired educators and school administrators Bob and Susie Thomas, who successfully launched a reading program to improve literacy in the Elgin School District.

The city of Elgin was originally called Fish Trap Ford after the habit of the local Native Americans, who built traps in the river to catch fish during the major runs. The early pioneers started to call the hill to the east of the river "Fish Trap Hill." The first bridge across the river was built in 1878, about 100 feet above the old ford. *(History of Elgin, Oregon, Bernal D. Hug, Sr. page 8)*

The name for this road was suggested by Scott and Katie Ludwig, preserving its historical reference to Fish Trap Hill. *(Scott Ludwig interview, Dec. 28, 2019)*

Five Point Creek Road - This road #3A runs 4.72 miles in Township 2S R37E Section 31 in the La Grande maintenance district.

The name comes from the Five Points Creek that was so named on the *1882 Government Survey Map*. The variant spellings of the creek on maps through the years have included: Five Point Creek, Fivepoints Creek, and Fivepoint Creek. The official name on the U.S.G.S. map is Five Points Creek. However, the official Union County road name is Five Point Creek Road. This name originated with the early settlers as they traveled up the "Old Emigrant Road" and crossed a creek where five mountain ridges come together, thus the U.S.G.S. name Five Points Creek.

"Five Points Creek empties into the Grande Ronde River at Hilgard, Oregon. In the 1920s and earlier, a fair-sized lumber mill produced railroad ties and general lumber. There are some concrete foundations remaining of the [Five Points] mill." *(Clayton Warnstaff 's handwritten memoirs donated by Dallas Hibbert, October 17, 2021)*

Fletcher Lane - This lane is designated as road #122 and is located in Township 3S R40E, Section 11 in the Union maintenance district. It runs 1.14 miles long and provides access to 10 residences. Only one house and shed on this lane dates back to 1900.

This lane is named after John "Jack" Riley and Margaret Elizabeth "Bessie" (Laird) Fletcher. Jack was born July 18, 1878 in Mobetie, Texas to James Preston Fletcher and Elizabeth Marshall. John married Bessie in 1907 in Weiser, Idaho. She was born July 24, 1873 in Blue Hill, Nebraska to William C. Hill and Margaret Ann Murdaugh. John and Bessie did not have children.

John died January 26, 1957 in La Grande and Bessie died May 1, 1961 in La Grande. Both are interred at the Cove Cemetery.

They originally came to Cove in 1924. Bessie got involved with the Cove Ladies Guild and was active in various groups throughout her lifetime. The first mention of Jack Fletcher in the La Grande Observer was on June 21, 1924, in which it mentioned that he had a large number of turkeys on their farm, and many of them would be sold for Thanksgiving. *(La Grande Observer, Nov. 21, 1924, pg. 7)*

In the *La Grande Observer of Dec. 18, 1925 pg. 9,* it noted that "Mrs. Bessie Fletcher will be absent from her place at school (in Cove) the rest of this week. She is taking examination at La Grande."

In 1926, it appeared that the Fletchers had a boarder in their home, Mr. Ayer M. Lightfoot, of Butte, Montana, who lived with the Fletchers for one year before he returned to his home on June 1, 1926 by train. *(La Grande Observer, June 1, 1926, pg. 5)* It appears that the Fletchers were hospitable, and numerous times they had house gatherings and guests. The couple started off the 1927 new year hosting a sleighing party. *(La Grande Observer, Jan. 6, 1927, pg 3)*

In the *March 31, 1927 La Grande Observer, pg. 6*, it stated that "a recent school board meeting had elected teachers including Mrs. Bessie Fletcher as a high school teacher."

Bessie was also actively involved with the Mt. Fannie Grange at Cove, holding various offices throughout the years.

In October of 1928, Jack bought 45 black-faced ewes to add to the 75 ewes he already had at the ranch. *(La Grande Observer, Oct. 18, 1928, pg. 9)* He was active in a local wool growers association and very knowledgeable about the business.

One of Jack's ewes gave birth to a 17-pound lamb, when the average weight of a newborn lamb was between seven and ten pounds. *(La Grande Observer, Feb. 1, 1929, pg. 9)*

Later that year, the *La Grande Observer* noted that Stewart French and R. H. Daniel were shearing sheep at the Arch Conley farm for Jack Fletcher and R. J. Baker. It was said that Mr. Fletcher had more than 30 years experience handling sheep. *(La Grande Observer, May 17, 1929, pg. 12)*

Although the lambing season at the Fletcher ranch had barely begun, out of the 18 lambs that had arrived, there were five pairs of twins. *(La Grande Observer, Feb. 15, 1930, pg. 6)* At this time Fletcher had 150 sheep on his ranch.

Bessie had quit teaching for a while and then accepted a position at Juntura, Oregon, where she held the post of principal. Mr. Fletcher planned to join her later to spend the winter there. They sent their livestock to brother-in-law Todd Bauer of Imbler. *(La Grande Observer, Sept. 8, 1942, pg. 5)*

At this point, apparently the Fletchers decided to downsize as they had purchased ten acres from Mrs. Lew Bloom of Cove. It was located about one mile east of Cove. The same article indicates that Bessie would finish teaching school at the end of April 1943 and had no plans to return to Juntura to teach. *(La Grande Observer, March 26, 1943, pg. 3)*

She accepted a new teaching post at the high school in Monument, Oregon in 1943 and continued there at least two years. She accepted the post of school principal during the 1944-45 school year. *(La Grande Observer, Sept. 9, 1943, pg. 3; March 18, 1944, pg. 3; and Sept. 9, 1944, pg. 3)*

During that same time period, the Fletchers sold part of their farm to relatives Eugene and Claude Laird of San Diego, California, who were planning to move onto the farm in 1945. *(La Grande Observer, Sept. 29, 1945, pg. 8)*

By 1946, she was again teaching in the Cove School District as a high school teacher. An article in February 1949 stated that residents of Cove's cherry orchards had become alarmed by the damage caused by roaming deer. They were trying to devise methods to minimize this damage. The hungry deer had been eating the young shoots of the cherry trees, including the old Fletcher place. Local people distributed baled hay and rabbit concentrate at the west end of the old Fletcher pasture. The food was provided by the state game commission. *(La Grande Observer, Feb. 2, 1949, pg. 7)*

Aside from teaching, Bessie also contributed as a La Grande Observer news correspondent for Cove society news. Her first column was printed on October 22, 1949, page 9 and her last column was printed on February 5, 1958, page 5. During her last year of writing, she was a widow, then she died on May 1, 1961.

Flevious Road - This private gravel road located in Township 4S R37E Section 1 departs Coombs Loop and sprawls southward in five directions. Today there are three different property owners on this road.

This road is named after a man named Flevious Glenn Knauber (1916-1997), who rented a trailer in that area, but he wasn't a land owner. *(Greg Tsiatos interview, Oct. 30, 2018)*

Flevious Knauber was born July 23, 1916 in Topeka, Kansas, the son of William and Florence Knauber. He was married to Alta Good (1913-2009) in Benton, Oregon, on July 3, 1959.

He was listed as living at 58504 Flevious Road in Union County in a 1996-1997 directory. It was his last residence prior to his death on May 9, 1997 at the age of 80 years. He was the only known person called Flevious to live on Flevious Road.

Fly Creek Road - This road leaves Starkey Road and leads to Fly Valley. According to local historian, Greg Tsiatos, the road is closed now. Fly Creek was named on the original *1882 U.S. Government Survey Map*. Fly Creek may have been named for fly fishing, a popular sport in Union County or the abundance of pesty flies.

Fly Ridge Road - This road is a continuance of Fly Creek Road, which leaves Starkey Road,. After it crosses Fly Creek, it does a lot of winding around and connects with Grande Ronde River Road. This is also on the *1882 U.S. Government Survey Map*.

Fly Valley Road - This road is the same as NF-5172 and NF-220. It curls around the forests of the Blue Mountains in the Starkey district, connecting to Tin Trough Road on one end and Fly Creek Road on the other end. It is noted on the *1882 U.S. Government Survey Map*.

Fly Valley is mentioned in the La Grande Observer as early as June of 1920, but it is mentioned earlier on the original *1882 U.S. Government Survey Map*. Long-time Starkey resident, Greg Tsiatos, who cut and cleared a couple of roads in the Starkey area, did not know where "Fly" originated in naming the three aforementioned roads. *(Greg Tsiatos interview, Oct. 30, 2018)*

Follett Road - This 2.22 mile-long gravel road #61A in the Elgin maintenance district is located in Township 1N R40E of Section 2.

It is named after Warren King Follett Jr., who bought 160 acres from Firandus Slack in 1905. Of that purchase, there was a 40-acre parcel still owned by the family in 2005 when the family applied for Century Farm status. *Deed from Union County, Century Farm Application, dated December 25, 2005.*

Warren Follett Jr. was born in Clover Valley, Nevada on May 17, 1873, the son of Warren Follett Sr. (1848-1907) and Mary Emily Hamblin. According to a family history narrative, Warren Follett Jr. visited relatives in the Minam area and liked what he saw, so he purchased land in 1905.

His widowed father, Warren Follett Sr., joined him in the Pine Grove district in the early summer of 1907. Sadly, Warren Follett Sr. died on the farm on August 17, 1907.

His obituary states: "Warren Follett (Sr.), a rancher of the Pine Grove section, was found dead in his field last Friday, shortly after the dinner hour.

Follett was running a binder and when he did not appear at the usual hour for dinner, his daughter went to ascertain the cause of the delay, and she found him crushed beneath the binder. The authorities were at once notified, and in the absence of coroner Hall, Justice of the Peace Gillmore acted in that capacity, and in company with Dr. Whiting and others, left immediately for the scene.

The following jury was empaneled to ascertain the cause of death: Hiram Wheech, Percy Chandler, F. C. Potter, A. Waelty, A. M. Bosell and Ed Chesnut. After a thorough investigation, the jury found the cause of death to be purely accidental and was accounted for as follows: While binding, the seat broke, letting the man fall to the ground behind the machine. The lines were tied around him, and when he fell backwards, his weight on the lines caused the horses to back the machine up and his life was crushed out by the farm equipment before he could get out of the way.

Deceased was 63 years old and came to this section from Utah several months ago. He leaves several grown children. The remains were interred on the home farm." *The Elgin Recorder, August 23, 1907* The cemetery on the home farm is called Pine Grove Cemetery, located on Follett Road.

Presently, there are 12 Follett burials recorded in the Pine Grove Cemetery, including but not limited to: Warren King Follett Sr., Warren King Follett Jr., Jesse King Follett and George Orien Follett. There may be more than the record states. *Findagrave.com*

On July 15, 1898, Warren King Follett Jr. married Hannah Encora "Cora" Batty (1875-1970). He was killed in a car wreck at the top of Minam grade on July 30, 1923, according to a Follett family history narrative.

Their firstborn was Jesse King Follett born in Pima, Graham County, Arizona on November 22, 1899, and he married Florence Monroe Hug in 1924. One of Jesse's daughters, Reta June Follett, married Billy Hindman, also of Cricket Flat.

The history of the Follett farm's ownership goes as follows: Warren K. Follett Jr. to Jesse Follett and then to George Orien Follett in 1963. George married Norma Tribbett in 1953 and they had a son Boyd born in 1954.

Boyd Follett and his wife Sheree took over the farm operation next. They have two daughters Kim and Shellea. Kim and her husband, Justin Shaffer, are now actively involved in the farming operation as is their son, Calvin Lee Shaffer.

Foothill Road - Today this road #12 runs 6.47 miles along the foot of the hills south of La Grande in Township 3S R38E Section 8. This was just one of several Foothill Roads in the county.

Located on Foothill Road is the Irwin D. Smutz Century Farm established in 1910. Smutz (1872-1928) came to Union County by train from Kansas in 1895. He married Dora Mae Gekeler (1872-1935) in 1897. Smutz taught school in La Grande and originally had a farm in Alicel.

In 1910, he traded this farm for W.R. Jasper's 750-acre Foothill Road farm. Both parties paid each other $16,000 for their respective properties and were satisfied with the trade.

Unlike other county roads, Foothill Road was reportedly a well-drained road, enabling residents to drive their buggies easily to and from La Grande without the challenges of deep, muddy ruts so common to other unpaved roads in the county.

Today, Foothill Road goes right through Ladd Marsh Wildlife Area (LMWA), one of the largest remaining hardstem bulrush wetlands in Northeast Oregon, thanks in large part to the clever tenacity of its project leader, Bill Brown (1914-2011), who fought to develop this wetland area despite opposition at the state level.

Brown was the supervisor of ODFW's northeast region from 1951 to 1976, encompassing nine counties. When he retired from his job in 1976, the LMWA had grown to 2,300 acres, and now it spans 6,200 acres, welcoming migratory birds to breed and thrive. *Union County Oral History Project, Bill Brown, Pierce Library Collection*

Foothill Road allows for year-round viewing of the Ladd Marsh Wildlife Area. Make sure to drive it and enjoy a state treasure of wildlife preservation.

Fox Hill Road - This road #7 runs 3.35 miles in Township 2S R38E Section 35 in the La Grande maintenance district. This road quickly becomes a gravel road with a 17% steep grade ascent, so if you're towing, a 4-wheel drive vehicle is a must.

Fox Hill Trail Head is on the right at the top of the hill. "Fox Hill commands one of the loveliest views of the prettiest valley in Oregon," so stated the *La Grande Observer, Sept. 12, 1914 issue, pg. 3*. It also is rich in history, far greater than the authors expected to discover.

The road was named after Charles Fox, who along with Stephen Coffin is credited with starting the sawmill at Oro Dell. *Bernal D. Hug's History of Union County, pg. 216* explains: "Late in the fall of 1861, George Fox came into the valley to build a sawmill for Charles Fox and Stephen Coffin. In 1862 the mill was finished on the Grande Ronde River at the foot of the [Fox] hill, which later was named after him.

Others joined these, and soon a trading post was developing, inappropriately called Speak Easy.

The town location was a little dell at the foot of the mountains which suggested to Captain Harlow, a resident of the community, the name Oro Dell, oro being the Greek word for mountains. This name was submitted to the Postal Department and was accepted.

By 1865, the little town was building along its streets in an orderly fashion with two streets running east and west and two running north and south. In 1873 there were several stores, blacksmith shops and wagon shops, two hotels, and a school house. The greater part of the business district was built on the north side of the river. The Hall Hotel was on that side also." (End of Bernal D. Hug excerpt)

"One of the early day sawmill men of the valley was named [Charles] Fox, and he operated a mill at Oro Dell. A large part of his lumber supply came from the northern hillside which has since been known by the name of the lumberman. In the early times, the Fox hill road continued on over the mountains, and most of the Grande Ronde settlers who came here from the Willamette came by way of the Fox hill road instead of the longer circuit necessary to come into the valley by way of the old emigrant road at La Grande." *(La Grande Observer, Fri. March 23, 1917, p. 7)*

The Fox mill was operated by water power from a water wheel in Grande Ronde River and was of a type known as a "sash saw." *(A Brief History of Union County, Oregon, by Lee C. Johnson, page 16)*

Fox Hill Road was created to allow access to and from the timber forest, but it was also a road that some emigrants used to shorten their journey to the Grande Ronde Valley. Fox Hill Road and its connecting Robbs Hill Road quickly became a neighborhood of families living in cabins and houses, some later abandoned and some were never owned in the first place.

Fox Hill area historian, Clayton Warnstaff, wrote his memoirs listing some of these old-time neighbors and places surrounding the Fox Hill Road/Robbs Hill Road neighborhood that he knew when he lived there between the years 1924 to 1941.

His list read: "Five Points Creek Mill, Carter cabins, Pitts house, a grave site, Clay homestead, Warnstaff home, John Stroeber home, Henry Stroeber house and mill, Honni Morgue cabin, Klintworth home, Looker home, McClure home, the school house, the Smith cabin, some Indian graves, another grave site, the State place, the Shirts home and mink farm."

The two brothers, John Stroeber (1878-1952) and Henry Stroeber (1885-1967), operated a high-production sawmill of their own at the top of Fox Hill Road. John's obituary read in part:

"Funeral services for John Stroeber, 73, retired sawmill worker who died suddenly of a heart attack at his home Thursday... Born in Bavaria, Germany, in 1878, Mr. Stroeber had lived here for 64 years. He operated a sawmill on Fox Hill for 24 years, retiring seven years ago. Surviving are a brother Henry, La Grande, and a nephew, Herman J. Stroeber, Elgin. Burial will be in the city cemetery." *(Obit in La Grande Observer, Sat. June 14, 1952, pg. 7)*

Warnstaff wrote this about the Stroeber brothers and their sawmill:

"John and Henry Stroeber operated a sawmill at the top of Fox Hill and produced lumber used to build most frame houses in the south side area of La Grande. John's place had a fair sized orchard and Henry's place had the sawmill. Ruins of that mill are still visible; however, nothing remains of John's place." *(Clayton Warnstaff's handwritten memoirs, donated by Dallas Hibbert, October 17, 2021)*

The schools in the Fox Hill district started their school term in March and classes continued through the summer months, closing in November. Weather conditions in this district made it necessary to hold classes in the summer instead of the winter months. In 1927, Miss Marion Fulkerson of Seaside was hired to teach the Fox Hill children. *(La Grande Observer, Mar. 3, 1927, pg 1)*

This school district was consolidated into La Grande School District after 1931.

"A one-room school house served the area for many years," Clayton Warnstaff said. "I've never heard any reference to exactly when it began. In 1915, my grandfather Edwin Looker and his son, Ray, rebuilt it and added a peaked roof. They also built another cabin for the school teacher. Two of my aunts, Gladys Crouser and Lola Murchison and my Uncle Ralph Looker attended there. It is now a summer type home." *(Clayton Warnstaff's memoirs)*

Winters on Fox Hill were described by Fox Hill rancher John Morge, who had one news briefly written about his life. It read: "Regardless of the weather John Morge comes down nearly every day from his Fox hill ranch with a load of cord wood. In reply to the query as to the condition of the snow on Fox hill, Mr. Morge said: 'It is all sizes; some places four feet and some places six, depending on which way the wind blows." *(La Grande Observer, January 24, 1916, pg 4)*

John Morge was born July 1861 in Germany, and he settled on Fox Hill. His house was known by neighbors as the "Honni" Morge cabin. (Imagine saying Johnny with a German accent, and you get Honni.)

Clayton Warnstaff said: "A bachelor of German descent lived here. He spoke very little English, and what he did for a living is unknown. His cabin is one of very few buildings remaining. I remember him as a visitor to my grandparent Lookers' place—especially at supper time!" *(Clayton Warnstaff's memoirs)*

Another Fox Hill neighbor was Rufus Clay (1838-1889), who came to Oregon around 1867 and settled at this location. "The Clay homestead originally comprised 360 acres, according to family members; however, land records reflect only a quarter section was actually homesteaded," wrote Clayton Warnstaff. "The house on the property was known as the "Red House" since it was painted bright red. Nothing remains of the house and outbuildings; however, some of the original lumber was part of a cabin built by Ted Crampton on the site. That cabin burned down in 1993."

Living there was the Rufus Clay family, including his wife Leah and two children initially. "He [Rufus] came from Kentucky with his wife Leah and two very young children. My grandmother Susan and my Uncle Albert were the children. The family returned to Kentucky after one year where six more children were born and subsequently returned here early in the 1880's," wrote Clayton Warnstaff, the great-grandson of Rufus Clay.

The *Findagrave.com* narrative for Rufus Clay stated: "Between 1875-1878, Rufus, Leah, and their six children moved from Carter County, Kentucky to Cooke County, Texas. They had three more children in Texas. In 1884 their last child, Callie, was born in Oklahoma. In the fall of 1888, they moved with their nine or ten children from Brown County, Kansas to take up homesteading on Fox Hill in Union County, Oregon."

They were on Fox Hill for just a year when tragedy struck their family: "In December of 1889, Rufus died and was placed in a snow bank over the winter and was buried in [spring] 1890 when the ground thawed. It has never been confirmed, but local history places a 10-year-old boy in the same grave, who has never been identified. The widow of Rufus filed a homestead claim in October 1895." *(Clayton Warnstaff's memoirs)*

Online research conducted after Clayton wrote his memoirs showed the 10-year-old boy was Rufus' son Willie Vernon Clay, the seventh child of nine born to Rufus and Leah Clay. Willie was born 1879 in Texas; died 1889 at home on Fox Hill at about the same time his father died. Rufus and Willie were buried in the same grave and another child, Daniel Clay (1872-?) was also buried next to them. The graves were encircled by a 4-sided wrought iron fence. Sometime later someone stole the fence and then three sides were recovered. They could never find the fourth section of the fence. Their burial were considered a "non-cemetery burial."

Great-grandson, Clayton Alfred Warnstaff (1924-1999) made a cement marker with Rufus Clay's name on it and placed it on the ground. Then he re-installed the 3 sides of the fence around it. It may not be the exact site of the grave anymore due to its earlier desecration by vandals.

This cemetery has no name, and their burials were recorded by Clayton so that no one would forget them. Someone from the cemetery association did get Clayton's information on these burials.

Clayton wrote about his "hill" neighbors, meaning Fox Hill and Robbs Hill roads, as follows:

"Many years from now, when my generation is long gone, much of the local history will have become lost. The time before the Great Depression of 1928 was as poor or worse than 1928 to 1933, when things began to improve somewhat," he wrote. "Life on Fox/Robbs Hill was one of just survival, large families, poor transportation and no luxuries. There were approximately 60 people living there, but they were able to survive. I shared in much of the poverty and hardship and have many memories, good and bad, of life on the hill." *(Clayton Warnstaff's memoirs)*

The following La Grande Observer news clipping showed that perhaps their fruit orchard helped them survive those lean years.

"J. R. Warnstaff, who resides on Fox hill will have an exceptionally fine fruit crop this year. As delicious fruit as we have ever seen grown anywhere was picked from his orchard last year." *(La Grande Observer, Thurs, July 14, 1904, pg. 4)*

Clayton enumerated some residents not previously mentioned that lived on the hill. His list read: "Ardie Lyman, a local taxidermist and trapper; Tom Haskins; Sam Brown, one of the first railroad men here; [Mr.] Heidenreich, a deaf and mute hermit; Fred Greeves, one of the first section workers; Harry Coalwell, a cattleman with an iron foot because of one short leg; Hairy M. Carthey, a one-legged Irish man with not much known about him; Dexter Eaton, the namesake for Eaton Ridge and an uncle of Fred Beeman in Island City; Marian Fulkerson, a handicapped school teacher; Gerald Pierson, a long time owner of Long Branch Café, formerly called Imperial; and Kenneth Pierson, a local railroader." *(Clayton Warnstaff's memoirs)*

As for the grave sites on the hill, Clayton related: "Located in a small grove of trees on the west side of the Smith Meadows were the graves of six children of the area, who died of diphtheria about 1925. It is reported but never verified, that some of the children were from the Leslie Shirts family, who lived close by. There are no remains left of the graves due to cattle movement in the grove."

What remains of the "State" place located on the hill is a lonely rock chimney that stands and a small building of a foreclosed farm and hence called the "State" place, Clayton Warnstaff said. The occupants in the 1920's and 1930's were the Haskell family and then the Halsey family. Nothing significant is known about the origins of the place. It was also owned by Dr. J. B. Gregory and the McFarlands.

In the Fox Hill and Robbs Hill territory, there lived the Leslie Shirts family in a large house at the extreme west end of the Smith Meadow, and they operated a mink and muskrat farm, Clayton recounted. The pelts of these animals were sold to Chris Miller, a furrier in La Grande, located on the corner of Adams Avenue and Greenwood street where the Texaco station is.

Miller then sold the pelts to the Hudson Bay Company of Vancouver, Washington. Clayton's father helped provide meat to the animals, and he also sold his pelts to Chris Miller; however, he began trapping in 1911 and since then sold directly to the traveling Hudson Bay representative.

The Smith cabin was another place on the hill that had special meaning to Clayton Warnstaff.

"At one time this was a working cattle ranch with hay barns and corrals, etc. My family lived here from 1927 to 1934," he said. "From here my father and I ran trap lines to the Eaton Ridge, Carter Ridge, Sugar Loaf, Black Mountains and Five Points creek area. We also trapped the three cabin ridge area, Mahogany Ridge, and Beacon Light area and the Grande Ronde River between Hilgard and La Grande."

Clayton remembered the Carter family on the hill during the 1930's. "I remember two cabins with a covered walkway. My father and I used to pass by it on our way to a trap line for coyotes. I remember especially two of the Carter boys, Harvey, a teacher of mine, and Jim, our mail carrier, who was a particular friend of my father for many years."

The Native American burials on Fox Hill were well known to its residents. Clayton explained: "At the far end of the Smith Meadow to the north were several Indian grave sites of people who came from Mission (Umatilla's, Cayuse, etc.), who came to this area for huckleberries and on over to Elgin for pow-wow at the Elgin fish trap on the Wallowa highway bridge leaving Elgin. These graves have been destroyed by later timber harvest and cattle. I recall many times seeing Indians passing by the Looker home. They followed generally the same trail that Marcus Whitman used in 1836, in which he came up the Fox hill road past the Looker home and on to Deadman Pass to Gibbons and Minam (as they are identified today)."

Clayton Warnstaff's Looker grandparents were Edwin and Cora Looker, who moved to Fox Hill from Canada in 1913 and lived there until 1927 or 1928.

He wrote in his memoirs: "Nothing remains of their house, ice house, two barns, machine shop and two hog houses. It was a local place for dances, socials, and feeding haying crews, while haying in the big meadows here. There were eight children who grew up there and went to school on Fox hill. Three of them married into other families living on the hill."

Residents on "the hill" developed into quite a community, rich with stories and lacking no element of intrigue. (See Robbs Hill Road entry)

Frances Lane - North of Elgin on Palmer Junction Road is this private lane, which leads to Ernest Road, and it is named after Frances Elizabeth Gilkison (1914-2004), also known as Mrs. Ernest Adams. *(See Ernest Road)*

Frances Elizabeth Gilkison was born on February 4, 1914, to Frank and Elizabeth (Beber) Gilkison in Keating, Oregon. She attended North Powder schools until her family relocated to Elgin, where she finished her senior year of high school. During that year, she played on the 1932 Elgin High School championship basketball team. *(1920 and 1930 Federal Censuses-Frank Gilkison Family)*

After graduation, she married Ernest Edgar Adams (1913-2006) in Union County on November 11, 1933. *(Oregon, County Marriages)* They relocated to Portland where Frances worked in the ship yards during World War II.

After the war, they moved back to Elgin and opened Adams Supply Store, where Frances was the bookkeeper and operator until her retirement in 1976. The two of them enjoyed many trips together, including trips to China, Hawaii, Alaska and Mexico.

She and Ernest lived in the area where Ernest Road and Frances Lane are located, off Palmer Junction Road. They had three daughters and one son.

During her life, Frances was involved in a number of clubs and organizations, including the Good Sam Club, the Women's Service Club and the Elgin Stampeders, where she was a member of the drill team.

Her favorite activities were hunting, fishing, camping, playing cards, riding horses and spending time with her family. She died at her home on December 11, 2004, at the age of 90, and she was laid to rest in the Elgin Cemetery in Elgin, Oregon.

French Corral Road - This road has a La Grande zip code, but it is located out in the remote hills west of Starkey where there is no settlement or post office.

It is believed that this road was named after cattleman and civic leader, Samuel G. French who came to this county about 1862, settling in the area now known as Cove.

On June 4, 1863, a post office was established there called Forest Cove. The first postmaster was Samuel G. French, who likely named it. In June 1868, the first part of the post office name was dropped due to the fact that it sounded too much like Forest Grove in Washington County, Oregon. Consequently, this area of Union County was referred to as "the Cove." *(Oregon Geographic Names, 1982 pg. 185)*

Samuel G. French set about buying grazing land, and he purchased four sections on August 20, 1869.

Although French lived in the Cove, he owned several stock ranches in Union County. This particular mountain road is believed to lead to one of his stock ranch properties, as he is said to have become one of the wealthiest cattlemen and farmers and most prominent citizens of the valley prior to 1884.

To help him manage his many stock ranches, he hired foreman W. R. Holmes, who he trusted so much that he appointed him as the executor of his will. Samuel French's estate was settled around 1884, and thereafter Holmes moved to Wallowa County to manage his own cattle operation.

During the first decade after his arrival to Union County, Samuel G. French played an important part in the development of the Cove and its surrounding area. About 1866-67, he hired builder Heman J. Geer to build a flouring mill along a tributary of Catherine Creek. It was still in operation in 1902, but with superior equipment than at its start. *(An Illustrated History of Union and Wallowa Counties, 1902, pg. 150, 230)*

Fruitdale Lane - This paved lane is designated road #125. It runs 2.24 miles in length and is located in Township 2S R38E Section 32 in the La Grande maintenance district.

The lane is well known as one of the access roads to the historic Riverside Park & Pavilion. The property was acquired in 1909 and the park was laid out in 1910. The pavilion was built between June 1913 and July 1914.

Jacob Nessly came to the Grande Ronde Valley in 1862 and lived the rest of his life on his homestead, which was the principal part of Fruitdale. He was the original nursery man of the Grande Ronde Valley, according to the *La Grande Observer, January 4, 1917, pg. 1*. The reporter quoted from one of La Grande's early newspaper editors, who included a note of thanks to Jacob Nessly for a fine lot of pears, which he grew by grafting on wild trees. Some years later, Mr. Nessly also started growing peach plums, the first of its kind in the Grande Ronde Valley. He later developed an apple that became know as the "Lucinda" which was named in honor of his daughter.

Fruitdale was first mentioned in the *La Grande Observer on Nov. 26, 1901, pg. 4*, where it mentioned that S. J. White, L. Oldenburg, W. M. Hall and Mr. Bougards received 2,600 Gano (apple) fruit trees to be planted at their Fruitdale orchards.

This area apparently had been known as Fruitdale for quite a number of years as the School District No. 27 had been known as Fruitdale since at least 1882. In the *La Grande Observer on Dec. 10, 1901, pg. 4,* had a community column called Fruitdale Findings. In that column there were several mentions of fruit farms and orchards, including the fact that there were about 8,000 boxes of apples still in the hands of members of the fruit association.

Also, in December 1901 an article noted that three tracts in Fruitdale of orchard land had sold for $300 per acre, and this was considered a good price. In January 1902, the Fruitdale column mentioned that S. G. White had received 200 more Gano apple trees that he will set out in the spring. This was to add to the 1,200 trees White already had on his 15 acre orchard. Mr. C. P. Thompson was getting ready to set out 700 trees on his acreage in the spring. A. Beldin had also purchased part of the Ladd farm in Fruitdale and will be setting out a fruit orchard.

From an article in the *Observer on March 5, 1902, pg. 3*, it indicated that Thomas Walsh sold 23 acres of orchard land to Bishop Jordon. This orchard was all set out in good commercial varieties, 12 acres in bearing trees from which Mr. Walsh harvested 1,100 boxes the past season.

In April 1902, C. W. Nessly was getting ready to set out a 10-acre orchard just north of Fruitdale, and S. J. White had received 5,000 more Gano and Roman Beauty apple trees recently to set out. At the end of the 1902 fruit season, the *November 8, 1902 issue of the La Grande Observer on page 2* stated that the quality of apples was excellent but the yield was rather light. The same column said that L. Oldenburg was shipping some apples to eastern points at very satisfactory prices.

Fruit men were beginning to think about orders for planting additional acreage the next year. Orchardists C. D. Huffman and E. Z. Carbine would each be planting 20 acre plots along with some other smaller areas.

The *La Grande Observer of February 26, 1903, pg. 1* had printed a letter to Mr. Thomas Kelly of Fruitdale from A. Miller and Sons, of Milton Nurseries as follows: "Dear Sir—Mr. Thomas of this place, who was at your place not long ago, handed us some sample varieties of apples grown in your orchard. They are typical specimens of the Gano, Mammoth, Black Twig, and Shackelford, all of which are first class commercial varieties. Anyone possessing land that will grow such beautiful colored and large-sized fruits as came from your orchard, surely need not look further for a location for the growing of first-class, marketable Big Red Apples."

A headline in the *La Grande Observer of September 24, 1903, pg. 3* stated, "Apple Buyers are after Fruitdale." The article stated that there were four large apple buying firms in the city trying to secure auctions on the 50 carloads of apples in Fruitdale. The crop is estimated at 30,000 boxes, grown on 280 acres. The price cannot be far from 75 cents per box, which means about $22,000, the article read.

The Fruitdale orchards eventually met the same fate as many other orchards in Union County. The trees were pulled out and the land was developed or used for more profitable crops.

Another historical feature of Fruitdale Lane was its nearby school named Fruitdale School, located on the southeast corner of Gaertner and Mount Glen Road. It was operated until its closure on September 30, 1960 after which the students were bussed to Greenwood School in La Grande. After its closure, the property was leased out to the Seventh Day Adventist Church as a parochial school. They used it until January 30, 1962, when it burned down. Due to a lack of available water, the fire was not able to be quickly extinguished.

One historical institution located on Fruitdale Lane was the Union County Poor Farm. The purchase of the land was noted in the *May 10, 1909 issue of the La Grande Observer, pg. 8*. It read, "County Court Buys Poor Farm near Island City—Union County has a poor farm. The county court and commissioners in a special session late this afternoon purchased the Charles Green 40-acre tract north of Island City, between that town and Fruitdale for $6,600. The buy was a splendid one. The farm has on it a full crop of grain, 10 acres in orchard, 2 wells, a 6-room house, a barn that will hold 20 tons of hay and horses and farm implements valued at $500 alone. The location is excellent and the court is to be complimented for seizing the opportunity presented."

Incidentally, this was not the first Union County Poor Farm in existence. There was one operated earlier that was located in Township 4S R40E in Section 19 in the city of Union, platt #73. Most of the property was located on the east side of North Main Street. It's south of the entrance of today's Buffalo Peak Golf Course. The land was surveyed for Union County, Oregon on April 3, 1889 by J. W. Kimbrell county surveyor.

There was an article about the acquisition of the Union County Poor Farm property in Union published in the *Oregon Scout of December 14, 1888, pg. 8*, stating in part:

"The property belonging to S. A. Purcell, south of Union was purchased by the court to be used as a county poor farm. Consideration, $1,700."

"Contract awarded to C. H. Day for medicine and medical attendants on the county poor at the poor farm and the prisoners in the county jail, for the ensuing year, for $550."

"Nelson Schoonover was appointed superintendent and manager of the county poor farm at a salary of $600 per year." (End of excerpts from Oregon Scout)

The *Oregon Scout* printed an editorial appeal to its readers as follows: "Clear Grit. Almost any day an old man, with one leg missing, may be seen hobbling around town encumbered with a buck-saw, seeking for work. When he finds it, he goes in with a will and never lets up till his work is accomplished. He is an inmate of the county poor house, and his name is Albert A. McLaughlin. We know not what brought him to this condition, but surely it is through no fault of his. In a conversation with him a few days ago, he informed us that he was hoarding all his little earnings for the purpose of buying a cork leg which he thought would enable him to work with greater ease, and that he would then be able to support himself. As the leg will cost nearly $100 it will be a long time before he gets it, unless he is assisted. Mr. Schoonover, the efficient and kind-hearted supervisor of the poor farm has drawn up subscription papers—subscribing liberally himself—for the purpose of raising money to buy the leg for the old man. One of the papers can be found at this office. If our charitably inclined people will drop in and contribute a very little, each, the old gentleman will have his desires gratified many weary months before he expects it." *(Oregon Scout, May 23, 1889, pg.*

The Union County Poor Farm in the city of Union became home to people who were seriously injured and could not support themselves. This poor farm operated until the new poor farm was built on Fruitdale Lane after 1909.

A grand jury inspected the poor farm property in 1939 and the outcome was published in the *La Grande Observer, June 2, 1939, pg. 1* as follows, in part:

"County Poor Farm needs cleaning, grand jury says. Further recommendations of the county grand jury which reported to circuit judge R. J. Green yesterday here (in La Grande) revealed today.

The jury recommended that the county poor farm be "generally cleaned"... elaborating on the poor farm, the jury said, 'We have visited the county poor farm and wish to recommend, if said poor farm is to be continued and maintained, that the farm be generally cleaned especially with respect to refuse and junk found lying on the premises and that a few minor repairs be made upon the buildings.'"

This property was located one-quarter mile west of McAlister Road and ran from Fruitdale Lane south to the Grande Ronde River. This county poor farm was discontinued in the 1940s.

Gaertner Lane - This public, unmaintained lane on the north edge of La Grande is officially located in Township 2S R38E Section 32 and runs for .45 miles east off of Spruce Street. It brings access to six property addresses.

This lane was named after a coal mining family, Emil and Lena Gaertner of Dresden, Germany, who came to America on Lena's winning lottery ticket that she won in a drawing held in Germany.

Prior to her good fortune, the family was struggling for work and food. They saw no relief to the economy in Dresden, so Emil wrote to tell his younger brother, Paul, who was then living in Enterprise, Oregon. Paul advised him, "Before your lottery money is all gone, come to America. I will send money for our mother and sister, Martha, to come with you."

So Emil and Lena, along with their children, Adolf, Hattie, Irna, Ella and Emil P.; and Emil's mother and sister Martha, left Dresden on May 1, 1901. They took a train to the coast of France, where they bought passage to America, using their lottery money and the money from Paul.

The Gaertners sailed the Atlantic and arrived at New York's Ellis Island on May 20, 1901. From there they took the railroad pathways across the plains to Pasco, Washington and then south to La Grande, Oregon. From La Grande, the railroad spur took them as far as Elgin's depot, where Paul was waiting to pick them up in a stage coach.

The stage was filled with grocer's supplies that Paul was hired to deliver to Joseph, but despite this, the womenfolk and children rode in the stage coach and everything else was piled onto the back and top. Emil walked in front of the stage, clearing the road of rocks that might stumble the horses.

When they reached Paul's place in Enterprise, Lena exclaimed with distaste, "Das ist ein vogelwiser!" (This is a birdhouse!) Her place next door was no better, she found out.

At first, the Gaertners lived in a two room house with an upper loft. Emil and Lena had the large bed, the children had bunk beds, and the two little ones had the loft. Clearly, Lena had grander expectations than this, but she made the most of what was provided for them through Paul. In 1907, Lena gave birth to one more child, Herman Gaertner, and after his birth, their large family moved onto their own homestead farm on the lower end of the valley outside of Enterprise.

They farmed there until 1912, when they relocated to Island City. While on their new farm, Lena stumbled upon another stroke of good fortune, which put their name in Union County's agricultural history.

It was 1914, and Lena had bought two milking cows. When she discovered she had more milk than her family could drink, she told the children to give the rest away to the neighbors. So she packed their little red wagon, and the children pulled it to their neighbors' homes to give the milk away to them.

To Lena's surprise, the children returned home with money given them by their neighbors for the milk. Consequently, each day, Lena put the extra milk in the little wagon, and the children sold it to their neighbors. Lena imagined how much more she could make if she bought two more cows, so she bought them, and this set the Gaertners on a new course that led to the establishment of Greenwood Dairy in 1921.

Their dairy farm and milking parlor were originally located on East L Avenue in Island City. While at this location, the Gaertners discovered that their cows produced 60 gallons more on days when they played concert music on their phonograph player. Thereafter, music became a regular feature in the milking parlor.

Emil Gaertner died in August 1939 due to complications of cancer, and Lena went to live with her daughter, Hattie Campbell, leaving the house and dairy to their son Emil P. Gaertner. He operated it until 1949, and due to several heart attacks, he retired. After that, the dairy was operated by a number of family members in turn.

The dairy ceased operation in late 1980 due to the costly pasteurization equipment required by the State of Oregon. Other dairy closures soon followed in Union County until there were no dairies left in operation.

Consequently, Greenwood Dairy and the Emil Gaertner name are among an elite and historic group of dairy producers and distributors in this county. *(Bill Gaertner interview, Union, Oregon, September 2002)*

Geiger Butte Lane - This private gravel road is not on the county list but it is located in Township 1S R40E Section 7 and exits Indian Creek Road, allowing access to eight properties.

It is named after John "Lute" Geiger, a farmer-rancher in Elgin for 38 years and his wife Lenina Geiger, who taught students at Indian Creek School.

His obituary was published in the *La Grande Observer, Thursday, Sept. 1, 1960, pg. 7* and it reads: "John Geiger of Elgin Dies. John Geiger, 68 year-old retired farmer of Elgin died at Spokane, Wash., on Monday, August 29, 1960. Funeral services will be held at 2 p.m. Friday at Daniels Funeral Home with burial in Elgin cemetery.

Born in Dixie, Wash., Feb. 15, 1892, Mr. Geiger had resided in Elgin for 38 years. Survivors are the widow, Mrs. Lenina Geiger, Elgin; two sons, Lewis Geiger, Gresham, and Wayne Geiger, Spokane; two daughters, Miss Grace Geiger, Pendleton and Mrs. Irene Gilliam, Elgin; a brother Fred Geiger of Walla Walla, Wash; three sisters, Mrs. Arva Dunlap, Waitsburg, Wash., Mrs. Effie Keve, Tekoa, Wash., and Mrs. Dora Spencer, Summerville and eight grandchildren." (End of obit)

Lute Geiger sold his ranch and moved to Walla Walla on August 31, 1958. He reportedly sold his Geiger Butte property to C. E. Redmen of Houston, Texas, according to the *La Grande Observer, August 18, 1958, pg. 3, Elgin Briefs.*

A later owner of the Geiger ranch was reportedly Scott A. Mitchek of Elgin. He also sold it, as the story goes. It may have been subdivided as well. *(Bob Scott Wiles, interview September 2021)*

Gekeler Lane - Road #116 in Township 3S R38E Section 8 runs 10.46 miles in length and is one of the longer county roads that exist. For this reason, county records say that it travels through both La Grande and Union maintenance districts.

This road is named after an early pioneer named George John Gekeler, who was born in Lancaster, Erie County, New York, on June 14, 1833, where he grew up on his father's farm and was educated in the public schools. As a young adult, he took up carpentry as a trade.

In 1859 in New York, George Gekeler, 26, married Miss Catherine "Kate" S. King, daughter of Louis and Fannie King. She was born May 11, 1840 in New York.

Together they ventured to Falls City, Nebraska, where they homesteaded for two years before deciding to pursue better fields in Oregon. They fitted out ox teams and entered their wagons in the McAlister-Yount train, which left on May 26, 1862 and arrived in the Grande Ronde Valley on September 30.

Once they arrived, Gekeler filed a claim for his first 160 acres that he purchased for $2.50 per acre, and he fenced it in by a rail fence he cut himself. Then he immediately borrowed $300 and started freighting between The Dalles and Silver City, Idaho, each trip consuming six weeks of work. But it was a lucrative business and enabled him to buy additional acreage for farming. Finally, by 1892, he acquired 598 acres. His hay crop alone yielded over 300 tons annually, in addition to cereals and other crops. *(An Illustrated History of Union and Wallowa Counties, 1902, pg. 369; Bernal Hug's*

When the Joe Yount family decided to move out of the valley, Gekeler bought his home, which has since been known as the Gekeler place. George and Kate Gekeler became parents to 11 children.

George Gekeler died October 25, 1901 at age 68; and Kate died July 10, 1926 at age 86. Their resting place is at Hillcrest Cemetery in La Grande.

Gilkison Road - Formerly Mann Road, this road #74 is about 8 blocks in length and connects Wolf Creek Road and Coughanour Lane in North Powder. It is located in Township 6S R38E Section 18 in the North Powder maintenance district.

This road was named after Socrates C. Mann (1866-1927) and his wife Ellen E. Powers (1856-1950). They had the following children: twins Cecil and Cecilia (1886-1886), Dora (1887), Leo (1892) and Charles (1897).

Socrates C. Mann was born March 12, 1866 in North Powder. During the 1880 Federal Census he was traveling between two work sites, so he was enumerated twice in that census. On June 3, 1880 he happened to be in the Baker County Census and in June 4-5, 1880 he was listed in North Powder as a farm laborer.

He was listed in the *1900 and 1910 Federal Census* in Baker County as a farmer, and in 1920, he was back in North Powder, where he stayed until he died on May 28, 1927. His wife moved back to Baker County, where she died on January 12, 1950. *(La Grande Observer, Jan. 13, 1950, pg. 3)*

Their son, Leo, appeared to have worked the Couch farm property next and also worked at different sites. In 1900, he was with his parents at a community called Willows. In 1910, he was listed in Baker County as a farm laborer; however, on another 1910 census, he was listed in Grant county on a grain farm. In 1920, he was listed on the census in Blue Eagle, Nevada as a ranch laborer.

He moved back to Union County, where he married Leona Leatha Maharry on September 26, 1923, and they started a family. By 1930, Leo was listed on the census as a farmer in North Powder. They had eight children, as near as could be determined. They included Clairellen Belle (1924-2004), Floy Dorene (1926-1978), twins Arel Leo (1929-1976) and Arlene Leona (1929-), Ella Nora (1932-), Ralph Vernon (1933-1933), John Emery (1934-1974), Cecil Socrates(1936-) and Letha Elizabeth (1938-).

In the 1940 Federal Census, Leo was listed as a farm manager in North Powder. Leo's wife, Leona was born September 16, 1895 in North Powder, and she died unexpectedly at her home on September 12, 1938 just short of 43 years. *(La Grande Observer, Sept. 14, 1938, pg. 6)*

Leo was born June 6, 1892 in North Powder, and he died from a long illness on November 23, 1948 in a La Grande hospital. Services were conducted in North Powder.

The Mann part of the road name was changed to Gilkison after James R. Gilkison and his wife, Mary Amanda McFadden, originally from Zanesville, Ohio and Mattoon, Illinois respectively. They were married on March 29, 1865 in Illinois and came to Oregon in 1866, settling first in the Pendleton area. Then they moved to the North Powder area in 1867. During their marriage, they had at least eleven children.

James was engaged in general farming pursuits, but he also worked as a bridge contractor on the Powder River bridge between Union and Baker counties, where he received $300 for his work. *(Oregon Scout, September 11, 1890, pg. 6)* Not only was he a contractor, but he was also interested in roads because in the *Oregon Scout, January 15, 1891, pg. 2* there is a list of persons appointed to serve as road supervisors for the year 1891, and he was on that list. J. R. Gilkison was appointed for district 27.

James Gilkison died on March 6, 1911 at age 72 and is interred in the North Powder cemetery along with his wife, who died on September 14, 1931 at age 84.

Glass Hill Road - Road #6 is another long road, 11 miles, and is located in Township 3S R38E Section 18 in the La Grande maintenance district. This road branches off Morgan Lake Road and was called by the name Glass Hill when Morgan Lake Road was first called Mill Canyon Road. (See Morgan Lake Road entry)

According to the late Bill Lovan of La Grande, the road was named this because in the winter, it was slick as glass and treacherous. That might be so, but it's not the reason for the name actually.

The road was so named for William Norman Glass (1834-1883) and his wife Mary Jane (Burnsides) Glass (1844-1920). Mary Jane Glass was buried in the Hillcrest Cemetery, but there is no record of a burial there for her husband, William. He may have had what they call a non-cemetery burial on land on Glass Hill Road because the Hillcrest cemetery was not started until 1895.

Mary Jane's memorial, written by a relative, was published on Findagrave.com, and it read in part: "Mary Jane Burnsides Glass was born August 26, 1844 in Ohio. She died April 6, 1920 in La Grande. Her husband, William Norman Glass was born April 30, 1834 in Ohio and died January 28, 1883 in La Grande."

William and Mary had four children, and all apparently stayed in the area and are buried in the Hillcrest cemetery. From homestead records, it is known that Mary Jane and William took up a homestead south of La Grande, and Mary Jane proved up on it April 5, 1890. She later took up two other homestead areas. Two of their sons, Charles F. and William W. also took up homesteads south of La Grande.

This road sounds like it would provide a nice Sunday drive experience, but we warn you it can be as slick as glass in the winter, so make the trip during fair weather.

Godley Road - This road #31 is located in Township 4S R39E Section 13 in the Union maintenance district. It runs for 6.62 miles north-south from Gekeler Lane on the north to Miller Lane on the south.

It is named after the Godley family who resided in Union County from about 1870 to 1893. The road definitely had its name before 1915 because it's used in the following briefly: "A bad mud hole in the Godley lane has been filled up and that road is now in good shape." *(La Grande Observer, June 1, 1915, pg. 1)*

The earliest Godley in that area was William Godley, a farmer. He was born in Pike County, Pennsylvania in 1831 to parents Mahlon Godley (1788-1870) and Mary Taylor (1789-1860). *(Ancestry.com family tree)*

He was listed in the *1840 and 1850 Federal censuses* with his parents in Lackawaxen, Pike County, Pennsylvania. Then on November 21, 1856, he married Catherine Virginia Poor (1839-1912) in Schuyler, Missouri. She was the daughter of Thomas Poor (1810-1862) and Anne Elizabeth Lockett (1819-1891).

In 1858, Catherine Godley gave birth to their son, Thomas, and the family was listed in the *1860 Federal Census* as residents of Wyacondah, Davis County, Iowa.

It was only after the *1870 Federal Census*, that the Godley family came to Union County, Oregon. On January 5, 1875, the father William Godley earned a homestead patent of 160 acres in the center of 4S R39E Section 23. *(Ancestry.com)*

William farmed in Union County near Catherine Creek for at least 20 years. Then he and Catherine relocated to a ranch, valued at $1,650, near Clear Creek on Anderson Road in Redding, Shasta County, California, where William continued farming and was noted in the *1906 Voters' Registration of Shasta County*.

The *1910 Federal Census* listed William alone in Redding California, and he died on April 13, 1913 in Redding, California. *(Ancestry.com; Miller Family Tree, Findagrave.com)* He was 82 years of age, but his gravestone reads 80 years.

Catherine Godley lived in Thomasville, Butte County, California, and she died there at the age of 73 on July 12, 1912. With the passing of both William and Catherine, their personal history ends.

The authors will now focus on their son, Thomas M. Godley, who was born 1858 in Schuyler, Missouri. He was named after his maternal grandfather, Thomas Poor. In 1860, Thomas, 2, was living with his parents in Wyacondah, Davis County, Iowa. *(1860 Federal Census)* He came to Union County with his parents after 1870.

At age 22, Thomas branched out on his own, living as a boarder in the William and Sarah Rees household in the Monroe Precinct of Benton County, Oregon, single and working as a teamster. There he met Mary Elizabeth Grant, the daughter of Elijah and Mary E. Grant. On February 17,

1881 in Benton County, Thomas Godley, 23, and Mary Grant, 16, were wed. *(Benton Co., OR Marriages, Book 5, page 206)*

Mary Elizabeth Grant was the direct descendant of Elizabeth Boone Grant, the sister of the famed Daniel Boone. Elizabeth and her husband, Elijah Grant, took Daniel Boone's wife and four children into their home and cared for them during the four years that Daniel Boone was held captive by the Indians. *(Ancestry.com)*

The Grant family, including Mary, crossed the plains to California in 1856, and came to Oregon in 1876 to settle in Benton County, the part which afterward became Lincoln County. *(Corvallis Gazette-Times, Jan. 19, 1940, pg. 1)*

One family tree noted: "Then Mary Grant became the bride of Tom Godley. His letter of proposal was extravagantly phrased, asking if she could bring herself to share the life of a 'cowboy riding over the billowy bunch grass hills of Eastern Oregon.'" *(Ancestry.com)* Mary Grant accepted her cowboy's romantic proposal, and she gave birth in April 1885 to twins, Charles William Godley and Gertrude Godley. Sadly, Mary died in 1885 after the twins were born.

On August 1, 1888, Thomas was married Mrs. Aurelia Belle (Lawrence) Holbrook in Union County. They were married by B. F. Wilson, Justice of the Peace. *(Marriage document in clear, legible handwriting on ancestry.com)* Belle had formerly been married to Owen A. Holbrook (1858-) on July 10, 1881.

Thomas and Belle's first child, a daughter, was born to them in Union County on September 16, 1890, according to the *Eastern Oregon Republican of Thursday, Sept. 18, 1890. (Accessgenealogy.com)* The baby was named Lillian Bell Godley (later Mrs. Silva).

The Thomas Godley family left Union County after Lillian's birth, ending their history there. For those who want to know what happened to them—Thomas relocated his family to Shoshone, Lincoln County, Idaho where another daughter, Anna Lulu Godley, was born on November 16, 1894, followed by sons Thomas Jr. in 1897 and Archie in 1902. *(1900 and 1910 Federal Census)*

Thomas Godley died on May 18, 1906 at about age 47 and was interred in the Shoshone Cemetery in Shoshone, Idaho. There are only two Godley graves on record at this cemetery: Thomas M. Godley died May 18, 1906 at about 47 years, and an unmarked grave lot that belongs to "Mrs. Godley" (no stone). *(USGenWeb Archives, Shoshone Cemetery)*

While researching the Godley family in Union County, the authors found that the facts on this family are conflicting with long held beliefs about how Catherine and Julianna creeks got their names.

The *Oregon Geographic Names book, Seventh Edition, page 180* states that "Catherine Creek was named for Catherine Godley, one of the daughters of Thomas and M.E. Godley, early settlers near Union."

Local historians have long held that Julianna Creek (later Little Creek) was named after Catherine Godley's younger sister Julianna. However, both Catherine and Julianna creek names have come into question for several reasons.

First, there are no known family tree records that prove Thomas Godley had daughters named Catherine and Julianna. His eldest children were twins, Charles and Gertrude.

Secondly, and more importantly, the creeks were named in 1862 when Thomas Godley was 4 years old. The names of the creeks are recorded on an 1863 original range and township map, 19 years before Thomas and M.E. Godley were married. Therefore, the creek names could not have been named after their daughters who were not yet born.

It is important to know that some early maps show the Julianna Creek was first named Elizabeth Creek. In that case, the authors looked for someone who might have a Catherine and Elizabeth in their families. (See Catherine Creek Lane entry for more details.)

On the other hand, Thomas' father William Godley had a wife named Catherine Godley, but again, they were not in Union County in 1862 when the creeks were named, so she is not the person after which Catherine Creek was named either.

William Godley is not registered on the 1870 Union County census, so he likely arrived just after the 1870 census was taken. His land patent in Union County was earned on January 5, 1875, and even if William spent the previous five years proving it up, that is still seven years after the creeks were named and put on the 1863 map.

After such a thorough look at this, we realized that the pioneer namesake for Catherine Creek by necessity had to be among much earlier pioneers, who arrived in Union County in either 1861 or 1862.

There is one Catherine that did arrive here in September 1862, Catherine Gekeler. Perhaps she is the namesake for Catherine Creek because the creek even ran through Gekeler property. Until more facts surface, the namesake for these two creeks will remain a history mystery.

Golding Road - Designated road #47, it runs 1.25 miles in Township 1N R40E Section 6 in the Elgin maintenance district.

It is named after Flora Elizabeth Golding (1882-1959) and Audas Ezra Golding (1884-1948). Flora is the landowner of record on the *1935 Metsker Map*, but it does not appear to have been a residential property since the Goldings lived in Elgin first and then in the Alicel area by 1928. After Audas' death in 1948, Flora returned to her Elgin home.

Flora E. Golding was the daughter of Joseph Andrew and Priscilla (Harris) Knight (see Knight Road entry). She was born in Elgin on September 11, 1882 and had been a resident in Union County, Oregon all her life.

She married Audas E. Golding on February 13, 1906 in Union County. It doesn't appear that they had any children during their marriage. In 1910, when they were married for 4 years, they lived in the South Elgin district and Flora's parents, Andrew (71) and Priscilla (68) lived with them. *(1910 Federal Census)*

Audas Golding was born February 11, 1884 in Greentown, Howard County, Indiana, the son of Leander (b. 1857) and Mary Zenetia Golding (b. 1861). His family came to Union County about 1898, including his older sister Mattie Golding (b. 1882).

While living in this county, he worked as a farmer and grain elevator operator in the Elgin area. On his WWI draft registration, he described himself as short, stout with blue eyes and dark hair. *(draft registration, Sept. 12, 1918)* At age 58, he was employed at the Pioneer Flouring Mill in Alicel, and his residence was in Alicel.

He died of a heart attack on Monday morning, June 28, 1948 at his farm near Elgin. He was a member of Elgin IOOF and the La Grande encampment.

Audas was survived by his wife, Flora; two sisters, Mrs. Ada Bechtel, Elgin and Mrs. Mattie Bishop, Madera, California, and an uncle, Charles Elliott of Milton-Freewater. *(La Grande Observer, June 29, 1948, pg. 5)*

Eleven years later, Flora died on August 13, 1959 at the Grande Ronde Hospital after an extended illness. The previous May she had been taken to the same hospital, following a heart attack at her home. *(La Grande Observer, May 15, 1959, pg. 5)*

She was survived by two brothers, William J. Knight of La Grande and Sam Knight of Joseph; two sisters, Mrs. Viva Ballen, Riverside, Calfornia, and Mrs. Dora Newell of Chula Vista, California.

She was interred with her husband, Audas, in the Elgin Cemetery. A red granite stone marks the place where they rest in peace together.

Good Road - Formerly Cricket Flat Road as listed on the *1935 Metsker Map of Union County*. It was known as Cricket Flat because of a serious infestation of crickets and their endless chorus of chirping that drove residents to the point of desperation. These crickets were attracted to the wild camas and the moist ground they grew in. This infested area was at the base of Stubblefield Mountain. Pioneer hog raiser Samuel G. French came to save the day, when he drove his herd of hogs from his flour mill in Cove to the flat to eat the crickets, and that managed the problem. *(Observations and Opinions, 2002, Dave & Trish Yerges, pg. 77-78)*

The name Cricket Flat Road was replaced with Good Road, also known as mail route #1 Elgin and county road #48 located in Township 1N R40E Section 5. Near the end of this 6.89 mile road is the Good Ranch, the earliest residence on the road and later a registered century ranch.

The road was named after pioneer settlers John Porter Good (1859-1942) and his wife Adaline

Arnold (1862-1938), natives of Luzerne County, Pennsylvania.

They were married on April 5, 1882, and worked a farm in partnership with a younger brother, William Good, in Jonestown, Columbia County, Pennsylvania.

However, when John developed tuberculosis from the dusty coal mines of that area and was given six months to live, he sold his interests in the farm, and he and Adaline, along with their children George, Lee, and Frank, left Pennsylvania and traveled to the western frontier for clean, mountain air.

That first winter, they stayed with John's uncle and aunt, Albert and Cordelia Good of La Grande, Oregon, and John's health started to improve. Progressively and miraculously, he became cured of tuberculosis, so he and Adaline decided to make Union County their home.

On May 16, 1890, John filed a homestead claim for 160 acres located about 11 miles northeast of Elgin with an awesome panoramic view of the Blue Mountains. That year he built the first of three homes on that property. Over the years, he and Adaline both purchased additional acreage in farm land and timberland so that in a matter of 14 years, the Good family owned 556 acres.

The Goods had two more children, Mae and Howard. The older children, George, moved to California; Lee was living and working in Montana; and Frank died in 1899 at the age of 15 in Elgin. Mae married, started a family and lived in Elgin, while Howard lived with his parents and helped on the ranch.

On June 9, 1934, Howard married Lillian, a former teacher from Shickshinny, Pennsylvania. They moved into the Good home with John and Adaline Good to care for them as they aged and help them with the ranch work.

Adaline Good, 76, died at her home on September 8, 1938 in the morning after a long illness. She had lived in the Elgin territory for 49 years, her obituary stated. She was born on February 2, 1862 in Pennsylvania. She was survived by her husband, John, daughter Mary Rasmussan, Elgin; three sons, Lee of Whitefish, Montana, George of Pacific Grove, California and Howard of Elgin. There were twelve grandchildren and eight great grandchildren. *(La Grande Observer, Sept. 8, 1938, pg 3)*

John Good died February 14, 1942 at the age of 82 years and 8 months. Both he and Adaline were interred at the Elgin Cemetery with their son, Frank J. Good (1883-1899). *(Findagrave.com)*

After their deaths, son Howard Good and his wife, Lillian, continued living on and managing the Good ranch. Howard founded the Good Saw Mill, which operated from 1933-1956 and employed 11 workers. He also started raising Herefords with his son, Richard, during the late 1940s.

Howard died December 30, 1968, but not before he worked to have Good Road put in and electricity brought to his ranch and his neighbors' homes. Lillian died July 8, 1974, a hard working partner on the ranch. During their marriage they had two sons, Paul and Richard. Paul had an accident that left him paralyzed, so Richard took over the operation of the ranch.

Richard married Sandra, a 39-year old, single teacher from Holland, New York, who had placed a personal ad in a science magazine. Richard answered that ad, and she agreed to come out for a 30-day visit to see if she liked rural Oregon and, of course, Richard. Their friendship turned into marriage vows on September 2, 1980.

Together they have been caring for their tree farm, and although they have no heirs to pass it on to, they have made a stewardship plan with the Oregon Department of Forestry that will ensure its care and management for years to come. *(Dick and Sandra Good interview, April 2001)*

Richard Irwin Good was born on December 22, 1937 in Elgin, and he died January 30, 2019 in La Grande. His public obituary posted on *Loveland Funeral Chapel's website* stated that he was educated musically, having taken piano lessons in elementary school and trombone lessons at Elgin High School. He also had a talent at wood-working, which he developed throughout his life.

He attended Oregon Technical Institute near Klamath Falls from 1956 to 1958, graduating with a major in farm mechanics. During his college years, he boarded and worked at the College Fire Department and learned fire fighting skills, his obituary read.

Known as "Dick" to family and friends, he spent his life doing what he loved most, cattle ranching and tree farming. As a young boy, he kept cattle records and joined 4-H. He started with Jersey milk cows, then Milking Shorthorns, Herefords and Angus in the late 1950s.

He also worked with Rod Brevig, the Boise Cascade Forester, to develop the first forest management plan for the ranch in 1975. The following year, Dick operated his own Cat logging using his forestry plan with careful selective logging practices, and in the mid 1980s, he used an Idaho Jammer lining machine to do his own log lining out of the steep canyons.

Dick deservedly won the recognition of Union County Tree Farmer of the Year in 1990 and 2012 from the Oregon State Forestry. His farm was also registered with the Oregon Historical Society as a Century Farm in 1990, and their history was published in the *April 26, 2001 issue of The Valley News*, written by Trish Yerges, who also contributed the story to the Oregon Historical Society's Century Farm files.

In 2008 at the age of 70, Dick set up a Timber King bandsaw mill and milled his own lumber, using it to build many structures on the ranch, including several calf shelters, corral fences and gates.

His cattle operation continued until his partial retirement in 2011. During his retirement, he enjoyed building projects on the ranch, gardening, hunting and fishing.

As his health declined, he left the home he put his heart and soul into and relocated to a care facility in La Grande, where he was cared for by staff and the Grande Ronde Hospital Hospice. He died on

Wednesday, January 30, 2019, and a funeral service was held at Loveland Funeral Chapel on February 8, 2019.

He was survived by his wife, Sandra; sister-in-law Ruth Good of Scio; a brother, Paul Good of Walla Walla; a sister Daisy Daw of Tigard; and nieces and nephews. He was preceded in death by his parents, Howard and Lillian, and by his brother Warren. *(Loveland Funeral Chapel website obituaries)*

The authors remember Dick Good as a soft-spoken, shy man with a hospitable, gentle personality. On the surface he seemed quiet, but any topic of a mechanical or engineering nature excited him, and his ranch was full of his own engineering productions that way. Certainly, if his ancestors were alive today, they would have been very pleased to see what he had accomplished with the family ranch in his lifetime.

Gordon Creek Road - This road #41 runs 5.96 miles northwest of Elgin in Townships 1-2N R39E Sections 33-34, 3-4.

The Indian Valley started to be settled in the summer of 1865, but the creek's name, Gordon Creek, came some years later. The earliest mention of Gordon Creek on any map the authors found was on the *Original U.S. Govt. Survey Map of 1882.*

The documentary history on this creek's name is sketchy at best, but the authors set out on a journey of discovery that led them to a reasonable namesake for Gordon Creek and Gordon Creek Road.

First, we examined what had been proposed by historians before us. *The Oregon Geographic Names, 7th Edition 2003, pg. 414*, states: "William Gordon, a rancher, had a place on the stream in the early 1870s, and it bears his name."

This is incorrect, says descendent Mort Gordon of Elgin. This William Gordon had a wife Priscilla Huffman, and they were the ancestors of Mort Gordon of Elgin. They were on the *1870 Federal Census* in Summerville as newlyweds and no kids at that point in time. The value of their residence was $200, and they had no acreage.

The authors asked Mort Gordon, 86, in 2021 if Gordon Creek was named after his great grandfather, William Gordon, and he replied, "I do remember asking my parents if the creek was named for our family, and the answer was always no. My 'Gordon Tribe' lived southeast of Elgin in the Elk Flat area of Cricket Flat and later moved to Pumpkin Ridge." Census records sometimes list Pumpkin Ridge as Elgin territory and other times as Summerville territory. However, neither of those residences are near Gordon Creek Road.

However, Bernal D. Hug leaves us the best clues about the elusive Mr. Gordon in his book, *The History of Union County Oregon, published in 1961, page 175.* He wrote: "A man by the name of Gordon came over the Walla Walla Trail with his horses. He built a cabin on the creek near, or a little below, the present location of Rock Wall Grange Hall [71562 Middle Road, Elgin] and pastured his horses in the meadows along the creek and then drove them back across the mountains in the fall. In the spring, he returned with his horses. The creek became known as Gordon Creek."

Bernal D. Hug's *Supplement #5 of The History of Union County, Oregon, pg. 1*, adds this information to that:

"The Old Walla Walla Indian Trail that was used by General Fremont when he explored through the country in 1843, and was later improved by Walla Walla merchants to reach the Snake River mines with their pack trains, made a logical route for emigrants into Indian Valley. They soon used it. A man by the name of Gordon brought horses over for summer pasture along the creek. This creek is now known as Gordon Creek."

This mention by Bernal D. Hug makes it very clear that Mr. Gordon was only a seasonal resident of Union County. He was like a squatter, who built a cabin along the creek on open range land, and he stayed only for the summer while his horses pastured there. Then in the fall, he drove them all back to his permanent home in Umatilla country, which in those years encompassed Walla Walla, Washington.

This mention by Bernal D. Hug was a good clue, and the authors started to search for a Mr. Gordon in the Walla Walla area.

The authors of this book believe they have found the Gordon gentleman after whom the Gordon Creek is named. His name was James A. Gordon Sr., an ambitious farmer and raiser of stock, who had easy access to the Walla Walla Trail to bring his horses over to Elgin to pasture in the summer.

James A. Gordon was born in 1825 in Kentucky, and he died June 21, 1876 in Milton-Freewater, Umatilla County, Oregon, what was once a Walla Walla precinct.

James Gordon married Rebecca Martin on July 10, 1851 in Davis County, Iowa. They settled and farmed in Soap Creek, Iowa (Harbour post office). His real estate was valued at $3,600 and personal estate valued at $1,200. Not bad for an ambitious 26-year-old man in 1860.

From Iowa James Gordon moved to what was then called the Walla Walla precinct with a post office in Cayuse, Oregon and then to the Milton [Milton-Freewater] precinct. Either location would have been very accessible to the Walla Walla Trail in order to herd his horses about 48 miles over the Blue Mountains to Elgin.

In the *1870 Federal Census of Cayuse, Umatilla County, Oregon,* it noted James A. Gordon Sr., 45, and his wife Rebecca Martin, 35, and the following children: John, 15, William, 13, James Jr., 11, Dana, 9, Alexander, 5, Nancy, 3, and Robert [George] 7/12 mos. Missing is an older sister Mary E. (Linville).

They were settled initially near the post office in Cayuse, Umatilla County, Oregon some time after 1862 but before 1865, when Alexander was born in Oregon. It may have been at this time that he was taking his horses to Elgin to pasture and fatten them up on well watered grass.

The Civil War was ongoing, and he might have been breeding and raising horses to sell to the U.S. military. Bringing them to Elgin as he did saved on feed and kept his horses in the best selling condition. Obviously, he did not need them on the ranch, so they were horses for sale. At the time of his death, he had 17 horses and colts on his ranch, evidence of a modest equine business.

Not too many years passed and the family moved to Milton, Oregon, a precinct of Walla Walla. There on June 30, 1874, James Gordon Sr. proved up three parcels of land close to the Walla Walla River which flows right through Milton. *(U.S. Land Records, ancestry.com)*

Tragedy struck the Gordon family when the mother, Rebecca, died sometime before June 21, 1876, the date of James A. Gordon Sr.'s death. This explains why she is not listed on the his probate paperwork at all as an heir. When James A. Gordon Sr. died, the county started probate action for the Gordon estate, and the administrator appointed was Lewis Bowles. There was no written will, so the court had to appoint an impartial administrator to take care of liquidating the ranch, paying debts and awarding the heirs.

On January 6, 1877, when the Gordon estate had been fully administered, the heirs of the estate were the nine living Gordon children: Mary E. Linville, 22, John, 21, James A. Gordon Jr., 18, Dana Gordon, 15, Alexander, 11, Nancy, 9, Allison, 7, William, 5, and George, 4.

Referring to the six minor Gordon children, Mr. Bowles said this to the judge, "The minors do not wish to have a guardian appointed for them." This is because their older brother, James A. Gordon Jr., wanted to keep the family together and act as head of the family thereafter. That's exactly what happened because in the *1880 Federal Census* in the family home in Milton, Umatilla, Oregon, the head of the house was listed as James A. Gordon Jr. with his siblings: Dana, 18, Alexander, 15, Nancy, 14, Alice, 11, William, 10, and George, 9.

So ends the story of an ambitious rancher and family man named James A. Gordon Sr., who came over the Walla Walla Trail with his horses to pasture them in the summers at what became a creek named in his honor. This is our best and most reasonable research that finally reveals "a man named Gordon" that Bernal D. Hug wrote about so long ago.

Government Gulch Lane - Almost 2-1/2 miles in length, this road #106 is located in Township 5S R40E Section 33 and is also in the North Powder maintenance district. This lane was curvy, and today it is part of a big loop that leaves and rejoins Highway 237.

The origin of its name likely came from the fact that in the early years prior to the 1930s much of this land was owned by various government agencies, including the Federal Land Bank, the State of Oregon and Union County.

The earliest mention of this area as Government Gulch was in an *April 24, 1923 La Grande Observer* article that stated that "Mrs. K. L. Burk of Baker had the misfortune to turn her car over on the turn at Government Gulch. Mrs. Burk and the young lady with her both escaped injury but Mrs. Burk had some trouble to get out of the wreck. The car was so badly damaged that they had to send out the trouble car (wrecker) from the Ledbetter Garage to tow it in. It is thought that trouble with the steering gear caused the trouble."

This was not the last time that automobile wrecks were mentioned in the paper in conjunction with Government Gulch Lane. There was a mention in 1930 of an automobile accident, and then in 1932, the *La Grande Observer* had an article about road work in the area, including Government Gulch Lane. It stated, "At Government Gulch, four crews of five men, are working in one week shifts, straightening out the sharp curve." Although one curve was straightened out, there were more curves on this road and the *July 18, 1936 La Grande Observer* noted another automobile accident.

All of these accidents may have precipitated more work on the roads in the area as noted in the *April 1, 1941 issue of the La Grande Observer*. It mentioned that the county was operating a rock crusher at Government Gulch near Telocaset Road. The county crew was working with the Works Progress Administration gang, fixing roads in the area.

According to a local resident, Janet Dodson, her father, who was born in 1930, said that "during WWII there were U.S. soldiers stationed along there to guard the nearby railroad tunnel. To reduce the chance of it being a target for enemy aircraft and bombing, the tunnel was deliberately demolished and the debris was cleared, leaving the tracks in place so that the trains could safely keep running." *(Janet Dodson interview, February 2021)*

Grande Ronde River Road - This road #149 is a scenic drive for 4.08 miles in Towsnhip 3S R35E Section 36 and turns into National Forest Road 51. It is geographically named because it follows the Grande Ronde River for many miles. It diverts from the Ukiah-Hilgard Highway 244 and runs south toward the Vey Sheep Ranch, an iconic landmark in the Starkey territory, and it ends when it intersects with National Forest Road 52.

Just before reaching the Vey Sheep Ranch on the Grande Ronde River Road is an old Forest Service Guard Station, and Greg Tsiatsos of Starkey, remembered that the father of one of his high school classmates named Larry used to work there as the only forest service man. "He used to stay at the guard station and handle all of this country," Tsiatsos said.

Tsiatsos recalled that the Forest Service sent a couple of employees to check the willows along the Grande Ronde, and they used to stay at the guard station when they were doing that work. As the owner of the Starkey Store, Tsiatsos said he owned 12 acres of the river across from the store, and one time, some Oregon State University students were out there studying green frogs. Tsiatsos and his wife eventually gifted their 12 acres to Oregon State University. The University kept it for 10 years, but then they wanted to sell it, so Tsiatsos bought it back from them.

Grandview Cemetery Rd - This is more like an approach to the Grandview Cemetery than it is a county road, but the tax assessor's office does list it as county road #89 in Township 3S R38E Section 17 in the La Grande maintenance district connected with 18th Street in the La Grande city limits.

Grays Corner Road - Formerly Grays Corner-Indian Creek Road #52. It runs 8.43 miles in length and is located in Township 2S R39E Section 13 in the La Grande and Imbler maintenance districts. It brings access to about 17 residences.

The "Indian Creek" name was later dropped, and it has since been called Grays Corner Road. It is easily accessed by taking Hull Lane on the south end of Imbler, going east until it intersects with Gray's Corner Road.

This gravel road meanders for miles along the base of Mount Harris and provides an elevated, scenic view of the Grande Ronde Valley. If you want a patchwork view of the fields, take this road.

It is named after the Gray family, including the patriarch Robert Doke Gray, his son George Grant Gray, his grandson Nathan Taylor Gray and great-grandson, Aldon Houx Gray.

Robert Doke Gray was born May 7, 1805 in Washington County, Tennessee, where on May 11, 1826, he married Agnes Chinneth. They had eight children, the first seven were born in Tennessee: Sarah (1828-1888), Melissa (1833-), Elizabeth (1835-1916), Joseph (1838-1917), George Grant (1840-1928), Cornelia (1843-), Robert L. (1845-1879). The seventh child, Nathan T. Gray was born in 1847 in Arkansas.

The family stayed in Arkansas until spring 1853 when they came to Benton County, Oregon. The Grays followed the trail that was later called Meek's Cutoff across central Oregon and the Cascade Mountains by way of McKenzie River to Eugene. The Grays, Taylors and others in the 20-wagon train were reportedly the first to make the crossing over the Deschutes River near Bend, Oregon.

When the Robert Gray family arrived in the Willamette Valley, they settled on a donation claim near Corvallis where they lived for the next 16 years. The family then included the parents, and children: Joseph, George, Cornelia, Robert L. and Nathan.

In 1869, most of them except for Cornelia and George, relocated to Union County, Oregon, and they lived on a farm on Sand Ridge, twelve miles from Cove. Son Joseph lived on a farm next door. Robert Gray and all his sons were listed as farmers on the *1870 Federal Census*.

Robert Doke Gray died on September 18, 1870 on his farm in Union County, and he was buried in Summerville. Hearing of his father's death, George Grant Gray, who had been away from home on his own adventures for nine years, relocated to the Grande Ronde Valley to be closer to his widowed mother.

He was fortunate to share the last 17 years with her. In the *1880 Federal Census*, his mother Agnes was living in George's household in Union County. She died in 1888 at 79 years of age and was buried at Summerville Cemetery.

Her death notice in the *Oregon Scout, Friday, February 3, 1888* issue stated:

"Died.—Jan. 23, [1888], at the residence of George Gray in Lower Cove, of pneumonia, Mrs. Gray, aged 79 years. Mrs. Gray was the mother of George and N. L. Gray and Mrs. J. H. Slater of La Grande." [Lower Cove is Grays Corner Road.]

The road history now focuses on George Grant Gray, who was born April 10, 1840 in Granger County, Tennessee. He married Sarah Sylvina "Vina" Jasper in Summerville on February 22, 1874.

They had ten children: Robert Nay (1875-1879), Ivie Jane (1876-1879), Sarah Agnes Conley (1879-1962), George Merrell (1881-1943), Anna E. Miller (1885-1949), Bessie Childers (1887-1963), Samuel Hughes (1888-1896), Joseph T. (1889-1963), Nathan Taylor (1892-1957), and Berdillie "Dillie" Mabel Millering (1898-2001).

"Mother lost the first two children in the 1879 diphtheria epidemic," Dillie said in a *February 2001 interview* with the authors.

Robert Nay, 4 years and 8 months, died on Sunday, November 16, and Ivie Jane, 2 years, died the next Sunday November 23, 1879. The children were laid to rest in the George Gray family plot at Summerville Cemetery.

While George predominately busied himself as a farmer, living a quiet and peaceful life, there was one year when he became part of something highly publicized and disturbing to everyone in the county. The story was covered by numerous newspapers across the state of Oregon.

George sat on the all male jury that heard and judged the Kelsey Porter case that occurred on Porter's farm in Pine in the panhandle of Union County, and it was tried in 1896 at the county seat in Union, Oregon. The Kelsey Porter case was known throughout the state as "the case of the century." In the end, Porter was convicted, some say unjustly, and the public outcry precipitated the reassignment of the county seat to La Grande and the redrawing of Union and Baker counties boundaries.

As disturbing as this case was to listen to, George had his own sorrows at home that year. His son Samuel Hughes Gray, who was born July 18, 1888, injured his spine in a fall, and from that time on, he developed a pronounced spinal curvature. He died September 17, 1896 when he was 8 years and 2 months old. He was buried in the family plot at Summerville Cemetery.

George continued farming a little longer. The *1920 Federal Census* noted that he was retired. His son, Nathan, who always lived with his father and mother, took over the farming operation. Then his father George died July 22, 1928 at his residence at 2:15 p.m. His burial took place in Summerville Cemetery. The widow Sarah continue to live at her homestead with her son Nathan until her death on January 7, 1940 at the age of 84 years. She lived 71 of those 84 years in the Lower Cove neighborhood. *(La Grande Observer, Jan. 8, 1940, pg. 1)*

The Lower Cove neighborhood was an informal term that included Grays Corner Road, and this is where the story focuses now on Nathan Taylor Gray. He was born on the family farm on January 19, 1892.

He married Miss Ada Alma Houx, who just happened to be the Cove Cherry Queen at the third annual Cove Cherry Festival on July 23, 1913. She was born August 6, 1895 in Strawn, Texas and came to Cove with her parents. On August 7, 1913, one day after she turned 18, Nathan and Ada tied the knot in matrimony.

During their marriage, they had three children: Delda Elizabeth Smith (b.1915), Donald Nathan (b.1918) and Aldon Houx Gray (b.1924). Initially, Nathan's family had been living in a house next door to the George Gray homestead, and they were noted that way in the *1920 Federal Census*.

Delda Gray Smith of La Grande related the family's residential history to the authors.

"My father Nathan got the farm after my grandfather died in 1928," Delda said. "Nathan always lived on the farm, and when he got married my mother and father made the farm their home. There were three generations living in that house [in 1930], my grandma, my dad and mother and us kids."

Nathan had plenty of experience at general farming, raising hay, wheat, barley and oats. However, in 1931 Nathan developed his farm into a dairy called Grays Red Star Dairy, and he built a milk house on the farm and raised a herd of about 100 Jersey and Holstein milking cows. He advertised in the paper, "You can whip our cream, but you can't beat our milk!"

"My dad ordered a truck from Seattle through Mr. Perkins automobile dealership in La Grande, and he had it fitted with refrigeration," Delda said.

His hired delivery drivers, dressed in white shirts and slacks who were on the road at 3:30 a.m. to make the many deliveries. Delda kept busy pressing the white outfits for the delivery boys and her mother and brothers were busy sterilizing jars and filling them. Quart glass jars bearing the Grays Red Star Dairy label were set on the doorsteps early each morning.

If extra milk was needed, Nathan purchased it from his brothers, George and Joseph Gray living nearby. Cream was also supplied upon the customer's request. If Nathan and his brothers didn't have enough cream to fill the orders, Nathan had another source.

Bill Howell of Imbler explained: "If Nathan ever fell short of his orders for cream, he called upon my dad, Oscar Howell, who farmed on Imbler Road, for his day's production to fill the gap. It was billed as grade A cream, but in those instances, it's highly questionable." *(Bill Howell interview, May 20, 2018)*

Nathan's life revolved around the Century Farm on Grays Corner Road until his death on November 5, 1957. Ada remained on the farm until son Aldon was married in 1966. Then Ada got an apartment in La Grande. She died on June 8, 1979 at 83 years of age. Both Nathan and Ada were buried at the Summerville Cemetery.

The Gray's farm was deeded over to Nathan's son Aldon Gray and his wife Dixie Lee Rayburn. Aldon was born on the farm and although the dairy was shut down, he was still engaged in general farming and stock raising. He raised about 100 head of Angus cattle during the years between 1957-1970s. In 1990, Aldon retired and sold the farm.

The Grays Corner Road sign attests to the lives of four generations of farmers, who lived decent lives and put farm-fresh milk and cream on many a breakfast table each day.

Greentree Road - This is a private road in Township 1N R40E Section 14 in the Elgin maintenance district.

Greiner Lane - This short gravel road #16A runs .51 miles in Township 2S R38E Section 1 in the La Grande maintenance district. It connects Sandridge Road to Webster Road and allows access to two properties.

The road is named after a farmer named Frank E. Greiner, the son of David Greiner (1837-1915) and Martha "Jennie" Frances Halley. David and Martha were married in Dayton, Columbia County, Washington, on December 6, 1883. *(Ancestry.com)*

The Greiner family moved to the Grande Ronde Valley in 1892. *(La Grande Observer, May 25, 1938, pg. 1, Mrs. David Greiner's obituary)*

Their son, Frank "Frankie" was born in Dayton on April 17, 1887. *(Ancestry.com)* He married Aldora "Nora" May Sheeks on November 5, 1913 in Alicel, Oregon. In the *1920 Federal Census*, Frank and his wife lived on and rented farm land on this stretch of road. They had three children at that time: Ethel, Edith and Dale F. Greiner.

By 1930, Frank owned his farm and had another daughter, Edna, making the family complete with three daughters and one son. On the 1930 census, Frank declared that he had a radio set in his home. The U.S. Government wanted to know how many Americans would be equipped to listen to President Franklin D. Roosevelt's fireside chats over their radio. Consequently, the census had a specific question about whether or not you had a radio in your home.

Frank died January 20, 1958 at age 70 years, and he's buried at Summerville Cemetery along with his wife, Aldora, who died March 19, 1965 also at 70 years of age.

Frank's obituary stated the following: "Frank E. Greiner Funeral Rites Set — Frank Edward Greiner, 70; a farmer living on route #1, La Grande, died in a hospital here on Monday, January 20, after a short illness. Funeral services at Summerville Chapel will be Friday, January 24, at 2 p.m. Daniels Funeral Home was in charge of arrangements, and burial took place in Summerville Cemetery.

Born at Dayton, Washington, April 17, 1887, Mr. Greiner had lived in Union County for 67 years. He was a member of Farmers Lodge 49, IOOF of Summerville.

Survivors include the widow, Mrs. Aldora May Greiner, La Grande; a son, Dale Greiner, La Grande and three daughters, Mrs. Ethel Hernandez, Seattle, Mrs. Edith Dixon, and Mrs. Edna Franklin, both of La Grande. A brother and sister, Ray Greiner and Mrs. Ona Woodell, also are La Grande residents. Eleven grandchildren and one great grandchild also survive." *(La Grande Observer, January 21, 1958, pg. 8)*

Gunnels Road - This is a private road off of Blackhawk Trail Lane in Township 2S R38E Section 31 in the La Grande maintenance district. It brings access to three private properties.

Hacker Lane - This lane designated road #144 is 2 miles in length and located in Township 1N R38E Section 33 in the Imbler maintenance district, exiting west off of Hunter Road and running along Strapping Creek.

It is named after John Hacker, who died Sunday evening on December 17, 1933 at his home in Summerville after a six month illness. He was born on June 13, 1862 in Bayreuth, Bavaria, Germany and came to La Grande from Germany in the spring of 1889.

He was married to Anna "Annie" Meyers on April 15, 1894 by Justice of the Peace J. W. Knowles. A year into their marriage, she gave birth to their first and only child, John Carl Hacker on June 16, 1895. In 1897, the family moved to Summerville where John Hacker Sr. resided until his death. In the *1900 Federal Census*, John is listed as a farmer and head of the household, age 37; his wife Annie, 30, born December 1869 and married for the past 6 years. Their son John Jr. was nearly 5 at the time of the census. He appears to have been an only child.

John Hacker Sr. was survived by his widow and a son John C. Hacker of Summerville; two sisters, Mrs. John Meyers of Elgin and Mrs. John Skilling of Portland; a brother, Charles Hacker of Elgin and other relatives.

The funeral services were conducted at the Summerville Chapel and burial took place at the Summerville Cemetery. The Walkers Funeral Home managed the care of the body. *(La Grande Observer, Dec. 16, 1933, pg. 4)*

Anna Meyers Hacker's gravestone in Summerville Cemetery reads 1867-1950. The *1910 Federal Census* stated that she came to America in 1893 and became a naturalized citizen.

She was age 82 upon death and her obituary stated that she as born in Kesees, Bavaria, Germany on December 31, 1867. She died in a local hospital Monday, March 13, 1950, and she was survived by her son, John C. Hacker and other relatives. *(La Grande Observer, March 15, 1950, pg. 9)*

John and Annie's son, John Carl Hacker was born June 16, 1895 in La Grande and was raised on his father's farm in Summerville. He helped his father in general farming and was a paid employee on his father's farm. *(Draft Card, June 5, 1917)* In the *1920 Federal Census,* he was 24 and listed as a member of his father's household. In December 1933, when his father died, the obituary read that he and his mother were from Summerville. John Carl Hacker married Oweda Alice Lilly (1903-

1996) on October 9, 1926 in Union County, and he died February 9, 1976.

Haefer Lane - Formerly named Mills-Haefer Lane, this paved road #121 is home to 50 property owners and is located in Township 3S R40E Section 15 in the Union district. It leaves the city of Cove and sprawls into the countryside for 2.77 miles intersecting with other roads such as Love Road, Wade Road, Sunday Drive and Stackland Road.

This road was named after John Christian Haefer, who died August 22, 1938 and is buried in the Cove Cemetery. His obituary states: "John C. Haefer of Cove Dies Here" — "John C. Haefer, long a resident of Cove, died at the Grande Ronde hospital Monday morning after a brief illness. Mr. Haefer has been in poor health for a long time. He was taken to the hospital Sunday, August 14 and was found to be seriously ill. He passed away Monday morning. He was born in Philadelphia, April 23, 1859.

He came west 60 years ago (1878) and to Cove, Oregon in 1918, where he has since made his home. He was united in marriage with Miss (Otilla) Killy Redmon in 1897. She preceded him in death a number of years ago (1928). Three sons, William, John and Herman of Cove and one daughter, Mrs. Bertha DeBorde of La Grande survive. One daughter passed away many years ago." *(End of Obit, La Grande Observer, Tuesday, August 23, 1938, pg. 3)*

He and his wife were married on November 17, 1880 in Mountville, Minnesota. They had six children, the first five children were born in Minnesota and the youngest was born in Washington. Their firstborn died in infancy. Otilla Haefer died March 5, 1928 at her home in Cove and is interred at Cove Cemetery with her husband.

The Mills part of this road name originates with James E. Mills (1879-1974) and his wife Mabel Alice Jones (1879-1975). They were married in Rock Springs, Wyoming in 1906, where James was a popular tea, coffee and spice merchant. They came to Union County in 1917, according to Mabel's obituary. *(La Grande Observer, June 25, 1932, pg. 3; Rock Springs Independent, January 5, 1906, pg. 4)*

Mabel's parents were from New South Wales and came to America, where she met James E. Mills. She taught for many years in several states, and then she trained as a nurse in Wyoming and was later appointed by the governor on the state examining board.

They had four sons and one daughter: Gordon, who graduated from Harvard; Dorothy, a student at Whitman College and head of her class; Allen, Lloyd and Gale. Mabel returned to teaching in 1922 in the Cove School District.

In 1931, James Mills donated a registered Jersey bull calf as a prize to a fair exhibitor owning the winning grade dairy cow. Mills was gainfully self-employed on his dairy farm and fruit orchard.

In August 1942, their son Lloyd J. Mills was one of the first casualties of World War II from Union County. *(La Grande Observer, April 2, 1943, pg. 5)* Another son, James Gordon worked in an art store as an artist and interior decorator in Los Angeles, California, prior to the war.

James E. Mills died February 23, 1974, and he is interred with his wife at Old Sunnyside Cemetery in Sunnyside, Washington.

Haggerty Lane - This lane is 1.32 miles in length, and designated as county road #111A in Township 4S R40E Section 2 in the Union maintenance district. It diverts off of High Valley Road.

This lane is named after the Leverett Bigwell Haggerty family. He was born September 11, 1839 in New York. He grew up there and became a dry goods clerk until age 23.

In 1864, he moved to Indiana where he married Celesta A. Etna on January 5, 1864 in Allen, Indiana, and during their marriage they had 13 children. In 1872, the family moved to Kansas, and in 1881, they relocated to Prairie City, Oregon. Their last three children were born in Cove, Oregon, in 1887, 1890 and 1891. There, he developed a dairy and was turning out a large amount of cheese. *(La Grande Observer, June 18, 1951, "In Former Years" pg. 4)*

In 1899, he and his wife, along with the younger six children moved to the Trout Creek area of Wallowa County. He died in Wallowa County on March 25, 1910. His wife died previously in May of 1904.

Their second oldest child, William Otis Haggerty, was born in Fort Wayne, Indiana in 1867, and in 1909, he proved up on his own homestead, where Haggerty Lane is now located near Union, Oregon.

"Mrs. S. J. Wilkinson has sold her Catherine Creek farm to W. O. Haggerty. This is one of the very best dairy ranches on Catherine Creek and would be a most valuable asset to one desiring to engage in that lucrative business. Mr. Haggerty will no doubt dispose of the farm as he has sufficient land besides for one man." *(La Grande Observer, March 15, 1915, pg. 6)*

His obituary states that he was a retired grocer in the city of Union, Oregon. The *July 23, 1929 La Grande Observer, pg. 3*, had a brief note that W. O. Haggerty improved the appearance of his grocery store with a new coat of kalsomine. In 1936, the Haggerty Grocery Company purchased a new delivery truck for use with their business. By 1939, he had sold his grocery store to Irwin Westenskow, and he re-opened it as Westenskow's Red and White Market.

In addition to W. O. Haggerty's interest in the grocery store business, he was also interested in the cheese business as noted by an article in the *La Grande Observer, July 18, 1921, pg. 1,* where it stated that he was the treasurer and on the board of directors for the Union Cheese Company.

He was also the owner of the Haggerty Apartments, which in May of 1939 was taken over by Georgianna Goodbroad.

He married Ida May Wilkinson, and they had three children, Grace, William and Emerson, and it appears that they were all college educated and had their own careers. Ida Haggerty died in 1918.

William O. Haggerty died on March 13, 1952 in Union.

Halley Road - This gravel road #15 runs 4.26 miles in Township 2S R38E Section 34 in the La Grande maintenance district.

It is named after the enterprising cattleman, Benjamin S. Halley (1835-1898), from Clark County, Kentucky. He founded this Century Ranch in 1864, when he purchased his initial 400 acres on this road. Other generations took their turns at the farm operation after Benjamin, including Edward and Maude Halley and then Henry and Edna Heyden. It was Henry Heyden that applied for Century Farm status in June 1970. Since then it has remained in the possession of Halley descendants, currently the Steve Stonebreaker family..

Benjamin S. Halley was born December 12, 1835, the eldest of seven children born to James Patton and Eleanor (Fisher) Halley, both natives of Kentucky. Benjamin's parents moved the family to Missouri, where in January 11, 1854 the father died.

On September 17, 1855, in Macon County, Missouri, Benjamin Halley, 20, married his first cousin, Elizabeth A. Halley, 20. The Halley couple made their home there and over the next ten years, Benjamin became known as an enterprising cattleman.

In Macon County, Missouri, Elizabeth Halley became mother to four children: Jonathan Presley "Press" (1856), Anna Belle (1859), later Mrs. James McAlister; Nancy (1861) and Edward Linn (1863). Following Edward's birth, the Halley family decided to migrate west for the virgin soils of Oregon in 1864. With a wagon outfitted with mule teams, 29-year-old Benjamin Halley, along with his wife and four children, commenced on the arduous trek of several months across the Plains, driving his stock behind the wagons. These were the start of his ranch in Oregon.

Making good time, the Halley family arrived in the Grande Ronde Valley of northeastern Oregon later that year (1864) and immediately made their claim to 400 acres located six miles northeast of La Grande on what was then called by several descriptive names, such as the Moss Chapel community; the Island precinct and the Iowa settlement. Today, the property is addressed as Halley Road, La Grande.

After settling there, Elizabeth gave birth to four more children: Winifred P. (1865), R. Estel (1868), Robert L. (1869) and Sanford Page, born January 27, 1870. In 1871, when Page was one year old, his mother Elizabeth Halley died. She was 37 years of age. Her burial took place at the Summerville Cemetery in a lot owned by a well-known Summerville blacksmith by the name of Jasper Bonnette. Her premature departure from the Halley family was felt by her husband and eight children, ranging in age from 15 to 1 year old.

Knowing that the children dearly needed a mother, Benjamin renewed his friendship with a recently widowed friend, Rebecca Jane (Anderson) McAlister (1836-1874), formerly the wife of Samuel H. McAlister, who died on April 5, 1870. Benjamin Halley and the McAlisters were once neighbors in Macon County, Missouri before each family migrated to Oregon.

Rebecca "Becky" Jane McAlister had six children of her own from her marriage to Samuel. Her three oldest sons, Daniel Jefferson "Jeff" 20, James "Jim" 16, and John, 13, tried to convince their mother to allow them to operate the farm and the horse breeding business. They thought they could manage this great responsibility, but their mother felt very insecure about it and did not agree to the idea.

"She sold off most of the stock and married Ben Halley. Sons Jeff, John and Jim McAlister refused to go with their mother and stayed on at the old home. In a year or two Jeff returned to his mother's people in Illinois." *(Bernal D. Hug's History of Union County, Supplement #8, pg. 24)*

Becky McAlister and Benjamin Halley were married on July 30, 1871. She brought her four youngest children with her to live on the Halley ranch and along with Benjamin's eight children, she suddenly had 12 children to manage and care for. It a all too much for her. In addition to this, Becky nursed some of those children through serious illnesses. *(Bernal D. Hug's History of Union County, Supplement 8, pg. 24)*

In 1873, Becky gave birth to an infant son, who died soon afterward; and on December 6, 1874, she gave birth to Eleanor Jane "Nora" Halley. About five months later in April 1875, Becky died, and the youngest Halley children were placed in other homes. The youngest, Page and Nora, were adopted by Mr. and Mrs. William Tillman.

The McAlister children, who were living in the Halley home, were taken in by friends for a few years. Becky's children, Susan McAlister married Samuel B. Williamson in October 1878 and Jim McAlister married Benjamin's daughter, Anna Bell Halley, in November 1879. The two McAlister siblings and their spouses took the younger McAlister children into their own respective homes to raise to adulthood.

After Becky's death and the placement of the children in other homes, the Halley house was uncomfortably silent and lonely for Benjamin, so he began to search for another wife. He knew of the Henderson family from Macon County, Missouri, and he traveled there to marry their 17-year-old daughter, Miss Kate Henderson, on July 21, 1875. He brought her back to Union County, where they made their home on the Halley ranch. There Kate became mother to a son, Freddie Halley.

Freddie died of diphtheria on September 27, 1877 in a camping tent at the Union County Fairgrounds, the first of 21 children in Union County to succumb to the dreadful, fast-acting disease. Fever was one of the first symptoms. It wasn't uncommon for a person to die within the week of contracting it because the disease quickly forms a membrane over the trachea and prohibits breathing. Diphtheria was highly contagious, and the virus lived on surfaces of all kinds for a long time. This is why it became a practice to burn everything that came in contact with the infected person.

To escape this plague, Benjamin and Kate Halley acquired a ranch from Wade Angus in 1878 near Enterprise, Wallowa County, Oregon. There Benjamin raised sheep, cattle and horses successfully until 1882. Moving to this isolated ranch quarantined them from the deadly disease and probably saved the Halley family. After little Freddie died, they had two more sons, J. H. and Charles Halley.

The Halley's early settlement in Wallowa County was also part of their county history. The pioneer arch outside the county courthouse lists Benjamin S. Halley as an early pioneer there. Life in Wallowa County was a refuge from sickness, but it wasn't without its trials that often make or break a rancher.

One winter in 1880, there were four nights when the temperatures were 38 degrees below zero. Benjamin rose the first morning after such a night and went out to feed the cattle in the field. He noticed how still the herd appeared to be as they stood huddled together. When he approached their frosty bodies, he pushed on each one with his gloved hand. The dead ones simply dropped over like stiff boards. Benjamin lost half his herd from that deep freeze.

His adult married daughter, Belle McAlister, wrote in her March 2, 1880 letter, "Has fell a foot of snow since the Chinook and cold... now the cattle and sheep failed... was 38 degrees below at Enterprise... had 4 cold nights."

After 1882, the plague had passed and the Halleys returned to Union County to continue ranching. They left their son, Robert L. Halley to manage the Enterprise ranch. In Union County, the Halley ranch included 25 acres in meadow, 25 acres in pasture and the balance in tillable fields for various cereals. In addition to the field work, Benjamin raised considerable stock, including thoroughbred sheep and horses.

His reputation extended beyond that of a successful cattleman and farmer. Benjamin was said to have been a civic minded gentleman, contributing when he could toward the good of the county. One notable achievement was that he participated in the creation of the Oro Dell ditch.

Benjamin ended his life of achievements on October 23, 1898 at the age of 62 years and 10 months. He was interred at Ackles Cemetery on Mt. Glen Road, where several other family members were buried. Thus ended the life of the namesake of Halley Road.

There is one thing for which Halley Road is especially known today—it's the only known site in Union County of a 20-acre meadow of never-plowed, native wild hay. It is as pristine as it was when settlers first came to the Grande Ronde Valley in the summer of 1862. *(Steve Stonebreaker interview, May 2003)*

Hallgarth Road - This road #81 runs 1.66 miles in Township 1N R39E Section 16 in the Elgin maintenance district. It exits Pumpkin Ridge Road in beautiful country territory.

"Hallgarth Road was called after my great granddad," said Ty Hallgarth of Elgin. "They settled that part of the country. If you go up Hallgarth Road to the end of it, it goes clear up around the side of the mountain. If you come down Hamburger Hill, and look east to the Lucas' place, across the river directly behind that house is where the Hallgarths settled when they came to the valley. They owned the land on both sides of the highway right there. The road led to their place." *(Ty Hallgarth*

"When Elgin had the big motel downtown that burned down (it was a pizza place at the time), there was a big block in the middle of the building that read "Hallgarth 1909," and my great granddad helped to build that building," he said. "There was a second block in the basement and when that building burned down, they actually got that second block out of the building and put it in front of Cowboy and Angel's Place. It reads, "Hallgarth 1909" on it." *(Ty Hallgarth interview, June 6, 2018)*

In the *October 28, 1912 Oregonian on pg. 11*, a death notice for Charles Hallgarth was printed. It read: "Union County Pioneer Passes" —La Grande, Oregon, October 27. Union County today suffered the loss of one of its oldest and wealthiest pioneers in the death of Charley Hallgarth, of Elgin. Mr. Hallgarth came to this country in the early days and has accumulated a fortune, most of which is invested in lands about Elgin. Mr. Hallgarth was also a heavy stock-holder in the Elgin Bank. He has been in poor health for some time, and his demise did not come unexpectedly."

Another history publication read: "Charles Hallgarth is one of the early pioneers of Union county, this state, having maintained his residence there continuously for the past thirty-eight years. After many years of activity spent in developing his large real-estate holdings in Oregon, he is now living a retired life in Elgin in the enjoyment of all his natural powers and, being still possessed of more than eleven hundred and twenty acres of fine Oregon farm lands, he is abundantly able to enjoy the good things of this life to which he is justly entitled.

He was born in Lincolnshire, England, July 19, 1838, and is the son of Nimrod and Sarah (Simcotes) Hallgarth, also natives of Lincolnshire, where they were reared, married and spent their entire lives. His father was by trade a butcher and followed that occupation for a livelihood.

Charles Hallgarth was reared at home and acquired his early education in the public schools. On reaching his majority, he became interested in farming. In 1857, he emigrated to the United States and on reaching the New World, he spent his first winter in the state of New York. In the spring of the following year he removed to Winnebago county, Wisconsin, and there remained for the three years immediately following his settlement in the Badger state, after which he removed to California and there was occupied for three years in mining in French Gulch, Shasta County.

Believing that his interests could be accelerated by employment in other fields, in the spring of 1873, he removed to Oregon and was here engaged in his former occupation, that of mining, in Canyon City, Grant county. At this employment he continued for three or four years and then severed his connection therewith and located on land in the Indian Valley near Elgin.

He located on this land at once and established his home and commenced farming and stock-raising, in which he continued for many succeeding years. Having brought his land to a high state of cultivation and receiving as a result a large annual income, he found it both possible and agreeable to retire from the active conduct of his farm interests and accordingly transferred the care and operation of his large farm, consisting of eleven hundred and twenty acres, over to his two sons, while he himself established his residence in Elgin, where he now resides. In addition to his home farm he also owns one hundred and sixty acres of fine timber land in this county.

Charles Hallgarth was united in marriage to Miss Jane Long, of Union county, Oregon, in the year 1875. Mrs. Hallgarth is the daughter of Jacob Long, who early removed from Indiana to Oregon, the family settling near Elgin in the early '70s. To Mr. and Mrs. Hallgarth thirteen children have been born, nine of whom are still living: John, Joseph, Nellie, Jessie, Samuel, Jacob, Frank, James and Carl." *(The Centennial History of Oregon 1811-1912; Illustrated Volume IV (1912) S. J. Clarke Publishing Company)*

Charles Hallgarth died October 26, 1912 in Elgin, Union County, Oregon at the age of 74 years, and he was buried at Elgin Cemetery. *(Findagrave.com)* His death notice spoke of him as "a prominent citizen and pioneer of Elgin, who passed away this afternoon." *(La Grande Observer, Oct 26, 1912, pg. 1)*

Charles Hallgarth's funeral was attended by 30 Elks from Elgin. He was a charter member of the La Grande Lodge. *(La Grande Observer, Oct 28, 1912)* Incidentally, Charles' son, Frank Hallgarth, was the Elgin city marshall from 1930-1937, and a good friend of the legendary mountain trapper Soapy Davis. *(Soapy Davis, The Legendary Mountain Man of Union County, Oregon, Dave & Trish Yerges, 2019)*

Hamilton Road - Formerly Miller-Hamilton road #34 lies on the east side of Highway 82, connecting Booth Lane to Market Lane. It is 2.09 miles in length in Township 2S R39E Section 26 in the La Grande maintenance district.

The Miller part of the road name came from George Washington Miller (1849-1932). George Miller was born September 18, 1849 in McComb, Ohio. He came to Union County with the Conley Train, which organized and departed from Fort Scott, Kansas on May 6, 1874, arriving in La Grande in September of that year. While traveling with the train, he acted as the scout.

Shortly after arriving, George Miller married Matilda Conley, the only daughter of A. B. Conley. They were married on January 1, 1875 in Union County.

Matilda was born December 28, 1858 in Mount Vernon, Illinois, and she died on March 30, 1951 in Cove, Oregon at her daughter Georganna's home, where she had been living for the last six years of her life.

Her obituary read, "She crossed the plains from Girard, Kansas to La Grande with her parents in a covered wagon in 1874." Girard is only 28 miles south of Fort Scott, Kansas, where the wagon train departed. Surviving her death were seven children, 27 grandchildren, 34 great-grandchildren and 9 great-great-grandchildren.

George and Matilda had the following children born in Union County: William Dudley (1876-1969), Effie Maude Smith (1878-1945), Mary Alma Gray (1884-1974), Joisa Eliza Clark (1876-1972),

Ernest E. (1881-1967), Frank (1891-1930), Arthur (1893-1973), Georganna Chadwick (1896-1980), and John Conley Miller (1900-1980).

George Miller worked for A.B. Conley's farm until he bought land on what is now Hamilton Road. He picked a good area, not only for farming because the Grande Ronde River ran through his property, but also the Boise to Walla Walla Emigrant Trail ran right through his property. The frequent wagons freighters coming through his property on this trail would have given him a way to receive supplies and sell and ship his cereal crops and livestock.

The story turns its focus now to William D. and his brother John C. Miller.

William D. Miller married Alice Maude Myers in 1899, and they had the following children: Edith E. (1900-1974), William W. (1906-1993), Leonard G. (1909-1964), Walter G. (1910-1994), Mary A. (1911-1974), and Alice M. (1917-).

John C. Miller married Marjorie G. Laird in 1919 and they had three children: Edmond Lewis (1921-2011), Alvin Lee (1924-1985), and Doris Letha (1927-2006).

Both brothers, William and John Miller, farmed in Union County around Hamilton Road. The *1930 Federal Census of Cove* shows George and Matilda Miller living in the same household with their son John and his family.

George Miller died on the morning of November 17, 1932 at his residence located two miles from Cove. He was buried with his wife in Summerville Cemetery.

The second part of this road name, Hamilton, is named after the Charles Wesley Hamilton family of the Lower Cove area where Hamilton Road is located.

Charles W. Hamilton was born to William Henry and Jane C. (Byers) Hamilton in Scioto County, Ohio on May 2, 1845. On Sept. 13, 1866 at Portsmouth, Scioto County, Ohio, he was united in marriage to Miss Sarah Frances Bridwell, daughter of James and Mary Bridwell. She was born in the same county on January 8, 1850.

To this union were born 11 children: Charlie (1867-1943); Lydia "Lettie" Pratt (1870-1948); Johnny (1871-1873); Harry (1872-1879); Irene (1874-1879); Ormina "Mina" (1879-1940); Hattie Wright (1882-1958); Sally Inez Gray (1884-1977); Shelby (1886-1887); Alma (1890-1893) and Anna Nora Cook (1893-1940).

The family suffered an unusual number of losses when five died in childhood: Johnny, 2, in Idaho; Harry, 7 years, 2 mos., in Island City; Irene, 4 years, 11 mos., in Island City; Shelby, 6 mos., La Grande; and Alma, 2 years, 11 mos., in La Grande.

In 1869, Charles Hamilton moved his family to Westralia, Montgomery County, Kansas *(1870 Federal Census),* where they lived until 1874. That year they came across the plains in a covered wagon to Oregon, settling first in Summerville *(1880 Federal Census)* and then east of Alicel on what was known as the Henry Young place. *(1900 Federal Census)*

Charles was known as "the threshing machine man of the Cove." *(La Grande Observer, Dec. 4, 1897)* In 1897, he was preparing to build a new house on his farm in Lower Cove. *(La Grande Observer, May 13, 1898, pg. 3)* For some reason, perhaps seeking medical relief for his wife's ill health, he decided to pull up stakes and move away.

In 1902 Charles sold his 200 acre farm near Wilholm bridge to son-in-law Walter E. Pratt, who married his daughter Lettie. *(La Grande Observer, Oct. 30, 1902, pg. 4; 1935 Metsker Map)* He first moved the family to Shasta County, California, and then in 1909 to Philomath, Benton County, Oregon, *(1910 Federal Census),* where they lived three years. After this, they moved to Lostine of Wallowa County and then to Stanfield, Umatilla County, Oregon *(1920 Federal Census).*

In 1921, Charles moved back to the Alicel area in the Grande Ronde Valley, where he lived the remainder of his life. His wife, Sarah, died on April 29, 1925 at her home near Alicel. She died at the age of 76 years, 3 months and 26 days.

In the decades preceding her death, she faced serious illness. She had been an invalid for 20 years from 1893 to 1913 with rheumatism, but she experienced a full recovery without the aid of crutches at Dr. Darland's chiropractic parlor in La Grande in 1913. *(La Grande Observer, Feb. 1, 1913, pg. 5)*

Charles died on May 5, 1933 at the advanced age of 88 years and 3 days. He had a serious heart attack three years prior to his death, but he hung onto life by virtue of his unusually strong constitution. He was interred with his wife at the Summerville Cemetery.

Six children were living at the time: Mrs. Hattie Wright of Joseph; Mrs. Sallie Gray of Bend, Oregon, Mrs. Mina Pratt of Lewiston, Idaho., and Charles Hamilton, Mrs. Lettie Pratt and Mrs. Nora Cook all of this valley.

Son Charlie Hamilton, 75, a farmer from Alicel, died Wednesday, June 9, 1943 at the Grande Ronde Hospital after a long illness. He was born August 25, 1867 in Scioto County, Ohio. He was a resident of Union County, Oregon for 70 years, his obituary stated. Surviving him were three sisters: Mrs. (Lettie) Walter Pratt, Mrs. (Hattie) J.G. Wright and Mrs. (Sallie) Charles Gray. *(La Grande Observer, June 11, 1943, pg. 5)*

Charlie Hamilton, pioneer farmer who recently died, transferred a 160-acre tract on the Grande Ronde River, approximately 15 miles from La Grande toward Alicel, to his nephew Wesley Cook of Alicel. Wesley was the son of the late Nora Hamilton Cook, who was Charlie's youngest sibling. *(La Grande Observer, June 19, 1943, pg 3; May 6, 1933, pg. 3; April 30, 1925, pg. 5; May 1, 1925, pg. 4; Findagrave.com; ancestry.com)*

In 1988, the county chose to retain the Hamilton name for this road and dropped the Miller name.

Hampton Court - This short public unmaintained road is located off of Fruitdale Lane on the edge of La Grande in Township 2S R38E Section 34. It is named after Don Hampton, who was born on May 21, 1935 in Hilgard. His grandson, Chad, lives on this road in 2018. *(Randy Hampton interview, April 19, 2018, Don's son)*

Hanging "S" Lane - This private lane is located in Township 1N R39E Section 4 off of Valley View Road outside of Elgin, named by its property owner, likely after his brand. This lane brings access to two residences.

Happy Walrus Road - This gravel road is another private road in rural Summerville off Wagoner Hill Road, located in Township 1S R38E Section 16. It allows access to three residences, including that of long-time artisan Judd Koehn and his wife, Kathy.

Judd was a potter at the time the county gave Koehn the opportunity to give his driveway a name thus christening it as an official road. His wordsmithing creativity stemmed from the custom of calling his two Basset hounds land walruses. He also liked the Beatles song, "I Am The Walrus," and since people name places Happy Valley or Happy something-or-other, Judd fashioned his version, "Happy Walrus".

At the road's entrance, Judd made two happy walrus mail boxes mounted on a fabricated metal stand. Their tusks are handles to open the face of the walrus to deposit mail inside. They are the only walrus mail boxes in Union County, and they make a good wallpaper pic for your cell phone.

This road has a second unique feature, that of three sculpted naked ladies walking up the road. It was an artistic series of sculptures Koehn called "The Walkers." He was interested in the nude form at that time, and each sculpture was a lady in a different position of taking a step. Koehn made three walkers initially, and there are two left now. One is bronze and the other is aluminum.

"At one time, we had one disappear. Someone took it," said Kathy. "But we got it back. I think they decided they didn't know where to put it or what to do with it. Where would you hide something like that?"

Koehn retired from teaching history and art after nearly 40 years. He was also chairman of the art department at Eastern Oregon University. He is currently making large sculptures for a future "Judd at 80" show. *(Kathy Koehn interview, July 6, 2018)*

Hardy Road - Formerly Roulet-Hardy Road #46 is accessed off Parsons Lane, and runs 3.88 miles and then dead ends. It is located in Township 2N R40E Section 31 in the Elgin maintenance district.

It is named after Royal "Roy" C. Hardy (1885-1971). The *1935 Metsker Map of Union County* lists this road as Roulet-Hardy Road after two long-time property owners. Roulet was later dropped from the name. *(See Roulet Loop)*

Royal "Roy" Clyde Hardy was from Coldwater, Kansas, the son of William Harrison Hardy (1863-

1928) and Mary Elizabeth Woodring (1863-1949), emigrants to Union County. Roy was the firstborn in their family, followed by siblings Harley Monroe (1887-1960), Olive Belle Walkins (1889-1966), Henry Hamilton (1893-1957) and Hazel Agnes Seward (1896-1975).

Roy married Mary Jane Rysdam (1885-1968), and they lived about one mile south of the John P. Good ranch on Cricket Flat. The "Rysdam Canyon" on Good Road is named after Mary Jane Rysdam's family.

In November 1950, the rural residences of Royal Hardy and Clyde Hardy on Hardy Road was serviced with electricity for the first time, according to the *La Grande Observer* of that date.

In 2018, Roy Hardy's grandson, Jeff Hardy, farmed land on Hardy Road, but he didn't reside on the road. Jeff L. Hardy, 66, died on March 6, 2022 at his residence on Good Road. *(Obit, La Grande Observer, March 7, 2022)* He was survived by brothers Don, David, Steven, and one sister Alice Hardy, all of Elgin.

Jeff Hardy's cousin, Gene Hardy, does reside on Hardy Road where he also actively farms. *(Union County Tax Assessor's website)*

Hardy Road's neighborhood cemetery is Highland Cemetery located on Good Road. Buried there are Rachel "Regula" (Hug) Roulet (1824-1910) and Florence Hardy (1899-1904).

Hartford Lane - Part of this lane lies within Elgin city limits and the west end of it is county road #42D, located in Township 1N R39E Sections 9 and 10. As a county road, it is only .68 miles in length.

The names of the streets or lanes north of Division Street in Elgin are named after U.S. cities, including Hartford. There are six residences on this lane. *(Joe Garlitz interview, August 25, 2018, retired Elgin City administrator-recorder)*

Hawkins Road - Formerly Peterson Lane, this is road #30, about 2.60 miles in length and located in Township 3S R39E Section 28 in the Union maintenance district.

This road was called Peterson Lane back in the 1980s after John E. Peterson, his wife Grace E., and their daughters Zelda and Velma. *(1920 Federal Census)*

In 1914, it appears that John and Grace Peterson lived in Union, and he worked as a teamster, but by 1920, they were farming on Hawkins Road in the Hot Lake territory of Union County. The Petersons moved off the road during the 1930s, according to Sherman Hawkins, who has lived most of his life on this road. The Petersons are not listed as property owners on that road on the *1935 Metsker Map. (Sherman Hawkins interview, March 14, 2019)*

By 1988, when the county wanted to rename the road signs, Hawkins Road was suggested and adopted as a replacement for the Peterson Road name since the Hawkins family had a long history with the road. The road was named after William "Will" Martin Hawkins, who farmed on this road and raised a family.

William was born December 21, 1876 in Oneida County, Idaho and died July 27, 1951 in this county. He married Ann Etta Halverson on September 8, 1915 in Weber, Utah, and moved to a farm on Hawkins Road about 1922 or 1923. Ann Etta was born January 13, 1878, and she died June 4, 1956. Both William and Ann Etta were interred in Hillcrest Cemetery in La Grande.

During their marriage, they had two sons, William "Bill" Martin Hawkins and Sherman Elwood Hawkins.

"My folks moved out here and bought 40 acres, and we just picked up property along the road as the years went by," said son Sherman Hawkins, who still resides on Hawkins Road, about 1 mile north of his parents' homestead.

"On this road my folks had 200 acres, and my dad was a boiler maker with the railroad. He worked nights for the railroad and days on the farm," said Sherman.

With the exception of his military service years, Sherman lived most of his life on Hawkins Road. He graduated from La Grande High School in 1941, and after the war, he returned to the family farm.

He married Hazel March on October 22, 1946. They were married 71 years before she died on June 9, 2017. They had two sons, Fred and Carl. The latter passed away several years ago. *(Sherman Hawkins interview, March 14, 2019)* They have grandchildren from both Fred and Carl, and Sherman hopes that one of them will carry on the farm on Hawkins Road.

After William Hawkins died in 1951, his son Sherman bought out Bill's share of the farm and continued farming. This allowed Bill Hawkins and his wife, Camille, to buy a residence near Hawkins Road on Hwy 203 where they have lived together from 1960 to January 2019, farming parcels of land in that area.

During his century-long lifetime, Bill Hawkins brought some historical record to the Hawkins name. He may be the only resident of Union County who could say that he personally saw and heard German Chancellor Adolf Hitler give a speech in Austria in 1938.

The young Hawkins was touring through this country leisurely with a friend when he unwittingly encountered a public assembly of villagers in the city square intently listening to Adolf Hitler addressing the people from atop a building, holding a megaphone to his mouth. Incidentally, *Time Magazine* chose Adolf Hitler as 1938's "Man of the Year".

Upon returning to Oregon, Hawkins worked for the Union Pacific Railroad since 1941, and from 1952-1960, he took a leave from this railroad duties to serve as a labor adviser, fostering commerce and reconstruction overseas as part of the Marshall Plan through the Foreign Operations

Administration. In this role, he was able to take his wife and children with him.

By 1960, Hawkins elected to resign from his role as labor advisor and take his family back to La Grande, at which time he bought his home and farm between Hot Lake and Union. He retired as a locomotive engineer with the Union Pacific Railroad in 1986, but he and Camille continued to farm their 630 acres on Highway 203.

Camille was born September 2, 1920. In January 2019, Camille was relocated to the Grande Ronde Retirement Center in La Grande, where she died on August 29, 2020, a couple days shy of 100 years old. Bill was born January 21, 1918, and enjoys exceptional good health and mobility. *(Bill Hawkins interview, Jan. 2018; La Grande Observer, Jan. 22, 2018, pg. 2A)*

Hays Road - (Hayes Road) This road #26 is 2.52 miles in length and is located in Township 2S R39E Section 7, running diagonally across Highway 82 and the railroad tracks. It connects on the south end to Alicel Lane and on the north end to Woodell Lane.

The road sign at one time was spelled historically correct, but in 2017, when new signs were made, it was reprinted incorrectly. It should be correctly spelled Hayes after its namesake, Ray Homer Hayes (1895-1948), interred at the Summerville Cemetery. (The tax accessor's website records are likewise misspelled.)

Interestingly, in a *1903 blueprint map of Imbler and the post 1983 Metsker Map*, it shows Hayes Road extending north of Woodell Lane and ending at Hull Lane. But the *1947 N.E. Oregon Forestry Map* shows the stretch of Hayes Road from Woodell north to Hull is gone, replaced by a field, and that's the way it is today. Consequently, some time between 1935 and 1947, Hayes Road was shortened by terminating it at Woodell Lane on its north end.

Ray Homer Hayes was born July 17, 1895 in Putnam County, Missouri. He married Mary Opal Ruckman on December 20, 1918 at the home of Mrs. Ada C. Ruckman in Seattle, King County, Washington. Opal was born February 23, 1900 and died in 1998. Her parents were William E. and Elizabeth Ruckman, land owners in the south Imbler-Alicel area.

In the *1920 Federal Census*, Ray Hayes and his wife were living in Lincoln, Walla Walla County, Washington. The couple had a daughter named Elenor born in La Grande August 31, 1926.

In a *1930 Federal Census* it enumerates them as living in the Imbler area, but by 1935 they had relocated to Wolf Creek Market Road in the North Powder-Haines area, and they were noted there in the *1940 Federal Census*. On February 24, 1948, Ray died at the age of 53 years, and he was buried in Summerville Cemetery.

After Ray's death, Mary and their daughter Elenor moved into La Grande, and while living there, Elenor attended Eastern Oregon College of Education (later EOU), where she earned her teaching degree. She thereafter had a teaching career for over 30 years.

While Mary was living in La Grande, her father, William Ruckman of Imbler, purchased land for her directly west of his own farm on Woodell Lane. Mary lived in the second white house on Woodell Lane thereafter. *(Elwyn Bingaman memoirs letter, April 30, 2019)*

On June 24, 1954, Mary was remarried in Weiser, Washington County, Idaho, to Otto Theodore "Bob" Robinette (1884-1974). Bob had been married previously to Lola Hayes. When Bob and Mary died, they were interred at the Summerville Cemetery.

Mary's daughter Elenor Hayes married Dale W. Pierson on July 24, 1948, and she died on August 12, 2013 in Salem, Marion County, Oregon. (See Ruckman Road)

Hayes Road is known for one other significant reason. It is the "Alicel Plant" of Blue Mountain Seeds founded by long-time grass seed growers and partners, George Royes Sr. and Creston Jay Shaw.

As a private grass seed grower, Shaw established a contract with the Scotts Seed company, and he brought that contract with him into the partnership with Royes in 1968. This is a significant reason for the company's success today. Their company has grown into a large grass seed cleaning operation regionally, as well as a warehouse and distribution center. Their grass seed is blended with others, packaged under the Scotts Seed label and sold around the world.

This business address on Hayes Road was formerly the Barenbrug grass seed warehouse until it was purchased by Blue Mountain Seeds in September 2015, following a fire in Barenbrug's east end warehouse. Blue Mountain Seeds has their headquarters in the city of Imbler. In its busy season, Blue Mountain Seeds employs about 22 men at this grass seed cleaning plant.

Blue Mountain Seeds celebrated its 50th year in business at the Alicel Plant at a reception and open house May 3-4, 2018. Many of their growers attended the May 3 reception. *(La Grande Observer, May 9, 2018, pg. B1)*

In 2018, the children of both of these men are members of the company's board of directors, including Creston Shaw, 96, and his two daughters Cresta May de Lint and Janet Rudd; and George "G" Royes Jr. and his son, Sam Royes, who has been the president for many years. The late Rein de Lint was also on the board of directors and acted as president before his death in 2007. *(Creston Shaw, 96, April 27, 2018 interview)*

Bill Merrigan joined the business in 1999 as general manager. He has a degree in plant science from the University of Idaho and has spearheaded the development of new varieties of grass seed at their Summerville experimental farm. He's also helped expand the buying contracts that the company held.

The staff at Blue Mountain Seeds is a loyal group of workers, many of them having been employed there for over 20 years. Creston Shaw said he likes to make the rounds at the Alicel plant and commend the workers there. This kind of hands-on management has served the company well for over 50 years.

Heber Road - This county road #23F runs .87 miles and is located in Township 5S R39E Section 28 in the North Powder maintenance district.

It is named after a well-known cattleman named Heber Parker Glenn (1914-1990). He was named after his maternal grandfather, Heber Thomas Riley Parker (1849-1914), who died the same year baby Heber Parker Glenn was born. *(Ancestry.com)*

The Glenn family came from Scotland and the Parker family originated in Lancashire, England. Henry Miller Parker (1807-1887) was born in Brindle, Lancashire, England and came to America in 1841 through New Orleans, settling and marrying in Nauvoo, Illinois. He and his wife traveled westward, residing for a time in Iowa. He then left Kanesville, Iowa with the Edward Hunter Company and arrived in Salt Lake City, Utah territory in 1850, where they farmed.

According to Parker family history, immigrant ancestor Henry Parker needed horses on his Utah farm, so he returned to his native England to acquire them. On his return voyage with a load of horses, the ship encountered a great storm, and in order to avoid sinking, they had to lighten the ship's load, so they put the horses over board. "Those horses swam behind that ship for two days," said Carol Glenn Pratt, great-great-granddaughter of Henry Parker.

This road's namesake, Heber Parker Glenn, was born in Wellsville, Utah on December 30, 1914, the son of Walter Lund Glenn and Christina Cooper Parker (1877-1955).

Heber is an unusual name and is of Biblical origin, being first mentioned at Genesis 46:17 as the name of Asher's grandson Heber, the ancestral head of the Heberites.

Heber Glenn worked his way into the cattle business while he was in high school in Hiram, Utah. At that time, he was renting land, milking cows on his own and growing diversified crops. His goal was to have a cattle ranch of his own after graduation.

That dream came true for him after he married Edythe Lakey on September 12, 1938 in Preston, Idaho. They settled on an unimproved farm in Caldwell Canyon, Idaho, where the Glenns raised row crops and milked dairy cows by hand. Edythe milked cows by hand twice a day and then helped Heber in the fields in between. He had to borrow money to prove it up and make it prosper, and Edythe worked hard alongside him.

In 1947, after a lot of hard work and some good yields on their row crops and cows milked by hand, the young couple were able to pay off their loan and sell their farm. They bought a 5,200-acre cattle ranch in the North Powder, Oregon area. It needed a lot of work, but the young Glenns were ambitious, and in time, they had it repaired and repainted so that it was a real eye-catcher of a ranch. *(La Grande Observer, Nov. 2, 1955, pg 4)*

Heber was frugal and was an early believer in reusing and recycling materials on the farm. He hardly ever bought anything new unless he didn't have any way to figure out how to use what he had on hand.

In 1948, Heber and Edythe welcomed their one and only child into the family, Carol. She was born in La Grande, but raised on the ranch and participated in 4-H club activities and contests. Carol's photo was included in the aforementioned La Grande Observer article, noting that she was a first grade student that year and assisted on the ranch with her mother.

At that tender age of 7 years, she was already riding a Shetland pony on the ranch. Over the years, Carol remembered having about 19 horses on the ranch. Heber had a mean stud, she said, that produced their ranch herd.

With just the three Glenns to operate the ranch, the family didn't have time to join organizations like the local grange. However, Heber was a member of the Elks Club and Cattlemen's Association, and Carol competed in some equine events at local rodeos. She was the first Queen at the Haines Stampede, and a Queen at Hell's Canyon Junior Rodeo at Halfway one year. "I spent a lot of time barrel racing at small rodeos around. I usually came home with money, usually finished first, second or third." She also rode in a lot of parades.

During Heber's ranching career, he made a name for himself as a progressive cattleman and rancher, being honored as Union County Cattleman of the Year in 1955. Carol remembered him as a man of integrity and honesty. "My folks worked hard and played hard," she said. "His word was what he lived by. He did not back out."

As Carol grew up on the ranch, she learned every facet of its operation and maintenance, including mechanical repairs. "My dad and I were really close. I was the son my father never had," she said. "I didn't spend a lot of time in the house. Those were the best years of my life." Edythe raised and butchered chickens, cooked and cleaned the home. She was active in calving, feeding them bottles and anything that was needed.

During 1962 through part of 1967, Heber, Edythe and Carol engaged in a new kind of farming, beaver breeding. An article printed on *page 10 of the Wed., Feb. 27, 1963 issue of the La Grande Observer* announced the Glenns new venture.

It was titled, "North Powder Cattleman Also Goes in for Domestic Beaver Farming." It read in part as follows:

"A new industry has caught on in Eastern Oregon, the raising of domestic beaver. Heber Glenn, North Powder cattleman, also raises beaver. Glenn is a member of the Weaver's Beavers, an association started by Mark Weaver of Salt Lake City in 1957 for the purpose of selling live beavers to different concerns for breeding. Weaver said the beaver today are sold as breeding stock and not for the pelts.

Six Ranches. Glenn's ranch is one of six located in the state of Washington and Oregon. Besides Glenn's, three are located on Whidbey Island in Washington and the other two in Salem." (End of excerpt)

Carol recalled those years of beaver farming. "I think we had 75 to 100 pairs of beaver, and we raised them as breeding stock," Carol said.

The domestic beaver industry came to a halt with the introduction of a tax law that prohibited people from investing in this kind of farming. "They were sold investors, and we got paid to feed and care for them," she said.

They required a lot of care. The Glenns made concrete dens located above the Heber home, and the beavers had their nest, where they kept their little ones. They also had a feeding platform and a swimming trench, about 2 feet wide by six feet long and water ran through it.

"To clean it, we had to go in it everyday and throw water up on the feeding platform because that's where they all pooped and then rinse that off down to the trench," Carol said.

When the platforms were rinsed off into the water trench, then she had to keep that water stirred up constantly so all the organic contaminants would flush through the drain hole when the plug was removed. "I hated cleaning those things," Carol recalled.

The beaver loved to eat quaking aspen, so Carol's job was to drive the truck up into the hills where they had aspen groves, and with her chain saw, she cut aspen trees into chunks about 14-16 inches in length, leaving the bark on them and brought them back to the farm. There she threw the logs into their pens along with young branches with leaves on them.

"They loved the limbs with the leaves on them," she said. "That was their candy."

The beaver typically ate all the young branches and all the bark, but anything left in the pens, Carol had to clean out with a pitchfork before she starting rinsing out everything each day.

"I love the animals. The baby beavers were so cute and they had a tail the size of a teaspoon, but you can't handle them. The females were mean, strong, wild animals, and they would bite the heck out of you," Carol said.

When beaver are raised domestically, their teeth grow long, and the Glenns used a hack saw to trim them down or they would get too long and bite into their lower jaw, preventing them from eating. Carol thought the beavers' teeth grew too long because they weren't cutting down their own trees, which kept their teeth at a certain length. Carol was doing that work for them.

Occasionally, Carol thought the beavers got beaver fever and diarrhea, so they had to treat them for that. She likened beaver farming to a dairy farm where the animals needed constant attention and their living area had to be cleaned daily. It was a high maintenance business.

Carol recounted how they had to build the concrete pens with cement block and install plumbing, and they required a lot of water, which was supplied by a spring up above. "They had good water and were as healthy as could be," she said. *(Carol Pratt interview, December 30, 2021)*

In the 1980's, however, ranches everywhere fell onto hard times, and so did Heber's ranch. "We had some crop failures due to frost and freezing, and the bank wanted their money. The interest rate then was between 18-20% and the bank wanted their money, so we went into bankruptcy," Carol said. "It was one of those times—the purging of family farms—another way to get farms into corporations."

Heber was wise, Carol said, and he saw this coming about five years beforehand, but there wasn't much to be done about it. They lost the ranch in 1989. At the same time, he was seriously declining in health, struggling with lung cancer until he succumbed to death on July 17, 1990 at the age of 75 ½ years. His burial took place at North Powder cemetery, the only Glenn belonging to her family to be buried in Union County, Carol said. (This Glenn family is not related to others in the county.)

After Heber's death in July 1990, Edythe was allowed to stay on the ranch for a short time. She rented the house she had called home for 40 years, and when it came time to move out, she relocated to her childhood home of Soda Springs, Idaho, where she lived in 2020 at the age of 100 years.

Today the former Heber ranch is part of Seven Diamond Ranches of North Powder. It is one more example, Carol said, of the small rancher being swallowed up by large farming corporations.

Carol married a local farmer named Ron Pratt in December 1966. His folks bought the neighboring McCanse ranch about 1963. (See McCanse Lane entry) Ron and his father grew cotton, but when the price of cotton dropped, it led to their losing the farm to the bank. The Pratts left their farm in the spring of 1990 and went into other occupations after that happened.

The Pratts had three children on the McCanse and Shaw farms, which they had purchased. Years later, they became proud grandparents to four grandchildren, none of whom currently live or farm in Union County.

However, there is one grandson, Jordan Pratt, who successfully farms in Hawaii, growing ginger and turmeric. "He has had farming in his blood every since he was little," Carol said. "He is a lot like his grandpa. He has a lot of the same characteristics as my dad."

Henderson Road - Formerly Henderson-Brugger Road #57 as noted on the *1935 Metsker Map*. It runs north-south off of Highway 82 on Cricket Flat, intersects with Witherspoon Lane and connects with Clark Creek Road. This road travels through Township 1N R40E Section 30 and is 3.78 miles in length.

It is named after the family of Joseph Franklin Henderson (1859-1939) and his wife Aletha E. (Barnes) Henderson (1869-1937) of Elgin. Joseph Henderson is shown as a land owner on the *1935 Metsker Map*. He retired from farming in Elgin and relocated to Caldwell, Idaho in 1929.

Joseph F. and Aletha had the following children: Lucinda Mae Windham (1884-1975), John Wesley (1886-1967), Charles William (1888-1906), Joseph Edward "Joe" (1890-1983), Andrew J. (1897-1917) and Leon Herbert (1905-1980).

Joseph's obituary reads in part: "Joseph F. Henderson, Caldwell—Joseph Henderson, 80, a resident of Caldwell for the past 10 years, died Tuesday morning at his home on College avenue. He was a retired farmer. Mr. Henderson was born in Springfield, Ill., November 17, 1859.

Surviving are three sons, John W. Henderson and Joe Henderson of Elgin, Ore., and Leon Henderson of Caldwell, and a daughter Mrs. May H. Hartley of Elgin, Ore.

The body is at the Peckham funeral chapel, but will be sent to Elgin, Ore., where funeral services will be held, burial will be in Elgin cemetery. Before coming to Caldwell, Mr. Henderson had lived 40 years in Elgin." *(End of obit, published in Idaho Daily Statesman in Boise, Idaho, Wed. Nov. 29, 1939, pg. 5)*

His wife Aletha's obituary states in part: "Aletha Henderson Buried on Monday—Mrs. Henderson died at her home in Elgin, Saturday, December 11, at the age of 69 years, 6 months and 19 days. She was born at Shaw, Kansas, May 20, 1868. With her parents, she came to Oregon at the age of five. Her parents, John P. and Mary Barnes, homesteaded on Cricket Flat near Elgin, and here Aletha with her brothers and sisters attended the district school. After her marriage, May 20, 1883 to Joseph F. Henderson, she moved with him to his homestead in Wallowa County near Joseph. Here the family lived about eight years and then moved to Elgin. The deceased had lived in this community for 45 years, during which time she made a large circle of acquaintances and a host of true and loyal friends. Interment followed at the Elgin Cemetery." *(End of Obit, Elgin Recorder, Dec. 16, 1937)*

Son Joseph Edward Henderson grew up on the family farm on what became Henderson Road. He was born October 8, 1890 in Alicel. In the *1900 Federal Census,* it records that his father, Joseph Franklin Henderson, was employed as a teamster for the lumber industry.

Following in his father's footsteps, Joseph E. Henderson was also employed in log hauling from 1910 to 1940, according to the federal censuses. In the *1930 Federal Census*, his farming occupation was also mentioned, all the while living on Henderson Road in the Elgin precinct #4.

Joseph E. Henderson was married twice, first to Clara Johnson (1895-1927) and after her death, to Nellie Coats (1903-1983). This concludes the history of the Henderson part of this road.

The second part of the road name, Brugger, originates with farmers John Jasper Brugger (1874-1939) and his second wife Mary Eliza (Wheeler) Brugger (1885-1947). They are shown as owning two adjoining parcels of land on the *1935 Metsker Map.* The land seen on that map, however, was first purchased by immigrant ancestor Peter Brugger, John's father, in 1878, according to official land records.

John Jasper Brugger was born December 12, 1874 in Elgin, Oregon. His parents, Peter (1833-1886) and Mary (Fanzey, Fahrni) Brugger (1847-1934) were both born in Switzerland and immigrated to America on July 16, 1853 from Tun, Switzerland, according to the *Early Oregonian registry in the Oregon State Archives*. Some census records state other years, but this registry had an exact date and activity by Peter in 1860 in Washington County, Oregon, so the authors feel the state archives have the true immigration date—July 16, 1853.

Peter settled first in the Willamette Valley and later came to the Elgin area. Peter was an interesting fellow, having sailed several times around the Horn before finally settling in Oregon. *(Brugger Part of Elgin History, October 2021 Newsletter, pg. 2 Elgin Museum and Historical Society)*

During the *1870 Federal Census*, the father Peter, 37, still lived in Forest Grove with his brother John Brugger's household. John was a miller and Peter was a sawyer, the census noted. Both equally possessed $5,000 value in real estate and $1,000 in personal estate value. Peter was issued his patent on what appears to be his last land acquisition in Washington County on June 1873.

His wife's obituary stated that she had lived in Elgin for 64 years [since 1870] and in 1873, their son Charley Brugger was born in rural Elgin. *(La Grande Observer, Monday, November 19, 1934, pg. 2, Mary Brugger's obit)*

In 1878, Peter was issued ownership of land on Cricket Flat of rural Elgin. He later acquired other parcels of land.

The *1880 Federal Census* showed their growing family residing on their farm on Cricket Flat, (territory northeast of the city of Elgin), including the parents Peter and Mary, and three children: Charley Brugger (1873-), John Jasper (1874-1939), and Benjamin Franklin (1879-1942). William T. (1883-1915), and Edward (1884-1976) came along over the next four years, but in 1880, the census stated that Peter was disabled and his brother Jacob Brugger, 20, lived with them and helped on the farm.

In the *1900 Federal Census,* Mary Brugger stated that she was mother to seven children and only four were living then. The authors could only identify the five aforementioned children, but could not identify the oldest two children, who were deceased. The five that are known and listed herein all appear to have been born on their homestead in Elgin, and they stayed in the Cricket Flat section of Elgin for their adult lives.

Interestingly, in that *1900 Federal Census*, the Brugger's neighbors on Cricket Flat were the Henry Hug family, also immigrants from Switzerland. Sometimes immigrants settled together where they felt comfortable with at least one other family that spoke their mother tongue, in this case German.

John Jasper Brugger spent his entire life in the Cricket Flat section of Elgin as a farmer and cattleman. He participated in the building of the first stockman cabin in 1906 on the east bank of the Minam.

"It was a log and shake building about 16 by 30 feet, dirt floor, no windows, door in the east, roof extended some ten feet past the door to make a shelter for wood and saddles, fireplace in the southeast corner, commissary in northeast corner, and two-story bunks across the west end. It was built by donated labor by the following cattlemen: Al Long, Harlan Long, William Roulet, Harry Hug, Arthur, Henry and Leonard Parsons, Bert Maxwell, and John, Ben and Ed Brugger." *(Bernal Hug's Supplement 1962 Annual to History of Union County, pg. 7)* The cabin burned down in 1920.

One interesting piece of trivia about Brugger's early childhood was mentioned in the *La Grande Observer Wednesday, July 5, 1939, pg. 1*. This account describes a fourth of July festival at which people gathered, who shared the experience of having been quartered in the old Indian fort in 1877. Those present at the gathering were introduced, and they included 64-year-old John Brugger. The 1877 Nez Perce uprising, as history calls it, frightened settlers, and they hid themselves inside the fort until it was safe to come outside again.

John's father Peter Brugger signed up for the draft in July 1878 for what the government called the 1878 Indian Wars, namely the uprising of the Bannocks, Snakes, Umatillas and Warm Spring Indians. Peter was enlisted with the Union County Oregon Volunteers with the Captain James K. P. Harris company. It was actually Peter's war pension document that provided his death date of December 12, 1886. His widow, Mary, applied for his pension on January 19, 1931. *(Application No. 1684955)*

After Peter's death, Mary lived on the homestead with son William T. until 1915 when he died suddenly of heart valve disease. In the *1920 Federal Census*, Mary Brugger let a 24-year-old Raymond Waelty board at her home, and he worked as a farm laborer for her. In the *1930 Federal Census*, Waelty was gone but Mary, 82, was sharing her home with her son Benjamin Brugger, 50. At that time, he was noted on the census as having worked as a trail builder for the U.S. National Forestry Service.

When Mary died on November 18, 1934 at her home, then her son John Jasper Brugger acquired the Brugger farm on the Hendersen-Brugger Road.

John Brugger was married twice in his lifetime. His first wife was Lucy Ellen Knight (1876-1963) on March 1, 1897. (See Knight Lane entry) *(La Grande Observer, Thursday, July 25, 1963, pg. 2)*

John Brugger's second wife, Mrs. Mary Eliza (Wheeler) Young, was previously married to Otto Young on October 28, 1903 in Union County. They had a daughter Neva L. Young, born about 1908, and she married Reid Hibberd of Imbler on January 31, 1926.

Mrs. Mary Eliza Young married John Jasper Brugger, 43, on August 28, 1918, when she was 32 years old. They apparently didn't have any children of their own, but Mary's daughter Neva Young became a member of their household as noted on the *1920 Federal Census*.

John Brugger's obituary relates this about his life: "J. J. Brugger, 64, Dies Near Elgin" — John Jasper Brugger, lifelong resident of the Elgin vicinity, died yesterday after a short illness, at his farm home nine miles east of Elgin. He was 64 years old and was an Elgin native.

Surviving him are his widow, Mary; a [step] daughter, Mrs. Reid Hibberd, Imbler; two brothers, Ben and Ed of Elgin, and a granddaughter. Interment will take place at the Elgin Cemetery. *(End of obit, La Grande Observer, Tues. Aug. 22, 1939, pg. 1)*

Mary Brugger's obituary states in part: "County Pioneer Dies Unexpectedly — Union county pioneers were saddened today by the death of Mary Eliza Brugger of Elgin, who died unexpectedly in a La Grande hospital Wednesday. She was 61.

Mrs. Brugger, who was born in Greenville, Texas, in 1885, moved to Union with her family when she was one year old and was a resident of the area for 60 years.

She is survived by her brother, Joe Wheeler of Elgin; daughter, Mrs. Reid [Neva] Hibberd of Summerville and a granddaughter, Shirley Hibberd, also of Summerville.

Mrs. Brugger will be interred at Elgin cemetery." *(End of obit, La Grande Observer, Friday, October 10, 1947, pg. 1)*

In summary, Peter and Mary Brugger of Switzerland came to Oregon in 1853, lived in Forest Grove until 1870, when they moved to Elgin to farm. Peter and Mary died at their Elgin home, and their son, John Jasper and his wife Mary (Wheeler) Brugger, farmed it until their own deaths. They had no son to leave the farm to, and the Brugger name was eventually dropped from the road sign, leaving the Henderson name alone to identify this 3.78 mile long gravel road.

Heritage Lane - This is a private lane in Township 1S R40E Section 16 in the Union maintenance district.

Hibberd Road - This is a gravel road about .34 miles in length. It is designated as road #151 and located in Township 1S R39E Section 21 in the Imbler maintenance district.

This road was named after the Charles and Carrie Louise (Wade) Hibberd family and their descendants. The road borders 175 acres of prime farm land north of Imbler, which Carrie Wade Hibberd inherited from her father Phares Wade.

Charles and Carrie left this land to their son, Dick Hibberd, who at the pinnacle of his ranching career raised upward of 200 registered Polled Herefords. Dick Hibberd established himself as the longest, continual Polled Hereford breeder in the Northwest and earned a place in the National Polled Herefords Hall of Fame.

Dick Hibberd was one of the charter members of the Elgin Stampeders organization, and won the wild and crazy suicide race a couple of times. "He was rough on horses. I mean he rode them for all they were worth. He loved to ride," said Bill Howell, an Imbler farmer who remembered Hibberd.

On one occasion at the Elgin Stampede suicide race, Hibberd came down over the hill and across the river on a hard gallop onto the race track. The track is sloped and he came up over the top of the slope and pulled his horse over hard coming around the race track. The horse lost its footing, and they went down. The horse got up and kept running. Hibberd also got up unharmed and got his horse and finished the race. *(Eye witness Bill Howell, 90, of Imbler, interview May 20, 2018)*

The Hibberd ranch was designated the Wade Century Farm in 1984. Today, Dick's children and grandchildren continue to operate the farm and ranch. His daughter, Mary West, lives on Hibberd Lane with her husband, retired Circuit Court Judge Russ West. They raised three children on Hibberd Lane and one of them, J.D. Cant and family, established his own home there and helps on the family ranch.

J.D. Cant, an FFA and agriculture teacher at Imbler High School routinely brings his Agriculture students to the Hibberd Road ranch for lessons on cattle raising.

Hidden Valley Lane - This road #156 is located in Township 3S R40E Section 22 and runs about one half mile in length, being located in the Union road maintenance district. It is home to 15 properties.

It is a gravel lane found southeast of Cove, departing from Mill Creek Road. Turning onto the lane, it immediately climbs sharply up a hill and at this elevation, the traveler is greeted by the sight of beautiful orchards.

There is a geographic ridge nearing the end of the lane, and behind this ridge is a hidden valley and home to Cove Cherries LLC. Also located on Hidden Valley Lane is cherry producer, Jubilee Farms LLC.

High Valley Road - This road is one of the longer county roads, being 12.53 miles in length. Designated as county road #66 it travels through the Union maintenance district, specifically located in Township 4S R40E Section 18.

This travels between Cove and Union, and it roughly follows Little Creek about 4 miles east of Union, then turns north toward Cove. The elevation of the valley, which is 2 miles in length, is roughly 700 feet higher than Cove or Union and thus the name "high valley" road.

High Valley Road is also known for the High Valley School about which the *Oregon Scout, July 11, 1885, page 5* had this to say: "Miss Himenia Sanborn, of the Cove, closed on July 2, a very successful term of three months school, having a picnic and exhibition on the last day. There was quite a turn out. The school house not being sufficient to accommodate the crowd, the exercises were held under the awning on the outside. The total number of scholars enrolled in the school was 34; average daily attendance was 16; number on the roll of honor, 7, as follows: Jessie Minnick, Josiah Davis, Charles Logsdon, Charles Baugher, Albert Wilkison, Thomas Wilkison, Mary Minnick. Our school has doubled in the last five years. The district is sadly in need of a new school house, as the one we have at present has served its time."

Also in that article, there is mention of the dairy industry in the High Valley. It reads: "The dairy business in this valley is at a stand still, owing to the low price paid for butter. This valley usually turns out about 6,000 pounds but this year it will not be much more than one-half that amount."

According to the *Oregon Scout of August 1, 1885, page 5,* "High Valley has a population of 158."

In the *Oregon Scout of April 24, 1886, page 5,* under the column, *"High Valley Hash"* it read: "High Valley is in need of a saw mill and a new school house. The school commenced a few days ago with 25 children in attendance the first day.

Perfect independence is the surest road to success in this world. Those who rely on others to give them a start, generally have to wait a long time.

We understand there will be a petition gotten up and presented to the people of the Cove and High Valley, for their signatures, to get a county road opened from Cove, to intersect the Pine Creek Road, at or near Rinehart's shingle mill. This is a good move and it will certainly meet with the approval and support of every well-disposed person living near the route. A public highway open for through travel is an absolute necessity. The road that is used now, was surveyed and laid out some years ago, but owing to mistakes made, it was not established and ordered opened, and the most of it is now fenced up with gates across the road." (End of article)

According to the *La Grande Observer of August 19, 1916, page 9*, a large part of the area in and around High Valley was originally populated by a colony of Canadian-French people. There were between 50 and 75 families of these people about 1880, and now there are about four families left.

Good roads and easy transportation was often on the minds of people around the county and High Valley as shown in a *La Grande Observer article of April 13, 1920, page 1.* It noted several roads in the area that were to be upgraded and made into market roads, including the one from Union to High Valley.

Another road close by that was getting upgraded was up Catherine Creek on the Union-Medical Springs Road. The county engineer was also surveying a portion of the Ladd Canyon Road and especially the Bees-Wax Hill with a view to upgrading under the Market Road Act.

In 1923, a delegation of High Valley residents were asking the Commercial Club for help in securing funds from the county to help with the upkeep of the road in High Valley to keep it in passable condition. The petitioners said that there were 1,600 acres of grain in High Valley and about 2,500 cords of wood were hauled from there into other parts of the Grande Ronde Valley each year. They stated that they used to have $1,000 a year to help with these roads, but now they get about $300, which is insufficient. A committee was appointed to investigate. *(La Grande Observer, April 28, 1923, pg. 5)*

Highway 30 - This road got its start in 1925 when the American Association of State Highway Officials started planning a federal highway system. The result was an organized, unified road system as compared to the previous era of named highways. These had often been identified by painted colored bands on telephone poles.

Once the secretary of agriculture approved the plan in November 1925, the names of all the roads were changed to a numbered system with major east-west routes numbered in multiples of ten, such as 30. Major north-south routes would end in either one or five, such as U.S. 1 between Maine and Florida or U.S. 101 between Washington and California.

U.S. Highway 30 was originally known as the Lincoln Highway, starting on the East Coast and going west to San Francisco. After several revisions, Highway 30 now starts in Atlantic City, New Jersey and heads east for 3,078.5 miles to Astoria, Oregon.

The Oregon part of Highway 30 is 477 miles long, making it the longest road in the state. Only a small portion of the road can be driven on, most of it currently being part of Interstate 84. *(Wikipedia; History of the Lincoln Highway: The End of Named Highways)*

Highway 82 - Originally the La Grande-Enterprise Highway No. 10, a primary state highway. The planning for the Wallowa Lake Highway 82 started in 1917, according to *History of State Highways in Oregon, Oregon Department of Transportation, March 2020, pg. 10-1.*

It travels roughly 70 miles starting from La Grande, and ending at beautiful Wallowa Lake in Wallowa County. The highway is part of the Hell's Canyon Scenic Byway. It will take you over and through the "Little Alps" of Northeast Oregon and the Wallowa Mountains. It's worth the afternoon traveling it.

Highway 82 travels right through the center of Imbler, and this section of the highway is called Ruckman Avenue. At the corner of Ruckman and Main Street is the Imbler Market grocery store situated on lot 1 and 2 of block 5 on the city plat map.

It was purchased by W. E. Anderson, who came to Union County from Utah in August 1902. Anderson was an ambitious developer, and in the spring of 1903, the Anderson Brothers built the red brick building that became Imbler Market. He leased the store to a Walter Stringham Jr., who turned it into a general mercantile, hardware and grocery store called Stringham's Store. By November 1904, it also housed the Imbler post office, and Mr. Stringham was appointed the eighth postmaster of Imbler.

On January 20, 1909, W. E. Anderson sold the store to Mrs. Walter Stringham, and it continued in their control until 1920. During the years 1903-2023, the store has been owned by 16 different people, and it was called by various business names, including Stringham's Store, Tucker's Grocery Store, Imbler Cash Store, Imbler Country Market and finally Imbler Market.

On December 20, 2022, it sold to Malinda and Johnny Gunnels of Imbler, just in time to ring in the 120th year as a grocery store. It is one of very few buildings of that era still in public use in Imbler, and that makes it a business icon worthy of mention. *(Imbler Market Has Long History, online story*

La Grande Observer, January 26, 2023 by Trish Yerges)

As you leave Imbler, heading toward Elgin, there is a section of the highway that was vacated and rebuilt up higher on the hillside. As you're climbing the grade of Hamburger Hill, as locals call it, look east and down at the remnant of the "old Highway 82" which follows the Grande Ronde River and railroad tracks through a short canyon.

According to road petition #50 dated about April 1, 1873, this canyon was described as the "Misener Gap" and one of the signatures on this petition was J. H. Misener, who would have had a direct interest in the construction of the road. His name was Joseph Hannah Misener (1833-1908), who married Carrie R. Holmes in Union County on April 21, 1872. He was a bookkeeper by trade, and he died on October 2, 1908 at 75 years, 8 months and 9 days.

The road petition described the original road now known as Highway 82 from the Grande Ronde Valley to Elgin. It read in full as follows:

"To the Honorable the County Court of Union County—We the undersigned citizens and householders living in Union County, State of Oregon and residing in the immediate vicinity of and along the line of the hereinafter described road respectfully petition your honorable body to lay out, locate and establish a county road as follows: to wit—Beginning at or near the George Allen house on the road leading from the Cove to Summerville via the pine tree—thence in a northerly direction on the east side of the Grande Ronde River passing through the Comduff Gap, thence a long the east side of the Messrs. Harris and Knight's enclosures and through the Misener Gap—thence over the best route to Indian Creek and crossing it at or near Joe Weaver's—thence over the most feasible route and terminating on the east side of said river at or near the Fish Trap—which road and all of which places are in Union County and State of Oregon." (End of petition, 26 signatures followed)

Dorothy Fleshman, 95 years old in 2021, stated that she remembered traveling that old section of Highway 82 when she was between 8 and 10 years of age, so about 1934-36.

"I do remember riding (northbound) in the car down that slope to reach the highway to Elgin with the river running along the left side of the road and the high rocky side on the right side that made it darker down in there," Fleshman said.

The old Highway 82 appears to have descended into the canyon starting about an eighth of a mile north of Rinehart Lane.

The county built a new section of Highway 82 up higher on the side of the hill above that canyon, and that's where it is today. This new section of highway is chronically threatened by water coming off the hillside causing drainage problems. Every ten years or so, the road has to be reinforced or repaved due to water erosion issues and shifting soil.

Along the old section of Highway 82, there was a stone fountain. Ed Botz, 87, of Elgin recalls that fountain and how he helped to relocate it to the Clarence Witty Park in downtown Elgin. *(Ed Botz interview, November 9, 2021 at his home)*

The wayside stone fountain, which was called "Hill Spring Fountain" by local residents, was fed by a spring on the hillside belonging to farmers Lynn and Etha (Huffman) Hill. They were the parents of Frederick "Fred" Huffman Hill (1920-2016), a well-known Elgin-La Grande photographer and historian, who lies in rest at the Summerville Cemetery.

This fountain and 29 others like it were funded by the Oregon State Highway Department and placed at 30 different sites along state highways. Two were placed on Wallowa Lake Highway 82, one near Minam and another south of Elgin on the old section of Highway 82.

In an article titled, "30 Fountains on State Highway" in the *La Grande Observer, Aug. 30, 1930, pg. 8* it read in part:

"Salem, Ore.,—While the maintenance division of the state highway department takes a lot of pride in the upkeep of the state highways in Oregon, it takes no less pride in a system of drinking fountains erected at roadsides in various parts of the state, particularly on the long stretches where habitation is scant. Oregon is credited with leading all other states in this accommodation for travelers.

The fountains are all of artistic design and add to rather than detract from roadside appearances. All of the cut stone work has been done by Italian workmen who are said to be skilled in this class of work.

In all there are about 30 fountains. Two are located on the Wallowa lake highway... The fountains cost from $200 to $300 each." (End of article excerpt)

In Irene Locke Barklow's book, *Gateway to the Wallowas on page 155*, under the subheading Wallowa Fountain, it read: "When the highway was surfaced and widened through the canyon, Oscar Victor, who worked all through it about 1922 or 1923 said, "The Engineers graft was ridiculous" and "the Engineers graft was predacious." He said, "The fountain in the canyon cost about $300.00 and they charged $2,000."

It's a reasonable assumption that the two fountains on Highway 82 were built about the same year, so the authors searched for any fountain news and found a news clipping from the *La Grande Observer, Oct., 13, 1922, pg. 4,* which read that "the Crow and Olsen families picnicked one afternoon at the Stone Fountain in the Wallowa Canyon (Minam) and enjoyed their camp-cooked dinner very much." Consequently, this shows that the stone fountain at Minam was built at least before October 1922.

Wallowa County Commissioner Susan Roberts stated in a phone interview on December 10, 2021 that Italian stone workers also worked on the Wallowa County Courthouse, when it was built in 1909. The stone was quarried out northeast of town and brought to the courthouse property to be cut. "The gentleman who designed this building was a Scotchman named Thorton, and he did some of the buildings in Union County too," Roberts said. "But some of the work crew were Italian stone workers, and on some concrete in the Wallowa County Courthouse basement, they all put their names on it. One of the first names was Geovanni."

Italian workmen on state highways were not uncommon, come to find out. The *La Grande Observer, May 13, 1921, pg. 3* explained.

"Two new road camps have been set up near Hilgard during the past week: one on the E. C. Gilbert ranch a mile out of town and another near the Hawes Bridge. This makes the third located near the Bridge. One (county road work camp) is filled with white laborers and two (state highway camps) are foreigner-filled—largely Italians... Three state camps in and near Casey are all foreign-filled."

One can understand now how it came to be that stone work was performed by Italians, who by the way, are world renown for their architecture. Oregon state highways are filled with their artistic stone work. It's a real privilege to have two fountains on Highway 82 made by these Italian craftsmen, and Elgin holds claim to one of them.

On the Hill Spring Fountain that was relocated to Elgin's downtown park, a plaque was mounted inside in 2014 by a committee of Elgin residents who participated in the Ford Family Foundation Leadership Development Institute training. The plaque stated that the fountain was made sometime circa 1920s. It also read that the fountain was relocated to the park from old Highway 82 in 1992/1994.

People driving along the old Highway 82 could stop and get a drink of the fresh spring waters. Fleshman said that when she was between the age of 8 and 10, she stopped to get a drink from that fountain and its water tasted very good.

Botz said that some Elginites wanted to rescue that fountain after the new Highway 82 was constructed and set it up in Elgin's downtown pocket park. City recorder/administrator Joe Garlitz said about this event, "After the city received ownership of the downtown park property from the county, city members were eager to adorn it with a water fountain. We took the 1920s-30s vintage water fountain from its former location on old Highway 82 and moved it to the park." *(La Grande Observer, Jan. 1, 2009)*

So with the city's approval, two fork lifts and a truck pulling a flatbed trailer were enlisted to go to the location and transport it back to town. Botz was one of the men helping that day as well as Ray McVey. He said that when they got the fountain where it could be lifted up, it had a bulky cement rock mass on its underbelly, which made it unlevel for setting on a trailer.

Their first attempt to place it on the trailer didn't work as it was positioned too far to the rear of the trailer bed, and that resulted in severe tipping of the trailer's rear end and lifting up of the trailer's tongue. This, in turn, lifted the rear end of the truck so it's hood was tipped to the ground.

Botz explained that they tried again to reposition the fountain on the trailer and this second time it worked. When they were ready to unload it at the pocket park in downtown Elgin, they had to dig a hole in the ground to accommodate the connected cement and rocks at its base. With some work, they were able to set it properly.

It was positioned over a city water pipe that was once used for service to a hardware store that was razed in a fire on January 27, 1986. That fire started when Odies Payne's former restaurant, under new ownership, was set on fire by that new owner. The fire spread to the hardware store, which had an upstairs apartment rented out. The tenant, Clarence Witty, died in the fire, and the city subsequently named the park after him. It seems almost ironic that a water fountain would be placed on the same city lot where a terrible blaze took a man's life.

Over time, Botz said that there were complaints that the kids were playing with the fountain water too much and making the grass too wet and muddy at the park. Although there was divided opinion on the topic of disconnecting the water to the fountain, that's what happened. Today, it's non-functioning, much to the disappointment of some who wanted this historic fountain to be a fully functional. Still, it is there, and it adorns the park---truly a piece of historic Italian architecture from the 1920s.

Highway 203 - This highway begins at an intersection with I-84 and U.S. Route 30 near La Grande, and goes southeast through Hot Lake to Union. The highway then continues southeast to Medical Springs, Pondosa and intersects with I-84 north of Baker City. *(Wikipedia)*

Highway 204 - On the *1935 Metsker Map* it was the Weston to Elgin Highway, also called Tollgate Road. The lower end of this highway follows Phillips Creek, which is named after Dan Phillips.

Highway 237 - This is the La Grande to Cove highway. Historically, it has frequently been snowbound in the winters.

Highway 244 - This is the La Grande to Starkey highway.

Hilgard Lane - This lane is designated as county road #3 and runs .90 miles in length in the La Grande maintenance district located in Township 2S R37E Section 31. Hilgard Lane leads to a rural community of about seven residences.

It is named after the community of Hilgard, and according to the *Oregon Geographic Names book, 7th Edition, page 467,* "Hilgard was apparently named for Eugene W. Hilgard, dean of the college of agriculture at the University of California. He was a cousin of Henry Villard, who built the railroad over the Blue Mountains, and was engaged by Villard in the early 1880s to make an agricultural survey of the area. While the above is probable, Villard was born Ferdinand Heinrich Hilgard and changed his name after coming to America. The cousins probably should share the distinction."

Hill Lay Road - This road #107 runs .91 miles and is located in Township 5S R40E Section 28 of the Union maintenance district. Interestingly, this road name retains its historical two-family name, whereas most road names were reduced to just one family name.

It is named after Charles "Charlie" Alfred Hill (1870-1961), the uncle of the well-known Union County photographer Fred Hill. Charles was born February 14, 1870 in Carson City, Nevada and died January 23, 1961 in Union, Oregon. He rests in peace at the Summerville Cemetery in Summerville, Oregon.

He married Nellie Ellen Hug on December 6, 1898 in La Grande. She was born September 5, 1874 in Utah and died January 1, 1944 in La Grande. They had six children together: Willard (1899), George (1901), Glen (1903), Juanita (1907), Mabel (1908) and Fern (1914).

They originally settled in Elgin, according to the *1900 Federal Census,* but by 1910 they were living in Antelope, Union County. Charles homesteaded and proved up his land in 1919 and some in 1923. The *1935 Metsker Map* showed some descendants still living on the Hill-Lay Road.

The Lay part of the road name originates with Joseph Colman Lay, born November 12, 1881 in Santa Clara, Utah. He was in Utah for the 1900 Federal Census, and that's where he met and married Katie Rosella Deuel on May 11, 1902 in Garfield County, Utah.

Joseph and Katie came to Union County soon after their wedding because their first son, Othello was born April 22, 1903 in Nibley, Union County, Oregon. Katie became mother to a large family of children: Othello (1903), Urdel (1905), Guild (1906), Clora (1908), Cleva (1909), Clara (1910), Laurel (1911), Deshler (1912), Gay, (1915), Masyl (1917), Beverly (1922), and Paula (1926).

Joseph was occupied as a farm manager, according to the *1940 Federal Census*. It appears his son Othello took over working the farm prior to 1935. Joseph Lay died in Union on May 15, 1971 and was buried in Baker City.

His wife, Katie, was born May 5, 1884 in Utah and died July 14, 1962 in Othello, Washington and was buried in Baker City.

Hindman Road - Formerly Hindman-Waelty Road #59, it runs 8.64 miles, located in Township 1N R40E Section 9 in the Elgin maintenance district. It's dual name is noted on the *1935 Metsker Map*, but the Waelty part was dropped in 1988 when the roads were renamed.

This gravel road was named after William B. Hindman, who in 1872, homesteaded 160 acres on this road.

He was called "Union County's statesman" since he served as a State representative during the 1880s. Considered a legal scholar, people came to him for advice, and he was known for bringing the first thresher and Model "T" Ford to this area.

To this day, Hindman Road is a curvy road in scenic Cricket Flat northeast of Elgin. One Hindman descendant, Billy Hindman, and his wife, Reta, were ranchers, equestrians and charter members of the Elgin Stampeders organization in Elgin.

They supported the Elgin Stampede Rodeo since it was established in 1946, and they were honored by this organization as Stampede Legends. *(Billy Hindman interview, January 2001)* Billy was 1963 Cattleman of the Year and very involved with stage coach racing at Pendleton Round-Up and other places.

The intersection of Hindman Road and Chumos is the location of the Hindman Century Farm and the Hindman family donated part of his homestead land for the Hindman School No. 36 located one quarter mile north of his home. The last class in Hindman School was held in 1937.

"My grandad came to this valley in 1864," said Billy Hindman in a January 2001 interview with the authors. His grandad, William B. Hindman, was born in Cedar County, Iowa in 1846 to Methodist preacher, John Hindman, and his wife, Emily Weeks Hindman. While living out East, John Hindman helped to start Cornell University. *(Billy Hindman interview, January 2001)*

When W. B. Hindman was 18 years old, he left Iowa with his uncle and cousin, and together they made the trek west to the Grande Ronde Valley, arriving in 1864. He stayed in the Summerville area for the first several years, where he procured a teaching position during the winter months and freighted during the summer recesses. The latter was a profitable occupation, but he was molded by his father's influence to be an educator.

Early historians recorded that W. B. Hindman taught in school district #17 long before the Dry Creek School was built in 1885. A 1940 *Elgin Recorder* noted, "He taught school in about 1865 or 1866 in a log house north of Summerville and a little west of where the [Rinehart] Flour Mill later stood." Some of his pupils described him as a scholar with special interests in mathematics and English. He always presented himself as a man of deliberate, well enunciated speech and perfect grammar.

W. B. Hindman was dedicated to farming, and he was honored as Conservation Man of the Year in 1959 by the Union County Wheat Growers Association. He was also honored as the state winner that year.

He eventually passed his farm onto his son, Luther, who in time, passed it onto Billy Hindman. The authors had the privilege of getting to know Billy and Reta Hindman through several interviews for publication in the *La Grande Observer*. Billy died on January 23, 2003 at the home of his daughter, Shirley, on Nine Mile Ranch in Touchet, Washington; and Reta June Hindman, 76, died November 12, 2008 also in Touchet, Washington. The Hindmans were laid to rest in the Hindman Cemetery on their ranch property in the soil they loved and spent their lives caring for.

The W. B. Hindman family and descendants left a memorable legacy as educators, rodeo participants, Elgin Stampede Rodeo members, century farmers and later in life, windpower investors. They had many friends in Northeast Oregon, especially through the Elgin Stampede Rodeo club and their association with the Pendleton Round-Up, where Billy engaged in some pretty wild stagecoach races.

The Elgin Stampeders' stagecoach teams included: Billy Hindman, Jerry Chandler, Sonny Weatherspoon, Odies Payne, and Jim McClure. They called themselves the "Wild Bunch from Elgin". The stage coaches belonged to the Pendleton Round-Up, but the horses belonged to Odies Payne. Later Billy and Sonny Weatherspoon and others were involved in making their own Elgin Stampeders' stagecoach which is still used for Elgin Stampede parades today.

The Waelty part of the road name originates with Adolph Waelty, born July 28, 1863 in Switzerland. He immigrated to America in 1880, according to the *1900 Federal Census of the south precinct of Elgin, Oregon*. He homesteaded property directly east of the Hindman one-room school house on Hindman Road and some farm land farther south of there. Combined he had about one section of land there.

Adolph married Mary Jane Gordon of Elgin on May 3, 1894 in Union County and they had eight children. (Ancestry.com) According to one detailed family tree maker, the children were: Henry (1895-1957), Raymond (1896-1983), Arnold (1898-1985), John (1899-1990), Mary A. (1901-1981), George (1903-1977), Rose (1905-1984), and Elva Lorene (1909-1998).

During their lives on their farm on Cricket Flat they enjoyed many socials at the Cricket Flat Grange.

One report from the *La Grande Observer, March 8, 1934, pg. 7* read in part:

CRICKET FLAT—Cricket Flat grange met Saturday in its hall with a potluck dinner at noon. A group of members met at the hall Tuesday and papered and painted the kitchen inside and out. The lecturer's program consisted of a recitation by Zetta Waelty, and Jack Patten, songs, Fish-for-Your-Hook contest and a debate upon the question, "Resolved that a broom is more useful than a pitchfork." Mrs. Mary Waelty and Mrs. Bernal Hug represented the affirmative and Mrs. Mary Breshears and Lois Witherspoon the negative. The latter won by a 2-1 decision of the judges, who were Emil Miller, A. R. Hill and Raymond Waelty. The H. E. C. Club discussed plans for a benefit social. The club is sponsoring refinishing the kitchen. The next meeting of the grange is to be held Saturday, March 10. (End of article)

Besides the grange hall socials, Mary Waelty was very active socially in a winter club called the "Cricket Flat Grass-hoppers" which met for their weekly ski with Mr. and Mrs. Leo Roulet. One report on a club outing read:

"The day was quite stormy and the snow was a little sticky, but everybody was in for a good time and the weather man was outwitted. Honors went to Rex Roulet for the best riding." Those present this time were ... Mrs. Mary Waelty... Mr. and Mrs. Raymond Waelty and daughter; and John and Arnold Waelty. *(La Grande Observer, Wed. Feb.3, 1932, pg. 6)*

Adolph was rarely in the newspapers or mentioned as a participant in these social events, but he was very active on his ranch and the field of agriculture. To say that he was a successful farmer would be an understatement.

After his death on September 28, 1926 in Richland, Baker County, Oregon, at age 63 years, his estate went through probate and the following notice was published in the *Idaho Daily Statesman (Boise, Idaho), Thurs. Oct. 7, 1926, pg. 6* as follows:

"BAKER BRIEFS. Estate Filed— The Adolph Waelty estate was filed for probate here Monday with County Clerk Combs. The property which will be divided among the heirs is valued at $32,000. Mrs. Mary Waelty, his widow, petitioned for appointment as administratrix."

Adolph Waelty's obituary was not found because the Baker County newspaper is not archived on newspapers.com, and since he died in Baker County, that's where the obit would have been printed.

However, the La Grande Observer did print Mary Jane Waelty's obituary because she died in Union County at the hospital in La Grande. She died on January 26, 1956 at a La Grande hospital. Her obituary read in part:

Mrs. Mary Jane Waelty, 80, a lifetime resident of Elgin, died in a La Grande hospital this morning after an extended illness. Funeral services were held at the Daniels Funeral Home and burial took place at Richland, Baker County, Oregon. She was survived by five sons, three daughters, two brothers, three sisters, 20 grandchildren, and 27 great-grandchildren. Mr. Adolph Waelty and an infant son preceded her in death.

Her sons are Henry of Central Point; Raymond, Arnold and John of Elgin and George of La Grande.

Daughters are Mrs. Anna Wood, Grants Pass; Mrs. Rose Evans and Mrs. Elva Williams, both of Richland. Brothers are George Gordon of Richland and William Gordon of Baker. Sisters include Mrs. Lottie Blank, Mrs. Lura Hoover and Mrs. Sarah Varah, all of Richland. *(La Grande Observer, Jan. 26, 1956, pg. 6)*

Hot Lake Lane - This road #12A runs 2.68 miles in Township 4S R38-39E Sections 1, 6 and 5 in the Union maintenance district.

Anyone who has lived in Union County would know where to find this road, and many outside the county and even the state perhaps would have heard of the lake that gives the road its name.

The first note of the lake was given by Robert Stuart in his journal in 1812. Since that time it has become a well known and often popular place. Throughout the years there has been a hotel and or a hospital (Hot Lake Sanitarium) besides the hot mineral springs. At one time it was Hot Lake Post Office and Hot Lake Railroad Station.

For extensive history of Hot Lake, read one of the books by Richard R. Roth that have been published in past years.

Howard Lane - This is a private lane off of Hunter Road in 1S R38E Section 4 in the Imbler maintenance district.

Howell Road - This gravel road #133A is .62 miles in length and is located in Township 1S R39E Section 19 of the Imbler maintenance district.

The road is an access between Summerville Road and Hull Lane south of Imbler. The only residence on this gravel road was that of William Fred "Bill" Howell and his wife Florence Irene (Carn) Howell. Bill farmed and raised cattle. His son Mark Howell and family live on the connecting Hull Lane.

"The county planning commission called us to ask if they could name this Howell Road," said Florence.

Bill Howell was the son of farmers Oscar W. and Helen (Green) Howell. He was born and raised on a nameless lane off of Imbler Road about a mile south of Imbler. This lane led to his grandparents' place, and then it belonged to Oscar, along the bank of the Grande Ronde River, where Bill grew up.

When his grandfather, Fred Howell, lived there, a pneumonia epidemic swept through the area and claimed Fred's life and nearly all his family. Surviving were Fred's widow and son, Oscar, 5 years old. When Oscar became an adult, he inherited the homestead property.

As a young child, Bill went out to the barn with his dad, Oscar, and learned to sing period songs like the "Preacher and the Bear." Then when Bill was 13, he learned to play the bell trumpet. The Imbler school band instructor noticed his talent and invited him to join the Dick Lindsey Band, so Bill got involved with the band, gaining experience performing in public.

Bill participated in a contest singing with KLBM radio station. He used to sing the 1950s love songs and dance tunes—the kind of songs that television singer Perry Como used to sing.

Bill performed with the band all through high school and graduated from Imbler High School in 1945. Following one year in the service, he went right back into entertaining, but this time as Billy Howell's Orchestra, which included a piano player, a bass player, a guitar player and himself as vocal and on trumpet. He played at all the Imbler High School proms, at the college and at the Sacajawea Hotel ballroom, among other places. He earned $12 per man for 3 hours of playing, Howell said.

Then on March 5, 1955, Bill Howell and Florence Irene Carn were married. Florence was born December 10, 1932 in Boise, Idaho to Stephen and Blanche (Johnson) Carn. She spent her youth growing up in Camp 58 at Starkey. She graduated from La Grande High School in 1951 and four years later married Bill Howell.

The newlyweds lived at the Howell homestead for the first six years of their marriage, during which time three of their four children were born: Curt, Kristy and Ann. Bill's grandmother Howell had remarried and was then living in Elgin, so the homestead on Imbler Road was occupied by Bill and Florence.

During that time, Bill's father Oscar Howell married a second time to Mrs. Dolly Dolstrum, a widow with three children, and for a short time they lived in La Grande. Discontented, they returned to the Howell homestead in Imbler, meaning that Bill and Florence had to find another place.

So in that same year (1961), Bill and Florence Howell bought their present 2-story home from a bachelor named Alex McKenzie. He was a jolly Scotsman, who, for two terms (1938-1947) served as county commissioner, and in 1957 was honored by the Masons, when they named their Elgin lodge "McKenzie Hall" after him. The building still stands today in downtown Elgin.

McKenzie had been living in the 2-story house with his aged mother when the Howells bought it from him. This farm property included nearly 200 acres, which Bill farmed. He also raised about 200 head of horned Hereford cows. There on their new farm, they welcomed their fourth child, Mark, in 1962, which completed their family.

Bill engaged in general farming, growing all types of grains and crops, including wheat, peas, garbanzo beans, bluegrass and fescue species of grass seed, sunflower seeds, mint and sugar beets. In 1976, Bill Howell was honored as Conservation Man of the Year.

In 2018, Bill, age 90, was still actively engaged in farming with the help of his son, Mark, who lives close by. Bill's wife, Florence, 87, died on August 23, 2020. She and Bill had been married for 65 years. Bill lived at Wildflower Lodge when he died on February 1, 2021 at 93 years of age. *(Bill and Florence Howell interview, May 20, 2018; Loveland Funeral Chapel obituary)*

Hug Road - Formerly Hug-McDonald Road #36 runs 3.29 miles in length in Township 1S R39E Section 8 in the Imbler maintenance district. Located north of Summerville in the foothills of the Pumpkin Ridge section, it is one of the most scenic drives in the north end of the Grande Ronde Valley.

The road was named Hug after a prominent family in this county. The oldest Hug pioneer to come to this valley was Henry Hug, born October 16, 1829 in Weiningen, Switzerland. He was married twice. He married his first wife on April 26, 1857 in Zurich, Switzerland. Her name was Anna Maria Wampfler.

They immigrated to America shortly thereafter and settled in Utah Territory where Anna gave birth to a son on October 14, 1860. She died from complications five days later.

On November 24, 1861, Henry married Anna E. Muller in Utah. During their marriage, they had the following children: Julius (1862-1941), Walter (1864), Anna (1866-1880), Henry H. (1869), Eugene (1872), and another daughter, name unknown.

The following story comes from Anna Hug's obituary as printed in the *La Grande Observer, August 3, 1934, pages 1, 3.*

"Hug Funeral Is Held at Elgin This Afternoon — Funeral services for Mrs. Anna Hug, who died Wednesday at the home of her son at Elgin, were being held at a Christian church this afternoon. Anna Muller Hug was born in the canton of Bern, Switzerland, in June 1836. She was the youngest of nine children and at the age of seven, her parents were both dead, and in poverty she was obliged to shift for herself in the big city of Geneva. Electric lights, telephones, street cars, automobiles and other modern city conveniences were unknown. Streets had cobble-stone pavements, if any, sewers and running water were rare. Amid these surroundings, she worked for various people and grew through her childhood and youth.

As a young woman she joined a band of people who were going to America. Six weeks on a little German sail boat brought them across the Atlantic. Days on the primitive railroad bounced them along until they crossed the continent as far as Omaha, Nebraska.

From Omaha the summer was spent in traveling by ox train to Salt Lake City. Miss Muller walked beside the train and earned her living by baking bread of evenings over a buffalo chip fire. Out of provisions, tired and with her three pair of tough leather shoes worn out and gone, the company reached Salt Lake as the first autumn snows were falling.

In Salt Lake, she met Henry Hug, who she married. Her first home was in a tent bought from an abandoned U.S. Army camp. An adobe house in Santa Clara, southern Utah, then became the pioneer home where her six children were born.

In 1879, the family loaded its belongings into a covered wagon and came to Oregon. The first winter in Oregon was spent on the old Norval place at the foot of Pumpkin Ridge in Union County. The next year, Mr. Hug bought the farm on Cricket Flat now owned by Albert Hill.

This became the Hug home until 1901, when Mr. Hug moved to Elgin and left the farm to his sons. He died shortly afterwards, and Mrs. Hug continued to live in the Elgin home until it was destroyed by fire in 1930, and she was obliged to start housekeeping anew in another house. She remained alert in body and mind until last September, when she suffered from a fall, probably caused from a light stroke. Since that time, her four sons arranged so that one of them has been constantly at her bedside.

From her century of strenuous life, Grandma Hug, or Aunt Ann, as she was commonly called, developed a cheerful disposition and a philosophic outlook on life. She spoke three languages, was a good cook, loved flowers and children and nearly always had a cheerful smile. When she lost her home and cherished belongings (among these a letter from President Wilson complimenting her on the number of pairs of socks that she had knit for the soldiers of the World War) at the age of 94, her friends offered sympathy. She told them that her house was rather old, and she guessed she needed a new one. Without complaining, she adapted herself to her new surroundings, planted herself a new flower garden and seemed quite happy.

She leaves five living children: Julius C., Walter Fridoline, Henry H., Eugene F., and Mrs. Andrew (Huldia) Tucker; all of Elgin; eight grandchildren and eighteen great grandchildren." (End of obit)

Walter Hug is the father of the well-known Bernal D. Hug, Union County historian and author of *The History of Union County, Oregon, 1961.*

The second part of the road name, McDonald, is named after Hiram McDonald, who purchased his first 40 acres of his 520 acre estate in this area in 1873, and the subsequent farm became a Century Farm, currently owned by descendants George and Carla McDonald.

Hiram was born on February 17, 1834 in Chariton County, Missouri. His mother died when he was just a child, and his father thereafter moved to Linn County, Missouri, and then in 1854 to Sullivan County, Missouri. Two years later, on June 9, 1856, Hiram married Margaret R. Taylor, 24.

In 1864, the Hiram McDonald family, along with their four young children, took an ox team and crossed the Oregon Trail with a caravan of 75 wagons.

"They settled in the Willamette Valley near Harrisburg where they remained for seven years. One son and another daughter were born there. In 1871, they moved to Pilot Rock, but stayed only a short time. In 1872, they moved to Union County. They lived on Dry Creek for a time, then in 1873, they moved into a lean-to that Hiram had built on 160 acres he was homesteading on Pumpkin Ridge." *(Memoirs of Harley C. McDonald)*

"That first winter they were here, Hiram spent his evenings planing boards for the house he would build the next year. Margaret spun wool. They worked by the light of tallow candles and the fireplace fire," wrote Harley McDonald in his memoirs.

There on July 14, 1875, Hiram purchased 80 acres from Isaac Gordon. Then he busied himself building the family's first home. Each board in the home was hand planed, and each was unique from the next in measurement. After building the home, there was some question in Hiram's mind as to whether or not the structure was sitting on his property.

To head off any possible legal problems regarding this matter, he asked his oldest daughter, Susan Elizabeth McDonald, to file a homestead claim for the land adjacent to his. She did and the McDonalds built her little home not far from Hiram's. On September 21, 1885, Susan and her husband, Albert Becker, sold this land to Hiram McDonald for $200.

For the next 17 years this pristine property was home to Hiram, Margaret and their children: Susan,

Sarah, Mary E., George W. and Ellen. Sadly, Mary E. died in 1880; three others died in infancy or early childhood: Annie, Lee and John. The surviving children included Susan Elizabeth (Becker), Sarah J. (Fisher), Ellen (Oswell) and their son George W.

They endured their losses so common in pioneer life by focusing on developing their property and moving forward with life. In 1893, Hiram hired a local carpenter, Silas Johnson, to build a spacious eight-room house. Meanwhile, their first home was moved to another place on the property for a bunk house.

By 1902, the McDonald estate included 520 acres of tillable ground, timberland, 25 acres in fruit of every kind native to this area. Hiram's daughter sold the fruit to mining camps, which brought in a little extra income for the family. The family also raised hogs, which served a dual purpose of providing bacon and hams for the smokehouse, but also they ate up the rattle snakes around the yard.

Hiram died on January 9, 1912. His widow stayed on the farm and her son, George W. and his wife Annie (Smith), who lived nearby on Hug-McDonald Road, looked after her until she died on October 1, 1921. After her death, George and Annie took ownership of the grand McDonald home built by Hiram. At first they rented it out to Wesley McDonald and his wife, but after they moved out, George and Annie moved in.

Under George's hand, the farm continued to be transformed. He cleared off brush, trees and blew up stumps. He also built two new barns, and to help him with this, he and his brother-in-law Columbus Fisher, ran a saw mill together on Pumpkin Ridge Road. That mill stayed in operation until sometime after 1905.

George W. raised wheat and the typical farm livestock. His stud horse and dairy products supplemented his income. He also did custom threshing, and he fed his crew on the meats from his smokehouse. Ruth Smith was the cook of choice for the McDonald threshing crew, and there were plenty of pies on the menu, made from the fruit of the McDonald's large orchard
.
All the years George W. farmed, he was accompanied by his son, Harley, who was next in line to operate the farm. Harley Cecil McDonald was born on the Hug-McDonald Road farm on July 31, 1901. He went to one room country schools and eventually met his sweetheart and bride to be, Miss Lottie Black, who taught school in Summerville. They knew each other for about ten years before they married on June 7, 1936.

Harley managed the farm when it went from horses to horse powered gas engines. He got rid of his horses in 1947, trading them in for a Model U Alice Chalmers, and in the forties he used a combine pulled by a 22 Caterpillar tractor.

However, in addition to farming progress, hardships also struck, as they often do. In 1961, the McDonalds suffered a serious fire, which destroyed their grass crop and damaged the neighbor's orchard. It was a costly mishap, but once again, the McDonalds endured.

Harley's son George was next to operate the farm with his wife Karla (Lund). They married in 1966, and initially lived in a small trailer that they set on the farm, and they raised six children: Jeanne Ann (Taylor), twins Scott and Jeff, Mary (Allen), Steven and Mark.

Harley retired from active farming in 1968, and during this retirement, Lottie applied for Century Farm status through the Oregon State Century Farm and Ranch Program. They were awarded their honors at the State Fair in Salem on August 31, 1976.

Harley Cecil McDonald Sr. died on January 18, 1983 and Lottie on March 11, 1996, and they were interred at the Summerville Cemetery, where 23 other McDonalds are resting in peace.

The grand McDonald home and century farm now belong to fourth generation farmers, George and Karla McDonald and their children.

Hulick Lane - This is a public unmaintained lane, which is only .75 miles in length and is located in Township 3S R40E Section 17 of the Union maintenance district.

According to Mary Jane (Conley) Johnson of rural Cove, this road was unnamed until 1988, when the Union County road names were assigned. At that time, it was given the name Hulick Lane after the creek that runs nearby. This creek was named after the John and Eleanor Hulick family that lived on the southeast side of Cove. The Hulick family lived about two miles from Hulick Lane.

Both John Hulick and his wife, Eleanor Farmer, were born in Indiana in 1815 and married prior to 1837. All of their children were born in Iowa, the last child being born in 1857. The family relocated to Union County, Oregon, sometime after 1860 and before 1870 because in the 1870 Federal Census the family was listed as farm residents in Cove.

Ten children are known: Elsia Ann (Mrs. John Martin), Sarah A., Isaac, William, James, Mary Ellen, David Trolonda, Cordelia, and John W. *(1856 Iowa State Census; 1860 Iowa Federal Census)*

John Hulick was a farmer in Cove until his death on July 7, 1871, at about 56 years of age. The homestead was put in Eleanor's name after John died. In 1880, Eleanor is shown as the owner of the farm and her sons, James, David and John, were living at the farm homestead and were listed as laborers, likely on the farm. *(1880 Federal Census)*

Eleanor Farmer Hulick was born June 11, 1815, and she died February 6, 1899. Her son John W. Hulick died in May 1899.

Eleanor's son, David Hulick, married Annetta Wright on March 6, 1878 in Cove. They had a son, William Albert, born November 1, 1880. David died May 10, 1897 in Cove.

Eleanor's son, James Hulick, married Clara Burford, and they moved to the Medical Springs vicinity, where they lived for the next 42 years.

Eleanor's daughter, Elsia Hulick, married John Martin on August 9, 1860 in Iowa. In 1865, they were living in Montana, and in 1867, they were farming in Cove, Oregon. John Martin died in 1910. *(Ancestry.com)*

The La Grande Observer apparently did not have any information on John Hulick Sr. because of his early death date. In spite of that, he has a creek and a lane named after him.

Hull Lane -   Formerly divided into two sections, Hunt Lane and Hull Lane. This road #133 runs 3.59 miles in length and is located in Township 1S R39E Section 19, creating the southern boarder road of the city of Imbler.

It's paved inside the Imbler city limits and then it goes to gravel. It is primarily a market lane, leading from outlying farm properties to Ruckman Road (Highway 82), which runs through the center of Imbler.

The Hunt part of this road runs on the west side of Highway 82, forming the southmost road of Imbler on a 1980's county road map. Oddly, the *1935 Metsker Map* of Imbler shows that Frederick Christopher Hunt owned about three-quarters of a section of farm land on the east end of the road where it intersects with Gray's Corner Road.

Frederick C. Hunt was born in Baker City in 1901. In the *1920 Federal Census of Baker City*, Frederick's occupation is listed as a brakeman for the railroad.

He married Iris Funk in 1927, and they had four children: Norma Jean Feik (1929-1986), Margaret Ann Hopkins (1931-2012), Elva Mae Quebbeman (1936-1996) and Fred C. (1944-). In the *1930 and 1940 Federal Census for Imbler, Oregon*, he was listed as a farmer.

Iris died October 5, 1948 in Imbler, the city where she was born 40 years earlier. She was interred at the Summerville Cemetery, and her husband joined her on June 17, 1966.

The Hull Lane part of the road is named after farm resident, William Hull, the son of Joseph Hull and Sarah J. Hardee. Joseph Hull was born on January 29, 1806 in Pennsylvania and died on April 5, 1882 with interment at Summerville Cemetery in Summerville, Oregon. Sarah was born in Ohio on December 24, 1809 and died on August 22, 1878 with interment in Summerville Cemetery. *(Findagrave.com)*

Joseph and Sarah began their married life in Sarah's birth state of Ohio. There she gave birth to six known children: Susanah, Sarah Ann, Mary, Martha Jane, William and Harriet A.

Then before 1846, the family relocated to Wapello County, Iowa, where Joseph, Sarah and 7 children were listed on the *1846 Iowa State Census*. That year baby Catharine M. joined the family. On January 27, 1850, Susanah Hull was married to Abner L. Johnson in Wapello County, Iowa. Then in 1852, baby Louisa F. Hull was born. *(1856 Iowa State Census of Pleasant Township)*

Consequently, over the years, the Joseph and Sarah Hull family started to grow and change. They remained in Pleasant Township, Wapello County for the 1860 and 1870 census years, except for William, who had left the area for Oregon.

William was born October 5, 1844 in Ohio and farmed with his father. At age 19, he left his family, then in Iowa, and ventured west by ox wagon to settle in Union County, Oregon in 1863. Later, his father, mother and siblings followed him and were counted among the Union County population in the 1880 Federal Census.

William married Sarah J. Neville on February 15, 1872 in Union County. She was born in Iowa on

February 19, 1853, and she came by wagon train to Union County with her parents, Edward and Jane Neville in 1871. She died in Imbler on November 18, 1924.

During their lives together, William and Sarah engaged in farming on property east of Imbler on what became Hull Lane. It appears that they had one child, a daughter named Lettie, who later became Mrs. Henry "Hank" McGoldrick, residents of Imbler. They had a son, Eugene "Gene" Omer McGoldrick, born in May 1896, who was listed as part of his grandfather William Hull's household in the *1900 and 1910 Federal Census. (*Eugene's full signature can be found on the 1918 registrar's report, *ancestry.com)*

In the harvest of 1897, William had a crippling fall that left one of his arms paralyzed. Being disabled now, he began looking at a property to buy for a retirement home. *(La Grande Observer, March 4, 1898, pg. 3)* Later in the December 24, 1897 issue of the newspaper, it said, "William Hull and Hank McGoldrick have moved to the (Sand)ridge." It appeared that after William's injury, he depended upon the help of his son-in-law and resident grandson on the farm.

In 1898, there was a newspaper mention of William Hull's farm.

"A new bridge is needed across a Grande Ronde River on the county road near Mr. Hull's farm. The old one is a private bridge and is very unsafe. While crossing with a load of wheat last week, John Hawthorn came near having a serious accident. His wagon began to slip and came near slipping off the bridge. John said, 'My hair stood on end, and I prepared to jump.'" *(La Grande Observer, January 6, 1898, pg. 4)*

Sarah Hull had siblings that lived in Turlock and Long Beach, California, where the Hulls no doubt visited and came to desire their mild winters.

"Mr. and Mrs. William Hull left last evening for Santa Anna, California, where they will spend the winter. Mr. and Mrs. Hull came to this valley in 1863, and this will be the first winter that they have spent out of the valley since coming here." *(La Grande Observer, November 24, 1903, pg. 8)*

William and Sarah moved in 1909 to the north side of La Grande, but they returned to Imbler to live just three weeks before his death on August 21, 1916. William was interred at Summerville Cemetery. Sarah survived her husband and lived with her daughter, Lettie McGoldrick, in Imbler until her death in 1924.

William's obituary was printed in the *La Grande Observer, August 22, 1916 paper on pg 1*. It read in part: "... the remains of the late William Hull who died in this city yesterday will be laid away at Imbler (Summerville Cemetery). Because of his wide acquaintance in this county and in Wallowa country as well, it is expected a large audience will be present to pay tribute to his sterling life."

The August 28, 1916 issue of the La Grande Observer, pg. 2, added: "Mr. Hull was a pioneer in the valley, coming here in an ox wagon. He was well known in the Grande Ronde valley."

Sarah Hull's obituary printed in the *November 21, 1924, pg. 4 issue of the La Grande Observer* stated in part: "Sarah J. Hull, widow of William Hull, passed away at the home of her daughter, Mrs. Henry McGoldrick of Imbler, Tuesday morning, November 18, 1924, at the age of 71 years.

Mrs. Hull was a Union County pioneer, having come to the county from Iowa with her parents, Edward and Jane Neville, in 1871, making the then long, adventurous journey across the Plains and through the mountains in company with many others, making the entire trip by wagon train.

She married William Hull, who was also one of Union County's early and well-known settlers and lived for many years on their farm near Imbler. In later years, Mr. Hull retired from active farm work and took up their residence in La Grande, where they lived for about 15 years and until the death of Mr. Hull. Mrs. Hull from that time until her death lived in the home of Mr. and Mrs. McGoldrick, her daughter and husband of Imbler.

She is survived by one daughter, Mrs. Henry McGoldrick; one grandson, Eugene McGoldrick of Imbler; four sisters, Mrs. George Ruckman of Imbler, Mrs. J. N. Rinehart of Portland, Mrs. M. B. Mitchell of Salem, Mrs. Flora Gelham of Turlock, Calif.; two brothers, William Neville of Long Beach, Calif.; Solomon Neville of Turlock, Calif." (End of obit) Burial took place at the Summerville Cemetery.

The Hull farm was passed onto Lettie and Henry McGoldrick. Lettie was born on December 11, 1875 in Imbler. On October 18, 1893 she married Henry McGoldrick. They had two children, but the eldest died young. The younger son, Eugene "Gene" Omer McGoldrick, grew to manhood, married in 1937 and was residing in Baker City in 1950.

Henry McGoldrick died in 1937; Lettie died in 1969 in Imbler, and their son Eugene died in Portland in 1974.

Hunter Road - This is county road #14, the second longest county road in Union County. It runs 12.83 miles in length in Township 2S R38E Section 34 in the La Grande and Imbler maintenance districts.

The name of this road has gradually shortened over the years from its early name, Hunter Lane Market Road in 1923 to Hunter Lane Road by 1946 to its current name of Hunter Road since 1988. Over the years, Hunter Road was extended north of McKenzie Lane until it connects with Dry Creek Road, where it ends. That northerly section of road used to be called Lewis-Dry Creek Road. This name was replaced with Hunter Road. (See Dry Creek Road entry)

In spring 1926, a road article appeared titled, "Extension of Hunter Lane to Summerville Market Road" It read in part: "The road is being built from the Hunter Lane end and will eventually extend to Summerville, where it will connect with the Summerville-Imbler road." *(La Grande Observer, March 6, 1926, pg. 7)* Today, that extension road that connects Hunter Road to Summerville Road is McKenzie Lane.

Hunter Road was named after the prominent family of John Thomas and Nancy (Gay) Hunter, and their son William Gay Hunter, former Mayor of Island City.

John T. Hunter was born October 9, 1818 in Maury County, Tennessee, and he married Nancy Gay on October 11, 1838 in Licking County, Ohio. *(Family Search website)* She was born 1816 in New Hampshire to Charles S. Gay and Rebecca Armstrong.

The Hunters made their home in Gentry County, Missouri where they had a large family. Their children included: Jason Smith (1840-1916), Emily A. (1841-1843), William Gay (1843-1907), Louisa J. (1846-1870), Mary Quintella (1848-1928), Irvin B. (1852-1877), Sarah Margaret Halley (1854-1896), Charles F. (1856-1895) and Julia Belle (1860-1940). *(1860 Federal Census; LDS Family Search)*

On August 21, 1865, John T. Hunter organized and became the captain of a wagon train carrying members of four families across the Oregon Trail with a goal of reaching the Willamette Valley. Among them were the John T. Hunter family, including William Gay Hunter, 21; a single man named Mansfield A. Harrison, and Al Good.

According to Bernal D. Hug's *History of Union County, Oregon, pg. 54-55,* the Hunter train started west on August 21, 1865 (presumably from Gentry County, Missouri). Their rigs were well stocked and food rationing began right from the start. "Supplies for the last half of the journey were placed in the bottom of the wagon bed and then a floor laid over them. Provisions for the first half of the trip were stored above this second floor, which would not be removed until the halfway point was reached on the trip."

They were careful not to kill the buffalo for food during their trip because this angered the Native Americans, often resulting in retaliation and sometimes the offenders were killed. Instead, other forms of game were sought. As they journeyed, the children were assigned to pick up buffalo chips for their camp fires.

In November 1865, the Hunter train entered the Grande Ronde Valley. Instead of driving on the valley floor, they took the road just east of Ladd Canyon, Hug wrote. Considering the snow accumulation and the fact that they were weary, the travelers on the Hunter train made their decisions to make this valley their home and forego traveling on to the Willamette Valley as originally planned.

John T. Hunter and family settled initially in the Mt. Glen area, where Ben Brown had homesteaded four years earlier. Also, settling there in the Mt. Glen settlement was the Moses Hawkins Mitchell family, he being the captain of his own train that started out from Hudson, Macon County, Missouri in June 1865 and arrived in October. Among his children was 14-year-old daughter, Eliza Weir Mitchell, who drove one of the wagons part of the way over the Oregon Trail.

Hug described the 1865-66 winter in the Mt. Glen area, when those families arrived. "That winter the Mitchell's cabin snowed so nearly under that they had to go in and out of a window, which was made of oiled paper and (they) kept a flag at the spring so they could find where to dig for water." *(History of Union County, Oregon, pg. 56)*

The Hunters did not waste time filing claims for donation land. According to his descendant Jeffry Zurbrick, John T. Hunter homesteaded 160 acres as did his wife. He purchased additional property in Union County in 1866 and bought even more over the years.

By the *1870 Federal Census,* the John T. Hunter family were residing on their new farm in the Oro Dell area of Union County not far from Mt. Glen.

It appears that another homestead claim was filed in the name of John's brother, William C. Hunter.

This may have been a relative claim or simply a misspelling of William G. Hunter, John T. Hunter's son.

Regardless, the 160-acre homestead was proved up, and on March 6, 1873 a patent was issued to William C. Hunter. He never lived on the homestead, because he lived nearly all of his life on his farm in Partridge, Woodford, Illinois, where he farmed and raised a family of his own until his death on April 10, 1898. *(Obit, Woodford County Journal, Eureka, Illinois, April 22, 1898, pg. 1)*

Consequently, this homestead eventually became the property of William G. Hunter and Eliza W. (Mitchell) Hunter. By 1935, it was owned by the estate of their son, Gilbert W. Hunter. *(1935 Metsker Map)* The property is located 4-1/2 miles north of Island City on what became known as Hunter Road.

The family patriarch, John T. Hunter, died November, 10, 1878 at his home. His descendant Jeffry Zurbrick stated that he died after his buggy tipped over on him during a run-away incident. *(Zurbrick interview, Oct. 2000)* His wife Nancy died November 9, 1891. Both were interred at Ackles Cemetery with other family members.

Much is written about their son William Gay Hunter, who built upon his father's estate, eventually acquiring 3,000 acres of farm land. In 1902, he planted 65 acres in sugar beets and became a principal promoter of the building of a sugar factory in La Grande. In 1903, he harvested his first crop of apples off his new orchard. Hunter and Charles Goodnaugh were also significantly involved in the Pioneering Flouring Mills Company.

In the *1900 Federal Census of the Island City precinct*, those residing and working on his expansive ranch included 22 Chinese men described as "servants" or clearly farm laborers. Their names will be enumerated here in the event that someone is searching for them.

The household of William G. Hunter in the census included his wife, Eliza, and their children: Edna E., Carrie B., Pearl F., Addie, Stella, Hazel, and William G. Jr., or Gilbert, as he was known. Then there were farm hands listed: John A. Glen, 29, William H. Ritter, 21, John Abele, 28 and Abbot J. Waite, 67.

Among the 22 Chinese farm laborers there were: Shuey Lee, 38, single, Onen, 46, single, Wah Mer, 56, single, Sing Ah, 56, single, Mon Ah, 52, single, Leeh Lee, 55, married, Ock Fohn, 58, married, He Fong, 61, single, Jim Ming, 64, widowed, Che Lee, 55, single, Tung Ah, 50, married, Chong Wong, 43, single, Tye Ah, 48, married, Jung Ah, 55, married, We Ah, 62, single, Song Kim, 57, married, Yeng Ah, 58, single, Yinget Ah, 38, single, Kour Lee, 50, married, How Chin, 52, single, Sun Lee, 55, single, and Louie Ah, 56, single.

William G. Hunter was no doubt the largest private employer of Chinese-born laborers in Union County in 1900. He was remarkably impartial for the time, considering the racial discrimination that existed in Union County and throughout Oregon against the Cantonese-Chinese immigrants seeking a livelihood in America.

Hunter was very influential, and he had his hand in nearly every important development in Union County. In fact, he represented the county at the Oregon Development League in August 1904, being referred to as "Honorable W. G. Hunter." *(La Grande Observer, August 1, 1904, pg. 4)*

He also was a director and major stockholder of the Morgan Lake Electric Company plant, owning two-fifths of the capital stock ($10,000).

Civically, he served as a county commissioner for a number of years. *(La Grande Observer, March 16, 1925)* At the time of his death in 1907, he was serving as Mayor of Island City and was highly esteemed by the community.

He died at the age of 63 in a terrible accident. His obituary explained in part:

"William G. Hunter, one of the most widely known and respected residents of Union County, was fatally injured by the explosion of a giant powder near his home at Island City Tuesday evening.

He had gone to a place on the river where some blasting was being done, and while standing near a fire, the explosion occurred. Mr. Hunter was thrown several feet in the air and his left leg and hip were frightfully mangled. As a last resort amputation of the leg was attempted by doctors Bacon, Molitor and Richardson, but the injured man could not survive the shock. Notwithstanding the severe injury, Mr. Hunter was conscious and was surrounded by members of his family.

Mr. Hunter was widely known as one of the most energetic citizens of the county, and his success was attained through his own efforts. He handled a large estate and was heavily interested in farming, stock-raising, merchandising and was one of the principal members of the Grande Ronde Light and Power Company.

He was 63 years of age and leaves a widow and family of eight children, three sons and five daughters. Interment will be at the Ackles Cemetery." *(La Grande Observer, Friday, January 25, 1907)*

The above obituary appears to have been in error as to the interment, as there is a grave monument in the Island City Cemetery bearing the name William G. Hunter and dates. The *Findagrave.com* website has a photo of him and his wife Eliza (Mitchell) Hunter. He appears to have been a very tall, slender man.

Descendant Jeffry Zurbrick offered the family's version of the tragedy in an interview with the authors in October 2000.

"In January 1907, William Gay Hunter was doing volunteer work with a group of men on the river channel near Island City," Zurbrick said. "They were doing some blasting, and the dynamite they were using had been frozen due to the cold weather. Someone had set the dynamite in a tin bucket by the warming fire to thaw."

"Apparently, W. G. Hunter bumped or kicked the bucket, which detonated the dynamite," explained Zurbrick. "He was carried on a door up to the family house and laid on the kitchen table where his leg was amputated. His daughter Stella and son Gilbert were assigned the job of burying the leg in the pasture behind the house. William Hunter lived for 1 or 2 days longer and then died. His buried leg was retrieved and re-buried with him."

The kitchen table was handed down to members of the family and eventually became the possession of descendant Jeffry Zurbrick. It was at this very table that the authors sat and recorded their notes during the Zurbrick interview of October 2000.

After W. G. Hunter's death, the Hunter farm faced some difficult times, Zurbrick said. Some of the ground was lost, some was split up among the children. Stella received 120 acres that became part of the Zurbrick Century Farm and Gilbert came in possession of the property on Hunter Road.

Hutchinson Lane - This lane is road #112 and runs 1.52 miles outside the city of Union in Township 4S R40E Section 6. It's named after brothers James Henry Hutchinson and William R. Hutchinson, two of the most prosperous farmers and stock raisers in Union County, owning 4,000 acres for cultivation and pasture.

The Hutchinson family history is quite extensively researched. For you genealogists, see the *JoJo Family Tree on ancestry.com* for great information. To be synoptic, William R.'s grandfather, James Wilder Hutchinson, born in Nottinghamshire, England, emigrated from the port of Liverpool and arrived in New York on June 18, 1833.

When the James W. Hutchinson family came to New York, they first settled near Elizabeth, New Jersey. After several years, the family moved to Illinois, where James Wilder Hutchinson died on September 22, 1877 in McLeansboro, Hamilton County, Illinois.

James Wilder Hutchinson had a son William Hutchinson Sr., and he married Margaret Young, who was born near Mount Carmel in Wabash County, Illinois. The couple married on December 20, 1842 in Mount Carmel, and they settled in Wabash County, Illinois. They had six sons (in birth order): James H.(1843-1917), William Rushton (1846-1923) Charles E. (1850-1862), Francis "Frank" Asbury (1855-1929), Stephen A. (1858-1911) and Gustavus A.(1861-1946).

The eldest three were born in Wabash County, Illinois, and the last three were born in Oregon. Young Charlie Hutchinson died in Rainier, Washington in 1862 at the age of 12, before his family came to Union County, Oregon.

Our subjects, James H. Hutchinson and William Rushton Hutchinson were born near Mount Carmel in Wabash County, Illinois. James was born October 15, 1843 and William R. was born February 14, 1846.

On May 1, 1852, when James was nine and William R. was six years old, their family joined a party with seven wagons, horses and oxen, and they left Illinois to cross the Oregon Trail heading to the Pacific Coast. With them were three other heads of families: John Campbell, Ransom Higgins and George Wright. In addition were the following single men: Samuel Taylor, Samuel Woods, and James and Henry Young.

They arrived in Portland on November 1, 1852, but they lost Samuel Woods in a drowning incident on the Snake River during the trip. Their first winter in Portland was hard, and all their stock except one horse died. It required all the resourcefulness the emigrants could devise to provide necessary food and clothing during that winter.

In the spring, William Sr. took up a claim of 320 acres in Cowlitz County, Washington, according to homestead laws. He remained on that claim for 4 years for ownership of a half section to legitimize, and then in late April 1864, he migrated to the Grande Ronde Valley, arriving there on May 1, 1864.

Upon their arrival to the valley, they noticed a small settlement of only a few cabins along the creek that had been built over the previous two years by earlier settlers. What "roads" existed were lined with freighting outfits carrying supplies to the Idaho mines. This work provided a living for many men who settled in the valley. Activity at the mines was going strong then, so supplies were freighted, being landed at Umatilla by boat and transported by wagon from there.

The young man William R. Hutchinson remained living with his parents in Union County for many years after reaching maturity. During his young manhood, he engaged in prospecting to some extent and during the various uprisings of the Indians, William R. frequently was called upon for scout duty and assisted in guarding the stock of the settlers from raids.

He eventually took up land southwest of Union and afterward purchased state school land and engaged in farming. On August 20, 1869, James bought land in section 23 and 26, Range 39E in Township 4S. This was just the beginning of the land acquisitions of these two brothers.

They increased their land, and along with their father, William Sr., they engaged in agricultural pursuits and stock-raising for a number of years in partnership. In 1870, the Hutchinson brothers moved their headquarters to North Powder, where James lived for a short time, and the partnership continued until 1900. It was a very successful business, and when the partnership was dissolved, they divided about 4,000 acres between them.

The *Eastern Oregon Directory, 1900, page 231*, enumerates a public listing of people living in North Powder. In it is listed Hutchinson Brothers with 1000 acres valued at $19,550.

Thereafter William R. continued farming and stock raising. By 1912, he was one of the largest landowners in Union County, with about 4,000 acres. A large section of that was under cultivation and the rest was in pasture.

William R. was considered a highly successful rancher and businessman. At the age of 39, he married Miss Isabelle Asbury of Baker County on December 2, 1885. She was the daughter of Wesley and Susan (Mitchell) Asbury, former natives of North Carolina and Illinois respectively.

To their union was added four children: Dora Belle (1886-1966), Ralph William (1888-1959), Stephen Asbury (1889-1976), and Mrs. Mabel Elsie Withycombe (1891-1959).

Siblings Stephen Hutchinson and Dora Hutchinson, apparently single all their lives, remained living at home with their father, William R., helping on the farm and assisting him, especially after the death of their mother, Isabelle, on September 25, 1918 at Hot Lake in Union County. William R. died on December 2, 1923 at his home in Union and was buried at the Union Cemetery in the family plot.

His obituary published on *January 29, 1923 in the La Grande Observer*, stated:

"William R. Hutchinson, 78, one of the early pioneers of Union County, died at his home north of Union early Sunday morning after a brief illness. Mr. Hutchinson and his daughter, Dora, both were ill with pneumonia at the same time, but the daughter is much improved in health and able to be up again." (End of obit)

As for James H. Hutchinson, he was a Union banker and a prosperous rancher. In 1912, he was chosen as county commissioner to replace a man who resigned, but in 1914, he also resigned, stating that he just did not have time to carry out the required duties because of his personal business affairs.

James Hutchinson, 74, died on September 14, 1917, and he left a wife, Mary Frances, and 8 children. He left land to his wife and son, William H. Hutchinson, in the Union area as seen on the *1935 Metsker Map* of Union.

Hutchinson Lane stands as a memorial to these two brothers, who worked hard as stock raisers and farmers. If they were alive today, they would be proud to know that the lane that bears their name is home to Grande Ronde Dairy, a thriving goat dairy farm run by equally ambitious ranchers and farmers Byron and Stephanie Rovey. They have set a national record as the first dairy in the United States with a GEA rotary milking parlor. *(Rovey Interview 2016; Oregon Pictorial and Biographical Deluxe Supplement, S. J. Clarke Publishing Co., Chicago, 1912)*

Igo Road - Formerly Whiting-Igo Road #88 runs 1.50 miles west off of Mount Glen Road and is located in Township 2S R38E Section 16 in the La Grande maintenance district.

The Whiting part of this road name originates with Edward Lucian Whiting (1846-1926) and his wife, Martha (Alleman) Whiting (1849-1936). Martha was born December 12, 1849 in Iowa and came to Utah with her parents in 1853. Edward L. Whiting and Martha were married on August 3, 1874 in Salt Lake City, Utah.

During their marriage, they became parents to four children, all born in Utah: Edward D. (1875-1964), John (1880-1954), Christiann "Ella" (1886-1967), later Mrs. Waite; William (1892-1894), and Charlotte Almyra, (1896-1977), later Mrs. Harvey Larsen.

The Whiting family came to Union County, Oregon in time to be on the *1900 Federal Census*. In the *1910 Federal Census,* it stated that he also worked as a saw mill worker. Edward engaged in farming until his death on December 31, 1926.

His obituary reads: "Blackhawk War Veteran Passes—E. L. Whiting, one of the earlier Utah pioneers dies at Mt. Glen. Edward Lucian Whiting, veteran of the Blackhawk Indian War and one of the earlier Utah pioneers, who crossed the plains to Springville with an ox team, died at Mt. Glen this morning.

Funeral services will be held from the Bohnenkamp Chapel, but the time is indefinite, awaiting word from relatives in California.

The deceased, who was born June 28, 1846, at Nauvoo, Ill., came west early in his life. After residing in Utah many years, he came to La Grande a quarter a century ago and made his home in the Grande Ronde Valley until his death.

He is survived by his widow, Martha Elizabeth Alleman Whiting, and four children: Edward D. Whiting of La Grande; John L. Whiting of Calpine, Cal.; Ella Waite of La Grande and Mrs. Harvey B. Larsen, of Perry, Ore." (End of obit) *(La Grande Observer, Dec. 31, 1926, pg. 1)*

From this point, the story turns to his son, Edward D. Whiting, born June 17, 1875 in Springville, Utah. He was a graduate of Brigham Young University in 1894.

Edward D. helped his father on the farm, and on February 10, 1904, he married Mary E. Olsen in Salt Lake City. Mary was born October 7, 1877 in Logan, Utah.

During the marriage of Edward D. and Mary Whiting, they had three children of their own. In addition, over the years, they fostered 34 other children in their home. Their children were Blanche (1905-1956), later Mrs. A. L. Quebbeman; Edward J. (1909-1911), and Anna Mae (1917-2004), later Mrs. J. C. Flower. In 1940, both of his daughters were single and still living at home and listed as teachers.

Edward D. was engaged in farming, but in addition to this, he was associated with the Whiting and Black Real Estate firm and also the Causey Real Estate firm. "Over a period of time, they sold over 100,000 acres of property in Union and Wallowa counties." *(La Grande Observer, Feb. 11, 1954, pg. 3)*

He died on October 31, 1964 in La Grande, Oregon and was buried at Hillcrest Cemetery in La Grande. Mary died September 19, 1970 in Pendleton and was also buried in Hillcrest Cemetery.

The second part of this road name, Igo, is the one that endured the test of time, and the Whiting name was dropped from the road sign.

Igo Road is named after Vernon Lester Igo, the second child of four children born to Charles Lewis Igo (1863-1915) and Atha Jane "Jennie" Veal (1859-1925). When Vernon relocated to Union County, he purchased the H. Warmholz barber shop in the new Foley building. *(La Grande Observer, May 26, 1937, pg. 8)*

It appears that he had been married more than once. He had a wife in 1937 and three daughters, LaVerta, LaVerne, and Lorene; and a son, Vernon Jr. The latter daughter stayed behind with her husband in Kansas, and the rest of the family joined Vernon in the Grande Ronde Valley in June 1937. He took on a partner, Roy Grice, in 1939, when the barber shop was called Vernon's Barber Shop. *(La Grande Observer, May 9, 1939, pg. 5)*

One of their daughters, Lorene, was visiting from Kansas. She married Doyle Myron Eisiminger, and Lorene died in Imbler, Oregon. *(La Grande Observer, Aug. 6, 1940, pg. 2)*

Vernon Igo, 49, worked in the ship yards in Bremerton, Washington in 1943, where he and Clysta "Iva" Neal, 42, were married on November 15, 1943 by a justice of the peace in Pierce County, Washington. *(Washington County Marriages)*

In 1953, he bought the Noel Bottling Company, 1408 Jefferson St., La Grande and changed the name to Igo Bottling Company. *(La Grande Observer, Jan. 7, 1953, pg. 6)*

They moved the business later that year to the corner of Fir and Madison Streets in La Grande, about a half a block from its previous location.

In 1954, Vernon bought a registered brown Swiss bull named Mount Fannie Gold Brick. *(La Grande Observer, June 28, 1954, pg. 5)*

Before August 1960, Vernon sold the bottling company to George W. Bruce. Iva died August 18, 1970, and Vernon died on April 1, 1988 at the age of 96 years. Both are interred at the Island City Cemetery.

Imbler Road - Formerly Imbler-Ruckman Road, this gravel road #35A runs north-south and connects with Hull Lane on the north end and Speckhart Road on the south end. It runs 4.01 miles through Township 1S R39E Section 29 in the Imbler maintenance district.

In 1988, Imbler Road was chosen as the permanent name for this road. (See Ruckman Road entry) Imbler Road is so named after successful farmers and stock-raisers, Jesse and Esther (Masiker) Imbler, who homesteaded land in the Imbler area in 1868. Modern-day family genealogists say the surname was spelled Imler without the "b" letter in it, but in Union County, it has always been spelled Imbler.

Jesse Imbler was born in Kentucky on May 26, 1842, and he came west with his parents to Iowa in 1845. In 1853, he came across the Oregon Trail with his father, who made his home near Eugene. *(Michael Imler Dopson interview, Feb. 3, 2019)*

After living in Eugene for a time, they relocated to Dufur, where they lived for a few years, engaging in extensive cattle operations.

In Dufur, Jesse married Miss Esther Masiker of Yamhill County on January 4, 1866. They had six children, two of whom died in early life. Four children survived to adulthood: Alfred E. (1867-1938), Ellis A. (1871-1934), Lillie Mae Greene (1877-1943), and Royal Ray (1881-1954). *(Ancestry.com)*

In 1868, the Imbler family moved to the Grande Ronde Valley. Each eligible family member took out a claim of land under the Homestead Act and started raising stock. Over the next 20 years, Jesse Imbler's success as a stock-raiser became evident in both his land holdings and in his stock. He acquired 1,000 acres for cultivation and pasture of his stock. He supervised his farming and stock-raising operation personally, which was another secret to his success.

By 1889, he had improved his herds to include 120 high-grade Hereford and Durham short-horn cattle and a considerable number of high-grade Norman Percheron horses, which he imported by himself and were the first of their kind in this district.

It was on his land that the town of Imbler was platted in 1891. Imbler Road was named in honor of Jesse Imbler, and within the city limits there is a street named after his wife Esther on which all of the Imbler public schools are located. *(History of the Pacific Northwest: Oregon and Washington, Vol. II, 1889)*

During his 33-year residency in Union County, Jesse Imbler served as a county commissioner twice. He also had the great misfortune of serving on the 12-man jury at the courthouse in Union from February 12-16, 1896, a jury that, some say, wrongly convicted bachelor farmer Kelsey Porter of Pine Valley.

At the time, Oregon newspapers called the Porter case the "trial of the century." Due to the distant sources of these newspapers and the imperfect conveyance of information by wire, their sensational trial coverage stirred up strong emotional opinions among residents of Union County. When a conviction was rendered by the jury, there was a great public outcry, and the case was appealed, but failed to be overturned. Neither did the Governor commute Porter's sentence, despite the petition of at least 400 Panhandle residents. *(Porter vs State of Oregon, Salem, trial transcripts 1896-1897)*

Historically, the outcome of the Porter case was one of the primary causative reasons for the annexation of the Panhandle to Baker County and the reassignment of the county seat from Union to La Grande in 1905. Union had been the county seat from 1874 until 1905, but without the support of the Panhandle residents following Porter's conviction, Union lost the county seat to La Grande.

The Porter conviction was such a pivotal event in Union County history that it ultimately redrew the map of Union County in 1905, yet it is barely mentioned in most history annuls. Only a few historians or journalists today have any notes on this case or realize how it reshaped Union County. It's almost lost history except for its brief mention herein. Despite its significant historical value, the new Union County courthouse in La Grande did not have the complete 300-page trial transcript in its attic. The bulk of the trial archives are held in Salem.

Kelsey Porter's grave is located in Union Cemetery, but both the spelling of his first name and his death date are incorrectly engraved on the grave stone. For the longest time, he rested in peace without a headstone, but a local historian, John Evans, led the effort to set one on his grave lot. Sadly, the information on it is not accurate. The authors have found Porter's complete signature in the trial transcripts, and this record has printed it just like he signed his name. The authors also informed the secretary of the Union Cemetery of the correct information, and she has made a record of it in her office files.

Articles written much later have called his death "the only legal hanging in Union County history." Commenting on this, some historians have stated that had this case gone to trial today with modern investigation techniques, crime scene processing and forensics, there would never have been a conviction. The truth will never be known in this world. What the authors did discover was Jesse Imbler's reaction to all of this.

Jesse Imbler, a man of strong moral convictions may have felt a twinge of conscience over the conviction or perhaps he felt personally unsafe after his involvement on the jury; but either way, soon thereafter, in 1897, he and his wife Esther (1849-1912) left Union County and did not return. Instead, they moved into the home of their son, Albert E. Imbler, near Talent, Oregon. Jesse Imbler died on December 17, 1908 at the home of his son.

"All four Imbler children were present by his side when he died. He was conscious to the last and bid his loved ones a fond farewell with the hope of meeting them again. Among his last words were "The Lord is my Shepherd, I shall not want." Burial took place in Ashland Cemetery. *(The Hood River Glacier, December 31, 1908)*

Jesse Jackson Imbler (1842-1908) was buried at Hargadine Cemetery in Ashland, Jackson County, Oregon. *(Family genealogist Michael Imler Dopson, email Feb. 4, 2019)* Esther died on January 12, 1912 in Grants Pass, Josephine County, Oregon. She was buried in the same cemetery next to her husband.

Indian Creek Road - This road is named after Indian Creek. According to Charlie Horn, Elgin Museum curator, Indian Creek was one of the first creeks named in the Indian Valley territory. *(Charlie Horn interview, September 7, 2021)*

Indian Creek Road exits east off of Highway 82 toward Elgin and takes a bend south at Dutton Road. Right at this juncture is the Indian Creek Cemetery with a few burials.

The southern most end of Indian Creek Road has long been called Klinghammer-McNab Road *(1935 Metsker Map)*. That stretch of the road #54 ran for 2.96 miles in length in Township 1S R39E Section 12 in the Imbler maintenance district. The northern stretch of this road, located in Township 1N R39E Section 27 runs 4.26 miles and is designated as road #53 in the Imbler maintenance district.

The Klinghammer portion of the road name came from John and Anna (Schenker) Klinghammer, farmers who had land along this section of the road. The Klinghammers came to Elgin in the fall of 1898, according to Anna's obituary. They had 10 children and 6 lived to adulthood: Charles, Hugo, Otto, Reinhold, Ida Hallgarth, and Walter. Their father John died on June 6, 1925 and their mother Anna died on September 16, 1948. They are both interred at the Elgin Cemetery.

The McNab portion of the early road name was taken from Charles Henry McNab (1866-1934) and his wife Louisa McNab (1873-1951). Charles immigrated to the U.S. from Canada, where he was born and later naturalized in 1885. His father was born in Ireland and his mother in Canada. Charles and Louisa were married about 1905, and they farmed. They had two sons, Francis "Frank" J. McNab (1906-1980) and Albert "Harry" McNab (1907-1960).

The Klinghammer-McNab road name was not chosen as the road's permanent name. Instead the road was renamed Indian Creek Road after a tributary which was given its name in the late 1860s by the first settlers, who discovered many Indian artifacts in the valley where Elgin is located today.

It was common to see the Nez Perce Indians along the creek and thus its name. One story about Indian Creek was told by Mickey Endicott Blemenstein, as she related about her father, Ulric Ernest Endicott, and his brother John Richard Endicott and their encounter with the Indians on Indian Creek.

"Quite early during their first year on Indian Creek, there was a warm spring day. Father, who was then 8 years old, and his brother John decided they should go swimming. They asked their mother's permission. She said, 'Decidedly not. It is too early and cold.' They did, however, gain consent to go to the creek and throw rocks in the water and to fish.

Out of the sight of the house they found an inviting hole that looked like an ideal swimming hole. They piled their clothing in two neat little piles and dove in. What a surprise! The icy water of the creek was not like streams in Missouri. They gasped for breath from the shock of the cold. Yet when they raised their heads above water and took a look at the creek bank, they received a greater shock.

Standing by each pile of clothes was a big Indian. Up to their necks in water they stood still, frozen with fear and freezing from the icy water. Soon their teeth were chattering like castanets.

To keep from freezing to death, they worked their way up the creek and then ran for their lives toward the house. The Indians did not chase them, only roared with laughter. Naked and blue from cold, they bolted into the house. Their mother started the warming process with a generous use of a paddle.

When their father went to look for their clothes, the Indians were gone and the two piles of clothing were just as the boys had left them. Father always said that no one could tell him that Indians do not have a sense of humor." *(Bernal Hug's 1961 Annual Supplement to History of Union County Oregon, pg 55-56)*

Industrial Lane - This road #152 is .19 miles in length and brings access to about several businesses in Township 2S R38E Section 35. It departs from Pierce Road to an industrial park area on the east side of Highway 82.

Island Avenue - This avenue travels through Island City, a city originally described as an island formed by a slough of the Grande Ronde River. As a result, prior to 1900, it was common for the city to be called "the Island" even on legal paperwork.

After extensive ditching by farmers and others, the land dried to create Island City, what some refer to as a suburb of La Grande. The city's post office was established on April 10, 1873, and Marshall B. Mallory was the first postmaster.

The post office was discontinued on October 31, 1959, after which it underwent a change of status to Island City rural station of La Grande, but that was also discontinued on September 30, 1972. Now the two cities share the same zip code, 98750. *(Oregon Post Offices 1847-1982, Richard W. Helbock)*

Island Avenue is a main thoroughfare through Island City and into La Grande's downtown area. There is a business district on both sides of this avenue, including banks, small businesses of all types and Walmart.

Janson Lane - This gravel lane designated county road #26A is .46 miles long and is located in Township 2S R39E Section 5. It exits Highway 82 heading east and ends when it intersects Imbler Road.

It is named after Sven Johan Janson, born in Sweden on March 23, 1853 and immigrated to the U.S.

in 1885 with Utah as his destination.

He married Charlotte J. Sandahl in Sweden. They had nine children: Enoch (1884-1973) born in Sweden; Aaron (1886-1969), Nephi (1887-1961), Sylvia (1890-1942), Linnea (1892-1983), Alva (1894-1910), Theodore (1896-1983), Victor (1898-1954), Ruth (1899-1980) all born in Logan, Utah, and George H. (1903-1988) born in the Alicel area on May 23, 1903.

Sometime between 1899 and 1903, the family relocated to the property on what became Janson Lane in the Alicel area. This property had one house and a barn, both built in 1890 by its prior owner. It is still the only residence on the lane.

In the *May 20, 1922 La Grande Observer, pg. 28,* he was noted as being paid $224.00 for a right-of-way through his property, making way for the construction of Highway 82.

Though the lane name is spelled by its Swedish form Janson, the family evidently decided to Anglicize their name to Johnson, as seen in their obituaries and cemetery records.

In early January 1940, Charlotte "Johnson" was mentioned in the newspaper. "Mrs. Johnson is critically ill at her home north of Alicel." *(La Grande Observer, Jan. 2, 1940, pg. 8)* A day or two later, she died of her illness. Some of her family had gathered around her at that time.

Swen Johnson, 90, died on November 24, 1943 at the home of daughter, Mrs. C. R. Gekeler of La Grande. Surviving children were Enoch and Victor of Alicel, Aaron of Los Angeles, California; Nephi of Pocatello, Idaho, Theodore of Cove, George and Ruth Johnson of The Dalles, and Mrs. C. R. Gekeler of La Grande.

Swen and Charlotte were interred in Summerville Cemetery under the name spelling Swen and Charlotte "Johnson." However, the Janson Lane spelling preserves their Swedish heritage to this day.

Jimmy Creek Road - This road #72 is 5.40 miles in length in Township 6S R39E Section 11 in the North Powder district.

This road is named after a stream called Jimmy Creek, which empties into the Powder River about three and a half miles northeast of the city of North Powder. It also feeds into the large Jimmy Creek Reservoir, which is located half way between Highway 237, the Union to North Powder highway and Interstate 84.

It turns out that Jimmy Creek is named after a pioneer settler named James "Jimmie" Dalton, who homesteaded about one quarter mile from the creek. He had become almost lost history because none of the old-timers in the area remembered him, but thanks to public records, the authors have found him.

On a September 4, 1863 Union County survey map, the creek was called Cove Creek, but a month later on an October 31, 1863 Union County survey map, it was noted as Clover Creek. Then there was a first mention of Jimmy Creek in a 1888 newspaper issue. That is also the year when the Jimmy Creek School district #53 was established for children in this section of North Powder. On a 1906 Telocaset quad map, it noted Jimmy Creek on it.

The namesake of Jimmy Creek was already a history that was not recalled by anyone the authors approached. Neither long-time cattleman Jack Wilson, 91, of North Powder nor Don George, 92, of Union, ditch digger for Wilson and Davis ranchers, had any remembrance about who Jimmy Creek was named after. Don George said he worked on 80 miles of ditches for Wilson, and although he knew exactly where Jimmy Creek was located, he never heard the story of how it got its name.

Consequently, retrieving the history of Jimmy Creek was looking bleak had it not been for donation land records and plat maps. Now with confidence, the authors can say that Jimmy Creek and Jimmy Creek Road were named after a pioneer homesteader by the name of James "Jimmie" Dalton, who was born March 27, 1864 in Tennessee, son of Thomas and Jeanette (Lawhanner) Dalton, and his obituary stated that he came to North Powder territory in 1883.

There he homesteaded and started buying land, including the NE 1/4 of the NE 1/4 of Section 11 in Township 6S 39E, which is one quarter mile from what is now Jimmy Creek. Over the next couple of years and as late as 1911, he added numerous other parcels of land totaling several hundred acres, some of which were adjoined to the Old Oregon Trail.

On October 20, 1886, he married Cora E. Nelson in Baker City. They had one child, a son, James "Wiley" Dalton, born February 9, 1893 in North Powder. *(Oregon U.S. County Marriage Records; Baker County Marriages, BYU Vol 1, pg 18)*

Apparently, he suspended his farming in 1889 and took up work temporarily in North Powder. "James Dalton has moved his family to town. Jimmie is mixing drinks at Schiedhauer's saloon." *(Oregon Scout, Oct. 3, 1889, pg. 1)* This news briefly revealed that he was commonly called Jimmie.

Later records revealed that he retained ownership of his farm lands even after moving into town in 1889. The *1900 Federal Census* indicates that he was back on his land as a farmer. James Dalton entered other business pursuits in addition to farming and ranching.

"Mill Sold—The North Powder flouring mill has been sold to a company consisting of James Dalton, Oscar Jacobson and others. We understand that the present owners will continue in control until next spring." *(La Grande Observer, Oct. 17, 1903, pg. 1)*

His wife, Cora, died August 21, 1904 and was buried at Mount Hope Cemetery in Baker City.

He appeared on the *1910 Federal Census* for the Haines precinct, and he operated his own farm with the help of two hired men, who lived in the same household, and a housekeeper, who he later fell in love with and married.

In 1915, James Dalton bought more land. "Summer home at Wallowa Lake. James Dalton, the well-known North Powder stockman and capitalist, is having a vacation in Wallowa County. The Joseph Herald reports that Mr. Dalton has purchased from E. T. Schleur seven acres at the head of the lake—formerly the Jack Humphrey place. He will erect there a neat, little bungalow and make it his summer home in the future." *(La Grande Observer, Oct. 16, 1915, pg. 4)*

On August 14, 1916, James Dalton married his second wife and housekeeper, Mrs. Rose Springer, and the following article noted their marriage.

"North Powder couple marry. North Powder, Oregon, August 17—James Dalton, wealthy rancher and stockman of North Powder and Mrs. Rose Springer of the same place were united in marriage at St. Anthony, Idaho, August 14th. Both the bride and the groom are well known people of this section, especially Mr. Dalton, who came here in his early boyhood from Tennessee, and by industry and business ability has become one of our foremost citizens. He is a self-made man in every respect and stands high in the esteem of the community, as does his wife. They have just completed a honeymoon trip to Yellowstone Park and have returned here to receive the congratulations of their many friends. Their trip through the park was made in company with Mr. and Mrs. H. A. Monday, also of this place." *(La Grande Observer, August 18, 1916, pg. 1)*

In 1917, it appears that the Daltons were renting out their farm land, slowly retiring from active farming. They also enjoyed seeing their new home completed that year at Wallowa Lake. It had spring water piped in from the nearby spring and electricity for heating and lighting. The home had a large fireplace in the dining room. *(La Grande Observer, August 9, 1917, pg. 3)*

The *1920 Federal Census of Portland* noted that James and Rose lived in Oak Grove, an unincorporated community in Clackamas County, Oregon, and part of the metropolitan Portland precinct. He was listed as a farmer and his household included his aged father-in-law, George Springer, 86, and his widowed sister-in-law, Lula Mays, 49.

On Wednesday, April 13, 1932, they came to conduct business and visit their son, Wiley, who was living on the Dalton Ranch in North Powder, when James Dalton lost control of his vehicle at the highway viaduct at Telocaset and struck the guardrail and concrete abutment. James and his wife died as a result of that crash, and their son Wiley, who was in the rear seat, survived with some injuries.

"Mr. and Mrs. Dalton, who owned two ranches in the vicinity of North Powder, resided there for 38 years, but in 1924, left for Oak Grove. She was about 60 years of age and he was about 75. They were visiting their son, who lives on the Dalton Ranch." *(La Grande Observer, April 14, 1932, pg. 1-2)*

Their combined obituary published in the *North Powder News, Friday, April 15, 1932* stated in part:

"James Dalton, universally known as 'Jim' Dalton, was born at Marshtown, Tenn., and his age is given at about 69 years. (d/c states 68 years and 16 days)

He came to North Powder a year before the railroad was built on from La Grande, arriving here in 1883. He purchased railroad land and was successful in a business way from the first, we are told. The present Dalton Ranch, joining for a mile or more the Old Oregon Trail two miles from North Powder, was acquired in the early days and has one of the older water rights from the North Powder River.

Mr. Dalton was married after coming to Oregon to Cora E. Mitchel, and J. Wylie, the injured son, is the only surviving child. Mrs. Cora Dalton was a native of Michigan, her birth occurring February

24, 1861. She died April 21, 1904.

Jim Dalton, married Rose Springer of Baker, who met death with her husband, Wednesday at the age of 54 years. Two sisters and one brother in Baker survive her.

Two brothers: Grant Dalton of Baker and C. R. (Curt) Dalton of North Powder survive. They came from their Tennessee home a few years after Jim came west.

North Powder was Dalton's home until a dozen years ago when he moved to Oak Grove. He arrived here Monday to attend to business matters.

Pall bearers for Jim Dalton will be the following well-known men of this city and Baker: Chris Johnson, H. F. White, H. A. Monday, J. B. Wilson, of North Powder and George Foster and J. C. Sturgill of Baker.

Judge C. H. McCollock of Baker and M. M. Gilkison and R. E. Haines of North Powder will serve as pall bearers for Mrs. Dalton, with three others yet to be selected at Baker." (end of obit)

The mysterious namesake for Jimmy Creek Road has finally been solved, thanks again to land records and newspaper archives. This history has been compiled and preserved in this publication should anyone need to know, "Who's Jimmy?"

Jones Road - Formerly Hallgarth Road #81A in Township 1N R39E Section 16 is a short one, only about an eighth of a mile and then it dead ends. Resident farmer Michael Hays stated that it was formerly called Hallgarth Road and was renamed Jones Road in 1988. *(Interview with Michael Hays, September 2, 2021)*

Jones Road is located off Highway 204 between Valley View Road and Middle Road.

The Jones Road was named after Joseph W. Jones (1868-1935) and his wife Agnes McNaughton (1869-1954), farmers in the area where Jones Road is located.

Joseph farmed until his death on January 25, 1935, and his obituary described his life this way: "Joseph W. Jones Dies at Elgin" — Joseph W. Jones, pioneer resident of Elgin, died at his home this morning after a long illness. Born in Deer Lodge, Montana, May 30, 1866, he came to the Grande Ronde valley 54 years ago, making his home at Elgin since. He was 68 years, seven months and 26 days of age.

Mr. Jones was survived by his widow, Mrs. Agnes Jones; a son, Glen, of Elgin; a stepson Robert J. Brack, of La Grande; five grandchildren; a sister, Mrs. Martha Shelton, of Elgin, and a brother, David Jones, of Lowden, Washington. *(End of obit, La Grande Observer, Friday, January 25, 1935, pg. 1)*

Agnes Jones was born at Knoxville, Iowa, November 9, 1869, the daughter of Dr. Thomas McNaughton. The family then moved to Elgin, Oregon, where her father practiced medicine. She married her first husband, Adam Brack, of Iowa City, Iowa, on September 10, 1890 in Island City. He contracted consumption (tuberculosis), so the young couple returned to his hometown of Iowa

City, Iowa, where he eventually died on April 21, 1892. He was buried in Saint Joseph Cemetery Old in that city.

Following his death, the widowed Agnes Brack and her son, Robert J. Brack, returned to Elgin to her own family. They were both counted in the *1900 Federal Census of Elgin,* as members of the Rachel Jones household, including the widow Rachel Jones, 67, son David M. Jones, 37, farmer and son Joseph W. Jones, 34, farm laborer. Joseph took a liking to Agnes, and they were married on February 13, 1905 in Union County

In 1939, Agnes' son Robert J. Brack died at the age of 45. She lived on another 15 years before she died at 84 years of age on Saturday, June 5, 1954. She died at the local hospital (La Grande) following a long illness. Services were held and interment was at the Elgin Cemetery.

All told, Agnes was a resident of Elgin for 69 years. She was survived by a son, Glen W. Jones, of La Grande, her stepmother, Mrs. Sadie McNaughton of Pendleton, five sisters, eight grandchildren, and 10 great-grandchildren. *(La Grande Observer, Monday, June 7, 1954, pg. 2)*

The Jones couple may have lived a quiet life on their farm, but as long as the Jones Road sign stands upright, there will be a public reminder that they once lived, laughed and loved here.

Kamela Highway - This road has one residence on it, and it leads to the tiny community of Kamela, where at one time it included a post office that operated from 1887 to 1949 and a train station.

"Kamela was, during the stagecoach period, known as Summit Station. This was unsatisfactory to the railroad company, and J. C. Mayo of Stayton informed the compiler in 1927 that Dr. W. C. McKay was asked to furnish a number of names of Indian origin which could be used at various points on the line. From this list, Kamela was selected. Mr. Mayo said it meant black pine, although as far as the compiler knows there are not many of these trees in the neighborhood.

The official interpretor at Umatilla Agency said in 1927 that Kamela was a Nez Perce word meaning Tamarack, and this ought to settle the matter." *(Oregon Geographic Names, 7ʰ edition, pg. 523)*

"James Riley Warnstaff [of the Fox Hill-Robbs Hill area] was one of the drivers on the horse-drawn stage between La Grande and Walla Walla via the Meacham--Deadman's Pass area. Remnants of the stage road he traveled are marked at the Oregon Trail Interpretive Site near the I-84 and Kamela junction." *(Clayton Warnstaff's memoirs, donated by Dallas Hibbert, October 17, 2021)*

Keen Cabin Creek Road - This gravel road #82 is 3.62 miles in length and is located Township 2N R39E Section 21 in the Elgin maintenance district. (Part of this was shown as Palmer Junction on the *1935 Metsker Map*.)

From the supplement to *History of Union County #6 by editor Bernal D. Hug, page 48*, there is an explanation on the "Cabin Creek Road" part of this name.

"Cabin Creek received its name because in early days some hunter or prospector built a cabin on its bank besides the trail to the Grande Ronde and Indian valleys. In later years, a little logging took place on this side of the valley, and loggers commenced building their cabins at this location. This added to the reason for the name."

As for the surname Keen in this road name, it refers to the family of William Isaac "Ike" Keen Jr. (1876-1955) and his first wife, Effie P. Walker (1873-1920).

Both William and Effie were born in Arkansas where they married on January 23, 1898. They had a son William Era Keen born in November 1898 and a daughter Alva Keen, born on October 27, 1902. The young family is noted on the *1900 Federal Census of Arkansas*. After this, the family moved to the Elgin, Oregon area by 1904, when the last of their three children, Albert T. Keen, was born on July 19, 1904.

In the *1910 Federal Census of Elgin, Oregon,* William's occupation was recorded as an edger in a saw mill. Little 8-year-old Alva was listed on the census, but she died on April 15, 1910 and was buried at the Elgin Cemetery.

By 1920, William was listed on the census as a farmer in the Elgin precinct #1 on what was then called Foothill Road, and Effie was a housewife. However, ten days after the census was taken, Effie died on January 31, 1920.

Their son, Era, and daughter-in-law, Frances Helen Craig, a native of Detroit, Michigan, were then living in the William and Effie Keen household during that census year. Era was occupied as a logger in a logging camp. Era and Miss Frances "Helen" Craig were married in Detroit, but made their home in Elgin, where Era accepted a position with a local lumber company.

In the *1930 Federal Census*, William was a laborer at odd jobs. In the *1940 Federal Census,* William was living with Era and Helen. William's youngest son, Albert, had been living in Los Angeles, California in 1941, and employed by California Lumber and Moulding Company.

In 1937, Era Keen had his own logging trucks and was employed by H. F. Reed Lumber Company in Elgin. Mention was made of him in the *La Grande Observer of July 30, 1937, page 7*. It read that after some community fund-raising for light poles and illuminators for the baseball field at the school playground, Era Keen's logging trucks hauled the six 90-foot-long poles from the mountains to the site, where they were peeled and set in 10-foot-deep holes. Each of the six baseball teams worked on one hole to accomplish this labor. It took them three evenings to set the poles with help and equipment owned by William "Bill" Moore, owner of Pondosa Pine Lumber Company. Nearly 100 men volunteered to work at erecting outdoor lights on the baseball field. This would have cost about $1,500 in labor had they paid someone to do this work commercially.

It is of note to add that William was married twice in his lifetime. On August 7, 1924, William married Flora J. McKenzie. She was born in 1864 in Canada. She came to this country in 1907, and this was her second marriage as well. She had a son, Murray Durham, by her first marriage. She died October 6, 1947 and was buried in the Elgin Cemetery.

William survived her and later died on July 12, 1955 in the La Grande hospital from an extended illness. He was buried in the Elgin Cemetery. At the time of his death, both of his surviving sons were living in California. This ended the Keen family residency on Keen-Cabin Creek Road.

Kerns Loop - This road #114 is 1.17 miles in length in Township 2S R40E Section 20 in the La Grande maintenance district. It diverts from and reconnects to Lower Cove Road, and it brings access to seven properties.

The loop was named after the Melvin Sr. and Emma Kerns family, who farmed there. Emma's obituary tells an interesting story about this pioneer family.

"Mary Kern, a Pioneer, Dead" — Crossed Plains with ox team in 1862, Many years a resident of Walla Walla, then Alicel." *(La Grande Observer, Monday, May 20, 1912, Pg. 7)*

It continues, "Emma Mary Kerns died May 14, 1912 at Alicel, Oregon. She was born in Iowa on November 20, 1861; crossed the plains in 1862 with her parents, Lewis and Mary Randall by ox team and settled on the foot hills of Walla Walla valley. In 1880, she was married to A.S. Turner of Richmond, Va., at Walla Walla, where they made their home until the spring of 1886, when they moved to Spokane. Mr. Turner being drowned in the Spokane river July 15, 1886.

In 1888, she was married to Melvin Kerns in Walla Walla, afterwards moving to the Grande Ronde valley on July 10, 1892, where she has made her home since. She leaves three sisters, Mrs. J. B. Kenney, Mrs. Wiley Shelton and Mrs. J. N. Boyd of Walla Walla and four brothers, John, William, Edward and George Randall.

She was the mother of nine children, six of whom are living (in 1912): Ross Turner and Melvin Kerns Jr. of Pine Valley, Lloyd Kerns of Medford, Oregon, Ethel, Mabel and Helen Kerns who are with their father, Melvin Kerns Sr. at their home in Alicel (Kerns Loop location); Lewis Turner, Maude and baby Kerns, who are laid to rest." (End of obit).

In 1926, Melvin Kerns Sr. died, and as noted in the *1930 Federal Census*, the three Kerns siblings, Ethel, 38, Melvin Jr., 36, and Helen E Kerns, 26, all single, were managing the farm together. Ethel Mae (May) Kerns had ownership of the land, about 400 acres on Kerns Loop, as noted in the *1935 Metsker Map.*

In late December of 1928, Ethel Kerns sued Union County and some individuals for damages due to their condemnation of her property on Lower Cove for a right of way for the market road. The Lower Cove market lane was built across her land in 1927 (likely creating the Kerns Loop section today).

The case was tried in Baker County, and in 1931, she won the case and $2,778 in damages. Union County appealed the case, and it went to the Oregon Supreme Court, but the *July 9, 1932 La Grande Observer, page 1* reported that the Oregon Supreme Court upheld the lower court's decision in favor of Kerns. She persevered, showing herself to be a woman of determination.

At some future time, Melvin Kerns Jr. moved to Portland, where he died in 1966. Ethel sold the farm, after which she and her sister, Helen, moved to Buena Park, California. Ethel died there in 1972 and Helen in 1984.

Kingsbury Lane - This road #78A runs 2.86 miles in length in Township 2N R39E in the Elgin maintenance district. It connects Darr road on the west and Palmer Junction on the east in rural Elgin.

It is named after Mr. Shirley Francis Kingsbury, who was born December 13, 1882 in Jacksonville, Indiana and died April 23, 1954 in the hospital in Pendleton and was buried in Island City Cemetery.

He married his first wife Margaret Kaziah Sutton in Idaho in 1906, and they had two children, Arthur (1909) and Alta (1910). According to the *1920 Federal Census of Portland*, Shirley Kingsbury was living there alone. At some point, he returned to Idaho, where on August 18, 1924, he entered his second marriage with Nora Marie Geer (1899-1983).

His obituary published in the *La Grande Observer, September 24, 1954 pg. 4* states in part: "Shirley Kingsbury Dies in Pendleton — Mr. Shirley Francis Kingsbury, 71 year old retired farmer of 1020 Y Avenue, La Grande, died in a Pendleton hospital yesterday following a short illness.

Funeral services are scheduled for 2 p.m. Monday in the Daniel's Funeral Home with burial in Island City Cemetery.

A native of Indiana, Mr. Kingsbury was born December 27, 1882 and had lived in La Grande (the county) for 27 years.

Survivors include the widow, Nora M. Kingsbury of La Grande, a daughter, Mrs. Loy Gossler, Stanfield; a step-brother, Dean Isaacs of Boise, a step-sister, Mrs. Lou Shaeffer of Caldwell and one grandchild." (End of obit)

The *La Grande Observer, October 15, 1927 page 6* states that Shirley and Nora Kingsbury recently moved from Idaho to the Catherine Creek area, where they had traded for the ranch formerly owned by Ed Gillispie.

The next move they made was noted in *the La Grande Observer, April 18, 1939, page 8*. It stated that the Kingsburys of Catherine Creek traded their interest there and moved to the Elgin area. Prior to August of 1942, they held a dinner party for several guests at their home in Cove. *(La Grande Observer, August 1, 1942, pg. 3)*

Their final move as a couple was noted in the *La Grande Observer, August 29, 1951 page 5,* which stated that they sold their property in Cove to Carl Elmer of Lower Cove and were moving to a home they purchased in La Grande. This appears to have been their final home. After Shirley's death, Nora moved back to Idaho, where she lived the remainder of her life.

Today, there are no residents living on Kingsbury Road in rural Elgin.

Knight Lane - This gravel lane, designated road #138 is .75 miles in length and is located in Township 1N R40E Section 14, exiting Roulet Loop out on the Cricket Flat of Union County.

There are three residents on this lane, and Patricia Ann Knight lived in one of those. She was the great granddaughter of the lane's namesake, Willard Boliver Knight (1849-1934).

Willard's ancestors were North Carolina stock, including his grandfather Joseph Knight (1772-1852) and his father William Woodson Knight (1805-1860).

Willard Boliver Knight had a son, Jesse Knight (1887-1953), a grandson Oscar C. Knight (1909-1997) and great granddaughter Patricia Knight (1944-2018), who are all part of the Knight Lane history.

The Knight's immigration story started after the Civil War in spring 1865, when Willard Boliver Knight and some of his brothers came to the Grande Ronde Valley. Willard was a teenager when they came across the plains with ox teams, and upon arriving, he helped on his father's farm. Several of his brothers acquired land in Union County.

Willard grew to manhood and eventually received the patent for his homestead in Union County in 1883. He and his wife, Mary Ann Smith, had four children: Emma, Lucy Ellen (Brugger-Allen), Jesse and George. She died in 1927, but he lived an additional seven years.

"Mr. Knight is one of the oldest residents of the Cricket Flat section and has lived in the same home for over a half a century." *(La Grande Observer, Dec. 2, 1931, pg. 8)*

Willard Knight died on Jan. 25, 1934 at his home eight miles east of Elgin after a short illness. He lived nearly 70 years in Union County. He was 84 years, one month and 30 days of age at death. He was buried at Elgin Cemetery beside his wife, who died on May 23, 1927.

Now we turn our focus to Willard's son, Jesse B. Knight (1887-1953). Jesse was born August 14, 1887 in Union County, and he married LaVonna Mason Page (1890-1984) on November 7, 1907 in Union County, according to the *Oregon U.S. Marriage Records film #001689581.* Jesse Knight died March 3, 1953 in La Grande, Oregon and was interred at the Elgin Cemetery.

Jesse's obituary from the *Elgin Recorder of March 5, 1953, pg. 1* stated in part:

"Jesse Knight, retired Elgin farmer, died at the age of 65 at a La Grande hospital on Tuesday, March 3. He had been in failing health for a number of years, and in the last few months his condition became critical.

He was born at Elgin on August 14, 1887, the son of pioneer parents who had homesteaded the Knight ranch nine miles east of Elgin at the foot of Stubblefield Mountain. Here Jesse Knight grew up and after his folks were gone, stayed on to farm the land, adding to the original homestead site with additional acreage. He retired from active work in 1942. Last fall, he moved to Elgin, where they would be near their son, Oscar C. Knight.

Jesse Knight and LaVona Page of Elgin were married Nov. 7, 1906. He was survived by his widow and their son Oscar; by two sisters, Mrs. Lucie Allen of La Grande, and Mrs. Emma Richards of Cove; one brother Roy Knight of Baker." [End of obituary]

His parents were William Bolivar Knight (1849-1934) and Mary Ann Smith Knight (1854-1927). His siblings were: Lucy Ellen Allen (1876-1963), George Leroy Knight (1878-1963) and Emma Rosella Richards (1891-1963). The siblings all died in 1963—a sorrowful year for the family.

Jesse's wife, LaVona Knight, was born September 8, 1890 in Polk County, Missouri. She died February 3, 1984 in Union County and was buried at the Elgin Cemetery.

Now we will turn out attention Jesse's son Oscar Clarence Knight, who was born March 29, 1909 in Elgin, Oregon. He was married twice: M#1 on March 23, 1934 in Union County to Cleora Leilla Frost; and M#2 on May 11, 1943 in Missoula, Montana to Elizabeth Ann Hoffner.

Oscar Knight received his pilot's license on January 12, 1940. The account was mentioned in an article as follows titled, "2 La Granders Earn Pilots' Licenses."

It read: "Two members of the La Grande Flying club have been granted solo flying licenses by the civil aeronautics authority, with seven others now flying solo and awaiting more solo tests by the CAA in March, Wesley F. Brownton, club secretary announced today.

Those who took the CAA examination and obtained licenses were Oscar Knight, Elgin, and William Arrivey, La Grande. Both were given their licenses Friday after both practical and written tests before Charles Walker, CAA inspector from Portland.

The club's training plane has been going up, under instruction by Art Walters, whenever weather permits. The club membership, he said, has grown to 22." *[End of article, La Grande Observer, Jan. 15, 1940, pg. 1)*

Knight purchased his own plane, and he flew in and out of Elgin on a regular basis. On December 18, 1941, Union County was planning a blackout night (all lights out), and Oscar was going to fly over the city of La Grande to see how effective such a blackout would be. *(La Grande Observer, Dec. 18, 1941, pg. 1)*

After the war, he got involved with the Elgin Flying Club and was instrumental in building a 3-plane hanger at the Chandler Air Field in Elgin. *(La Grande Observer, July 19, 1946, pg. 1)*

He also had a service station in Elgin. One of his advertising post cards read: "Stalled Again and not a service station in sight! You won't have to cuss and fuss if you will have your car regularly service by us. With our King Motor Testers all motor troubles are quickly and accurately located. O. C. Knight, Standard Stations, Inc., Elgin, Oregon, Authorized Distributors."

Another advertising card read: "We can Increase Your Motor Efficiency. You will marvel at the big improvement we can make in your motor after our 'King' Tester has checked up on your motor and ignition system. It is a 'Sherlock Holmes' when it comes to locating trouble. Drive in and let us check your car. We will increase your motor efficiency. O. C. Knight, Standard Stations, Inc., Elgin, Oregon."

Oscar Knight died August 26, 1997 in Bothell, Washington and was buried in Kent, Washington at the Tahoma National Cemetery.

Oscar's second wife, Elizabeth Ann Knight, was born in Pilot Rock, Oregon, August 23, 1913, the daughter of Jim and Elizabeth Hoffner, one of eight children. She was an athletic woman who climbed Mount Rainier for one ski run and tried out for the Women's Olympics in swimming. She died April 17, 2003. She had four children: Patricia, Douglas, James and Frank. *(Seattle Times,*

Next in line on the farm was Patricia Knight, a professional photographer, who lived on Knight Lane in a rustic wooden cabin. The structure was at least 100 years old, and in it, she surrounded herself with art, photography and Native American crafts. She was well known in Northeast Oregon, and she organized the "Art Rocks" community art show at Stella Mayfield School during one of the annual Elgin Riverfests. She had many friends, including Scott and Katie Ludwig of Elgin, her neighbors who made themselves available to help her when needed. As Pat declined in health, she received home health visits at her cabin. Pat died following a lingering illness, and she was mourned by many friends.

Her obituary stated in part: "Patricia Ann Knight was born June 6, 1944 to Oscar and Elizabeth Knight. The oldest of four children, Pat attended school in Elgin and Milton-Freewater, where she was active in ballet and was crowned Pea Festival Princess and Miss Walla Walla. She attended Eastern Oregon College and the University of Portland where she studied to be a social worker.

Pat was very involved in the Native American community and considered the Umatilla tribe her extended family. Pat spent most of her life as a working photographer, both freelance and in commercial studios. Her work has been featured in galleries and publications throughout the Northwest including Native American cultural centers. Her biggest joy was teaching photography to aspiring artists of all ages.

Pat returned to the Knight ranch outside of Elgin, Oregon and had spent the last two decades teaching photography, showing in galleries (in La Grande and Pendleton) and selling specialty food products. It is here she felt the most at home.

Pat passed away in Milton-Freewater on October 9, 2018 and is survived by her son Michael Stinnett of Soldotna, Alaska, and grandchildren Joshua, Aiden and Caileigh; and daughter Mary Lee of Bellevue, Wash., and grandson Dylan Gary. She is survived by her three brothers, Douglas, James and Francis, as well as many nieces and nephews. The family will host a memorial service in the Elgin/Pendleton area in honor of Pat's 75th birthday in June 2019." *[End of obituary, East Oregonian, Oct. 15, 2018]*

Pat was a frequent art client at the Mitre's Touch Gallery in Pat's Alley, La Grande, where her work was always on display for sale. She had a showing of her photography there, and through this association, the authors came to know her and support her work. Over the course of 20 years, the authors made frequent visits to see Pat at her cabin home where our conversations revolved around art, the Bible, creation and spirituality, all topics of personal intrigue to Pat.

Kofford Road - This gravel road #66A is short, only .39 miles in length, located in Township 4S R40E Section 20 in the Union maintenance district.

This road is named after James Arthur Kofford (1880-1957). James was born November 19, 1880 in Paris, Bear Lake County, Idaho. to Christopher and Nancy Kofford.

Christopher Anthon Kofford was born February 19, 1841 in Barnholm, Denmark, coming to America in April 1857 on the ship West Moreland. He arrived in the port of Philadelphia in May

1857 and arrived at his destination in Utah by 1860. James' mother, Nancy Rich Kofford, was born 1853 in Utah, and married Christopher on November 21, 1876. *(La Grande Observer, Nov. 18, 1929, pg 1)*

The subject of this road story, James Kofford, married Julia Pearl Stevens (1884-1929) in 1905 in Big Horn County, Wyoming. They made their first residence in Otto, Big Horn County, Wyoming, where they started their family: Vivian (1906), Florence (1907) and Kenneth (1908).

After Kenneth's birth, the family relocated to rural Union, Oregon, to continue farming. There, they welcomed baby Beulah on July 14, 1909, followed by sons Don (1911) and Edwin (1913). Their daughter, Miss Florence Kofford, 16, a junior at Union High School fell sick with influenza and died of pneumonia at her home in January 1923—a sad day for the family. There was also a baby girl Kofford, who was born and died on January 17, 1926 in Hot Lake, Oregon.

James Kofford was a farmer all his life, and his family appeared on the *1910 Federal Census* in what was described as Union Precinct #2. By 1920, they were listed on the Union Precinct # 3 & 4 Federal Census, where they were owning a home with a mortgage.

In 1918, he registered for the draft for World War I. In the paperwork, he described himself as able-bodied, having blue eyes, brown hair, medium height and build. He stated that he was self-employed as a farmer and married to Julia Pearl Kofford at the time.

Sadly, Julia Kofford died on April 24, 1929 at Hot Lake Sanatorium. On June 10, 1936, James Kofford married his second wife, Mildred Lindsay Bean in Logan, Utah. The next year on January 21, 1937 about 3 p.m., a fire broke out at their farm home. Most of the furniture was saved, and the relatively new house was insured for $1,100. *(La Grande Observer, January 22, 1937, pg 1)*

By mid-March 1937, the Koffords were in the process of rebuilding a new residence to take the place of the home which was completely destroyed by fire a few months earlier. *(La Grande Observer, March 16, 1937, pg 6)*

The Koffords shared another 20 years together, and then on April 2, 1957, James Kofford, 76, died at his home as a result of a heart attack. He had lived in Union County for 47 years. He was buried in the Union Cemetery. Surviving him was his widow, Mildred, two daughters and three sons. He had two brothers, Fred and Wilford, who lived in Pendleton.

After James' death, Mildred moved to La Grande and then to Los Angeles near her daughter, where she died at the age of 74 on September 26, 1963. She was born in New Zealand. Her burial took place at Hillcrest Cemetery in La Grande.

Ladd Creek Road - This road and for that matter Ladd Creek were named for John R. and Rachel Ladd, who "in 1862, during the gold rush to Auburn near Baker City, built a cabin and hotel at the foot of the hill, where the wagon road entered the Grande Ronde Valley. By the time of John's death 25 years later, he owned 4,500 acres of the valley." *(The La Grande Observer, March 18, 2011, pg. 1B Travel, "Portion of valley's original wetlands come to life at Ladd Marsh" by Mark Highberger.)*

John Ladd was born in New York on October 25, 1838, and in 1852, he came with his father to

California. He returned to Illinois to marry Miss Rachel Knapp on October 12, 1860 in Henry County.

Rachel Knapp was born October 7, 1843 in Illinois. At the time she married John Ladd, she was living as a tenant with relatives in Cambridge, Henry County, Illinois. *(1860 Federal Census)* During her marriage, she became the mother of two children, Eva (Ladd) Andross (1861-1949), who was born in Illinois and Charles W. Ladd (1863-1932), who was born in Oregon.

In 1862, John and Rachel intended to relocate to the Salmon River mines, but instead, they settled in what became Ladd Canyon in the Grande Ronde Valley. At this spot, they built a cabin and due to its location on the direct route to the mines, they saw great potential for a livelihood as a hotel.

As such, there were times when John and Rachel Ladd fed a hundred men at a meal, and they charged a handsome price of a dollar each. They turned a good profit feeding people at a time when a pound of beef soup could be purchased for just four cents and a dozen eggs for twenty cents.

He and Rachel spent the year1865 in Walla Walla after which they returned to their Ladd Canyon home. John Ladd engaged in the lucrative business of freighting for the next five years. Then he settled down into raising stock and farming.

"In 1867, he bought one hundred and sixty acres of land for three thousand dollars, which one freighting trip to Idaho paid for, and took one hundred and sixty more of government land. In 1877, he put on a stage line from Wallowa to Grande Ronde, and in after years owned several other stage lines in other East-of-the-Mountains regions." *(History of the Pacific Northwest: Oregon and Washington, Vol. II, 1889.)*

John Ladd acquired 4,500 acres by 1887, all in the Grande Ronde Valley. He was quite the entrepreneur, operating a livery stable, raising stock, including large flocks of sheep. Beside ranch lands, he owned quite a bit of city properties in both La Grande and Pendleton.

John Ladd died October 14, 1887, at the age of 49 years. For this era in history, 46 years was the average lifespan, so he fit into the normal parameters of the time. As he was a prominent man in Union County with a wide association of business contacts, his death was duly noted and mourned by many. He was interred in the Hillcrest Cemetery in La Grande, joined later by his wife, Rachel.

Following his death, Rachel Ladd continued living at their home in Island City, Oregon, and has the care of his estate. Her daughter Eva is the wife of M. D. Andross of Island City; and her son, Charles W. Ladd, is a stock-raiser and farmer of the Grande Ronde. (See Alicel Lane)

Rachel was remarried briefly, after John Ladd's death, to David Benjamin Hilts, a native of Ontario, Canada, then living in Baker City, Baker County, Oregon. He lived in Union County with Rachel, where he died on Jan. 28, 1890.

Sometime after 1914, Rachel relocated to Portland where she lived with her companion Rozina White, 73, until her death on November 22, 1922 at the age of 79 years. *(1920 Federal Census)* Her remains were transported from Portland to La Grande for funeral services at the Bohnenkamp chapel. *(Obit, La Grande Observer, Nov. 24, 1922)*

Lakeview Lane - This is a private lane located in Township 3S R38E Section 17 in the La Grande maintenance district.

Lampkin Lane - This road #73B runs .44 miles in Township 6S R39E Sections 4-5 in the North Powder maintenance district. It comes off the relocated Old Oregon Trail Highway on the west side of North Powder.

This lane is named after William Thomas Lampkin (1877-1936), a native of Missouri, and his first wife, Bertha (1879-1913) of Pennsylvania. She died in Malheur County, Oregon.

During their marriage they had three children born to them while living in Colorado: Thomas Ethelbert, born 1902; Ruth, born 1903; and Thelma, born 1905.

After Bertha's death, William Lampkin married Susan Wilson (1877-1971). She died in North Powder. In 1920, they lived in Council, Idaho. Between then and 1927, they came to settle in the North Powder area.

On his ranch, he grew 100 acres of flax to see how well it would do. He also owned a gravel pit, and in 1932, the Wolf Creek Road was surfaced with gravel from the Lampkin's pit. *(La Grande Observer, July 25, 1932, pg. 1)*

In 1936, he shipped a railroad carload of fat cattle to Portland along with five other local ranchers. On April 29, 1936, he died unexpectedly in an automobile accident. He was 56 years of age at the time of his death. He was buried in Ontario, Oregon. Details of his accident were published in the *La Grande Observer, April 30, 1936 on page 1.*

Following his death, his son, Thomas E. Lampkin, who had a successful career as a pharmacist in a Seattle drug store, came home to operate the family ranch. He did use his education to fill in for local pharmacists when they had a need for time off.

In 1948, Thomas filed to run for Union County commissioner, but he lost the race to Ray Baum. However, he did win the hand of Mrs. Blanche Morris in marriage on October 13, 1948. Together, they continued working the wheat and cattle ranch. In 1949, Thomas was elected to the North Powder School District Board, where he was quite active as chair of a school study group.

Thomas Lampkin was honored as the Conservation Man of the Year in 1960 by the Union County Wheat Growers Association. The ensuing newspaper article read:

"Before Lampkin initiated soil and water conservation practices much of the land was gutted. He seeded four miles of sod waterways in alfalfa and grass and then turned his attention to his roving hills.

In 1957, he tried a three-point subsoiler on 221 acres. He estimates today that 90% to 95% of future run off drains into the soil after the hardpan was broken down. Proof of this is his increase of ten bushels of wheat per acre.

Lampkin also has turned his attention to weed control, and he worked for five years on one hard to kill thistle patch." *(La Grande Observer, August 10, 1960, pg. 1)*

His step-mother, Susan Lampkin, was still active on the family farm, taking delivery of a Cat-6 tractor for use on the ranch. *(La Grande Observer, August 10, 1957, pg. 4)* Susan died on August 10, 1971 in North Powder, where she was interred at the city cemetery there.

Thomas died in 1987 and is buried in North Powder Cemetery. Blanche died 1994 and is also buried there.

Lantz Lane - This road #120 runs 1.11 miles in Township 3S R40E Section 10 in the Union maintenance district. It is named after J. K. Lantz, Cove orchardist who came to the area in 1902 and purchased a 55- acre fruit ranch. *(La Grande Observer, Feb. 28, 1902, pg. 4)*

He came here from Woodburn, Oregon. He called his place "Fairview Fruit Farm." *(La Grande Observer, Dec. 20, 1912, pg. 4)* In 1914, he was paid by the county $36.60 as a fruit inspector. *(La Grande Observer, May 26, 1914, pg. 2)*

J. K. Lantz was born October 20, 1860 in Pennsylvania and died at his home in Cove on January 28, 1922. He married Miss Lydia Lantz in Illinois and they had five children: Harvey, Roy, Louis, and daughters Mabel and Bessie. *(La Grande Observer, Jan. 31, 1922, pg. 4)*

Lariat Drive - This is a private drive in Township 1N R39E Section 15 in the Elgin maintenance district.

Lark Road - This private road in Township 3S R38E Section 4 in the La Grande maintenance district. It is one in a series of five roads named after birds and a mobile home park community that is located off Fruitdale Lane.

Leffel Road - Formerly Chandler Road, according to Dale G. Chandler. (See Chandler Loop) This gravel county road #13 is 2.40 miles in length and located in Township 2S R38E in Section 32-33 in the La Grande maintenance district.

Leffel Road was named after Homer Volney Leffel, who was born November 9, 1895 (or 1896) in North Manchester, Wabash County, Indiana. *(1917 Draft Registration says 1895; grave stone says 1896)*

His parents were Alvin W. Leffel (1867-1938) and Mary Catherine Blood (1869-1952). He had a sister, Vera Kimenia (Leffel) Wattenburg (1893-1933).

Homer's family left Rochester, Indiana and moved to La Grande in 1902, where his father Alvin W. Leffel became occupied as a railroad conductor for years. In Homer's primary grades, he attended the old White School, located on the corner of Second Street and K Avenue in La Grande. *(La Grande School District #1, pg. XII, Dave Yerges, 2009)*

In the *1910 Federal Census*, when he was 15, he was a boarder living in La Grande. It was common for rural students to board with families that lived close to the school they wanted to attend. If not for that provision, many rural students would not have gone to high school.   In this case, it was La Grande High School (LHS). Homer V. Leffel graduated from LHS in May 1914. *(Class photo in La Grande Observer, May 16, 1914, pg. 7)*

Homer continued his education, attending one year at University of Oregon, where he was a member of the Phi Delta Theta fraternity. There he took classes in formal dancing, something that he enjoyed for decades to come.

After college, in December 1915, he started working for J. C. Penney Store in La Grande as a stock clerk, rose to manager in 1931 and retired in 1956. For seven years, he worked at other   J. C. Penney stores. In 1924, he managed the store in Washington, Pennsylvania. Then he was sent to Dickinson, North Dakota, and about 1930, he worked at the store in Kokomo, Indiana.

Merchandising was very different in 1915, according to Homer in a newspaper interview. He said, "clothing was displayed on wires strung across the salesroom and hung from the ceiling. Merchandise (in the window) was placed in piles either in the shipping boxes with the cover removed or outside the boxes folded neatly. No mannequins were used and considerable care was exercised in displaying 'unmentionables' since it was considered poor taste to permit them to be seen."

Homer told a reporter that business advertising in the *La Grande Observer* cost 15 cents per column inch in 1915. A good men's suit cost $15, and a cheaper one ran $10. These suits were always blue serge, and every gentleman owned one that he wore to all functions of importance, including weddings, funerals, parties and dances.

Homer loved to spend time on weekends dancing. He was one of five founders of a dance group in 1916 called Watch Your Step Club, and they hosted dances at the Riverside Park Pavilion. The war interrupted his dancing for a year or so, but when he returned, he resumed working at   J. C. Penney and dancing.

In the 1920s and 1930s, there weren't too many things for young people to do for group recreation, Homer recalled, so they went to dance halls. Dance halls were all the rave, and Zuber Hall on Washington Avenue just behind Goss Motors store was one of four dance halls in La Grande in addition to the Riverside Park Pavilion, where dances were held in the summers.

His dance group held dances regularly. "They were very formal, and we'd send out invitations and had tally cards as was the standard. Tally cards were to keep track of your dances. You sign up and should always dance every other dance with the girl you took. That was mandatory, but you still traded dances that way."   Most of the dances were fox trots, waltzes, two-steps and three step dances.

But when Homer tried to dance these styles at Zuber Hall, he ran into some trouble, when he didn't meet the standard of moral dancing. La Grande was designated as having the cleanest dancing in the Northwest and dance floor managers were policing dancers to keep it that way.

A front page article of the *La Grande Observer of December 16, 1921* explained this era of clean dancing. "During the past few weeks, P. J. Powers has investigated conditions in Walla Walla,

Pendleton, Baker and La Grande, making a visit to every dance hall in these cities and as the result of his investigation, he announced today that there is no doubt that La Grande has the cleanest dances of any city in the Northwest."

Dancing master P. J. Powers of Medical Springs was the self-proclaimed dance hall investigator, and he explained his criteria of clean dancing in this article.

He said, "Dances are good and clean if they are danced as they should be danced. If dancing is taught in this manner there can be no objection, but individual styles creep in and these usually result in corruption. No reputable dancing master will allow such demoralization of dances under his direction, and it is to the credit of the floor manager of the dances in this city that they have succeeded in putting into effect a code of behavior that places La Grande far above the cities surrounding her."

He went on to suggest that "practically all the signs of objectionable dancing could be eliminated if the floor managers of dances were required to post the names of all dancers ordered off the floor for improper dancing."

Had floor managers followed such strict procedures, Homer would have been on that list. Homer said, "I remember I took a friend of mine down to Zuber Hall, and they kicked us off for indecent dancing. We were dancing too close. They gave me my money back and told us 'we don't want you here.'"

Homer said he took dancing lessons at the University of Oregon and that explains his close dancing. "All I was doing was what the university dances looked like," he said. "Everybody did them, and I didn't think anything of it."

Throughout his life in La Grande, Homer was active in the community. He was a member of the City Commission for six years, two as president and was also very involved with other civic groups in the area. He also enjoy fishing and hunting as time permitted it.

In his personal life, Homer was married twice, first on August 1, 1924 in Kokomo, Indiana to Lois Jane Comstock (1900-1941). He and Lois had three children, Lorna J., Janet C. and a son John A., who was born on May 13, 1933. *(La Grande Observer, May 15, 1933, pg. 1)*

Homer's father died in 1938, so he took his mother into his family home, and she was noted on the *1940 Federal Census for La Grande.* Then sadly, his wife, Lois, 41, died on June 29, 1941. She was buried in the family lot in the Masonic Cemetery in La Grande. *(La Grande Observer, June 30, 1941, pg. 1, obit.)*

Then Homer married his second wife, Mrs. Leona Ethelbert (Newlin) McNamee (1896-1965) formerly of Seattle, Washington. They were married in Vancouver, Clark County, Washington, on July 9, 1942. He and Leona made their home in La Grande immediately following their wedding, and together they finished raising Homer's three children. Leona was also involved in civic organizations during her marriage to Homer, and she died August 22, 1965.

Homer V. Leffel died in Pendleton, Oregon on June 7, 1986 at the age of 89 years and was buried in Hillcrest Cemetery, La Grande, Oregon. It could be said of him that he was a committed individual, loyal to his community and a generous volunteer.

Leopard Drive - This is a private drive in Township 3S R40E Section 22 in the Union maintenance district.

Lester Road - This private road runs north off of Igo Lane in rural La Grande in Township 2S R38E Section 17.

It's named after Russell "Glenn" Lester, who was born May 22, 1914 in Liberty Township, Clarke County, Iowa, the son of Lathette and Myrtle (Young) Lester.

Glenn Lester's first marriage was to Geraldine Ethelda Beymer on January 12, 1939 in Iowa. She died September 5, 1945 in Iowa. Then he became engaged to Marie Cleaver in La Grande, and they were married on April 3, 1949 in La Grande.   She was born January 16, 1927, and was a well-known La Grande girl. *(La Grande Observer, Jan. 21, 1949, pg. 3)*

His third and last wife was Martha "Marty" H. born July 25, 1931. After being widowed, she lived in Blaine, Washington in 1993.

Glenn died September 30, 1985 in La Grande and was buried in Grandview Cemetery in La Grande. The data base lists "Martha H." as his last wife.

Glenn and Marie Lester of Swan River, Iowa, made annual trips to this area with their six children. *(La Grande Observer, Aug. 6, 1956, pg. 4)* During Glenn's 1957 visit to Union County, he bought a 200-acre farm in the Igo Lane area—he liked the area so well. In 1959, he planted cherry trees on this property. *(La Grande Observer, July 3, 1959, pg. 7)*

In 1962, he was a board member of the Grande Ronde Symphony. *(La Grande Observer, Oct. 2, 1962, pg. 1)*

In a 1963 advertisement, he was listed as a salesman for Ranch-N-Home Realty on 1103 Adams Avenue in La Grande. *(La Grande Observer, Dec. 5, 1963, pg. 5)* It was after this work experience that he founded his own realty business, Lester Real Estate. As a realtor, he developed several properties and owned buildings in La Grande.

When he retired, his son, Russell L. Lester took over, renaming the building Coldwell Banker Lester Real Estate. *(Russell L. Lester interview, June 26, 2018)*

Levi Lane - This is a private lane in Township 1N R39E Section 9 in the Elgin maintenance district.

Little Creek Lane - This public, unmaintained lane is very short, only .53 miles in length in Township 4S R39E Section 12 in the Union maintenance district.

Its name has gone through a bit of a transformation. It was named after a creek east of Union called Little Juliana Creek. *(1863 Map and 1935 Metsker Map)* The legend about its early name states it was named after the younger sister of Catherine Godley. However, that story seems improbable for the main reason that they were not in Union County when the creek was given its name. (See Catherine Creek Lane entry)

It has always been held that Catherine Creek and the smaller tributary, Juliana Creek, were named after sisters from the same family; however, Juliana Creek has, at different times, been shown on road petition maps and county maps by other names. The county surveyor on all these road petitions was consistently Mr. Willis Skiff, but the road viewers were different people, who may have used other creek names at various times on documentation they generated.

The following road petitions show the Juliana Creek with different names. Road petition #36 in April 1871 called it Elizabeth Creek. The various documents making up road petition #75 in February 20, 1876 refers to the same creek by three different names: Little Creek and July Ann Creek and Julia Ann Creek. Road petition #77 in March 7, 1876 called the creek again by the name Elizabeth Creek, and the documents making up road petition #81 in April 4, 1876 called the creek Little Creek and Juliana Creek.

All of the aforementioned petitions, except for #36, have the same legal description of starting and ending points of the road, so there is no doubt they are also talking about the same creek.

Perhaps the Juliana in this creek name was a young girl or woman from among the Canadian French community that settled in the territory before other pioneers did.

In any case, the name Little Juliana Creek did not endure the test of time. In place of that name, the creek was renamed Little Creek and the road, Little Creek Lane. *(Donna Patterson interview, Feb. 2, 2019)*

Livestock Road - This private road brings access to the Intermountain Livestock Company property in Township 3S R38E Section 15 in the La Grande maintenance district. Unless you are looking to sell or buy livestock, this road would probably not be a good choice for a Sunday drive.

Lizabeth Lane - This is a public unmaintained road located directly west of Ackles Cemetery on Mt. Glenn Road in Township 2S R38E Sections 21-28. It brings access to three properties and runs only .47 miles in length. It was a long driveway flanked regally on either side by some mature black locust trees.

One of the residences at the end of Lizabeth Lane is the Monte and Teri Carnes home and farm, which was purchased in 1937 by Monte's parents, George Lester and Gladys (Scott) Carnes. Monte lived in the same house since the age of two. He raised hogs and grain on his family's farm until his death at home on November 4, 2005.

Teri Carnes recalled when the county contacted them, explaining that they needed to select a name for the road leading to their home. They had never thought of their long driveway as a county road before, but under the definitions of the new ordinance #1988-3, any road bringing access to three or more buildings must be named for the purpose of directing emergency services with expediency.

Consequently, after considering a lot of names, and excluding Carnes Road and any words having to do with their pig farm, Monte and Teri Carnes were baffled at what to call it. Finally, they decided to name their lane after a little girl, Lizabeth Garten, who lived next door to their home for a short time. That's how the name Lizabeth Road came into existence. "It has no historical significance," Teri Carnes said.

The Carnes' home is a lovely turn-of-the-century bungalow built in 1919 by Frederick and Emily (Chadwick) Zaugg. The stones mortared into the flanks of the front staircase were taken from the farm fields.

According to the Federick Zaugg oral history, published by the *Union County, Oregon History Project*, he was born April 26, 1869 in Colombier, Switzerland, and he emigrated to America in May 1884. He married Emily Chadwick on March 5, 1891 in Logan, Utah, and they were noted in the *1900 Federal Census* in Box Elder, Utah.

Frederick Zaugg stated in his oral history that he came to Union County in 1911. They chose a beautiful property to farm on Mt. Glen Road, built a house in 1919, and farmed the land during the 1920 and 1930 censuses. By the mid-1930s, the Great Depression made it impossible for them to operate the farm. They were one of many farmers facing foreclosure because of the widespread financial collapse of the economy.

As a result, they lost the farm—just four months before the U.S. Government decided to assist struggling farmers, explained Teri Carnes. Up until then, banks were holding title to too many foreclosed farms, so the U.S. Government was on the verge of giving farmers a little relief so they would not lose their farms. That relief came too late for the Zaugg family, however. *(Teri Carnes interview, October 30, 2021)*

As a result, Frederick Zaugg, his wife and large family, relocated to West Point, Utah, to farm there, according to the *1940 Federal Census*. Frederick must have reflected often on his misfortune in Union County, Oregon, leaving behind a house and outbuildings he constructed, not to mention the beautifully cultivated fields around his home. These were the things that spoke about the Zaugg family after they left. All memory of their life there slowly faded into the limbo of forgotten things, that is, until their long driveway needed a road sign and name.

In 1988 when Monte and Teri Carnes chose Lizabeth as the road name, they had no awareness that Lizabeth was a variant spelling of Frederick Zaugg's mother's name, Elisabeth Zaugg. Teri Carnes thought Lizabeth Lane had no historical significance, but, in fact, she and Monte inadvertently created a memorial sign to the Zaugg family.

Elisabeth Zaugg (1842-1887) of Erlach, Bern, Switzerland lived just long enough to hug and kiss her son Frederick goodbye as he left Switzerland for a new life in America. Perhaps the Zaugg family would find some comfort to learn that Lizabeth Lane does honor their pioneer ancestor, Frederick Zaugg, and if he were living today, he would be very pleased to see this.

As for Lizabeth Garten, the little neighbor girl—Teri Carnes does not know her whereabouts, but this little girl, now a grown woman, might be very surprised to learn that her lovely name is on a green metal road sign at the residence where she lived briefly once upon a time.

Longview Lane - This private lane near Cove brings access to five properties.

Lookingglass Road - This private road is located in Township 3N R40E Section 29 and diverts off of Moses Creek Lane north of Elgin and runs north about 2 miles following Lookingglass Creek all the way to Lookingglass Fish Hatchery.

The name Lookingglass has two sources, one being the Nez Perce Chief Lookingglass, whose Indian name was Apash-wa-hay-ikt. The second is a geographic description.

"The confluence of the creek and Grande Ronde River was a favorite picnicking spot in the 1870s and 1880s. There was a large tree with a hole in its trunk. One could look through this hole, and when the light was right, see reflections on the water." *(Oregon Geographic Names, Seventh Edition, pg. 590; Horner papers, pg. 954)*

According to local history, Lookingglass country had three unofficial mayors: Frank Baker, mayor of Lower Lookingglass; Frank Killian, mayor of Palmer Valley; and Soapy Davis, mayor of Upper Lookingglass. *(Elgin Recorder, Oct. 28, 1954)* This entry will expound on the legendary Soapy Davis (1884-1954), Elgin's Mountain Man of Lookingglass.

"Soapy Davis" was born Ira Cleveland Davis in Athens, Athens County, Ohio on September 1, 1884, the son of Lysander K. Davis (1853-1918) and Lillian Ann Mansfield (1861-1896). He was the fifth of thirteen children born to his parents.

At the time of the *1900 Federal Census*, the Davis family was still living in Athens, Ohio. Ira was 15, working as a cook in that city, a skill that he used extensively in his adult life in Oregon.

In 1902, Ira's father remarried twice in Muncie, Indiana. The Davis family was living in nearby Eaton, Indiana, from 1902 to 1918. Ira and his siblings are noted in the Eaton city directory during the years 1909 to 1913, each gainfully employed. Ira was listed each year as a laborer.

Then in 1913, Ira asserted his independence from the family and moved to Elgin, Union County, Oregon, where he immediately forged hunting and trapping friendships with locals, Frank Hallgarth, John Shelton, Jay Johns and James Hallgarth. *(See 150 Photographs of Elgin and North Union County, pg. 140)*

He used his savings to buy a saloon in Elgin. As people saw him frequently washing his saloon windows with soapy wash water, they began calling him "Soapy Davis," a nickname that stuck with him the rest of his life.

He operated the saloon from 1913 through 1915. On January 1, 1916, Oregon "went dry" due to the enforcement of the state prohibition on alcohol and saloons. While some saloons in Elgin morphed into soda fountain stores and pool halls, Soapy decided to close up business in December 1915.

At this juncture, Soapy decided to visit his father and siblings in Eaton, Indiana. His father was in his mid-sixties then, proprietor of a shoe repair shop in Eaton, living there with his third wife, Dora. Soapy's visit there was timely because his father died about two years later on May 8, 1918 while Soapy was still out East.

After visiting his father, he traveled to Hackett, Washington County, Pennsylvania, where he found work as a labor foreman. In that county, he met a woman 20 years his senior, a widow named Mrs. Anna Belle (Lutes) Chase. They were married on April 24, 1917 in Hackett, Pennsylvania.

(Pennsylvania marriages, ancestry.com) Anna was born May 17, 1865 and was nearly 52 years old at the time of her wedding, and Soapy was 32.

It wasn't long and Soapy was missing the Blue Mountains of Elgin, Oregon, but Anna was not interested in moving there. She lived 52 years of her life in Washington County, Pennsylvania, and everyone she knew and loved lived there in that mining country. She did not want to give up her life there for the primitive and isolated life Soapy wanted to live in the Blue Mountains of Northeast Oregon. Soapy and Anna had been married such a short time, maybe three years, and they were at an impasse. She would not go, and he would not stay.

The July 7, 1948 La Grande Observer told the story with diplomatic delicacy. "His young wife preferred to stay in Pennsylvania. So Davis told her goodbye and headed west. He hasn't seen or heard of his wife since."

By then it was 1921, and he packed up his belongings and moved to an abandoned cabin that he knew about from his earlier years of hunting and trapping in the Lookingglass country. He became a squatter on this property at first.

The cabin was built in 1883 by Ed Alexander, located about 100 feet from Lookingglass Creek and 19 miles north of Elgin and about five miles west of the Rondowa train stop. The cabin was on part of a 30,000 acre sheep ranch owned by Enoch Pearson and his wife Tillie Pearson of Pendleton. Following Enoch's death in 1935, it was owned by their son, Laverne Enoch Pearson.

The Pearsons admired Soapy's independent personality, so they allowed him to stay at the cabin free of rent if he would maintain the property for them. They also paid him to pack in supplies from Elgin to the sheep camp during grazing times of the year.

He was living off the grid at the Alexander cabin with no telephone service. He engineered piping to bring in running water from a nearby spring, and he made improvements to the cabin. With the help of two friends, he packed in a Kalamazoo five-hole stove and oven for cooking. He covered the floors on the second story bunk rooms of the cabin with bear hides, and made the cabin as efficient as possible with a hide-away wall ironing board, a Murphy bed and a hidden kitchen table in the wall that sat 15 people in the great room.

Near the Alexander cabin, up in the hills, he had a well hidden still, and he produced "Lookingglass moonshine." He used seven of his burros, ranging in size from a horse down to an oversized dog, each packing liquor kegs appropriate for their size.

"In the dark, he would load up his mule train, head for civilization (Elgin) and peddle his merchandise. He never got caught, being a little too slippery (or soapy) for the law to nail the evidence on him." *(Elgin Recorder obituary, Oct. 28, 1954)* Of course, it helped when the police chief was his personal friend too.

"Whenever Soapy came to town with his moonshine, it was like a holiday," Richard Cason of Elgin said. "All the men would rush down to the back of The Brunswick and buy moonshine from him. He unloaded his burros and let them roam freely in town with his mare while he handled business."

With frequency, Soapy came into the city of Elgin for supplies, mail and to do necessary business or to pick up visitors. Otherwise, he had no use for city life. He said, "Town life and I simply could not get along." Still, Soapy was well liked by just about everyone he met. (See Moses Creek Lane entry)

When he did come to town, he didn't stay at the Sommer Hotel. Roy Hills of Island City explained, "I remember when Soapy Davis came in from the Lookingglass, he'd stay overnight doing his business. Now, Soapy never had a place to stay overnight, so the police chief let him sleep overnight in a cell. Now, that's the kind of Elgin I would like to see again." *(La Grande Observer, Feb. 12, 2012, Roy Hills' Letter to the Editor)*

In 1946, Soapy received mail advising him that he was going to get a visit from his brother, Frank C. Davis, sister-in-law and 17-year-old niece, Miss Goldie Nagey. It was an overdue reunion, 29 years in the waiting, but they stayed with Soapy for most of the summer at the Alexander cabin. While with him, they saw just how occupied he was, checking and setting traps throughout the mountains each day. He was a self-sufficient man in many ways and a great host and cook whenever company arrived.

The newspaper article covering this news stated that the two Davis brothers last visited together in 1917, when Soapy traveled to the East Coast to visit relatives after a lapse of many years and to see his brother off to war in Europe. Another brother, James "Hugh" Davis and his wife, Nellie, also made the trip from DePue, Illinois, to join the family reunion with Soapy.

Soapy enjoyed the mountain man lifestyle, and he had no regrets. He said, "Some people consider me crazy for living way out here all alone, but I like it. Wouldn't live anywhere else." *(La Grande Observer, July 7, 1948, pg. 1)*

Though very satisfied with his lifestyle, there was one thing that he showed some concern over. "He wonders if his friends—the sportsmen whom he entertained so much—will see that he gets a respectable funeral some day." *(La Grande Observer, July 7, 1948, pg. 1)*

"In March 1953, Soapy suffered a heart attack that just about laid him low," stated his obituary in the *Elgin Recorder*. He had to leave his beloved cabin so that he could be cared for by dear friends in Elgin. Initially, Mrs. Lena Wilson was his nurse maid as he stayed at the home of his old buddy Jay Johns, and then Soapy moved to the old folks' home at Hot Lake where his last days were spent in visiting with old friends who went there to see him. Then about mid-October of 1954, he suffered another heart attack and was taken to the local hospital where he died. *(Elgin Recorder, Oct. 28, 1954 and La Grande Observer, June 2, 1953, pg. 2)*

Soapy died at the Grande Ronde Hospital in La Grande, on Saturday, October 23, 1954 at the age of 70 years. He had a funeral in Elgin and a burial at the Elgin Cemetery. It was a respectful funeral, just like he wanted, and his gravestone reads as it should, "Soapy" I. C. Davis 1884-1954.

His obituary stated that he was survived by two younger brothers, Frank C. Davis of Columbus, Georgia, and Charles D. Davis of Eaton, Indiana. *(La Grande Observer obituary, Oct. 25, 1954, pg. 2)* Overlooked in the list of survivors was his youngest sister, Rosa B., of Jacksonville, Florida, who later died in 1980.

Soapy was preceded in death by his parents, eight siblings and his wife, Anna Belle (Lutes) Davis of Venetia, Washington County, Pennsylvania, who passed away 18 years earlier on October 24, 1936 at the home of her sister and caregiver, Mrs. Bessie Lewis. Anna and Soapy did not have children. According to the Elgin Recorder, Soapy did try to reconcile with his wife, but the same issues about residency, lifestyle and values proved to be beyond mediation for them. They remained married, but lived separate lives.

For 17 years, Anna heard nothing from Soapy, so she assumed he was dead. Though Soapy was dismissed as dead and forgotten by folks in Washington County, Pennsylvania, he was not treated that way in Oregon. Soapy was loved and deeply respected by many throughout Northeast Oregon, where he spent over 40 years of his life guiding hunters, packing supplies to the sheep camp, and hosting hunters and other guests at his isolated cabin home. As a result, many colorful tales were created among such company, and he would not have wanted it any other way.

Soapy was a man of many ironies. He lived in a cabin that he never rented or owned, craved solitude yet ran his cabin like a hunters' resort, invented things he never patented, bought and sold products but never paid taxes, had little wealth but was always generous, lived hidden in the mountains, yet was dubbed mayor by the Lookingglass community. He lived the life of a trapper and hunter, yet he became the epitome of a legend. He died 68 years ago, but the Soapy tales are still alive today.

This was the adventurous life of Soapy Davis, the unofficial mayor of Lookingglass, and the legendary mountain man of Union County, Oregon. He certainly earned his place at the Elgin Museum and Historical Society, where at least one of his diaries is kept. *("Soapy" Davis, The Legendary Mountain Man of Union County, Oregon, 2019, Dave & Trish Yerges)*

Lookout Mountain Road - This road #43 is 5.75 miles in length and is located in Township 3N R40E. It runs north from Fry Meadow to Lookout Mountain and on into Wallowa County. The lookout that it was named for was developed in 1935 with a 60 foot, wooden observation tower, the present 82 foot treated timber tower with L-4 cab, built in 1948, was staffed until 2001. The tower was refurbished in 2004 and was staffed once again in 2005. Lookout Mountain is at an elevation of 5,229 feet.

Love Road - This road #64 runs 1.27 in total length north and south in Township 3S R40E Section 10 in the Union maintenance district. On the north end it connects with Lantz Lane and Stackland Road and on the south it connects with Haefer Lane.

According to the *1935 Metsker Map*, J. B. Love owned land on both ends of this road. Apparently, he was a cherry grower and liked to engage in the cherry contests in Cove. His wife also entered vegetable contests, submitting dry lima beans, peppers, and green pod beans in competition with other Cove growers.

The *La Grande Observer of September 10, 1932, pg. 3* had a nice write up about him. Here is a paraphrased version of the lengthy writeup.

"J. B. Love, Cove" — J. B. Love one of the prominent orchardists of the valley. His parents were William Love, who married Sarah Jane Pickens. Their son, James Boston Love was born August

31, 1869 in Athens, Tennessee. He was the second of 12 children born into the William Love family.

James came to Cove in 1912, and although he was a jeweler and optician by profession, became owner of one of the finest fruit ranches here. He lived in Cove for 20 years, much of that time being spent in travel.

James married Blanche M. in April 1893 in Lincoln County, Nebraska, and their first son, Chester "Chet" was born in Cambridge, Nebraska. They also had a second son, Leonard, and one daughter, Ione. In the *1900 Federal Census* the family was living in East Pagosa, Archuleta County, Colorado with the two oldest sons. James B. Love was employed as a jeweler there.

In the *1910 Federal Census* James and Blanche and their three children lived in Kerrsville, Kerr County, Texas. James was a jeweler, and he owned a shop there. In the *1920 Federal Census* James and Blanche lived in Cove with Ione, age 16. The two oldest boys were grown and out of the house.

In March 1932 in Sacramento, California, he married his second wife, Grace Evangeline Jamieson.

"With all his love of growing things, he is a great lover of music. The guitar is his chosen instrument, but he has a voice of great charm, and he has also the gift of writing music," the article read.

James B. Love died June 3, 1953 at age 83 years in Stayton, Marion County, Oregon. He was interred alongside his wife Grace Love at the Fox Valley Cemetery in Lyons, Linn County, Oregon.

Lowell Road - This is a private road in Township 4S R39E Sections 13-24 in the Union maintenance district.

Lower Cove Road - This road #128A is 7.67 miles in length and is located in Township 2S R39E Sections 13 through 9 in the La Grande and Union maintenance districts.

It connects with Market Lane (road #128) which heads west to Highway 82. Market Lane used to be a part of Lower Cove Road. The road sign on Highway 82 used to say "Lower Cove Road" but now it reads, "to Lower Cove Road."

Lower Cove Road is a section of the Cove-Union Farm Loop tour where visitors can tour participating farms and market sites. The farm loop brochure can be acquired at the La Grande Chamber of Commerce each summer. It's a self-guided tour, where you can buy fresh, in-season produce at farms and produce stands along the route.

Historically, Lower Cove Road was home to the Rascellas and Lydia (Elmer) Morris Century Farm, established in 1896. They came to the Grande Ronde Valley from Farland, McPherson County, Kansas. Their pioneer story is rich with tales of adventure, risk-taking, resourceful tenacity and compassion.

The authors present their story from an *interview with Manford and Wilma Morris in December 2000.* Manford said he wanted to tell his family's story because "the younger generation ought to know about the sacrifices and work it took to tame this land." Their dramatic story begins in

Wisconsin.

"My grandfather, Rascellas Morris, was a real salty guy," began Manford. He was born in Stevens Point, Wisconsin in 1858 and nicknamed, "Mike"—a name that stuck with him the rest of his life. When he was a young boy, his mother died, and his father remarried. Mike and his step-mother contended with a less than amicable relationship.

"One unforgettable day, in a fit of rage, she tied Mike's dog 'ole Bob' to a pole in the barn and beat it to death," Manford said. Terribly angry and hurt, the 11-year-old Mike packed some food and a few personal belongings and ran away from home, leaving his father, step-mother and two half-sisters behind him for the next fifty-six years.

For a year, he found a temporary home with a childless couple, who cared for him and sent him to school. Resistant to their guidance, he left their care, ending his formal education. Then he heard of jobs out West building railroad beds and laying track for the Santa Fe Railroad. He impulsively rode the rails to Albuquerque, New Mexico, where he became employed as a chore boy, caring for the horses used in building the railroad. Over time, he saved his wages of 25 cents a day and bought his own team and slip scraper. Equipped as a youthful business man for the first time, he proudly earned $2.50 a day.

In 1879, Mike was employed driving Texas long-horned cattle to railroads along the route to Kansas. At a stop in McPherson County, Kansas, he met Miss Lydia Elmer at a neighborhood dance. They corresponded by letter over the next two years, letters that Lydia saved and tied with a ribbon.

On July 4, 1881, Lydia, 21, and Mike, 23, were married at the home of her parents, Harvey and Amelia Elmer. The newlyweds established a farm near the Elmers, and a year later, Lydia gave birth to their son, Elmer Story Morris.

Despite frequent Kansas hail storms, drought, grasshoppers and pestilence, Mike and Lydia were able to save enough money to make the payments on the farm. On the day when that final payment was in hand, Mike rode off to the land office in McPherson. Before he got to the land office, he was persuaded instead to buy a team of fine looking horses, an investment he could double easily if he found the right buyer. However, not only did buying the horses delay the last payment on the farm, but it led him on a marketing search westward and eventually to the Grande Ronde Valley.

While in the valley, he was struck by its awesome beauty. It was a verdant jewel amidst a sage brush wilderness. When he finally returned to his Kansas farm, he eagerly shared his memories and experiences of the Grande Ronde Valley with his wife, son and Elmer in-laws. After a little planning, the Elmer and Morris families decided to move to the Grande Ronde Valley in October of 1888, eager to leave behind a hard life in Kansas.

Lydia and Story, who left Mike behind until he could sell the farm and join them later, traveled with her parents and four siblings. It was a time of mixed emotions for Lydia, as she left her home and her husband behind.

"My great-grandparents and Lydia came to Imbler in 1888," Manford said. Arriving in late October, they spent their first winter near Imbler. Soon afterward, Lydia's father found a farm just west of

Imbler, and he bought it without a second thought.

By March of 1889, Lydia and Story moved near Island City, where she worked as a cook and housekeeper for Mr. John Frazier. While there Lydia wrote about her first impressions of this valley in a letter to Mike in Kansas. She wrote:

"I think the soil is as good as you thought it was. It don't look quite like I thought it would here. The mountains are steeper than I expected to see them. You said you was thinking of leaving your accounts and coming out here this spring. I won't advise you to do anything rash, but we would be glad to have you come. You could make more than $15.00 per month. There is some raw land on the ridge for sale at $18.00 per acre and people that have bought land say they can pay for it the first year. I will never live any place but the West again. It seems more like home than it ever did in Kansas."

When Mike arrive in 1889 to rejoin his family, Lydia's employer, Mr. Frazier, helped them to homestead 160 acres five miles from Elgin on the Palmer Junction Road. Lydia was delighted to have a nice two-story frame house and a place for a garden. Mike was also pleased with the natural spring on the property and a good meadow for hay.

Story was six years old when he came to the Grande Ronde Valley. He attended a one-room school about a mile from their rural Elgin farm. When he was ten, his mother called upon him in an emergency to run 1.5 miles to the neighbor's house for help. Mike was away on business when Lydia went into labor in her bedroom. She tied a rope to the bed post and delivered the first of the twins on her own. By then Story brought the old neighbor lady with him, and she helped deliver the second baby. Over the course of two days, the twin infants died, and they were buried in the front yard. Story was sad that he was going to remain an only child.

The Morris family would have stayed on this homestead had it not been for the persistent and violent harassment from their neighbors. The threats came to a head one day in 1896, when one of the neighbor's sons shot Mike with his 45-70 caliber rifle, while Mike was working in his garden. The shot lodged in his hip and Lydia and Story brought him into the house, where Lydia performed a crude surgery to remove the bullet. In time, Mike healed, albeit with a permanent limp.

In the fall of 1896, while yet on crutches, Mike started looking for another home. He found a 320 acre ranch to rent six miles north of Cove, just below the foothills of Mt. Harris. With a wagon load of possessions, including the exhumed coffins of their twin girls, the Morrises moved from Elgin to their new farm. The farm was complete with a house that was actually two houses joined together, a horse barn, a shop, a granary and other outbuildings.

In January 1900, Mike began making payments to buy the farm, and after seven years, it was paid off. During those difficult years, Mike resourcefully raised hogs, which were always a good investment, and mules, which he sold for $175-$225 a pair. This extra income, especially from the mules, helped the Morris family pay off their farm, after which Mike was able to pursue his true love, raising and selling beautiful horses. Mike's annual grain crops and hay helped feed the horses.

Lydia, who was concerned about making ends meet, planted an orchard and took care of the 13 milking cows, marketing their cream and butter weekly in La Grande. Meanwhile Mike was often away from home, carrying on business, sometimes over a game of high stakes cards. But often, after a long absence, he would come home with some significant acquisition that made Lydia wonder just where he had been and how he managed these things.

He had a knack for orchestrating money-making deals, and over time, he made enough deals to increase his land holdings to 3,000 acres. Some of those acres were adjoining his homestead property and other acreage was in the Ladd Canyon and Pyles Canyon.

Story was 14 years old when he moved with his parents to the Lower Cove farm, and during that first year he spent all his daylight hours plowing on the 160 acres. He attended school sporadically, riding horseback 12 miles round trip to Cove and back.

In 1909, when Story was 27 years old, his mother took in a family of five motherless children, including the eldest, Agnes Merony, who was then 15 years of age. Lydia volunteered to take them into her home temporarily as a favor to the father.

Months turned into years, and on December 1, 1912, just one week before Agnes turned 18, she married Story. The newlyweds initially lived with Mike and Lydia after their marriage. By 1918, Story and Agnes were making their home a half mile northeast of the Mike Morris farm.

There Agnes gave birth to Manford, and when he was two years old, his mother Agnes contracted the Spanish Influenza. She survived, but it weakened her heart, and she could not care for her children for a time. By then, Story and Agnes lived across the road from Mike and Lydia, and the children lived with their Morris grandparents. When Agnes recovered, Mike and Lydia sent the children back to their mother, all but little "Manie."

Manford had the best of two worlds, playing across the road with his siblings, but going back to grandma's hot suppers and his grandpa's doting attention. That was his home. During those years, Manford attended "Frosty School" the one room school house located one and three quarters mile away.

In 1931, Mike Morris died, and in 1935 Lydia died. They were buried in the Summerville Cemetery, where their twin baby girls were eventually laid to rest. After their deaths, Manford lived and worked alongside his father Story. They got their first tractor in 1935. Manford graduated from La Grande High School in 1938, and on August 31, 1941, Manford married Miss Wilma Burch.

"After we married, we moved into my grandparent's home here, and we've been living here ever since," Manford said. The home had been vacant since Lydia's death, so Manford and Wilma rolled up their sleeves and painted the walls and did a little remodeling in the kitchen. Regarding their future goals together, Manford told Wilma, "I want to have something in life, something to call our own." To that, Wilma replied, "Me too, and I'll help you."

Manford developed the farm into a dairy, milking 29 cows a day by 1950. Wilma said, "We milked 29 cows to pay the utility bills and the gas man." They improved the farm over the years, using very frugal means. Manford cut his own lumber and made his own concrete with sand from the river. "We made everything but the nails," Manford said.

On the farm they raised barley, oats, grass, and Austrian dry peas. In 1965, they started to irrigate their grass crops. They sold their blue grass to O. M. Scott & Sons, and they got a good price because Manford and Wilma spent eight weeks of meticulous field hoeing.

Looking back over the past 60 years, Manford, then 82, said, "The challenge of farming and the love for the land is what keeps me here. I love the freedom and the fresh air. I wanted to farm and stay with the land, and I did. If I had to do it all over again, I'd stay with the land. It's been good to us. If I leave this place, it will be because the sheriff locked the gate because of back taxes or because the mortician came."

The realities of advanced age did catch up to them both. Wilma May (Burch) Morris died September 1, 2006, and Manford died on July 25, 2008 at 89 years of age at a local care center. They were buried next to each other at Summerville Cemetery.

Note: The authors vividly remember the interview at the Morris home that December evening of 2000. Unbeknownst to us, a snow storm developed while we were inside the house talking with the Morrises, and upon leaving, everything was covered with a heavy blanket of snow. It was a nail-biting experience getting home in a little Pontiac Sunbird that night, when not even the road was distinguishable from the shoulders, ditches or fields on either side. Only a few tall weeds on either side of the road warned us if we were veering too far to the left or right on the road.

It was a privilege to meet Manford and Wilma and to relate a homestead story they felt the younger generation "ought to know."

Lower Palmer Junction Road - This road #44 is 2.36 miles in length and is located in Township 1N R39E Section 3 in the Elgin maintenance district. This shorter section of the greater Palmer Junction Road lies closer to the city of Elgin. (See Palmer Junction Road entry)

Lower Perry Loop - This loop (road #5) of .36 miles comes off of Upper Perry Lane in the Perry area of Union County. It is a rectangular-shaped loop that gives access to about 21 residences.

Perry is an unincorporated town located about five miles west of La Grande on the Grande Ronde River and Interstate 84. The town was once unofficially called Stumptown due to the operation of the sawmill there over the years, but in 1890 its post office name was registered officially as Perry, it being named after DeWitt Clinton Perry, commonly called D. W. C. Perry, a civil engineer and the first assistant superintendent of the Oregon division of the railroad. (See Upper Perry Lane for a full account of Perry's life.)

The Smith-Stanley Lumber Company that was built in 1890, was later sold to Charley and Jim Mimnaugh and again in 1900 to C. W. Nibley and George Stoddard, who renamed the mill the Grande Ronde Lumber Company. The mill town was bustling during those sawmill days (1890-1931), even having a Chinese Restaurant among other businesses operating there.
In 1927, the Grande Ronde Lumber Company merged with the Stoddard Lumber Company of Baker City and moved across the valley to Pondosa, taking most of the town of Lower and Upper Perry with it. The Perry post office was discontinued in 1931. *(Wikipedia)*

At the close of its sawmill days, a section foreman by the name of John Elmer Gray brought his family to live on the outskirts of Lower Perry. His son John Gray, now 96 years of age living in Hilgard, was about 5 years old when they moved there. He said, "We were living in a railroad company house then and my brother attended school there. I was a little too young to attend first grade, but the teacher said I could come along with my brother anyway."

There were two school houses side by side in Lower Perry, Gray recalled. "One school house was for the first through fourth grade kids, and the second school house was for fifth through eighth grade kids. I went to school there during the 1930-31 school year, and then we moved to Hilgard in 1932," he said. "But when I lived there, I remembered the sawmill dam washed out, and the water was pretty high that year in Lower Perry."

The sawmill in Perry was one of many in Union County. After all, the settlers needed lumber for homes, barns and outbuildings of all sorts. Saw mills served a practical, immediate need as brought out in the following excerpt of an article entitled, "La Grande Picture 53 Years Old." It read: "The very first buildings were of logs, but a saw mill was established at Oro Dell in 1862, and then board houses became the rule." *(La Grande Observer, June 17, 1916, pg. 20)*

Those sawmills were supplying a local market usually, but not the Smith and Stanley operation. They were true capitalists from Wisconsin, and their vision was to use the timber resources here to fill orders from large companies in other states. To accomplish that they needed a railroad man in their pocket, one they could work with to make sure their orders were shipped to their out-of-state customers. That man appears to have been D. W. C. Perry at the dispatcher's office.

When the company officers felt they exhausted the timber supply here, they closed up or sold the saw mill to others and moved elsewhere, which is what happened to the Smith-Stanley sawmill in Perry. The town's namesake, D. W. C. Perry, was here only briefly, perhaps six months before he was transferred to The Dalles. Likewise Smith and Stanley sold and moved on about 1900.

Market Lane - Formerly Lower Cove Road #128 diverts east from Highway 82. It's name was changed to Market Lane. Residents didn't like the change much because the old name provided clearer signage to Cove, so in time the county added another sign that read: "To Lower Cove."

At one point in the history of Union County, there were many market roads. They were sometimes referred to as "farm-to-market" roads, and basically they were a county road that connected rural or agricultural areas to market towns. They were often better built and maintained roads, meeting state standards and used to transport farm products and livestock to destinations such as mills, stock sales, farmers' markets, grain cleaners and other places of "market" to buy and sell.

Marks Road - Formerly Starr Road, this straight-as-an-arrow gravel road #129B runs north and south for a half mile off Starr Lane in Township 2S R38E Section 9 in the La Grande maintenance district.

On the 1978 Union County map, this road was first called Starr Road, which was intersecting Starr Lane. Due to the duplicity of the road names, the county renamed this road in 1988.

Jane De Clue and her sons of La Grande nominated "Marks Road" as its official name in 1988. They chose "Marks" to honor a pair of single brothers who were members of the Ben Brown party of 12 that settled in the Mount Glen area of the Grande Ronde Valley in October of 1861.

Their names were Richard E. "Dick" Marks (1830-1905) and William "Willie" Marks (1832-1905), both born in Stark County, Ohio. Their parents were John and Mary A. Marks, both Pennsylvania Germans, who settled in Stark County, Ohio to farm and raise a family. This was a county settled predominately by Pennsylvania Germans and others from Germany and France. The county had at least one newspaper printed in the German language for these settlers.

The authors first grasped the Marks family profile from examining the *1850 Federal Census of Mifflin, Ashland County, Ohio.* This was a small town, and every Marks living there in 1850 were part of the John and Mary A. Marks family. The only ones missing were the deceased father, John Marks Sr., and his one married daughter, Julia Ann Marks Bishop, living in the neighboring county of Crawford. She was discovered later by the authors.

Compiling the mother and all siblings together, the family profile looked like this in birth order: widow Mary Marks, 53; and children: George (b.1819), Julia Ann Bishop (1821-1907), John (b.1823), Abraham (1826-1884), Eve Bushong (1827-1905), Richard E. (1830-1905), William (1832-1905), Adaline Hoover (b.1836-1905), Israel (1840-1903), and David (b.1842).

All ten Marks children were born in Stark County, Ohio, but it wasn't the only county in Ohio they lived in. As brought out in Israel Marks' biographical sketch published in the *Counties of La Grange and Nobel, Indiana, 1882, pg. 301,* the father, John Marks Sr., died in Stark county. Israel was born there on June 7, 1839 and reared and educated principally in Wyandot County, Ohio. Then they finally lived in Mifflin, Ashland County, Ohio during the 1850 census.

According to the aforementioned biographical sketch, Israel told the compiler that "I came to Indiana when twenty years of age." So it appears that Mary Marks and the rest of her family that lived in Mifflin, Ohio in 1850, all left in 1859 and relocated to La Grange County, Indiana. The 1860 Federal Census of Mifflin showed absolutely no Marks living there. They had all left, which corroborates Israel's narrative.

In the *1860 Federal Census in Bloomfield, La Grange County, Indiana,* Mary Marks, 65, was found living with her youngest child, David, 18, who was the head of the household. Mary Marks died there on March 11, 1865 at 72 years of age, and she was buried in the Greenwood Cemetery in a part of it called "Big Old" where some of her sons and grandchildren later rested in peace.

Interestingly, in Richard E. Marks' guardianship court papers of 1891, he mentioned that he once lived in La Grange County, Indiana—likely that was in 1859 when all the John and Mary Marks' children left Mifflin, Ashland County, Ohio for La Grange County, Indiana.

By early 1860, the brothers, Richard E. and William were lured by a desire for adventure and gold mining possibilities, so they traveled to northeastern Oregon. Richard especially had the mining bug in him, but William was happy to marry and settle down, if he could find the right lady in the isolated wilderness where he was heading.

As things turned out, the brothers met a man by the name of Benjamin Brown, who was employed as a freighter between the newly established Umatilla Indian Agency and The Dalles and Walla

Walla. Ben's family (Frances and two small girls) lived at the agency for a year, and Frances was the cook at the Agency with G. W. Abbott as agent. *(My Oregon Trail Families, Oregon State archives; Supplement #7, the Diary of Ben Brown by Bernal D. Hug. pg. 45)*

By September 1861, Abbott and all the officers at the agency, being Democrats, resigned in protest that Abe Lincoln was elected as president. Those officers and Ben Brown and his wife had to find other work to do as a result. Some of them, along with Ben Brown, decided to seek land in order to farm, and among those men were Richard and William Marks. Since the land in Umatilla was mostly claimed by then, Benjamin Brown looked to the Grande Ronde Valley for potential homesteading possibilities.

He organized a scouting committee to spy out the Grande Ronde Valley. The committee included himself, William Marks, William McCauley, Jake Reeth and Job Fisher. They came over the Blue Mountains from Umatilla to spy out the geographic features and natural resources of the Grande Ronde Valley.

They specifically wanted to know if the valley was suitable for farming, had a good water supply and natural protection from marauding Indians. On determining this to be the case, they returned to the Pendleton area to give their favorable report to those waiting there, filed several initial land claims and started to pack their wagons to leave.

Brown then led a group of 12 men plus his wife Frances and two girls to the Grande Ronde Valley, arriving there in October 1861. *(Supplement #7, Diary of Ben Brown, pg. 35-36; La Grande Observer, Aug. 15, 1902, pg. 6)* The settlers coming to the Grande Ronde Valley included Benjamin and Frances Brown and their daughters Ada and Esther; the brothers Richard E. and William Marks; William Chaffin, Job Fisher, S. M. Black, E. C. Crane, R. Alexander, William McCauley and Jake Reeth.

However, a couple of parties beat them to the valley first, namely, the Henry W. Leasy family who were already there since September 5, 1861. They came by wagon from Iowa, and they stopped for a two-week layover along the Grande Ronde River to refresh themselves before moving on their way to the Willamette Valley. In their party was Henry W. Leasy and wife Emily (Moorehouse) Leasy, and their children Frances Caroline, Will, John, Columbus, Joseph and James.

After their rest, they started out again on the trail heading toward the Willamette Valley, but they were struggling on the hill leaving the valley with their wagons. Just then, coming toward them on the trail from the Umatilla direction were three men with supplies, Daniel Chaplin, Green Arnold and Charles Fox. They explained they were going to start a settlement in the Grande Ronde Valley and sell supplies to the Native Americans and emigrating settlers passing by. These men convinced the Leasy family to turn around and join them, which they did.

Now when the Ben Brown party finally arrived in October, they were probably surprised to be greeted by the Leasy family. They also discovered Stephen Coffin and four or five other men camped out in what was known later as Old Town La Grande. Clearly, people were starting to settle in this valley, and they were converging on the valley as early as September of 1861. *(An Illustrated History of Union and Wallowa Counties, 1902, pg. 138; see also Miller Lane entry)*

The Diary of Ben Brown described the first winter of 1861-62, and he mentioned the Marks brothers often in his journal because they contributed so much toward the well-being and survival of the colony during the first and second winters there.

He wrote about how the settlers hastily built log houses in the form of a square. They were provided with loop holes and were to serve as a fort. The idea was to connect them with a stockade, but some members got distracted with tempting employment and began hauling freight so the fort never got built. These houses constituted the colony at Mount Glen with the intentions of becoming Brown's Fort, but that never transpired.

In this colony, the cabin farthest east and south belonged to Ben Brown and his family. The house west of Browns was occupied by William McCauley and E. C. Crane. A bit westward was the home of three other single men, including brothers Richard and William Marks and their friend, Job Fisher. North of this was the cabin home of the Leasy family, and east of the Leasy family was a cabin occupied by Black, Chaffin and Alexander. *(Supplement #7 to Bernal D. Hug's History of Union County Oregon, pg. 44)*

Bernal D. Hug sometimes used the variant spelling, Leasey, in his diary except when it came to the official wedding certificate between William Marks and Caroline Frances Leasy, so the spelling, Leasy, will be used in this publication.

Thanks to the Marks brothers and their whipsaw that they brought with them to the valley, the cabins were made more secure and warm with doors. The Marks brothers were also good cooks because located in the center of the colony was a baking unit, and the Marks brothers busied themselves with a great deal of baking on a community plan. There was no doubt about it, the Marks brothers were team players and worked for the well-being of the colony as a whole.

The Marks brothers weren't all work and no play, however. To bring some entertainment to the early settlement, Richard Marks made two violins during that first winter.

"The tops and backs were made of pine and the side walls of the instruments were fashioned from alder wood. Strings were fabricated out of sinews of beef, the bows were made of Indian arrow wood and the hair for the bows was procured from horses' tails. Glue to put the instruments together was manufactured from beef hoofs. Although undoubtedly not of the finest tone, it is probable that the music from these homemade instruments sounded as sweet to the ears of the lonely little group as any they had ever heard." *(oregongeneology.com)*

William Marks had his eye on the young Frances Leasy, as other bachelor men did too, but she gave her approval only to William, and within a three month period they decided to wed.

On January 8, 1862, the first wedding in the valley took place between William Marks and his bride, Frances "Fannie" Caroline Leasy, officiated by S.M. Black, who had previously been a justice of the peace and was familiar with marriage law.

"According to the (wedding) statute, in the absence of anyone duty empowered to perform marriage ceremonies, a marriage could be legally made if both parties would ratify a written agreement to become husband and wife. In the Marks-Leasy marriage this was properly attended to as a part of the wedding ceremony. Such an event, of course, called for a real celebration, and Mr. Brown in his diary remarks 'that we had quite a time dancing' and that 'some of the boys got a little tight.'" *(oregongenealogy.com)*

The wedding certificate was signed by all in attendance except the Browns. *(My Oregon Trail Families, Oregon State archives)* It was recorded "Marks, William and Frances Caroline Leasy, 8th day of January 1862." William was 29 and Frances was 15 at the time of their wedding.

"Know all men by these presents that we, William Marks and Frances Caroline Leasy of the County of Wasco,* State of Oregon, do agree and solemnly engage and by these presents have engaged to enter the bonds of Matrimony and to live as husband and wife in conformity with the laws of the State of Oregon during our natural lives." (Note: * Wasco County then included a huge area, including what was later called Union County in 1864.)

"In witness whereof we have hereunto set our hands and appended our signature at Rondeville,* Grand Ronde Valley, Wasco County, this 8th day of Jan. 1862." The groom William Marks signed his name, and the bride, Frances Caroline Leasy, put her X by her name in the presence of G.H. Abbott, Byron N. Dawes, E.C. Crane, S.M. Black, William W. Chaffin, Ross Smith, W.I. McCauley, and R.E. Marks. Recorded April 19th, 1862 (pages 37-38). Richard Marks signed his name R. E. Marks on this document.

Note: * Rondeville was quickly renamed Brownsville, but because there was already a Brownsville post office registered in Linn County, Oregon, the settlers in the Grande Ronde Valley had to choose another name for their community. A Frenchman named Charles Dause suggested the name La Grande. (See also Moses Creek Lane entry) Therefore, it's very likely that the Marks wedding certificate is the only document that bears the colony's unofficial name of Rondeville on it.

During their marriage, William and Frances had twelve children. Listed in birth order: James Israel (b.1863, La Grande), Christopher Columbus (b.1865, La Grande), Ruth Adeline (b. 1868 Astoria), Sarah Elizabeth (b.1872, Castle Rock, Wash.), Clarence Sylvian (b. 1875, Bellevue, Oregon), William Ebenser (b.1879, Willamina, Oregon), Thomas Jefferson (b.1882, McMinnville, Oregon), Emma Osborne; Nora M. (b.1885, Sheridan, Oregon), and Albert Owen (b.1889, Willamina, Oregon). The twelfth child is unknown to the authors.

From this list of dates and birth locations, it's apparent that William and Fannie Marks left the valley sometime after March 17, 1865, when their son, Christopher, was born in La Grande. They moved around a bit, staying in the region west of Salem for many years, except for their move to Astoria, Oregon and Castle Rock, Washington.

William and Frances' final residence appears to have been Monmouth, Oregon, southwest of Salem. William died there on May 3, 1905 and was interred at the new Smith Cemetery in Monmouth, Polk County, Oregon.

A simple death notice was all that the family researchers could find published in that county. It was printed in the *Itemizer-Observer newspaper, 1905, of Dallas, Polk Co, Oregon* as follows: "Old Mr. Marks died in Cooper Hollow last week." Talk about getting right to the point—.

Almost nine years later on March 29, 1916, Frances (Leasy) Marks married again, this time to Willard Lewis, native of Independence, Missouri.

Frances was born in Indiana on January 16, 1847 and died on February 5, 1922, at the age of 74 years 20 days at her home near Salem, Oregon. Interment was made in the Smith cemetery where her late husband William Marks was buried. Her brothers James Leasy of Baker County and John of Astoria were with her when death came, her obituary stated. Her funeral service was held at the home of her son, Christopher Columbus Marks, on February 7, 1922 in Elkins.

As for William's brother Richard "Dick" Marks, *Bernal D. Hug's "Diary of Ben Brown #7" page 23* shed some light on him. "January 24, 1862—We went over again this morn to finish raising (my new log house). It snowed a little last night... We got home a little after dark. Richard Marks was taken awful sick. He had spasms so bad that it was all six men could do to hold him. He has been ailing for the last few days. He is but an ailing man anyhow, his liver has been very much affected. He came to himself after about two hours. January 27, 1862—R. Marks is getting well again."

Another fact about Richard Marks was that he made trips back and forth for supplies from Walla Walla. On one holiday party occasion, there was a "great bowl of nuts, raisins, hard candies and red apples brought by Dick Marks from Walla Walla, set on one end of the table." *(Supplement #7 to Bernal D. Hug's History of Union County, Oregon, pg. 46.)*

Richard Marks left the Grande Ronde Valley to pursue mining in Meagher County, Montana. It's uncertain if his older brother, George, was there first and invited Richard or vice versa, but in any case, George was residing in this county by 1870. Sadly, George suffered from a psychosis involving hallucinations that drove him to take his own life on April 3, 1870 in the city of Helena, Meagher County, Montana. *(The Sacramento Bee, April 16, 1870, pg. 3)*

Richard also inherited a mental illness, which led to two hospitalizations and an appointed guardian in Montana. He was discharged from his last hospitalization after 1880, and although he filed another land patent for mining in 1882, it appears that he was convinced to leave Montana and live with his sister Eve (Marks) Bushong of Sherwood, Branch County, Michigan. His brother-in-law was John Bushong.

In July 1891, Richard, who still lived in Sherwood, Michigan, was again assigned a legal guardian by the court and officially assigned to a state hospital in Kalamazoo. However, in the final analysis, Richard was transferred to Long Cliff Hospital in Cass County, Indiana, only a county away from Richard's two brothers Abraham and Israel and their families of La Grange, Indiana.

After 13 years residency at Long Cliff Hospital, Richard E. Marks died on February 18, 1905 of broncho-pneumonia and melancholia. His death certificate states he was a laborer in his working years and was 73 years old at his death. Other documentation shows he was 75 years of age.

He was buried at the Long Cliff Hospital cemetery. The cemetery was a mess after some years passed. The stone memorial markers were piled up in the corner of the cemetery and records were gone. There is an effort being made to reconstruct the Long Cliff cemetery records and the authors made sure to provide the recorder of all the details to include Richard E. Marks on their new files. Now family researchers can find him if they are searching for him. Today the hospital is called

Logansport State Hospital. May he rest in peace until the resurrection on the last day.

Authors note: The research for this entry was a story in itself and is at the heart of the history of La Grande, Oregon. The data presented in this road entry was just a fraction of what we actually found, and everything we collected was gifted to the Marks family, who always wondered what happened to Richard E. Marks after leaving La Grande in the 1860s. With this new data they now have, they are eagerly analyzing its details with a zeal that only genealogists understand. *(Kimberly Marks interview, October 3, 2021)*

Marley Creek Lane - This private lane diverts from Ukiah-Hilgard Highway 244 and follows Meadow Creek. It's located in Township 4S R35E Section 8.

It is named after Marley Creek, a tributary of Meadow Creek. There are two segments of Marley Creek Lane all on the north side of Highway 244 on Camp Elkanah property.

Marley Creek Lane leads to the headquarters of Camp Elkanah and its large, centerpiece building. It also provides access to 18 recreational cabins south of Marley Creek Lane. Fifteen of the 18 recreational cabins were built in 1925.

According to one cabin owner, the cabins were originally old, wooden railroad cars, and people turned them into living quarters by building exterior walls around them and remodeling from the inside out. Cabin owners lease their lot of land from Camp Elkanah. *(Cabin owner Doreen Pierce interview, Dec. 3, 2018; www.union-county.org)*

Almost all the cabins up there were boxcars, and they were moved to those individual locations to have the logging workers stay in them for 2 or 3 years, and then they moved them up the railroad line. So they were originally railroad cars that were taken off the track, and the wheels were removed. They set them on large logs that were much more durable. Then the individual owners that lived in them would add onto them, such as lean-to's. Those cabins at Camp Elkanah, Hickler's camp, Hollywood Camp, all those different parts of Camp Elkanah were moved into place in 1938.

Marley Creek runs south from Highway 244, and it is named after Leonard Marley, who came to the Starkey area about 1885 and took up government land in 1890 where Marley Creek flows into Meadow Creek. *(Oregon Geographic Names, 1982, pg. 471)*

His full name was Leonard California Marley, and he was born December 21, 1850 in Indiana. *(Grave stone date)* He was the son of an Irishman named Leonard Halton Marley (1826-1895) and Mary A. Lynch (1829-1857).

Leonard C. Marley married Mary Ella Williamson on November 23, 1881 in Union County, Oregon. She was born on November 7, 1860 in Illinois, the daughter of Isaac and Elizabeth Williamson. *(1900 Federal Census; Ancestry.com)*

Their history in Union County began in 1881 and seems to have ended about 1889. It is a short lived history, but on account of their early land ownership, they have been honored with the naming of Marley Creek, and Marley Creek Lane.

After they settled in the Starkey area in 1885, they started a family: Leonard Harrison Marley, (1886) and William Joseph Marley (1889). Their next child, Ellen Caroline Marley, was born in Oregon (place unknown) in April 1892.

It appears that after Ellen's birth, the family moved to Forestville, California, where Mary Ella Marley gave birth to twin daughters on October 15, 1893: Libbie Ethel Pentney and Frances Bliss Stone. Both died just months apart in 1987 at 93 years.

Also living in the Forestville Precinct was Leonard C. Marley's father, Leonard Halton Marley. The senior Marley had registered as a voter there on July 31, 1896 and was described as 6-foot tall, dark complexion, hazel colored eyes, dark hair, and born in Indiana. Likewise, on June 22, 1898, Leonard C. Marley had become a registered voter in Forestville, and he was described as 5-foot 11-3/4 inches tall, medium complexion, grey eyes and brown hair, also born in Indiana.

According to the *1900 Federal Census,* the Leonard C. Marley family was living in Kelseyville, (District #5) in Lake County, California, where he was occupied as a farmer, owning his own farm and where the children were attending school. Shortly after settling there, daughter, Ellen Caroline Marley, died on January 12, 1911 at the age of 18 years.

From there, they lived in the following Oregon cities: Fairlawn (1910), Dayton (1920) and their last residence in Unionvale (1930).

At the age of 87 years, Leonard C. Marley died on December 15, 1938 at his home in Unionvale, Yamhill County, Oregon, and he was buried in the Masonic Cemetery in McMinnville, Oregon.

His wife, Mary Ella Marley, 81, died at her home on November 7, 1941. She had been a resident of the Unionvale district for the past 24 years.

Surviving her were two sons, William J. Marley of Dayton and Leonard H. Marley, Hillsboro; one daughter, Libbie E. Pentney, Salem; and five grandchildren.

Marley Circle - This is also named after Leonard C. Marley, a brief resident of Starkey, Oregon. (See Marley Creek Road)

Marley One Road - Also named after Leonard C. Marley, a brief resident of Starkey, Oregon. (See Marley Creek Road)

Marvin Road - Formerly called Clark Drive, but due to the fact that there was a Clark Creek Road, the county wanted to avoid any duplicity in road names, so they decided to use Marvin Jay Clark's first name instead of the last name for this road.

This public unmaintained road is a gravel road that runs .83 miles and branches off of Morgan Lake Road. It is located in Township 3S R38E Section 13 in the La Grande maintenance district.

Marvin Jay Clark had a dairy on this road called Clark's Dairy, and later he founded Silver Hill Dairy.

This story gets a little complicated, so read slowly as we cover the following members of the Clark family: Henderson Clark (father), Martin Luther Clark (son), and Marvin Jay Clark (grandson). It is the latter who is the namesake of this road.

Marvin's history here started with his grandfather, Henderson Clark, who was born November 15, 1840 in Missouri, and he died August 29, 1916 in Union County, Oregon. Marvin's grandmother was Mary Magdaline Shobert, and she was born September 8, 1843 in Pennsylvania, and she died March 1, 1923 in Union County, Oregon. They were both buried in Grandview Cemetery in La Grande. *(Findagrave.com)* They were married in 1861 in Pennsylvania. *(ancestry.com)*

The Henderson Clark family moved around a bit, but came to Union County by 1887, according to the obituaries of his sons, Martin and Jacob Clark. By then all six of their children were born. *(newspapers.com)*

They are as follows in birth order: Harriet Caroline "Hattie" Waldrop (1865-1941), Joseph (1870-1947), Jacob (1871-1944), Jeanette "Nettie" Montgomery (1873-1962), Martin Luther (1876-1947), and Harvey Lee (1883-1955). *(La Grande Observer, Aug. 29, 1916, pg. 1 obituary; ancestry.com)*

Henderson's son, Martin Luther Clark, was born May 9, 1876 in Roseburg, Oregon. He married Ida May Farris on May 28, 1906. *(Oregon, County Marriage Records)* She was born November 25, 1886 and died June 7, 1959 at 72 years of age.

Their son, Marvin Jay Clark, the subject of this history, was born in La Grande on January 4, 1913. *(La Grande Observer, Jan. 6, 1913, pg. 1)* Marvin was married Josie Luton (1918-2004), on November 17, 1932 in Baker City, Oregon, and they raised two sons.

Marvin adopted Josie's baby, Martin Robert Clark, who was born April 29, 1933 in La Grande, and he died at age 62 on September 28, 1995 in Richland, Washington. Marvin and Josie also had one son together, Allen Marvin Clark, who was born on April 27, 1934, and he died at age 58 on August 2, 1992 in Morrow, Oregon, according to one family tree. *(ancestry.com)*

Marvin J. Clark sold out his share of Clark's Dairy to partners Gertrude S. Weiss and Miss Nelle Grimmett in 1957. *(La Grande Observer, Sept. 4, 1957, pg. 2)* The two women modernized the plant for many thousands of dollars, got a new fleet of delivery trucks and held an open house at their plant on Second Street in La Grande.

The business seemed to prosper, but then six years later, Clark's Dairy was renamed Clark's Superior Dairy, according to Arvid Brown, plant manager and spokesperson. *(La Grande Observer, Dec. 17, 1963, pg. 3)*

After Marvin J. Clark pulled out of the Clark's Dairy partnership, he went back into the dairy business, founding Silver Hill Dairy on Marvin Road. Marvin J. advertised himself as the sole proprietor, and the ad said that he purchased a New Jersey herd of cows at Caldwell, Idaho. The dairy sold Grade A raw milk, homogenized milk, and pasteurized milk and advertised home deliveries. *(La Grande Observer, Sept. 6, 1957, pg. 2; and Nov. 24, 1962, pg. 3)*

It does not appear that any of his children continued in the dairy business. Marvin Jay Clark, 64, died January 17, 1977 in Malone, Grays Harbor, Washington. *(Washington Death Index)*

Mathson Road - This private road comes off of Lower Perry Loop in the area of Perry in Township 2S R37E Section 35, and it is named after dairy farmers Ole and Rosie (Walmer) Mathson.

Ole Mathson was born on August 8, 1870 in Norway. At age 18, he immigrated to the U.S. on April 13, 1888, and at age 29, Ole married Rosina (Rosie) Barbara Walmer on August 28, 1899 at the bride's mother's home in La Grande, Oregon. Ole spoke fluent Norwegian and Rosie spoke German.

On the *1900 Federal Census,* Ole and Rosie resided in Perry, stating Ole had been living in the U.S. for 12 years at that point. That year, they welcomed a daughter Olga Rose Ripley (1900-1969). After this baby, there was an apparent pause in childbearing for about 6 six years, and during this time, an Ole Mathson of identical age was working as a farm laborer in Foxhome, Minnesota, (a village comprised of 27% Norwegians) according to the *Minnesota Territorial and State Census of 1905.* Why he temporarily left Perry to work there was not discovered—perhaps a relative was in crisis, and he helped out.

Whatever the case, he returned to Perry by January 1906 when more children started to come along: Alfred M. (Oct. 4, 1906-1968), Christina (1909-1911), Theodore Ole (1912-2001) Alvin Louis (1916-1991 and Neva Witten (1919-2001).

The *1910 Federal Census* placed the Mathson family in Perry, and a year later little Christina Mathson died.

An interesting story of Ole Mathson's home life was printed in the *La Grande Observer, April 30, 1915, pg. 1.* It read: "An evening or so ago a coyote came to the home of Ole Mathson and began to fight the dog. Mr. Mathson heard the noise and ran out to find the dog and coyote were fighting furiously. Ole got a club and struck the coyote and parted them. The coyote then turned and started in his direction, but Ole ran into the house to get his gun. While after his gun, the coyote ran out in the field and on account of the darkness disappeared. Later in the evening, however, the beast returned and was after the dog again. Mr. Mathson was successful in killing the coyote after an exciting chase in the yard and fields. The beast was shot several times before it was killed."

Ole Mathson had limited outside interests because dairy farming was a very time consuming occupation as was raising a family.

In the *La Grande Observer, March 6, 1935, pg. 5* issue it read: "Ole Mathson, who has been to Clarkston, Washington, since last November for the treatment of cancer, has returned to his home in Perry. Mrs. Mathson and son, Ted, made the trip down by car to bring him back. He is reported to be doing as well as could be expected."

Ole Mathson died three months later on June 28, 1935 at 64 years of age. He was interred at Hillcrest East cemetery in La Grande, Oregon. His headstone gives only his year of death.

Rosie died at her son Theodore's home in Haines on July 26, 1962. She was also interred at Hillcrest East cemetery in La Grande. Rosie was born in Switzerland in 1879 (alt. 1880). Her obituary states she was 82 at the time of her death. Surviving her were three sons, Alfred, Louis, and Theodore; and two daughters, Olga Ripley and Neva Witten. *(Findagrave.com; ancestry.com)*

May Lane - Listed as county road #204, it runs 1.23 miles in length and is located in Township 3S R38E Section 4 in the La Grande maintenance district. At first glance, it appears to be in the city, but it actually borders the county and is listed as an official county road.

This lane was named after Miss May Belle McWhirter in 1892. May McWhirter was born in La Grande on May 1, 1873, the daughter of Joseph A. McWhirter (1833-1904) and his second wife, Miss Katherine Elizabeth "Kate" Tatlinger (1838-1920).

According to Joseph McWhirter's obituary, he was born on December 25, 1833 in Mercer County, Pennsylvania, where he was educated in common schools. There he learned the harness and saddlery trade. In 1853, at the age of 20, he decided to explore the opportunities of the Western Frontier. Consequently, he embarked on an ocean voyage to Oregon, landing first at Portland, which was then a small village in the woods.

"Portland presented no inducements in his line, so he moved up the Willamette River to Corvallis then called Marysville, where J. B. Congle was then operating the largest harness and saddle making establishment in Oregon," the obituary read. Joseph found employment there and a good wage, so he stayed for several months. But aspiring to self-employment, Joseph left and soon opened up a shop of his own, where he worked for some time successfully.

From there, he visited places like Sacramento, San Francisco, Stockton and other places before getting involved in mining in California for at least four years. Then he relocated to the Auburn mines in Baker County, Oregon. There he got the idea of freighting, so he bought his own rig and horses and started freighting from Walla Walla to the Auburn mines.

The freight trail led him right through the Grande Ronde Valley each time, and he loved the green, meadowy land and fertile farm soil there. So he sold out of freighting and purchased 240 acres of wild prairie a few miles from La Grande. He also started a harness and saddle shop in Old Town La Grande in 1865, and worked both occupations for the next 30 years successfully.

Two years before his retirement, on November 23, 1892, he donated some of his land to create May Park. It was platted and designed by Arthur Philbrick, civil engineer of La Grande, Oregon, and named after Joseph's daughter, Miss May McWhirter. The park was dedicated and acknowledged in the presence of Joseph and Kate McWhirter, along with their daughters, Fannie and May McWhirter. In May Park there was a May Street and River Street, along with 16 subdivided lots.

Two years later, in 1894, Joseph McWhirter retired from his harness and saddle shop, and by this time in his life, he had become quite well known in the community.

He lived in a comfortable house in La Grande and residents showed their support of him, when they elected him to the office of mayor of the city. He reportedly performed his duties with honesty and skill. *(An Illustrated History of Union and Wallowa Counties, 1902, pg. 271-272)*

Joseph had been married twice in his lifetime, first to Miss Helen M. Henderson (1848-1870) of

Iowa in about 1868. Helen died shortly after their daughter was born. The daughter also died prematurely at the age of 17 years.

In 1872, Joseph married again, to Miss Kate Tatlinger, and she became mother to their two girls, May and Fannie. May became the wife of Alvaron V. Andrews (1863-1942), and Fannie became Mrs. William Woodard "Wood" Berry.

Joseph's daughter May B. McWhirter grew up in La Grande, and finished her education through her sophomore year at La Grande High School. *(1900 Federal Census)* On February 5, 1896, in La Grande, May McWhirter, 22, married Alvaron V. Andrews, 31. *(Western States Marriage Record Index, Vol. F, pg. 228)*

A later newspaper did shed some light on their wedding day. "Thursday evening Mr. and Mrs. A. V. Andrews celebrated their 17th wedding anniversary by entertaining La Grande people, who were present at their wedding. With the exception of Mr. Andrew's brother and family (E. T. Andrews), all the guests were among the original wedding guests. Cards were played and refreshments served and a very pleasing evening spent in commemoration of that eventful day for Mr. and Mrs. Andrews." *(La Grande Observer, Feb. 7, 1914, pg. 8)*

On November 25, 1896, May gave birth to their only child, a son named Jesse Varon Andrews, who served in France in World War I at a field hospital. After his discharge in 1919, he enrolled in college in Corvalis, Oregon, with a focus on commercial business. After his graduation in 1922, he came back to La Grande to buy an interest in The Toggery with his father. Jesse married Martha Eileen Morelock on July 14, 1934 in Union County. *(ancestry.com/family tree, Polk City Directories, 1946)*

May McWhirter Andrews enjoyed the luxury of being a homemaker in their home at 1516 Adams Avenue in La Grande, and she devoted herself to the raising of their son. May's widowed mother, Kate McWhirter, lived next door at 1520 Adams Avenue, and May also looked after her well-being, no doubt. May's father, Joseph McWhirter, died September 9, 1904, according to his published obituary. *(1910 Federal Census, ancestry.com)*

While May lived a rather quiet life, her husband was quite the opposite. He was well-known and a member of several civic clubs throughout his life. He supported his family by various successful enterprises. Andrews came to La Grande in 1890 as a professional baseball player to play with the La Grande baseball club. In those days La Grande had a good ball team. He was a conductor on the railroad in La Grande for about 13 years. *(La Grande Observer, August 31, 1927, pg. 93 special edition)*

According to the *La Grande Observer of Nov. 28, 1901*, Andrews belonged to the Order of Railway Conductors, and at a regular meeting at that time, he was elected as the assistant chief railway conductor. In that same organization, he was also elected on the committee of adjustment, along with J. C. McCreary and H. C. Grady.

In February of 1902, the newspaper mentioned that Alvaron V. Andrews was also on the La Grande Commercial Club, serving on the social committee with W. J. Church, Dr. L. D. Reavis and E. E. Kirtley. The paper read, "The social committee is already formulating plans to make this the banner social season in the history of the Club, and some royal entertainments will be given to Club members." *(La Grande Observer, Feb. 4, 1902, pg. 4)*

While Alvaron and May resided in La Grande, Alvaron owned some prize fruit acreage between La Grande and Island City. His yield in November of 1903 was impressive, so he sent some apples to show his father, T. J. Andrews, of the historic East End of Cincinnati, Ohio.

The *Evening News Review* of that town made mention of the apples he received from his son. "T. J. Andrews, of the East End, has in his possession an apple that weighs 31 ounces, or one ounce less than two pounds. It was raised on a tree five years old in the orchard of his son, A. V. Andrews, at La Grande, Ore. Mr. Andrews has 10 acres of fine fruit trees. He selected 21 apples which filled a 50-pound box. The giant apple is perhaps the largest ever seen in Ohio. An apple weighing half as much is considered large in this state (Ohio). This one measures 18 x 17-1/2 inches in girth."

In addition to raising prize apples, A. V. Andrews also occupied himself as a merchant of men's tailored clothing and accessories. His partner, J. V. Ross, was a long-time tailor in La Grande, who was hoping to retire soon. Their partnership was published on the front page of the *September 13, 1903 issue of the La Grande Observer*, and it read that the two men were expanding Ross' tailoring business to now include "a complete line of gents furnishing goods and men's shoes."

The article boasted, "Mr. Ross for a number of years has conducted in this city one of the largest tailoring establishments in Eastern Oregon. Mr. Andrews has been one of the popular O. R. & N. employees with headquarters in La Grande for over 13 years and enjoys a large acquaintance."

In that day a suit could be tailored at prices from $28 to $65 for the smart looking gent. The Ross and Andrews store advertised in a way that would probably not be printed today. It read, "You fat man, long arm man or short arm man, we will take your measure and guarantee shirts to fit you from $1.75 to $2.50." They also sold Knox hats, Hannan & Son dress shoes, Regent shoes, neck wear, and fancy suspenders and winter underwear.

In 1904, Ross did retire and Andrews bought out his interests in the business, then called "The Toggery." It was located in the 1200 block of Adams Avenue, La Grande. Andrews hired eight tailors and advertised that he would make a custom suit for gents from as low as $18.50, which was $10 lower than when Ross was working with him. He also advertised suits for women as well.

In 1905 he bought his first automobile, an Oldsmobile, and he joined the Union County Automobile Association. In April 1913, he was the secretary of that organization. At that time, the sign posts on Foothill Road between La Grande and Hot Lake were being vandalized and destroyed. The Automobile club was offering a $50 reward to whoever could identity the vandal.

The Automobile club was also a significant donor toward the costs of laying new gravel on what is now Highway 237 to Cove and the road from La Grande to Hot Lake. Andrews was a spokesman for that project and donation drive in 1914.

He and Fred Myers also led an auto party with picks and shovels to improve roads between La Grande and Hot Lake. "Whenever the party comes upon bumps or holes in the road, they do not complain about the condition of the lanes, but get out and remedy the trouble at once. Bridges that cause the party to leave their seats will be smoothed over and this popular driveway will be in excellent condition before they return this evening." *(La Grande Observer, August 9, 1912, pg. 1)*

Clearly, Andrews was a man of action. He was the same with his business. In June 1913, he introduced a partner in his business, his brother, Ealy Taylor Andrews of Ohio. The store's new signage now read: "The Toggery, Andrews Brothers proprietors." Ealy Andrews' investment of $10,000 doubled the present stock in the store. A. V. Andrews said, "This will make our shop the best tailoring establishment in the Northwest outside of the very largest cities." *(La Grande Observer, pg. 8, June 26, 1913)*

One of the 1913 ads for The Toggery stated, "We make all our suits in our own shop. Nothing is sent out of town to be made by sweatshop men." Obviously, locally made products was an important selling point for the business. In 1921, Andrews was a member of the Wing, Fin and Fleetwood Club, and an avid fisherman on Catherine Creek.

Alvaron Andrews, 79, died on December 28, 1942 and was buried at Hillcrest Cemetery in La Grande. May Andrews died June 25, 1958 in a Pendleton hospital at age 85 years. She was likewise interred at the Hillcrest Cemetery.

Her obituary stated, "Mrs. Andrews was born in La Grande on May 1, 1873, and she had lived here all her life. Survivors include a son, Jesse Andrews, Pendleton, and a grandson, Matthew Andrews, also of Pendleton." *(Obituary, La Grande Observer, June 26, 1858, pg. 6)*

She may not have been a famous woman in the community, but she will now be remembered for May Park and May Lane.

McAlister Road - This road #14A runs 3.58 miles in Township 3S R38E Section 22 north and south through Island City, 2 miles east of La Grande. It is named for early pioneers Samuel "Harvey"and Rebecca Jane (Anderson) McAlister, who filed a land claim in this area and homesteaded it.

Harvey was the son of Daniel Jefferson McAlister (1780-1836) and Susan Emmaline Cowan (1793-1834) who moved to Coles County, Illinois to ranch. *(Bernal D. Hug's History of Union County, supplement 8, pg. 2)*

Following his return from the war in Mexico, Harvey married a neighborhood girl named Lettitia Franklin Ashmore (1828-1851) on October 24, 1848 in Coles County, Illinois. She bore him a son, Daniel Jefferson "Jeff" (1851-1918), named after Harvey's father. Lettitia died unexpectedly on August 8, 1851. (See Halley Road entry)

The widower, Samuel H. McAlister, 29, then married another neighborhood girl named Rebecca Jane Anderson, 16, on March 8, 1853 in Coles County, Illinois. Their first son, James William (1854-1943) was born there, but then the McAlisters and Andersons moved to Terre Haute, Putnam County, Missouri, where Harvey engaged in stock breeding and farming.

There the following children were born: John Washington, Susan Lucinda Williamson, Jerusha Ann Huffman, and baby George Anderson.

When baby George was just 6 weeks old, a train of 20 wagons was organized at the McAlisters' farm, preparing for their migration to Oregon. Harvey McAlister was appointed as captain initially.

They left Terre Haute, Putnam County, Missouri, on May 7, 1862 for Oregon. When they reached the east side of Fort Kearney, Nebraska, the U.S. Calvary held them up, saying their train was too small and indefensible against Indian attacks, so the McAlister train waited to form a larger train.

They didn't have to wait long because that evening another train from Kansas and Missouri showed up to combine with the McAlister train. They agreed that Joseph Yount would become captain of the 42-wagon train henceforth to Oregon. Harvey McAlister was second captain of the stock during the rest of the journey.

The Yount train arrived to the Grande Ronde on September 13, 1862 (alt. Sept. 20) for a brief respite before journeying on to the Willamette Valley. However, they liked the Grande Ronde so well that they decided to stay.

The McAlisters brought six children with them: Daniel Jefferson "Jeff" (1851-1918) James William (1854-1943), John Washington (1856-1912), Susan Lucinda Williamson (1858-1941), Jerusha Anne Huffman (1860-1935) and George Anderson (1862-1864). George died in 1864 of measles in the Grande Ronde Valley. The others lived to adulthood and had full lives.

"Four long weary months were spent dragging across the plains," Susan McAlister Williamson said. "People, cattle and horses were worn out. When the company reached the top of Ladd hill and gazed down on the beautiful vari-colored bowl, the Grande Ronde valley, they were delighted with what they saw." *(La Grande Observer, Oct. 15, 1941, pg. 1)*

The McAlisters saw the beginning of a settlement where Old La Grande now stands, including three houses, one being a log cabin built by Ben Brown. Also, there was a packers and traders post operated by John Quinn, and a number of tents. Some single men decided to weather out the winter in their wagon.

Others from the Joseph Yount Train also decided to remain in the valley with the McAlisters, including the following family heads and their families: Joseph Yount, George Gekeler, Thomas Williamson, Joe Goodman, Thomas Elledge, Sol (Saul) Gerkin, and the following single men: George Horsepool, Arthur Hemming, Ike Elledge, the brother of Thomas; and D.A. "Uncle Bud" McAlister, a teacher and the nephew of Harvey McAlister. *(La Grande Observer, April 13, 1918, pg. 8)*

"Two wagons went along to The Dalles, the nearest source of supplies to get provisions for the winter. They accompanied the travelers who decided to push along to their original destination," Susan McAlister Williamson said.

Joe Williamson and Bud McAlister took the wagons to The Dalles, and it took 32 days there and back to bring needed supplies for the winter. As things turned out, the winter of 1862 was mild, much to the relief of the new emigrants. The homes of the settlers that first winter were not much more than wind breaks, Williamson said, "(They were) one room log huts with dirt floors, sod roofs, fire places for heat and tallowed paper for windows."

The McAlister's cabin roof leaked so badly that by spring it was necessary to erect a tent inside the house to keep the beds and provisions dry. Over the next few years, things improved rapidly.

The first year, Harvey McAlister had the only grindstone in their end of the valley. People came from as far as Cove to have their cutting tools sharpened by him. He offered sharpening services, and this brought many to the McAlister house. It was not uncommon for the McAlisters to have other settlers and their families come a long distance and stay all night with them.

Besides this tool sharpening business, Harvey engaged in breeding horses, which also brought scores of people to their ranch. For this reason, there was seldom a meal served at the McAlisters that didn't include guests at the kitchen table.

"After the Harvey McAlisters came to Grande Ronde, four more little boys were born to them: Thomas H. (1864-1940), Pleasant P. (1865-1920), General Price (1868-1918) and Samuel Ellison (1870-1920).

Baby Samuel was born on April 3, and two days later his father, Harvey, died of lung fever caused by a terrible chill after going out to round up strayed stock without a coat on. Harvey died on April 5, 1870 from his acute illness, and was interred in an unnamed cemetery on the hill in Old Town La Grande. This is where Eastern Oregon University is now located.

Shaken by her loss and great family responsibilities, Rebecca "Becky Jane" married a recent widower, Benjamin S. Halley, of La Grande, and she moved to his home outside La Grande. (See Halley Road) With his six children and her own young ones, she was overwhelmed with the care of 12 children. She died on April 5, 1874 and was buried in Ackles Cemetery on Mount Glen Road.

Her oldest sons, Jeff, John and James, stayed on at the Harvey McAlister homestead. Jeff eventually returned to his mother's kin in Ashmore, Coles County, Illinois, and he received his mother's share of his grandfather's estate. *(Findagrave.com)*

John and James continued working their father's farm. In 1879, James married Anna Belle Halley, his legal step-sister, and by 1880, they established their own ranch 3-1/2 miles east of Enterprise. James died in 1943, and was interred at Hillcrest Cemetery in La Grande. John McAlister remained on the family farm. *(An Illustrated History of Union and Wallowa counties, 1902; Bernal D. Hug's History of Union County, supplement 8, pg. 1-24)*

In 1890 and 1896, John was elected to the state legislature and earned the title, Honorable John W. McAlister. His political life ended there, but he started a new life with his bride Grace Cronkite of Hillsboro, Oregon. By 1902, he was a successful and prominent stockman in Union County.

Today, McAlister Road is heavily traveled by residents, commercial and Island City Elementary School traffic, and it is the location of Island City Cemetery and the golf course.

McCanse Lane - Noted as road #105A, it travels 1.07 miles in Township 5S R39E Section 29 in the North Powder maintenance district.

This lane is named after Edson Rodney McCanse (1900-1982), who was born on September 10, 1900, in Pataha, Washington. He spent some years in southern California before moving to the North Powder area before June 1924. In 1924, while he was a single man, he seeded about 400 acres of fall grain. *(La Grande Observer, October 25, 1924, pg. 10)* The authors will say that he wins the prize for the most mentions in the newspaper compared to any other person in this book.

The following year, he married Lydia Bertha Sailer in Canby, Oregon. She was born on December 20, 1898. After marrying Edson on November 2, 1925, she made her home with him on his farm in North Powder. According to Ron Pratt, who later bought the McCanse homestead, Edson McCanse put together his homestead from several other homes, the Dolstrums being one of them. *(Ron Pratt interview, September 29, 2021)*

During their marriage, they raised five children: Donald, Margie Lou, James Edson, Bonnie, and Audrey.

In 1931, the prices for wheat were so low that much of it was fed to pigs and cattle on the McCanse ranch. *(La Grande Observer, August 29, 1931, pg. 1)* Many of his neighbors did the same. Not only was that a bad year for wheat prices, but their house also burned in September, which they soon rebuilt.

McCanse raised not only wheat but he also had pigs, cattle, and sheep that he raised. In 1935, he shipped a railroad car full of lambs to eastern markets.

Then in 1944, his father, James McCanse, died in Jackson County, Oregon.

In 1945, the McCanse couple bought a house at 1502 First Street in La Grande. They regularly entertained at this home because Lydia was active in many organizations and clubs, and she enjoyed playing bridge with other women.

By 1948, the younger McCanse children were all attending Oregon State College, and they came home on school breaks. *(La Grande Observer, March 17, 1948, pg. 3)* A year later, 1949, Edson's mother, Margaret, died. In the *1935 Metsker Map*, it is noted that Margaret owned parcels of land next to ones owned by Edson. It is very possible he acquired those parcels after her death.

In 1950, Edson and Lydia took a rather unusual vacation. They flew in their small, personal plane in a group of 69 other planes to Cuba, and they stopped along the way at various places coming and going. They returned in about three weeks. *(La Grande Observer, March 2, 1950, pg. 1; March 21, 1950, pg. 4)*

After their trip, Edson went right back to work on the farm and had a sprinkler system installed because of the small amount of spring rain that year. Later that summer, the state was working on upgrading the Ladd Canyon highway and used 340,000 yards of cinder rock acquired from the McCanse property nearby. *(La Grande Observer, September 5, 1950, pg. 1)*

Also, in 1950, McCanse received the honor of Conservation Man of the Year from the Union County Wheat Growers Association. This was decided upon by a committee that toured his 13,000-acre ranch near North Powder before making the selection. Conservation played a key role in McCanse's 27-year task of building a sparse 880 acre holding into one of the most outstanding ranches in the state.

He was active in grain, seed and livestock operations on his ranch. He was one of the pioneers in the use of nitrogen for heavy straw growth. His range management and irrigation water handling have become models for all of Eastern Oregon. *(La Grande Observer, December 7, 1950, pg. 1)*

McCanse was always interested in improving things, so he participated in several seed trial plots, using 16 varieties of spring wheat to see which kinds of grain would grow best in his soil. *(La Grande Observer, May 6, 1953, pg. 4)*

For all of his efforts at various kinds of conservation practices, he became the Conservation Man of the Year for the state of Oregon. *(La Grande Observer, December 5, 1953, pg. 1)* McCanse not only had interests in farming and ranching, but he also had a part interest in the Union Lumber Company, which he sold in 1954. He did, however, continue with a sawmill that he owned.

Some of the improvements McCanse made on his land were shown and talked about during a tour of his operation in 1954. It was mentioned that he purchased a 1,700 acre tract of rundown, weed-infested and eroded landed west of North Powder. The better soil had been cropped continuously to wheat, since the first water rights were filed in 1880.

Nearly 700 acres had been abandoned, and this land was growing Canada thistle. He told that the previous year more than 2,700 tons of top quality alfalfa, alfalfa grass and mixed hay were harvested from the 700 acres of what used to be covered with Canada thistle. The value of the year's crop alone was more than the cost of the place plus irrigation improvements.

Also a highlight of the tour was his sprinkler system, which irrigated 1,500 acres and the livestock operation. At noon, the members of the tour enjoyed a luncheon at the Powder Valley High School (just like they do today). *(La Grande Observer, May 26, 1954, pg. 1, 6)*

McCanse believed in passing along his agricultural knowledge to another generation. He did this under the Youth Farmer Exchange Program through the Farm Bureau. In April 1955, a 26-year-old Turkish farmer, Haluk Ozsoy, arrived to live with the McCanse family for one year to study farming methods in the area. This farmer had 600 acres in Turkey, and was eager to learn American farming practices. He attended the English college in Istanbul, Turkey, so he could speak English fluently.

Haluk said that it takes 60 people to run his 600-acre farm, and he has two tractors. He raised tobacco, wheat, corn and other cereal grains. He was especially interested in cattle because he didn't have any. *(La Grande Observer, April 18, 1955, pg. 4)*

McCanse was a forward-thinking farmer and business man, who had several interests going at the same time. "He had the first CAT in the Powder Valley, from what I heard," said Pratt. "He was also involved with the big saw mill in Union and was a partner in that for numerous years."

As for the road itself, Pratt said, "That was called Shaw Lane or Shaw Road in the early days before the freeway was put in, and all the roads got named, when they put Highway 30 in and again in 1988, when they renamed all the roads."

There was a Shaw Creek Road in the north end of the valley, so Shaw was dropped near North Powder, and McCanse took its place. "When you went up the road, McCanse's place was on the right and about a quarter mile back in to their homestead," Pratt said.

Pratt remembered that the road just became known as McCanse Road since Edson was "quite a figure around here," he said. That wasn't an overstatement either because by 1964, McCanse accumulated between 14,000 and 15,000 acres in multiple places, said Pratt who bought the

McCanse homestead that year.

"By that time, Boise Cascade bought the timber off of about 4,000 acres of ground on Shaw Mountain behind the ranch house," Pratt said.

After the sale of the McCanse homestead to Pratt, Edson McCanse moved to Canada. His daughter and son-in-law moved ahead of him as did one of Edson's partners in the Union saw mill. When Edson joined them, they started to develop large farms there. While clearing a lot of land there, Edson injured himself in an accident with his Caterpillar tractor, and he was laid up for a while.

Ron Pratt owned the original McCanse homestead for about 15 years, and then he sold to Don Burkel, who has since passed away. It's gone through a couple of owners since then. As for Ron, he retired in 1990 and lives with his wife, Carol (Glenn) Pratt, in North Powder. *(Ron Pratt interview, September 29, 2021)*

Edson McCanse died July 20, 1982; and Lydia died November 22, 1985. Both were interred at the Union Cemetery. McCanse Road stands as a tribute to one of the more successful ranchers and farmers in the state of Oregon.

McDonald Lane - Recorded as road #16B, it runs 2.28 miles in Township 2S R38E Sections 12-13-14 in the La Grande maintenance district. On the east end it intersects with Halley Road and on the west end it intersects with Sandridge Road.

It was named after Peter Alexander McDonald (1860-1925), an immigrant from Shieldaig, Scotland, and it is the location of the McDonald Century Farm.

On May 24, 1882, Peter and his brother, John Jr. purchased a 320-acre farm on what is now McDonald Lane. John Jr. sold his ½ interest to Peter in January 1903 and moved with his wife, Maggie, to Wallowa County to farm with another brother, Hector McDonald. They prospered well there. Meanwhile, Peter and his wife, Emma (Krone) McDonald, developed the farm on McDonald Lane and two other parcels.

The land was deeded to their son, George K. McDonald, and then to George's widow, Lyla E. McDonald, in 1958. Lyla deeded the property in 1971 to their daughter Barbara, who was married to Elwyn D. Bingaman. Barbara died in 1998, and in 2004, Elwyn deeded the original 1882 property to their son, Gregory L. Bingaman, who in 2015 gained Century Farm status.

Gregory is the farm's owner and does business under the name Bingaman Enterprises in 2018, and he operated a mint distillery operation with his father, Elwyn. On July 11, 2019, Elwyn died and with him went a great memory of Imbler's history. *(Elwyn Bingaman interview, June 2016)*

His son, Greg, has two daughters, Jessica and Hailey, with his first wife; and with his second wife, Chandra, he has a son, Kale. Greg Bingaman also owns and operates "Pioneer West," a farm implement and supply business in La Grande.

Elwyn's obituary relates his life in the pages of the *July 2019 La Grande Observer*:

"On July 11th, 2019, Elwyn D. Bingaman of Imbler passed away at his home, which was the only home he had lived in for almost 83 years. Elwyn was born on August 9, 1936 to Franklin Harold Bingaman and Leona (Witty) Bingaman. Elwyn attended Imbler School and was proud to graduate from the "Red Brick Building" in 1955.

While in high school, Elwyn enjoyed judging animals and competing with his FFA team where they won the PI (Pacific International) in Portland. Elwyn had fond memories of traveling by train to the National FFA Convention in Kansas City, Missouri. He was president of the Imbler FFA Chapter his senior year. Elwyn briefly attended what is now Eastern Oregon University and Oregon Institute of Technology, but his heart quickly drew him home to his life-long passion of farming.

As a generational farmer, Elwyn started farming at a very young age. When he returned from college, he and his brother, Howard, were farming on the McDonald property near Alicel where he met his future wife Barbara. They wed in 1964, and they had two children, Kathleen and Greg. Barbara passed away in 1998. He later married Louanne McDonald, and they shared the next 18 years together.

Throughout his life, Elwyn served on various boards, and he enjoyed his tenure on the Imbler School Board, where he served when the new high school was built in 1977.

In 1965, Elwyn was awarded the Young Farmer of the Year for Union County. In his earlier farming years, he enjoyed working on the farm with his family, especially nephews, Russell and Ross. Being a progressive farmer and seeing the value of irrigation, he drilled three deep artesian wells in the Grande Ronde Valley. Elwyn was always aware of the farming history of this valley and those who homesteaded and farmed before him. Elwyn was a historian and had a passion for retelling these stories.

He had a love for growing grass seed, and he enjoyed working fallow ground for the next year's crop. Even when Elwyn wasn't physically in the field, he continued to be a huge part of the day-to-day farming operations with his son Greg. He was a mentor not only to Greg, but to many others." (End of obit)

Elwyn was preceded in death by his parents, wife Barbara, daughter Kathleen, sister Maxine, and brother Howard Bingaman. He was survived by his second wife Louanne, son Greg and grandchildren. He was interred at the Summerville Cemetery.

McIntyre Road - (MacIntyre Road) This road holds two titles. It is county road #1, and it is the longest county road in Union County, measuring 15.22 miles in length in Township 3S R35E Section 16 in the La Grande maintenance district. This road was not the original #1 county road, but that distinction belonged to Blackhawk and Booth Lane combined. At some point, the roads were re-numbered by the county.
It runs northwest off of Ukiah-Hilgard Highway 244 and becomes NF-21, which leads to Indian Lake Campground. There are seven addresses on McIntyre Road today. It used to be called Starkey Road. *(Greg Tsiatos interview, Oct. 30, 2018)*

The road is named after McIntyre Creek which runs in the same Township and is a tributary to the Grande Ronde River. The road generally runs in a parallel direction, but not real close to the creek, when viewed aerially or topographically.

This road is named after a lumber man named James Charles MacIntyre (1855-1916), who lost his life on the job. MacIntyre is how the family spelled their surname, having strong Scottish ancestry. Both the creek and the road sign are misspelled, but that has happened a few times, as the authors have discovered in writing this book.

The MacIntyres were not in Union County prior to 1900. There's no mention of them in the *An Illustrated History of Union and Wallowa counties* book and nothing in the history books of Bernal Hug and no mention of McIntyre Creek in the Oregon Geographic Names book.

However, the authors did find someone in the land records, a James Charles McIntyre, who proved land up in Union County on March 19, 1906. He was born on December 29, 1855 in Charlottetown, Queens, Prince Edward Island, Canada. He immigrated in 1875 and became a naturalized citizen. His parents were both natives of Scotland.

He married Eva A. Longway, a nurse, on September 6, 1892 in La Crosse, Wisconsin. Eva was born September 5, 1876 in Syracuse, New York. She became mother to Helen M. and Kenneth Arnold. There is an older child, Edith Sarah Grace, who was born January 1884 in Canada, who is possibly James' daughter from a previous first marriage.

In 1905, it appears that the family lived in Neillsville, Clark County, Wisconsin on a farm that James was paying a mortgage on. At the same time, he was also improving land he bought in Union County, Oregon.

In 1910, the family made its way to Baker City, where James was working as a timber cruiser. Then in the *Union and Wallowa County Directory of 1914*, the family was listed as residing in Union County and that James worked as a laborer with Nibley-Mimnaugh Lumber Company. Eva worked as a nurse; Helen worked as a stenographer and Kenneth was a student in school.

Edith was not listed in their household, but she became Mrs. Willis M. Peacock on January 12, 1915 in Cook County, Illinois, and she resided in Fennimore, Wisconsin with her new husband.

James McIntyre was 21 years older than his wife, Eva, and he passed away first on June 7, 1916 at about 60 years of age. A death notice was printed in the *Fennimore Times, Wednesday, June 14, 1916, pg. 10,* published out of Fennimore, Wisconsin.

It read: "Mrs. W. M. (Edith) Peacock received a telegram Wednesday evening from Wallowa, Washington (Oregon), conveying the sad news of the death of her father, James MacIntyre, who was killed by a log that afternoon. Mr. MacIntyre was 60 years old and had been superintendent of a lumber camp there for many years. His body was taken to Neillsville, Wisc., his former home for burial under the auspices of the Masonic order. Mr. and Mrs. W. M. Peacock and little daughter, accompanied by Miss Grace Horton, left Friday afternoon for Neillsville."

He was survived by his wife, Eva, and his three children, Mrs. W. M. Peacock, Helen and Kenneth A. MacIntyre.

The *Fennimore Times, Wednesday, June 21, 1916 issue, pg. 12* made mention of Eva in the following social briefly:

"Mrs. James MacIntyre of Wallowa, Wash., (Oregon) came yesterday from Neillsville, where she recently buried her husband (James), for a few days' visit with Mrs. W. M. Peacock before returning home."

After James' death, Eva and daughter Helen relocated together to live closer to Eva's son, Kenneth Arnold MacIntyre, who lived in Englewood, Los Angeles County, California. Helen was single then, and she found work there as a court room stenographer. The *1920 Federal Census* enumerated them as boarders with the William Edwards family, including his wife Martha and their 30-year-old son Joel Edwards. Eva was then 43 years old and Helen was 25 years old.

Eva lived an additional 36 years until her death on December 9, 1952, and she was buried in Englewood Park Cemetery in the Los Angeles area. *(Ancestry.com; census records)*

McKennon Lane - Formerly Gaskill Road, this road #132 runs 2.02 miles straight as an arrow east and west, connecting on its east end with Gray's Corner Road and on its west end with Imbler Road. It is located in Township 1S R39E Section 32 in the area south of the city of Imbler, which abuts the Alicel district.

According to a 1978 Union County map, this road was called by the name Gaskill Road. It was named after Ebeneezer D. Gaskill (1846-1923) and his wife Susannah Stroup (1847-1937). They were both buried at Summerville Cemetery.

They were married on August 12, 1867 in Almont, Michigan. They had six children, four of whom were born in Michigan. They were: Frederick (1868-1947), Jesse Allen (1870-1953), Samuel (1873-1877), Samuel B. (1878-1952). Daughter Maude (1885-1976) was born in Kansas. In November 1886, the family arrived to the Grande Ronde Valley in Union County, Oregon, where their son Wilfred (1902-1912) was born in Alicel, where they resided.

The story now focuses on their second son, Jesse Allen Gaskill, also called "Jet". He continued living with his parents until he married his wife, Jennie Armintha Woodell. They married on January 6, 1896 in Union County, and had four children: Ralph, born March 5, 1897 and he died September 15, 1897; Lola, (1901-1985), LaNita (1906-1995) and Wilma (1908-1988).

Jesse operated a 220-acre farm southeast of Imbler and raised a variety of cereal crops. About 1922, he allowed part of his land to be used for crop experimentation conducted by men from the Umatilla and Moro station. The bulk of the work was being done by the Pendleton office. *(La Grande Observer, September 27, 1940, pg. 13)*

Jesse died on August 11, 1953; his wife died December 14, 1971 and both of them are buried in Summerville Cemetery. So the Gaskills were in this area from 1886 until 1971.

Gaskill Road was eventually changed, presumably in 1988, to McKennon Lane. It is named after a prominent agriculturalist named Frank McKennon (1889-1974), the son of Leonidas Lafayette "L.L." McKennon (1853-1945) and Allie Elizabeth (Patterson) McKennon (1854-1922).

In 1897, Leonidas and Allie brought their family to the Grande Ronde Valley from Prairie, Carroll County, Arkansas.

The McKennon family farmed in Alicel, according to the *1900 Federal Census*. Leonidas retired from farming and moved into La Grande, where he lived at 1311 N. Avenue. He had married Allie on October 15, 1875 in Berryville, Carroll County, Arkansas. She died May 5, 1922.

Then he married again, this time to Mrs. Alice (Barrett) Beckwith on August 5, 1923 at the home of William Crosby Ross of La Grande. This was her second marriage as well. She was born in Parkersburg, West Virginia on May 19, 1873. She was 20 years younger than Leonidas McKennon, and she died on January 10, 1939 at age 65 in their La Grande home after a long period of illness. She was interred at Hillcrest Cemetery in La Grande, and her husband survived her for six more years.

Leonidas McKennon, 92, died at his home on January 10, 1945. He was born in Arkansas on January 11, 1853 and had come to the Grande Ronde Valley in 1897, where he lived for the past 48 years. He had an older brother named Archibald McKennon who lived in Cove.

Leonidas was interred at the Hillcrest Cemetery in La Grande, next to his first wife, Allie. Surviving him were four daughters: Mrs. Nora Webb of Spokane, Mrs. Alice Wright and Mrs. Fannie Sackett of Sheridan, and Mrs. Ina E. Keltner of La Grande; and four sons, Floyd of Seattle, Bliss of Oakland, Routh of Portland and Frank McKennon, then living in Salem.

Frank McKennon was born on September 10, 1889 in Berryville, Arkansas, when his father was 36 and his mother, Allie, was 34. He came to the Grande Ronde Valley with his parents at the age of 8 years. He grew up on his father's farm, and as an adult, he acquired his own farm, located near the bridge where the county road crosses the Grande Ronde River east of Alicel. *(La Grande Observer, Oct. 18, 1945, pg. 4)*

On September 9, 1908, when he was 18 years old, he married Elva Montana Smith (1887-1960), and they had two children, Russell Melville born May 17, 1909 and Frances E., born in 1912.

The *1915 La Grande Observer*, refers to his ranch as the "McKennon-Ledbetter ranch near Alicel." *(La Grande Observer, Aug. 25, 1945, pg. 2)* On this ranch McKennon and his son-in-law (W. R. Ledbetter) raised some fine Clydesdale horses that were shown at the Union Livestock Show in 1917. *(La Grande Observer, June 13, 1917, pg. 1)*

An *October 28, 1927 La Grande Observe (pg. 7)* carried an article, "McKennon Farm is Known As One Of Most Progressive". The article points out that this 400 acre ranch is right at the foot of Mt. Harris and is a handsome property. Frank McKennon is described as an open-minded man, ready to be convinced of any good project.

In fact, the article praises the fruitage of his open-mindedness in that "Many of the farm practices which are today considered as standard over the valley were first tried out on the farm by Mr. McKennon."

He experimented with wheat Hybrid No. 128 seed that he bought from Mr. Nelson of Pendleton, and by 1927, about 60 percent of the fall wheat was of this type, and all because of the experiments of McKennon, the article read. He also introduced Hard Federation wheat and had the biggest acreage of this wheat in the state of Oregon. He shipped this wheat all over Eastern Oregon, Washington and Idaho.

Grimm alfalfa also found its way into the valley through the testing and experimentation on the McKennon farm, the article read. McKennon believed that the answer to decreased fertility of the soil was to plant alfalfa and sweet clover crops.

On his ranch, he raised hogs, 130 fine Plymouth Rock chickens, a large flock of purebred Hampshire sheep, cattle, and horses. He always had an experimental mind, when it came to ranching and stock raising. He loved to enter competitions to see how well his stock would do. To that end, he raised Holstein cows and even won state championship for one of them.

During his life, he was involved in a number of organizations, including being a member of the agriculture and health committee of the Union County Chamber of Commerce; a farm member of the La Grande Rotary Club; a member of the Imbler school board; and the master of Pleasant Grove Grange in 1931.

Frank McKennon died on January 11, 1971 in Salem, when he was 84 years old. His wife Elva Montana died earlier on September 26, 1960 in Pendleton at age 73. They had been married 52 years, living a good part of it on their ranch in Union County. *(ancestry.com)*

McKenzie Lane - Formerly Hunter Lane on the *1935 Metsker Map*, this paved road #14B connects Hunter Road to Summerville. It runs 2.27 miles east and west and is located in Township 1S R38E Section 12 in the Imbler maintenance district.

McKenzie Lane is named after father and son, Clyde and Glen McKenzie, who both took their turns at operating the Glenn Century Farm located on land originally settled on by Clyde's father-in-law, Tolbert T. Glenn in 1868.

"For that matter, this road should be called Glenn Lane," said Glen McKenzie, grandson of Tolbert T. Glenn.

Tolbert Glenn, 18, arrived in the Grande Ronde Valley and staked a claim for 160 acres in Summerville on January 5, 1875. He married Sarah Meyer. They had 8 children, the youngest being Myra Glenn, who married Clyde McKenzie in 1913.

In 1918, after Sarah Glenn died, Clyde and Myra inherited the home place and bought out all but three of the other heirs. Henceforth, the farm was known as the McKenzie farm. Glen McKenzie gave the farm a more personal name, Glenwood Ranch. *(Noted on the back of one of Glen's aerial photos in his own handwriting.)*

In 1934 during the Great Depression, Clyde decided to build a new house on the property and set his parents' home toward the back of the property. He hired a Summerville carpenter, John Lewis, to do the work.

The construction of the new house was called "crib built" or "horizontal plank-on-plank construction." As a result, the walls were so immensely solid and thick, Glen said, "that there's enough wood in this house for two houses." The window sills were 8 to 12 inches deep because of this style of construction. By 1935, the house had electricity.

Their only son, Glen Roderick McKenzie was born on August 22, 1917 in the original Glenn house and delivered by midwife, Frieda Fries. His mother, Myra, was also born in this same house, incidentally, but in 1888.

Glen McKenzie attended Pleasant Grove School about 2 miles west of Summerville, Central School in La Grande and then graduated from La Grande High School in 1934. He graduated from Eastern Oregon Normal School in 1936.

During his college years, he met Jean Williams through their mutual love of theater, but WWII separated them. After the war, they reunited and a romance bloomed.

On July 4, 1947, Glen married Jean Williams, and they took over operation of the family farm in 1960. Glen's mother Myra died in 1971 and his father Clyde died in 1976. The McKenzie farm was given Century Farm recognition on September 6, 1970 at the Oregon State Fair in Salem. It is registered with the Oregon State Historical Society.

Glen earned other recognitions, including Oregon State University (OSU) Extension Cooperator, OSU 75 Year Club and the OSU Agricultural Hall of Fame, Chamber of Commerce Service to Farm Community and Man of the Year in 1974. He was Cattleman of the Year in 1989, and the Master of Ceremonies for the Farmer-Merchant Banquet for 35 years. *(McKenzie Obituary)*

Jean and Glen McKenzie had no children, but they were very involved with the theater at Eastern Oregon University. One of the two theaters there was later named "McKenzie Theater" in their honor. In 1992, the McKenzies established the Oregon Agriculture Foundation, a subsidiary of the Eastern Oregon State College Foundation, which was entrusted with ownership of the McKenzie farm under a hired manager after McKenzie's death.

Jean died in 1993, at which time the McKenzie Memorial Scholarship was established. Glen McKenzie's death occurred on August 14, 2006 at age 88. Their home on this lane was sold in 2011 to William and Karen Gamble, who take immaculate care of the property and value its Century Farm status. The Century Farm sign hangs in a prominent place on the property today on McKenzie Lane.

The farm acreage is managed by EOU's Oregon Agriculture Foundation. Glen said that he wanted to "keep the farm in one piece." *(Glen McKenzie interview, November 2000)*

McNeill Road - This road #142 travels 3.91 miles in Township 3S R40E Section 26 in the Union maintenance district and is located off Mill Creek Lane near Cove.

This road is named after John Archibald McNeill (1856-1925) and his wife Sytha Virginia (Bell) McNeill (1856-1938), farmers from Erath County, Texas, who came to Cove, Oregon in 1901. Here they became orchard growers and fruit farmers.

John A. McNeill was born November 27, 1856 in Stephenville, Erath County, Texas, the son of Dr. William Wallace McNeill (1819-1902) and Mary Abrilla Stephen (1840-1864). John married his wife Sytha on September 3, 1878 in Erath County, Texas. They were noted there as a family in the *1880 Federal Census,* when he was a 23 year-old married man and father.

They had ten children: Winifred Bell (1879), William Archibald (1880), Anna Margaret (1882), Rosa Ora (1884), Charles Volantine (1886), James Marvin (1890), Mary Ann "Lulu" (1892), Susan

Ophelia "Suda" (1894), and twins Louine Sena and Louis Sidney (1897).

John A. McNeill was a fruit grower in Cove for 18 years, and then he moved to Baker City, where he did general farming, but lived in the city limits on 1515 Valley Street. John died at the hospital in La Grande on June 23, 1925 and was buried at the Cove Cemetery. Sytha died in 1938.

Their eldest son, William Archibald McNeill, grew up on the family fruit farm, learning the business, and after his father died, he received ownership of the orchard land his father owned. The land on the *1935 Metsker Map* indicates a transfer of land ownership from the J. A. McNeill estate to his son and daughter-in-law W.A & S. McNeill. The latter would be William Archibald McNeill and his wife, Stella McNeill of Cove.

He and Stella Alvereta Warner were married on September 24, 1912. They had two children, a baby that died at birth in 1916 and a daughter named Margaret Ruth McNeill, born 1919.

Sadly, Margaret died at the home of her aunt, Mrs. C. W. Thompson, at 804 Washington Avenue, on the morning of May 31, 1934 after a long illness, "during which she suffered greatly," her obituary stated. "Ruth was born April 21, 1919 in La Grande and was 15 years, one month, and 10 days of age. The McNeills made their home in Mill Creek Canyon above Cove. Ruth was a student in Cove High and very popular and talented." *(La Grande Observer, Friday, June 1, 1934)*

William retired from cherry farming, and his obituary states that he died at the age of 82 years at a local hospital. He was born in Stephenville, Erath County, Texas on October 8, 1880, and he lived in Cove for 60 years. He was survived by his widow, Stella McNeill, Cove; a brother, Charles McNeill, Willamina, Oregon, five sisters, Mrs. Winnie Ayars and Mrs. Annie Ryan, both of Nampa, Idaho, and Mrs. Lula Rutter, Mrs. Suda Comstock and Mrs. Louine May, all of Baker; and several nieces and nephews. He had no living children to carry on the orchard business that came through the McNeill family. This concludes the history of McNeill Road, home to a cherry business run by father and then by his son.

Meadow Cow Camp Road - This is a private road off of Ukiah-Hilgard Highway 244 at the end of Meadow Creek.

The camp located there was for private use by cowboys, who rode the range and needed a lodging place for the night. There were five or six people who had reserved rights to use the camp, including Ray Strike, sheep operator John Correa of Echo; and Ted and Mary Stickler.

Meadow Creek Road - This is a "Private Property" road off of Highway 244 at the end of Meadow Creek. There are 8 addresses on this road. *(Greg Tsiatos interview, Oct. 30, 2018)* It is located in Township 4S R35E Section 8 in the La Grande maintenance district.

According to the *Oregon Geographic Names, 1982 edition, pg 487*, "Meadow Creek is a good sized stream flowing eastward in the Blue Mountains and draining into Grande Ronde River near Starkey. Some old maps show this as Starkey Creek, but letters from the postmaster at Starkey in 1933 and from the USFS say that Meadow Creek is the correct name and the one in general use."

Melody Road - This is a private road in Township 3S R38E Section 3.

Merritt Lane - Formerly called Witty Road, this road #139 runs 5.72 miles in Township 2N R30E Section 21 in the Elgin maintenance district. This lane starts at Highway 82 east of Elgin near the Minam Summit, and it intersects with Yarrington Road and ends at Good Road. It runs through a northeast precinct of Elgin called "Cricket Flat" or "the Flat," as it was often called in newspaper clippings.

It was called Witty Road after the Quintus Vandicus Witty family, wheat farmers on the Flat. He had married Mary Ann Scott, the daughter of Joseph and Sarah Scott, Elgin farmers.

Quintus had a big red and white barn, which was standing in 2011. Mr. Deb Rysdam bought the Witty property and moved the house down into Rysdam Canyon. *(Joe Bechtel interview, Aug. 29, 2018)*

After the Witty land was sold, the lane was known only as Merritt Lane after Clarence Edgar Merritt (1885-1974), and the Merritts lived at the beginning of the road. Highway 82 used to run past his residence before the highway was re-routed to its present course.

Clarence Edgar Merritt was born November 1, 1885 in Ringgold County, Iowa to William Reuben Merritt (1852-1915) and Nancy Ann "Nannie" (Jackson) Merritt (1854-1932). The Merritt family lived in Prairie, Wallowa County, Oregon in 1900, when Clarence was 14.

On October 1, 1905, he married Margaret Elizabeth Barnes in Union County. The year 1905 was a record year for marriage license applications—145 of them. The Merritts were part of that historic record. *(Newspapers.com)*

According to the *1910 and 1920 Federal Censuses*, Clarence and Margaret were grain farmers, living in Haines, Baker County, Oregon, and in 1930, they were living on C Street in Elgin, where he was a proprietor of a warehouse.

His mother, Mrs. Nancy Ann Merritt, died at her home at Elgin on the evening of May 25, 1932 at the age of 78 years, one month and eight days. Burial was at the Elgin Cemetery. Mrs. Merritt lived at Elgin the last 21 years. She was born in Indiana on April 17, 1854. She was survived by the following children: Clarence E., Mrs. Nora A. Bussear and Mrs. Gleana Taylor, all of Elgin, besides other relatives. Her husband (William R. Merritt) preceded her in death several years ago. *(La Grande Observer, May 26, 1932, pg. 1)*

Clarence's father, William Reuben Merritt, was born October 9, 1852 and died March 14, 1915 in Elgin. "He was dangerously ill with stomach trouble," stated the *La Grande Observer, March 9, 1915, pg 2.*

Clarence's grandparents were Daniel David Merritt (1750-1831) and Nancy Jane (Johnston) Merritt (1762-1837). Daniel died in Belmont County, Ohio on January 18, 1831 and was buried in Crabapple Cemetery in Wheeling, Belmont County. Nancy also died in that county and was buried in the family plot with her husband.

Besides the Elgin farm, Clarence owned a vehicle that he sported around in. "Clarence Merritt drove in his auto to Joseph one day last week," stated the *September 22, 1913 issue of the La Grande Observer, pg. 7.* He liked his Fords, and sold a Model A to Joe Bechtel in 1953.

On October 16, 1913, Clarence and Margaret had an infant who died and was interred at the Elgin Cemetery. *(Findagrave.com)*

The La Grande Observer, Oct 31, 1914, pg. 2 mentioned that Clarence E. Merritt was born on a farm in Iowa. He worked in the Grande Ronde and Wallowa valleys for the last seventeen years, and he was currently working for Union County Co-Operative Association. Hundreds of good citizens in both counties knew him.

He and his wife, Margaret, got into the business of building houses that were advertised as artistic, different and yet affordable.

"Mr. Merritt is a builder and architect of New York City but as a side line and on his own hook he and his wife are putting up the most adorable and artistic little houses for people of moderate means. It is a labor of love that pays exceedingly well. Mrs. Merritt is artistic to her finger tips and most of the quaint little touches in their delightfully different domiciles emanate from her." *(La Grande Observer, Aug. 24, 1917 pg. 7)*

On January 13, 1921 in Elgin, Margaret gave birth to a daughter, Ruth Josephine Merritt. She survived all the perils of childhood and married twice, once to Philip G. Preston and then to Donald Lee Reynolds. Clarence Merritt let his son-in-law take a hand at farming the land, but this did not work out for either of them, and the son-in-law abandoned that occupation. *(Joe Bechtel interview, Aug. 29, 2018)*

Clarence's wife, Margaret Elizabeth Merritt, 64, died January 5, 1953 at Harrisburg, Oregon following an operation. She was born in Elgin on February 28, 1888 and had lived in that community all her life. She was survived by her husband, Clarence, and a daughter, Ruth J. Reynolds of Salem. Margaret was laid to rest at the Elgin Cemetery in the family plot.

On February 22, 1953 in Boise, Idaho, Clarence married his widowed sister-in-law, 67-year-old Olive Viola Briggs (1885-1973). They were married by Cecil Warner, and the witnesses were Glen R. and Myrtle Ballard. *(Idaho county marriage records)*

Following their marriage, they took a 10 day honeymoon and visited relatives in the Willamette Valley, The Dalles and in Selah, Washington. *(La Grande Observer, March 2, 1953)*

Olive (Barnes) Briggs was the widow of Alvirtus "Bert" S. Briggs, who died in 1950 at age 78 years. Olive and her late husband, Bert, farmed acreage in section 35 directly adjacent to Clarence Merritt's property and also in section 25 next to the Bechtel farm.

On November 8, 1953, a young couple by the name of Joe and Phyllis (Phippen) Bechtel were married and following a honeymoon to Portland, they returned to make their home in the Clarence Merritt ranch home. *(La Grande Observer, Nov. 21, 1953 pg. 1)*

Clarence had sold his farm about 1952-53 to Dick Waller, and Clarence and Olive lived in their newly built cement block home not far from the former Merritt home that the Bechtels rented.

"We rented the home for $30 a month," Joe Bechtel said. "It had two bedrooms, a bath, a kitchen and living room. We rented for about 3 months and then moved because our landlord was just a little too close, and we wanted more privacy." *(Joe Bechtel, 84, interview, Aug. 29, 2018)*

Joe knew Clarence Merritt well, having grown up on a 580-acre farm on Merritt Lane about a mile from Clarence's place. Joe's parents, Ora and Sadie (Thompson) Bechtel had a farm and "part of the acreage they bought had once been called the Witty place, but I can't remember which Witty owned that," Joe Bechtel said. Ora Bechtel's farm boundary joined in one area to Clarence Merritt's land.

"My dad was one of the first ones to have a combine out there," Joe said. It was an old Holt combine that he pulled with an old CAT. He did a lot of custom cutting."

When Ora was 58 years old, he suffered a stroke, so he and his wife moved into Elgin and Joe bought the home place. After Joe sold it, he and Phyllis moved to their present ranch south of Elgin on Highway 82.

Clarence's second wife, Olive (Barnes) Briggs Merritt was born June 30, 1885 and died July 10, 1973 in Union County at the age of 88 years *(Oregon Death Index)*. Olive was buried in the Briggs family plot at Elgin Cemetery. She had three children with her first husband, Alvirtus S. Briggs (1872-1950).

After Olive's death, Clarence's daughter Mrs. Ruth J. Preston arranged for him to relocate closer to her at 614 Dearborn Avenue in Salem, where he died on September 23, 1974 at the age of 88 years. He was interred at the Elgin Cemetery next to his first wife, Margaret.

Michaelson Drive - This is a private road off from Watson Street in Township 3S R38E Section 4 in the La Grande maintenance district that brings access to seven properties.

Middle Road - This road #42B was pragmatically called "Middle" because it lies between Valley View and Palmer Junction roads. It travels 2.70 miles in length in Township 1N R39E Section 16 in the Elgin maintenance district.

This is why the *1935 Metsker Map* called it "Elgin-Palmer Junction Road" because it led from the edge of Elgin near Boise Cascade Lumber Mill to Palmer Junction Road leading north of Elgin into the rural territory.

Today, Middle Road lies between Hartford Lane and Gordon Creek Road. According to resident Mary Lou Martin, Middle Road was once a gravel road and was called "Grange Hall Road" and "Galloway Road" after the William Harrison Galloway family. He and his wife, Sarah Ann Lawson, came to the Grande Ronde Valley in 1878.

William H. Galloway was born on May 3, 1821 in Tennessee. He was in the shoe business in Spencer, Owen County, Indiana. In 1858, he relocated to Charleston, Coles County, Illinois and operated his business until 1865, after which he moved to Mount Ayr, Iowa until 1873. It was then that he desired to move out West, and so he migrated to Cowlitz County, Washington, where he took up farming until 1878. Then he moved to Pine Grove, Wasco County, Oregon, farming there for four years before relocating to Elgin. *(An Illustrated History of Union and Wallowa counties, 1902, pg. 340)*

During his life in Elgin, he donated land for the Thorny Grove School, about three miles north of Elgin. *(150 photographs, Elgin and North Union County, 2009, pg. 134, photo of William H. Galloway)* Elgin was his last place of residence, and he died on June 21, 1892.

After his death, his widow, Sarah, moved in with her son, H.S. Galloway in Cove. Sarah was born January 10, 1824 and died Sept. 26, 1903. She and her husband were interred at the Elgin Cemetery. *(ancestry.com; An Illustrated History of Union and Wallowa Counties, 1902, pg. 340-341)*

Their son, John Tilford "Til" Galloway (1848-1911) had his farm in the Gordon Creek area of Elgin, and his name was in the paper for owning the largest cow. It read, "J. T. Galloway, the well known Gordon Creek rancher, claims to have the largest cow, considering her age, there is in the county. The animal in question is a full blood shorthorn, three years old, and recently tipped the scale at 1570. Who can beat her?" *(The Elgin Recorder)*

There was a newspaper report about J. T. Galloway in *The Weekly Republican Newspaper of 1888,* which explained how he got into the sawmill and planing business. It read as follows:

"About four miles north of Elgin is the saw and planing mill of Mr. J. T. Galloway. Some three years ago or a little more, he returned from a wild goose trip back to Iowa, having gone back there believing that Oregon was not the place to live, but in less than a year, thoroughly repenting of his folly, he saw that Oregon for him, at least, was better than Iowa. So he returned and set up the aforesaid mill."

The article continued, "Out of this enterprise, which is a remarkable accommodation to the neighborhood, he is building up an enviable business and realizing that honest work pushed with industry will build up a reasonable competency. His mill is run by steam and has a capacity of 10,000 feet per day of ten hours. It is in the midst of a fine body of timber in abundance apparently all around him."

Galloway's products were high quality, and his business ethics were praiseworthy as the article stated: "It is possible that he can furnish as good, if not better, lumber than any other mill in the valley. Though having the compass of the lower part of the valley and Elk Flat has his patronage without competition, yet he has seemingly not taken advantage, but sells his lumber at a fair living price and so low that he can cut lumber and deliver it even in Union though thirty miles away at a lower price than we are able to get it from other mills nearer us." (End of article, as published in the *Elgin Museum & Historical Society's newsletter, May 2021, pg. 2)*

John T. Galloway's son, Jewell W. Galloway (1872-1935), also lived on this road, he being the grandson of William H. Galloway. Jewell's spacious Victorian home was located across the road from the Rockwall Grange Hall, but was torn down and replaced with a manufactured home in the 1970s. It was no doubt built from lumber milled at the Galloway Brothers Mill in Elgin. *(House photo in 150 Photographs of Elgin and Union County, 2009, pg. 73)*

The Galloway Brothers Mill was no little operation. The newspaper printed an article titled, "A Large Carload of Lumber" and it read as follows: "The largest carload of lumber that ever came over the Elgin Branch and probably the largest that ever came into La Grande, arrived in this city last evening. The car was loaded at Elgin by Galloway Bros., the lumbermen, and consisted of 51,000 feet of lumber." *(La Grande Observer, Nov. 25, 1904, pg. 6)*

Jewell was married to Emma Hathron in Union on Wednesday, May 25, 1898. *(La Grande Observer, May 28, 1898, pg. 3)* He died on January 4, 1935, and his obituary stated that he was a pioneer resident of the Elgin community, arriving in that section in 1878. He was occupied in farming and sawmill work since that time, and he had made quite a few friends in the Grande Ronde Valley as a result. He was a member of the Elgin Lodge No. 98 A. F. & A. M. He was interred in the family plot at the Elgin Cemetery. *(La Grande Observer, Jan. 5, 1935, pg. 4)*

Not to be overlooked, but Middle Road is home to a small country cemetery, well kept. It's known as the Galloway Cemetery, but there is a sign there calling it the Jacob Long Cemetery with at least 12 burials. Among them were three from the Long family.

Mill Creek Lane - This road #65 is 3.76 miles in length in Township 3S R40E Section 22 in the Union maintenance district. Due to the prevalence of saw mills in the county, there were about four Mill creeks in Union County, one in Elgin (later renamed Shaw Creek), one in Summerville, another in La Grande and the one in Cove, after which Mill Creek Lane was named.

The saw mill on this stream was built by James M. DeMoss. *(Oregon Geographic Names, 7th edition, pg. 643)*

James McElory DeMoss was born in 1837 in Greensboro, Indiana, and he married Elizabeth Ann Bonebrake in Marion County, Iowa, on November 25, 1858. He and his family settled initially in North Powder in 1862, where he built a small hotel and put in a toll bridge over the Powder River. These two structures enabled him to make a good living.

Then the DeMoss family moved to Cove prior to 1866, where James built a toll bridge over the Grande Ronde River and erected the first sawmill on Mill Creek near Cove.

While living there, James M. DeMoss and family formed a musical group called the DeMoss Concertists of Oregon and performed from 1872 to 1933, starting in Union County, Oregon. As they became more popular, they toured throughout the United States, Canada and Europe.

In Eastern Oregon, they put on concerts in remote mining camps and frontier towns, bringing culture, music and entertainment to these Pacific Northwest communities. James and Elizabeth had seven children and five lived to adulthood: Henry, George, Minnie, Lizzie and May.

The children were all under the age of 12 when they became a touring music group. Each of the children showed extraordinary talent in reading, writing and performing music. They collectively were trained to play 41 different instruments. Later, the family moved to DeMoss Springs in Sherman County, Oregon. Their 1,200 acre ranch there was their family retreat from their busy performing schedule. *(Online biographies)*

As for the saw mill built on Mill Creek, it changed hands a few times. According to the *Oregon Scout, June 19, 1886, pg. 5*, "James F. Kelley has sold his sawmill two miles above town on Mill Creek to T. J. Deborde, who will take possession on the 15th of July."

Readers might want to take this next news clipping about Mill Creek and Fred E. Corpe (1863-1944) of Cove with a grain of salt, but this appeared in the *Oregon Scout, July 23, 1887, pg. 5*:

"It isn't every place that can afford a *true* snake story, but Cove is so favored, for we have the necessary papers certifying to the correctness of the foregoing. A few days ago, Fred Corpe, a man whose reputation for voracity is A-one, was on Mill creek just below town cutting some willows, when a rustling in the bushes attracted his attention to one of the most hideous reptiles ever appearing to mortal sight. Although a person of undoubted nerve, Fred, concluding discretion the better part of valor, lost no time in leaving the serpent in the rear. Having been so near, he had a good opportunity for observing and says at the lowest estimate, the snake was ten feet in length, of a spotted color and with immense head and jaws raised at a considerable distance above the ground. Chickens and pigs have been mysteriously disappearing along the creek for some time in the past and now it is thought this snake is responsible for the loss. The owners of poultry have offered $5.00 reward for the scalp of the serpent."

Mill Creek is nicely described in the *Oregon Scout, May 23, 1889 on page 1:*

"Mining and Lumbering Business—Mill Creek, which flows through the village and carries a good volume of water, with an average fall of 150 feet to the mile, has its source in the mountains to the northeast, and flows through a body of fine saw timber, which could supply the whole country for years to come. It has but one sawmill upon it. A shingle mill and planing mill are also located at the edge of the timber. There are opportunities here for lumber men who can command capital.

The development of this section has only commenced. The O. & W. T. Road is an assured fact and will pass near the Cove; and it is only four miles to the head of the Sand Ridge, so widely celebrated for its last production of grain.

Mill Creek would furnish the necessary power, and at little expense to propel a hundred different factories, mills, etc., of large dimensions. But the men of the Cove, though by no means poor, have their money invested in other industries and to acquire these things, money must be had from abroad.

The enterprising citizens here offer great inducements to men of means, who would embark in any of the many manufacturing enterprises which a careful examination of the surroundings could but convince almost anyone, would prove successful. Correspondence is already being had with Eastern parties looking to the erection of a woolen mill here." (End of article)

There was also an article dealing with hydro power in the *La Grande Observer, March 14, 1905, pg. 5* as follows: "The Cove will have electric lights by June (1905). Active work is going on at the power plant at the head of Mill creek, which power will be transmitted through different parts of the county by the Grande Ronde Electric Company." (End of news briefly)

Water rights to various creeks in the area, including Mill Creek, were hot items of discussion, starting in June of 1909, as shown by the many articles appearing in the La Grande Observer.

One such article relates that the Caldwell Ditch Company, Claude N. Ogilbie and T. G. Wilson were contesting who had the water rights for water from Mill Creek. It is the first of the hearings in Union County resulting from the new water law passed by the last legislature. The Honorable F. M. Saxton, superintendent of water division No. 2 heard the case. It took several months of witness statements and testimony before the case was decided. *(La Grande Observer of June 29, 1909; November 23, 1909)*

On the topic of water—not having it is a terrible thing, but so is having too much of it, as the following article brings out.

"Cove Streets Flooded. Cove, May 28—"Special"—Mill Creek is on a rampage and several streets of Cove are under water, as the result of the highest waters in that stream in the present generation. It is likely that a cloud burst caused the sudden swelling of the stream. Farming land at Five Points, three miles from town, is under water, and certain streets here are inundated. The stream is still rising. Hail, falling Monday and yesterday, did damage to the cherries but the exact amount or scope is not known." *(La Grande Observer, Wed., May 28, 1913, pg. 1)*

Now for some good news from Mill Creek to finish up. "Good catches of trout are being made between Cove and Borkgren's sawmill, reached from Cove by auto, wagon, trail, railroad or stage." *(La Grande Observer, May 2, 1920, pg. 7)*

Miller Lane - This road #109 is 3.19 miles long and connects with Curtis Road on its west end and on its east end it turns into W. Bryan Street entering the city of Union. It's located in Township 4S R39E Section 10 in the Union maintenance district.

This road is named after a prominent Union pioneer named Simon Edward "Ed" Miller. The *1935 Metsker Map* shows that he owned quite a bit of land in the abovementioned township and surrounding area.

Ed Miller was born on a homestead near Union on September 26, 1876, the son of Simon Miller of Shaafhausen, Switzerland (1832) and Juliet Ann Galloway of Indiana. (1841) They arrived to the Grande Ronde Valley in 1863, commencing in general farming and stock raising.

Ed Miller's obituary continued, stating that he was a "prominent Union County stock raiser." During his life he earned the honor of "Man of the Year" by the Union County Livestock Association in 1949. He was one of the most featured individuals in the La Grande Observer in this book. This speaks of his character and community involvement.

He was also featured in the *Western Livestock Reporter*, stating "At the age of 18, he started in business for himself, renting from the other heirs a part of his father's estate in the Clover Creek district four miles north of North Powder. In 1894, he purchased 100 head of cattle on the John Day and drove them 100 miles back to his ranch."

The *Reporter* went on to report, "In 1897, Mr. Miller embarked in the sheep business and the second year he and a brother had about 4,000 head which they kept at Eagle Valley. Later they moved the bands to Wallowa county and still later brought them to the upper end of Catherine Creek." He went out of the sheep business after WW II.

Ed Miller was civic minded and a great volunteer in his community, becoming a member of the Union School Board for 30 years, a member of city council and director of the Eastern Oregon Livestock Show and president of the association in 1920-21. In addition he was a charter member of the Catherine Creek Grange.

On February 5, 1905, Simon Edward Miller married Miss Elida A. T. Stackland (1877-1963), and they celebrated 50 wedding anniversaries by the time 1955 rolled by. The *1920, 1930, and 1940 censuses* showed that during their marriage they lived on Bryan Avenue, which turns into Miller Lane.

He died February 17, 1958 and was interred in the Union Cemetery. His survivors included his wife and four adult children: Elida S., Bethene M., Rodney E. and Odin E. He also had three married sisters, May, Alice and Margaret, six grandchildren and other relatives.

Mink Lane - This private lane is located off of End Road in Township 1S R38E Section 16 in the Imbler maintenance district, and it is named after the mink breeder who lived on this road. At one time, mink fur was quite popular in the making of coats and coat collars.

Mitchek Lane - This is a private lane developed in the early 1970s, and it's located in Township 1S R40E Section 6 in the Imbler maintenance district, but the mailing addresses are in Elgin. This lane brings access to about seven properties, none of which are old enough to hold historic significance.

The road was named Mitcheck in 1988, after landowner Scott A. Mitchek. He does not currently own land or live on this lane. *(Resident Bob Scott Wiles interview, September 25, 2021)*

Monroe Lane - Formerly Sidehill Road in the 1930s. *(La Grande Observer, December 26, 1930, pg. 7)* Enumerated as county road #10B, it runs 2.28 miles through Township 2S R38E Sections 2-3-4 in the La Grande maintenance district.

This road is named after Otis Schweicker Monroe, born December 1881 in Idaho. In 1900, he was working as a plumber and living in Lewiston, Idaho, with his father and two brothers, Charles (1878) and Walter (1891). Otis was the second of the three boys.

He married Elma M. Clarke, who was born July 21, 1880 in Anderson County, Kansas. They apparently never had children. In 1910, he was still following the plumber's trade. Sometime between then and 1920, they moved to Linn County, Oregon, where he was listed as a farmer in the *1920 Federal Census*.

The *La Grande Observer of October 9, 1929, pg. 5* reported that Otis S. Monroe purchased a ranch near Mount Glen known as the Durland place (near Iowa School). He expected to move to that ranch shortly and make his home there. He accomplished his move to the ranch before December 1929.

"Happy Days" — "Mr. and Mrs. Otis Monroe, who own one of the orchard farms on the Sidehill Road in the Iowa district, have returned from Corvallis. They had taken Mrs. Monroe's parents, Mr. and Mrs. W. B. Clarke, to their home after having spent the past two months with the Monroe's at Mount Emily Orchards. The Monroe home has been the gathering place of many relatives and friends for the last few weeks. On one occasion, four generations were represented, and this was the first time that Mr. and Mrs. Clarke had seen their great grandchildren. Mr. and Mrs. Clarke were delighted with our valley and expressed the hope that they might spend other summers in the shadows of Mt. Emily." *(End of article, La Grande Observer, August 29, 1931, pg. 6)*

In October of 1931, Grant Tucker was packing apples under contract with Pacific Fruit and Produce Company. They were working on the crop of Jonathan apples grown in the Monroe orchard and the first car was going to leave this week for export and others will soon follow. This was the first car of apples out of Imbler this season. The Monroes picked more than 7,000 boxes of this variety. *(La Grande Observer, October 13, 1931, pg. 6)*

In the *La Grande Observer, October 2, 1941, pg. 9,* it reported that Otis paid 5 cents a box to apple pickers, however, by 1943, wages paid to pickers per box increased to 15 cents.

Mrs. Elma Monroe died on August 27, 1947 at the hospital in La Grande after an illness of several months. She was a resident in the county for nearly 20 years. She was the president of the Happy Circle Club of the Iowa district and active in civic affairs. She was buried in the Island City Cemetery.

Otis Monroe died August 8, 1953 at the hospital in La Grande. He was buried beside his wife in the Island City Cemetery.

Morgan Lake Road - Formerly Mill Canyon Road #118, it was renamed Morgan Lake Road #118A after the lake. This road travels 2.82 miles through Township 3S R37E Section 23 in the La Grande maintenance district.

This road is named after Morgan Lake, which was named after Thomas Morgan (1870-1965), a sheep drover, who pastured his family's bands of sheep on the pastures in that area and watered them at the nearby creek. But before the authors explain this part of the history, let's first consider the road's original name, Mill Canyon Road.

One early reason for this road name is mentioned in the *La Grande Observer, Oct. 8, 1948, pg. 1* as the namesake for Mill Canyon itself.

"A second industrial establishment which the early settlers found desirable was a grist mill. The earliest inhabitants had made flour by grinding whole wheat in coffee mills, but as more and more people began to established themselves on farms near La Grande, the need for a flouring mill became very real. To turn the virgin soil of the valley, the Rynearson brothers had begun the manufacture of plows, these probably being the first satisfactory agricultural implements manufactured in Oregon. By using these plows, more land was brought under cultivation and the primitive methods of grinding flour was no longer sufficient.

The first flouring mill was built in 1865 by a Mr. Woods, who located it at the mouth of Mill Canyon in south La Grande, the canyon taking its name from that early structure. The mill was of a stone burr type and was placed in operation sixty days after construction was commenced. When completed it was capable of milling 25 barrels of flour a day. Mr. Woods sold the mill in 1866 to John R. Wilkinson, who, in turn, disposed of it in 1874 to Augustine I. Gangloff, who operated it for many years." (End of article excerpt)

Early on, Mill Creek was the source of La Grande's first regular water system, but it was privately owned by Daniel Chaplin. The supply coming from Mill Creek was delivered via pipes of logs, bored out in La Grande. Originally, the log pipes were laid out to supply water to Chaplin's house.

"They were extended so as to cover the most of the Arnold & Dray addition, a fractional part of what is now South La Grande. The receipts were scarcely ever more than $30 per month and the most of this was paid to Jack White, long since deceased, for doing the work of collecting and keeping the system in repair." *(La Grande Observer, Oct. 1, 1915, pg. 3)*

"When La Grande's center of gravity shifted toward the railroad, the wood pipes were extended down Fourth and along Depot streets. They were continually bursting and the whole system was finally abandoned." *(La Grande Observer, Oct. 1, 1915, pg. 3)*

Historian Dorothy Fleshman, 95, of La Grande once lived on Mill Canyon Road, as did her grandparents, Fritz and Mary Hofmann, immigrant farmers from Switzerland. Fleshman said, "It was called Mill Canyon Road because Fred and William Arnold had a sawmill on that road in the 1880s, but it wasn't there very long." *(Dorothy Fleshman interview, October 22, 2021)*

Fleshman researched the county road files, particularly file #300, which revealed a county road petition initiated by F. M. Bartmess and others for the construction of a road through Township 3S R36E in Section 15, starting from "Old Town" of La Grande and running to the top of the hill and beyond to Rock Creek. It was surveyed on July 20, 1888.

The approved road petition was filed on September 7, 1888, with the official name of Mill Canyon Road. File #311 further verified that this road was the location of a sawmill owned by Fred and William Arnold. Mill Canyon Road was initially designated road #6, commencing at the fork in the road where Glass Hill diverts left and Mill Canyon Road proceeds forward. Sometime later Mill Canyon Road was reassigned as road #118 and remained that number for the duration of its county road status. *(Dorothy Fleshman email, October 23, 2021)*

Mill Canyon Road did not take its travelers to the shorelines of Morgan Lake because the Morgan Lake property was state school land, and then privately owned from 1873 to 1959. The road traveled uphill about 1,200 feet to the top of the hill and then it bypassed the southern end of the lake with a wide berth. Today, Morgan Lake Road at the top of the hill runs only a quarter mile more past the lake's south end and stops at a cattle gate that reads, Elk Song Ranch.

Historically, Mill Canyon Road was printed on an early *1880 Survey map* despite not being an official county road at that time. It was simply the common name used due to the presence of the mills. After the road gained official status as a county road in 1888, then, of course, it was noted on subsequent maps like the *1978 Union County map* and the *1981 Union County survey map of the Morgan Lake Estates.*

On January 24, 1980, Fleshman saw Mill Canyon Road on a state highway *Code Index Map of Union County* that had been revised on February 20, 1979. She explained that this map showed Mill Canyon Road starting from the city of La Grande and running past (not to) Morgan Lake to the Hilgard Highway #341. This road was listed as #679. The left fork partway up the hill was called Glass Hill Road, as it is today, while the right fork became Mill Canyon Road #118A.

Mill Canyon Road was officially a county road from 1888 to 1988. In the latter year, the century-old Mill Canyon Road name was replaced by another equally historic name, Morgan Lake Road, and one that was more appropriate for a road allowing public access to Morgan Lake Park.

From Morgan Basin to Morgan Lake

Prior to 1900, Morgan "lake" did not resemble anything like it does today. It was not a recreational area or a clean source of drinking water for the city. In fact, its original appearance was described in the following *1915 La Grande Observer article*:

The lake was originally described as a "depression in the mountains that was so enticing that the original builders of the lake looked no further for a place to impound water to be used for power purposes." *(La Grande Observer, Oct. 15, 1915, pg. 1)*

For this reason, *The Morning Oregonian, November 14, 1901* article titled, "Big Water System Planned" described it in more geological terms than other newspaper articles had in the past. It read: "Morgan Lake, or rather Morgan Basin, is situated in the hills above and about two miles southwest of La Grande."

Lakes are often formed in the basins of land. A basin is a dip or depression in the surface of the earth that could be formed by various geological reasons. In the case of the Morgan Basin, water collected there annually, although the natural accumulation of water was very shallow in depth. Nonetheless, it was fed by rain water, snow melt, and two nearby creeks. When rainwater is collected in a basin, or creek water flows into a basin, it becomes filled and produces a lake.

The "lake" was a shallow, swampy marsh prior to 1900. It wasn't until after January 1902, when the 322 foot dam was built, that the basin was sufficiently excavated and water was conveyed from Sheep Creek that the water level started to rise to four feet in depth. Prior to that, Morgan Basin had steady leakage on its north end onto the meadow and down into Deal Canyon. As a result its water level was very low and marshy.

This fact actually corroborates the sheep man story about how Thomas Morgan likely watered his sheep at what became known as Sheep Creek instead of Morgan Lake. Back in 1867 when a survey was done of the land around Morgan Lake, it was ranked as excellent pasture land. Fleshman remembered that was prime sheep pasture up there, as long as she has known it.

Morgan Lake is located in Township 3S, Range 37E, Section 13 on the plat map, and a gravel access road diverts from Morgan Lake Road and runs along the west shoreline of the lake. The gravel road continues to travel over the northwest end of the lake right atop the dam structure itself, which is 30 feet wide supporting a roadway in that section. The roadway does not go around the entire perimeter of the lake, but it stops and turns around at the north end. However, there is a walking trail that completes the circuit around the lake's perimeter.

To learn more about Morgan Lake, the authors turned to La Grande Parks and Rec Director Stu Spence to see what the city files revealed. He submitted the following:

"On September 20, 1873, James Mason (1844-1923) purchased from the State of Oregon, 320 acres of a school section for the price of $400. Eventually after a series of sales, it was sold to the Grande Ronde Electric Company for one dollar and other good and valuable consideration in 1905. This company and other companies that would follow used Morgan Lake to supply water to the local power plant at the bottom of Table Mountain that served the City of La Grande.

The Grande Ronde Electric Company sold this property to the Eastern Oregon Light and Power Company on September 24, 1909 for $100, and other good and valuable considerations. Eastern Oregon Light and Power, in turn, sold the land to California Pacific Utilities in 1946.

California Pacific Utilities then in March, 1959, sold the Morgan Lake holdings to the City of La Grande for $7,500.00 for the purpose of making it into a recreation facility. Today Morgan Lake Park is still managed by the City of La Grande Parks & Recreation Department. The 205 acres of park land includes various amenities including vault restrooms, trails, camping, and fishing." *(La Grande Park and Rec files)*

*Morgan Lake Name*sake

Since the La Grande Parks and Rec Department files did not reveal the namesake for Morgan Lake, the authors continued their search. Something that was written in the *La Grande Observer, Sun., Sept. 27, 1903 on pg. 3* made them wonder if Morgan Lake was given a geological name.

The article read in part: "The bottom of the reservoir is a clay formation and holds the natural seepage water the year round, hence its name, Morgan Lake." In the *Lexicon of Geologic Names of the U.S., pages 1420-1421*, there is an entry called "Morgan formation" having to do with soil formation and composition.

However, Deric Carson, a water shed conservationist with the Union County Soil and Conservation District said that he checked his geologic maps for that area and found nothing indicating any Morgan formation. He said that the ground around Morgan Lake has a silty composition. Carson suggested that Morgan Lake was most likely named after a person.

Historian Dorothy Fleshman offered two possible namesake candidates, ones that she jotted down on small pieces of paper and put among her Morgan Lake files.

The first story Fleshman heard was told to her on September 30, 1996 by the late Howard Fisk (1916-2009) of La Grande. He said that the lake was named after Enoch Morgan, who was said to be the foreman on the crew that built the dam on Morgan Lake. The dam construction began in the summer and fall of 1901 and continued through at least July of 1903.

However the name Morgan Lake was known long before the dam was built, according to the *La Grande Observer, Sept. 17, 1903, pg. 3* which stated: "The principal reservoir is located at an elevation of 1,500 feet above La Grande, known for years as Morgan Lake, where the main body of water will be stored." So Morgan Lake was known by this name "for years" prior to 1903, and this fact alone would eliminate Enoch Morgan as a candidate for the lake's namesake.

What about any person named Enoch Morgan around that time frame? There was only one in La Grande by that name, and he was born in 1895 in Riley County, Kansas and came to La Grande in 1926 to work for the railroad. Later there was a county engineer by that name in the 1930s. Both of these men weren't here early enough to be the namesakes for Morgan Lake, so the authors moved on to investigate the next theory.

The second story that Fleshman was told was that Morgan Lake was named after Thomas Morgan, a sheep drover who pastured his sheep at the top of Mill Canyon Road and likely watered them at the creek near the marshy lake. This Thomas Morgan was born in 1870, so could he be old enough to have pastured his family's sheep in the 1880s and early 1890s?

"Yes," said well-known stock raiser and rancher Janie Tippett of Wallowa County. "It wasn't unheard of for a young boy, age 10 or 12, to be herding a band of sheep away from home for long periods of time." *(Janie Tippett interview, Dec. 8, 2021)* It was common for sheep operators as far away as The Dalles to drive their sheep to Union County for pasturing.

Fleshman recalled how every year in her childhood, great bands of sheep, cattle and horses were driven from Umatilla County through La Grande on their way to Cheyenne, the nearest railroad station leading to the Eastern market.

"There was just one way for them to pass through La Grande and that was right down main street, whether it was B or C Avenue at the time," she said. "They were on B Avenue when we saw them being driven up the hill past our house. It would take nearly the entire day for them to pass. The children would watch the flocks of sheep go by, but when the long-horned cattle went through, the children were kept inside." *(Dorothy Fleshman email, Dec. 4, 2021)* Those kind of drives stopped sometime in the 1960s.

The Morgan Family

The subject of this entry, Thomas Morgan, has a descendent named Donna Morgan Lewis, Cove's city clerk, who provided some of the following family history.

Combining Donna Lewis' family tree information with that found in the *An Illustrated History of Union and Wallowa counties, 1902; ancestry.com, Findagrave.com, and newspapers.com,* the authors present the following Morgan family history.

The Morgan family story begins with Daniel and Rachel (Woodsides) Morgan, married in Lewiston, Fulton County, Illinois on July 29, 1841. They had four children born in Fulton County, Illinois: Thomas (1842-1918), Ann (1844-1899), Seth (1846-1915) and a baby girl (1847-1847) that was born in Wyoming.

In 1847, en route over the Oregon Trail, the Daniel and Rachel Morgan family reached Natrona County, Wyoming, near Independence Rock where Rachel gave birth to a baby girl, name unknown. Due to some complications, Rachel died there and was buried on the trail. The bereaved father, Daniel, took the infant and his small children Thomas, Ann and Seth and continued their journey to Corvallis, Oregon. Sadly, on October 24, 1847 at age 3 or 4 months, the baby girl also died from some kind of accident. She was buried at Government Camp, Clackamas County, Oregon.

On July 27, 1848, Daniel married Mary Jane Taylor in Benton County, Oregon, and she became step-mother to the three Morgan children. She also gave birth to Minerva Jane Morgan, born July 28, 1850. That same year, by some awful twist of time and unexpected events, Daniel died, leaving four young children to the care of his 22-year-old widow, Mary Jane Morgan (1828-1877). She married John Sylvester (1814-1891) in 1851. The two step-parents then raised all the Daniel Morgan children, including Seth, to whom we will now turn our attention.

As a young man Seth must have returned to Fulton County, Illinois because he married Margaret Jane Hamilton there on January 23, 1868, and then he brought her back to Corvallis, Oregon to build a life together and raise a family. On February 28, 1869, their first child, Daniel, was born; and then Thomas (1870), Albert (1873), Rachel (1876), Sheppard (1880) and Ben (1883). The kids were raised on a stock ranch first in Forest Grove and then in The Dalles, in sight of Mt. Hood, and were taught everything about raising and herding sheep.

Their father, Seth Morgan, sold his farm 4-1/2 miles outside of The Dalles and retired to his residence in town in 1901, but not before helping Thomas, Albert and Sheppard get started ranching on their own. For the next 14 years, Seth enjoyed his retirement, including prospecting for placers on the east fork of Mount Hood River. He died on July 22, 1915, and his daughter Rachel and son Thomas were the executors of the estate. The authors now focus on Thomas Morgan, the namesake for Morgan Lake.

As a young boy Thomas Morgan was familiar with herding sheep, and it's believed that he pastured them around the lake southwest of La Grande for many years for his father. By the age of 18, he was equally determined to be prosperous like his father Seth. At age 20, Thomas was ranching in Umatilla, and within three years, he made himself among the prosperous farmers there. Thomas Morgan then went to The Dalles, where his parents lived, and he worked as a stock raiser there.

By 1900, the Morgan brothers, Thomas, Albert and Sheppard all moved to set up their individual ranches in Wallowa County. Brother Daniel was well established in northeast Washington State. However, Thomas lived in Joseph; Sheppard and Albert owned land in Imnaha and Fruita. In time, Thomas purchased a half section near Fruita, quickly adding to it other parcels until he alone owned 680 acres. All three Morgan boys were incredibly prosperous, adding more and more land to their ranch holdings.

"Thomas Morgan is to receive a band of sheep of J. H. Dobbin soon, which he expects to run in connection with his cattle." *(Wallowa Chieftain, May 22, 1902)*

In all the land records, however, Thomas Morgan never purchased or sold property in the vicinity of Morgan Lake or Sheep Creek. He may have leased the land, but he never owned any in that area where sheep were pastured. At this present day, the meadow land near the lake is terribly rocky and silty, so hard to cultivate, but great for pasture.

A historical article appeared in the *La Grande Observer, Oct. 1, 1915, pg. 3* that lends credibility to the Morgan sheep story. The canyon spoken of in this article is the one where Mill Creek runs along what later became Morgan Lake Road.

"In June 1881, a band of a couple hundred sheep stampeded and piled up in the canyon a mile above town. The dead carcasses formed a fill twenty feet deep from one bank to the other. For several months thereafter the people refused to use "city" water." Prior to this incident Mill Creek had been providing La Grande with drinking water.

This certainly verifies that sheep did graze atop the mountain in the vicinity of the lake and that they came off the mountain by way of Mill Canyon Road. The article did not mention the owner of the sheep, unfortunately. Since Mill Canyon Road was more narrow then than it is today, it's very understandable how stampeding sheep could fall over the edge of the road into canyon below and Mill Creek.

On November 1894 in Pendleton, Thomas Morgan married Miss Etta B. Smith, daughter of Levi P. And Laureandia A. Smith. She was born in North Salem, Indiana on January 28, 1871. Her father was a prosperous farmer of Indiana, who came west in 1878, settling in Umatilla. The young married couple were held in high esteem by their community. *(An Illustrated History of Union and Wallowa counties, 1902)*

At one point, he took on a dairy farm in addition to his sheep operation. "Mr. Morgan is a well known sheep man and so is used to making good money. That he sees a big profit in the dairy business is evidenced by his purchase." *(La Grande Observer, Thurs., Nov. 21, 1907, pg. 4)*

He bought the first milking machine east of The Dalles in March 1908, which milked two cows in seven minutes. He owned farm properties simultaneously in Union and Wallowa counties, and he was noted in the newspapers often for his land purchases.

In August 1908, Morgan bought a 320 acre ranch from Dr. A. F. Poley on Prairie Creek in Wallowa County, known as the old Watson Place for $14,000. Morgan will superintend all of Dr. Poley's places on Prairie Creek, consisting of about 1,000 acres. *(Enterprise News Record, Aug. 6, 1908, pg. 4)*

Then in March 1912, Morgan purchased the J. D. McKennon place on Cove Road, 720 acres for $52,000 located midway between Cove and La Grande. "The deal is one of the biggest turns in realty of the present year." *(La Grande Observer, Mar. 7, 1912, pg. 1)* A follow-up article stated that "This purchase makes Mr. Morgan one of the large farm land owners of this city. It gives him about 1400 acres all told, in three lots, his Prairie Creek ranch, his Alder Slope tract and the Grande Ronde valley farm." Morgan had farm managers placed at each of these properties to carry out his business. *(La Grande Observer, Apr. 5, 1912, pg. 1)*

Readers got familiar with article titles like this: "Morgan Buys More Land". This time he traded land in Wallowa County for Home Independent Telephone stock. His farming equipment was among the best. "Mr. Morgan has a big traction engine which pulls 12 plows, turning over a strip 15 feet wide at a time. He is thinking of bringing the power plowing outfit to Wallowa County next summer. Enterprise Record-Chieftain" *(La Grande Observer, Sat. Jan. 11, 1913, pg. 6)*

On the sheep scene, Morgan and his brother Albert were making news too. "Seventeen carloads of spring lambs purchased for C. L. Buell of Chicago were weighed Wednesday for shipment east to go out on Thursday's train. The lambs were bought by W. H. Graves for Mr. Buell. Mr. Graves has purchased about 3,200 lambs in the last week. He got ... 500 of Thomas Morgan and 650 of Albert Morgan. Thomas Morgan's are Merinos, but all the others are coarse lambs. The Merinos probably will be resold for feeding here, but the others will be shipped out for early fattening in the east." *(La Grande Observer, Sat., Sept. 27, 1913, pg. 1)*

After his father died, Thomas and his wife did live with his widowed mother for a time and took care of her. Thomas and his wife apparently did not have children of their own. He lived a long life, centered around a cherished western lifestyle, not to mention lots of wheeling and dealing in his pursuit of prosperity.

Even at age 84, Thomas was making news for the local paper, and it wasn't his obituary either. He decided he would climb up icy Mt. Hood, something on his bucket list. Consequently, on August 11, 1955, he fulfilled this life-long dream "and then he hurried back down in time to herd his flock of sheep," the article read, titled, "Oldster Climbs Icy Mt. Hood to Get New Angle on Country."

"Thomas Morgan, who had lived in sight of the mountain since boyhood, said he wanted to climb the mountain to view the land where he was raised 'from a new position.' So with the company of guides and two Oregon State college students, Thomas Morgan, made the climb successfully.

"A check of lodge records after his ascent showed that no one approaching Morgan's age had ever registered as making the tough climb, part of it over ice," the article read. "In addition to raising sheep near Maupin, Morgan recently published a book locally called, 'My Story of the Last Indian War in the Northwest.'" *(La Grande Observer, Mon., Aug. 15, 1955, pg. 4)*

Thomas Morgan, the ambitious sheep man makes a plausible, not to mention colorful namesake for Morgan Lake, Morgan Lake Road and even Sheep Creek.

Morgan Lake's development—1901

The city of La Grande was looking for a source of water to supply fire protection, sewerage and hydropower to its residents, and the Morgan Basin on top of the hill southwest of La Grande looked like it might be the solution to their needs if waters could be conveyed from Rock Creek and Sheep Creek to keep Morgan Lake full.

This reservoir proposal was published in the *La Grande Observer* newspaper on November 4, 1901, pg. 4 as follows: "To be changed—A corporation has just been formed by La Grande men capitalized at $10,000 for the purpose of converting the waters of Sheep Creek into Morgan Lake, which is situated at the head of Deal Canyon, 1,200 feet above this city."

At the turn of the century, the lake was not created for public recreational use, but rather "for the purpose of supplying water for the generation of electricity at Morgan Lake power house. At that time the power output of the project was sufficient to satisfy the electrical demand of all the City of La Grande and some of the other towns in the valley," stated an article by City Manager Fred J. Young in the *La Grande Observer, Sat. March 8, 1958, pg. 5.*

The corporation was called La Grande Water Storage Company. They filed their corporation papers with the state of Oregon on October 28, 1901 with $10,000 in capital stock, according to the *Biennial Report of the Secretary of State of the State of Oregon, 1903 edition, pg. 74, covering January 1, 1901 to September 30, 1902* filings of new corporations.

F. E. Enloe was the city water superintendent in November 1901 and also the secretary of the aforementioned corporation.

"The company states that the proposed reservoir, —80 acres 20 feet deep—when filled would furnish 500 horse power for five years without any additional water running into it baring evaporation." *(La Grande Observer, November 6, 1901, pg. 4)*

The corporation also built a dam, 322 feet long on Morgan Lake. *(La Grande Observer, December 11, 1901, pg. 4)* "Just what the cost of the dam will be is yet largely conjecture. H. W. Stoner for a number of weeks had a force of from ten to thirteen scrapers at work and thinks he has about one half of the dirt in position, which requires 35,000 yards, each team handles about 40 yards per day. The dam is 160 feet at the bottom, 30 feet high and 30 feet wide on the top. Mr. Hunter states that they are putting twice as much dirt in the dam as there is any necessity for, but to make it doubly safe they are taking every precaution, as in case it should break it would endanger the city. The dam will be five feet higher than the 25 foot water mark which they expect to reach." *(La Grande Observer, Sun., Sept. 27, 1903, pg. 3)*

The expressed purpose of Morgan Lake was stated in the *La Grande Observer, November 6, 1901 issue, page 2* as follows: "In addition to an abundance of water and power, the Morgan Lake storage proposition would also provide for a much needed sewerage system."

Well, the city's hopes were very optimistic, but during the winter of 1907, reality came to light when the power turned off to the city. Morgan Lake had run out of water. Consequently, after this unpleasant experience, the city knew they had to find an additional reservoir and water sources that would not go dry on them during the winter.

In September 1909, the Grande Ronde Electric Company sold the Morgan Lake property to the new Eastern Oregon Light and Power company. Then in 1927, a transmission line was built between Baker and La Grande, an interconnection with Idaho Power company at Baker. *(La Grande Observer, Feb. 24, 1961, pg. 9)*

In 1946, Eastern Oregon Light and Power Company sold the Morgan Lake property to the California Pacific Utilities Company, and in March 1959, the City of La Grande bought it from them for $7,500 for the purpose of making it a possible future water supply. *La Grande Observer, May 5, 1960, pg. 1; Feb. 24, 1961 pg. 9)*

"Morgan Lake contains about 76 acres of water. The city recently purchased 200 acres and the lake. The lake was bought from California-Pacific Utilities Company for use as a reserve water resource for the City of La Grande," read an article in the *La Grande Observer, Thursday, May 7, 1959, pg. 1 issue.*

With the city's purchase of this property, the Morgan Lake plant operation discontinued as it was no longer needed for electricity. Instead, a city commission was formed to develop a road to the lake so people could start using it for recreational purposes and the grounds became a city park.

"The discussion (of the commission) centered on the quarter-mile of road going from the main county road down to the lake and the parking lot at the lake." *La Grande Observer, May 5, 1960, pg. 1)*

Regarding Morgan Lake Road itself, some repairs are being planned. In April 2021, the County Commissioners' Board initiated a matching grant application with the State of Oregon for funds to widen the narrow, gravel road and put up guard rails. If the matching funds are raised by 2022, then construction will begin on the county road in 2023.

This beautiful blue water lake is open when the water temperature rises in April. There are some boat landings available, some picnic tables and spots to park your recreational vehicles, campers and trailers for an overnight stay. Camping visitors should stop at the registration kiosk and complete a registration form and proceed to a marked camp site.

No motor boats are allowed on the lake, but other motorless craft are allowed such as canoes, paddle boats and floating devices. Fishing is permitted, and the lake is stocked annually with 23,000 finger length and up to 2,000 legal size rainbow trout. Besides trout, there are catfish and crappies.

Lastly, make sure you ask the camp host or city parks and recreation department about using a camp fire. The campground is open from April 22 through October 31, and each night the entrance gate is closed at 10 p.m.

Moses Creek Lane - This lane was named after Moses Creek, formerly called Shoddy Creek. This lane was part of Palmer Junction Road. It is enumerated as road #42C which runs 3.96 miles in length in Township 3N R39E Section 26 in the Elgin maintenance district.

The present day Moses Creek Lane is located 13 miles north of Elgin via Palmer Junction Road. It is the connecting road between Robinson Road on its west end and Palmer Junction Forest Boundary Road on its far east end. In between are intersecting roads like Lookingglass Road, Yarrington Road and Bowman Loop. It's incredibly scenic out that way and makes for a good weekend drive during late spring, summer and fall seasons.

To learn the name origin for Moses Creek Lane, the authors had to research the namesake of Moses Creek. The authors scoured the territory for landowners by this name but found none. However there was a historic character named Mose De Motlette La Grandeur (abt. 1837-1900).

The 1860 Federal Census states he was living in Curry County, and it is believed that he came to eastern Oregon in 1862 because of the gold rush. He settled in the Grande Ronde Valley, got married and engaged in raising horses in Union. This was where there was a French Canadian community started. Among them were the Beauvais, Brouillot, Le Boeuf families, who had eventually migrated to Alberta, early pioneer settlers of the Pincher Creek District.

Union County researcher and historian, the late Jack Evans, stated on this subject, "There is a strong tradition in the family that La Grande was named for Mose La Grandeur. Green Arnold, close friend and brother-in-law of Daniel Chaplin, has also been given credit for naming the community." *(Evans, Powerful Rocky, pg 311-12)*

In light of this, Moses Creek might have meant Mose's Creek, much like Phys Road should have been written Phy's Road in the possessive form.

There is only one other significant historic figure in Union County History, who may be the namesake for Moses Creek and Moses Creek Lane. His name is Moses Lore, another French Canadian. He's spoken about in an article written in the *La Grande Observer, Aug. 19, 1916, pg. 9* as follows:

"Perhaps one of the best known characters of the French settlement above Union was Moses Lore, whose death occurred but a few years ago. Mr. Lore was considered to have been Union county's oldest resident, his age being placed at 102 years at the time of his death. The Canadian French were known principally for their neighborly hospitality and as a rule for their integrity in business affairs." (His stated age was mistaken in this 1916 article.)

His obituary published in *The Oregon Daily Journal of Portland, Oregon, Friday, Feb. 21, 1908* and posted on Genealogy Trails website stated this:

"Four Years Past Century Mark
Moses Lore at Champoeg in 1842
Came to Oregon country in 1836

UNION, OR., Feb. 21 — Moses Lore, aged 104 years, an Oregon pioneer of 1836 and a survivor of the party of French Canadians who at Champoeg opposed the adoption of an organized territorial government for Oregon on May 2, 1842, died at his home on Catherine creek, four miles from this place, Wednesday night. Lore was born in Montreal in 1804, and when but a small boy joined the Hudson Bay's trapping and hunting expeditions to the west.

He left St. Louis with a party of trappers in 1824 and came up the Missouri river to the headwaters, where he left the party and joined the Flathead Indians, with whom he lived until 1836, when he went to the Willamette valley and joined the French settlement near Salem. At the Champoeg convention on May 2, 1842, when the first steps towards a territorial government were taken in Oregon, Lore, with his Indian wife, stayed at his home and did not take part in the discussions or voting on that memorable day. His squaw wife, thinking there would be trouble, kept him in the cabin until the meeting at Champoeg had dispersed.

In 1862, he moved from Champoeg to Catherine creek, a mountain stream flowing through his place, and was one of the first of a large French settlement there. He had been engaged in farming on a small scale and in stock raising. Lore was a most interesting character. He knew personally Whitman, Spalding, Dr. John McLoughlin and other pioneers of the northwest. His Indian wife is yet living in the Blue mountains. She separated from him many years ago." (End of obit)

According to the *An Illustrated History of Union and Wallowa counties; Western Historical Publishing Company; 1902, pg. 301:*

"Mr. Lore was born near Montreal, Canada, in October, 1804, nearly one hundred years ago, being the son of Henry and Margaret Lore, who were agricultural people, natives of France, and early settlers of Canada.

He was occupied in his younger days on the ranch with his father and in the winter went to the timber and rafted down to Quebec for two springs. When he arrived at the age twenty-six years he went to St. Louis and there worked on a boat for one winter and in the spring engaged as overseer of the stock with the American Fur Company, which was starting an expedition to the Rocky Mountains. For two years, he was with this company traversing the wild regions of the mountains in search of fur, and trapping and hunting. He became very expert in these arts and also while enjoying the thrilling adventures attendant thereupon was well acquainted with the hardships and dangers that so thickly bestrew the path of the hunter and trapper.

At the end of his two years' service he engaged with a party led by one Jarvey to go to the mountains near Salt Lake, but on account of the uprising among the Indians the trip was abandoned and our subject, in company with Jaguerie, a member of the former party, trapped and hunted for two years more in the territory adjacent to Fort Hall, in Idaho. They were within one hundred miles of this station and were successful in their endeavors. They went north from there to the Payette river country and hunted buffalo, then returned to Fort Hall and wintered, then went to the Clearwater country and on to the Flathead territory, all the time hunting and trapping.

Then they started for California, but the partner became afraid of the Indians, and so the trip was abandoned, and Mr. Lore went to work for the noted Henry Spalding where he continued for ten months.

After this he crossed the Cascades and took up a ranch of six hundred and forty acres in the Willamette valley and remained twelve years or until 1852, when he went to California and operated in the mines but without much success except to incur the discomfort and pain of enduring an attack of fever and ague and the scurvy, after which he returned to the Willamette valley, sold his ranch, took up another and bought enough more to make five hundred acres in all.

There he remained until 1862, when he crossed the Cascades to Union county and was occupied for a time in peddling among the miners, and once was attacked by robbers when he was returning home. For two years he wrought here and then sent for his family from the Willamette valley and bought his present place of one-quarter section, where he has given his attention to farming and stock-raising. Success has attended his efforts and he is now enjoying a competence that his thrift and energy gathered for him.

In 1853, the marriage of Mr. Lore and Mary Ann Sanders was solemnized and to them have been born six children, one of whom is living. Joseph, who resides with his parents on the farm. Mrs. Lore is seventy years of age. Mr. Lore is over ninety-seven, and is active and takes interest in the farm and in business generally. He is highly esteemed by all and in a county where many pioneers dwell there is perhaps not another with so extended and interesting a career as has been passed by the worthy and venerable gentleman who is now spending his golden years in the county where he has labored long and faithfully." (End of 1902 narrative)

Naming one road to honor the French Canadian residents of Union County, may have been the intent of Union County officials during the 1988 road renaming program.

"A large part of the country along Catherine Creek above Union and a portion of High Valley was originally populated by a colony of Canadian French people. There were between fifty and seventy-five families of these people at one time—along about 1880—and now there are but about four of the original families left. They are Peter Goyette, Henry Moyette, Arthur Celia and "Frenchy" Taylor. All these are old men, approaching eighty years. Of the other original settlers in this district a number went to Montana, a few to Umatilla County, and others to various localities in Eastern Oregon." *(La Grande Observer, Aug. 19, 1916, pg. 9)*

Moses Creek was formerly call Shoddy Creek, according to historian Robert C. Bull of La Grande and author of *A Little Bit of This & A Little Bit of That, Union County Historical Society, 2007. On page 8* he wrote: "Cabin Creek and Shoddy Creek drain this flat country. I cannot find Shoddy Creek on any of the current maps I have. However, in the book *The History of Elgin, Oregon by Bernal D. Hug Sr.*, there is a hand-drawn map of the area, which shows Shoddy Creek. Comparing that map with current maps it appears that Shoddy Creek is now labeled Moses Creek."

He also related in his book, page 8: "The Palmer Junction Lumber Company first built a spur line up Shoddy Creek into the heavily timbered Palmer Valley. Each day from 1908 to 1914, an average of about 16 carloads of logs pulled by a Shay engine would come from Palmer Valley down the steep winding grade on Shoddy Creek to Palmer Junction."

From this historical account, we understand that the creek name was still called Shoddy in 1914, and likely beyond that into the 1950s, as pointed out by Berta Lou Gerber, 92, the wife of Lee Gerber of Umapine, Oregon, who lived in the Palmer Junction territory between 1939 and 1980. Berta said that Moses Creek Lane was first a part of Palmer Junction Road until 1988 when the county road names were changed.

Maps as early as the *1935 Umatilla National Forest Map* called the creek Moses Creek, but Berta did verify that the creek had an earlier name, Shoddy Creek, and she heard this from a lone trapper, who knew the area like the back of his hand. Referring to him, she said, "Soapy Davis used to call it Shoddy Creek."

Soapy (Ira) Davis (1884-1954) was Elgin's legendary mountain man, trapper and moonshiner, who was the caretaker of the Alexander hunting cabin in the woods near Lookingglass.

He had the custom of coming by Berta's parents' home about once a week to pick up his mail from a row of mail boxes there, she said. Whenever he came for the mail, he would stay at a cabin nearby, a place he called his headquarters camp, and he spent two or three days there. As soon as the neighborhood kids learned he was there, they all came running to see him. *(Berta Gerber interview, November 23, 2021)*

"He was a nice old man, and a great cook," Berta said. "My sister and I and others went to his cabin in the woods, and he made us some of the best sour dough bread I ever tasted!" *(Soapy Davis, the Legendary Mountain Man of Union County, Oregon, 2019, Dave and Trish Yerges)*

Berta admitted that those who would know the details of Shoddy Creek and later Moses Creek have now passed away. Still, she remembered Shoddy Creek and verified its existence. As far as Moses Creek and Moses Creek Lane go, the authors have presented their most historical candidates for the namesake. Without more conclusive archival documentation to nail it down, Moses Creek remains a history mystery.

Mountain View Drive - This is a private drive off Love Road near Cove that brings access to eight properties. It offers a good view of the mountains from this location.

Mt. Emily Road -   This road #9A is both a county road and a public unmaintained road. It runs 5.54 miles in Township 2S R38E Sections 18 and 19 in the La Grande maintenance district.   It is named after the iconic Mt. Emily on the west side of the Grande Ronde Valley.

Historian John Evans wrote in his book, *Powerful Rocky*, that there was a story about how Mt. Emily was named after a little pioneer girl, who died and was buried at the base of the mountain; however, a more plausible story is generally accepted as its namesake, as follows:

Mt. Emily was named after one of the very earliest pioneer women, Emily Leasey, wife of Henry W. Leasey, emigrants from Iowa. But before you read any further, it must be stated that this name is not the original name of this mountain. Before the Leasey family ever set foot on this soil, the Native American people called it "Keen Moteen." Consequently, Mt. Emily is second in place when it comes to the name of this great mound of dirt and rock. *(1962 Annual to History of Union County, Bernal D. Hug Sr., pg. 68)*

The Leasey family came by wagon from Iowa and arrived to this valley in September 1861 on their way to the Willamette Valley. They planned a layover to rest, so they made camp along the Grande Ronde River. After a short recuperation, they packed up their wagons, but they were struggling to get their wagons up the hill on the old emigrant road back of La Grande.

Just as they were struggling up the hill, they met three travelers heading the other way toward La Grande with supplies from the government post in Umatilla. They explained to the Leasey family that they were planning to establish a permanent settlement in the Grande Ronde and sell supplies to those in wagon trains passing through.

They urged the Leasey family to turn around and join them in this settlement. Since the season was late and their journey ahead was still a very long one, they were easily convinced to go back to the Grande Ronde Valley.

The Leasey family were joined by the Ben Brown party who brought assets with them from the Umatilla Landing. Together these first settlers built five log cabins. The Leasey family's first home was built on what became Black Hawk Trail, and their household included the father Henry W. and his wife Emily; their five children: Caroline, Will, John, Columbus, Joseph and James. (See Marks Road entry)

"The great mountain which dominates the north end of the valley was named for Mrs. Emily Leasey," stated Bernal D. Hug in his book, *History of Union County*, page 28.

Mount Glen Road - This road #10 is an abbreviation of Mountain Glen Road, and it runs 5.4 miles along the base of Mount Emily through a narrow glen of residential homes before turning east onto Standley Lane. The road is located in Township 2S R38E Section 32 in the La Grande maintenance district.

The full road name was abbreviated to its current rendering, Mt. Glen Road, to fit the road sign. *(Glen McKenzie interview, November 2000)*

One historic landmark on this road is the Ackles Cemetery, so named after George Ackles, who was born on May 30, 1832 in Clearmount County, Ohio. He crossed the plains in 1865, settling near La Grande, where he made his home until about 1910. He then moved to Portland, where he lived until his death on September 21, 1917. He was interred in the Ackles Cemetery on Mt. Glen Road.

During his life in La Grande, he became a prosperous businessman, being one of five directors of the National Bank in that city. He held extensive business interests in La Grande that his wife periodically attended to in person in the years after their departure to Portland. Surviving him were his wife in Portland, a son, Neri Ackles of Portland and a daughter, Mrs. Viva Little (later Daley, 1939) of Toppenish, Washington. *(La Grande Observer, Sept. 25, 1917)*

By 1916, Ackles Cemetery had been badly neglected, and for a time, there was a cemetery association organized to try and keep it in good condition. That eventually disbanded, and today the cemetery is not much improved. The cemetery is now under the supervision of La Grande Cemetery District.

Noteworthy among the burials in Ackles Cemetery are Union County pioneer homesteaders, John

McDowell (b. July 31, 1828 - d. Jan 10, 1899) and his wife, Lucinda Viola (Mitchell) McDowell (b. Oct. 18, 1842 - d. May 21, 1885), a couple who came across the Oregon Trail by ox team and wagon from Prairie Township in Mahaska County, Iowa.

Almost as soon as they arrived to Union County, she gave birth to a daughter, Lydia Ruth McDowell, who some say was the first white girl born in Union County.

Pioneer James Rinehart who came to this county on July 11, 1862 wrote in his personal diary: "...the first white child was born this month (referring to July 1862, when he arrived in the county), Liddie McDowell, and Mrs. Mary Nessly was the only person to act as the doctor at the birth of this little girl."

The John McDowells first lived in the Oro Dell area *(1870 census)* and then they homesteaded near Island City *(1880 census)*.   In 1868, John was nominated and elected as Union County Commissioner. *(An Illustrated History of Union and Wallowa counties, 1902, pg 196)*   He served as such through at least 1870.

His migration to Oregon, however, started long before this. In 1852, when John McDowell was an adventurous, single man in his twenties, he came out to western Oregon. He fought as a soldier in the Indian wars of Rogue River, and after that was over, he farmed in the Willamette Valley.

However, John eventually decided to return to his widowed father, James McDowell, in Mahaska County, Iowa. While there, he married Lucinda Mitchell on September 13, 1859. They had a daughter there, but she died at 7 months of age. Then about April 1862, John, his pregnant wife, and his father left Mahaska County to take advantage of the homesteading opportunities in Union County, Oregon. His father, James, took a place in Alicel.

John McDowell's obituary states, "Now after 71 years of life well spent, he sleeps with his father, leaving in death no spot on his name. He spent his last years among his grown up children and grandchildren and like a true Scotchman, he loved his bairns and their prattle was soothing music during his declining years." *(Dave Yerges family documents)*

Mt. Harris Loop -   This road #62 is 2.85 miles in length, and it is located in Township 2S R39E Section 11 in the Imbler maintenance district. It is named after one of the earliest pioneer settlers to the county, Joseph Harris, a native of Stokes County, North Carolina.

He was born in North Carolina on March 19, 1821, the son of Charles and Priscilla (Collins) Harris. When he was two years of age, the family moved to West Virginia and then again later to Sullivan County, Missouri where the parents died.

In 1840, Joseph married Miss Mary Ann Sturgill (1819-1888), and commenced farming as a livelihood. Soon the children started coming: Priscilla (1841), Rachel Catherine (1843), James Knox Polk (1845), Rebecca Jane (1848), Martha Ellen (1850) John (1853-1854), and Sarah Elizabeth (1856).

The Civil War was well underway when Joseph Harris, 43, enlisted. He was actively serving for less than one year when the war ended. Soon after his discharge and while it was yet spring time, he decided to leave Missouri with his wife and all of his grown children, moving as far away as they could from the traumas of that war. What was admirable was that they all stayed together and relocated together. That says something for their unity and the love they felt for each other.

Consequently, the Harris family fitted their wagons and joined a 100 wagon train led by Captain Joe Knight, pulling out of Missouri the spring of 1865 and anticipating a six month journey.

The Harris family members included: Joseph Harris and his wife Mary Ann (Sturgill); their daughter Priscilla (Harris) Knight, her husband Andrew Knight, their small daughter and a baby, Bill, born just the February before leaving; a second daughter Rebecca (Harris) Morelock, who was pregnant, and her husband Ned Morelock; a third daughter Rachel (Harris) who was single at the time, but she married John McKinnis in 1867 in the Grande Ronde Valley; a fourth daughter Ellen (wife of Robert Knight); a fifth daughter Sarah (wife of William Fine); and the only living Harris son in the family, James Knox Polk Harris.

Their journey across the Plains brought typical hardships including: a shortage of grazing grass at times and cattle that were stampeded by renegades dressed in bear skins, hoping to steal some of the cattle. As a result, wagons and equipment were broken, some livestock died or were lost, and some people on the train were injured. They lost two weeks of valuable traveling time repairing equipment. Due to the loss of work stock, some people used their remaining cows to bring their wagons the rest of the way. *(History of Union County, Bernal D. Hug Sr. page 57-59)*

Finally, the train arrived to Union County, Oregon in the fall of 1865.

"When they got here, Harris found a green meadow at the foot of a mountain on the east side of the valley. He arranged to spend the winter by the big spring that kept the meadow green.

When spring came, Harris' cattle ranged on the bunch grass of the sunny mountain side and soon grew fat. Before many years, he was growing "bid red apples" for his family and neighbors and becoming prosperous as a stockman. Neighbors were calling the mountain where his cattle ranged, Harris Mountain." *(History of Union County, Bernal D. Hug, pg. 59)*

Joseph had a prosperous life in Union County, but not without sorrow. His wife, Mary, died November 8, 1888 and is buried in the Summerville Cemetery. Joseph retired from ranching and farming in 1890 and moved to Elgin, where he married his second wife, Mrs. Martha "Mattie" (Wilson) Hughs on October 24, 1893.

Joseph, 94, died on June 4, 1912 in Elgin, and his wife Mattie preceded him in death just a month before he died. At the time of Joseph Harris' death, he had seen five generations of his progeny, and he had purchased many large farms so that his worth accumulated to $100,000 at the time of his death. *(Findagrave.com obituary)*

Today, the most beautiful scene over Mt. Harris is when the big, white, harvest moon sits just above its rocky summit in the twilight of an August evening. One never tires of looking at that majestic view, and it becomes easy to understand just why Joseph Harris called this place home.

Mountain View Lane - This lane is not on the county road list. It's a lane that lies outside of Cove and leaves Love Road. It bring access to eight properties. Besides the residences on the lane, there is also farm land. This road has a geographic name, bringing attention to the mountain view it offered those living in this area.

Mud Spring Road - The road meanders a long distance west of North Powder and is named after Mud Spring. Its name simply describes its physical characteristics.

Myers Road - Formerly Myers-Burnaugh, this gravel county road #38 is 3.02 miles long and travels through Township 1S R38E Section 1 in the Imbler maintenance district.

This road was named after the John J. and Edna D. Myers family. They came from Jefferson, Scotland County, Missouri where they were noted on the *1860 Federal Census,* and then they relocated to Summerville, Oregon in 1865.

During their marriage John J. and Edna D. Myers had five children: Margaret, Charles A., John A., Mary, and Thomas W. Myers. From all indications, the youngest four children came to Union County with John J. and Edna Myers.

Some time later, Thomas died and was buried at the Summerville Cemetery. John A. appears to have married and resided in Iowa.

The focus of this history now turns to Charles Arnet Myers, who farmed on what became known as Myers Road.

Charles was born on December 23, 1843 in Scotland County, Missouri. At age 21, he came to Summerville, Union County, Oregon with his parents and some siblings. He farmed with his father on the family farm.

He married Rachel Margaret Wade of Imbler on August 20, 1871, and they made their home on the Myers farm. His father John J. Myer died the previous January of that same year.

During their marriage they had the following children: John I. (1872-1941), Robert (abt 1873), Edgar "Clyde" (b. June 13, 1876) with his twin sister, Edna Clair, and Belle Eilers (1879-1961).
Charles A. Myers retired from farming, and he and Rachel were living in the city of Summerville in 1910. He and Rachel moved to La Grande in 1918 and resided at 1902 First Street with his daughter Belle, who was a chiropractor with her own office. *(1920 Federal Census of La Grande, Oregon)*

The obituary for Charles A. Myers states:

"C. A. Myers, one of the pioneer residents of the Grande Ronde Valley, passed away this morning at his home on First Street at 12:30 o'clock at the close of a long illness. The funeral arrangements have not yet been announced. The remains are in care of the Reynolds and Zimmerman funeral service parlors.

C. A. Myers was born in Scotland County, Missouri December 23, 1843 and was 70 years, 3 months and 4 days of age at the time of his demise. With his parents, he crossed the Plains in 1865, first locating at Summerville, where he made his home until five years ago when he moved to La Grande. He was married to Rachel M. Wade on August 20, 1871 and to this union five children were born. He is survived by: John I Myers of Portland, Robert R. Myers of Tepic, Mexico; Clyde Myers and Clare Hamilton, of Summerville and Dr. Belle Myers of La Grande. He is also survived by one brother, Reece Myers, and a sister Mollie Myers of Napa, California, and a host of friends and other relatives who today sadly mourn his passing on." (End of obit; *La Grande Observer, March 27, 1923, pg. 1*)

Rachel died March 17, 1929 at her home at 1902 First Street in La Grande after a long illness. She was born in West Virginia in 1841, one of 12 children born to George Irvin and Ann (Eakin) Wade.

Following Charles Myers' death, it appears that two male relatives took over the operation of the Myers farm, his son, Clyde Myers and his son-in-law Fred C. Hamilton, who was married to Edna Clare Myers.

The *1935 Metsker Map* shows that Clyde, Edna and Belle all owned part of the Myers property, even though Belle was not actively farming her share. There was quite a bit of acreage between the three heirs.

Clyde was born June 13, 1876 in Summerville and married Millie Elmer on May 14, 1905 in Summerville. They had three children: Charles H. (1906-1987), Edna Belle (1908-1982), and Lawana (1917-1986).

Clyde's wife, Millie, died on July 13, 1940 in a hospital in La Grande and was buried in Summerville Cemetery.

On May 17, 1944, Clyde died at his home in Summerville, and he was buried in Summerville Cemetery. He served as a county commissioner for several years and operated the farm until his death. All the Myers children were living outside of Union County; his son lived in California and his two daughters were both in Portland.

That was the end of the Myer family farm, but the family name has endured on the road sign. The farm was next sold to Lawrence Starr, the father of Donald Starr, currently of Island City. Donald, 77, lived on this farm his entire life, he said in an *October 2021 interview.*

The second part of the road name, Burnaugh, originates with Joseph "Merrell" Burnaugh, born in Elgin on February 25, 1880, to pioneer farmers of Elgin, Samuel Lynch Burnaugh (1843-1923) and Susan Elvira (Jasper) Burnaugh (1858-1885). Merrell was named after his paternal grandfather, Joseph Burnaugh.

Susan was Samuel's first wife and mother of their five children: Samuel L. Jr. (1877); Dora F. (1878); Joseph Merrell (1880-1943); Andrew (1882-1904) and George (1885-1885; 4 months). *(1880 Federal Census of Indian Valley, Oregon; Willena Velma Burnaugh's birth certificate; World War II Draft Registration)*

Susan Elvira (Jasper) Burnaugh died in 1885, and then in 1895, Samuel married Mary Savannah Patten (1858-1942). Samuel lived the remainder of his life farming in Elgin, and he died at 9:20 p.m. on November 1, 1923 at 80 years, 9 months and 19 days old. His death certificate states that his father was Joseph Burnaugh and his mother was Lydia Black.

The history now focuses on Samuel's son Joseph "Merrell" Burnaugh. He married twice in his lifetime. His first wife was Mabel Mary Kerr, born January 7, 1885 in Sheridan, Wyoming.

She married Merrell Burnaugh on July 5, 1903 in Union County, Oregon, and they made their initial home in the north Elgin precinct where they are noted in the *1910 Federal Census*. At the time, Merrell was employed at a planing mill. Elgin has always been a mill town and remains so to the present day.

By the *1920 Federal Census*, the Merrell Burnaugh family lived in the Imbler precinct with their three children: Willena (1905), Walter (1910) and Margaret (1911). The census indicated that Merrell was engaged in general farming.

However, two years later on April 28, 1922 his wife Mabel died at the Grande Ronde Hospital following an operation performed on April 18, 1922. Following her funeral, she was laid to rest in the Summerville Cemetery.

On December 12, 1923 Merrell Burnaugh married the widow Mrs. Emma F. (Slack) Hug, formerly Mrs. Benjaman F. Hug. Mr. Hug had died at age 39. Emma was born near Summerville, Oregon. (See Slack Road entry)

During the *1930 and 1940 Federal Censuses*, Merrell and Emma Burnaugh were living in Summerville, their final residence.

Merrell, 63, died Sunday, December 26, 1943 at Grande Ronde Hospital after a long illness. He lived in Union County all his life. The funeral was held at the Summerville Chapel and burial took place at the Summerville Cemetery.

A family portrait of the Burnaugh family shows Merrell, a very handsome, tall and slender man, with a long mustache, oval face, white hair, and brown eyes that were crescent shaped and reminiscent of the actor Paul Newman's eyes.

In 1988, the county decided to shorten the name of the road sign to Myers Road, but this publication will keep the memory of the Burnaugh's from being forgotten.

Nice Road - This road #75 is .90 miles long and travels through Township 6S R38E Section 12 in the North Powder maintenance district.

This road name originates with John Nicholas Nice, whose parents came to America from Germany before his birth in 1853. Several censuses state that John Nicholas Nice was born in New York. Then about 1858, the Nice family settled in Portage County, Wisconsin. They were counted on the *1860 Federal Census of Stevens Point, Portage County, Wisconsin,* and John Nicholas Nice was 7 years of age at that time.

In the *1870 Federal Census of Portage County, Wisconsin*, John Nicholas Nice was living in the village of Sharon (Ellis post office) with his family: his father Nicholas, 59, mother Elizabeth, 41, and children born in New York: Elizabeth, 18, John Nicholas, 17, Margaret, 14, Peter, 12, Amelia, 7, Helena, 3; and the baby born in Portage County, Wisconsin, Frederic, 1 year old.

When John Nicholas Nice was about 23 years old, he married Elizabeth Simonis on June 4, 1876 in Portage County, Wisconsin, and they immediately came west to Island City, Oregon, where Elizabeth gave birth to their first child, Mathias "Matts" Nice on March 2, 1877.

From there they made their home permanently in the North Powder district of Union County, specifically in the Wolf Creek area. There, they had four more children: Mary M. Magdalena (1880-1882), John Henry (1883-1964), Joseph Aloysious (1884-1981) and Harry Louis (1892-1981). Their toddler daughter died, but all the boys lived into adulthood and became farmers.

The sons of John and Elizabeth Nice became well known in the North Powder district of Union County. According to the *1935 Metsker Map*, John Henry Nice and Mathias "Matts" Nice had property on the road, and Harry Louis Nice lived nearby on Wolf Creek Road as early as 1916. Joseph A. Nice is spoken of as being a North Powder farmer in the *La Grande Observer, September 15, 1932 issue, pg 5.*

Harry Nice's farm was located five miles west of North Powder and three miles off U.S. 30 on Wolf Creek Road. He raised wheat and one news briefly wrote about his yields this way. "We have been having some terrible electric storms, but no damage has been reported in this vicinity. Wolf Creek district boasts of the largest yield of winter wheat, 40 bushels per acre being threshed for Harry Nice." *(La Grande Observer, Aug. 19, 1921, pg. 3)*

Harry held annual threshing days toward the end of August, and the first of such events started in 1957. He advertised the threshing day in the La Grande Observer so that others could make plans to join in the old-time threshing day event, one of the largest of such affairs in the West.

The Nice family has kept the old fad of threshing and plowing with steam traction alive, since it has long since died out throughout the country.

"The old steam engine, clunking slowly but surely along and with an occasional sharp whistle blast that heralded its approach to the next farm of ripened wheat, long since has been a victim of progress." *(La Grande Observer, Aug. 28, 1959)*

The Nice family said they had 2,500 people in attendance for their 1958 Threshing Day, and predicted 3,000 for the 1959 annual event. Admission was free, as was parking. The ladies from the Wolf Creek Grange had a lunch stand set up for the guests.

Matts Nice died on August 20, 1965 at 88 years of age; John Henry Nice died July 3, 1964; Joseph Aloyious Nice died March 30, 1981; and Harry Louis Nice on October 11, 1981.

All of the Nice brothers were buried in the North Powder Cemetery. Today, a road sign stands as a reminder to everyone that the Nice brothers made their mark on the land and on their community.

North Powder River Lane - This county road #101 is named after North Powder River, a tributary of Powder River. *(Oregon Geographic Names, 7th edition, pg. 547, 780)* It runs 9.54 miles in length in Township 6S R39E Section 22 in the North Powder maintenance district.

The North Powder River is a branch of the Powder River, which historical sources say was probably named by Donald McKenzie. Dr. William C. McKay, born at Astoria in 1824, grandson of Alexander McKay, a partner of John Jacob Astor, wrote that the name Powder came from the Chinook expression *polallie illahe,* meaning a sandy or powdery ground used to describe the soil along the stream.

North Powder River Lane has long been associated with the James B. Wilson Century Farm that was founded in 1889. It was officially registered as a Century Farm with the Oregon Historical Society's Century Farm and Ranch Program in June 1998.

That year, a total of 23 farm and ranch owners, including the Wilson family, submitted Century Farm applications and all of them met the requirements for Century Farm status. With these additional 23 names on the state register, it brought the total of Oregon Century Farms to 921. *(Oregon Historical Society letter dated June 5, 1998)*

John S. "Jack" Wilson, 91, is the principal owner in a family of owners of Wilson Cattle Company, established in 1950, and of Beef Northwest Feeders, established in 1991. His grandson, Zach Wilson, is the ranch manager, and represents the sixth generation of Wilsons in America. He's proud of his family's cattle operation, and his video clip can be seen on their business website.

Historically, the Wilson family story begins with James Bruce Wilson Sr., who was born in Glasgow, Scotland and immigrated to the United States prior to 1857. While in Massachusetts, he met and married Jane McGavin on March 23, 1857. There they welcomed their first child, Jennette (Nettie) in 1858.

Moving west, the family arrived to the Utah territory where they had seven more children after Jennette: James B. Wilson Jr., Robert, Grace, Clarence, Jane, Sarah and Elmer.

According to An Illustrated History of Union and Wallowa counties, 1902, pg. 305-6, James Bruce Wilson Jr. was born in Salt Lake City, Utah on July 28, 1860. He came with his parents to Baker City. In 1879, the entire Wilson family relocated together to a household in the North Powder territory of Union County. There they were all accounted for on the *1880 Federal Census of the North Powder precinct:* James B., 45, and wife Jane, 44; with children: Nettie, 22, James, 19, Robert, 17, Grace, 16, Clarence, 14, Jane, 11, Sarah, 7, and Elmer, 2.

Breaking out on their own, brothers, James B. Wilson Jr. and Robert M. Wilson settled on land in 1884 that they later purchased through a Bond of Deed contract dated October 8, 1889. The land parcels were described as follows:

The W ½ of Section 29 (state school lands); E ½ of the E ½ of Section 30; the E ½ of the NE 1/4 of Section 31; and the N ½ of NW 1/4 of Section 32 in T6S R39E in Union County, Oregon. *(Oregon Historical Society's Century Farm Program's archives)*

The Bond for Deed was fully satisfied on November 21, 1891, and the deed was sent directly from the State, being made to James B. Wilson Jr. and his brother Robert M. Wilson. *(Bond of Deed record, Book A of Misc. pg. 126)*

About this, Jack S. Wilson stated, "My grandfather came here in 1884 and homesteaded part of our ranch here, 320 acres with his brother. Then he bought his brother (Robert) out, and we still have my grandfather's 320 acres."

James B. Wilson Jr. married Dora Alice O'Bryant on January 22, 1892 in Union County, Oregon, and they had three children: Bessie Wilson, James Albert Wilson, and Doris M. Wilson.

On May 18, 1893 James B. Wilson Sr. died in Baker City, and his wife Jane died on September 17, 1919. They both rest in peace in Mount Hope Cemetery in Baker City in Baker County, Oregon.

The unbroken thread of family ownership of the James B. Wilson Century Farm begins with James B. Wilson Jr., then to James A. Wilson, followed by John "Jack" S. Wilson Sr., and his sons and grandchildren.

Throughout the first three generations of Wilson men, three of them bore the name James B. Wilson. Jack said, "My deceased brother was the third James B. Wilson." Known as Jim, he and his wife, Jean, moved to Walla Walla, Washington. Jim supervised the Nine Mile Ranch near Touchet, Washington, which he and Jack purchased as part of the Wilson Cattle Company holdings. Jim died in 2020 at age 93 years.

"We have cattle ranches here in Oregon and Washington, and we have feed lots in Oregon, Washington and Idaho," Jack said. "We go under the name Wilson Cattle Company on our land holdings, and then our feed lots are under Beef Northwest."

Jack S. Wilson said that their family business employs 27 people at their office. His second office, which is undergoing expansion in 2021, is located about two miles out of North Powder on Anthony Lake Road. Jack S. Wilson often spends his time at this location as he continues to have an active role in their cattle operation. *(Jack S. Wilson interview, November 4, 2021)*

Olsen Lane - Registered as county road #105, it runs 2.18 miles through Township 5S R39E Section 27 in the North Powder maintenance district.

It is likely named after Albert Olsen who farmed 8 miles northeast of North Powder ever since the 1900 Federal Census. The *1935 Metsker Map* shows that some land remained of the Albert Olsen estate.

Albert Olsen was born May 20, 1863 in Black Earth, Dane County, Wisconsin to Norwegian parents Ole Oleson (1828-1867) and Geennild Kundrak (1840-)   Ole Oleson was born in Oslo, Norway, according to one family tree maker. *(Ancestry.com)*

Albert Olsen married Nellie Frew Shaw (1875-1940) on September 27, 1894 in Baker City, Oregon. He did pretty well for himself as a North Powder farmer, and the land records show that he acquired land in September 1907, August 1908, June 1910 and October 1923. He is noted on the North Powder censuses of 1900, 1910, 1920 and 1930, so he stayed put in North Powder for 30-some years.

On the *1920 and 1930 Federal Censuses*, he moved into the city of North Powder on Second Street, no doubt retiring from the farm operation.

During their married life, Albert and Nellie raised seven children, all born in North Powder: Tillman August (1895-1965), Harry Dean (1896-1961), Thomas O. (1905-1952), Helen M. (1908-1959), Robert Alexander (1910-1989), Ernest Albert (1913-1996) and Alvin (1916-).

Throughout the year 1917, Albert Olsen and others kept petitioning the county court for an official county road. Eventually that happened, but it is interesting to see him taking the lead in that petitioning process.

He otherwise lived a relatively quiet life, working hard, dedicated to the farm and his family, so there weren't many occasions when he was in the newspaper. There was one mention of him outside the road petition, where he was reporting for jury duty. *(La Grande Observer, September 25, 1919*

Albert Olsen died on August 26, 1930 in North Powder at the age of 67 years. He was buried at the North Powder Cemetery. *(Findagrave.com Memorial ID#76989430)* Nellie Frew (Shaw) Olsen was born January 8, 1875 in Kilsyth, Stirlingshire, Scotland and died April 21, 1940 in North Powder, Oregon. She rests with her husband.

In 1961 at the time of Harry Olsen's death, there were four surviving Olsen brothers, Robert and Ernest Olsen in North Powder, Tillman Olsen in Newberg and Alvin Olsen in Portland. It appears that Tillman, Robert, Ernest and Harry all farmed during their adult lives.

One-O-One Road - This road is about 1.5 blocks in length, located in Township 6S R38E Section 27 in the North Powder maintenance district. It is named after its official county road #101A.

Orchard Road - Road #10A on the county records, Orchard Road is descriptive of the old commercial orchards growing in this area. The road runs .99 miles in Township 2S R38E Section 9 of the La Grande maintenance district. Its orchards remaining there are a shadow of their former glory. *(See Monroe Lane)*

Oregon Trail Road - Enumerated as county road #23B, it runs 9.41 miles in length in Township 6S R38E Section 15 in the North Powder maintenance district. It basically follows Interstate 84 from North Powder heading north.

Orodell Road - This is a private road that is located in Township 2S R38E Section 31 in the La Grande maintenance district.

According to the *Oregon Geographic Names book, 7th edition, pg. 731,* "Orodell is a locality, a ghost town, on Grande Ronde River just northwest of La Grande. It is where the river leaves the canyon and enters the valley.

Paul Van Scoy of La Grande wrote the compiler in January 1944 that a man named Fox started a saw mill at this point in the early 1860s, the first mill in Grande Ronde Valley. A store and a post office followed in due time. The post office was named Orodell, and the name apparently originated by a Captain Harlow, who worked for W. J. Snodgrass, storekeeper and for a time the postmaster. The name was coined by taking part of the Greek word *Oros,* meaning a mountain, and adding the English word *dell* as a suffix. The place is still known as Orodell, but there has been no community there for many years. Orodell post office operated from October 1867 to October 1878." *(End of Oregon Geographic Names narrative)*

Otten Drive - This drive used to be outside the La Grande city limits but is now a city street. This secluded neighborhood of 12 properties is served by this street.

This road was named after general practitioner, Dr. Frederick R. Otten, who resided on this road. He died May 16, 1962 at his home in La Grande. His obituary read:

"Physician Killed—La Grande, Ore., Dr. Frederick R. Otten, 50, a member of the State Board of Health, was killed Wednesday when his tractor overturned on a hill near home. Otten was preparing soil in an orchard when the tractor overturned.

Otten was appointed to the board of health February 12, 1961. Born in Cavalier, N. D., he had lived in La Grande 21 years. Survivors include his widow, Florence, a son, three daughters, his father and two brothers who are also doctors.

The funeral is scheduled Saturday in La Grande." *(End of Obit; The Eugene Guard, May 18, 1962, pg. 6)* Dr. Otten was buried in Hillcrest Cemetery in La Grande.

Outback Lane - This private gravel lane turns east off Summerville Road to bring access to three properties. John and Tracie Wick, who live on this lane were given the opportunity to name it. They decided upon "Outback" which was borrowed from a business John's father started in Wallowa County called Outback Outfitters. John later purchased the business from his father. The Wicks purchased their land on this lane in November 2006, and that's when the lane was named. *(Tracie Wick interview, September 22, 2021)*

Overlook Drive - This is a private drive in Township 3S R40E Section 15.

Owsley Canyon Road - This gravel road is 3.28 miles in length and is located in Township 2S 38E Section 31 in the La Grande maintenance district.

It was first called Owsley's Lane and is named after the Owsley family, who came to Union County in 1862. The landowners on this road were brothers William "Lee", Benjamin Franklin and Charles Owsley, all sons of Thomas Owsley (1834-1898).

The Owsley family can impressively trace their heritage back at least 12 generations to John Owsley (1524-1592) of Misterton, Somerset, England.

Five generations after him, the first Owsley was born on American soil, Thomas Owsley II (1698-1750) who was born in Stafford County, Virginia. His son, Thomas Owsley III (1730-1796) was a Revolutionary War soldier, according to *Findagrave.com*.

Yet another descendant, Thomas Owsley (1834-1898), was the father of our subjects, Lee, Benjamin and Charles Owsley. This Thomas Owsley was born in 1834 in Jefferson Township, Missouri, when his father, Moses, was 24 and his mother, Mahala, was 21.

Thomas married Catherine Louise Dryer on December 15, 1853, in Jefferson City, Johnson County, Missouri. They had nine children in 15 years, including: Lyda Jones (1860-1909), Arminta Copp (1861-1909), William "Lee" (1864-1933); twin sons Francis Harvey "Bart" (1866-1923) and Benjamin Franklin (1866-1938); Ann Catherine (1869-1878), Charles L (1871-1936), John (1873-1878) and Joseph Edward (1875-1875). *(Ancestry.com)*

By 1860, Thomas and Catherine were living in Lake County, California, northwest of Sacramento. Here their two oldest children, Lyda and Arminta, were born. Then, in 1862, Thomas moved his family to Union County, Oregon and was listed on the *1870 Federal Census* there. The rest of his children were born in Union County.

Thomas Owsley lived in Island City and, according to family trees, he died on July 14, 1898, in La Grande, Oregon, at the age of 64, and he was buried at Hillcrest Cemetery in that city.

Thomas Oswley's death was mentioned as a side note in the obituary of former Senator James H. Slater, which stated, "This makes the sixth pioneer in (Union) county buried within 60 days. They were James H. Slater, Mrs. M. B. Rees, W. W. Welman, John McDowell, Thomas Owsley and Benjamin Hawley (Halley)." *(The Dalles Times-Mountaineer, Feb. 4, 1899)*

Three of Thomas' sons farmed on Owsley Canyon Road: William "Lee" Owsley, Benjamin Franklin Owsley and Charles Lycurgus Owsley.

This history now focuses on the eldest son, Lee Owsley, who was born on April 13, 1864 in Union County. He eventually established a fairly large farm on what locals called Owsley's Lane.

A small newspaper clipping about his life on the farm stated: "Lee Owsley killed a genuine possum on his farm north of the city." *(La Grande Observer, March 25, 1955, pg. 4, "50 Years Ago")* Lee was a bachelor all his life, and he died first before his other adult brothers. Afterward, his surviving brothers Benjamin and Charles were shown as landowners on the *1935 Metsker Map.*

Apparently, sickness was among members of the family in 1932 as the La Grande *Observer, July 7, 1932, pg. 7* article pointed out: "Lee Owsley and his brother, Charles Owsley, of La Grande have changed places. The latter who was in the hospital for several months is now living at home in comparative good health while the former, Lee Owsley, is now in the hospital recovering from a sudden and severe illness which came upon him last week."

The *La Grande Observer, March 13, 1933 pg. 1* had the headline: "Native Son of County Dies at Hot Lake Today"— "Lee Owsley, native son of Union county and a brother of B.F. and Charles Owsley, died this morning at Hot Lake after a long illness. The body was taken to the Snodgrass and Zimmerman mortuary. Funeral arrangements have not been completed."

The next day's paper had this to say about Lee Owsley's funeral services: "Professor John B. Horner, of Oregon State college and a friend of Lee Owsley in his youth, will come to La Grande to officiate at the services. The burial will take place in the Masonic cemetery. Mr. Owsley, very well known over the county, was born at Union April 13, 1864 and was 68 years and 11 months of age at the time of his death. He made his home in this county throughout his life." *(La Grande Observer, Oct. 26, 1938, pg. 1)*

Upon Lee's death, his farm went to his working partner and brother Charles. Consequently, Charles Owsley's name is on the *1935 Metsker Map* as the farm's landowner.

This history now focuses on Charles Lycurgus Owsley, who was born on October 10, 1871, in Island City. He engaged in farming this land until 1916, when he married and subsequently moved to Washington.

"Charles Owsley is Married" was the headline, and the subtitle read, "Bachelor Rancher North of La Grande Will Live at Montesano Hereafter." Apparently, the marriage of a long-time bachelor was news for the paper back then. An announcement was published and read in part:

"Charles L. Owsley, for many years a bachelor living in the vicinity of La Grande, has been married at Aberdeen to Mrs. Hattie Hewett of that place. The wedding took place Monday, November 20th in Aberdeen. The only attendant was the bride's little eight-year-old daughter. Mr. and Mrs. Owsley will make Montesano, Washington, their home for a time, the *Grays Harbor Post* says. Mr. Owsley has visited Aberdeen frequently and for a time lived there but rated La Grande as his home, he having ranched north of town for several years." *(La Grande Observer, Nov. 29, 1916, pg. 4)*

He was back at his La Grande home the next year as he was listed in the *Polk's 1917 Union County Directory,* and he was also listed in the *1920 and 1930 Federal Census* of La Grande as a single man living with his brother Lee on Lee's farm on Owsley Canyon Road.

In January 1930 an article came out explaining Charles Owsley was ill. "Mr. Owsley Ill"—Charles Owsley of Fruitdale who has been ill for months and a patient at the Hot Lake sanitorium is reported as being worse again. Mr. Owsley is suffering from some nervous trouble." *(La Grande Observer, Jan. 17, 1930, pg. 7)*

Charles died at the age of 64 on March 3, 1936 in La Grande. He was buried in the city's Hillcrest Cemetery. His obituary read as follows:

"Charles L. Owsley, native of Union county and the son of pioneer parents, died at the Grande Ronde hospital this morning after a long illness. He was a prominent farmer in this valley and was actively engaged with his agricultural work until he became ill. Mr. Owsley was well known throughout this section. Born on Oct, 10, 1871, he spent all his life in this country. He was 64 years, four months and 22 days of age at the time of his death. Survivors include his brother, B. F. Owsley and other relatives." *(La Grande Observer, March 3, 1936, pg. 1)*

This Owsley history now focuses on the surviving brother, Benjamin, who was born July 8, 1866 in Island City. He was the twin brother of Francis "Frank" H. Owsley, who passed away August 30, 1923 at 11:30 p.m. from pneumonia. Frank was 57 years, one month and 22 days of age at the time of his death.

Benjamin married Louella Owsley, and they had 7 children: Gilbert Frank (1897-1978), Alfred Thomas (1898-1980), Helen (1903-1995), Elma (1906-2001), Ruth Ann (1909-1970), Howard Lee (1915-).

During his life, his home caught fire, but no lives were lost because of it. "B. F. Owsley Home Damaged by Fire"—" Between $200 and $300 damage was caused when fire broke out this morning in the home of B. F. Owsley, near La Grande. Mrs. Owsley and her son were alone in the house when the flames broke out in the chimney, and called neighbors who succeeded in extinguishing the blaze." *(La Grande Observer, Dec. 13, 1932, pg. 1)*

Benjamin Owsley died October 26, 1938 in La Grande. His obituary was printed in the *La Grande Observer, Oct. 26, 1938, pg. 1,* and it had a full accounting of his life's achievements and family history in Union County.

"Benjamin Owsley Longtime Resident Dies Early Today—Benjamin Franklin Owsley, 72, born in Union county and a resident here for many years of his life, died early today at a local hospital (likely Grande Ronde Hospital)."

The obituary article continued, "Mr. Owsley had been ill for about two weeks and succumbed to pneumonia. He had been in the grain business for many years and, as a young man, hauled ties from the Blue Mountains for the construction of the railroad when the line was built through the valley in 1884.

One of twin sons born to a pioneer family, Mr. Owsley was born about half a mile north of Island City on July 8, 1866. Thomas Owsley, his father, came to Oregon from California in 1862. The twins were the last of nine children." The latter sentence is incorrect because four more children were born after the twins, including Charles (1871-1936).

Benjamin Owsley first attended school at Moss chapel. He also attended Oregon State college in Corvallis. When he was 10 years old, the Owsley family moved to what is now known as Owsley Canyon, two miles north of La Grande. It is likely called that because they owned the canyon.

He first entered the grain business as a youth with Frank Brothers, a La Grande firm. He then was employed by Hamilton and O'Rourke Grain company. He then became an employee of Kerr Gifford Grain Company as manager for about 40 years, working at Dayton, Colfax and Walla Walla, Washington.

The La Grande Observer announced this occupation in the March 22, 1903, pg. 4 issue as follows: "Mr. B. F. Owsley and family will leave on Monday morning's train for Dayton, Washington, where Mr. Owsley will establish headquarters for Kerr Gifford Company grain buyers of Portland. Mr. Owsley has many friends here who regret very much his leaving, but wish him unbounded prosperity in his new home." As things worked out, he and his family returned to Union County in 1918.

"He was school director for 18 years in the Fruitdale district," read his obituary.

He met and married Luella Jaycox on November 11, 1896 in La Grande. They had seven children. Mrs. Owsley died in 1935.

Their children who survived Benjamin Owsley's passing were Alfred T. of Arlington, Mrs. Helen Hood of Spokane, Marjorie Wright, Elma Eckley, Ruth Price and Gilbert and Harold Owsley, all of La Grande. There were also three grandsons, Jerry Owsley of Arlington; and Dick and Donald Wright of La Grande besides other relatives.

Benjamin Owsley was a long-time member of the Masonic lodge. Members of the Elks lodge had charge of the services at the Snodgrass and Zimmerman funeral home. Interment occurred at Summerville Cemetery beside his wife.

The *1935 Metsker Map* does show Benjamin Owsley's son, Gilbert Owsley as a land owner on Owsley Canyon Road.

Palmer Junction Road - This road #42 is 10.10 miles in length, running through Township 2N R39E Section 34 in the Elgin maintenance district.

This was the Elgin-Palmer Junction Road on the *1935 Metsker Map*. The first part of the road north of Elgin was called Galloway Road. (See Middle Road entry) This road is a continuation of Palmer Road running north out of Elgin, and it ends at Moses Creek Lane. It roughly parallels the Grande

Ronde River.

Palmer Junction Road was home to three well-known actors. Two of them, Roy Rogers and Don Blocker (played Hoss Cartwright on Bonanza), time-shared a log home on this road in a section that locals referred to as "the millionaire's hill." Neighbor Carleta Ashburn stated that Rogers had a horse on this property, the offspring of Trigger, as the story goes, and when it died, Rogers buried it on this property. *(Carleta Ashburn interview, Palmer Junction Road resident)*

The current property owners, the Donigians, purchased the property in 1978, but they said they have not heard this story, and they haven't located any burial site for a horse yet. They did confirm that Rogers and Blocker resided in the log home when it was corporately owned and used as a time-share residence. *(Diane Donigian interview, Feb. 2022)*

The third actor who resided on this road was Kevin Costner, along with his wife, Cindy, who in 1991, had a residence on the Cabin Creek ranch property. This Palmer Junction property was complete with a heli-pad and backyard pool and lots of fenced in pasture land. It appears that the Costners sold the property about 1996. One La Grande resident that the authors know personally spoke to Costner at this address.

Putting aside all the star-studded hoopla, this road was originally named after the George Palmer Lumber Company, who had extensive timber holdings in the area. George Palmer was born in 1849 in Northfield, Vermont. *(Ancestry.com Federal Census of 1850, Northfield, VT)* In 1860, he was living with his parents in Chicago, Ill., and in 1870, he was enrolled in Whitewater College in Whitewater, Wisconsin.

His wife, Emma, was born in 1854 in Wisconsin. They married in 1877, and their only child, Edith, was born in Iowa in 1878. According to the *1880 Federal Census*, they were living in Page, Iowa. They came to the Grande Ronde Valley in 1904.

In 1907, George founded the Palmer Lumber Company and continued operating it until his death on July 11, 1922. The business was then sold and became Bowman-Hicks Lumber in 1923. It was located on the current fair grounds in La Grande. The fair office there used to be the lumber company office. For more information, see *A Little Bit of This & A Little Bit of That, Vol. 2, pg. 1-26, by Robert C. Bull.*

Park Road - This is a public unmaintained road in Township 3S R35E Section 36 in La Grande maintenance district, and it runs off Coombs Loop. It was called Flevious Road on the *Coombs Addition plat* dated 1996. *(Union County land records, See Flevious Road)*

Parsons Lane - Formerly Parsons-Hug Road, this county road #45 runs 3.78 miles in length through Township 1N R39E Section 12 in the Elgin maintenance district.

This road was named after the Arthur H. Parsons and W. F. Hug families living on this road. The Hug name was eventually dropped, leaving only Parsons Road printed on the road sign. (See Hug Road entry for Hug information.)

The *1935 Metsker Map* shows that on this lane, both Arthur H. Parsons and his son, Leonard Parsons (1889-1969) owned farm land. Arthur and his wife Nellie came with their children from Utah and settled initially in Cove in 1899. They were listed on the *1900 Federal Census* as living in Cove.

In 1905, the family moved to the south precinct of Elgin, and they were listed as residents there in the *1910 Federal Census*. Likely that same year, they moved to Cricket Flat and stayed.

Arthur Parsons was born in Iowa, and he brought his widowed mother, Mary, with him. She is listed on the *1900 Federal Census* with Arthur and family, she being 82 years old at that time. Nellie Parsons was listed on the census as an immigrant from New Zealand.

Their son, Leonard R. was 11 years old when they came to Union County. As an adult, Leonard was honored as the 1959 Union County Cattleman of the Year and his story was published in the La Grande Observer as follows:

"Leonard Parsons, Elgin, came to Union County in 1899, and started running cattle in the Cove area, where Brazille Brothers ranch is now located. Parsons ran cattle up Little Minam to the meadows on Big Minam. In those days, due to snow, cattle had to be trailed from Cove, around through Elgin. At this time Leonard ran around 700 to 800 head.

He stated that "Grief Ridge" was named then because in trailing in, the leaders would feed clear to the top, and when you got there with the drag, you would have to ride to the top to gather everything up to go on.

Parsons came to Elgin in 1905, and (later) located where he is today, still engaged in farming and the cattle business.

He has run his own brand on the Minam for 46 years. He also has the oldest forest permit that there is on the Minam. *(His brand was — L, Union County Brands, 1966, pg. 14)*

Parsons has helped and guided all stockmen that have run cattle on the Minam through all these years and has been the wheel horse on all the roundups every fall when the gather comes.

He has been a member of the Elks for 40 years. It is due to cattlemen of this caliber that have stayed in the industry and given guidance to younger men that has made it the great industry that it is today." *(La Grande Observer, Oct. 18, 1958, pg. 1)*

On December 14, 1910, Leonard married Elsie Marie Aldred, who was born December 14, 1890 and died May 29, 1968. They are interred at the Elgin Cemetery along with a dozen family members.

During their marriage, they had a large family, Dell being one of the last, born February 26, 1929. He died December 8, 2016. His online obituary read, in part:

"Dell Earnest Parsons, 87, of Elgin, passed away on Thursday, December 8, 2016, at Grande Ronde Hospital in La Grande. A Celebration of Life was held at the Elgin Stampede Hall on Saturday, December 17, 2016, at 2:00 p.m.

Dell was born February 26, 1929 at the Parsons Farm on Cricket Flat, outside Elgin, Oregon to Leonard and Elsie (Aldred) Parsons. Dell spent his entire life on the Parsons Family Century Farm established in 1896. (The farm is not yet registered with the Oregon Century Farm and Ranch

Program.)   He attended Elgin elementary school and graduated from Elgin High School. Dell married his high school sweetheart, Sallie D. Lorsung, on September 17, 1949. It was a double wedding with her twin sister, Allie and Raymond "Buzz" Farmer. Dell and Sallie were married for 67 years.

Dell was self-employed as a farmer and rancher on the Parsons farm all his life. In his earlier years, he also worked for various gas stations and logging jobs to make ends meet. In 1964, he started the night shift at La Grande Boise Cascade Sawmill and retired after 26 years.

Dell and Sallie were chosen co-grand marshals of Elgin Stampede in 2008. He enjoyed hunting, fishing, camping, dancing, flying and wood working.

Dell was survived by his wife Sallie; son Earnest R. Parsons and daughter, Jill M. Parsons-Chaffee (Rod) both of Elgin; a brother Dick Parsons (Laura); and a sister, Phyllis Bechtel (Joe) both of Elgin; grandson, Brock Hindman of Redmond, Oregon and many nieces and nephews. Dell was preceded in death by his parents, Leonard and Elsie; sisters, LaRue Parsons, Chloe Phippen, Ruby Kuhn, Alta Hunt, and June Gray."

At the time of this writing, Sallie was still alive and residing with her daughter, Jill, in Elgin. Earnest and Jill do the farming at the homestead on Parsons Lane.

Peach Road - Registered as county road #28, this travels 8.33 miles in Township 2S R39E Section 29 in the Union maintenance district.

This road was first called Peach Lane but was changed to Peach Road because it runs north and south. At its north end is Booth Lane and on its south end is Highway 237 to Cove.

The road was named after the Peach family of Vermont, namely, brothers John (1829-1894), William George (1833-1908) and Thomas Peach (1835-1887). The Peach residence was located 10 miles east of La Grande toward Cove. John and William G. Peach formed Peach Brothers Dairy.

In the *1882 Oregon Papers and Sketches in Union and Baker Counties, page 35*, it mentions the John Peach Dairy, and he had over 70 cows and 840 acres. There was also a mention in the newspaper of William G. Peach, stating that he had been in the dairy business for over 20 years. *(La Grande Observer, Feb. 8, 1898, pg. 3)* His son, James Seaver (J. S.) Peach also became involved in the dairy.

In 1898, J. S. Peach of Peach Brothers had 200 acres of grain that had good prospects. *(La Grande Observer, April 22, 1898, pg. 3)*

The third brother Thomas G. Peach married Augusta Nutt about 1872, but he died early in life on May 9, 1887, and he was apparently not involved in the Peach Brothers dairy.

The elder brother John Peach died on May 3, 1894, and afterward it appears that the Peach Brothers business was operated by his younger brother William G. and William's two sons, James S. and George W. Peach. Then in 1904, William G. retired.

A notice of business dissolution was printed in the *Nov. 28, 1904 La Grande Observer* stating:

"Notice is hereby given that the co-partnership heretofore existing between W. G. Peach, J. S. Peach and G. W. Peach under the name of Peach Bros., has this day been dissolved by mutual consent, W.G. Peach retiring. J. S. Peach and G. W. Peach, who will continue the business, as Peach Bros., will pay all outstanding debts and collect all accounts due the old firm. Signed: W. G. Peach, J. S. Peach and G. W. Peach"

William G. Peach was born on October 15, 1833, and he died December 5, 1908, four years after retiring from Peach Brothers. His burial took place at the Island City Cemetery. Interestingly, W. G. (William George) Peach started the cemetery when it was called by its original name, Peach Cemetery. *(La Grande Observer, Aug. 10, 1959, pg. 5)*

James Seaver (J. S.) Peach died prematurely from cancer on December 29, 1917 at a sanatorium in Portland. James' brother, George Peach, died on July 14, 1954.

George had two sons, Lester and Leonard but neither of them carried on the operation of the dairy. Lester Peach (1905-1959) lived in the vicinity of Peach Road and raised chickens and turkeys, and Leonard Peach lived in Walla Walla, Washington.

One interesting note about the Peach Brothers farm was that in November 1912, two dozen China pheasants were released on the Peach farm in the Pierce reserve for preservation. *(La Grande Observer, Nov. 23, 1912, pg. 1B)*

Also, in 1913 a new metal bridge called Peach bridge was completed over the Grande Ronde River on Peach Road. *(La Grande Observer, Feb. 6, 1913, pg. 1)* Over the years, ice jams formed at the Peach bridge, and this became problematic for local residents.

One notorious mention was made of the "Old Peach Place" long after the dairy dissolved and the Peach family left the property. On the front page of the *February 23, 1925 La Grande Observer*, the headlines read, "Officers Seize 85-Gallon Still - Believed to be the largest ever taken in East Oregon by enforcement agents."

The article continued, "The apparatus for making whiskey, which was found by the officers was complete in every detail with the largest capacity of any still ever confiscated here. The net haul, besides the arrests follows: an 85-gallon copper still, eight barrels of fig mash, two barrels of raisin mash, a vat containing 200 gallons of corn mash, 14 gallons of whiskey, 25 gallons of first run whiskey."

This raid was engineered on information obtained by Carl Helm, district attorney, and three men who were on the scene at the time of the raid were arrested, the article read. The arrests were made by George M. Pierce and John Stricker.

Even though whiskey has its loyal patrons, in the end, it was milk that was legislated as Oregon's official state beverage in 1997. The Peach brothers had it right—"Milk does a body good."

Peacock Road - This private road is located in Township 2S R38E Section 33 in the La Grande maintenance district and is one of five bird roads off Fruitdale Lane on the north edge of La Grande. There is a mobile home park community there.

Philberg Road - This paved road #148 runs about 1.12 miles along the Grande Ronde River in Township 1N R39E Section 27 in the Imbler maintenance district. It dead ends with huge boulders of rock so that a traveler cannot go onto the canyon remnant of old Highway 82.

This section of Highway 82 was repositioned higher up the hillside. That hill was known by locals as "Hamburger Hill" because of the frequent vehicular hits of deer trying to cross the highway. It's not a name on a map and only locals seem to refer to it, but this was where the new stretch of Highway 82 was engineered and located. However, right along that section of the highway, there is constant water drainage problems and without maintenance, this part of Highway 82 could collapse or wash out. Every few years, that stretch of road has to be worked on by the Oregon Department of Transportation (ODOT) work crew.

Philberg Road is one of a very few examples of "designer road names" that were created by borrowing letters from two personal names to make one new one. The namesake for this road name was Philip James Bergstrom or "Bergie" to his friends and neighbors. He was born on June 2, 1943 in Los Angeles, California. He died at age 40 on October 19, 1983 in a vehicular crash on the freeway between Ukiah and La Grande. He owned a bar in Ukiah, and he is buried in the Ukiah Cemetery.

He was married to Rosalie Pulido in Los Angeles, California on September 4, 1965; then to Cheryl Stoll, and lastly to Sharon Estrada on December 31, 1981, who became his widow almost two years later.

After his death, a friend, Mike Caldwell, nominated Philberg for the name of this road, in memory of his friend. *(Contributor Steve McClure, retired county commissioner, May 23, 2019)*

Bergstrom's home is on the south end of this road, and it was built in 1974. Next door to the north, Becky Churchill lives. She was married to Cecil Churchill, and they owned and operated C-zers Drive In on 14th and Division Street in Elgin. This historic business is an icon in Elgin. *(Becky Churchill interview, November 23, 2021)*

He also bought a bar in Ukiah, and on the way home from Ukiah one night, he was killed on the freeway in an auto crash. *(Scott Ludwig interview, May 21, 2019)*

La Grande historian Dorothy Fleshman had a childhood memory of traveling the old Highway 82 section to Elgin, which is now Philberg Road. She wrote: "I just remember as a child riding in our car and heading for Wallowa County. We crossed a bridge and went down to where the Grande Ronde River flowed and followed the river at bank level to Elgin.

There were a lot of rattlesnakes down there so we never went there to swim or picnic. Later they took out that part of the road and the bridge and made a new road up higher, where it is now.

If you went all the way to Elgin you would pass this drinking fountain that was made waist-high of concrete blocks with water coming up from a spring." *(Dorothy Fleshman contributor, October 24, 2021)* For more details on these drinking fountains, see Highway 82 road entry.

Phillips Creek Road - This gravel road is not included on the county roads list because it probably started as a logging road. It departs off of Tollgate Highway 204 about 3 ½ miles outside of Elgin's city limits.

It is named after Phillips Creek which flows alongside the road and through the south end of Elgin, and it empties into the Grande Ronde River. Phillips Creek is fed by melting mountain snowpack, producing a robust stream flow until May when it starts to go dry.

It's early history traces back to about 1872, when a man by the name of Dan Phillips took up a claim, and the creek that ran by his place was soon called Phillips Creek. *(The History of Elgin, Oregon, Bernal D. Hug Sr., pg. 21)*

People do enjoy camping along Phillips Creek, but in July 2015, a large wildland fire started. Its cause was identified as an escaped camp fire from a dispersed camp site along Phillips Creek. Freelance correspondent, Trish Yerges, broke the story in *the La Grande Observer on August 11, 2015* and on the paper's website.

The fire was a careless act that exposed hundreds of fire fighters to over 70,000 hours of fire exposure. The fire burned over 2,600 acres of forest land and was 79% contained by mid-August. A level I evacuation notice was issued for about 60 homes on the outskirts of Elgin.

An incident command post was set up at the Elgin Stampede grounds, a rather historic use of the Stampede Hall at the time. For a couple of weeks the air quality from that fire was suffocating for those living in the townships of Elgin, Summerville and Imbler. At night the distant sky was lit up with an orange-yellow glow and billowing clouds rose like an atomic bomb exploded. We all welcomed the fall rainy season that year and fresh air again.

Philynda Loop - This private loop was named by Phil and Lynda Peterson, owners of AC Electrical Construction. They combined their first names to make the hybrid Philynda. It is located in Township 3S R38E Section 10 in La Grande maintenance district.

Phys Road - Historically called Phy's Point Road, this road #32 runs 1.20 miles in Township 3S R40E Section 18 in the Union maintenance district. This road name has reference to a man's name but also a geographic feature of a ridge that comes to a rocky point and ends. Sometime prior to 1884, this point was known as Hendershott's Point, according to road petition #223.

The road petition #223, dated July 22, 1884 was initiated by E. T. Neville and A. B. Conley, but the petition did not suggest a road name at that time. The surveyor's description of the road's location was as follows in part: "...and running to Phy's Point, formerly known as Hendershott's Point, all of said road being in said county." This petition makes it clear that Phy and Hendershott were land owners of the same area, and that the name should be printed in the possessive as shown in the aforementioned road petition.

Phy's Point Road is named after John Marshall Phy, born January 28, 1840 in Alabama. He married Margaret Ann Shoemaker on May 19, 1866 in Ada County, Idaho. She was born November 22, 1853 in Polk County, Oregon.

During their marriage they had seven children: John Franklin (1867-1930), Marshall H. (1870-1892), Dr. William Thomas (1873-1931), John A. (1876-1886), Mary M. (1878-1938), Margaret L. (1881-1966), and Hester Caroline (1884-1968).

Many readers of Union County history are aware of the well-known Dr. William Thomas Phy, who practiced medicine at Hot Lake. However, he had an older brother, John Franklin "Frank" who was also well known as a Union County sheriff and also a Union County judge.

The subject of this road entry, John Marshall Phy, was living in Union County by 1870. Ten years later he was working as a farmer in Cove, according to the *1880 Federal Census*. His wife Margaret passed away March 6, 1891. John remarried on December 3, 1896 in Union to Lydia Scott Jackson, and they had one child in 1898.

By 1900, they moved into the city of Union, and John was a stock raiser, according to the *1900 Federal Census*. About 1904, John and his family left Union to relocate to a small town in southern California called Highland.

There he engaged in real estate, raising sheep, and he also bought an orange orchard. He died in Highland, California on November 27, 1914.

The authors felt that since this ridge was formerly called Hendershott's Point, and it was often used as a reference to this road in road petition documents, it would be appropriate to include some history about the family. Its namesake, James Hendershott (1829-1887), was the son of David and Catherine Hendershott. He was born in Lebanon, Saint Clair, Illinois on September 11, 1829.

As an adult man, he had a strikingly dignified appearance, broad in the shoulders, strong and extremely good looking with dark hair, a mustache and well-groomed beard. He married Harriet Jane Vincent on December 7, 1848 in New London, Henry County, Iowa. During their marriage, they had four children: Minerva Ann (1850-1924), Mary Josephine (1857-1905), Harriet Orzilla (1858-1860), Selena Grace (1861-1863), and two adopted children, Robert E. "Lee" Vincent (1863-1915), and Mollie Bonn (1872-1935).

In the *Plain Dealer of Roseburg, Oregon, March 1, 1897, pg. 3* an obituary for James Hendershott was printed that stated in part:

"Jim Hendershott Dead—According to a dispatch from Union, Oregon, dated Saturday last, James Hendershott died at his home at Cove Friday night, after a protracted illness of several months. Mr. Hendershott was one of the earliest settlers of this part of Oregon, and is well known throughout the state. He held a number of official positions in the state, the last of which was that of commissioner of horticulture. The deceased was a resident of Southern Oregon in the 1850s and was once sheriff of Josephine County."

Hendershott's migration to Josephine County, Oregon was made by the Asa McCully wagon train from Iowa, which left in 1852. Hendershott's wife, Harriet, and two daughters, Minerva and Mary Josephine, apparently remained behind with Harriet's parents at their home temporarily in Youngstown, Ohio. Then in 1857, the women made a fantastic journey west to meet up with James Hendershott.

Author Alan Hill tells the story this way: "They traveled by stage to New York, then by boat to the Isthmus of Panama; then overland the Isthmus (the canal was not yet built); then by boat again to San Francisco; and finally by stage to Josephine County, Oregon." *(Alan Hill, The Honorable James Hendershott: Oregon Pioneer and Early Civic Leader, pg. 4)*

Another brief obituary from the *Statesman Journal of Salem, Oregon, March 9, 1897, pg. 7* gives the highlights of his life's achievements: "James Hendershott, who died at his home in Cove February 26, at the age of 67 years, came to Oregon in 1852; was sheriff of Josephine County from 1854 to 1860; followed mining for a short time on Salmon River and in 1862 settled in Grande Ronde Valley; was a member of the state legislature in 1866, and in the Senate in 1868-1872." *(Ancestry.com family tree document)*

The earliest mention of James Hendershott in an Oregon newspaper, that the authors could find, was in the *Table Rock Sentinel of Jacksonville, Oregon Territory, December 6, 1856, pg. 3.* It stated in part that there was going to be a sheriff's sale of the portion of stock owned by Jonas W. Garrison in the Sailor Diggings Water, Mining and Milling Company of Scotch Gulch in Josphine County. At the end of the printed newspaper notice of sale it read "James Hendershott, Sheriff of Josephine County, O. T." (O. T. stands for Oregon Territory)

Hendershott's daughter Mrs. Minerva Eaton gave a presentation to the Union County Pioneer's Association in which she told the dramatic story of her family's migration from Walla Walla to the Grande Ronde Valley. She was traveling with her mother and sister to Union County as her father had traveled separately ahead of them. Mrs. Hendershott and children traveled by wagon until they reached the base of Crawford Hill, where they had to get out of the wagon and walk because the hill was so steep. Minerva continued with the story:

"Finally reaching the top, we again seated ourselves in the coach and bounced over the rough and rocky country, for there was no road, until we got to the top of the hill just above old Lagrande. Then we thought we had come to the jumping off place, for we could see no way to get down the mountain. After much deliberation on the part of the driver and a torrent of suggestions from my mother, we had about concluded to camp, when two pert looking young men came to our rescue.

After felling a big pine tree they tied it to the back of the wagon so we were safely landed at the foot of the hill into the most beautiful valley we have ever seen. We turned to thank our benefactors, asked their names, and it was none other than our old pioneers, J. L. Caviness and Roe Rogers. We camped quite near the little town of old Lagrande, which consisted of a tavern, blacksmith shop, feed corral and saloon. Later in the fall was added a small dry goods and grocery store. December 18, 1862, we arrived at our destination, Forest Cove. (The first name of Cove, Oregon.)

It was here our father had located our home, known as Hendershott's Point. This old stand was a welcome sight to many a weary traveler, for it was our business to make them as comfortable as possible with the material at hand." *(An Illustrated History of Union and Wallowa counties, 1902, pg. 669)*

Another published biography for James Hendershott follows:

"James Hendershott, who became known to the state as a member of our legislature in both branches during the years 1866-72, is now residing upon a beautiful and well-improved farm upon the gently sloping lands described as a "territorial paradise," lying east of Hendershott's point, near The Cove, Oregon. He is engaged in farming and fruit-raising, and in the culture of fine stock and poultry. His is a farm somewhat rare on this coast, where a flock of pea fowls may be seen. His residence is described as "palatial," and is known as "Forest Home." His mode of life is upon a liberal scale. Many of his experiments are conducted with a view to public improvement and information, since he holds the position of state horticultural commissioner for the fifth district. He is evidently fulfilling his duties in this line with fidelity and efficiency. His three children and six grandchildren live near.

Mr. Hendershott is, as the name implies, of German extraction, and was born in Illinois in 1829. His parents became early settlers of Iowa; and at Burlington young James received his education.

While but a youth of nineteen he was married to Miss Harriet J. Vincent, of Iowa, and in 1852 crossed the plains to our state in the company of Asa McCully, who was in the lead of the other trains, and thereby escaped the plague and disasters for which that year was notable. As salesman for J. L. Starkey, at Salem, in 1852; as pioneer, auditor and sheriff of Josephine county from 1854 to 1860; as scout in the Indian war; as miner on the Salmon river, and as settler of the Grande Ronde valley, whither he first came in 1862; as state legislator in 1866, state senator 1868-72, and state land registrar 1872-74, and now as horticultural commissioner, Mr. Hendershott has made an honorable record, and has served the state with efficiency. He and his excellent wife are noted for their hospitality, and are honored by their neighbors. *(History of the Pacific Northwest: Oregon and Washington, Volume II, 1889, compiled and published by the North Pacific History Company of Portland, Oregon)*

James Hendershott was buried in the Cove Cemetery next to his wife Harriet Jane Hendershott.

Pierce Road - This county road #23 runs 9 miles in Township 2S R38E Section 25 and 26 in the La Grande/Union maintenance district.

This road is named after Walter Marcus Pierce (1861-1954), member of the Oregon State Senate (1903-1907 and 1917-1921); Oregon's 17th Governor (1923-1927); and member of the U.S. House of Representatives from Oregon's second congressional district (1933-1943).

Pierce was born May 30, 1861 in Morris, Illinois. He moved to Portland, Oregon in 1883, but eventually settled in Pendleton of northeastern Oregon, where he raised beef cattle, taught school and served as a school superintendent.

At age 26, he married one of his students, 18-year-old Clara Rudio in 1887. Three years later in Pendleton, she died giving birth to their baby daughter, Clara R. Pierce. On September 3, 1893, he married Clara's sister Laura Rudio, and they had five children: Lloyd, Lucille, Helen, Edith, and Lorraine.

In the mid-1890s, he relocated his family to Illinois, where he earned his law degree in 1896 at Northwestern University. Thereafter, the Pierce family returned to Pendleton, Oregon, where Pierce raised Hereford cattle, practiced law and invested in real estate.

Around 1900, he turned his attention to business ventures in Union County, including the development of the Hot Lake Sanitorium Company. He was involved in this company for about 15 years. He owned a lot of land in the Hot Lake area.

At the same time, Pierce was also the principal investor in the development of hydro power in Cove with a goal of supplying La Grande with electricity.

Walter Pierce and associates were developing the Cove hydro project at about the same time as William G. Hunter was leading the Morgan Lake development in 1902.

"A potential rivalry loomed as to which plant would serve La Grande. The two systems were consolidated some time before 1908 with Walter Pierce as president and William Hunter as vice president." *(La Grande Observer, Feb. 24, 1961, pg. 9)*

Eventually, Walter and Laura left La Grande for western Oregon. Laura died of cancer in Marion County, Oregon in 1925. In 1928, Pierce married Cornelia Marvin, Oregon's first state librarian. She had to give up her career to marry him. *(Wikipedia)*

In his retirement, Pierce moved to his new home near Salem. He died there on March 27, 1954, at the age of ninety-two. *(oregonencyclopedia.org)*

Pine Grove Loop - Enumerated as county road #61, it travels .85 miles in Township 1N R40E Section 2 in the Elgin maintenance District.

It's found on the *1935 Metsker Map* as Pine Grove Road. This loop used to be Highway 82, and it was the address of a few families. This road brought access to the Pine Grove church (now burned down) and cemetery where there are 30 marked graves recorded.

It also brings access to the historic Pine Grove School. This school was called Pine Grove School District #26 and was organized in 1880. During the winter of 1881-82, a log school house was raised on land donated by William Galloway. The door and windows and possibly the desks were made by G. J. Wagner of Indian Valley. Some of the first students were Sherman, Jewel, Cecil, Maggie, Pete and Dick Galloway. One of the first teachers was Kitty Goodall of Union.

In the 1890s the following families had arrived to the Pine Grove area: Michaelson, Shoemaker, Richards, Daron, Taylor, Henderson, Bishop and Scott. Later in the early 1900s, the following families arrived: Walch, Weech, Chandler, Boswell, Follett and Ransome. The Pine Grove School consolidated with Elgin in July of 1945. *(School Districts of Union County, Oregon, 1965, Stella M. Edvalson, pg. 95-96)*

Ponderosa Lane - This is a private lane off of Comstock Road in Cove. It runs through Township 3S R40E Section 26 in the Union maintenance district.

It's a descriptive road name, drawing attention to the Ponderosa pine trees that are abundant in this territory. They can tower upwards of 200 feet with a three or four foot diameter at the base of its trunk, not to mention its ponderous (heavy) wood. Their bark is reddish brown with a deeply creased texture. They are majestic to look at and worth a Sunday drive to go see. As you do, roll your windows down and smell the awesome pine scent.

Pumpkin Ridge Road - This road #37 is 7 miles long and runs in Township 1S R38E Section 12 in the Imbler maintenance district. It travels north of Summerville, winding over the foohills between Summerville and Elgin. This is a very scenic drive or bicycle ride if you are up for a cardiac workout.

A farmer named James Riggs found the climate on Pumpkin Ridge to be mild and relatively frost free, so one year he planted a field of pumpkins on the south slope to be used as hog feed. They grew to huge sizes and their bright orange color could be seen for miles from the floor of the valley. It is thought that this is the basis for the name "Pumpkin Ridge."

The Johnson Fruit Farm has a commercial pumpkin patch that grows on the slope of the mountain near Pumpkin Ridge. The Johnson Fruit Farm is owned and operated by two brothers, Mark and Michael Johnson. They are both employed by the U.S. Forest Service, but they still spend their spare time caring for the farm their grandfather gave them. Pumpkins, being a fruit, are part of the crops they raise.

In early October, they set up their pumpkin stand at the edge of the pumpkin field and wait for customers to come and buy a variety of pumpkins that have grown there. When the customers stop coming, the Johnsons open their field up to the farmers who want cattle feed. Nothing is wasted.

Quail Road - This is a private road in Township 2S R38E Section 34 in the La Grande district. It may seem like just another street in Island City, but it is on the county road list, and there are four properties on it, a business and three residences. Its name reminds everyone of a very common bird in Union County, one that always wears her Sunday's best, complete with a stylish feathered hat.

Railroad Drive - This is a private road in Township 5S R40E Section 28 in the North Powder maintenance district.

Ramo Flat Road - This road #69 runs 4.27 miles in Township 4S R40E Section 30 in the Union maintenance district. It resembles a loop, leaving Highway 237 and returning to it on the other end.

It is named after the geographic territory of Ramo Flat. Both the flat and the road were named after a couple, who farmed the flat prior to 1870. On the *1870 Federal Census* were listed P. Ramo, 55, a farmer born about 1815 and his wife M. Ramo, 50, housekeeper born about 1820, along with A. Moray, 18, a farm hand, who lived with them. P. Ramo's land was valued at $1,000 at that time. The Ramo couple were French Canadians, who settled here.

The *Oregon Geographics Name book, 7th Edition, pg. 798* states: "This flat is southeast of Union. Dunham Wright of Medical Springs informed the compiler in 1927 that it was named for a Frenchman, one Raymou, who lived thereon." (This is a variant spelling of the name Ramo.)

The paper trail went cold on the Ramo couple with no further mention of them in the newspaper, no burial records or no family tree makers on ancestry.com to shed light on the rest of their story. There was a Peter Ramo found on the Lane County, Oregon 1900 census, who was born in 1844 in Canada, and the census states his parents were from French Canada.

About Ramo Flat, the *La Grande Observer, July 20, 1914 issue, pg. 5* reprinted an article from the *Union Republican*:

"A Productive Section"— Ramo Flat, a piece of high land that lies from four to twelve miles southeast of Union, is one of the most productive high-land farming sections of the county. Only last week Milton Cunningham, who lives on the flat, was in the city with as fine a lot of Dunlap strawberries as one will see in a day's journey, and he informs the *Republican* that other kinds of fruit, vegetables, and hay and grain, also potatoes grow perfection up that way. In addition to all these, comes dairying, and Ramo Flat will not take a back seat for this or any other section. Mr. Cunningham has been milking a small bunch of cows and last month's creamery check amounted to $111.60—not a bit bad at this period of hard times. One naturally wonders where a man will go to beat the natural conditions that prevail at Ramo and many other places in this part of the world. Sheep, hogs, cattle, horses, hay, grain, fruit, potatoes, all thrive up that way—and where can one beat it for an industrious man.—*Union Republican*."

This territory has been called Ramo Flat since at least 1889, and the name carries on to this present day.

Rankin Road - This road #2 runs south off of the Ukiah-Hilgard Highway 244 for 1.68 miles in Township 3S R36E Section 11 and leads to the forest lands. It is in the La Grande maintenance district.

Two barns were built first on the family home place in 1900, followed by the old family home, a basement and two stories above in 1903. Ownership of the Rankin family property was handed down from William Rankin to George Rankin, then to George's brother Earl Rankin, and to Earl's son Patrick Rankin and to Charlotte Rankin in trust. *(Charlotte Rankin, 88, interview, July 12, 2018)*

William Rankin was born March 1, 1839 in Tuscarawas County, Ohio, and he died March 21,1920 at the home of his sons Earl and Thomas Rankin, who live near Hilgard. William had been ill for several months before his death. He was age 82 years.

He married Jannette Morrison (1838-1902) on November 22, 1860 in Pandora, Putnam County, Ohio. In 1880, they resided in Jackson, Paulding County, Ohio. His wife, Jannette, was born in Scotland on August 18, 1830 and died January 5, 1902 in Union County, Oregon.

In 1898, he and Jannette, along with their children moved to Oregon, and they made their home near La Grande until his death. *(La Grande Observer, March 22, 1920, pg. 1 obit)*

During their marriage, they had eight children, according to family tree researchers. They include: James A. (1862-1878), Robert M. (1864-1926), Thomas M.(1867-1937), Abbie Euphemia (1871-), Cora Louella (1872-1939), George W. (1878-1945), Minnie (1881-1960) and Earl C. (1884-1969).

At the time of William's death his sons Thomas and Earl still lived in Hilgard. Earl Rankin married Mary Finley (1896-1979), and they had a son, Patrick Rankin.

Patrick married Charlotte, and they lived just outside of Island City. Charlotte was 88 years old when she was interviewed in 2018 for this information. At that time, Paul Rankin lived in a mobile home on the family property on Rankin Road. *(Charlotte Rankin interview, July 12, 2018)*

Rawhide Lane - Formerly Rusau-Gawith Road, which diverts east off of Merritt Lane about 9.7 miles east of Elgin. It is designated as county road #51 and runs .78 miles in length, being located in Township 2N R40E Section 36 in the Elgin maintenance district.

It was originally called Rusau-Gawith Road on the *1935 Metsker Map*, named after three area landowners: Enock Arden Rusaw, Jackson Gawith and Harry Gawith. Later, those names were dropped and a property owner on that road suggested the name Rawhide for no historical reason.

The Rusau (Rusaw) part of this road is named after Enock "Arden" Rusaw, who was born December 13, 1898 in Moscow, Idaho. By 1918, according to his WW I registration card, he was farming in rural Elgin, Oregon. This is where he met and married his wife on October 5, 1921. Her name was Clytie "Esther" Clippenger. She was born July 11, 1906 in Lakeview, Oregon.

They had three children, all born in Elgin: Harriet M. (1923), Clyde (1928) and Emma (1931).

Harriet married a neighbor named Leo Lester Kennedy (1914-1998) on September 15, 1938 in Walla Walla County, Washington. They had a child, Kimber, in 1940 and they lived on B. Street in Elgin. About seven months later, her family sold the farm and moved away. Harriet died January 30, 1982 in Umatilla County, Oregon, after her second marriage.

There was a briefly in the *La Grande Observer, April 5, 1939, pg. 5* that described the family's departure from Union County. It read, "Mr. and Mrs. Arden Rusau left Monday evening for their new home in the Williamette Valley."

Arden and Esther Rusaw took their two youngest children and moved to the Williamette Valley, according to the *1940 Federal Census of Yamhill County, Oregon*. After their deaths in Yamhill County, Oregon, they were buried there.

Jackson Gawith was born near Wichita, Kansas on September 19, 1877, the son of English immigrant John Gawith I (1847-1928) and his wife, Mary Jane Wise (1839-1906). John was born in Liverpool, England and Mary Jane was born in Tennessee.

John Gawith married a widow, Mrs. Mary Jane (Wise) Rogers. Her first husband, Irvin K. Rogers, died young, and they had one son, George J. Rogers (1868-1941) that she brought with her into her second marriage.

John and Mary Jane (Wise) Gawith had five additional sons together: John II (1872-1917), Charles W. (1875-1932), Jackson (1877-1951), Harry (1880-1948), and William (1882-1900).

John Gawith migrated from Iowa, where he married Mary Jane, and then they moved to Wichita, Kansas, where on June 10, they were listed on the *1880 Federal Census of* the Township of Seventy Six, Sumner County, Kansas. The listed included: John Gawith I, 36, a farmer, and his wife, Mary Jane, 40, with children: George E., 12; John II, 7; Charles, 5, Jackson, 3, and Harry 5 months. William came along in 1882.

Then sometime before 1900, the Gawith family moved to Union County, Oregon. Son Jackson Gawith became a young man and was stepping out on his own.

The *1900 Federal Census* found Jackson, 22, still a single man, living in Elgin as a boarder and day laborer. He met Mabel Clare Bond (1886-1973), and they were married on September 30, 1906 in Union County at the home of J.H. Taylor. Witnesses to the marriage were his brother Harry Gawith and friend Mattie Goff.

Now a married couple, Jackson and Mabel started farming together in Elgin. They homesteaded on land at Township 2N R40 E, the south half of Section 36. The *1910 Federal Census* listed the young family, including: John, 32, a farmer, wife Mabel C., 24, and their children, Keith E, 2, and newborn Lyma I. Gawith.

As a homesteader, Jackson had to prove up the land, so the following newspaper article recorded that accomplishment.

"Jackson Gawith of Elgin was in the city today appearing before the officials of the local land office, making final proof to his homestead. He was accompanied by Celeste Nascinbeni and Edward Chestnut, also of Elgin, who were witnesses in the case." *(La Grande Observer, Dec. 14, 1914, pg. 5)*

About 1917-18, Jackson moved his family to Freewater, Umatilla County, Oregon, where Jackson worked for the Oregon-Washington Railroad and Navigation company as a road laborer. In time, Jackson and Mabel had seven children: Keith Edwin, Lynn Irvin, Ray Arthur, Leroy Gillis, Arden Loren, Gerald Harry and Thelma.

After Pearl Harbor on December 7, 1941, the U.S. was digging deeply into its pockets for every able-bodied man. A registration form designed to record and count American men age 45 to 64 was printed on April 1, 1942. The required registration started after that.

Consequently, in 1942, at the ripe age of 64 years, Jackson Gawith (no middle name), signed up for the World War II draft registration. He stated on the form that he lived in Milton-Freewater, Umatilla County, Oregon, was a Union Pacific Railroad employee, and that he was born September 19, 1877 near Wichita, Kansas.

During WWII, however, railroaders were often given exemption from the armed forces because keeping the railroad operational was a high priority, so many employees of the railroad stayed on the job. Jackson retired from the railroad.

Jackson Gawith died in 1951 and was interred at the Milton-Freewater IOOF Cemetery. Mabel died in 1973 and was laid to rest next to him.

There is a Gawith family plot in Highland Cemetery on Good Road east of Elgin, where John, Mary Jane, Charles and William are buried.

Red Pepper Road - This county road #33B runs 1.52 miles, connecting Cove Highway 237 with Gekeler Lane outside La Grande. It travels through Township 3S R39E Section 2 in the Union maintenance district.

It is named after Red Pepper School, which was first organized and called Valley Centre School on February 10, 1877 as Union County District No. 73. It was renumbered school district No. 40 after Wallowa County was created in 1887.

Then on July 19, 1919, the district was divided, and part of it was assigned to District No. 12. The other part to District No. 9. This closed one of the most noted country schools in Union County—Red Pepper School.

The school's name is a humorous tale published by Bernal D. Hug in his history books and written by district clerk, Mr. M. L. Carter, describing how the name "Red Pepper" was given to the school and District No. 40.

"On the (wintry) evening of the first dance at the new school, the attendants found, among other deterrent pranks (like sulfur in the stove and sacks in the pipe), that red pepper had been generously sprinkled about (and the broom was taken away). Nevertheless, after dragging a blanket (with two persons sitting on it) over a snow-sprinkled floor, the dance went on accompanied by much sneezing. Red Pepper caught on as a name and Valley Centre waned."

The school attracted a healthy enrollment due to its good teachers, though spring floods and snow-socked roads to the school did interrupt classes some years (1913).

"A number of the well-to-do farmers in the Red Pepper school district have subscribed $10 each towards keeping the subscription school going, which O. M. Gardner is so successfully teaching." *(La Grande Observer, May 26, 1898, pg. 3)*

To raise money for the school, the district directors allowed "basket suppers" to be sold there as a fund raiser. The aforementioned newspaper article stated, "Owing to the rain Saturday night, only 20 baskets were taken to the basket social at the Red Pepper school house. These however, enriched the treasure $5.25, besides the pleasant meeting of those who attended."

No tuition was charged to pupils enrolled from surrounding districts. The school was popularly known for its good teachers, its orchestra with an organ and stringed instruments, its dances, basket suppers and its literary society entertainment led by its president M. L. Carter.

In November 1892, Carter wrote a comic but scathing poem about the failings of district clerk, W. H. Madison, who was just a little too straight-laced for the likes of the fun-loving, dancing enthusiasts of Red Pepper School District. Madison resigned and high-tailed it out of Dodge, returning to Kansas from whence he came, never to return.

About Madison's departure, Carter wrote: "Hurrah boys! Hurrah! Deliverance is near. And when our trouble vanishes, we'll never shed a tear." *(School Districts of Union County, Oregon, pg. 121, Edvalson; "Over the Valley" column by M.L. Carter in the La Grande Evening Observer, Aug. 2, 1927; Supplement to History of Union County, No. 8, Bernal D. Hug, pg. 41-42.)*

Riddle Road - Formerly River Road on a 1978 *Chamber of Commerce* map, this very short road #210 departs from Island Avenue and runs toward the Grande Ronde River. It travels .39 miles in Township 3S R38E Section 4 in the La Grande maintenance district.

Frankly, River Road has no mystique to it, but Riddle Road absolutely makes a person puzzled about its origin. So then, how is a riddle better than a river? Let's find out.

Riddle Road is named after Charles Mortimer Riddle, who was born November 17, 1850 in Genesee County, Michigan, the son of Jesse (or Jose) Merrick Riddle (1809-1855) and Caroline Hayden (1815-1889).

His wife, Marcia E. Stone, was born in Newbury, Ohio, on May 30, 1858. They were married in

1879 (alternate 1880) in Cleveland, Ohio, and they came to the valley in 1893. They first lived in Perry, where he was a saw filer for Stanley Lumber Company.

They then moved to May Park (the Riddle Road area) before their fourth daughter was born in 1896. In the *1900 Federal Census*, Charles Riddle was listed as a farmer. He was active in promoting the Union County Fair, as superintendent of "Division F" (fruits) at the fair. *(La Grande Observer, Sept. 2, 1914, pg. 2)*

In October 1914, Riddle and Attorney C. H. Finn entered a partnership in making vinegar and apple cider. They also wanted to put into production a canning line to can fruits and vegetables. This idea was born to make use of the fruit waste from less perfect specimens of the fruit harvest.

During Charles and Marcia's marriage they had four children: Mollie (Aug. 1880); Sarah H. (Oct. 29, 1887); Mildred (1893); Katherine (1896 in La Grande). Mollie married Charles Ruckman, and Sarah was an unmarried school teacher, who died on December 27, 1925.

Mildred Riddle married Justice William O. Douglas, who sat on the U.S. Supreme Court for more than thirty-five years (1939-75), longer than any other Justice. *(The Nation, biography, April 2003)* Mildred was married to him in 1923, and the marriage ended in 1953, the first of his four wives. Katherine Riddle married Lloyd Pierce, the son of Governor Walter M. Pierce, on May 18, 1919.

Charles Riddle died on October 19, 1927 and Marcia Riddle died on October 26, 1942 at her May Park residence. Both are interred at Hillcrest Cemetery in La Grande, along with their second daughter, Sarah.

Ridgeway Lane - This is a private lane off of Middle Road in Township 1N R39E Section 16 near Elgin that was subdivided in 1980 by Ed and Laveta Botz of Elgin.

Rinehart Lane - Designated as road #135A, it runs 3.46 miles in Township 1S R39E Section 10 in the Imbler maintenance district.

This road has been misspelled as Rhinehart Road on the *1935 Metsker Map*, but it was changed to Rinehart Lane to conform with the road naming ordinance in 1988 and to correctly reflect the family name which it honors.

This lane is named after Henry Rinehart (1842-1917). He was a man of many overlapping and ambitious enterprises, including freighting, mercantile affairs, farming, cattle-driving, stock-raising, and politics. He established his home on the corner of what became Highway 82 and Courtney Lane, but the train stop on the Union Pacific Railroad was located on Rinehart Lane.

He was born in Adams County, Illinois, on February 1, 1842, one of 13 children born to Lewis Ludwig and Elizabeth (Ellis) Rinehart, both of Tennessee. Lewis and Elizabeth's migration west led them to Mahaska County, Iowa in 1845, then by ox team and wagon to a place near Eugene, Lane County, Oregon in 1854. There Lewis obtained a donation land claim.

Leaving his family home, 19-year-old Henry Rinehart and his brothers James Harvey and Lewis Bird ventured east to Walla Walla in 1861 before coming to La Grande in April 1862. Henry continued on a bit farther to the Powder River, prospecting there through the summer, and then he returned to

La Grande in the fall of 1862, making this his future home. At that time, the land was wholly unsettled, unsurveyed and covered with bunch grass.

Of course, the town was not yet called La Grande (incorporated in 1885), and there was no post office until 1863. The area was first called Brown's town or Brownsville after Benjamin Brown, one of the earlier settlers. The latter names were dropped due to a duplication of names in Linn County, Oregon. Thus, in 1863, La Grande was born as the post office name. *(oregonencyclopedia.org)*

Henry Rinehart staked a claim and started planting with seeds he brought with him from Walla Walla. In the meantime, he also busied himself in the business of freighting to the Idaho mines. He did a little mining and prospecting himself.

He also engaged in cattle driving between the Willamette Valley and La Grande, bringing with him from Lane County pack animals and cattle for stock raising. On one occasion, Henry was involved with a long cattle drive from Union County to Granger, Wyoming and on to Chicago.

In 1866, Henry and Lewis joined their brother James (proprietor) in the operation of the Anna-Lulu Flouring Mill in Summerville, the first grist mill in Union County. This mill was named after James' two daughters, Anna and Lulu.

In 1868, Henry sold his share of the milling business and bought a farm three miles east of Summerville, returning to raising crops and livestock while continuing in the freighting business.

The growth of Union County was developing rapidly in the 1860s and 1870s with mining activities in nearby areas and because of the Homestead Act of 1862. Trains of immigrants were arriving steadily each year, so in 1865, Henry and Lewis built the first mercantile house in what later became known as Summerville. From then on until 1874, Henry remained in the mercantile business in both La Grande and Summerville.

In 1893, he was appointed by President Cleveland as registrar of the U.S. land office in La Grande. He served in this post for four years.

As a farmer, he had 600 acres of improved land where he lived, farmed and raised stock. He was the president of the creamery association and served within the Pioneer Association as its recording secretary.

On March 30, 1865 near Creswell in Lane County, Oregon, he married Miss Margaret Ann Martin, the daughter of Even and Mary Martin, of Missouri. Immediately following their wedding, they came to Union County, traveling overland to the Columbia River, then by boat to Umatilla, and by stage to Meacham, where the newlyweds visited overnight with the Meachams. There they heard the joyous news that the Civil War was over at last. Bidding the Meachams farewell, they journeyed by horseback to La Grande and settled in Summerville.

During 1868 to 1909, they established the Rinehart farm, where they lived busy and fulfilling lives. They had nine children: Henry Lee (1867-1870), James Thomas (1869-1878), Martin Luther (1867-1876), Nellie May Eubanks (1872-1938), Lloyd Watson (1880-1882), Eugene Edwin (1880-1915), Franklin Clay (1884-1970), Bertha Ethel Chappell (1887-1970) and an infant son, who died April 5, 1880. All but Nellie and Bertha were interred at the Summerville Cemetery.

Though the Rineharts retired to Walla Walla, they celebrated their 50th wedding anniversary with their family and friends in the Grande Ronde Valley, a place they considered home.

Henry Rinehart died April 8, 1917 in Walla Walla, Washington. His wife, Margaret, died August 21, 1921 in Elgin. They are interred at the Summerville Cemetery along with about 35 other Rinehart relatives. *(An Illustrated History of Union and Wallowa counties, 1902; ancestry.com; Biographical Sketches, pg. 536-7)*

Riverside Road - This public unmaintained road is .41 miles in length and located in Township 2S R38E Section 32 in the La Grande maintenance district. According to the 1978 *Chamber of Commerce* map, the current Riverside Road goes north off of Fruitdale Lane to Gaertner Lane, but in reality the northern part is not used and has brush on it.

Robbs Hill Road - This road #7A is 5.22 miles in length and travels through Township 2S R38E Section 35 in the La Grande maintenance district.

It runs northwest from the Lower Perry exit 257 and connects with Hamilton Canyon Road, running almost parallel with Fox Hill Road. Back in the day, Robbs Hill Road and Fox Hill Road comprised "the hill neighborhood." Today, there are six property owners on Robbs Hill Road, but none with the Robbs surname.

This road is named after a lumber man named Henry C. Robbs, who with his new bride, Sarah Jane (Alley) Robbs, came to Union County in 1862 from California.

Not much is written about Henry C. Robbs, but the authors identified him as the namesake by comparing two newspaper clippings. Here's an excerpt of one from the *La Grande Observer, Sat. Sept. 8, 1917, pg. 1.*

"Daniel Elledge came to the Grande Ronde valley in 1864. He was a farmer and lived most of the time near Summerville, although he spent a few years on the Sandridge and a short time in the Grange Hall neighborhood on the farm now owned by W. H. Hughes. He also worked a few seasons at Stumptown (Perry) at the Robbs' sawmill. He married Miss Lucy Robbs, daughter of the lumber man."

As it turned out, Lucy Robbs was the adopted daughter of Henry C. Robbs, the "lumber man" mentioned in the earlier news briefly. This was confirmed in Henry Robbs' obituary where it listed Mrs. Lucy Elledge as one of his surviving children.

Consequently, the authors identified the road's namesake as Henry C. Robbs and his wife was Sarah Jane (Alley) Robbs.

Henry C. Robbs was born in Tennessee on August 9, 1832. He married Mrs. Sarah Jane (Alley) Williams in California, and they came to the Grande Ronde Valley in 1862, according to *An Illustrated History of Union and Wallowa Counties, 1902, pg. 181 and his obituary.*

Sarah was an Oregon Trail pioneer, as she came across the trail at the age of 15, being the eldest of five children in the family of Andrew Jackson and Louisa Elizabeth (Perkins) Alley.

She was born January 18, 1837 in Tennessee, and then she moved to Missouri from where, in 1852, her family departed for the Oregon Territory. When they reached the Snake River in Oregon, her mother Louisa Elizabeth (Perkins) Alley, died at 35 or 36 years of age.

Louisa's death was among the one in ten, who set off on the Oregon Trail and did not survive. Most commonly people died on the trail from two causes, accident or cholera. It is not known what took Louisa's life, but she was buried along the trail near the Snake River. Likely, a few words were said over her grave, and then father and his five children had no choice but to leave her behind and press on. For the Alley family, it was a journey of tears from that time forward. *(Findagrave.com)*

With Louisa's absence in the family, the widower Andrew Alley needed a wife to care for his children, the younger two being just six and three years of age. So that same year, in 1852, he married Mary Adeline Moore. They reached western Oregon and eventually traveled south to California, where they settled and where Mary gave birth to a daughter and son.

Andrew and Mary Alley lived the remainder of their lives there. He died in Upper Lake, Lake County, California on December 11, 1885 at age 74 years.

When their daughter Sarah Alley reached adulthood, she married Jason L. Williams. They lived in Linn County, Oregon, and she gave birth to two children: Lucy Ann Williams on July 2, 1856 and William Andrew Williams on February 25, 1858. The marriage ended, so Sarah and the children returned to California before the 1860 Federal Census was conducted. There, she married again, this time to Henry C. Robbs, and they came to the Grande Ronde Valley in 1862. *(La Grande Observer, Sept. 8, 1917, pg. 1)*

Together, Henry and Sarah raised ten children, two from her first marriage and five girls and three boys of their own. From all that the authors could find about him, he was a beloved father, who loved his children. Sometime after the 1870 Federal Census but before the 1880 Federal Census, Henry Robbs adopted Lucy and her brother William, and henceforth they were referred to as Lucy Robbs and William Robbs.

Henry Robbs died at his residence on Saturday at 9:40 p.m. on September 9, 1899 at 67 years and 1 month old. He was buried in the family plot at Hillcrest Cemetery in La Grande, where his wife Sarah joined him 17 years later.

After Henry's death, Sarah (Alley) Robbs rented houses in La Grande, and later moved in with her son Thomas Robbs.

Sarah's obituary stated that she passed away September 6, 1917 at 8:45 p.m. after a short illness at the home of her son, Thomas Jefferson Robbs at 1620 Sixth Street, La Grande. Her husband and seven of her ten children had preceded her in death.

At the time of her death, there were three surviving sons: William Robbs of Summerville, Thomas Robbs of La Grande and Benjamin Robbs of Barber, Idaho. *(La Grande Observer, Sat., Sept. 8, 1917, pg. 1)*

Robbs Hill Road was known by this name ever since Henry C. Robbs (1832-1899) started his sawmill operation there. The earliest mention of the Robbs Hill Road in the newspaper was in 1916 as follows:

"J. H. Blumenstein has been engaged with a crew making some improvements on the Robbs Hill Road. At several points, the road has been widened and otherwise put in shape for travel. The work will probably be completed today." *(La Grande Observer, March 31, 1916, pg. 6)*

Robin Road - This road is one of five roads named after birds, comprising a mobile home park community located off Fruitdale Lane on the edge of La Grande.

Robinson Road - This county road #42A runs 1.30 miles in Township 3N R39E Section 35 in the Elgin maintenance district. It's the connective road between Moses Creek Lane on the north end and Palmer Junction Road on the south end.

It's located about 12 miles north of Elgin, traveling on Palmer Junction Road to get there. When the *1935 Metsker Map* was printed there was no Robinson Road as it was all called Palmer Junction Road.

Robinson Road was named Elmer Horace Robinson (1894-1930), son of George Elmer Robinson (1858-1932) and Hattie Amelia Green (1866-1945). His parents were married January 4, 1890 in Lewis County, Washington.

They had three children: Elmer Horace (1894), Frank Seba (1895) and Hattie Irene (1899). By the time little Hattie was born, the family was living in La Grande, Oregon. Their father was supporting the family as a logger.

On July 1, 1908, when Elmer was about 13-1/2 years old, his mother remarried to Norman Lewis Swikert of Proctor Meadows (Palmer Junction territory) in Union County, Oregon. The new Mrs. Hattie Swikert took her Robinson children and moved into his home. In time, Norman Swikert adopted little Hattie Irene Robinson, who later became Mrs. Roy Henry Kennedy.

The *1920 Federal Census* of Palmer Junction precinct of Union County noted that Norman, 43, and Hattie, 47, had her children in the household: Elmer, 28, Frank, 25, and Irene H., 18. Norman Swikert was a sheep rancher and no doubt his step-sons, Elmer and Frank, were helpful ranch hands.

Elmer Robinson, 32, married Violet Addie Cook, 17, of Palmer Junction territory, Union County, on June 18, 1926. On the wedding certificate, Elmer described himself as a farmer from rural Elgin. Violet was born in Nebraska in 1909. They were married for 4-1/2 years and just had a baby boy when tragedy struck.

The *La Grande Observer, Friday, December 5, 1930, pg. 1* article read that Elmer Robertson, who lived near Palmer Junction, passed away suddenly early on December 4, 1930. He had complained of not feeling well and his wife started to fix an onion poultice for him, but he died before she could give him any aid. Since their home was a considerable distance from any other ranches, his wife Violet strapped her baby [Larry Elmer] to her back and trudged a mile and a half in snow 10 inches deep to get help. His body was taken to Elgin and is in charge of Snodgrass and Zimmerman. Funeral services were held at Elgin on Sunday, December 7, 1930, and burial took place at the Elgin Cemetery.

After Elmer's premature death, Violet was alone with a very young baby. Elmer's brother Frank was single at that time, so Violet married him on April 21, 1931. It was a type of brother-in-law marriage for Violet, and now she had someone to help her raise Elmer's son. Everyone stayed in the family this way, and young Violet had some security for the next 32 ½ years. After Frank died on August 8, 1964, she married Mr. Harris. Violet died in Walla Walla on July 21, 1988 at age 79 years. She was buried in the Elgin Cemetery.

The patriarch of the family, George Robinson, outlived his son Elmer by about 2 years. George had also remarried and moved to the Milton-Freewater area, where he farmed and ranched until his death from a sudden heart attack on April 30, 1932 at 73 years of age, his obituary stated. He had adopted his step son, the child of his second wife, Hattie Rosana (Carroll) Bray. The child's name was Ben Bray, born 1905 in Missouri. *(The Spokesman-Review, Spokane, Washington, Tue, May 3, 1932, pg. 8)*

George E. Robinson was interred at the Milton-Freewater IOOF Cemetery and was joined later by his second wife, then Mrs. Hattie Irons, who died November 30, 1963 in Junction City, Oregon.

Elmer's mother Hattie Swikert, 79, died December 7, 1945 at the hospital in La Grande following a long illness. She was born July 14, 1866 in Illinois, and had been a resident of Union County for 35 years. She was buried in the Elgin Cemetery beside Norman Swikert, who died in August 1939.

The Robinsons were well known in the Palmer Junction precinct, and now a road sign will remind everyone that they once lived, laughed and loved there.

Rock Creek Road - This road, named after Rock Creek, is located in Township 3S R37E, Section 6 and is 4.51 miles long. It is also known as Road #118 in the La Grande maintenance district. (In the Anthony Lakes area.)

Rock Ridge Road - This is a private road off Mt. Glen Road, located at Township 2S R38E, Section 32. It is a geographic name for the rocky ridge formation that the road climbs up and onto a plateau, accessing 3 residences there. From this elevation, there is a great view of La Grande.

Roe Drive - This is a private drive that exits south off of Gekeler Lane and opposite of Anson Road, bringing access to the farm residences of the Roe families.

Rose Ridge Road - This road is located in Township 3S R40E Section 42 on the edge of Cove. On this road, there are two property owners with county addresses and three property owners with city addresses.

Land owner John Robinson bought his land in 1962 or 1963 from Royal Borkgren, who Robinson thought was a relative of the original homesteaders James and Ellen Bloom, one of the earliest pioneers to Cove. *(John Robinson interview, October 24, 2021)*

Robinson subdivided his land, calling it Rose Ridge subdivision, named in fashion, after the historic Rose Ridge Cemetery (Cove Cemetery). In 1883, pioneers, James M. and Ellen (Chrisman) Bloom, donated some of their land to the newly formed cemetery board. It was a parcel of land on the rocky hills south of Cove, enclosed by a rail fence with an abundance of wild roses growing there, hence the name Rose Ridge Cemetery.

The cemetery's earliest burial stone is dated 1864 for Selena Grace Hendershott, the daughter of another early Cove pioneer. One of the first mentions of the name Rose Ridge in the La Grande Observer was in an 1898 obituary for Mrs. Maria (Goodspeed) Corpe of Cove. It read in part: "The last sad rites were conducted by Rev. Thompson, of Union, and the remains were laid to rest in the Rose Ridge cemetery, Cove, May 3, 1898." (*La Grande Observer, May 4, 1898, pg. 3*)

The Rose Ridge Road was so named to remain consistent with the Rose Ridge Cemetery and the Rose Ridge subdivision names.

Robinson said that the former owner of his property, Royal Borkgren, built and operated the Cove swimming pool. Research shows that Royal Borkgren and his father Martin L. Borkgren (1864-1933) were well known for developing the spring-fed Cove pool in the 1920s. Their history was written up in the *La Grande Observer, June 25, 2005, by Dick Mason.*

The article read: "It was just a large hole with sloping sides surrounded by willow trees before the Borkgrens went to work. There were large boulders around the spring that the Borkgrens made short work of. They dynamited the boulders, sending pieces of rock flying throughout Cove. Breaking up the boulders allowed the two to build a pool 62 feet long by 55 feet wide."

After Martin Borkgren's death in 1933, his son Royal Borkgren assumed ownership of the pool.

"It was his life each year from April through September." He served as the only lifeguard 12 hours each day and then would drain and clean the pool. Borkgren also slept in the back room of the pool building, providing a measure of round-the-clock security. Sometimes it was needed. Running the pool was a family affair for the Borkgrens, who operated it through about the mid-1960s. Esther Borkgren, Royal's wife, sold admission tickets and rented caps and suits." (End of article excerpt)

Roulet Loop - Formerly called Parks-Roulet Road, this county road #137 is 4.45 miles in length in Township 1N R40E Section 9 in the Elgin maintenance district.

On the *1935 Metsker Map* it was called the Parks-Roulet Road. This road wasn't a loop originally, but two straight roads, one called Parks and the other Roulet. Later, the roads were connected to make Parks-Roulet Loop. *(Norma Jean Roulet Elmer interview, age 92, April 2018)*

Norma Jean Roulet, who grew up on this road, only remembered calling it Hindman Road. The Parks-Roulet name was later simplified to Roulet Loop, and its beginning and end both intersect with Hindman Road northeast of Elgin.

The first part of the name, Parks was named after Kendrick "Kinder" Parks, who was born in Jackson, Orange County, Indiana on July 14, 1847, where he lived with his parents, William and Nancy Parks.

He continued to live with his parents until he married Malinda Jane Byers in Orange, Indiana in April of 1866. Malinda Jane Byers was born March 18, 1846 in Kentucky. They had four children: Nancy (1868), William O. (Sept 1872), Thomas E. (Oct. 1876) and Ruth A. (Jan. 1880).

Sometime between 1880 and 1900, they moved to Elgin, Oregon. He had a farm there but apparently, he also had a lumber mill that he operated with his sons, William and Thomas. "Kinder

Parks & Sons sold their lumber interests to the Elgin Lumber Company late last week." *(La Grande Observer, November 23, 1902, pg. 1)*

Kinder moved away and lived in Umatilla County *(1910 census)* and in Seattle, Washington *(1920 census)*. It appears that his son, Thomas, took over the farm and lived there. He married Florence Idella Atteberry on May 4, 1908 in Elgin. They had two children, Vera E. (1909-10) and Floyd E (July 16, 1918). They were still in Elgin in the *1920 and 1940 Federal Census*es.

Floyd Parks, 24, died on October 9, 1942 on Guadalcanal, Solomon Islands during the war. His body was brought back to Elgin Cemetery for burial.

Thomas sold his farm, according to the *La Grande Observer, Oct. 2, 1945, pg. 10* in preparation for moving. He was in his sixties by then and wanted to retire from farming, especially now that Floyd was gone.

In 1946, Thomas and Florence along with their daughter, Vera, went to Portland, where Vera lived. Then the parents had plans to travel south to find a more healthful climate for Florence. *(La Grande Observer, June 26, 1946, pg. 3)*

It was reported in the *La Grande Observer of July 30, 1946 on pg. 3* that Thomas and Florence were in Medford, Oregon. Floyd's name was placed on a bronze plaque at the Whitman College student center building where Floyd had studied. *(La Grande Observer, June 14, 1947, pg. 8)*

Florence Parks died in 1954 and Thomas in 1967; both are buried in Portland, Oregon.

The second half of the early road name, Roulet, was named after the Roulet family, Swiss settlers from Santa Clara, Washington County, Utah. They settled on land about 8 miles northeast of Elgin, locally called Cricket Flat, where they engaged in farming and raising cattle.

The patriarch of the family, William Henry Roulet was born November 29, 1865 in Santa Clara, Utah, the son of Francis Frederick Roulet (1816-1885) from Payerne, Vaud, Switzerland and Rachel "Regula" (Hug) Roulet (1824-1910) from Weiningen, Zurich, Switzerland.

William Roulet settled and farmed on what is now called Parsons Lane for 73 years until his death at the age of 93 on August 6, 1959. During his lifetime, he had three wives: Julia F. Kirschner (1872-1926), who died in a car accident. Then he married Nancy Alice (Morton) Gorden (1880-1974), formerly Mrs. Willis E. Gorden (1897 marriage). After the marriage ended, he married Mary "Cordelia" Davis-Rhine (1880-1968) on October 30, 1939.

William Roulet's son and daughter-in-law, Leo and Nellie (Parsons) Roulet, settled on a ranch in 1919 on the then Parks-Roulet Road *(Metsker Map)*. They had three children: Frederick "Fred" William Roulet and Norma Jean, who married Russel Elmer. Their third child, 3-year-old Arthur Leo Roulet, born February 10, 1928, was butted by a cow, and he died soon afterward at the hospital on July 29, 1931.

Fred was born November 24, 1922 and grew up on the Roulet ranch, being a good friend of Billy Hindman. The boys hitched rides to high school together, he said. He graduated with the Elgin High School class of 1941, and his wife Helen E. Van Blokland of La Grande graduated in 1940.

Fred and Helen were married on November 7, 1942 in Walla Walla, Washington. In the spring of 1944, he actively farmed on Roulet property, earning the honor of Union County Cattleman of the Year in 1979. *(Scott Ludwig interview, May 21, 2019)*

Together, they attended almost every one of their Elgin High School alumni banquets. They were married 73 years before Helen died on January 14, 2016, and she was dearly missed by Fred.

Fred died at age 95 on March 15, 2018 as a result of an accident he had while feeding his cattle. He had broken his hip when a 80# bale of hay fell on him, pushing him against his truck. He was rescued, but died a few days later in a nursing facility. *(Fred Roulet interview, June 2017; Norma Jean Roulet Elmer interview, April 2018)*

Ruckle Road - Formerly called Finley Creek Road, this county road #22 runs 4.26 miles in Township 1N R38E Section 28 in the Imbler maintenance district. The former name Finley Creek Road is on the *1935 Metsker Map*. Before that, it was called the Thomas and Ruckle Road or Ruckles, which was a wagon road over the Blue Mountains.

"George Thomas was a stagecoach driver who came west to California in 1849, before moving to Walla Walla. Colonel J. S. Ruckle arrived in Oregon in 1855 as a steam boat pilot for the Oregon Steam Navigation Company (OSN) along the Columbia River. Eventually Ruckle left the OSN and ran his own boat along the river. The two men planned and built the road in 1864 and 1865, as well as a stage line from Walla Walla to the Idaho Mines. The road ran from the northwest to the southeast, offering a more direct connection to Walla Walla, despite being longer than the Meacham Road." *(Wikipedia, Thomas Ruckle)*

The Ruckle Road, as well as others over the Blues, charged $3 to $5 per wagon. Several towns were platted along the road: Summerville in 1873, and Cove sometime in the 1870s. Mail was delivered over the road, causing it to bypass La Grande in favor of Union and Summerville, helping Union become elected as the county seat in 1872.

The road washed out in 1886 and was never rebuilt. However, Ruckle Road was surveyed in 1917, and in December 1926, the Union County Chamber of Commerce Good Roads committee discussed a proposal by H. H. Huron of Imbler to build a highway over Ruckle Road connecting with the Pendleton-Walla Walla road at Weston.

The argument in favor of this was that it could be built $25,000 cheaper than any other route over the mountains. It was also argued that it could be kept free of snow in the winter and that the highest elevation would be 4,500 feet, which is much less than via Toll Gate.

Summerville residents were also in the discussion, declaring that Ruckle Road could start from the Pleasant Grove school house corner or from Summerville, both distances being about equal. If it started at Pleasant Grove, the proposed highway could follow Hunter Road to Island City. If it started in Summerville, then the road would connect to the La Grande-Wallowa Lake Highway. Either way, a 7 mile road could be built to connect Elgin to the highway. *(Newspapers.com)*

Ruckman Road - This road #35B runs 3.98 miles in Township 2S R39E Section 9 in the La Grande maintenance district, and it is located two miles east of Alicel, running north and south.

It is named after the George Washington Ruckman family, who farmed in this district.

George W. was born April 2, 1848 in Wapello County, Iowa, the son of William and Mary (Miller) Ruckman, natives of Pennsylvania and Ohio respectively. William was a farmer and blacksmith, two trades that pair well together for a self-sufficient life.

He was educated in the district schools of Iowa and assisted his father on the farm until he was age 23. Five years earlier on April 15, 1866, at age 18, George married Miss Lucretia Cassanna Neville in Agency City, Wapello County, Iowa, daughter of Edward P. and Margurette J. (McGuire) Neville.

They welcomed their firstborn, William Edward Ruckman, in 1867, and in 1871 they traveled by train from Iowa to Ogden, Utah, where they supplied a wagon and bought a team of oxen for their journey to Walla Walla, Washington. They arrived there on June 18, 1871.

After working on a farm there for 2-1/2 months, he moved to the Grande Ronde Valley on September 4, 1871. He bought a half section of school land, remained there a year and sold it before moving to his permanent home two miles east of Alicel on the Sandridge. *(An Illustrated History of Union and Wallowa Counties, 1902, pages 384-385)*

During their marriage, George and Lucretia Ruckman became parents to six children: William Edward (1867-1974), John H. T. (1874-1891), Robert Jasper (1877-1910), Samuel G. (1880-1964), Mary Jane Peal (1883-1935), Hattie Opal (1885-1902).

He was successful enough to increase his acreage to about 680 acres in one body, producing beets, alfalfa and cereals. In addition to these crops, he had a 3-acre orchard that included 300 trees. He also purchased 80 acres of timberland west of Summerville.

His stock raising efforts were successful because he imported five full-blood shorthorn animals from Missouri and raised a good herd from them. He also raised good Poland China and Berkshire hogs.

He took special interest in raising mules, importing them from Virginia to produce the finest jack in Union County. Each year, he raised 15 mules. In like fashion, he raised good horses, roadsters and working animals, using a well-bred Hambletonian stallion. He even sold one of his finest working horses to Senator Slater.

When he retired from farming, sometime between 1910 and 1915, he moved into the city of Imbler, and his son, Samuel G. Ruckman, who had always assisted him in farming, took over the operation of the homestead ranch. At this juncture of his life, George accepted a position as deputy sheriff of Union County.

He was also interested in school affairs. As a result, he was on the school board for a number of years. He had a charitable heart and was reportedly very generous to those in need.

George died at the age of 66 from a sudden heart attack on the evening of January 5, 1915 while driving his wife home after a pleasant visit with their son Samuel Ruckman at the homestead ranch earlier that evening. Lucretia died at her Imbler home on October 18, 1929. Both are interred at the Summerville Cemetery. *(An Illustrated History of Union and Wallowa counties, 1902, pg. 384-385;*

Their firstborn, William "Bill" lived in the first white house as one turns west on Woodell-Ruckman Road, as it was called then. Bill married Elizabeth Elenor Endicott, and they had three children, Harvey Edward, Mary Opal and Hattie "Wave" Ruckman.

Mary Opal Ruckman (1900-1998) married a man named Ray Homer Hayes (See Hayes Road entry). An insightful memorial on *Findagrave.com* read: "Mary's first husband, Ray Homer Hayes was her love. Ray died and several years went by after which Mary met Otto Bob Robinett. They married, but Mary chose to be buried under her first married name of Hayes. Bob died before Mary."

Hattie Ruckman (1909-1989), who was known by her middle name "Wave" married Carl D. Friswold (1907-1958). *(Findagrave.com, Summerville Cemetery)*

Harvey Ruckman was born October 31, 1896 in Alicel and died January 29, 1974. He lived in the big white Ruckman family house. He broke his leg in the 8th grade, playing football. He never went back to school. He farmed in Alicel during his adult life. He married Goldie Belle Hayes (1895-1992) in Weiser, Idaho, and they lived a prosperous life here in Union County. Both are interred at the Summerville Cemetery.

Harvey and Goldie had a daughter, Mary Elizabeth Ruckman, who was born in 1926. She married Richard Bennett on December 1, 1951. He was a graduate of the University of Oregon and was stationed at Fort Ord, California. He completed his course in law at the university shortly before being called to the service. The couple made their home in California. *(La Grande Observer, Dec. 10, 1951, pg. 3; Ancestry.com; Oregon Marriage Index)*

Mary and her first cousin, Elenor Hayes, had an especially close friendship during their lives. Elenor stood up as matron of honor at Mary's wedding to Richard Bennett. Elenor's husband, Dale Pierson, was the best man for the groom.

"Many generations back," wrote informant Elwyn Bingaman, "a great grandmother who married a Ruckman, had a brother that was at Sutter's Fort (near Sacramento, California) when gold was discovered (in January 1848). He sent money to his sister back here to buy the ground with the tree (still standing) on the corner of Woodell-Ruckman Road and Highway 82." *(Elwyn Bingaman memoirs letter, April 30, 2019)*

Ruth Lane - This private lane runs off Mill Creek Lane and is located in Township 3S R40E Section 22 in the Union maintenance district.

It is named after Ruth Comstock. She and her husband Roy D. owned the area that was sub-divided in 2007. *(Union County land records)* They bought the property in 1949, and the lane was originally a long driveway to the Comstock residence. The original house is still there. Roy had a big cherry orchard. Quite a few acres are still in cherries and owned by Galloway.

"This lane wasn't named until three people lived on it, so when my Dad sold the property and they built houses and had addresses, they had to name it. So my Dad, Roy D., named it after his wife, Ruth Comstock. It was probably in the 1980s that this happened. There are four permanent residences on the lane now, but there will be more later." *(Nancy Comstock, daughter of Ruth*

Ruth's obituary on the website of Daniels Chapel read in part: "Ruth W. Comstock, age 91, of Cove, died Monday, May 7, 2007. A celebration of life will be held on Friday, May 11, 2007 at 2:00 p.m. at Daniels Chapel of the Valley, 1502 7th Street. Committal and interment will follow at the Cove Cemetery.

Mrs. Comstock was born on May 27, 1915, the daughter of Henry Odd Willhoit, Sr, and Emma Josephine (Mahler) Willhoit in Iowa Park, Texas. She graduated from high school in Kilgore, Texas and then attended Kilgore State College. During World War II she worked for the Goodyear Tire Company in Pensacola, Florida and was a United Service Organizations singer.

On August 23, 1945 she married Roy Comstock in La Grande. They lived in Tulsa, Oklahoma and in Iowa before returning to the Grande Ronde Valley in the spring of 1949. She loved to sing and sang for many weddings over the years. She enjoyed crafts, crocheting, ceramics and sewing. Her social memberships were many, including a bowling league, Mt. Fanny Grange, the Cove Sportsman's Club and Cherry Chapter and other groups.

Survivors include her husband, Roy Comstock of Cove; children, John Comstock of Salem, David and Pam Comstock of La Grande, Nancy Comstock of Albany and Joyce and George Hyland of Sandy. She was preceded in death by her parents, brothers, Jack and H. O. Willhoit and sister, Nell Carpenter." [End of obit]

Sammyville Lane - This private lane exits Gordon Creek road, and it leads to an unincorporated community called Sammyville. Both the lane and the community are named for its landowner, the late Samuel Isaac Horrell, also called Sam or Sammy. The lane is located on Township 2N R39E Section 29 in the Elgin maintenance district.

Sammyville was a tenant community, part of Sam Horrell's rental business as well as the location of his personal residence. He also owned properties in and around Elgin city limits. His rent was low enough to allow tenants of little means to have housing, and for this, many felt he was a generous man. As local legends go, Sammyville was also a dark woods sanctuary for people who wanted to live in anonymity.

Horrell had an eccentric personality and for that he gained some notoriety after a movie was made about him in 1999 called "Sammyville" (later "Dark Woods"), depicting him as a gun-slinging, spiritual leader and law officer of a self-made community called Sammyville on Gordon Creek Road. His signature line in the movie is "I am the Law!"

It's true he routinely carried a holstered pistol over his overalls. No matter how much he denied it, his step-daughter, Daryl Logan, confirmed that he really did shoot a bullet through the Elgin Opera House movie theater screen during a John Wayne movie. He got a little carried away watching that movie.

He seemed to have a thing for dynamite too, so on one July 4th at 5 a.m., he startled everyone in Sammyville when he lit dynamite to blast a tree stump. Eventually, Logan had to lock up his stash of dynamite, and Horrell wasn't happy about that. *(Richard Cockle, The Oregonian, July 17, 2011 pg. 1)*

For these reasons and others, he has become a legend of sorts in Union County. With his passing, and legendary status, he has earned a place in the Elgin Museum and Historical Society at 180 N. Eighth Avenue in Elgin.

Samuel "Sambo" Isaac Horrell was born February 13, 1930 in Halfway, Oregon to Samuel "Martin" Horrell and Sylvia May Mills (1906-1990).

Samuel Martin Horrell married Mrs. Sylvia May (Mills) Hoffman on December 5, 1928 in Grant County, Oregon. Sylvia had a son, Earl Hoffman, from a previous marriage, who came into the Horrell household with her. *(Findagrave.com, Elgin Cemetery)* Samuel Martin went by "Martin" but also by "Ike" which is engraved on his memorial stone "Ike Martin Horrell."

Our subject, Samuel Isaac Horrell, spent the first 8 years of his life living in Halfway (Pine Valley) of Baker County. In 1938, he moved with his family to Elgin where he attended school to third grade.

He grew to adulthood and founded Sammyville on part of his 88 acres of land, but it had no electricity until 1953 and no telephones until 1958. The town has a centralized water system and a network of surprisingly good dirt streets. The dwellings have indoor plumbing and electricity, and he maintained a fire truck and snow plows capable of dealing with 8 feet of snow, which he insisted the town occasionally gets. *(Richard Cockle, The Oregonian, July 17, 2011)*

Sam was married twice, first to Shirley Cox on June 17, 1961 at the home of Sam's parents, Mr. and Mrs. Martin Horrell. The wedding was held on the lawn with an arch made of evergreen, purple locust and elkhorn flowers. They had guests from La Grande, Elgin and other areas in attendance. *(La Grande Observer, July 5, 1961 pg. 5)* They were married until September 1966. *(Ancestry.com)*

He married his second wife, Mrs. Annabelle Rosetta (Matters) Yeager (1928-2016) on December 8, 1973. Annabelle was born August 19, 1928 in Sharon, Pennsylvania to Walter and Ada (Shacklock) Matters. She resided in Greenville, PA and Elgin, OR. She graduated from Sharpsville High School in Sharpsville, Pennsylvania.

Her marriage to Sam Horrell was her third one. She had previously been married to Howard Carroll Stephens on June 4, 1948, and they had six children. She then married John Arnold Yeager on March 6, 1962, and he died in 1972. Then a widow, she married Samuel Isaac Horrell on December 8, 1973, a marriage that lasted over 41 years. *(Ancestry.com)*

Sam was employed at Boise Cascade as a faller and later in the mill for a total of 30 years. He then busied himself as the landlord for Sammyville residents. As pastimes, he enjoyed fishing and hunting. He earned recognition as a horse shoe player champion and was honorary deputy sheriff.

Sam Horrell was good to his tenants, even hosted picnics for them in Sammyville. He didn't allow liquor to be consumed at the picnic, but the tenants enjoyed playing card games, horse shoes and eating plenty of food. Elgin Museum curator Charlie Horn said that Sam Horrell wasn't the man so many portrayed him to be. *(Charlie Horn interview, May 25, 2019)*

Sam Horrell, 84, of Elgin, passed away at his residence on Monday, June 16, 2014. He had no biologically related children.

For more online reading on Sam's ancestors, the Horrell Brothers of Lampasa, Texas, the authors suggest you search under "The Horrell-Higgins Feud" if you want to read how the Horrells went down in Texas history and how Sammy's branch of the family escaped to Oregon.

For you genealogists, please note Sam's family descent as follows: great-great-great grandfather Benedict D. Horrell (Harrell), great-great grandfather Samuel M. Horrell Sr. (1820-1869); great grandfather Samuel M. Horrell Jr. (1837-1936); grandfather John Samuel Horrell (1871-1927); father Samuel Martin "Ike" Horrell (1896-1975) and then our subject Samuel Isaac Horrell (1930-2014).

Samuel and Annabelle Horrell are buried in the Elgin Cemetery on Cemetery Road.

Sanderson Road - This gravel county road #80 is 1.58 miles in length in Township 1N R38E Section 23 in the Imbler maintenance district.

On the *1935 Metsker Map* it was labeled McKenzie Road, but later renamed Sanderson after Willis Sanderson, the father of Bill Sanderson. Walt and Elizabeth "Liz" (Sanderson) Sullivan of the Sanderson Century Farm on Summerville Road are related to Willis Sanderson. *(Thelma Oliver interview, 2005)*

Elizabeth (Sanderson) Sullivan wrote a narrative about the Sanderson Century Farm in 2003, in part as follows:

My grandfather, Mathew Sanderson was born in Lanark, Ontario, Canada on March 27, 1852. He was one of nine children born to David and Betsy (Deachman) Sanderson. Mathew married Euphenia Young. Their first two children, Epsie and David, were born in Howick, Ontario, Canada.

A physician told Mathew that they should seek a warmer climate for Euphenia's health. They went first to California and worked their way up to Oregon. In Oregon they first moved to a homestead in the Flora area, but then moved to the Grande Ronde Valley near Island City, where they worked for a butter and cheese factory for several years. After saving money, they sold their Island City property and purchased what is now the Sanderson Springs Ranch.

Mathew and Euphenia purchased the Sanderson Springs Ranch from Turner and Anna Oliver in 1900. They settled there with their eight children: Epsie, David Lunham, Bessie, Deachman, Willie Wilson, Mary Ellen, Annie Rachel, Charles Mathew and Stuart Alexander. Their farm produced hay and grain and they raised cattle. Near their house, they grew a vegetable garden.

David Sanderson purchased 180 acres from his parents when he married Silvia Neiderer in 1907. They had two sons, Virgil David and Lyle Gale Sanderson. In addition to the same crops that were raised on his parents' farm, David put in a large trout pond fed by the springs. They enjoyed the trout they caught there.

Virgil Sanderson married Theresa Gietlhuber in 1939, and they had two daughters, Georgene and Elizabeth Sanderson. After David's mother Silvia died in 1943, and David in 1951, then Virgil and Lyle inherited the land. Virgil bought out Lyle's share of the farm in 1957. During the next 20 years, the land produced grass seed, meadow hay that was in high demand by the Native Americans for horse feed and provided pasture for horses owned by Peterson Mink Farms.

In the early 1960s Virgil and Theresa Sanderson moved the original barn and built their new ranch style home with a full daylight basement in 1964. The original farm house was moved to End Road where it was used as a residence.

The barn was raised with house jacks and tamarack skids were placed under it. Several neighbors came with their logging Caterpillar tractors and pulled the barn to the north of its original location. The barn was constructed with mortise and tenon joints, and it was restored and repainted.

Virgil Sanderson farmed the land and raised cattle while he worked full time as a senior postal clerk at the La Grande post office on a 3 p.m. to 11 p.m. shift. He spent his vacations haying, harvesting grain and stud logging.

Upon Virgil's death in 1982, his wife Theresa had assistance with ranching the land from a relative Steve Craig. The land produced hay and pasture for cattle. Upon Theresa's death in 1997, Elizabeth and Georgene inherited the 180 acres. Elizabeth purchased Georgene's share in 1998 and resided in the newly remodeled home with her husband Walt Sullivan and their son Dallas. They finished the remodel of the house in 2002. They also jacked up the barn and poured a new foundation under it.

When they were excavating for the new house, the original hydraulic ram was uncovered. This was used to deliver water to the house from the spring from 1907 until 1951 when electricity was made available to the ranch.

The other three quarters of the original Sanderson ranch was owned by Dorothy (Sanderson) Craig. Dorothy Craig's son Steve and Elizabeth Sullivan's son Dallas have farmed the land. *(Taken from Elizabeth Sullivan's century farm application narrative, 2003)*

Sandridge Road - This unpaved, sandy gravel road #25 runs 7.88 miles in Township 2S R38E Section 25 in the La Grande-Union maintenance district.

It veers north off Highway 82 about two and three-fourths miles north of Island City at an intersection historically called "Conley Corner." That history has been all but lost except by resident farmer and area historian John Cuthbert, who was one of two owners of Conley Corner.

Conley Corner is really a bend in Highway 82 and not a right-angled corner, per se. Regardless, this marks the southern entrance onto Sandridge Road. From there it travels about 8 miles until it intersects with Summerville Road opposite the Summerville Cemetery.

Sandridge Road is named after one of the valley's most significant geological features, a large swath, hump or ridge of sandy soil that begins at Conley Corner, straddles both sides of Highway 82, occupying a large portion of the north central area of the Grande Ronde Valley.

The north-most border of the sand ridge is prominently visible at Summerville Cemetery and then the elevation drops rapidly as Summerville Road continues northbound into the city of Summerville. Geologists believe the sand ridge was formed by the forces of water, bringing and leaving sedimentary material in the valley.

For a spectacular view of this geological phenomenon, travel one mile east of Summerville on Courtney Lane and look directly south toward the Summerville Cemetery. This gives you an amazing wide-angle view of the sand ridge, and you'll see just how waters must have flowed around it, carving the land and leaving this elevated and sweeping ridge of sand behind.

Sandridge Road is more easily traveled than dirt or gravel roads in the county because of its ability to drain away moisture. However, in the dry season, one's vehicle will be covered with fine sand after traveling it. This road is just part of the larger "Sand Ridge" district.

As a district, the Sand Ridge had its own post office from April 6, 1875 to July 9, 1877, with Cyrus G. Enloe as its first postmaster. There were several months during this time when it did not function, but it was located at a station on the stage route from Union to Summerville on the Creston Shaw and Rudd farms on Ruckman Road.

Sand Ridge also had its own one-room schoolhouse called Sand Ridge School, which closed in 1888. The retired school building was reused as a machine shed and was relocated 100 yards off the road in one of Will Ruckman's fields. After the school closed, the pupils went to a new school called Lone Pine near the railroad tracks at Imbler. That school was later consolidated in the Iowa district of Union County. *(La Grande Observer, Sept. 4, 1951, pg. 1-2)*

As for the soil quality of the Sand Ridge, it was recorded in 1863 by government surveyors as "rich, level, bottom land, prairie, soil first rate." *(Government survey map of Sept. 3, 1863)*

Apparently, not all held that opinion of the Sand Ridge, according to the *Baker Democrat Herald of January 13, 1930, pg. 8.* The article was titled "Dunham Wright Tells how Local Places Were Named." Wright was a well-known pioneer resident of Medical Springs, and he said this about the Sand Ridge of Union County.

Wright wrote: "Then we have the name Sand Ridge, indicating a dry desert waste and was so recognized by the first settlers and visitors to the valley as the first settlement was around the margin of the valley or foothills. It was a common expression of both settlers and visitors 'what a pity it was that so much of such a beautiful valley should be one half a lake or swamp and the other half a desert.'"

Wright's newspaper article continued, "Both these, considered worthless tracts of land by an act of congress, fell to the state. The Sand Ridge was a part of the 500,000 acres grant for internal improvements selected by Governor Gibbs, whose name was frequently discussed...for selecting such a worthless tract of desert land that the state could never have the benefit from the sale of it." (End of Wright's article)

Interestingly, this assessment of the productivity and value of the Sand Ridge district could not have been more wrong. This so-called desert, which was sold by the state for $1.25 an acre under the Homestead Act, became the million-dollar grain, mint and hayfields of the Grande Ronde Valley by 1930.

Well drilling, irrigation systems, improved farming methods, crop rotations and soil conservation practices all helped to transform the Sand Ridge district into very productive soil.

Sandridge Road which travels through this district is home to very successful farmers and land owners, including John Cuthbert, the Bingamans, Matt & Melanie Insko, Cresta DeLint family, Samuel Royes, David Hafer, Doug Wright and H. L. Wagner and Sons to name a few.

The Sandridge Road sign therefore stands as a testimony that sandy soil can still grow crops bountifully.

Seventh St. Alicel - This is a public unmaintained county road that runs .14 miles in Township 2S R39E Section 7 in the La Grande maintenance district. (See Alicel Lane)

Sharp Road - This road is a public unmaintained road that runs .27 miles in Township 3S R40E Section 16 in the Union maintenance district. It diverts off of Chadwick Lane near Cove. It is named after Steven J. Sharp, who subdivided a parcel there in 2002. *(U.C. Tax Accessor's site)*

Shaw Creek Road - This county road #53A runs .71 miles in Township 1S R40E Section 7 in the Imbler maintenance district. It is named after Shaw Creek.

On the *1935 Metsker Map* and the *1978 Union County map*, Shaw Creek Road was called Indian Creek Road. It appears that the Shaw Creek Road was probably given its name in 1988 when the roads were renamed.

This road is named after Shaw Creek, which is a stream that originates in the forested mountains northeast of Imbler and meanders through the south precinct of Elgin emptying from the east into the Grande Ronde River at a junction just south of Philberg Road on Highway 82.

Shaw Creek and by extension Shaw Creek Road were named in honor of the Angus Shaw Sr. family, prominent farmers and land holders in the north valley area. This history will now focus on him and his family.

Angus Shaw Sr. was born June 12, 1816 on the Isle of Skye in Scotland. There he met Elizabeth Murchison, who was born December 15, 1817 in Alisky Locharon Ross-shire, Scotland. *(Tombstone inscription; Summerville Cemetery burial records)*

They were married on December 15, 1850 in the parish of Contin, in the region of Ross and Cromarty, Scotland. *(In the Scotland, Select Marriages, 1561-1910)* Elizabeth (Murchison) Shaw was the daughter of John Murchison (1786-1867) and Elizabeth (McKenzie) Murchison (1778-1877) of Ross and Cromarty, Scotland.

In the 1851 Scotland Census in the household of John and Elizabeth (McKenzie) Murchison were adult children Ann Murchison, 36, Elizabeth (Murchison) Shaw, 33, Murdo Murchison, 28; with visitor Roderick McKenzie, 57, Flora (Murchison) Macrae, 21 and baby daughter Kate Macrae, 1; servant Flora Macrae, 15. The authors believe these people were all related to one another.

Angus Sr. and Elizabeth Shaw had three children born in Scotland: John Shaw (1852-1932), Christina Shaw (1853-1940), later Mrs. James H. Standley; and Angus Shaw Jr. (1855-1940).

The Shaws immigrated to America in 1856, and they settled in Elmira, Stark County, Illinois, where they stayed for seven years. During these years, they had two more children, Sarah "Sallie" Shaw (1857-1917), later Mrs. Jasper Bonnette; and Elizabeth "Bettie" Shaw (1859-1930), later Mrs. H. Clay Humphrey. *(La Grande Observer, Mon., Oct. 21, 1940, pg. 1, Christine Standley's obit)*

After the Homestead Act of 1862 was passed, the Shaw family wanted to move to Oregon, as did many others living in Illinois at that time. Some of those families included the Murchisons, McKenzie, and McRaes. In fact, the aforementioned names were Summerville pioneer settlers. Murchisons became active Summerville farmers and Mrs. Murchison ran a restaurant; the sailor Roderick McKenzie operated "the Anchor" a busy livery in Summerville from 1880 to 1953; the John and "Belle" McRaes took their turn at operating the hotel on main street in Summerville in 1906, calling it Hotel McRae.

In any case, all these Scottish families rendezvoused in Illinois and from there they formed what later was called the Scotch Train that left Illinois in May 1863. All of them were looking forward to the homesteading deals in Oregon.

Enroute in Omaha, Nebraska, they joined up with others to form a 100-wagon train. This train was to have a government escort of 36 mule teams and 150 men under the command of Captain Crawford. *(Bernal D. Hug Supplement #3 to History of Union County, Oregon, pages 73-74.)*

The McDonald family history book mentions the Angus Shaw family as being part of the train heading for Oregon. It recorded that the Shaws brought with them all their young children: John, Christy, Angus Jr., Sallie, and Bettie. Of course, the nicknames Christy was for Christina Shaw, Sallie was for Sarah Shaw and Bettie was for Elizabeth E. Shaw. *(The McDonalds from Shieldaig, Scotland, Ellen Lopez and Mildred Nystrom)*

After six months of traveling the Oregon Trail, the Scotch Train arrived to the Grande Ronde Valley in Union County, Oregon on October 5, 1863. For the Shaws, Murchisons, McKenzies, and others, it was their final stop. The McRaes and Camerons went on to Walla Walla, Washington, but came back to Summerville later as their activities are preserved in Summerville history.

Angus Shaw Sr. homesteaded in Summerville in 1865, a tract of 160 acres, which adjoined land owned by William H. Patten, the first homesteader in Summerville. Patten owned the ground that most of the village of Summerville was built on. He laid out its streets and opened the doors to the post office on May 30, 1865 as its first postmaster.

He is the person who named the post office and community in honor of his close friend, Alexander Sommerville, who was Patten's neighbor when he lived near Harrisburg in the Willamette Valley. Although the U.S. Post Office registered the post office as Summerville, it had some brutal winters and that's why other settlers wanted the name to be registered as Winterville. However, the post master won out, he being the one to fill out the papers and the one who owned the ground that the settlement was going to be built on.

The Shaws were in the Grande Ronde Valley less than four years when on June 5, 1867, Elizabeth Shaw died at the age of 50 years, 5 months, and 7 days. Elizabeth's burial was the second one on record at the Summerville Cemetery, which was established in 1866.

This place of rest was situated on an elevated sand ridge one mile south of the village. Though it was chosen with some haste by settlers in response to the drowning death of 18-year-old Mary Stevens in 1866, it was an excellent choice in hindsight. It was a peaceful place with an awe-inspiring, panoramic view of the Blue Mountain range to the west. Mary Stevens (18) and Elizabeth Shaw (50) were its first two sleepers, casualties of pioneer life, but now preserved in death. *(Summerville Cemetery burial records)*

This newly inaugurated cemetery was a lonely place back then, but it was visited regularly by the afternoon breezes and the orange and pink sunsets. During the dark, wintery nights, one has only to be still to hear the sound of yipping coyotes in chorus and the mournful crying of the winds that chase after mad-dashing tumble weeds, the cemetery's only evening visitors.

Today, there are over 3,300 burials at Summerville Cemetery, and the grounds are being expanded to allow for more. It's very well groomed and still the loveliest of all of Union County cemeteries.

Three years following Elizabeth Shaw's death, during the *1870 Federal Census* of Summerville, four of her children were living together in a house. Her firstborn, John Shaw, 18, was the head of the house, along with his siblings, Angus Jr., 15, Sarah, 13, and Elizabeth E. Shaw, 11.

It appears their father Angus Shaw Sr. was securing another donation land claim, but in Alicel. He was living in a farm home with two male boarders in their late twenties. Angus was described as head of the household and as a farmer, but the men were described as "servants." It's possible that this farm was the one that his son John Shaw took over in 1909 when Angus Shaw Sr. died.

Angus Shaw Sr. also homesteaded 160 acres in Summerville, part of which is called the Shaw Addition today. In the *La Grande Observer, Thurs., June 15, 1939 issue, pg. 1* there was an article entitled, "74-Year-Old Summerville Homestead Tract is Sold".

"This last tract of the 160 acres of land homesteaded at Summerville by Angus Shaw I was sold a few days ago by Angus Shaw II to H. L. Wagner. The tract consists of 100 acres and has been vested in the Shaw family since the date it was homesteaded by Angus Shaw I in 1865, 74 years ago."

"Wagner, purchaser of the land is a prominent seed grower of the Summerville district. He has done much to promote the growing of seed on a commercial basis in that district. The land adjoins the village of Summerville. In fact, part of the village is located on land originally included in the homestead.

It is understood that the purchase price was $10,000 or $100 an acre. Angus Shaw II received the 100 acre tract as one of the heirs of the estate and has farmed it continuously, although he moved to La Grande a few years ago to reside. He is now over 80 years old." (End of article)

Since his arrival to Union County in October 1863, Angus Shaw Sr. purchased other parcels of land and increased his land holdings steadily. His sons, John and Angus Shaw branched out to establish their own farms in the Alicel area and inherited some lands from their father.

Their sister, Christina Shaw, married James Henry Standley, who arrived in this valley with his parents and siblings on the Standley train in 1864. Christina was working as a cook at the Ruckle stage stop, when she met James, a teamster, running his wagons with freight from La Grande to Walla Walla. She must have reached his heart with her cooking because they were married on March 18, 1869. In 1870, they established their farm that later became the James H. Standley Century Farm on Standley Lane in Union County.

Angus Shaw Sr. outlived his wife Elizabeth (Murchison) Shaw by 42 years. He apparently did not remarry after her death. As tragic as this loss was, he did suffer another of a different kind, that also had serious consequences.

"A. Shaw, one of the pioneers of Summerville, while driving home from La Grande on last Saturday evening had the misfortune to freeze both hands. While the hands are badly frozen the family think with proper care they can be saved." *(La Grande Observer, Sat. Feb. 1, 1902, pg. 1)*

Then there seemed to be improvement. "Mr. A. Shaw, who had the misfortune to freeze his hands, is slowly recovering." *(La Grande Observer, Feb. 14, 1902, pg. 4)*

The next report, however, dashed those hopes for Angus. "Since last weeks items were written, the attending physicians found it necessary to amputate all of the fingers on both hands of A. Shaw, whose hands were so badly frozen a short time ago. While the patient is quite weak, he seems to be doing as one could expect under these circumstances." *(La Grande Observer, Fri., Feb. 21, 1901, pg. 1)*

Despite his disability, for the next 8 years, he continued to operate a saloon in Summerville. Older maps show the saloon on main street Summerville in 1888, but not on the 1910 Sanborn map, which seems to corroborate the memories of living relatives today and reflects Angus' death in 1909.

Angus Shaw Sr. died on the anniversary of his birth at 3 p.m. on Saturday, June 12, 1909 at 93 years, 0 months and 0 days at home in Summerville. He was interred in the Shaw family plot at Summerville Cemetery, and a tall, engraved obelisk marks their resting place.

The physician from Elgin, Dr. F. W. Whiting attended him for the last month and a half in his ill state. The death certificate also states that he was born in the Isle of Skye, Scotland, and that his mother's name was Mary Baton, also born there.

Afterward, Angus Shaw Jr. handled his estate and took over the operation of the large Shaw farm business. Angus Shaw Sr. only had two sons, John and Angus, who were both recognized as prominent and progressive farmers in this county.

The eldest, John Shaw, married Vesta Iola Heskett on November 22, 1881, and they had three children: Edward Hartford Shaw, Jasper "Jay" Shaw and Angus "Wilbur" Shaw. The John Shaw farm was located one and a half miles east of the Iowa school and about two miles west from Alicel. He farmed until 1926 when he retired to Pasadena, California. In April of 1932, feeling ill, he came to Twin Falls, Idaho to be with his son, Wilbur A. Shaw, for the last four months of his life. He died at age 80.

John Shaw's obituary was titled, "Formerly Prominent Valley Farmer - Funeral to be Held on Sunday." It read in part: One of Union county's oldest pioneers, John Shaw, died August 23, at the Twin Falls county hospital after a major operation. He was visiting his son, Wilbur Shaw, in

Twin Falls, Ida., and his body has been brought here for burial at Summerville. Born in Kirktown, Scotland on March 12, 1852, he came to the Grande Ronde valley in 1863, at the age of 11 years and made his home here until 1926, when he went to Pasadena, Calif. He went to live with his son in Idaho in April (1932).

Mr. Shaw, who was at one time a prominent valley farmer, was 80 years, five months and 11 days of age at the time of his death. He is survived by two sons, Wilbur, of Twin Falls, Ida., and Jay, of Roseburg, both of whom will attend the funeral; a sister, Mrs. Jim Standley of La Grande, and a brother, Angus of La Grande. *(La Grande Observer, Fri., Aug. 26, 1932, pg. 1)* Jay Shaw of Roseburg is the father of Creston Jay Shaw, 99, of Alicel, who is a well known farmer in Union County, and a partner in Blue Mountain Seeds Inc. of Imbler.

John Shaw's younger brother, Angus Shaw Jr., died May 30, 1940, and his obituary was titled, "Angus Shaw Dies in Heart Attack". It reads in part: "Funeral services for Angus Shaw, who died after a heart attack here yesterday will be held at the Summerville chapel Saturday at 2 p.m. with burial in the family plot there. He was born in Scotland, Nov. 15, 1858, being 81 years of age.

(This year date should read 1855 since the family immigrated in 1856. That would have made him 84 years old at the time of his death.) He came to this country with his parents and settled near Summerville where he had since made his home.

Survivors include: one sister, Grandma Standley; two nieces, Mrs. Etta Welch of Imbler and Mrs. McAllister; three nephews, Louie Standley of the valley, Jay Shaw of Roseburg, and W. A. Shaw of Twin Falls, Ida." *(La Grande Observer, Fri., May 31, 1940, pg. 1)* Angus Shaw Jr. was unmarried. Preceding him in death was his older brother John Shaw of Pasadena, Calif., the brother Angus wintered with for many years; and his parents Angus Shaw Sr. and Elizabeth (Murchison) Shaw.

Angus Shaw Jr. led a very interesting life as an adventure-seeking, gold miner, and a progressive farmer.

"Angus Shaw is now preparing to start for the Klondike about May 1st. He is going overland via Spokane to Lake Teslin, (Canada), a distance of about 1,500 miles. From there he will proceed 500 miles by water. He will take 8 or 10 pack ponies with him, and thinks it will require him about two months to make the journey." *(La Grande Observer, Tues, Feb. 22, 1898, pg. 3)*

"Mr. Angus A. Shaw Jr., of Alicel, made the Observer a pleasant call yesterday. Mr. Shaw is a mining man of many years experience and intends to start for the Alaskan gold fields in a short time. He intends to go by the overland route, as he says he will be able to prospect more territory than if he was to go by the water route." *(La Grande Observer, Tues, Feb. 22, 1898, pg. 3)*

Angus also did more than gold mining, he also traveled to places like Portland and Chicago to do business, and he wintered in Pasadena, California with his brother John Shaw.

The *July 1, 1901 issue of the La Grande Observer, pg. 5* stated: "Angus Shaw, who owns considerable property in the Grande Ronde valley, returned to La Grande last night after spending the winter in Pasadena, California. Mr. Shaw always spends his winters in California."

"Big Crop of Wheat is Sold—Probably the last deal in 1913 Crop." Draft for over five thousand rewards for last year's efforts. The last big wheat crop in the Grande Ronde has been sold and will soon be in Portland, the property of Balfour & Company. The sale and purchase covers the 8,200 bushels of forty fold, grown and owned by Angus Shaw of Summerville. The owner has his draft for over $5,000 from the company issued through the local agent, Dave Clark, and will soon thresh another crop of like proportions if the weather is propitious." End of article. *(La Grande Observer, Thurs., May 28, 1914, pg. 3)*

The following members of the Angus Shaw Sr. Family are buried at Summerville Cemetery: Angus Shaw Sr., Elizabeth (Murchison) Shaw, and children John Shaw, Christina Shaw Standley, Angus Shaw Jr. and Sarah Shaw Bonnette. Their sister Elizabeth "Bettie" E. (Shaw) Humphrey was buried in Eugene Pioneer Cemetery.

Shaw Mountain Road - This road exits Ladd Canyon Road and creeps around Shaw Mountain extensively. Both the mountain and the road are named after a Shaw family, who are unrelated to the Angus Shaw Sr. family mentioned in the preceding Shaw Creek Road entry in the Imbler district.

This road and mountain are named after William Shaw (1831-1900) of Scotland, his son John Shaw (1858-1946) and grandson Alex J. Shaw (1905-1997) and a relative named Louellen Shaw, who owned land and ranched in the North Powder territory of Union County.

The history of the Shaw family starts in the Glasgow area of Scotland with William, the son of John Shaw and Mary Laing of Scotland. William married Hannah Frew (Eaton) Shaw (1832-1902) on November 6, 1857 in Kilsyth, Stirlingshire, Scotland.

On March 6, 1858 in Kilsyth, Scotland, just 16 miles north of Glasgow, Scotland, Hannah gave birth to twin boys, John and William II. John was named after his paternal grandfather and William II was named after his father. Soon the twins were joined by younger siblings: Robert M. Shaw (1861-1948), Farquhar Tunnick Shaw (1866-1956), and Helen Frew "Ellen" (1869-1948).

The seven of them emigrated to America on the ship Europa from Glasgow, Scotland, arriving in New York City on July 2, 1870 when the twins were 12 years of age. The family came directly to Union County, Oregon, where, as it turned out, William Sr.'s older brother Robert Shaw (1829-1900) was already farming by July 21, 1870 when the census was taken. *(1870 Federal Census)*

William Shaw homesteaded 320 acres in 1870 on Clover Creek near North Powder, and two years later in 1872, Hannah gave birth to their first American-born child, a daughter, Mary Laing Shaw (later Mrs. Frank Stickney). Baby Mary was named after William's mother, and with this baby the family was complete.

In time, others in the family became naturalized U.S. citizens, including William's son John Shaw in 1887.

William died February 12, 1900 in Baker County where he was buried in Mount Hope Cemetery. He was 68 years of age when he died. His older brother Robert died in 1900 also and was interred in the Union Victorian Cemetery in the city of Union, Oregon.

Taking over the ranch after William's death was his son, John Shaw. John married Mary Nicholson on December 13, 1884 in Baker County, and they had a daughter Lelah Ire Shaw (1889-1981). The *June 19, 1900 Federal Census* indicated that John, 41, was widowed, making it clear that Mary Nicholson Shaw had passed away, and Lelah, 12, was living with and being supported by her father on the Shaw ranch.

Also listed in the Shaw household on the *1900 Federal Census* were two single siblings, Andrew H. Fugit, 49, (servant) and his sister Lida Fugit, 31, who was working as housekeeper. They were the grown children of their deceased parents, Reuel Custer Fugit (1818-1887) and Rebecca Washer (1824-1880).

Lida E. Fugit was born October 15, 1864 in Emporia, Lyon County, Kansas, being one of the youngest in a large family. Her mother died when she was about 16 and her father when she was about 22 years old. She and her older brother Andrew came to Union County, Oregon and worked together for John Shaw.

On December 26, 1900, John Shaw married Lida Elizabeth Ann Fugit, in Baker County, and they had two children: Ruth Luise (1901-2001) and John "Alex" Shaw (1905-1997). In 1912, daughter Lelah Shaw married Reinhart C. Pedersen in Wenatchee, Washington and was thereafter living in that city.

The paper trail produced by John "Alex" also called him by a variety of other names such as: Alex J., John Alexander, J. Alex, John A. and just plain old Alex Shaw. Despite the name variances, his gravestone gets the last eternal word, and it reads, "John A. Shaw" not to be confused with his father John Shaw. One name the authors did not see for Alex was John Jr., but that would have been appropriate too. Note how he is recorded in the census below.

In the *1910 Federal Census,* the John Shaw family is enumerated as follows: John Shaw, 52 (head), Lida Fugit, 42 (wife), Ruth L., 8, (daughter), Alex J., 4, (son), Jennett Fugit, 20, single (niece) and two farm laborers. Lida's brother Andrew Fugit was no longer in the household.

John Shaw and only son Alex Shaw worked together on the family ranch. Occasionally cattle from their herd would wander and mix with a neighboring herd.

One such instance was noted in the newspaper, and it stated that George Pierce drove some cattle to North Powder to return some strays to John and Alex Shaw. The cattle strayed over the mountains and joined the Pierce herd. Pierce will bring back some of his stock that had mingled with the Shaw herd. *(La Grande Evening Observer, Oct. 10, 1910)*

In June 1917, the newspaper reported that John Shaw had bought an engine and "will use it for farming on his large farm on Clover Creek." *(La Grande Observer, June 4, 1917, pg. 3)*

Ruth L. Shaw married Axel Ludwig Dahlstrom, whose parents Andrew and Britta Dahlstrom and an uncle, Olaf P. Dahlstrom, immigrated to America about 1892-93 and bought land near Shaw Mountain and Clover Creek in Union County, Oregon. *(1935 Metsker Map)* Since the Shaws and the Dahlstroms were living in the same Shaw Mountain territory, it was convenient geographically for Ruth and Axel to get acquainted. They were married on September 10, 1930.

In 1934, John and Lida Shaw retired from their farm, and they moved to La Grande, where he was a member of the Blue Mountain grange, Union County pioneers and the La Grande I.O.O.F. lodge for more than 50 years.

The Shaws' retirement was announced in the *La Grande Observer, Fri., Aug. 25, 1933, pg. 2.* "Move to La Grande—Mr. and Mrs. John Shaw, well known farmers of the southeast part of the county, have recently moved to La Grande where they plan to make their home in the future. Their farm near North Powder will be operated by their son, Alec Shaw."

There was another relative named Louellen Shaw, and she sold her land to Edson Rodney McCanse in 1944. This property is shown on the *1935 Metsker Map* in Township 5S, R38 E, Section 14 at the base of Shaw Mountain. *(La Grande Observer, Dec. 1, 1944)*

John Shaw died March 19, 1946 at the hospital in La Grande at the age of 88 years after an illness of two months. He was interred at the North Powder Cemetery. *(La Grande Observer, March 19, 1946, pg. 1, obit.)* His wife, Lida, died in 1950 and was interred in North Powder Cemetery also.

Their son, John Alex Shaw was born February 5, 1905 in North Powder, and he built quite a reputation for himself as a conservationist and rancher on the 2,100 acre Shaw ranch. In May 1958, he was named "Union County's Conservation Man of the Year" and there was an extensive write-up in the *La Grande Observer, May 17, 1958, pg. 1* in which he is called John Shaw. (By then his father John Shaw was deceased, so no more confusion of identity.)

John Alex Shaw of La Grande and North Powder was awarded this honor by Wren Case, president of the Union County Wheat League. The announcement was made by the 1957 recipient, Larry Starr. Shaw's conservation practices won him the award, including range management, stubble mulch farming and pasture management.

One innovative measure he instituted on the farm was the storage dams he built to conserve water, precious to the productivity of the North Powder area. His father began the work in 1890, when he brought water from the North Powder River 18 miles by ditch to feed his parched acres, the account read.

Since then three dams have been built, two for stock water and diversion ponds and the latest and largest was the construction of a reservoir that holds 500 acre feet of water and covers an area of 55 acres. The water is used as supplemental water to the original ditch and has enabled Shaw to double the productivity of his soil.

Another way Shaw increased his farm productivity was through his careful selection of grasses and legumes in his vast seedings of alfalfa. The article said that he was able to increase his alfalfa yield from one to two tons of hay per acres to three and four tons per acres with good pasture available for his 600 feeder cattle after the last crop is taken off the fields.

He followed a 10 year rotation schedule, seven years of alfalfa, one year of summer fallow and two years of grain, and he claimed this practice improved his soil and increased his yields.

In 1958, Shaw was renting 8,000 acres of range land and applying the proverbial "conservation thumb" to this land. He is deferring at least 25 percent of the land each year, a practice that enables range grasses to re-establish themselves, turning this range into a fertile, renewable resource.

"His home range is getting the same treatment with deferment, seeding, and sage brush control and turning brown hillsides to green, lush growth of improved grasses and legumes," the article read.

John Alex Shaw married Pearl Laurel Wicks on July 29, 1929 in Union County. They had four girls: Margaret, Patricia, Betty Jane, and Jacqueline. Pearl Shaw died on July 19, 1997, and John Alex Shaw died three days later at age 91 on July 22, 1997. They were both interred at the North Powder Cemetery. Their stone reads "Forever Together." *(Findagrave.com)*

Simonson Lane - This public unmaintained county road is .11 miles in length in Township 1N R39E Section 9 in the Elgin maintenance district. It is located off Middle Road northwest of Elgin. It's named after Terry Simonson, who put the road in so that he could subdivide his property, and it was later named for him by the county. *(Terry Simonson interview, April 19, 2018)*

Skyline Lane- Located in Township 3S R38E Section 18. This private road runs in an eastward direction off Tollgate Highway to Langdon Lake toward Bald Mountain. It follows part of the ridge, thus the name.

Slack Road - This county road #76 runs 1.02 miles in Township 1S R38E Section 11 in the Imbler maintenance district. It is located northwest of Summerville and connects McKenzie Lane and Behrens Lane. There are currently three property owners living on this lane.

Slack Road is a gravel road, and in hard winters, it's used as a bypass when McKenzie Lane is closed by severe snow drifts. The year 2016 was the hardest winter since 1947 in Summerville, and Slack Road resembled a tunnel with huge snow walls on both sides of it to Behrens Lane.

Slack Road is named after pioneer settlers Abraham J. Slack (1816-1889) and his wife, Susan Salome Lull (1817-1892). They married on March 25, 1838 in Muskingum County, Ohio. At the time of the *1840 Federal Census*, they were living in Washington, Muskingum County, Ohio with one child.

In the *1850 Federal Census*, the Slack family lived in Liberty, Jefferson County, Iowa with two Ohio-born children Fidelia (11) and Philander (5); and in the *1860 Federal Census*, they were living in Caldwell, Appanoose County, Iowa with five children: Phidelia (22), Filander (15), both born in Ohio; and Frances (7), Nancy (5) and James (3), all born in Iowa.

The family came across the plains to La Grande, Oregon, in 1864 when James M. Slack was 7 years old, and there were only a handful of houses in town. *(La Grande Observer, April 15, 1929, pg. 1)* The Slack family were counted there in the *1870 Federal Census,* including the parents and their two youngest children: Nancy (14) and James Monroe. (12).

James Monroe Slack (1857-1929) and Nancy Ann Hawk (1852-1931) of Illinois were married on June 3, 1879 in Union County. The couple were listed in the *1880 Federal Census* living in Summerville along with their son William Hawk Slack, age 2.

James Monroe made many friends during his residency in the county, but a long illness coupled with blindness caused a despondency which overcame him, said an article titled, "Oregon Pioneer of 1864 Takes His Own Life." His death occurred on April 13, 1929, and he was survived by his wife and three sons. Interment took place at Summerville Cemetery. *(La Grande Observer, April 15, 1929, pg. 1)*

His son James Abraham Slack (1881-1955) and wife Ruia Elizabeth (Tiffany) Slack (1888-1953) purchased land from James Monroe Slack on Slack Road. At their home on Slack Road, Ruia gave birth to a son Clifton "Duck" Leroy Slack on January 1, 1913. *(Duck Slack interview, July 2003)*

For the first 10 years of Duck's life, he lived on the family farm on Slack Road during which time Duck attended the Dry Creek one-room school on Summerville Road with neighbor kids like Grover Hardy, the Craig kids, the Oliver kids, Zack Pugh, Roy Niederer, Clifford Royes, and the Sandersons. *(See Sanderson Road)*

Then his family moved into the city of Summerville for two years, and he attended the Summerville one-room school in town. His family moved to Elgin after that, and he finished eighth grade in Elgin.

After finishing eighth grade, he started his working life as a ranch laborer. Later he also worked for Bill Moore's Pondosa Pine Lumber Company (1922-1944), which kept men working and supporting their families during the Great Depression years when others were unemployed and going hungry.

At the time of the *1930 Federal Census*, Duck was living in Elgin. It was here in 1948, Duck met Irene (Gentry) Talbott and her three children, Lenore, Franklin and Donna in Elgin. They moved to the Tyler ranch west of the La Grande Truck stop, where they lost two sets of twins. In 1950, they moved to Lower Perry, and then to a farm home in 1959 in Perry along the river, where they had two children, Vicki (McLean) and Teri (Walker). *(Duck Slack's obituary, La Grande Observer, Fri., Dec. 7, 2007)*

He worked at Boise Cascade for 23 years before retiring at age 65. Irene died in 1990 and Duck died on December 5, 2007 at age 94 in Upper Perry, Oregon at the home of his loving caregivers and friends, Dave and Brenda Hickey. This was an adult foster home just up the road from where Duck used to live, and he moved in with the Hickeys on February 14, 2006, until his death. Otherwise, he had the joy of living in his own home. *(Brenda Hickey interview, November 2021)*

His obituary mentioned that he loved horses. "He broke his first horse at the age of 10 and continued until the age of 82. He also loved to hunt, and at the age of 93, he had two deer tags that he filled while using his walker to get around. With the help of his daughter and two good friends, he went on two more hunts, and he was able to fill both tags, taking only one shot for each. He planned a third hunt for cow elk, but his health declined, and he was unable to go. He dreamed of more hunting in the weeks that followed."

The authors had the privilege of meeting Duck at the Dry Creek School reunion while covering this event for the La Grande Observer. When teasingly asked if he was a "slacker in school," he said no, but he liked to be a practical joker. He was filled with stories of the past and enjoyed being among his other classmates that day.

Today, there are no Slack descendants living on Slack Road, but the road name endures to honor this hard-working farm family and 1864 pioneer settlers.

Smith Loop - This is county road #155, and it runs .64 miles in length through Township 3S R38E Section 24 in the La Grande maintenance district. It is located off Airport Lane, and runs into Downs Road. This was originally a loop, but part of it was vacated in 1999. The part left now is Eastern Oregon Court, which is a general geographic name.

Speckhart Lane - This county road #131 runs .75 miles in Township 2S R39E Section 5 in the La Grande maintenance district.

The road is named after John Speckhart (1869-1955) and Josephine Johanna Katherine Uhlenbrock (1870-1938), who arrived in Union County, Oregon from Illinois in March 1905. *(La Grande Observer, Oct. 24, 1955, pg. 1)* John was a farmer in Illinois, according to the *1900 Federal Census* of Fall Creek Township, Bluff Hall, Illinois.

John was born November 1, 1869 in Quincy, Illinois, and he married Josephine in about 1890. Josephine was born August 15, 1870 in Quincey, Illinois.

They brought four children with them: Elmer, Herbert, Bertha, and Flora. They made their home on a farm near Alicel. They farmed there for 13 years before John and Josephine retired to La Grande in 1918.

The *1920 Federal Census* of La Grande stated they lived on Fifth Street, and John worked as a express messenger for the railroad. By the *1930 Federal Census*, he was working as the county assessor.

John was widowed on May 15, 1938, after which he married Blanche Spears about July of 1939 in Boise, Idaho. A wedding announcement stated that they went to Yellowstone for their honeymoon. *(La Grande Observer, Aug. 4, 1939, pg. 2)*

John died October 22, 1955 in La Grande at the age of 85 years. He and his wife were buried at Hillcrest Cemetery in La Grande.

The farm was next operated by Herbert Speckhart. He was born January 4, 1894 in Fall Creek, Adams County, Illinois, coming to Union County with his parents when he was about 11 years old. He was married January 28, 1917 to Mayme Virginia Snider in La Grande. She was born November 12, 1895 in Union County, and she died December 2, 1940 and is buried in Hillcrest Cemetery in La Grande.

During their marriage, they had one daughter, Hellen Jean, born February 24, 1923. Herbert was listed in the 1920, 1930 and 1940 censuses as a farmer in the Alicel precinct. In addition to farming, Herbert was also a county commissioner.

Herbert married Mrs. Irene (Wagoner) Conrad on January 10, 1942 in Nampa, Idaho. They made their home together on Herbert's farm in Alicel until her death on May 24, 1949 in La Grande. She was interred in the Summerville Cemetery.

After her death, Herbert married an elementary school teacher named Velma from Illinois on February 2, 1952. She died October 13, 2003 and was buried in Payson, Illinois.

Herbert died on June 7, 1974, and the farm went to Hellen Jean Speckhart and her husband Harlow A. Speckhart.   Harlow A. Speckhart was from Payson, Illinois and was born January 18, 1918. Hellen and Harlow married in La Grande on September 9, 1942, and they had two daughters, Mary (1944-2018) and Joanne-Lowry-Parsons.

Both sisters applied for Century Farm status with the Oregon Century Farm and Ranch Program on May 10, 2004, and they received this elite status later that year. The Century Farm continues to be operated by the Speckhart descendants.

Spooner Road - This is a private road that is found in Township 2S R38E Section 33-34 in the La Grande maintenance district. It is located off Fruitdale Lane, and it is named for residents, T. Dwain and Darlene F. Spooner. Historically, their home, two sheds, and a barn were all built about 1930, according to county records.

Sporting Lane - This private road is off of Leffel Road on the north side of La Grande, specifically in Township 2S R38E Section 32 in the La Grande maintenance district. Mr. and Mrs. William R. Willis, older residents on this road, enjoyed a variety of sports and so the road was named Sporting Lane. *(Neighbor Shirley Vanderzanden interview, July 5, 2018)*

Spout Springs Road - This road is directly across from Spout Springs ski area, and it's all on National Forest land. This road is not officially listed on the county's road list, but it is inside Union County and has 21 residences on it.

Historian Bernal D. Hug states in his 1961 book, *History of Union County, Oregon,* page 225:

"At an elevation 5,200 feet, where the Old Walla Walla Trail follows the top of the mountain is this spring. In early days it was piped into a trough into which it spouted its crystal clear waters under a slight pressure, and people thought of it as the spring that spouted forth.   The National Forest Service erected the spout springs lookout on a hill east of the spring, but otherwise it had little prominence. It was just a refreshing spring handy for travelers, a place to picnic, and well located for huckleberry pickers.   The trail that led past it had become a road, and then it became a paved highway."

He continued, "In 1934, Umatilla and Union county ski fans organized the Blue Mountain Ski Club with Pat Mansfield of Milton-Freewater as president. For two years they skied about 8 miles up on the Weston side and a few miles above Elgin. As the roads could be kept open, they moved from time to time higher up until in 1940 some reached Spout Springs."

"Members of the club from both side cooperated in 1936 in an effort to have Highway 204 kept open during the winter. In 1940, this was accomplished."

"On March 5 and 6, 1949, the first National Cross Country Championship was held at Spout Springs. In the summer of 1955, standard jumping hills were built, and that December the United States Cross Country Olympic Team stayed at Spout Springs and trained for the Olympic games to be held at Cortina, Italy." (End of quote)

Spring Creek Road - This road exits Interstate 84, and it is not on the county road registry.   It crawls and curls around for miles in the forest and turns into NF-605.

Squire Loop - This loop, created in 2003, is in the Westview Heights subdivision outside of Cove and runs off of Lantz Lane near Cove. It is a public unmaintained road that runs .48 miles in Township 3S R40E Section 10 of the Union maintenance district. There are 14 property addresses on this loop.

The road name was proposed by Ron Morris and Thomasine A. Morris, the people who sub-divided this area and knew the Squires. The loop was named after their friends, Doug and Louise Squire, who were both educators. *(Squire Loop resident Barney Brooks interview, Nov. 19, 2018)*

Louise Squire explained, "My late husband, Doug Squire, and I built the house at what is now 69424 Squire Loop in 1982. It was not a loop when we built the house but a driveway for our house and the next house in. The loop was developed a few years after my husband died. Ron Morris came up with Squire Loop. I was very touched by that."

At the time Louise was a high school teacher at Cove High School. Doug, who passed away in 1998, was a professor at Eastern Oregon University, working in the Department of Education.

"We were living there when he died," she said. "I moved to La Grande in 1999, renting the house on Squire Loop. I retired from Cove High School in 2007, and I moved back to Squire Loop in 2008. I lived there until I sold the house in 2014. It was fun living on a road with my name. People were always puzzled when I'd fill out my name and address on a form, and they noticed that the two names were the same."

Ron Morris was a good friend of Doug Squire, and so he ultimately proposed Squire as the road name to honor Doug and Louise. Speaking of her late husband, Louise said, "He was a wonderful person."

Louise Squire taught math, accounting, Spanish and home economics at Cove High School. In 2001, she and another educator, Sharon Freeman, traveled to Finland, Russia and Estonia to tour those countries and observe their educational systems and resources, among other things. *(La Grande Observer, Oct. 25, 2001 "Teachers Tour Russia)*

In 2012, Louise Squire of Cove enjoyed a road tour with Anita and Kim Metlen, covering several hundred miles on bicycles in Vietnam in March 2012, during their eight-day cycling venture. This remarkable story and photos can be read in the *La Grande Observer of March 23, 2012.*

Squire is currently retired in La Grande and devotes herself generously to various civic and community interests.

Stackland Road - Formerly called Stackland-Lieurance Road, this county road #120A is listed on the Buena Vista subdivision dated 1981 on the Union County Platt map. It runs 1.89 miles in Township 3S R40E Section 11 in the Union maintenance district.

The name Lieurance originates with a man named Joshua Lieurance (1822-1910). Joshua was married twice, first to Elizabeth Michael, and after her death in 1894, he married Mary Batty.

Joshua's first marriage to Elizabeth Michael occurred on February 24, 1842 in Warren County, Illinois. She was born February 11, 1811; died December 24, 1894 at 83 years of age.

Joshua and Elizabeth (Michael) Lieurance had the following children born in Wisconsin: Lemuel (1843-1905), Frederick (1845-1925), David (1847-1924), Marvin (1848-), Allen C. (1850-), Orlando (1852-1928), Hiram (1853-1946) and Lucinda "Alice" (1856-1941). *(1850 Federal Census of Willow Springs, LaFayette County, Wisconsin;1860 Federal Census for Viroqua, Bad Ax County, Wisconsin.)*

Family tree makers relate that Joshua left the Midwest and came to Cove, Oregon prior to 1890. Some of his grown children followed him to Oregon. His former wife, Elizabeth, remained in Wisconsin with some of their other grown children. She died in 1894 and was buried in Brush Hollow Cemetery in Viroqua, Vernon County, Wisconsin. There are a number of other Lieurance burials in that same cemetery.

On Joshua's travels west, he lived for a time in Norton County, Kansas, where there is a record of him farming, growing corn in 1874. *(History of the Early Settlement of Norton County Kansas, pg. 36)*

On January 18, 1880 in Kansas, Joshua married Mrs. Mary (Batty) Edwards, the mother of 10 Edwards children. According to the *1900 Federal Census*, Mary was born March 28, 1827 in England; died September 14, 1905 at age 88 years in Cove, Oregon. She and Joshua had no children together.

Joshua Lieurance was born December 25, 1823 [alt.1822], in Economy, Wayne County, Indiana. He came to Union County prior to 1890 and was mentioned on the *1890 Special Schedule of Surviving Soldiers, Sailors, Marines and Widows etc.* as a resident of Cove in Union County, Oregon.

The *1900 Federal Census* mentions Joshua as a farmer in the Cove area. It appears that three of his children, Marion, Hiram and Lucinda "Alice" Van Vlack also came to the Cove area.

The father Joshua Lieurance died on April 2, 1910 according to *ancestry.com,* just a month prior to the 1910 census. In the *1910 Federal Census of Cove,* his sons Marion and Hiram Lieurance were living together and working as farmers. By the *1920 Federal Census of Cove* area, their sister, Alice VanVlack, had joined their household, which was located near Shoppat Road on Foothill Road. This road was later renamed Lower Cove Road.

Hiram was born in Vernon, Wisconsin, on September 23, 1853. He never married. He was 92 years old at the time of his death on June 11, 1946. He was a retired Cove farmer. His brother Marion Lieurance married Lucinda Dennis.

Their sister, Lucinda "Alice" (Lieurance), married Francis Van Vlack, and they had the following children: a daughter name unknown, James Milo, Valda McGee, Thurlow Guy, Edward Burt, Verna, Ola, Vesta, Harold Dewey and Mina Stella, according to one family tree maker.

Ed Van Vlack was the only one of Lucinda's children mentioned as a surviving relative in Hiram's obituary, although his sister Valda was yet living. *(La Grande Observer, June 12, 1946, pg. 3)* Hiram and his siblings had died and were all buried in the family plot in Cove Cemetery.

In 1988 when the county roads were renamed, the name Lieurance was dropped, and the road was known only as Stackland Road henceforth.

The Stackland part of the road name originates with three Stackland brothers, Karl J. Stackland, Christopher Muller Stackland, and Gerhard Stackland, who came to the Cove area in Autumn of 1891 and engaged in fruit farming.

Their widowed mother, Bertha M. (Mauritsdatter) Stackland immigrated from Norway to the United States in 1882 with seven children: Karl Johan (1863-1944), Alexander (1865-1932), Paulina (1867-1952), Christoffer (1869-1942), Gerhard (1872-1937), Elida (1877-1963) and Constance (1879-1948).

They joined up with Bertha's father, Maurits Rosseland, in South Dakota, where he had immigrated in 1864-65. From South Dakota, Bertha and children moved to Kansas, where her three sisters were living.

Bertha (Mauritsdatter) married Peder Stakland in 1860 in Haugesund, Norway. She was a mother of ten children. Elida (1874-1876) died at the age of less than three years; and a premie baby girl unnamed died in 1880. Bertha's husband, Peder, and oldest son, Kornelius, died in June 1881, which left her with seven surviving children, ages 2 to 18 years. *(La Grande Observer, March 7, 1912, pg. 7)*

Due to repeated crop failures in Kansas, Bertha and three of her sons and two daughters migrated to Cove, Oregon in Autumn of 1891. The other two married children followed within two years.

When Bertha and the children came to Cove, they acquired 80 acres of farm land. In 1912, Christopher and Gerhard owned Grand View Fruit Farm and Park View Farm. At the same time, Karl owned the Orcheim Fruit Farm, the Glendell Fruit Farm and the Pear Angou Fruit Farm. *(La Grande Observer, Dec. 20, 1912, pg. 4)*

The Stackland brothers received a railway car filled with empty berry boxes. *(La Grande Observer, June 11, 1898, pg. 3)* Then in 1902, Karl Stackland put in at least 2,000 new fruit trees, roughly half apples, half cherries. *(La Grande Observer, June 29, 1902, pg. 3)*

Later in 1902, at the La Grande carnival's agricultural display, Christopher Stackland won the award for best exhibit of fruits of all kinds. *(La Grande Observer, Sept. 30, 1902, pg. 1)*

In 1904, Stackland brothers of Cove had negotiated to sell a carload of fancy graded apples to Norwegian dealers. This was their second shipment as the Norwegian buyers were so pleased with the quality of their apples. *(La Grande Observer, Dec. 20, 1904, pg. 5)*

In 1912, Gerhard and Christopher Stackland advertised that they wanted at least 50 cherry packers and pickers for their orchard and packing house. *(La Grande Observer, July 8, 1912, pg. 3)*

By 1920, Karl owned a fourth farm called the Blue Mountain Fruit Farm at Cove. He was the grower, shipper and owner of this operation. He left in mid-December on a business trip to Europe where he spent four months trying to sell apples and dried fruit from the Grande Ronde Valley. His business agenda took him to Britain, Holland, Belgium, Germany, Sweden, and Norway. *(La Grande Observer, Nov. 24, 1920, pg. 1)*

In an article in the *January 25, 1921 La Grande Observer, pg. 3,* Gerhard and Christopher Stackland were called "the cherry kings of the Cove region."

In 1935, Karl Stackland was the Mayor of Cove. *(La Grande Observer, Sept. 5, 1945, pg. 2)* His son, Karl Stackland Jr. took over the operation of the fruit farms.

"Due to lack of a market this fall and winter (1931) for his crop of cabbages, Karl J. Stackland Jr., of Cove, has rigged up and equipped a plant for making sauerkraut on a commercial scale and will compete in this county with products from outside points. His plant is at Cove, and he has made approximately 20,000 gallons of sauerkraut, which he regards as sufficient for the meat market trade in this county for one season." *(La Grande Observer, Jan. 4, 1946, pg. 2)*

In 1946, Karl Stackland Jr. made a generous donation of a few hundred books to the Cove Public Library. *(La Grande Observer, June 10, 1946, pg. 6)*

The Stackland brothers had a fourth brother, Alex M. Stackland, who worked as a commercial painter in La Grande before moving to Portland, where he died March 16, 1932. Karl Stackland Sr. and Gerhard Stackland were buried at Cove Cemetery. Their brother Christopher was buried at Hillcrest Cemetery in La Grande.

Standley Lane - This road #130 runs 4.70 miles in Township 2S R39E Section 7 in the La Grande maintenance district, and it connects Mt. Glen Road to Highway 82 at Alicel.

It is named after James Henry Standley (1843-1934), who came to this valley on the "Standley Train" over the Oregon Trail with his parents, Jeremiah and Mary "Polly" (Wilson) Standley from Missouri in 1864.

In 1865, at the age of 22, James Standley worked in the Bannock mines and afterward engaged in a freighting enterprise, running his wagons between La Grande, Oregon and Walla Walla, Washington.

While doing this, he met Christina Shaw (1853-1940) at the Ruckel stage stop where she had been working. She was the daughter of pioneers Angus Shaw (1817-1909) and Elizabeth Shaw (1817-1867), who came to the Grande Ronde Valley in 1863.

James married Miss Shaw on March 18, 1869, and they purchased a quarter section of farm land on this road in 1870 and immediately engaged in growing wheat, feed grains and raising stock.

Their first home was built in the 1870s, framed with milled lumber from nearby forest land. This home used two framework construction styles, vertical plank and stacked plank construction, very popular building styles in those years before studded walls and insulation became the construction standard. By building in this way, it took about twice as much lumber as it would take today to build a home, and it often created thick walls and wide window sills. (See McKenzie Lane entry.)

The Standley farm was handed down to James' son Louie Standley and then to Louie's son, J. Dale and to Dale's son, Jim Standley. The property was recognized in August 1974 as a Century Farm by the Oregon State Historical Society.

Staples Street - This private road is located in Township 2S R37E Section 31 in the La Grande maintenance district. It exits off Five Point Creek Road near Hilgard. It was shown on the original plat of the Town of Hilgard dated August 11, 1888. It is one of very few roads on the county listing that is called a street.

The post office in Hilgard was first established on August 23, 1883 under the name Dan, which is what they called the town before it was called Hilgard. The post office was discontinued May 21, 1884 and re-established as Hilgard on December 20, 1887 with Edwin P. Staples as postmaster. He was postmaster for several years before moving to Island City.

Starkey Cow Camp Road - According to *Trails,* "This road is a hiking, biking, and horse trail in Union County and is within Wallowa-Whitman National Forest. It is 2.3 miles long and begins at 4,208 feet altitude. Traveling the entire trail is 4.5 miles with a total elevation gain of 590 feet. This trail connects with the following: National Forest Development Road 2120."

Starkey Headquarters Road - This road diverts off of Meadow Cow Camp Road and wanders about in the forest land. There are no residences listed with the county on this road.

Starkey Unit #52 is home to the Experimental Forest Headquarters not far from Meadow Cow Camp, which may account for the name of this road.

Starkey Road - This road diverts south off of Ukiah-Hilgard Highway 244 right before reaching Camp Elkanah, and on the other end, it connects with McIntyre Road. In between, it meanders through the national forest land. It is not listed on the Union County road register, but the authors discovered an interesting history about it worth relating.

Starkey Road and Starkey Creek are named after the unincorporated community of Starkey, 17 miles up the Grande Ronde River from La Grande.

The Starkey community is named after its first postmaster, John Starkey, who served for two years from December 10, 1879 through January 3, 1881. On the latter date, the post office was discontinued because he resigned, possibly due to ill health. It was re-established with the second postmaster, Willis Nail, on February 2, 1881. *(Appointments of U.S. Postmasters, 1831-1971, pg. 397)*

However, before the post office was established in 1879, the locals called that section by the name, Starkey Prairie, as noted in the following newspaper article.

"Starkey Prairie was the former name of the locality up the Grande Ronde River, which has gone into the postal guide as just plain Starkey. Starkey was named in honor of John and William Starkey, who were among the first settlers in that section. They were brothers and both have been dead for upwards of thirty years." *(La Grande Observer, March 23, 1917 issue, pg. 7)*

While there was hardly a paper trail for William Starkey, there was sufficient information on John Starkey (1829-1881). He was a native of Colerain, Belmont County, Ohio, where there is a large population of Starkey relatives living. We might add that Starkey is as common a name as Smith in that part of the country, and everyone wanted to name their Starkey baby John, of course. So what you're about to read is one of the more comprehensive histories written on postmaster John Starkey.

John Starkey's history begins with his parents, John Starkey Sr. (b. Virginia) and Sarah Collins Starkey (b. 1793 Ohio -1851). This couple were married on March 23, 1815 in Belmont County, Ohio, and the father died before 1850. He was survived by his widow Sarah and the children we know of: George, William, John and Martha (McClara, Huntsman).

The *1850 Federal Census* of Colerain, Belmont County lists the following family members: Sarah Starkey, 57, mother (b. 1793 Pennsylvania), son George, 24, (b. 1826 Ohio), farmer, $800 in real estate; John Starkey, 21, (b. 1829 Ohio), and widowed sister Martha Starkey McClara, age 23, (b. Nov. 2, 1827 Ohio); and her McClara children: Angeline, 8, (b. 1842 Ohio), George W., 7, (b. 1841 Ohio); and Sarah, 1, (b. 1849 Ohio).

The mother Sarah Collins Starkey died shortly after the census on October. 26, 1851. She was buried in Saint Clairsville Union Cemetery in Belmont County, Ohio. She was 57 years, 2 mos and 11 days old at death. *(Findagrave.com)*

On June 14, 1861 John Starkey, 32, married a widow, Mrs. John M. Carter, 32, of Union Township, Des Moines County, Iowa. Her maiden name was Eliza Lucas, born December 3, 1828 in Ohio to parents William Lucas (1805-1853) and Hester (Bull) Lucas (1800-1854).

Eliza Lucas' first marriage to John Miller Carter occurred on October 27, 1844 in Iowa, and they had five children: Seraphina (1845-1850), Ervin (1848-1921), Flora Alice (1851-1937); Iowa (1853-), Laura May (1856-1928). Only Ervin, Flora and Laura survived to adulthood.

Their father, John M. Carter, died prematurely at age 37 on March 29, 1859, and left Eliza with a real estate value of $3,000 and personal property in the amount of $400. *(Iowa Marriage Index 1758-1996; the 1860 Federal Census for Iowa; and Findagrave.com)*

The following year, she relocated 84 miles north from Green Bay Township in Clarke County, Iowa to Union Township in Des Moines County, Iowa. Besides her children, two others lived in her home, her 21-year-old sister, Caroline Lucas and a hired farm hand.

In 1861, when Eliza married her second husband, John Starkey, she brought her children into the marriage with her: Ervin, 13, Flora, 10, and Laura, 5 years old. John and Eliza also had their own child together, Aurora, born in 1862, the year after their marriage.

This research agrees with Aurora's obituary, as printed in the *Medford Mail Tribune in Medford, Oregon, dated May 25, 1921, pg. 2,* where it reads that she had two sisters and one brother—a sister in Portland and a sister and brother living in Twin Rocks, Tillamook County, Oregon. Those siblings were Aurora's half sisters Flora and Laura and a half brother, Ervin, since they shared the same mother but not the same father.

In a June 1863 enumeration record, John Starkey is listed in the *Civil War Draft Registration of 1863-1865*. Therein, he states that his age at July 1, 1863 was 35 years, born in Ohio and that his occupation in Des Moines, Iowa, was a ferryman.

During the 1860s, John and Eliza decided to pull up stakes and go to Cove, Union County, Oregon to take advantage of the homesteading opportunities there.

By the *1870 Federal Census*, John, Eliza and Aurora were residents of Cove, Oregon. Enumerated on that census were: John, age 41, b. 1829 Ohio, occupied as a hotel keeper; wife, Eliza, 40, b. 1830; and daughter, D. Starkey, b. 1862.

In the *1880 Federal Census*, the Starkey family profile changed significantly with added members in the household: John Starkey, age 51, a farmer; wife Eliza, 51; daughter Aurora, 18, b. 1862 single at home; John's married brother George, 54, b. 1826, a laborer; Eliza's widowed son Ervin Carter, 32, b. 1848, and his daughter Elma Carter, 3, b. 1877.

This is the last census in which John Starkey was listed because in 1881, at the age of 52, he died. This was a few years short of the average lifespan of 56 years for males living in the 1880-90 decade.

Gratefully, his isolated grave location has been recorded for posterity. A Union County historian, the late John "Jack" Evans, author of "Powerful Rocky" did make a notation "Starkey's Grave" on his book's 1961 map.

With a little further searching in Access Genealogy, isolated grave listings, John Starkey's grave location was described as "north of the Ukiah-Hilgard Highway #244 at a point 13.5 miles S.W. of its junction with I-80 N, between Highway 244 and the old railroad grade (In S.W. 1/4 of S.W. 1/4 of Section 35, T.3S., R.35E), on Starkey Creek."

After his death, it appears that the family dispersed and no other Starkey graves are found in Union County.

After considerable searching, the authors found Eliza again, as Mrs. Nicodemus, 71, whose third husband died before 1900. In the *1900 Federal Census*, she was listed as a widow, living with her son Ervin Carter, 51, in Garibaldi, Tillamook County, Oregon. In 1910, she was living in Clackamas County, Oregon with her widowed daughter, Flora A. Garrison; and in 1915, her final residence was in Aurora, Marion County, Oregon.

Eliza died in Aurora on July 21, 1915 at the age of 85-86 years, and her burial took place in Butteville Cemetery in Butteville, Marion County, Oregon. Her stone reads "Eliza Lucas, wife of J. M. Carter, 1829-1915".

Eliza and John Starkey's daughter, Aurora, married James Allen in 1884 in Walla Walla, Washington, and her cousin William Collins Starkey (George Starkey's son) signed the marriage certificate as a witness to the ceremony. In 1905, Aurora and her husband relocated to Phoenix, Oregon where she died in 1921. She was survived by one son, Walter E. Allen of Phoenix, Oregon. *(ancestry.com)*

So ends the history of the John Starkey family and one of the more difficult histories to research and compile for this book.

However, there is a secondary road story to tell related to John Starkey's postmaster application that opens a very interesting part of Union County history, and the authors wish to include this in this road entry as follows:

On November 11, 1879, John Starkey applied for a post office, and in the process, he made several requests of the post office department: (1) that the post office name be "Daleyville," (2) that it be located at the Daley's Ranch along mail route #44190 (at Starkey Prairie), and (3) that his daughter Aurora be appointed as the postmaster. Why did he initially recommend Daleyville as the official post office name? We did some digging.

Daleyville was suggested to honor David Dealy Jr. (1824-1892), son of David Dealy Sr. and Elizabeth (Mills) Dealy. David Dealy Jr. lived six miles west of North Powder, and he also owned and operated Dealy Ranch, also called Dealy's Station on Starkey Prairie, headquarters of the Dealy Wagon Road Company established in 1864.

His name, Dealy, was often misspelled by his contemporaries, and the variant spellings included: Daley, Dailey or Daly, but Dealy is how the family spelled it and what is found on his family plot of gravestones in Baker City, Oregon and Bellingham, Washington. The misspellings are mentioned here because a prominent wagon road built through Umatilla, Union and Baker counties in 1863-64 is sometimes recorded incorrectly as Daley.

On a personal note: David Dealy was a strikingly handsome man from Jackson County, Missouri, who married three times: Diana Tucker (m. January 7, 1847, Jackson Co., Missouri, died on the Oregon Trail in 1852); Mary Jane Ray (m. October 3, 1852, Marion Co., Oregon); and Martha A. Clearwater (m. August 13, 1865, Walla Walla, Washington).

Dealy was father to eleven children by his wives. With his wife, Diana Tucker, they had Jonathan Thomas (1847-1908) and James Daniel (1850-). With his wife, Mary Jane Ray, they had William Joseph (1853-1906), Mary Jane York (1855-1882), Susan Davis (1857-1952), and Rebecca Frances Johnson (1861-1937). With his wife, Martha A. Clearwater, they had: Elsie Beidler (1866-1961), Belle (1868-1920), Florence Lillie Johnson (1870-1952), David M. (1874-1897) and George W. (1877-1916).

According to the *1860 Federal Census*, Dealy and his second wife Mary Jane were living in Lebanon, Linn County, Oregon in 1860, and their last child Rebecca was born in 1861. Then they were listed in Union County for the *1870 Federal Census*, but in between those censuses, Dealy was involved with the building of what became the historic Daley Wagon Road, his greatest legacy in northeast Oregon.

In 1863, he was hired by the Blue Mountain Wagon Road Company to oversee the project of building this toll road that would carry freight from Umatilla Landing (city of Umatilla, Oregon) to the Powder River mining district, about six miles north of Baker City and to more distant points. The place of business was located at the Dealy Ranch. *(The Dealy Road by Forest Ranger Gerald J. Tucker of Pendleton, Jan. 14, 1946)*

However, in the spring of 1864, the 3-man partnership of Blue Mountain Wagon Road Company was dissolved. One partner (Vaughn) dropped out and in his place, David Dealy stepped in. A new company was formed, the Dealy Wagon Road Company, incorporated by David Dealy Jr., Attorney James H. Slater and S. Ensign. Again, the business was headquartered at the Dealy Ranch.

Work on the Dealy Wagon Road started in 1863 and the road was largely useable by the following July of 1864 "...for the first wagon to pass over the road was that of James H. Slater, one of the incorporators of the road, who moved his family over the road from Walla Walla to Auburn in July 1864." *(The Dealy Road by Forest Ranger Gerald J. Tucker of Pendleton, Jan. 14, 1946)*

Ranger-historian Gerald J. Tucker wrote that some work remained on the road at lower elevations in 1864, but generally speaking, the road was ready for use. Tucker wrote that the Dealy Wagon Road, also called the Starkey Route, shaved about 25 miles off other commutes over the Blue Mountains to the Powder River mining district.

The Dealy Wagon Road was a toll road located on Townships 4, 5 and 6 S, R. 36, 37, and 38 E. "It was built in 1864 as a short cut for a portion of the Birch Creek-Grande Ronde Military Road. It was used heavily by pack trains to supply gold mines at Auburn and the Baker area." *(Wallowa-Whitman National Forest, Burnt Powder Palnning Unit, a Land Management Plan, pg. E2)*

"The starting point on the Powder River Valley side was at the old Doc Anthony homestead, where the toll gate was located. Doc Anthony collected the toll from the wagon drivers. There was a halfway station located at Whiskey Hollow, (Jordon Creek) where there was a saloon and lodging house run by Tom and John O'Bryant." *(Historical Data on the Daley Road by W.E. Barnett)*

"The old Dealy Road was a favorite route for pack trains and was used heavily for a few years during the summers by freight wagons, but when the Meacham Toll Road was built across the Blue Mountains about 1867, the Dealy Road gradually faded out of existence. One of its chief disadvantages was that it crossed the mountains at high elevations, being blocked for many months each year by snow," Tucker wrote.

Another historian wrote that "due to the steepness of the road, it was never used as extensively as the builders hoped." *(W.E. Barnett, Whitman Historical Data on the Daley Road)*

Thus came and went the Dealy Wagon Road, forever noted on historic maps and the legacy of David Dealy Jr. He's the man that John Starkey had in mind when he proposed "Daleyville" as the name for the 1879 post office in the Starkey Prairie locality.

Starkey pioneer families started to celebrate their community heritage at annual picnics, starting in 1925. It gained in popularity so that by 1926 there were 100 Starkey pioneers in attendance. On June 12, 1927, there were 300 people in attendance. W. S. Burnett emceed the gathering, suggesting that a permanent organization be formed and that future picnics be held the second week of June each year at Emigrant Springs. *(La Grande Observer, June 4, pg. 1 and June 13, 1927, pg 1)*

Some of the pioneer family names in attendance were Burnett, Sullivan, Tompkins, Beaumont, Griffin, Williams, Loftus, Kennedy, McMillan, Gavin, Moore, Carroll, and Dunn.

Starr Lane - This county road #129A runs east and west for 2.57 miles in Township 2S R38E Section 10 in the La Grande maintenance district.

This gravel road connects Aspen Road on its west end and Halley Road on its east, and it intersects with Hunter Road, Marks and Mt. Glen Road.

Starr Lane is named after Samuel Elias Starr (1875-1969) and Catherine Scheel (1882-1950). Samuel E. and Catherine Starr are noted as land owners on this road on the *1935 Metsker Map*. They are the grandparents of Donald Starr, a well-known farmer in the county, now residing in Island City.

Samuel Starr and Catherine Scheel were married on April 25, 1906 in Pendleton and made their home initially in Helix, Oregon, where Sam had been living.

Sam was born March 20, 1875 in Beaver, Ohio. Apparently he came to Oregon prior to 1900, where he was listed on the *1900 Federal Census* in Helix, Oregon as a "servant" in the household.

However, in the years following his marriage to Catherine, Samuel became a skilled druggist, and the *1910 Federal Census* of Helix, Oregon revealed that he owned a drug store in Helix.

The Starr couple seemed to relocate a few times in the following years. Samuel's son, Lawrence "Larry" Robert was born August 30, 1911 in King Hill, Idaho.

In the *1920 Federal Census* in Lind, Washington, Samuel was engaged in farming on land he was purchasing. Catherine's obituary mentioned that they came to Union County in 1927. The *1930 Federal Census* noted Samuel was farming in the Alicel precinct where Starr Lane is located today. He continued there through the *1940 Federal Census* period, probably the longest he had lived in any one area.

His wife, Catherine, died August 25, 1950 in a La Grande hospital after a long illness, and she was buried in the Summerville Cemetery about one mile south of Summerville. She was born in Germany on August 12, 1882 and lived in Union County with her husband for 23 years. Catherine was survived by her husband and their son, Larry Starr.

The history now focuses on Larry Starr, who came to Union County in 1927 as a young child and farmed with his father Samuel until 1934. He married Eleanor Elizabeth Squire on June 26, 1937 in Kettle Falls, Stevens County, Washington, and they initially made their home in Portland. However, in 1941, they returned to Union County and then bought a farm on Myers Road in 1943 where they farmed 560 acres. Here they raised two children: Beverly (b.1943) and Donald (b.1946).

During those years, Larry was honored as Union County Conservation Man of the Year in August 1957 by the Union County Wheat Growers Association. Then in December of that year, Larry was awarded the Oregon State Conservation Man of the Year. At that time, he farmed 2,067 acres in Union County. He was the second man in Union County to win this state award, the first being Ed McCanse of North Powder, who won the state award in 1953. (See McCanse Road entry)

Larry's farm was unique in that each field was rated as to its fertility, location, erosion potential and other capabilities. Grass was sown on steep, hilly land; alfalfa was used to restore nutrients to the soil and stubble mulching was practiced to control wind and water erosion.

He also installed two miles of drain ditch, five miles of diversion ditches, a mile and a half of sod waterways, plus four miles of tile drainage to assist in the productivity and conservation of the soils on his land. *(La Grande Observer, December 7, 1957 pg. 1 and photo)*

Larry Starr died on October 24, 1999 and was buried in Summerville Cemetery.

Eleanor Starr, 94, died on May 30, 2007 and was survived by her children, Bev and Larry Knouse of La Grande and Don and Karen Starr of Summerville; six grandchildren and four great-grandchildren; and other relatives.

Her obituary read, in part: "Eleanor was born June 11, 1912, to Archer and Carrie (Mahler) Squire in Kettle Falls, Washington. She graduated from Kettle Falls High School in 1930 and from Washington State University in 1934. She worked for the Resettlement Administration in Pullman, Wash., which moved to Portland in the fall of 1935 and became the Farm Security Administration, where she met her future husband." (Obit on Ancestry.com family tree source)

Now the history turns to Larry's son Donald Starr. He was born in a La Grande hospital in 1946, and until 2005, he lived on the Starr farm, the former Myers farm on Myers Road in Summerville.

He married Karen L. Smith on May 19, 1984, and they became a blended family, including children Blake, Jeana (Starr) Bingaman, Ryan and Nathan. Karen's two children were adopted by Donald.

In 1982, Donald was honored as Conservation Man of the Year in Union County. In his soil conservation efforts, he also invented a flotation device for pivot irrigation systems and started Starr Trak LLC located in the Industrial Park on the south edge of Elgin off Highway 82. He operated the manufacturing business for a short time and then sold it. *(See La Grande Observer, Sept. 8, 2001, online article written by staff reporter Tina L. Peterson)*

The Starr Trak system was invented by Donald, and he received a patent for his tire assembly for mobile irrigation structures. The patent abstract explains that the invention involves a flexible belt wrapped around the two tires to reduce soil compaction by providing a greater area on the ground to evenly distribute the weight of the equipment. The patent date is September 9, 2003, U.S. Patient No. US6,616,374 B2. *(Inventors of Union County, Oregon and Their Inventions, 2010, by Dave Yerges.)*

Donald retired from farming and sold the farm in 2005. Currently, he and his wife, Karen, live in Island City. Donald works for Goss Motors of La Grande, and Karen helps manage the White Barn Estate, a wedding and party venue on Hunter Road, owned by Jeana (Starr) Bingaman and her husband Austin Bingaman.

Stonehaven Lane - This lane is a public unmaintained road off Watson Road, which is off May Lane in Township 3S R38E Section 4 in the La Grande maintenance district.

Striker Lane - This road #39A runs 2.17 miles through Township 1S R39E Section 22 in the Imbler maintenance district. It is located on the northeast end of Imbler and connects Highway 82 with Gray's Corner Road.

It is named after Henry Striker, who was born in 1839 in Germany and immigrated to the United States in 1851. *An Illustrated History of Union and Wallowa counties, 1902, pg. 181* reads that he came to Union County in 1865.

He married Johanna Rysdam on December 7, 1870. He was single again by the time of the 1900 Federal Census. He then married Mrs. Margaret J. (Foster) Aster on June 25, 1903.

In association with Jacob Zuber, Henry Striker built a brewery in Union and operated it for five years before selling.   The 1900 Federal Census thus called him "a brewer." *(An Illustrated History of Union and Wallowa counties, 1902, pg. 373-4)*

The old Striker place of 480 acres near Imbler was sold in March 1904. *(La Grande Observer, March 11, 1904, pg. 1)* There was a steel bridge purchased by the county for $2,450 to replace the old Striker bridge over the Grande Ronde River. The bridge was located near the Hibberd farm, and it flooded in 1917. *(La Grande Observer, Sept. 18, 1912, pg. 3; and April 30, 1917, pg. 5)*

Johanna and Henry Striker had two children, Hellen (b. Nov. 15, 1872) and John (b. Jan. 15, 1876). Hellen died April 14, 1905 and John died Jan. 8, 1926.

Henry Striker died March 5, 1910 and his second wife, Margaret "Maggie" died April 6, 1939. Henry and Margaret are buried in the Elgin Cemetery, but their headstone reads Stricker instead of Striker.

Summerville Road - Formerly called Dry Creek Road on the *1935 Metsker Map,* this county road #39 runs 9.93 miles through Township 1S R39E Section 20 in the Imbler maintenance district.

This earlier Dry Creek Road started at the Imbler city limits and ran past the Summerville Cemetery and through the city of Summerville and north another five miles to Sanderson Springs, turning sharply at the pond until it connected with Highway 204. At Highway 204, the traveler has first crossed a small bridge over Phillips Creek, what Elgin residents call Three Mile Bridge because it is three miles from the Elgin city limits.

Today, that same road route is called Summerville Road, and it passes by the iconic Summerville Store and Tavern at 301 Main Street. Back in 1910, that property was a harness shop. That was torn down and locals recall that the store was built sometime after 1947. It had several owners, including Irv Pratt, who in 1966 sold it to Jay and Carolyn Howard. The store was one of two income sources for the Howards, who were living with their four children in a home nearby on Patten Street.

Summerville Road is named after the city of Summerville, "first settled in the spring of 1865, being a stage station on the George Thomas line of coaches. The station was operated by William H. Patten, whose homestead was the town site. Mr. Patten was also the first postmaster of the town giving it the name Summerville in honor of his friend and neighbor Alexander Sommerville, who had lived near Mr. Patten in the Willamette Valley near Harrisburg. The Summerville post office was established on May 30, 1865." *(Oregon Post Office 1847-1982; Oregongenealogy.com)*

The U.S. Postal Department mistakenly spelled the post office Summerville rather than Sommerville.

Local resident Emery Oliver tried for years to get the county to correct the road sign from Patton to its correct form, Patten. Not long before he passed away, Emery Oliver accomplished his mission, and today the sign correctly reflects the name of the first postmaster of Summerville, William H. Patten.

In 1967, the Summerville Store owner, Jay Howard, was appointed as postmaster, and he operated the post office that was located inside the store, much as it is today. The Howards had a full line of groceries in their convenience store, and they catered to the farmers who wanted case lot sales and migrant workers who wanted shrimp, canned corn and burritos.

The Howards had a small bar room, but no dining tables or grill service. Instead they had ready-made sandwiches and deli meats and cheeses. In 1972, they remodeled the store, enlarging the tavern area, which allowed for greater storage of their wine and beer inventory.

Then one evening in 1980, the store was held up by two masked, armed robbers. Owner Carolyn Howard was mopping up, waiting for her last customer to leave so that she could close the store for the night. It was a frightening experience. Inventory and purses were stolen, but no one was hurt, and thankfully that was the last time the Summerville Store was ever robbed.

Then in 1995, Jay Howard retired at age 65, and the store was sold to Jim and Sheri Rogers. Sheri contracted with the U.S. Postal Service to continue delivering into the post boxes and offering limited postal services at the store.

"When we bought the store in 1995," Sheri Rogers said, "I was employed full time at Boise Cascade as a bookkeeper, a job I retired from in 2011 after 27 years. We ran the store with the help of employees, and I worked weekends and on quieter nights so our employees could have the busy nights and the tips."

Since 2000, Sheri Rogers has been the sole proprietor of the store. She expanded her food menu to cater to families, and she hired Laurie Young and Jodi Hafer, "two of the best cooks in Oregon," Rogers said.

Today, Summerville Store serves as a post office, gas station, quick mart, tavern, family restaurant, weather station, live band venue, pizza parlor, information hub and three summers as a water stop for Cycle Oregon bicyclers.

The restaurant has a strong patronage that has carried it through the dark months of the COVID-19 pandemic of 2020, when there was no vaccine and in-house dining was prohibited by law. It continues to be supported in 2021 albeit with social distancing and mask wearing. *(Mayor Sheri Rogers interview, 2019)*

Some of the early pioneers who settled on Summerville Road included the Hiram Oliver family, the Craig family, and the Sanderson family whose Century Farm is near Sanderson Springs. Summerville Road led to Wesley Oliver's sawmill, established in 1865; and it brought access to Dry Creek Road where the John L. McKinnis sawmill was established in 1884.

Also on Summerville Road and Dry Creek Lane stands the one-room schoolhouse called Dry Creek School. Summerville pioneer Joseph T. Woodell was hired by the school board to build the school house in July 1885. Though Woodell received $312 for his part in its development, the "total cost of the school house, fence, toilets, walks and ground was $1,052.69," stated Edna Teter Rush, author of *The One Room School*. He had help putting up the structure from local carpenters like John Lewis, who built quite a few homes in the area over the years.

Dry Creek School was added to the National Registry of Historical Places in 2000. Marshall J. Kilby, a farmer who also lives on Summerville Road, owns the schoolhouse and hopes to get grant funding for its restoration. Presently, it serves as a storage building for him. It is painted red and has a historical sign on it.

The school provided area children with academic instruction through eighth grade until July 10, 1945 when the school consolidated with the Imbler School District No. 11, and the children were thereafter bussed to the main school on Esther Street in Imbler.

The earliest Dry Creek School teacher on record was Elijah Moore in 1877. From first to last, there were 37 teachers on record at Dry Creek, each having fulfilled the two year Teacher's College training course.

A partial list of those teachers prior to 1899 were: G. W. Moore (1878), Zella Rees (1880), J. S. Roe (1882), Allie Reese (1882), J. R. Laramore (1886), E. D. York (1886), T. A. Rinehart (1886), H. E. Gilliam (1886), C. E. Oliver (1890, 1891), Ida Brooks (1890-1892), Lydia M. Hug (1894), W. L. Tucker (1894-96), R. A. Wilkerson (1896-1897), and W. J. Case (1898).

The high school students attended Imbler High School after 1925, but the grade school continued through the 1944-1945 school year with Frances Downing as the last Dry Creek school teacher. *(School Districts of Union County, Oregon, Stella M. Edvalson, 1965, pg. 73-74)*

Other memorable teachers were Inez Fries, the 31st teacher at Dry Creek, teaching three school years, concluding in spring of 1934. She drove her Model-A vehicle and gave Stanley Rhoads a ride to school. She began teaching September 1, 1930 for a term of thirty-six weeks. The school board paid Fries $95 per month as a wage for the first three years, but in 1933, due to the Great Depression, her wages dropped to $70 per month.

Following her was Miss June Hug, who taught the 1934-35 school year. "She made us kids hot cocoa during the cold winters," Dorothy Craig said in an interview in 2000. Those families who had milk would send some with their children to school in glass jars, and others would bring the cocoa and sugar. The kids all looked forward to this treat.

Also teaching there was Mary Elmer during the 1923-24 school year and Bonita Teter during the 1924-25 school year. Wanda (Sanderson) Pointer recalled being taught by Mrs. June (Hug) Wagoner for fifth grade and Naoma (Twidwell) Perry in her sixth, seventh and eighth grade classes.

"I walked two and one half miles to school, and the first kid there had to start the wood stove," Pointer said. "There was a hole in the wall of the school, and I stuck my hand in there to get the door key, unlocked the door and walked in."

Outside on this two-acre school property was a wood shed where cut wood was stacked for the school house wood stove. There were two outhouses, a boys and girls outhouse by the back fence and three horse barns and an old well. "Some of us kids were so little, we couldn't get on our horses by ourselves, so the teacher would lift us onto our horses so that we could ride back home after school," student Stanley Rhoads said.

There were a few Ponderosa pine trees there and two deciduous trees by the school house's front porch. Donald Sanderson planted a tree by the porch, Pointer recalled.

Teacher Mrs. Inez Fries, made her own toothpaste for the students with peppermint to teach them dental hygiene.

Stanley Rhoads said that the kids played outdoors for recess, games like "Fox and Geese", "Hop Scotch" and "Circle Stomp". When they heard the teacher ring her hand bell, they came indoors for classes. Classes included penmanship and the three-Rs—reading, writing and arithmetic.

Rhoads was misbehaving one day, he said, and Mrs. Inez Fries made him sit under her desk for discipline—completely out of view of the other students. Another time he sat in a chair facing the corner of the room. "Duck" Slack, another lad who earned his teacher's special attention, said that his teacher Bonita Teter kept him at school till 8 p.m. for not getting his homework done."

"I wanted to leave with the other kids at 4 p.m., but she locked the door and told me to stay until I was done studying," Slack said. "She ended up expelling me and Zach Pugh—I was an ornery kid."

It was no wonder Slack didn't have his studying completed. "I did the farm chores before school and more chores after school until 7 or 8 p.m. After that I did my homework by kerosene and gas light," he said. Slack wasn't the only student who was expected to milk the cows before and after school each day.

In the hard, windy winters when Pointer could not walk to school because the roads were drifted shut, Bill "Willie" Sanderson and her Uncle Charley Sanderson hooked up a team of horses to a sled wagon and picked up all the school children who lived along Summerville Road and delivered them to Dry Creek School. *(Wanda Sanderson Pointer interview, 2007)*

"That was for real bad weather when the snow drifts were so high that the horses and sled went right over the snow-packed fences and clothes line. The snow was so hard that it withstood the weight," Pointer recalled.

For lunches, kids wore a kind of shoulder strap purse that held a cannister where lunch foods were stored. Inside was usually a metal collapsible cup, so everything fit snugly into the metal cannister.

In those early years there was no kindergarten instruction. Kids entered school as first grade students and finished as eighth grade students. Between all the grade levels, Dry Creek instructed between 24-26 students each year. If they went on to high school, that depended upon if they could live close enough to get to school daily. If not, then eighth grade was where a student finished his or her formal schooling.

If there was a breakout of measles or chicken-pox, children were supposed to stay home until they were well again. There weren't any vaccines to protect anyone, not even the teacher, and although rare, "Mrs. Inez Fries got mumps twice from sick kids," recalled Wanda Pointer.

Also located on Summerville Road is the Summerville Cemetery, established in 1866 with the burial of 18-year-old Mary Stevens, following an accident in which she drowned in the Grande Ronde River. The second burial was Elizabeth (Murchison) Shaw, 49 ½ years, died on June 5, 1867, she being the wife of Angus Shaw Sr. who owned the ground that the west half of the town of Summerville was built on. The third burial was Mary "Polly" Standley, 59, who died on October 26, 1867. She was related to Elizabeth Shaw through the marriage of their children James H. Standley and Christina Shaw. *(Emery Oliver interview, 2000, Summerville Cemetery secretary and local historian)*

Considering that Summerville started to be settled on May 30, 1865 with a post office and settlers began to stake donation claims for homesteads, it was just a span of less than two years, and the cemetery already had three burials.

The late Emery Stuart Oliver (1912-2005), who lived on the corner of Summerville Road and Behrens Lane was the secretary of the cemetery for over 50 years. He started this job on his honeymoon, when he and his wife Thelma Grace (Kennedy) Oliver (1926-2015) started reconstructing the fragmented, mouse-nibbled records of this old cemetery to create a burial log.

Thelma remarked, "Of all the things to do on your honeymoon! But somebody had to do it, and that was Emery." Of course, she provided 50% of the help, but the restoration of these records was very important to the Olivers, as these were their neighbors and contemporaries of their parents.

Emery improved the cemetery grounds so significantly that it became one of the most well-groomed cemeteries in Union County with a breath-taking view of the Blue Mountains. In 1952, it was listed on the tax roll so that taxpayers would continue to fund its maintenance. Emery said that it was the first cemetery in Oregon to go on the tax roll, and after it, others followed. Living in the Summerville district, the authors paid $20.49 of their 2021-22 property taxes toward the support of the Summerville Cemetery.

By 2011, there were no more burial lots available for sale, but in 2016, the cemetery was expanded as part of a senior project by an Imbler High School student named Tyler Bales. Fill was brought in to level out a deep ditch near the road, the soil was seeded in grass, trees were planted, and parking space was developed with gravel.

Additional land was added to the cemetery, when Randy and Pam Glenn's large barn was disassembled on the property adjacent to the cemetery. During *an interview with Pam on October 27, 2021*, she said that she and her husband had up to three years to take the structure down, which was first built in 1995. As things turned out, the barn was totally removed from the property by summer 2022, and the land was graded. Top soil was added starting in January 2023 in preparation for seeding. The changes really opened up the cemetery and improved its park-like appearance.

Sunday Drive - This private drive is off Haefer Lane in Township 3S R40 E Sections 14-15 near Cove and part of the Union maintenance district. It allows access to seven properties. This residential area is not historically old or significant, but it probably makes for a scenic Sunday drive.

Syrup Creek Trail - This trail is 11 miles northwest of Camp Elkanah in the Starkey district and is also called NF-170. It follows Syrup Creek and dead ends into the forest. There are no residences on this trail. This road is not listed on the Union County road register, but the authors thought it had a sweet sounding name, so there you go.

Tamarack Springs Lane - This county road #147 runs .93 miles in Township 1N R38E Section 28 in the Imbler maintenance district.

It is named after Tamarack Springs. The tamarack or western larch grow plentifully in the Blue Mountains. Each fall their needles turn a beautiful mustard yellow and fall off, only to grow back again in the spring in a light green shade. Each fall, they provide great color contrast in a forest of blue and green colored firs and pine trees. The older tamaracks are particularly sought after as fuel for those who heat their homes with wood stoves.

On Tamarack Springs Lane is a thriving party and wedding venue called The Barn at Tamarack Springs. The red barn has never been used for livestock, and it provides an Oregon country ambiance that makes it a popular choice for any type of gathering. Its awesome backdrop of the Blue Mountains can't be beat when it comes to wedding photos.

Tamarack Springs Lane is all gravel, so drive slowly and enjoy the view of the country and mountains.

Telocaset Lane - This lane is 14 miles in length, designated road #70 in the county listing. It's located in Township 5S R40E Section 29 of the North Powder maintenance district.

According to the *Oregon Geographic Names* book by Lewis A. McArthur and Lewis L. McArthur, Seventh Edition, page 941, it explains:

"This place was once called Antelope Stage Station. When the railroad was built through the Blue Mountains, Dr. William C. McKay was asked to suggest new names for stations that had names duplicating others in Oregon. Among those he suggested was Telocaset. This word is from the Nez Perce language and means 'a thing at the top, or put on top' such as a tree growing on a hill, summit or plateau overlooking a valley. The Indians pronounced the word *taule-karset,* according to O. H. Lipps of Fort Lapwai Indian Agency, Idaho, in a letter dated March 2, 1927."

The *Oregon Geographic Names* book continued, "Telocaset post office was established February 25, 1885, with William A. Cates, first post master. The office was closed November 22, 1975."

Thew Loop - This loop is off of Mill Creek Lane near Cove and has no designated county road number. It is .19 miles in length and is considered a public, unmaintained road located in Township 3S R40E Sections 22-23 in the Union maintenance district.

This loop is named after Henry Prior and Emogene Thew, who came to Cove in 1957 from southern California. During his life in Cove, Henry became the vice chairman of the Cove Farm Bureau in 1958. His wife, Emogene, was the secretary-treasurer. *(La Grande Observer, October 16, 1958 pg. 1, photo)* Henry and Emogene both worked as adult 4-H leaders. *(La Grande Observer, November 22 and 26, 1960, pg. 1)* Henry was also occupied as a school bus driver.

Henry Prior Thew was born in Portland, Oregon on May 19, 1911 to Richard Henry Thew (1881-1957) and Ester Grace Prior (1887-1979). He died on March 24, 1994 at the age of 82 in Cove, Oregon. He married Emogene Welch on December 13, 1935 in Los Angeles, California

Emogene was born on September 14, 1912 and died on November 5, 2014 at the age of 102 years. Henry and Emogene were both interred at the Willamette National Cemetery in Portland, Oregon.

Henry and Emogene had four children: Henry W., Richard H., David and Lucy Strandlien. When Henry and Emogene came to Cove in 1957, Richard, David and Lucy were still in school. All three children were involved with 4-H in Cove and supported by their parents who were adult 4-H leaders during the years their kids were involved.

Richard graduated from Cove High School in May 1958; David in May 1960 and Lucy shortly thereafter. In 1960, David was then acting as reporter for the Cove Livestock Club.

After earning degrees from Eastern Oregon University, he spent time teaching in Eastern Oregon. He also served as Cove's mayor for over 20 years and dedicated about 30 years to the Cove School District as a teacher and football and track coach.

Richard Thew and his wife, Kathy, raised three children: Jennifer, Rebecca and Rick. *(Alice Alexander interview, August 25, 2020; Mary Jane Johnson interview, August 27, 2020)*

The Thew family will always be known as civic-minded, service-minded and educators, who made a positive difference in their community.

Thief Valley Road - This road is named after Thief Valley east of North Powder, where John Wetherly was hanged by vigilantes on December 1864. He was accused of stealing four mules from an emigrant at Boise. *(Oregon Geographic Names, 1982 edition, pg 726; La Grande Observer, Nov. 11, 1948, pg. 5)*

Thompson Road - Formerly called Thompson-Miller Road, it is county road #50 and runs 3.78 miles in Township 2N R40E Section 10 in the Elgin maintenance district.

The Thompson family lived on one end of the road, and the Miller family lived on the dead end of the road, where there is a breath-taking view of the canyon with the Wallowa River winding through it. In 1988, the county decided to retain the name Thompson on the road sign and drop the Miller name.

This gravel road was named after Albert Emmett Thompson and his wife Lillie Lavon Carroll. Albert died November 28, 1961 in La Grande.

His obituary relates that Albert Thompson, 84, retired farmer of 2009 East X Avenue died Tuesday, and following his service at Daniels Funeral Home at 2 p.m. Friday, he was buried at the Elgin Cemetery.

Albert E. Thompson was born September 11, 1878 in Appleton City, St. Clair County, Missouri. He resided in Wallowa and Union counties for 60 years. He married Lillie Carroll on March 18, 1900 in Missouri and came to Oregon shortly afterward where he homesteaded near Elgin.

Surviving him were his widow, Mrs. Lillie Thompson, La Grande; two sons, Clinton Thompson, La Grande, and Emmett Thompson, Elgin; a daughter, Mrs. Vallie Kingery, Saratoga, Calif., and two brothers, seven sisters, 9 grandchildren, 22 great grandchildren and two great-great-grandchildren. *(La Grande Observer, Thurs, Nov. 30, 1961, pg. 6; Vallie Thompson's birth certificate)*

Larry Thompson is a member of the Emmett Thompson family, who lived on this road, and he said, "My granddad was Albert Emmett Thompson, and his wife was Lillie Lavon (Carroll) Thompson. They homesteaded the land for five or six years, and then my granddad went back to Missouri. I think the Joplin, Missouri area," Larry said.

When Albert finally returned from Missouri, he and his wife retired at 2009 East X Avenue in La Grande. He never lived out on Thompson Road again, Larry said.

Larry's father was Emmett Carroll Thompson, and he married Eva Mae Rollins on June 20, 1924. They made their home on Thompson Road.

"My dad, Emmett, bought a place up Thompson road about a mile and a half from my granddad's homestead. It was called the old Harriman Place," he said. "We lived there from 1939 until 1960."

Emmett and Eva Thompson raised five children: Peggy Mae Kennedy, Lawrence "Larry" E., Barbara Janet Horn, Dixie Lee, and Virginia C. Thompson. Larry is the only surviving member of the Emmett Thompson family in 2021.

Rural mail carrier Mort Gordon of Elgin remembered the Thompson family who lived out there because Mort delivered mail out that way for about 15 years. *(Mort Gordon interview, October 8, 2021)*

"After my dad [Emmett] moved to town in 1960, I moved back to Thompson Road after I got back from the service," Larry said. "I was in the Korean War. I lived on Thompson Road for three years 1955-1958."

There were other Thompsons who have come to that area, some from California, but Larry said none of them are related to Albert Thompson or have a connection to the historic origin of Thompson Road. *(Larry Thompson interview, October 13, 2021)*

The second part of this road name, Miller, originates with the Herman Miller (1841-1911) family, including his son Emil Miller and grandson Francis Miller.

Hermann Gottlieb Balthasar Miller was born on November 23, 1841 in Ole, Berent, Westpreussen, Germany. He married Florentine "Flora" Gehrke on January 5, 1871 in Marinsee, Westpreussen, Germany. *(Findagrave; ancestry.com)* Flora was born February 14, 1842, and she became mother to two sons, Emil and Willie Miller.

They emigrated to America on the ship Strassburg, departing from the port of Bremen and arriving in Baltimore, Maryland on March 5, 1881. They settled in Dane County, Wisconsin, where their eldest son Emil was born on February 4, 1881. Their second son, Willie, was born in March of 1883 in Wisconsin.

About ten years after Willie was born, the Miller family migrated to Elgin in 1893. Seven years later Flora Miller died on October 28, 1900 at 58 years of age. After her death, the *1900 Federal Census* shows the widower Herman Miller, 70, lived with his son Emil in the south side of Elgin. Herman died on August 7, 1911, and he was buried with Flora at the Highland Cemetery on Good Road on Cricket Flat.

When Emil married Ora Huffman on February 25, 1903 on Cricket Flat, they made their home out there. They lived all their married life, over 50 years, on their home ranch. Ora (Huffman) Miller was the daughter of Mr. and Mrs. J. H. Huffman, and she was born on Cricket Flat.

Emil and Ora had three children born in Elgin: Francis Doyle, Fern V., and Myron. Fern died October 13, 1932 in Gridley, California, and Myron died as a teenager in an auto accident on October 19, 1931 in Elgin.

Francis Doyle Miller married his first wife, Mary Shelton, on September 1, 1927 in Hood River, Oregon. Mary was born December 1904 and died March 4, 1973.

On June 17, 1974, Francis Doyle Miller remarried. His new wife was Mrs. Beth Krause of Coeur d'Alene, Idaho. She was born June 30, 1912 to George and Dora Jewett in McLaughlin, South Dakota. She came to Elgin with her first husband, and he died in 1969.

Francis and Beth Miller had three children: Kenneth Max, (1929-2011), Ronald F. (1938) and Ted Shelton (1939).

Francis Miller died June 26, 1991 in Elgin and Beth Miller died May 24, 2004 at 91 years of age. *(Obit, Findagrave.com)*

Timberline Road - This road is a private road in Township 1S R38E Section 9 in the Imbler maintenance district. This road is home to six residences.

Tin Trough Road - This road is not on the county list, but it had such an unusual name that the authors had to include it in this book.

It is also called NF-5160, which departs from Ukiah-Hilgard Highway 244, thirty-one miles from La Grande and connects on the other end with Fly Valley Road. Like other National Forest roads, it is a gravel road, and it may be off limits to public traffic.

It is probably named after Tin Troughs Spring west of NF-200. In the early years, a tin water trough was used for livestock. Most were made from wood or hollowed out logs, but a tin trough would likely stand out as different in comparison.

Some years, like 1930, were dry in the mountains, and the stockmen had difficulty watering their cattle, sheep and horses on the range. So the forest service went to some expense in 1931 to develop springs and set up watering troughs as quickly as the funds were available. This work was done with the cooperation of the stockmen, who volunteered their labor in many instances. *(La Grande Observer, Jan. 21, 1931, pg. 1)*

Tucker Flat Road - This county road #102 is 4.4 miles in length and runs through Township 6S R38E Section 28 in the North Powder maintenance district. This road exits off of North Powder River Lane and passes by the west side of Pilcher Creek Reservoir, northwest of North Powder, Oregon.

A bachelor farmer by the name of Nemo E. B. Tucker took up a homestead outside of North Powder in Union County at Township 5S, R38E, S1/2 of NE1/4 and N1/2 of SE1/4 in Section 11. This property was sold in 1945 to Edson R. McCanse of North Powder.

Having no other namesake candidates in the area and in Union County, the authors believe Tucker Flat Road was named after Nemo E. B. Tucker, landowner and farmer in the North Powder territory from 1913 to 1945. He described himself as a thresher man and a lumber man, and in those occupations, he would have made many friends among the local ranchers and farmers.

Nemo was born January 21, 1887, in Sidney Center, Montcalm County, Michigan, the son of George Wellington Tucker (1860-1934) and Hannah Victoria Doddridge (1869-1945). Nemo became known by his friends as "John."

His family moved from there to Snohomish, Washington, according to the *1900 Federal Census*. Here George supported his family as a shingle weaver at a local shingle mill. A shingle weaver was a skilled cutter and packer of wood shingles. In the *1910 Federal Census*, Nemo's brother George also worked at the shingle mill.

When Nemo was 26 years old, he moved to North Powder, Oregon, where he homesteaded 160 acres on February 12, 1913. In the *1920 Federal Census*, Nemo, 39, and his younger brother George H. Tucker, 29, lived together and worked the farm together. Nemo was described as the head of the household and the farmer, and George H. was noted as his farm laborer.

On November 6, 1921 in La Grande, George married Edna "Isabel" Counsell from Foot Hill Road in the Hot Lake precinct of Union County. She became mother to two daughters, Maxine Tucker born on December 26, 1922 in La Grande; and Victoria Lulu, born on July 23, 1924 at the Counsell home in Hot Lake.

In 1926, according to George Tucker's obituary, the George Tucker family and his brother Nemo Tucker moved to Orchard Home, Jackson County, Oregon. *(Oregon, U.S. State Marriages; 1930 Federal Census of Orchard Home, Jackson County, Oregon)*

As for Nemo's North Powder homestead, it appears that he held onto the deed when he left Union County, Oregon. He most likely leased his 160 acres and rented out the house.

Looking back on Nemo's life, he lived with his brother George and family for the last 25 years of his life, starting first at his homestead in Union County and then at George's house in Jackson County, Oregon.

The *1930 Federal Census in Jackson County, Oregon* noted that both Nemo and George were self-employed as carpenters. It appears that the elderly Tucker parents were living in the Medford, Oregon area until their respective deaths, George W. Tucker in 1934 and his wife Hannah Tucker in 1945.

The year 1945 was one of big change for the family. Not only did Hannah Tucker pass away that year, but according to the *La Grande Observer, February 1, 1945,* Nemo sold his 160 acre homestead to Edson McCanse, a well-known rancher of North Powder.

About six months after the sale of his homestead, Nemo was admitted to the Veterans' Hospital in Fort Miley, San Francisco for treatment, but he died there on October 5, 1945 at the age of 58. He was a bachelor all his life.

Probably the most that was ever written about this bachelor man was in his obituary published in the *Medford Mail Tribune (Medford, Oregon) Mon. October 8, 1945, pg. 3*, which reads in part:

"Obituary— Nemo E. B. Tucker (familiarly known as John) passed away Friday at the Veterans' Hospital in San Francisco. Mr. Tucker was born in Montcalm county, Michigan, Jan. 21, 1887. He was a carpenter and had followed that trade throughout the valley for the past 19 years. He was a veteran of World War I, having served in France with the Engineer's Corps.

Mr. Tucker leaves to mourn his loss two brothers, George H., of Medford, with whom John had made his home for the past 25 years and Frank G., of Arlington, Wash., two nieces, one nephew, one cousin, also a host of friends throughout the valley and elsewhere.

Funeral services will be held at the Conger-Morris funeral parlors at 2 p.m. Tuesday, Oct. 9. Interment at Memorial Park, and will be conducted by members of the Eagles Lodge, with which Mr. Tucker had been affiliated for 18 years." (End of excerpt of obituary)

By all appearances, Nemo Tucker lived a productive life, contributing to his community and maintaining strong ties to his family and friends, both in North Powder and later in Medford, Oregon. His name on the Tucker Flat Road sign will honor him as a homesteader in North Powder from 1913 until 1945.

Turnbull Lane - This lane is county road #111 and exits Union-Cove Highway 237, traveling through Township 4S R40E Section 7 for 1.03 miles in the Union maintenance district.

It is named after John Stewart Turnbull (1847-1901) and his wife, Mary Ann (Flatt) Turnbull, natives of Canada.

He was born on January 11, 1845 (gravestone dates) in Canada. Most of the U.S. censuses indicate John was born in 1847. Mary was born July 18, 1849 in Canada. They were in the *1900 Federal Census* residing in Wisconsin and in 1901, they were living in Union, Oregon.

John died October 31, 1901, and his wife, Mary, died 1902. (ancestry.com)

John Turnbull had a son, Milton Stewart Turnbull, who was born November 19, 1875 in Simcoe, Ontario, Canada, and he moved to Union, Oregon with his parents. The *1940 Federal Census* stated that he finished school through third grade, later became a naturalized U.S. citizen, and supported himself as a farmer.

On December 24, 1907, Milton married Mrs. Nena Nina (Paddock) Andrews. Nena was born July 22, 1877 in Bonhomme County, South Dakota, the daughter of Charles Albert Paddock and Sarah Jane Barnes. Milton was of medium height and weight with light brown hair and brown eyes. *(ancestry.com, draft registration Sept. 12, 1918 , WWI)*

In 1922, Milton built a 6-room home north of Union. *(La Grande Observer, Dec. 14, 1922, pg. 3)*

Milton operated Turnbull Dairy about a mile northeast of Union. *(La Grande Observer, Oct. 23, 1929, pg. 5)* However, on June 25, 1932, a fire destroyed the large dairy and horse barn, along with several tons of hay, harnesses, tools and equipment. A small amount of insurance coverage was held on the lost property, but "appearances were said to point strongly toward incendiarism as a team of horses left in the barn had been turned out into an adjoining lot." *(La Grande Observer, June 27, 1932, pg. 1)*

Not quite a month later, Dell Irvin, who last spring had leased the Fred Ratz place near Union, purchased the Turnbull Dairy equipment and took over the milk route in Union. *(La Grande Observer, July 30, 1932, pg. 3)*

Milton and his wife apparently had no children. Nena died on November 5, 1946 in Union and is buried at the Union Cemetery. Milton died on April 4, 1959 in St. Louis County, Minnesota, where he possibly had relatives living.

Union Junction Lane - This road #12C runs 1.52 miles in length, traveling through Township 4S R39E Section 23 in the Union maintenance district.

According to *The Central Railroad of Oregon, by Richard R. Roth, 2014, page 22*, Union Junction is the place where the Central Railroad of Oregon rail line from the town of Union connected to the main line of the Oregon Railroad and Navigation Company (later Union Pacific Railroad). The first trip over the new line to Union was on November 1, 1892.

On this lane was the Union Depot Hotel owned by A. C. Craig. It had rooms for rent and it served meals for travelers. The hotel had hot water piped from Craig Hot Springs. (pg. 5-6) Electric power was brought to Union Junction in 1913 by the Eastern Oregon Light & Power Company. (pg. 117)

Upper Perry Lane - This county road is oddly not on the road registry, but it held such rich history for the area that the authors had to include it among the road entries in this publication. This lane brings access to ten residences. It's about five miles west of La Grande, taking Highway 30 and exit 257, the lane veers sharply to the right.

This lane is named after the namesake of the community, D. W. C. Perry, who in April 1890 assumed his new appointment as the first incumbent assistant superintendent based out of the La Grande railroad dispatcher's office.

The *Morning Oregonian (Portland, Oregon) issue of Wed. April 2, 1890, pg. 6* stated: "D. W. C. Perry is appointed assistant superintendent of the Oregon division, with office at La Grande, Oregon. He will have charge of all matters pertaining to operation on the Oregon division, and all employees of that division will report to him for orders."

But to better understand why he became the namesake of the post office, the community and subsequently, the Lower Perry Loop and Upper Perry Lane, one must understand the story about the Smith-Stanley Lumber Company and their officers Robert Smith and Fred C. Stanley, who founded the mill town in 1890 known as Perry, Oregon.

The community of Perry has two distinct precincts, one upstream (Upper Perry) and one downstream (Lower Perry). The bustling sawmill originally called Smith-Stanley Lumber Company used to be the centerpiece of this mill town, but when that sawmill was sold and relocated in 1927, it took half the people with it, and left a gaping emptiness between the two sections.

Thereafter, the local residents referred to this split community as Upper Perry and Lower Perry. Mail to these residents is now sent to the La Grande post office and rural mail carriers deliver to individual residences.

However, in its heyday (1890-1927), the Perry community was built and economically supported by the Smith-Stanley Lumber Company. The sawmill owners developed its operation alongside the Grande Ronde River and built a dam upstream to create a pond for their mill-log transport operation. Teri Walker, who lived in Lower Perry said, "The dam in the river for the mill-log transport was changed. They used to ride the logs from up Starkey way to the mill, stopping just above the dam."

It was one of the largest mill operations of its day in Union County. It provided many steady jobs to family men, and they brought their families to live there. Businesses came to the town, such as a Chinese Restaurant among others. Lower Perry had a school house and teachers. One of them, who taught there in February 1898 was Miss Anna Stevenson. In March 1898, line men were setting up poles and stringing wire for the Inland Telephone Company because they had moved from C. E. Wilson's boarding house in Oro Dell to Perry. *(La Grande Observer, March 10, 1898, pg. 3)*

The Smith-Stanley Lumber Company was financed by its president, the Honorable Lemuel Castle Stanley of Chippewa Falls, Wisconsin. He was a banker there and the mayor for a time. Now, with the help of his ambitious son and son-in-law, he was ready to expand into the lucrative lumber business in Union County, Oregon.

To structure this lumber company, L. C. Stanley appointed his son, Fred C. Stanley to act as secretary-treasurer for the lumber mill, and his son-in-law, Robert L. Smith, as business manager of the Smith-Stanley Lumber Company. The newspapers in their hometown area referred to them as "the Chippewa boys."

Stanley's son-in-law, Canadian born, Robert L. Smith, immigrated to the United States in 1882 and lived in Chippewa Falls, where he had happily captured the heart of L. C. Stanley's only daughter Lenore Stanley. The couple had a private wedding ceremony on February 14, 1888 at the estate of her parents, after which the couple took a honeymoon to Ontario, Montreal and other eastern destinations familiar to Smith. *(Chippewa Herald-Telegram, Feb. 15, 1888, pg. 3)*

Upon returning from their honeymoon trip, Robert and Lenore Smith made their home at the Stanley mansion on Bay Avenue in the city. In April 1888, Robert completed his naturalization process, thus preparing him to conduct Stanley's business as a legal citizen of the United States.

The newlyweds didn't stay in Chippewa Falls but a year, when they moved to Union County, Oregon with Fred C. Stanley in 1889, where they organized and managed the Smith-Stanley Lumber Company. For the sake of convenience, they lived on location where the mill was built and where Robert and Fred could locate their offices and perform their respective duties.

Mr. L. C. Stanley and his wife came out to Perry in November 1890 for three months to carry on business and promote the mill operation personally. Trips between Chippewa Falls, Wisconsin and Perry, Oregon were repeated over the years by the president and the officers.

L. C. Stanley and his wife made another extended trip through the West in August 1891 with Perry as their destination to check out the mill operation that "the Chippewa boys" had been developing in the last year. On this occasion, they brought their daughter back with them "for a long visit among old friends, who will be glad to welcome her." *(The Weekly Herald, Chippewa Falls, Wisc., August 21, 1891, pg. 5)*

Together the Robert Smith and Fred C. Stanley team managed so successfully that the company grew from small beginnings to a business of $1,000 per day. *(The Weekly Herald, Chippewa Falls, Wisc., Fri., June 5, 1896, pg. 3)* Business got even better two years later at the annual log drive.

"...Manager of the company Robert Smith, considers the company exceedingly fortunate, at a few days more would have on account of the rapidly falling river would have been fatal to the enterprise as it was only possible at this time by the use of a large dam above Starkey, which they used to flood the river with. 13,000,000 feet of logs scattered long the banks of the river would have greatly crippled the output of the mill during this season, as it is, this will be the banner year since its existence." *(La Grande Observer, Mon., May 2, 1898, pg. 3)*

Also, in that same year, a news article stated that Robert Smith not only managed a mill that put out 10,000,000 feet of lumber each year, but he was also "the president of the La Grande National bank, and was the organizer of the Blue Mountain Natural Ice Company, which subsequently became the Portland Ice and Fuel Company." He also brought to the attention of Misters Eccles and Nibley that the people of Union County wanted a sugar factory, an idea they accepted and brought to fruition.

As far as the lumber mill, 1898 was the boom year for new orders for wood products. Smith was conducting extensive business and landed a very large contract for orange boxes used in California and another order from the Standard Oil Company. "In all these transactions, his efforts have been awarded with the highest success." *(Chippewa Herald-Telegram, Dec. 4, 1898, pg. 5)*

It was this ambitious business manager, Robert Smith, who in 1890, applied to the U.S. Post Office to be appointed as the first postmaster at the mill, and with that request, he also applied for an official post office name.

He originally requested the name, Stanley, after his father-in-law, L. C. Stanley, the company president and owner of the mill. However, there already existed a Stanley post office in Clackamas County, Oregon, so Robert Smith's second choice for a post office and community name was Perry, after a key railroad man who played a significant role in transporting Smith-Stanley wood products to their contracted buyers. The company needed D. W. C. Perry and the rail line to conduct business outside Union County.

In any case, when Smith recommended the name Perry as his second choice for the post office name, it was accepted by the U.S. Post Office, since it had not been assigned out to any community before them. Once Smith's appointment as postmaster was official on August 26, 1890, the mill's post office was open for business.

The following record verifies the post office name and first postmaster from the *Oregon Post Offices 1847-1982, Richard W. Helbock, pg. 78.*

"Perry—Established 26 August 1890. Discontinuance 14 March 1931. Papers forwarded to: La Grande. Located about 4 miles west of La Grande on the Grande Ronde River and the O. W. R. & N. Co. RR. The community was originally known as Stanley, but the POD is said to have selected the name Perry due to duplication of the suggested name. *Robert Smith, first postmaster.*"

Since many of the residents of Perry worked at the mill, they could conveniently pick up their mail there too.

The *Oregon Scout, October 30, 1890, pg. 3* read: "A post office has been established at the Grande Ronde Lumber Company's sawmill. It is called Perry in honor of the former railway superintendent in La Grande. W. L. Smith is postmaster." (The postmaster's name is mistakenly printed in this article and conflicts with the U. S. Postal Record)

Discovering the full identity and character of the railroad man named Perry was the authors' next challenge. The newspapers and railroad publications offered the first clue as to his full name, albeit with a lot of initials.

In 1890, Mr. Perry, 49, was consistently referred to in newspapers as D. W. C. Perry, first as a train master in The Dalles and then as an assistant superintendent of the Oregon Short Line in La Grande.

According to *The Dalles Times - Mountaineer, March 29, 1890, pg. 1,* "Mr. E. B. Conan, train master for this division, has resigned his position, and Mr. D. W. C. Perry has been appointed to the vacancy."

"Oregon R & Navigation Company — D. W. C. Perry has been appointed assistant superintendent of the Oregon division of the road." *(The Railway Review, July 5, 1890)*

Even a historical recounting published in the *La Grande Observer, Wed., June 22, 1932 on page 5* referred to him by his initials: "In 1890 La Grande's office was given an assistant superintendent, D. W. C. Perry being the first incumbent and J. P. O'Brien the next. A. J. Borie, the third, was made superintendent, but under the receivership of 1894-6 the office was removed to Pendleton."

The whereabouts of Mr. Perry, after he left the La Grande dispatcher's office was puzzling at first, until the authors found the following write up in the *September 2, 1893 issue of The Railway Review, Volume 33, pg. 545:*

"Mr. D. W. C. Perry has succeeded Mr. W. A. Nettleton as superintendent of terminals of the Kansas City, Fort Scott & Memphis and associated lines at Memphis, TN." This was generally known as the KATY rail line and was quite a promotion for Mr. Perry, and he accepted it.

Further research finally revealed the names behind his initials, DeWitt Clinton Perry (1841-1914), and to learn about him, the authors had to take a virtual trip 3,000 miles east to New York, where the story of his life begins.

DeWitt C. Perry was born March 9, 1841 in Norfolk, St. Lawrence County, New York, the son of Daniel and Eleanor Perry, both natives of New York. They had six children, the first four were also born in New York: Ellen (1836), DeWitt (1841), Esther (1842), and Sophie (1845).

On February 1, 1848, the father, Daniel Perry, relocated his family to the town of Herman, Dodge County, Wisconsin, where he and his wife homesteaded and had two more children, Mary (1846) and Melissie (1849).

Their only son, DeWitt, was raised and educated in Wisconsin and then he returned to Canton, New York. After the Civil War ended, he gladly retired his uniform and pursued an education in civil engineering. Perhaps after seeing so much senseless destruction and demolition, he wanted to make his life's work one about purposeful design and construction. So he became a civil engineer, and about 1870, he married Charlotte "Lottie" A. Slorah in Norfolk, New York.

His adult life was just launching with a new bride and a position with a construction company, when an exciting engineering project came along. In the early 1870s, "he was among the officials of the construction company which put the long tunnel through the Andes mountains of South America, and it was in this country that his only son, George David Perry, was born" in 1871. *(The Parsons Daily Sun, Sat., July 25, 1914, pg. 1)*

In October of 1877, the young Perry family moved to Parsons, Labette County, Kansas, where DeWitt went into the employ of the KATY, which is the Missouri–Kansas–Texas southern Midwest line that connected St. Louis with much of east Texas. With his engineering background, he started at the KATY as roadmaster, and after several years, he was promoted to division superintendent, a job which he held for several years.

Just when life seemed to be on a progressive track, tragedy visited the Perry family. On Friday morning, September 4, 1885, Charlotte Perry died of typho-malarial fever at their home in Parsons, Kansas. Her death was anticipated for several days in advance, but this forewarning did not relieve the grief that this family felt. She was so young—her obituary states she was 37 years, 3 months and 10 days old at the time of her death. Surviving her was her husband and their son, George D., who was about 14 years of age, surely a lad still in need of his mother's presence and affection.

DeWitt continued to raise his son while taking an active part in the construction of the KATY from Parsons to Coffeyville and from Parsons to Paola during the years of 1886 and 1887. From the KATY, DeWitt Perry accepted work in The Dalles, where he became the train master, and in April 1890, he came to the newly opened La Grande dispatcher's office, where he became the first incumbent for the position of assistant superintendent. This is when he met Robert Smith and Fred C. Stanley of Smith-Stanley Lumber Company.

The office relocated eventually to Pendleton between 1894-96. In 1893, Perry was transferred to the KATY and in 1897 or 1898, he retired from the railroad service after 20 years of employment. He was listed in the 1899 and 1901 Kansas City, Missouri directory, working as a civil engineer, not the railroad. As a civil engineer, he was invited to be part of the executive superintendents of the upcoming St. Louis World's Fair to be opened May 30, 1904 through December 1, 1904. It was going to be the fair to beat all fairs.

"The Louisiana Purchase Exposition, informally known as the St. Louis World's Fair, was an international exposition held in St. Louis, Missouri, United States, from April 30 to December 1, 1904. Local, state, and federal funds totaling $15 million were used to finance the event. More than 60 countries and 43 of the then-45 American states maintained exhibition spaces at the fair, which was attended by nearly 19.7 million people." *(Wikipedia)*

Perry was honored with the enjoyable work of designing and constructing the grounds for that fair. According to the *Official Directory of the Louisiana Purchase Exposition at the World's Fair, St. Louis 1904,* there were 25 executive work divisions and listed under Superintendent of Landscape Department was DeWitt C. Perry.

Along with this honor came a huge responsibility. Google the photos, and you'll see that his landscapes rival any monarch's garden in Britain. This wasn't his only legacy in St. Louis. During the years he lived there, Perry designed and constructed some of the finest bridges in that section. *(The Parsons Weekly Eclipse, Wed., July 29, 1914, pg. 6)*

While living in St. Louis, he made the acquaintance of Anna Cunliff, and she had a room in her home for rent. So he lived as a lodger at the Elizabeth Anna Cunliff family home on Euclid Avenue, St. Louis, from May 1902 until June 1912. She was a widow six years his senior, and she had two adult children living with her. He did odd jobs for her around the home and property, and she gave him a comfortable place to live that didn't involve the hotel atmosphere or costs.

He wrote in his will that he wanted to bequeath her something because she kindly cared for him, even at times of illness in his retirement. *(Missouri Wills and Probate Records)*

The *1910 Federal Census,* Perry, 66, confirms that he was living with the Cunliff family, doing general work. However, in June 1912, he left their home and in 1914, he was living in a rented room at the Hamilton Hotel in St. Louis. His health was declining, and he sensed it was time to close up shop in St. Louis and return home to Parsons, Kansas to see his son George. George was the proprietor of the Hotel Kimball there, so when DeWitt arrived in March of 1914, there was a room waiting for him. *The Parsons Daily Eclipse, March 4, 1914* announced his arrival to town. "D. W. C. Perry of St. Louis is visiting in Parsons, the guest of his son George Perry."

Soon another announcement was published, "D. W. C. Perry has been ill at the Hotel Kimball during the past few days." *(Parsons Daily Eclipse, April 2, 1914)*

DeWitt's physical condition was deteriorating and a physician was called to his room. "He had been confined to bed only a short time, and it was thought that he was recovering from his illness. The doctor visited him this morning and had just left the room when death took place." *(The Parsons Daily Sun, Saturday, July 25, 1914, pg. 1)* His interment took place at Oakwood Cemetery in Parsons.

DeWitt Clinton Perry had three passions in life, railroading, civil engineering and family. He was an accomplished civil engineer and construction designer, even traveling to exciting places to perform historic work. Everywhere he lived and worked, he left signs of his presence there, tangible legacies for others to enjoy and benefit from. But besides his professional identity, he was a family man, who loved his wife, his son George David Perry and grandson Henry Cory Perry.

To George he bequeathed his personal belongings that had special meaning to him. He wrote: "I give my watch, engineering tools and other personal effects to my only son."

His railroad watch and engineering tools were the things that symbolized his greatest accomplishments in life, and he wanted to bequeath those extremely special things to his son George. He also left an inheritance in trust to his only grandson Henry.

This wraps up the life's story on DeWitt C. Perry, but after coming to know this family through their paper trail, the authors got curious as to what happened to George and Henry after DeWitt died.

To be succinct, George married a local attorney's daughter named Maud Cory on February 17, 1893 in Parsons, Kansas, and they moved to their home in Memphis, Tenn., where George had a job on the Memphis railroad. In 1911, they went to work for the Northern Pacific dining station in

Anaconda, Montana. This experience led them into a life-long career in the hospitality industry.

They owned and operated the Kimball Hotel in Parsons, Kansas (1914), the Jefferson Hotel in Wichita, Kansas (1917), the Chalmers Hotel in Hutchinson, Kansas (1919) and one in Kansas City, Kansas (1921), another hotel in Memphis, Tenn., and one in Pineville, Missouri (1935-1940). The latter was foreclosed due to the financial climate of the Great Depression. After this, they immediately retired to a farm property near Anderson, Missouri.

George's wife, Maud, died on April 20, 1941 at their farm home in Anderson, Misouri at 71 years of age. She had been ill for two years prior. George also died at their farm home in Anderson on March 27, 1942 at the age of 72 years.

Their son Henry, who had a disability, always lived with his parents and clerked at the hotels or labored on their farm. After his folks had passed away, the farm foreclosed, but Henry stayed in the Pineville area. On February 16, 1948, Henry, 49, married Mrs. Ethel E. Syverson, 47. They shared about 30 years together and then he died November 5, 1978 at 80 years of age in Pineville, Missouri. They had no children together.

In George's obituary, its final paragraph read, "He was the son of D. W. C. Perry, superintendent of the KATY in Parsons many years ago and at one time was a resident of Parsons." *(The Parsons Sun, Parsons, Kansas, Friday, March 27, 1942, pg. 7)*

So we have come full circle with the Perry story. It started out with a D. W. C. Perry newspaper clipping, and it ended the same way, but sandwiched in between those initialed book ends was a full life of satisfying work, adventure, and many legacies. If DeWitt Clinton Perry's life taught us anything, it was to always leave your world a better place than you found it. The residents of Perry, Oregon, can be proud that they have a man of such legacies as their namesake.

USFS Road 2036 - This road goes along part of Little Catherine Creek, east of Union.

USFS Road 21 - This road runs partially along Peet Creek in far western Union County.

USFS Road 31 - This road is also known as the Mount Emily road and goes from Interstate 84 to Highway 204 toward Tollgate. In the 1930s, Mount Emily Lumber Company owned much land in the area.

USFS Road 63 - This road is near Little Lookingglass Creek in northern Union County.

USFS Road 64 - This road is in the Little Lost Creek area of northern Union County.

Valley View Road - Formerly called Foothill Road, this road #40 is 2.89 miles in length and is located in Township 1N R39E Section 16 in the Elgin maintenance district. As you climb in elevation, there are some gorgeous views of Indian Valley surrounding Elgin. Its foothills and beauty have attracted about 40 families to reside on this road.

Due to the fact that there could only be one Foothill Road in Union County under the new county road naming ordinance of 1988, this road was given its new and lovely name Valley View, which much better describes its scenic value.

Before the county roads were sorted out in 1988, there were several Foothill Roads, leading to some confusion for emergency services. Consequently, today there is only one Foothill Road in the county, and it begins off 20th Street in La Grande, running south to connect up with Interstate 84.

Viewpoint Lane - This private lane travels through Township 6S R38E Section 23 in the North Powder district.

WAAS Road - This road #233 is located off Airport Road southeast of La Grande. It runs an eighth of a mile in length and is located in Township 3S R38E Section 24 in the La Grande maintenance district. It's named after WAAS avionics, and it's the only county road with an acronymic name.

"The Wide Area Augmentation System (WAAS) is a satellite technology that has become essential in making air travel safer and more efficient for both private and commercial travelers. WAAS represents an enormous leap forward in air navigation. When it was first activated on July 10, 2003, WAAS allowed pilots for the first time to rely on the Global Positioning System (GPS) as a primary means of navigation. That means that pilots can use WAAS alone to navigate and land, in most instances. It is important that pilots have as accurate information as possible when landing; WAAS collects, processes, and corrects the GPS information to ensure that the data the pilot receives can be trusted." *(FAA.gov website)*

Wade Road - This private road is located in Township 3S R40E Section 23 in the Union maintenance district. It is about one mile east of Cove and is a continuance of Haefer Lane. It goes in two directions, dead-ending at each one.

It is named after Richard J. Wade, born July 9, 1855 in Rochester, New York. He came to Oregon at the age of 22 years. His wife was Margaret M. Cullen, possibly born 1857 and married in Walla Walla on December 2, 1892. They then made their home in Cove, Oregon, where they became strawberry growers. *(La Grande Observer, June 10, 1913, pg. 8)*

Their daughter married in 1917 a Mr. Baudoin of Joseph. *(La Grande Observer, May 2, 1917, pg. 8)* In April 1930, their house burned down, and they decided to rebuild. *(La Grande Observer, Aug. 7, 1930, pg. 6)* In the *September 4, 1930, issue of the La Grande Observer, pg. 9,* the Wades built a Madison-style home, which is ready cut in pieces like a kit home, and the owner assembles it.

In 1931, Richard Wade and ex-governor Walter Pierce attended an annual dairy co-op meeting. *(La Grande Observer, May 19, 1931, pg. 2)* Wade also had a saw mill below his home on Mill Creek. *(La Grande Observer, June, 11, 1931, pg. 4)*

Not long after that the Wades moved to Baker City, where Richard died on October 4, 1932. *(La Grande Observer, Oct. 5, 1932, pg. 1)*

Margaret relocated to Elgin and died there March 7, 1940. *(La Grande Observer, March 8, 1940, pg. 1)* Both are buried in Hillcrest East Cemetery in La Grande.

Wagoner Hill Lane - This road #17A is 1.08 miles long and runs west of Summerville off of Hunter Road in Township 1S R38E Section 9-16 in the Imbler maintenance district. It is named after James Wagoner (1911-2003), who came to this area as a young man.

According to his obituary printed in the La Grande Observer online, it read in part:

James Wagoner, age 92, of Summerville died Friday, November 14, 2003 at his home. A graveside service was held at 2:00 p.m. Tuesday, November 18, 2003 at the Summerville Cemetery.

Mr. Wagoner was born on October 6, 1911 to Henry C. and Rebecca E. Wagoner in Unicoi, Tennessee. He came to the Grande Ronde Valley as a young man and married Leva Lockie Street. After her death in 1945, he married Essie May White on September 17, 1949 in Weiser, Idaho.

Essie died at her home on that road on April 14, 2016 at the age of 92 years. A funeral service was held at the Summerville Cemetery Chapel, and a social gathering followed at the Odd Fellows Hall in Summerville.

Essie was born May 26, 1923 in Henryetta, Oklahoma to Mack and Elva (Cox) White. When she was 7 years old, she and her parents moved to Oregon. They resided in Perry and La Grande. She attended Greenwood Elementary School and graduated from La Grande High School.

She married James Wagoner in 1949, and they remained together until James passed away in 2003 at the age of 92. For the past 67 years, she lived on Wagoner Hill three miles northwest of Summerville, Oregon.

Essie and James had 10 children that grew up in Summerville and attended school in Imbler, Oregon. A lot of the Wagoner kids worked for Imbler farmer Bill Howell. *(Bill Howell interview, May 20, 2018)*

Wallsinger Road - Originally called Ingle Road, this gravel county road #79A is 1.52 miles in length and is located in Township 2S R39E Section 19 in the La Grande maintenance district.

Ingle Road was named after Dr. Joseph Lombard Ingle, who owned property on this road. After graduating from La Grande High School, he went to Los Angeles, California where he completed a 4-year medical course at the College of Osteopathic Physicians and Surgeons. *(La Grande Observer, July 12, 1915, pg. 1)*

Shortly after returning to La Grande, he went to Portland where he successfully passed the examinations of the Oregon State Board of Medical Examiners. He took over the practice of Dr. Ralston in La Grande at the new Foley building. *(La Grande Observer, Sept. 14, 1915, pg. 8)*

Dr. Ingle wasted no time in advertising his practice in the La Grande Observer as it appeared two days after taking over the practice. It wasn't long until the public learned of some exciting changes in the Ingle family following his marriage on September 30, 1915. His advertisement in the paper indicates a novel partnership.

OSTEOPATHIC PHYSICIANS
DR. J. L. INGLE — Osteopathic physician. Dr. Margaret Ingle, Diseases of women: care and feeding of children. Offices rooms 37-38-39, New Foley Building. Office hours: 10-12 a.m.; 2-5p.m. and by appointment. Office phone: Red 3181; Residence phone: Red 601.

Dr. Margaret Catherine (Ransome) Ingle was born June 16, 1892 in Illinois. She was mother to two children, Stella Jean and Mary Marjorie. She died May 20, 1978 in La Grande.

Dr. Joseph L. Ingle was born June 13, 1891 in Wisconsin. He moved La Grande in 1901 with his widowed mother, Stella J. (Nason) Ingle and younger brother, Clayton Nason Ingle, who was born August 1, 1899. Clayton died in Germany in 1953 while in the military.

Stella Ingle was born June 11, 1867 in Nasonville, Wisconsin, and married Joseph S. Ingle on September 24, 1890 in Wood County, Wisconsin. Her husband died in 1900 before the June 20th census was taken.

Stella died on Saturday, November 14, 1953 in La Grande and was buried in Hillcrest Cemetery. She passed away in a local hospital, and her obituary stated her death was the result of a fall down a flight of stairs in her home on October 23, 1953. She received a fractured arm, spine and internal injuries from which she finally died, the account read. She was 86 years of age at the time of her death.

Stella was an educated woman, who opened the first kindergarten in La Grande in 1902, and from 1906 until 1937, she taught first grade at the La Grande Central School.

"She was a member of the original Neighborhood Club committee, which was active in getting a grant from the Carnegie Foundation for the public library in La Grande. She served as president of the library board and as a member for many years.

Mrs. Ingle was the author of several plays in verse for primary children. She wrote the words for one of the neighborhood club songs and for a pioneer song used in the public schools. She appeared many times on the program of the Oregon State Teachers Association, Eastern Division, and in 1913 was the first woman to be elected president of that association.

Mrs. Ingle was an honorary member of Zeta Chapter, Delta Kappa Gamma, a charter member of the American Legion Auxiliary, a member of Chapter 1, PEO, Hope chapter, Order of the Eastern Star, and a member of the Neighborhood Club for 52 years." (Excerpt of obit) *(La Grande Observer, Nov. 16, 1953, pg. 1)*

The name Wallsinger replaced Ingle in 1988 when the county was renaming roads with historic pioneer names wherever possible. Dale Case of Cove, who currently owns the Wallsinger home on this road, nominated Wallsinger as the road name. He told the authors that he recommended their name because they had lived many years on that road, whereas Ingle was property owner but not a resident. The county accepted his recommendation and Wallsinger Road was established.

Pioneer settlers, John Quincy and Eliza (Woodell) Wallsinger, who along with Eliza's father, James E. Woodell and four brothers left Bladensburg, Wapello County, Iowa and migrated to Oregon to homestead.

Factors that led them to Oregon included the Homestead Act of 1862 and the developing Civil War, which father Woodell did not want any part of. His two older sons wanted to pursue the homesteading opportunities in the Willamette Valley, so the family prepared to make the six-month journey in two wagons with six big yoke of oxen and four milk cows.

Numbered among the sojourners were the widowed father, James E. Woodell and sons: William, 21, Joseph, 19, James L., 13, Junius "Doon", 9; a married daughter Eliza and her husband John Quincy Wallsinger and their children Maggie, 4, and "Sallie," 3 weeks. According to a well-developed family tree on Ancestry.com, this Sallie is actually Sarah Florence (Wallsinger) Shafer (1862-1886).

Friends urged Eliza Wallsinger not to leave with such a young infant, reasoning that the baby would not survive the deprivations and sicknesses that they heard threaten such a journey, but Eliza was determined to leave with her family.

As it was, there was plenty of sadness felt when Eliza left behind her beloved sister Mrs. William (Mary Margaret) German, who occupied the family homestead. Incidentally, Mary Margaret German and her husband eventually did migrate to Oregon and they resided in Portland. Eliza had such a close bond with her sister that Eliza named her first daughter Mary Margaret "Maggie" Wallsinger.

In preparation for the trip, Mary Margaret German helped Eliza Wallsinger make homemade clothing, linsey spun and woven from flax. They also baked loaves of bread, dozens of cookies and made jars of jam. At first it seemed like there was plenty, but quickly their provisions and baked goods were eaten up. Eliza was described as a "frail little woman" and yet she labored as camp cook and clothes washer for the entire six-month journey.

"You can imagine that with Eliza being the only woman in the Woodell party, she had a lot of work to do cooking and washing on the Oregon Trail for all those men in addition to taking care of her babies," said family historian Jean Masse of Imbler. *(Jean Masse interview, September 2000)*

Under the first spring wagon's white canvas cover, two decks of necessities were tightly packed. The lower deck held necessary provisions such as many sides of bacon, bins of flour and sugar, paraffin-sealed Peoria Pottery jars filled with apple butter and prune butter. They also packed grain and corn seed for spring planting and a few Midwestern flower seeds to remind them of home. All of these things were on the lower deck for easy access, whereas household furnishings such as rolled bedding and some equipment were packed on the upper deck.

"We still have the flour bin that they brought with them on the trail and a pottery jar that I think is from that era too," said Masse.

Behind the spring wagon was the second Woodell wagon, a cargo wagon carrying Eliza, Maggie and infant Sallie. This wagon was pulled by six yoke of oxen in the wheel and four milk cows in the lead. Bedding was spread out on the upper deck of the wagon so that Eliza and the girls could rest conveniently during the trip. Eliza's father, James E. Woodell, walked alongside the wheel oxen and drove them with his long whip.

At the head, walked John Wallsinger, a tall, energetic and physically fit man. It seemed he never tired of walking and his good sense of direction was an asset to the party as he acted as scout for the train, walking several miles ahead of it looking for a water source for their night camp. Most noon camps sites did not provide water, but after a long, hot and dusty day of traveling, it was a necessity to find water in the evening for washing, watering animals and cooking.

As they traveled, they were joined by other wagons until they had about 30-35 wagons. In eastern Utah, they were getting into hostile Indian country. Since there was safety in numbers, more wagons joined in the train and Mr. Manville was chosen as captain. He had traveled the Oregon Trail twice before and was esteemed by all to be a very capable man. Everyone on the train respected him, and his word was law.

When the train reached the Grande Ronde Valley about September 12, 1862, they stopped for a rest. The Manville train was going to continue on to the Willamette Valley, but the Woodells and Wallsingers were tired, and it was late in the year. The trip across the bleak sagebrush wilderness between Boise and Ladd Canyon was discouraging, and the Grande Ronde Valley seemed like a lush oasis in comparison.

"To see such contrasting grasslands in the valley was like heaven to them," said Masse.

Consequently, the Woodell-Wallsinger wagons departed from the Manville train, and they wintered in Union County. Though they intended to start westward again in the spring, they didn't feel the need because they were very satisfied in Union County.

John Quincy Wallsinger was born October 17, 1835 in Scioto County, Ohio to a farmer named John Wallsinger Sr. (1810-1869) and his wife Sarah Clifford (1803-1860). He married Eliza Woodell on June 28, 1857 in Wapello, Iowa. They made their home in Buffalo County, Iowa and then met up with father Woodell and sons in Wapello County, Iowa. From there they left to come to Oregon in 1862. *(Findagrave, Eliza Wallsinger bio)*

Upon arriving in Union County, they made their immediate residence 3 miles northwest of Summerville, but by 1870, they had relocated to a farm 4 miles south of Summerville on the Sand Ridge, where John Q. Wallsinger lived the remainder of his life. *(Biography of William T. Wallsinger)* In the *1880 Federal Census*, John Q. Wallsinger's occupation was described as a music teacher.

John and Eliza Wallsinger had a large family of children: Mary Margaret (1858-1936) and Sarah F (1862-1886), both born in Iowa; and the following born in Union County, Oregon: Martha Jane "Jennie" Moss (1864-1949), Anna A. (1866-1879), Lucy Catherine Woods (1868-1957), William Thomas (1870-1943), Cynthie E. (1872-1878), Bertha May (1877-1941), Marshall Everett, (1881-1941) and Jesse H. (1884-1885).

Those that lived to adulthood were: Mrs. Mary Oliver, Mrs. Jennie Moss, Mrs. L. Catherine Woods, W. Tom Wallsinger, Miss Bertha Wallsinger, and M. Everett Wallsinger.

Following John Q. Wallsinger's death on July 25, 1897 in Summerville, he was laid to rest at the Summerville Cemetery. Eliza lived the remainder of her life between three last residences: first with daughter Lucy and son-in-law Joseph Woods, then with her unmarried daughter Bertha Wallsinger at 1404 9th Street in La Grande and lastly with her eldest daughter Mrs. Mary Oliver of Portland, Oregon.

Eliza Woodell was born in Virginia on June 3, 1841. At age 5 she came with her parents to the state of Iowa where she met and married John Q. Wallsinger and then migrated west with him and their two children. She lived almost all of her adult life in Union County, Oregon.

Eliza died in Portland with her surviving children present on March 20, 1913 at 72 years, 9 months and 20 days of age. Her remains were brought back to Union County and laid in wake at the home of Miss Bertha Wallsinger on 9th Street in La Grande. Her obituary stated, "Her remains were laid to rest in Summerville cemetery, there to await the resurrection day." *(Findagrave.com)*

Annually, the Woodell-Wallsingers gathered for a reunion at the Riverside Park in La Grande. Their respective road signs will memorialize these two early pioneer families, who were industrious families in the Grande Ronde Valley.

Waltz Loop - This section of road is about .21 miles in length, and it's a public unmaintained road located in Township 3S R38E Section 16 in the Union maintenance district. It leaves Chadwick Lane northwest of the city of Cove.

It's name was originally suggested by John C. Courtney, who sub-divided lot 4 of Cove Orchards Tract Addition in 2000.

However, since there already existed a road named Courtney Lane two miles north of Imbler, the Courtney Loop road had to be renamed. Consequently, John C. Courtney named it after his mother Elizabeth J. "Betty" Waltz. The Waltz family settled in Baker County before 1900 and were a railroad family.

Betty Waltz married Burl Elmer Courtney on December 23, 1940 in Weiser, Idaho, and moved to La Grande. Betty and Burl both military careers.

Wapiti Lane - This private lane is in Township 3S R40E Section 15 and exits off of Love Road near Cove. Wapiti means "elk" in the Algonquian languages.

One online source states this: "Wapiti as a word dates back to about the 19th century. Like the word moose, wapiti is an Americanization of a First Nation's word. It comes from waapiti. Waapiti, in turn, came from the word wap meaning white. Wap referred to the white tail and rump characteristic of the wapiti. The words moose and waapiti actually have similar origins: the Algonquian languages. Waapiti was used by both the Shawnee people and the Cree nation."

Watson Street - This is one of few county roads called a street on the county listing, and it is four blocks in length, being located in Township 3S R38E Section 4. It is a public, unmaintained road in the La Grande maintenance district.

To be clear, this is not named after Sherlock Holmes' best friend, Dr. Watson, but it is named after Joseph Franklin Watson and his wife Mary (Whalley) Watson. Information was sparse about them, but they lived in the Portland area prior to 1880. It is not known how or when they acquired their property in what became La Grande, Oregon because at the time it was outside the city limits.

However, when the Home Investment addition to the city of La Grande was platted on May 31, 1904, the name Watson appears on one of the streets. That street was on the west border of the Watson property. At some point they extended that street across Island Avenue and past May Lane. Later the southern part of the street was renamed 21st Street, and the northern part was left as Watson Street.

Weaver Lane - This road #67 is 1.17 miles in length and located in Township 4S R39E Section 12 in the Union maintenance district. The lane runs parallel with Hwy 237 and leads to the city of Union.

It is named after John B. Weaver, a native of Illinois. He was born September 18, 1864 in Sterling, Illinois, the son of Benjamin Snavely Weaver and Barbara Rebecca Book. Both parents died in Illinois and did not migrate to Oregon.

John B. Weaver and Mina E. Eyster were married in Whiteside, Illinois on September 5, 1889. They had six children: John, Earl, Horace, Fred, Miss Alice Weaver, and Mrs. Gertrude Osburn.

Apparently, the family came to Union County just prior to 1898 because in the *La Grande Observer of January 3, 1898, pg. 3* it noted that J. B. Weaver purchased a small farm from the Ames estate.

In 1903, Weaver was the proprietor of Union Nurseries. To prepare for orders already placed for the 1904 season, he planted about 40,000 apple trees and 10,000 cherry trees for resale. He remarked in a newspaper article that the way orders were coming in, he may not have enough to carry him through the season. *(La Grande Observer, Feb. 19, 1904)*

Apparently by 1912, some of Weaver's sons were involved with the business because a newspaper advertisement listed that J. B. Weaver & Sons had a variety of roses, fruit and shade trees for sale. *(La Grande Observer, Feb. 23, 1912, pg. 6)*

Sadly, a blow came to the family when John B. Weaver was notified that his son Fred was kicked by a horse at Mount Vernon, Washington and died about May 18, 1914 as a result. In time, the other Weaver sons moved away from the valley to pursue their own lives and ambitions.

His son, John, moved to Spokane, Washington and later became Dr. John Weaver, president of Pacific Union College, Angwin, California. Horace moved to College Place, Washington, and Earl moved to Buffalo, New York. Alice remained single and lived in Portland and Gertrude Osburn lived in Baker City, and by 1951 she was in Salem.

John B. Weaver expanded his nursery to having a producing orchard because in 1927, he was going to ship about 5,000 boxes of apples. *(La Grande Observer, Nov. 8, 1927, pg. 3)*

By the next year, Weaver had diversified and was going to ship four or five carloads of spuds. *(La Grande Observer, March 16, 1928, pg. 7)*

In 1946, the newspaper noted that Weaver was the second man to have faith in the commercial value of a prune orchard in the valley. *(La Grande Observer, Sept. 18, 1946, pg. 2)*

During his life, Weaver was the president of Eastern Oregon Fruit Growers Association for several terms, according to his obituary.

John and Mina moved to Portland to live with their daughter, Miss Alice Weaver, about 1945. This is where John, 84, died on May 25, 1949; and Mina, 84, died on November 29, 1950. They were buried in Lincoln Memorial Park in Portland.

Webster Road - This gravel road #16 runs 3.53 miles in Township 2S R38E Sections 11-12 in the

La Grande maintenance district. The road is unusual in that it runs north-south and east-west, and it is located on the Sand Ridge.

The road is named after William Martin Schuyler Webster and his descendants. He was born on November 17, 1872 in Iowa and died in Union County, Oregon on July 3, 1925 at the age of 54 years, 7 months and 16 days. *(Findagrave.com; Lawson Webster's birth certificate; obit La Grande Observer, July 8, 1925, pg 5.)*

He came to this valley about 1895 and remained a resident here for about 30 years. On May 27, 1901, he married Johannah "Hannah" Van Blokland.

Her father, John Van Blokland, brought the family over to Oregon on the Oliver Train that left Iowa on May 10, 1864 and arrived to the Grande Ronde Valley on October 10, 1864. The train encountered some trouble with the Indians along the way, and they lost a lot of their stock. The Van Bloklands were left with one ox and one mule to pull their wagon as a result. *(Bernal Hug's History of Union County, Oregon, pg. 53-54)*

When William arrived to the valley, he served as a deputy sheriff for his brother Wesley Webster. Then he went to work as a bridge foreman for the railroad. William also was involved in the building of the bridge near Orodell just to the west of La Grande.

William got into farming when his father-in-law, John Van Blokland, gave him 160 acres with a homestead house on it that John acquired from a single Dutchman by the name of Henry Booker. Booker came to Union County with high hopes, started working his homestead, but without the prospect of a wife, he grew lonely and returned to The Netherlands. *(Union County Oregon History Project, Webster oral history)*

William and Hannah lived on their ranch on Webster Road on the Sand Ridge and built a new home in 1916. William died in 1925 of cancer. Hannah continued living on the ranch until her death on January 12, 1943. William and Hannah Webster rest in peace at the Island City Cemetery.

During their marriage, they became parents to two sons, Lawson and Carl; and three daughters, Ina Mae, Mildred and Lilly Bell. A sixth child died from diphtheria.

Lawson Arthur Webster was born June 19, 1903 and died July 3, 1989. He lived on the family ranch and was a landowner noted on the *1935 Metsker Map* on this road.

He married Goldie Belle Redman on October 27, 1926, and after a 2-week honeymoon to California and Idaho, they made their home at the Webster ranch 15 miles west of Alicel. *(La Grande Observer, October 28, 1926, pg. 3)*

Goldie was born July 13, 1906, and she died March 12, 1997. She and Lawson had one child, a son, Gary Lawson, who was born November 19, 1934 on the family ranch on Webster Road. He attended Iowa School, a one room school house, then Imbler and Greenwood Elementary schools before attending La Grande High School.

Gary married Bernice Mae Howard on September 4, 1955, and they had two daughters, Victoria Lane and Stacia Jo. Bernice and Gary met at La Grande High School where they graduated in 1952.

Gary enrolled at Eastern Oregon College and Bernice got a job at a shop in downtown La Grande. Gary received a bachelor's degree in general studies from college in 1956. He enjoyed history and liked to relate it to others.

He supported his family as a rancher-farmer at the family ranch on Webster Road. It was the life he knew and loved, passed down by tradition and following the lifestyle of his father and grandfather. He and Bernice shared 55 years together there. He died from cancer on September 5, 2010 at age 75 at his home. He was buried in Island City Cemetery. Bernice died on April 21, 2020 after a short battle with cancer. *(Source: obituary)*

Gary and Bernice's daughter Stacia Jo Webster continues to reside on the Webster ranch today.

West Road - This road #210A runs for .37 miles and is located in Township 3S R38E Section 4 in the La Grande maintenance district. Oddly this West Road travels east off of Riddle Road.

This was originally named West Avenue when the Middletown Addition was platted by J. L. Caviness and his wife, C. E. Caviness on April 18, 1894. The road name does make sense because when you look at the original plat, West Avenue was on the west side of the addition.

Wheeler Lane - This road #86 runs 1.38 miles in Township 2N R40E Section 23 in the Elgin maintenance district. It is located off Yarrington Road northeast of Elgin in the Cricket Flat territory.

It is named after Milton Jackson Wheeler (1836-1920) and his wife, Charlotte Harris (1856-1934).

Milton Wheeler was born on June 9, 1836 in Miami, Saline County, Missouri, the son of Samuel and Mary Ellen Wheeler, natives of Kentucky and Tennessee respectively. In the *1860 Federal Census*, he lived in his parents' household in Jefferson, Saline County, Missouri with his siblings: Mary J., 34, Clarinda, 32, Margarett A., 28, Cynthia, 26, Milton, 24 and Susan, 21.

He married Charlotte "Lottie" Harris on April 18, 1875 in Saline County, Missouri. She was born January 19, 1856 in Sullivan County, Missouri. In the *1880 Federal Census* Milton and Charlotte were recorded as a married couple living in Carroll County, Missouri. They lived with Charlotte's brother, where Milton was a farm laborer.

According to the General Land Office records for Union County, Oregon, Milton bought land in 1894 on what later became Wheeler Lane. In the *1900 Federal Census* he was renting his home, but on the *February 10, 1920 Federal Census*, Milton, 83, owned his home free and clear. He died February 29, 1920 in Elgin, Oregon. Charlotte died on March 6, 1934. They are both interred in the Mount Pleasant Cemetery on Yarrington Road.

During their marriage, they moved to various states, including Hunt County, Texas, where their son, Joe E. Wheeler was born on February 19, 1881.

Joseph Wheeler married Alta M. Stowe, who was born in 1883 in Manti, Utah. They were married on June 10, 1908, and they made their residence on Wheeler Lane. Joseph died in February of 1970; Alta died on August 31, 1955. Both are interred in the Elgin Cemetery.

During their marriage, they had three children Anoma, Halstead, and Joseph Jr. He was born June

29, 1919 in the Elgin area, and he married Joy Dailey on May 27, 1954. "I got out of high school, got married, and moved out to the homestead, where I still reside," Joy said. *(Joy Dailey Wheeler interview, age 82, September 27, 2018)*

Joe died November 8, 1990, and his cremains were given to the family. Joy and their oldest daughter, Carrie Gerber, still live on the Wheeler property in 2018.

White Horse Road - This road is not on the county road list, but it exits from the Grande Ronde River Road by Starkey. The road closely follows White Horse Creek. On topographical maps it is written as Whitehorse Creek, and it meanders through the mountains heading toward Wallowa Whitman National Forest. It is a tributary to the Grande Ronde River. The Oregon Geographic Names book offers no explanation for the White Horse Creek name, but it may have a Native American origin.

Wickens Lane - Formerly Wickens-Rysdam Road, it is county road #143 and is 2.24 miles in length in Township 2N R40E Section 34 in the Elgin maintenance district.

The Wickens-Rysdam Road connects Good Road to Yarrington Road. Later, the name Rysdam was dropped, and the road became Wickens Lane.

According to the *1935 Metsker Map*, there were several parcels along this road labeled J. H. Wickens Estate. Long-time Cricket Flat resident, Dick Good, said that Wickens Lane was named after James Henry Wickens. In 1899, 32-year-old James purchased 160 acres of land on what became known as Wickens Lane on Cricket Flat. *(Dick Good interview, April 2001)*

James Henry Wickens (1867-1922) was the son of an Englishman named William Wickens and Sarah Ann Kimber, who were married on December 23, 1853 in Shinfield, Berkshire, England. William and Sarah Wickens and their children: William W., John Thomas and Rosetta emigrated to America in 1862.

They initially settled in Utah, where two more children were born, Flora A. Wickens and James Henry Wickens. James Henry Wickens was born August 21, 1867 in Cache County, Utah. Then the father, William Wickens died in 1869 at the age of 39 years.

His widow, Sarah Wickens married John Hill, and they had two children of their own: Sarah H. (b. 1872) and Walter L. Hill, born in Utah. The blended family arrived to Cricket Flat in time for the *1880 Federal Census*. John Hill was a farmer on Cricket Flat.

The *1880 Federal Census* shows five Wickens children living with their mother and step-father, John Hill. The family included: John Hill, 38, wife Sarah (Kimber) (Wickens) Hill, 42, and children: William W. Wickens, John T. Wickens, Rosetta Wickens, all born in England; Flora Ann Wickens and James Henry Wickens, both born in Utah. Also on the census were two Hill children: Sarah H. Hill and Walter L. Hill.

Sarah died on February 18, 1887 and was interred at the Highland Cemetery.

James Henry Wickens married Mary Isabell Cunningham (1882-1967) on November 16, 1898. They had the following children together: their first child, Rosie Ann Wickens, was born August 17, 1899, and she died young on March 11, 1910. Following her birth were William Henry (1901-1953), John Ray (1902-1976), James Lloyd (1905-1982), Jesse Albert (1906-1922), and Sara Frances Wickens (1908-1993).

In the *1900 Federal Census*, siblings John, William and Flora lived together in a household they shared that was separate from their mother's home.

Also listed on that census on a separate farm was James H. Wickens and his wife, Mary Isabell and their daughter Rose Ann, born August 1899.

The *1910 Federal Census* showed James H. Wickens, Mary I. and children: William H., John R., James L., Jesse E., and Sarah F.   Mary I. Wickens' mother, Lucy A. Cunningham was also living with them. Daughter Rose Ann died in 1910 before the census was taken. A very similar profile of the family could be found in the *1920 Federal Census*.

James supported his family as a farmer, and he owned his farm on Wickens Lane. In the *1920 Federal Census*, James and his family were still residing at the same farm, and all the children were still at home. The census noted that his eldest son, William Henry, helped out on the farm.

James Henry Wickens died October 28, 1922 and was interred at Highland Cemetery on Good Road on Cricket Flat.

In the *1930 and 1940 Federal Censuses*, Mary I. Wickens, a widow, was living in the household of her eldest son, William Henry Wickens, who was apparently farming the homestead farm. Mary Isabell Wickens died June 2, 1967.

James Henry Wickens was buried at Highland Cemetery with other relatives listed below:

Sarah (Kimber) Wickens	b. Oct. 22, 1834, England; d. Feb. 18, 1887
William W. Wickens	b. June 19, 1854; d. Dec. 14, 1907
John Thomas Wickens	b. Aug. 17, 1856; d. Oct. 16, 1920
Rosetta Wickens	b. Dec. 4, 1861; d. Jan. 5, 1882
Flora Ann Wickens	b. Aug. 4, 1864; d. Sept. 18, 1900
James Henry Wickens	b. Aug. 21, 1867; d. Oct. 28, 1922.
Mary Elsie Wickens	b. May 31, 1873; d. May 1, 1953 w/o John Thomas Wickens
John H. Wickens	b. May 21, 1910; d. March 27, 1966
William Henry Wickens	b.1901; d. 1953
Johnnie Ray Wickens	b. Oct. 16, 1902; d. June 14, 1976
Jesse A. Wickens	b. Nov. 25, 1906; d. Oct. 16, 1922
John Hill	d. 1909 @ 72 years, 2nd husband of Sarah Wickens

As for the Rysdam part of this road name, the *1935 Metsker Map* indicates that four Rysdam family members owned land along this road. The patriarch Arie Rysdam and his firstborn, William Henry Rysdam had the smallest parcels of land. Whereas Arie's younger sons, Albert and John "Egedius" Rysdam owned the larger parcels of land on this road.

Their story begins with Arie Rysdam, an early pioneer to Oregon from Marion County, Iowa. He was born August 23, 1849 to Gerrit and Magdalene (van Velzen) Rysdam. The parents were born, raised and married in The Netherlands, and they came to America in 1847 and settled initially in Marion County, Iowa.

Gerrit and Magdalene purchased their Iowa farm for $1.25 an acre under the Preemption Act of 1841, and they lived there until 1864, when the family planned to claim a homestead in Oregon under the Homestead Act of 1862. The father, two daughters and one son were going to leave with a wagon train first, and the mother would follow afterward, but in 1867, she fell ill and died, so she never joined them as planned.

The father and children's journey over the Oregon Trail involved their packed wagon and a mule team to pull it. Arie was 14 going on 15 years of age when they started their overland journey to Oregon.

"Gerrit and Arie began the journey with a team of mules which were stolen by Indians near Deer Creek Station on the North Platte River in Nebraska. The train stayed at Deer Creek until such time as Gerrit was able to purchase a team of oxen and a team of cows." *(Gerrit, a Dutchman in Oregon, Tony Rysdam-Shorre, 1985, pg 173-174)*

When they reached Union County, they immediately settled in the Island City precinct at first. This is where Gerrit Rysdam, 75, died in 1880. His son Arie was raised at home and educated at the schools common there at that time. Upon reaching manhood, he began farming and did so for several years, while also working as a freight driver for John Creighton.

Arie customarily drove a ten-mule team, bringing supplies from the Umatilla Landing to the mining camps in different parts of Idaho and Harney County, Oregon. Freighting like this paid a good wage and many pioneer men did this to earn enough to purchase farm land and settle down. Freighting was a means to an end until the train came in and modernized freighting.

In 1882, Arie filed on a homestead on Cricket Flat, about eight miles northeast of Elgin. The land had meadows for grazing, fields to plant grains, and timber to harvest the wood needed to build a house and outbuildings. He had earned enough to homestead 800 acres of land on the flat, and this is where he stayed for the next 26 years. His sons helped him operate the farm, and they took over the operation by 1909, when Arie retired to the city of Elgin.

The father, Arie Albert Rysdam Sr. (1849-1922) was married to Louisa Ball (Cruikshank) Rysdam (1851-1936). After Arie Rysdam Sr. died in 1922, his sons continued as land owners on this road. In 2022, Norma Rysdam owns land on Wickens Lane, but lives on Yarrington Road. Whereas, Larry Rex and Janice L. (Rysdam) Thompson reside on Wickens Lane.

Wilkinson Lane - This county road #115 is 1.52 miles long and travels through Township 3S R39E Section 28 in the Union maintenance district. This lane leaves Peach Road and connects to Hawkins Road about 6.5 miles from the city of Union.

On the *1935 Metsker Map #40*, the lane is located in Township 3S T39E, Section 28, where Jacob "Jake" Henry Wilkinson was a landowner in that section. He was the son of Thomas Wilkinson (1837-1922) and the grandson of Union County pioneers Jacob Sr. (1807-1893) and Matilda (Cox) Wilkinson (1808-1893).

His grandparents, Jacob and Matilda, were both born in Ohio, and after their marriage, they settled in Jackson County, Ohio. They had ten children: Polly Ann, Jacob, Nancy and William, all born in Ohio; Thomas and John, born in Peoria, Illinois; Andrew and Merritt, born in Cedar, Missouri; and Joseph and Eliza, born in Illinois. *(Ancestry.com)*

Obviously, the family moved around a bit from Ohio to Illinois to Cedar County, Missouri (1841-1848), then back to Illinois and finally settling in Salem, Richardson County, Nebraska (1859-1863).

In 1863, according to the record, they went to the mouth of the Platte River, and the following spring on May 9, 1864, the Wilkinsons started across the Oregon Trail, arriving in Union County, Oregon five months later on October 9, 1864. Jacob settled on his homestead located seven miles east from Union in High Valley.

There, they were listed on the *1870 Federal Census:* Jacob Sr. and Matilda Wilkinson and the six younger children of their ten, including Thomas, John, Andrew, Merritt, Joseph and Eliza, the latter listed as 17 years old. They all lived together and were farming in Union County.

In 1893, sorrow struck the family twice in one year when the family matriarch, Matilda Wilkinson died January 5, 1893 followed by her husband Jacob Wilkinson Sr. on November 11, 1893. *(An Illustrated History of Union and Wallowa counties, 1902, pg. 321-322)*

Two years prior in 1891, Jacob and Matilda sold their homestead property to their son, Thomas Wilkinson, and he made that his residence for the remainder of his life.

Thomas Wilkinson, was born on January 24, 1837 in Peoria, Illinois. On November 27, 1879, in Union County, he married Lydia A. Rundall, and during their marriage, they had four children: Jacob Henry, Matilda Ann, Mary Etta, and Philip Edgar.

During Thomas' life, he engaged in several enterprises, including grain, hay and orchard farming, as well as stock raising with his brother Merritt.

When Thomas finally retired, he turned the farming over to his children. His obituary stated that he was an honorable, upright citizen, a kind father, a good friend and neighbor, always aspiring to live by the Golden Rule.

Thomas Wilkinson died Thursday, March 23, 1922, age 85 years and 27 days. There was a 1 p.m. graveside service held on March 25, at the Union cemetery where he was interred next to his wife, Lydia, who had died January 13, 1918. *(Obituaries and Other Vital Records of Union County, Oregon. 1890–1930, Access Genealogy)*

The Wilkinson Ranch in High Valley was auction off on November 7, 1918 to the highest bidder.

The subject of this narrative is Thomas' son, Jacob Henry Wilkinson, who lived on Wilkinson Lane northwest of Hot Lake.

Jacob was born July 27, 1885 in Union, Oregon and named after his grandfather, but he went by "Jake". *(Sherman Hawkins interview, March 15, 2019)* Jake married Miss Gladys M. Dennison on

January 1, 1913 in Union by Justice of the Peace Williams. *(La Grande Observer, Jan. 2, 1913, pg. 5)* Gladys' mother was Mrs. A. M. Dennison of Freewater, Oregon.

During Jake and Gladys' marriage, they had three daughters: Irene, Eunice, and Ethel. *(1920 and 1930 Federal Censuses)* Jake became occupied in the dairy business on his farm north of Hot Lake.

In August 1928, Jake and Gladys were building another high grade dairy herd of Guernseys on his farm located northwest of Hot Lake. "The Wilkinsons were among the very first in the whole valley to believe in the Guernseys as suitable for this climate and purchased some of the very first Guernseys owned. They are building up their herd gradually and hope to some day have none but the highest grade animals. They are at present milking about 12 cows." *(La Grande Observer, Aug. 3, 1928, pg. 7)*

Along with this effort, "a second cutting of alfalfa was just completed and a good crop of a good quality of hay was reported. The Wilkinsons are firm believers in the dairy herd as one undertaking for profit in this county." *(La Grande Observer, Aug. 3, 1928, pg. 7)*

In 1932, Jake's family moved off the ranch to the city of Union. *(La Grande Observer, May 21, 1932, pg. 6)* He died October 25, 1972 in Baker City of Baker County, Oregon, and the home was eventually owned by their youngest son, Phillip "Edgar" Wilkinson (1894-1984). *(Ancestry.com)* There was a Wilkinson family reunion on October 14, 1934, according to the La Grande Observer of that date.

Willowdale Lane - This private lane is located in Township 4S R40E Section 7 in the North Powder maintenance district, and it runs east off of North 1ˢᵗ Street on the north edge of the City of Union and dead ends. It provides access to four residences.

Willowdale (Willow valley) is a descriptive name featuring the willow trees that grow abundantly on the land that is flooded each season from snow melt-off. Due to the moisture, willows like to grow alongside this lane. The county cuts them down to maintain the road but they are native to this area.

Due to the prevalence of willow trees/shrubs in this area, people have called this territory the Willowdale district of the city of Union as far back as 1918. In that year there was an Observer newspaper column titled "Willowdale News" and in that society column, the residents of this area were proposing to call the Hot Lake school in District No. 61 by the name Willowdale School. *(La Grande Observer, Jan. 22, 1918, pg. 4)*

The proposed name was adopted, and references to Willowdale district, school and community were all widely used since then by people in Union and the Hot Lake territory.

Consequently, the name Willowdale Lane was both historical and descriptive for the Union area residents.

Witherspoon Lane - This lane is nearly 2 miles in length and known as county road #58, located in 1N R40E Section 16 of the Elgin maintenance district.

It is located in a region called Cricket Flat east of Elgin and was named after its earliest settler, James

"Elvis" and Bertha Lieumender (Witty) Witherspoon. *(Judy Witherspoon interview, April 18, 2018)*

Elvis was born September 4, 1879 in Murray, Calloway County, Kentucky, the son of Daniel Rumsey Witherspoon (1828-1907) and Dora C. (Dunaway) Witherspoon. Elvis Witherspoon and Bertha Lieumender Witty (1883-1972) were married December 14, 1902 near Murray, Kentucky, and they moved to Oregon in 1904.

At first they lived in the Summerville area, but then moved to this road where they farmed. Incidentally, Bertha's brother, Clarence Witty is the man that the Elgin pocket park is named after following his tragic death in an apartment fire downtown on Eighth Avenue in Elgin.

Elvis and Bertha had six children: Jewel Marie (1903-1905); Perry Glascoe of Elgin (1905-2002); Mrs. Lois Cowan of Wallowa (1912-2006); Buford Lee of Irrigon, Oregon (1918-1984); Buren Dee of Elgin (1918-1991); and James Delbert of Downey and Ventura, California (1921-2012).

Elvis and Bertha celebrated their 60th wedding anniversary with some of their children and about 80 guests. *(La Grande Observer, December 19, 1962)* During their marriage, they belonged to the Cricket Flat grange hall and the Rock Wall grange hall. Elvis won a jelly making competition held at the Cricket Flat grange hall in 1942.

Elvis died Tuesday, April 25, 1967 at 87 years, 7 months and 21 days at a local hospital. Funeral arrangements were handled by the Crippin and Daniels Funeral Home in La Grande. He was buried at the Summerville Cemetery. *(La Grande Observer, April 26, 1967)* Bertha was born July 1, 1883, and she died February 4, 1972.

Wolf Creek Lane - This 8.66 mile long road #104 is located in Township 6S R39E Section 9 in the North Powder maintenance district.

Wolf Creek Lane is mentioned in the earliest of the La Grande Observer archives. dating back to 1897, and in those early years, it was common for newspapers to refer to rural communities as sections, "the Wolf Creek section" or even as an unofficial city called "Wolf Creek, Oregon."

In this Wolf Creek section there is a century ranch established in 1889, owned by Jack S. Wilson, 91, and he has lived his entire life there. He didn't think Wolf Creek was named after wolves in the area. "The only wolves back then would have been mistaken coyotes," said the cattle man. "Growing up I never saw wolves in this country at all."

With that possible explanation off the table, the authors searched for a pioneer settler by the name of Wolf, and there was one.

Wolf Creek and Wolf Creek Lane are named after a pioneer settler from Bavaria named Casper Wolf, who lived about three miles from the creek. According to his own handwritten signature, he spelled his name in its German form, Kaspar Wolf—the same way Wolf Creek is spelled.

Following his paper trail, it appears that Casper Wolf emigrated from Bavaria, Germany via the port of Antwerp, Belgium on a ship called the Jenny Lind, which arrived at the New York port on April 20, 1854. According to the passenger list, Casper Wolf, 49, was accompanied by his wife Mary, 42; and children: Irene Marie, 17, Margareth, 9, and Jacob, 5.

From there it appears that Casper may have settled in Dane County, Wisconsin, where there were well established German communities and where he later enlisted with the Wisconsin Volunteers in the Civil War.

Surviving that, he made his way west to the Yamhill, Oregon, where he claimed donation land (patent #6725) under the provisions of the Homestead Act of 1862. In addition to claiming donation land, he also purchased four more parcels of land. All of these transactions were done on May 1, 1866. Since he lived there in between censuses, it's difficult to relate anything about his wife and children.

The authors do know that he relocated to the North Powder, Oregon territory, where he was noted on the *1870 Federal Census of the Union, Oregon precinct.* He lived alone, then age 65, and without his spouse. It's possible that his wife didn't want to move anymore at her age.

Regardless, Casper Wolf relocated to Clover Creek Valley, near North Powder, buying four parcels of school land in 1871 for $400 and a fifth parcel for $75 in 1878 in Township 5S, R39E Sections 28, 29 and 32. He proceeded to farm that land for the next 13 years.

The *1880 Federal Census of North Powder precinct* showed that he was still farming these five parcels. His personal stats were mixed up on this census, stating he was 71 (75), born in 1809 (1805) in Bavaria. By this time, the census taker noted that he was single and living alone.

By 1884, he sold his land in this precinct and relocated to the city of Summerville, where he purchased two city lots. Lot #2 in block 14 cost him $25.00 and for lot #1 in block 14, he paid $260.00.

The third purchase in 1886 was lot #2, block 2 for $260.00. By the price of the lot, one can reasonably assume there was a structure on it, perhaps a business. This exact same lot in the *1888 Sanborn Map*, lot #2, block 2 was the site of a cobbler's shop.

At this point, Casper Wolf's paper trail in Union County disappears like a wolf into a dark forest. He was never one to let grass grow under his feet, so it's anyone's guess where he went next, but the authors did not find any burial site for him in Union County.

Regarding the Wolf Creek section near North Powder, its residents participated in the Wolf Creek grange hall, farming organizations, a school, and an American Sunday School.

Ron Roethler of La Grande recalled the days when that grange hall was a center for great entertainment. "There used to be a grange hall down below Wolf Creek reservoir, and that used to be a hot spot back in the 1930s and 1940s," he said. "They used to have dances there every other Saturday night."

The newspaper wrote about grange work that was taken up in the Wolf Creek section. "The farmers of the Wolf Creek district near North Powder have organized a Grange Patrons of Husbandry organization being effected on Wednesday with 31 charter members. J. E. Gilkerson was elected master, Mrs. Dorsie Standley, lecturer and J. A. Nice, secretary. W. R. Gekeler of La Grande did the organization work." *(La Grande Observer, February 12, 1921, pg 1)*

Regarding their school, the newspaper stated, "The progressive people of Wolf Creek are planning to build a new brick schoolhouse before another school year comes." The former schoolhouse building could not house more than one-half of the pupils attending the school, so the grange hall was being used as a school.

"The new building being planned will be a two-room brick building, and if the district keeps up its present growth, they will soon need three rooms. However, two rooms will do for the present," read the La Grande Observer article. The new building would be supported through bonds.

Interestingly, the article's author ended this news story with some editorial counsel to the Wolf Creek residents: "If Wolf Creek could see their way clear to join the North Powder school and send their children to the town school, it would be better for all concerned. The country school with two rooms and each teacher with four grades cannot hope to compete with the town school, where each teacher has only one grade and never over two." *(La Grande Observer, April 3, 1923, pg. 1)*

The Wolf Creek school did eventually join the North Powder public schools, and a school bus service helped the children get to and from school.

Today, Wolf Creek is also known for its Wolf Creek Reservoir, where people like to go and recreate. Though some visitors to this "lake" said it can be windy there and not exactly safe swimming for small children, it is agreed that it is a great site for boating, fishing and splashing around. *(Google, Wolf Creek Reservoir)*

Wood Road - Formerly Woodland Drive, this is a public unmaintained road in part of the Morgan Lake Estates and is one-half mile in length and breaks off of Morgan Lake Road. Its entire length runs through Township 3S R37E Section 13 in the La Grande maintenance district. There are six homes on this road, none of historic significance.

"My dad, Glenn Lester, named it that because it went through the woods," Russell Lester of La Grande said. Glenn Lester was instrumental in developing the Morgan Lake Estates subdivision. *(Russell Lester interview, October 16, 2021)*

Before it was subdivided, there were big fir trees on the property, but they got logged off. The property still has plenty of timber on it. *(Lanetta Paul interview, October 17, 2021)*

Wood Road is one that branches off of Morgan Lake Road, which was originally called Mill Canyon Road. Keep this in mind as you read the associated history below:

The name Wood Road aptly fits into the history of Mill Canyon Road (now Morgan Lake Road). A historical figure named "Mr. Woods, had the first flouring mill built in 1865 located at the mouth of Mill Canyon in south La Grande, the canyon taking its name from that early structure. The mill was of a stone burr type and was placed in operation sixty days after construction commenced. When completed it was capable of milling 25 barrels of flour a day. Mr. Woods sold the mill in 1866 to John R. Wilkinson, who, in turn, disposed of it in 1874 to Augustine I. Gangloff, who operated it for many years." *(La Grande Observer, Oct. 9, 1948, pg. 1)*

So whether Mr. Glenn Lester knew it or not, he picked an appropriately historic name for his road. It fit the general locality of the original flouring mill, and it honored a man, who founded the second industrial establishment in the history of La Grande.

Woodell Lane - This lane is registered as county road #134 and runs 4.24 miles east and west from Hunter Road at the foot of Mt. Emily and intersects with Highway 82 on its east end. It's located in Township 1S R39E Section 29 in the La Grande and Imbler maintenance districts.

It was first called Woodell-Ruckman Road because the oldest residents were James Lorenzo Woodell (1849-1931) and William Edward "Will" Ruckman (1867-1960).

William Ruckman and his wife, Elizabeth Elenor (Endicott) Ruckman, lived in the first white house, as one turns west off Highway 82 on Woodell Lane. They had a son, Harvey E. Ruckman (1896-1974) and two daughters Mary Opal (Ruckman) Hayes (1900-1998) and Hattie Wave (Ruckman) Friswold (1909-1989).

Daughter Mary Opal Ruckman married Ray Homer Hayes, after whom the intersecting road "Hays" was named, albeit misspelled today. Later the Ruckman name was dropped and Woodell Lane remained. *(Elwyn Bingaman letter, April 30, 2019)*

According to county records, the two story William E. Ruckman house was built in 1906 and its floor plan included a kitchen, dining room, living room, utility room, bathroom and four bedrooms. Today, the two-story home is occupied by Carl D. and Hattie Wave (Ruckman) Friswold's descendants, Scott and Deborah Friswold.

Woodell Lane was named after James Lorenzo Woodell, who was born in Bladensburg, Wapello County, Iowa on April 22, 1849. He arrived in Union County, Oregon across the Oregon Trail by ox team on September 12, 1862 when he was 13 years old.

He came with his widowed father James E. Woodell and siblings, William, 21, Joseph, 19, Junius, 9, and sister Eliza, her husband John Q. Wallsinger, and their children Maggie, 4, and 3-week-old Sarah called "Sallie." One sister, Mary Woodell German initially stayed behind in Iowa with her husband, William, but they later also came to Oregon, settling eventually in Portland. *(Supplement to History of Union County, Vol. 4; Ancestry.com)*

At age 17, James L. Woodell entered into the profitable freighting business for two years, and in 1868, he bought his first 160 acres of farm land for $200. In 1870, he built a barn on his property, and he acquired timberland three miles west of Summerville for his building purposes.

He was married on August 20, 1870 to Isabelle Murchison and their union produced nine children, four of whom died in 1876 in a diphtheria epidemic. Isabelle was born May 4, 1850 and died January 7, 1907 at age 56 years. James Lorenzo Woodell died on October 1, 1931 at age 82. He and his wife were both interred at the Summerville Cemetery.

Each of their surviving sons received a quarter section of land as inheritance, and son James Duncan Woodell received the homestead property.

James Duncan Woodell was born May 5, 1874 and became a 1895 graduate of Eastern Oregon College, formerly called O. B. Carper's School, which was a private high school with an emphasis on business education. *(Oregongenealogy.com; La Grande, a Unique Glimpse Into the Way it Was,*

"It was a private school conducted by Mr. O. B. Carper in La Grande from 1892 to 1898. This institution offered a complete curriculum particularly in the high school subjects. Many prominent residents of Grande Ronde Valley attended this school, and its graduates were accepted in any college or university." (Oregongenealogy.com)

As an adult, James Duncan Woodell became one of the earliest grass seed growers in the area, along with farmers, George Royes Sr. and Howard Wagner. Woodell was "one of the most prominent grain farmers in this county and one who is interested in farm relief for wheat growers." *(La Grande Observer, April 6, 1931 pg. 5)*

James Duncan Woodell died September 12, 1963 at 89 years of age. He had a daughter Pauline Howard and before her death, she set up a trust for her grandchildren that allowed the farm to be worked through leases.

The 1868 James Lorenzo Woodell farm received its Century Farm status with the Oregon Historical Society, and the homestead still stands in good shape at 64021 Woodell Lane.

Woodruff Lane - Formerly Keys-Woodruff Lane, this county road #113 runs 3 miles east of Hot Lake in Township 3S R40E Section 31 in the Union maintenance district. *(1980 Metsker Map)*

The Keys part of the road name originates with Arthur Harley Keys, who was born on September 18, 1901 in Oklahoma. *(WWII draft registration form)* He grew up in Oklahoma, and in the *1920 Federal Census* for Roland Township, Oklahoma he was listed as a farm laborer.

He was married September 19, 1923 to Alma Anna Mattes, who was born in 1903 in Merrell, Wisconsin. By 1930, they had moved to Baker City, Oregon and were raising three children, Lucille Kathleen, Arthur Jr. and Margaret Keys.

On October 15, 1932 Arthur married Ellen George, 22, in Baker City. She was born April 2, 1910 in Oregon. They had three additional children: a daughter Cleda Edwina; and two more sons Cody and Lynn.

In the *1930 Federal Census* in Baker City, Arthur was a delivery driver for a hardware store. Sometime between 1930-1935, he landed a job with the state highway department and moved closer to work, somewhere in the Fruitdale section of La Grande. He was also on the school board of directors for Willowdale School in the 1930s.

Around 1937, he moved his family to the Hot Lake area, where they were noted on the *1940 Federal Census*. The census stated that he was a farmer there in the Hot Lake precinct of Union County.

In April 1941 Ellen Keys was the school district clerk for Willowdale School District. In July 1941, there was an auction at the Arthur Keys' farm where he had milk cows. "Many of the milk cows were sold to buyers out of the state." *(La Grande Observer, July 7, 1941, pg. 1)*

After the auction of 1941, Keys placed an ad in the paper which read: "200 Ton Meadow Hay—has not been wet, with pasture. May be fed on ground, house accommodations. Art Keys, Hot Lake,

Oregon." *(La Grande Observer, Dec. 26, 1941, pg. 4)*

In 1944, the Keys family had a house fire that was reported in the newspaper.

"Hot Lake Ranch Home Destroyed by Evening Blaze—The farm home of Mr. and Mrs. Art Keys near Hot Lake was completely destroyed by fire of unknown origin which started under the back porch about 5:15 p.m. July 31."

The story continued, "The house, owned by Dr. A. J. Roth, was a modern story and a half log structure comprised of seven rooms and bath. Keys, who is recovering from a broken leg which he suffered earlier in the month while baling hay, was alone in the house with some of the small children when the fire occurred, and before help could be obtained, the fire was beyond control.

The hired men and older boy were in the hay field and Mrs. Keys and two of the other children were at the barn milking and did not see the conflagration start.

The Keys family was taken to Hot Lake by Dr. Roth. They will remain there until living quarters can be established at the ranch. The house and contents were partially covered by insurance." (End of article)

In 1947, the Keys family relocated to the Spokane, Washington area. Arthur Keys died on September 5, 1974 at Nine Mile Falls, Washington; Ellen Keys died at age 91 on October 18, 2001 at Spokane.

The Woodruff part of the road name is after the Woodruff family, including ranchers Emmett E. and Mary A. Woodruff. They were natives of Canada, where they married on September 12, 1881.

In the *July 11, 1913 pg. 1 of the La Grande Observer* he was said to have the second largest artesian well in the county. His obituary in the November 8, 1929 La Grande Observer said that he had been a resident of Union County since 1892 and was a prominent rancher and dairyman. His wife, Mary, died in 1947.

They had seven children, the first three being born in Canada. Their eldest child, William Hawkins Woodruff was born August 24, 1884. He married Pearl Williams, and they took over Emmett's ranching operation.

In a *June 28, 1926 article in the La Grande Observer, page 1,* William Hawkins Woodruff's dairy herd was the highest milk producing herd in the county.

In November 1941, his 3-year-old Jersey cow, Lulu, was the highest producer of milk and butter fat in Union County. Her production records for the month of November show she produced 1,074 pounds of milk and 61.2 pounds of butter fat as compared with the average for tested cows of 469 pounds of milk and 20.5 pounds of butter fat.

The 1940 census revealed that William Woodruff had four years of college education. He helped raise Pearl's son, William Hyrum Cooper (b. 1916).

An *April 19, 1948 La Grande Observer, pg. 1* article mentioned a soil conservation project constructed on farms owned by three farmers, including William Hawkins Woodruff. A canal system was dug to drain about 200 acres of land to make it tillable for crops.

In 1949, W. Hawkins Woodruff farmed 3,400 acres and had a herd of 100 Jersey cows. He used soil conservation practices to boost his hay yield from 1 to 3 tons per acre. He projected that he could raise that yield to 5 tons by installing a border irrigation system. *(La Grande Observer special edition, Oct. 1, 1949, pg. 60)*

That same year, Woodruff wondered why his milk production was down, and finally discovered that his pigs were suckling at the cows' udders. A fence was then built to keep the little critters away from the cows.

In 1951, Woodruff was honored as "Grass Man of the Year." His ranch included 3,400 acres of cultivated bottom land, 7,000 acres of range land, a 130-cow dairy and a 200-cow breeding herd for milking stock. He sold 20,000 bushels of wheat this year. He also raises oats, barley, alfalfa, and wheat grass. *(La Grande Observer, Aug. 27, 1951, pg. 1)*

In 1952, he bought a new water pump to supplement the Catherine Creek water to irrigate his land. He and his neighbors also put up 10 miles of dikes along Catherine Creek to control it.

He died June 11, 1965 at the age of 84 years and was buried in the Union cemetery. Pearl died December 15, 1984, and thereafter, it appeared that the ranch was operated by Woodruff's stepson, William Hyrum Cooper. The property is owned by the Hawkins family.

Wright Road - Once called Wright Lane, this gravel road #27 runs 2.24 miles in length in Township 3S R39E Section 19 in the Union maintenance district. It runs north and south between Gekeler Lane on the north end and Airport Lane on its south end. In its middle, it intersects with Bond Lane. Wright Road is located between Highways 203 and 237 and lies about 7 miles east of La Grande. Residents on this road have a rural La Grande mailing address.

Wright Road is named after Lazarus Franklin "Frank" Wright (1872-1965), whose second farm property was located on this road. His name is listed on the *1935 Metsker Map*, but ownership was presumed earlier than that. The current address of his farm property is 59915 Wright Road, owned at one time by Erhman Bates.

Lazarus Franklin Wright was born February 9, 1872 in Jacksonville, Oregon to Jackson and Marinda Jane (Richardson) Wright. He married Cora Ann Jones of Wallowa County on June 10, 1896, and they had six children together.

Frank's history was written up in the *August 13, 1932 pg. 3 La Grande Observer* and includes some family history as follows:

"Lazarus Franklin Wright, Valeria. In Oregon have been born many of her enterprising citizens, and one among them is Lazarus Franklin Wright, better known as Frank Wright, he having been born in Jackson county, Feb. 9, 1872 to Jackson and Miranda (Richardson) Wright. The mother was pioneer to the Willamette valley in 1848 and is still living there, residing in Forest Grove and being numbered among the oldest of Oregon's pioneers. She was 82 years of age the 5th of June, 1932.

The father (Jackson) crossed the plains in 1852, at the age of 10 years in company with his parents (Lazarus Wright Sr. and Mary A. Giles), and on the journey across the mother (Mary) died and was buried on the emigrant trail. The family settled at Myrtle Creek. In this section Jackson grew up.

Following his marriage, Jackson and his wife Miranda moved to Jacksonville, Ore., where their son, Frank was born. In the summer of 1874, Jackson took his family and moved to the Grande Ronde valley with a team and drove a band of sheep. He located in Lower Cove and raised sheep and cattle. In 1880 he bought a farm of 320 acres, later adding a section to that.

It was on this farm Frank passed his youth and remained until after he attained his majority. In 1882 (at age 10 years), he herded sheep in the middle of the valley, when the space was open from the John Smith farm to the Old Stage station at the Lower Ditch bridge, one way and from the Will Miller place to the Ed Jasper farm, on the other. At Hardscrabble School District No. 9 he received his education.

About 1895, he went to Wallowa county and engaged in stock raising. For 12 years he remained there, then he came to the Grande Ronde again. He lived at Island City three years, and in 1910 he purchased the old Jim Hawley place near Valeria school where he now resides. In addition to the 240 acres in his home place he owns 320 acres near Lone Pine, making all told 560 acres. Mostly cereals are grown on the two farms.

On June 10, 1896, Frank Wright married Miss Cora, daughter of John and Mary Jones and to them have been born the following children: Eva, wife of E.G. Greiner, and living on a farm in Fruitdale; Orville, married and living in La Grande; Hazel, wife of George Brickell, of Grants Pass; Ruth, wife of William Helvey of La Grande; Deane, wife of Frank Counsell, of Ladd Canyon.

The parents of Mrs. Cora Wright were pioneers, having settled in the Grande Ronde valley in 1879. Four years later they moved to Wallowa county. The mother, native of New York, crossed the plains three times; once was during the Gold Rush of 1849, when she crossed the continent, going from New York to California. She was a cousin of Harriet Beecher Stowe and Henry Ward Beecher.

Frank and Cora Wright are prominent in grange work. He has held the office as member of state executive committee. He was the master of Blue Mt. Grange three years. She has been chairman of the county home economic committee for the last five years." [end of La Grande Observer article]

Frank was also featured in an article from the *April 25, 1940 pg. 7 issue of the La Grande Observer*, which states in part:

"Mr. L. F. (Frank) Wright was born near where Medford, Ore., is now situated, Feb. 9, 1872, being 68 years old. His father crossed the plains in early days and his mother was a native of Oregon, born near Monroe June 5, 1850.

Mr. Wright moved to Union county in 1874, where he was educated in the public schools moving to Wallowa county and entering business in 1894. In 1896 he married Cora Jones, a Kansas pioneer of covered wagon days, who came to Oregon in 1878.

Five children were born to the Wrights in Wallowa county: Eva Edith, Orville Guy, Hazel May, Ruth Helen and Amy Florence, who died at the age of 3. A sixth child, Deane Etta was born in Union county, where the Wrights moved in 1908 because of Mrs. Wright's health. The children all live near La Grande except Hazel, who is a resident of Grants Pass.

Mrs. Wright died in April 1936 and is buried in the family plot in Enterprise. Mr. Wright has been a member of organized agriculture for more than 20 years, having served as county president of the Farmers' union for two terms and as master of the Pomona grange for six years. He also was appointed to the state grange executive committee. He served as chairman of the board of directors of a co-operative creamery at Union and represented the creamery in Payette, Idaho and Portland.

He has farmed except for two years with the Pioneer Flouring mills at Island City, been an Odd Fellow for the past 35 years." [end of article]

Other sources expound and say that Frank's wife, Cora died on April 23, 1936 at the home of her daughter. She had not enjoyed good health for a long time, and her last illness began before the holidays of 1935 and led to her death four months later.

During that time she had been cared for at the Grande Ronde Hospital and at the homes of her two daughters, Eva Greiner of Fruitdale and Ruth Helvey of La Grande. Cora's funeral was heavily attended, and five grange members were pall bearers: Clarence Carter, Frank Jasper, Tom Wallsinger Sr., Ralph Chenault and Tom Bates, and a neighbor, Charlie Gray. Cora was widely known and active in many civic circles. *(La Grande Observer, April 28, 1936, pg. 5)*

One significant legacy left by Frank Wright was described in the *La Grande Observer of March 3, 1938, pg. 1* which stated that he sold 120 acres of his 320-acre Wright Road farm to Union County for the purpose of developing an airport. Two other landowners did likewise: the Grandy estate (200 acres) and Emil Muilenberg (300 acres). The airport was finally finished and rededicated on October 10, 1942. (See Airport Lane entry)

Then in 1950, Frank sold the remaining 200 acres on Wright Road to his long-time friends, Thomas "Tom" and Laura Bates, who resided at their home place in the Hot Lake area. Tom Bates and Frank Wright were both farmers and members of the Blue Mountain Grange Hall. Frank Wright was the past Pomona master and a former member of the state executive board. *(La Grande Observer, Oct. 28, 1939, pg. 3)*

At the time of the sale, the Bates' son Charles "Erhman" Bates was serving in the Korean Conflict, but when he came home in 1953, he stayed to help his parents farm the old Wright property thereafter.

"Dad bought the Wright land when I was over in Korea," Erhman Bates said. "I remember the old house (on the property) and cattle ran through it. When my brother Ed got married, they cut it up and remodeled the house and lived there for about a year. They moved away to Carlton, Oregon, and I came home from Korea and helped Dad farm the Wright Road property. Our home place was still down toward Hot Lake."

Erhman Bates was born November 27, 1925 at the old Ferguson home place in Hot Lake, and he graduated from Union High School in 1944. In November 2019, he said he will mark his 94th year of life. *(Erhman Bates interview, Sept. 19, 2019)*

Frank Wright died July 19, 1965 in La Grande at 93 years and 5 months of age. He lived a long and fulfilling life. He is buried in the family plot in the Enterprise Cemetery of Wallowa County with his wife, Cora.

Frank's grandfather was Lazarus Wright Sr. (1810-1885) and his history is described in *An Illustrated History of Union and Wallowa counties, 1902, pg. 401-402.*

The Lower Cove Cemetery is named "Wright Cemetery" where some of Frank's relatives are buried, including his brother William who died February 12, 1969. There are many other Wright families in the Union, Cove and High Valley area, but some are not related, and Frank Wright is the only one on Wright Road historically.

Yarrington Road - Correctly, Yarington, this gravel county road #49 is 11.14 miles long, one of the longer Union County roads and a gorgeous drive. It is located in Township 1N R40E Section 2 in the Elgin road maintenance district.

On the *1935 Metsker Map*, part of this road was called Palmer Junction and the other part was called Scott. It later became Yarrington Road from Highway 82 to Merritt Lane; and then Scott Road to the Thompson-Miller Road. Consequently, it was called Scott-Yarrington Road. In 1988, the road was given one name, Yarrington Road, because compound names were generally discontinued under the new ordinance #1988-3.

The road was named after George Harland Yarington (with one "r"). The road signs and the Union County tax accessor's website have written it with two "r's" and it is frequently mispronounced, according to family members still living in 2020. The correct pronunciation, according to family sources is Yair-ing-ton.

George Harland Yarington was born in Wisconsin on June 2, 1858 and died in Elgin, Oregon, on June 13, 1933. His parents were George Washington Yarington (1822-1904) and Melissa Miranda Elizabeth "Lizzie" Cooper (1822-1904). *(Ancestry.com family tree)* George Washington Yarington homesteaded 1888-89, and the photo of his homestead is found in *150 Photographs Elgin and North Union County, published by the Elgin Museum and Historical Society, 2009.*

George Harland Yarington and his wife Minnie Mae Reed (1869-1946) were married in 1891 in Union County, Oregon, and they established their residence on this road, where their son, Donald M. (d. 1971, age 68) also lived until his death.

"Donny Yarington had the first house on the right after turning onto Yarrington Road," said Cricket Flat farmer Joe Bechtel. "We also called it the 'Scott District' down below because all the Scotts lived down there, so I'm surprised they didn't call it the Scott Road."

Several Yaringtons are buried at the Highland Cemetery on the neighboring Good Road, including two infant girls, Isabelle Yarington, born March 11, 1908, died March 30, 1908; Florence Yarington, born January 20, 1911, died February 9, 1911; as well as Donald C. Yarington, born August 2, 1903, died August 2, 1971; and Ivan "Ike", born March 11, 1908, died February 25, 1984.

George Harland Yarington's published obituary reads: "George Yarington, 75, pioneer of Cricket Flat where he has been a resident for the past 48 years, died Tuesday night at 11 o'clock at his home from heart trouble. Mr. Yarington was born in Wisconsin on June 4, 1858, and at the age of five years moved to Minnesota. In March, 1885 he came to Oregon and took up a homestead at Cricket Flat where he has lived since. He was married to Minnie M. Read (Reed), July 25, 1891.

Eleven children were born to Mr. and Mrs. Yarington, three of whom died in infancy. Mrs. Cora Moulton, a daughter, died 12 years ago.

He is survived by seven children, Horace B. Yarington, Moberly, Miss.; Mrs. Joe Miller, Caldwell, Idaho; George Harlen Yarington, La Grande; Thuron D. Yarington, Miller, Oregon; Donald C. Yarington, Elgin; Virgil L. Yarington, of Caldwell, Ivan Yarington of Elgin and 12 grandchildren.

Funeral services were held this afternoon (June 15, 1933, Thursday) at 2 o'clock at the Highland cemetery where interment will be made. Snodgrass and Zimmerman were in charge." End of Obit *(La Grande Observer, June 15, 1933, pg. 8)*

His wife, Minnie Mae (Reed) Yarington died at the age of 76 in Pendleton at her daughter's home on February 17, 1946 following a long illness. She was born on September 27, 1869 in Kansas City and lived in Elgin for 55 years. *(Obit, La Grande Observer, Feb. 18, 1946, pg. 1)*

The Scott part of the road name originated with Joseph Scott, who was born July 13, 1846 in Monitor County in the northern part of Missouri. Shortly after, the family moved to Mercer County to a farm in a timbered section laying along Medicine Creek.

He was one of nine children born to his parents. They lived in a primitively made one-room house. All necessary articles of life were hand made by the family. He lived with his parents until 1867, when he married and settled in St. Clair County, in the southern part of Missouri. He and his wife Sarah Ellen had eight children, one died in infancy.

In 1889, they moved to Oregon and settled on Cricket Flat of the Elgin district. Joseph rented land there until 1893, when he homesteaded a timber claim and cleared it up with much hard labor for cultivation. He and Sarah remained on the Flat for 43 years. He died at his daughter's home, Mrs. U. F. Weiss of Elgin on the evening of January 28, 1932 at the age of 85 years, 6 months and 15 days.

His wife, Sarah Ellen Scott, was born in Missouri on August 31, 1852. In 1907, she suffered a paralytic stroke, and in 1917, she had a second stroke that rendered her speechless and paralyzed. Her husband became her caregiver for 24 years until his own health deteriorated from diabetes in 1931. Sarah died at her home on January 12, 1934. She was survived by their seven children, more than 70 grandchildren, and great grandchildren.

They rest in peace at the Mount Pleasant Cemetery, also known as the Scott's Cemetery on Yarrington Road. *(Harlan Scott interview, January 2017; Dick Good interview and issues of The La Grande Observer dated: Jan. 29, 1932, pg. 1; Feb. 3, 1932, pg. 3; Feb. 17, 1932, pg. 6 and Jan. 13, 1934, pg. 3)*

Yerges Road - Okay, so this is just a 30-foot-long driveway to our garage, and not a Union County road name *yet*, but it really does exist in Dodge County, Wisconsin, where the authors' German immigrant ancestor, Heinrich Yerges, founded what became the Yerges Century Farm.

Six generations ago, Heinrich Yerges engaged in dairy and crop farming, and it was a busy farm until about 1995 when the dairy was closed, the barn was razed and the land was leased out to other farmers.

How we ended up in Union County, Oregon is a story about one of Heinrich's great grandsons, who rode the rails west in the 1930s, desperately looking for work like everyone else. He found work with the CCC in the Seattle, Washington area. Then he made his way to the Sacramento, California area, where he met a cute young woman at a dance hall, married her and raised a family of four children.

His youngest child is my history partner and husband, Dave Yerges, who, in 1993, came to Union County, Oregon, home of his great-great-grandparents, John and Lucinda (Mitchell) McDowell.

John and Lucinda McDowell were married on September 13, 1859 in Mahaska County, Iowa. After losing their firstborn child there in 1861, they decided to relocate to Oregon with their aged father, James McDowell (1789-1870). They equipped their wagon and left Mahaska County, Iowa over the Oregon Trail by spring 1862, arriving to the Grande Ronde Valley in the summer of 1862. Lucinda was pregnant with her second child at the time.

According to an early La Grande newspaper called the *Morning Star* and the *La Grande Observer, June 5, 1926, pg. 1,* Lucinda McDowell gave birth in July 1862 to the first white girl born in Union County. Mrs. Mary (Frederick) Nessly (1822-1906) acted as the midwife in the absence of a doctor and helped Lucinda bring Lydia Ruth McDowell into this world. James H. Rinehart provided this history in his public address to an audience at the Union County Pioneer meeting sometime before 1909 when he moved to Portland.

His granddaughter, Wilma C. Rinehart, the daughter of Henry C. and Jennie Gilham Rinehart stated in the 1926 article that her mother had the old news clipping from the *Morning Star* in a scrap album. The *Morning Star* (published 1907-1911) was once one of five newspapers that were concurrently printed and distributed in La Grande. It was purchased by the La Grande Observer in 1911, thus ending its circulation.

The *Oregon Pioneer Obituaries website* had this to say about John McDowell in his posted obituary dated *January 11, 1899 in the Oregonian, pg. 6,* after dying in La Grande on January 10, 1899:

"John McDowell, one of the oldest pioneers of Union county, died here this morning, aged 71 years. Mr. McDowell settled in Union county in 1862, coming from the Willamette Valley, where he had settled in 1852. He was a man of sterling worth, and was active in pushing the interests of the county. He served as county commissioner in 1866-68. He left two sons and one sister, Mrs. Warnick. The funeral will take place tomorrow." (end of death notice)

Incidentally, Mrs. Warnick was born Charity A. McDowell on February 14, 1837, and she married Arthur Warnick in May 1870.

Oddly, John McDowell was overlooked when the county started assigning road names, but then so was Emily Leasy and Benjamin Brown, among others.

My husband, Dave, brought me over the Oregon Trail in early January 1998, and yes, our wagon was a modern-day U-Haul truck rented from our relatives, the Yerges Vanlines Company of Fort Atkinson, Wisconsin. They didn't fail to tell us we were insane to drive across country in January, but they knew it was useless to try and talk sense to a pair of newlyweds.

So I left everyone I loved 1,875 miles behind to come to the beautiful but isolated Grande Ronde Valley. I felt the courage and hope that pioneers felt 150 years earlier as they pulled up stakes and traveled to build a new life. After arriving to Union County, I said to Dave, "If I'm going to make a life here, I must learn to love this land and its people, and the best way to do that is to write about them." Of course, I volunteered Dave to help me.

With this motive and sentiment, the Yerges history detectives began to research and publish Union County history for the next 24 years. This publication has incorporated much of that prior work, and without a doubt, it's been our greatest pleasure to publish. This is a Who's Who of Union County roads with all its "I didn't know that!" facts, revelations and a few discoveries that uprooted formerly held beliefs. We hope these have surprised our readers as they have us also.

As you have noted by reading this book, not everyone's ancestral story was like a box of perfect chocolates. There were some sweet characters and then there were a few nutty ones too. There were some chocolates where you knew what was inside them and others where you got a surprise. It's the same with people. Their many differences make life stranger than fiction at times. We don't judge. We just tried to compile and present histories respectfully, yet still tell the story. The biographies are not meant to be complete, but we tried to hit the highlights of their lives.

There were many times in the preparation of this book that we didn't know what direction all our research was going to lead us, and maybe we got detoured once in a while, but hasn't it been an amazing ride? The fun is in the journey of discovery, time travel, and ultimately rescuing history before it sinks six feet deep. Those we interviewed all expressed an appreciation for our work and cooperated so kindly in this venture.

Please forgive us if there are any errors. We relied heavily on public records of all sorts, historical resources and interviews with county residents and errors may creep in. This was a huge undertaking, probably the largest Who's Who in Union County publication since *An Illustrated History of Union and Wallowa counties* was published in 1902.

Following this page is the index, which includes about 7,800 entries scrupulously enumerated for the advanced historical researcher. You will find it organized by the name of the person you're seeking in the left column and the road entry name it will be found in the second column. There are two sets of columns on each page.

We truly hope you will enjoy this historical and entertaining book. Take it along on your Sunday drives as you explore Union County roads and give it a prominent place in your personal history library.

The Authors
Dave & Trish Yerges
Summerville, Oregon
February 2022; 2023

INDEX

SUBJECT OR NAME	ROAD NAME	SUBJECT OR NAME	ROAD NAME
"61" brand	Benson	Aldred, Elsie Marie	Parsons
"Body"	Bodie	Alexander (cabin)	Lookingglass
"Little Alps"	Highway 82	Alexander, Alice	Thew
"Old Jake"	End	Alexander, Ed	Lookingglass
"Y L" brand	Benson	Alexander, R.	Marks
1620 Sixth St., La Grande	Robbs Hill	Alexandria, VA	Badger Flat
1878 Indian Wars	Henderson	Alford Cemetery	Curtis
1902 First St., La Grande	Myers	Algonquian (language)	Wapiti
1918 Influenza	Alicel	Alhambra, CA	Bagwell
21st Street	Watson	Alicel	McDonald
614 Dearborn Ave., Salem	Merritt	Alicel Lane	Hays
Abbott G. H.	Marks	Alicel School	Case
Abbott, G. W.	Marks	Alicel, OR	Dorthy M
Abbott, Mr.	Eagle Creek	Alicel, OR	Foothill
Abele, John	Hunter	Alicel, OR	Golding
Aberdeen, WA	Owsley	Alicel, OR	Greiner
Able, Pete	Coombs	Alicel, OR	Hamilton
Able, Thomas M.	Coombs	Alicel, OR	Janson
Able, Urania Pamela	Coombs	Alicel, OR	Kerns
AC&R Advertising	Elgin Cem.	Alicel, OR	McKennon
Ackles Cemetery	Booth	Alicel, OR	Mt. Glen
Ackles Cemetery	Couch	Alicel, OR	Ruckman
Ackles Cemetery	Halley	Alicel, OR	Shaw Creek
Ackles Cemetery	Hunter	Alicel, OR	Speckhart
Ackles Cemetery	Lizabeth	Alicel, OR	Starr
Ackles Cemetery	McAlister	Alisky, Scotland	Shaw Creek
Ackles Cemetery	Mt. Glen	Alleman, Martha	Igo
Ackles, George	Mt. Glen	Allen, Aurora	Starkey
Ackles, Neri	Mt. Glen	Allen, George	Highway 82
Ackles, Viva	Mt. Glen	Allen, IN	Haggerty
Ada Co., ID	Phys	Allen, James	Starkey
Adams Avenue	May	Allen, Lucy Ellen	Knight
Adams Co., IL	Rinehart	Allen, Mary	Hug
Adams Supply Co.	Ernest	Allen, Mrs. Lucie	Knight
Adams Suppy Store	Frances	Allen, Walter E.	Starkey
Adams, Emily Jane	Ernest	Alley, Andrew Jackson	Robbs Hill
Adams, Ernest "Ernie" Edgar	Ernest	Alley, Louisa Elizabeth	Robbs Hill
Adams, Ernest Edgar	Frances	Alley, Mary Adeline	Robbs Hill
Adams, Frances Elizabeth	Frances	Alley, Sarah Jane	Robbs Hill
Adams, J. W.	Ernest	Almont, MI	McKennon
Adams, OR	Bagwell	Althiser, Sadie	Bowman
Agency City, Wapello Co., IA	Ruckman	Altlantic City, NJ	Highway 30
Airport Lane	Wright	American Fur Co.	Moses Creek
Airport Road	WAAS	American Legion Auxiliary	Wallsinger
Alabama	Phys	American Sunday School	Wolf Creek
Alaska	Frances	Ames (estate)	Weaver
Alaska (gold fields)	Shaw Creek	Ames, George	Catherine Cr.
Albany, NY	Conklin	Ames, Mr.	Draper
Albany, OR	Dorthy M	Amita, LA	Comstock
Albany, OR	Ruth	Anaconda, MT	Upper Perry
Alberta, Canada	Benson	Anchor, the (livery)	Shaw Creek
Alberta, Canada	Moses Creek	Anderson Co., KS	Monroe
Alder Slope	Morgan Lake	Anderson County, KY	Bond

Anderson Mark H.	Evergreen	Antles, Archer	Antles
Anderson Road	Godley	Antles, Averill A.	Antles
Anderson, MO	Upper Perry	Antles, Floyd	Antles
Anderson, Rebecca Jane	McAlister	Antles, Harry	Antles
Anderson, SC	Bagwell	Antles, Lulu May	Antles
Andes (mountains)	Upper Perry	Antwerp, Belgium (port)	Wolf Creek
Andrews Brothers	May	Apash-wa-hay-ikt (Lookingglass)	Lookingglass
Andrews, Alvaron V.	May	Appleton City, St. Clair Co., MO	Thompson
Andrews, E. T.	May	Arizona, steamer	Deal Canyon
Andrews, Ealy Taylor	May	Arkansas	Keen Cabin Cr.
Andrews, Jesse Varon	May	Arlington, OR	Owsley
Andrews, Martha Eileen	May	Arlington, WA	Tucker Flat
Andrews, Matthew	May	Armstrong, Rebecca	Hunter
Andrews, May Belle	May	Arnold & Dray (addition)	Morgan Lake
Andrews, Mrs. Nena Nina	Turnbull	Arnold, Adaline	Good
Andrews, T. J.	May	Arnold, Fred	Morgan Lake
Andross, Eva	Alicel	Arnold, Green	Marks
Andross, Eva	Ladd Creek	Arnold, Green	Moses Creek
Andross, M. D.	Ladd Creek	Arnold, William	Morgan Lake
Angus, Wade	Halley	Arrivey, William	Knight
Angwin, CA	Weaver	Art Rocks (art show)	Knight
Ann, Aunt	Hug	Asbury, Isabelle	Hutchinson
Anna-Lulu Flouring Mill	Rinehart	Asbury, Miss Isabelle	Hutchinson
Annsburg, ME	Coombs	Asbury, Stephen	Hutchinson
Anson Road	Roe	Asbury, Susan	Hutchinson
Anson Ski Shop	Anson	Ashland Cemetery	Imbler
Anson, Amelia	Anson	Ashland Co., OH	Marks
Anson, Claude	Anson	Ashland, Jackson Co., OR	Imbler
Anson, Claude	Blackhawk Tr	Ashland, OR	Dry Creek
Anson, Ella	Dial	Ashmore, Coles Co., IL	McAlister
Anson, George Joseph	Anson	Ashmore, Lettitia Franklin	McAlister
Anson, James	Anson	Asla, Amelia	Asla
Anson, Jody	Anson	Asla, Amelia	Asla
Anson, Joseph	Anson	Asla, Eudora	Asla
Anson, Joseph	Blackhawk Tr	Asla, Felicia	Asla
Anson, Leola Dot	Anson	Asla, Felix Sr.	Asla
Anson, Mabel	Anson	Asla, Francessa "Frances"	Asla
Anson, Margaret (Dinning)	Anson	Asla, Grace Vincento	Asla
Anson, Minnie	Anson	Asla, Josephine	Asla
Anson, Mrs.	Blackhawk Tr	Asla, Major Felix, Jr.	Asla
Anson, Nellie	Anson	Asla, Marian Aurora	Asla
Anson, Newell	Anson	Asla, Mitchell	Asla
Anson, Orlin	Anson	Asla, Pedro	Asla
Anson, Wilbur	Anson	Asla, Ralph Cedric	Asla
Anson, William	Dial	Asotin, WA	Dry Creek
Antelope Stage Station	Telocaset	Aspen Road	Starr
Antelope, Union Co., OR	Hill Lay	Aster, Mrs. Margaret J.	Striker
Anthony Creek	Anthony Lake	Astoria, OR	Highway 30
Anthony Lakes	Rock Creek	Astoria, OR	Marks
Anthony Lakes Highway	Ellis	Athens, Athens Co., OH	Lookingglass
Anthony Lakes Road	Antelope Peak	Athens, TN	Love
Anthony Lakes Ski Patrol	Anson	Atteberry, Florence Idella	Roulet
Anthony Lakes Ski Resort	Anthony Lake	Auburn (mines)	May
Anthony, Doc	Starkey	Auburn, Baker Co., OR	Ladd Creek
Anthony, William "Doc"	Anthony Lake	Auburn, OR	Starkey

Aurora, Marion Co., OR	Starkey	Ballard, Glen R.	Merritt
Austrian dry peas	Lower Cove	Ballard, Myrtle	Merritt
Ayers, Mrs. Winnie	McNeill	Ballen, Mrs. Viva	Golding
B Avenue, La Grande	Morgan Lake	Baltimore, MD	Thompson
Bacon, Dr.	Hunter	Bannock (mines)	Standley
Badger (state)	Hallgarth	Bannocks, the	Henderson
Badger, Bessie Thelma	Badger Flat	Barenbrug	Courtney
Badger, Ebeneezer	Badger Flat	Barenbrug Grass Seed	Hays
Badger, Erna	Badger Flat	Barklow, Irene Locke	Highway 82
Badger, Francis Marion	Badger Flat	Barnes, Aletha E.	Henderson
Badger, Lt. Col. Ralph	Badger Flat	Barnes, John P.	Henderson
Badger, Maude	Badger Flat	Barnes, Margaret Elizabeth	Merritt
Badger, Ross "Jinks"	Badger Flat	Barnes, Mary	Henderson
Badsky, Mrs. Elizabeth	Bond	Barnes, Olive	Merritt
Bagwell, Bertha	Bagwell	Barnes, Sarah Jane	Turnbull
Bagwell, George Joseph	Bagwell	Barnett, W. E.	Anthony Lake
Bagwell, John Chritopher	Bagwell	Barnholm, Denmark	Kofford
Bagwell, Joseph Arthur	Bagwell	Barnsville, OH	Deal Canyon
Bagwell, Mabel	Bagwell	Barrett, Alice	McKennon
Bagwell, Mary A. Cison	Bagwell	Bartmess, F. M.	Morgan Lake
Bagwell, Thelma Josephine	Bagwell	Barton, Mrs. Lois	Bean-Coffin
Baker City, Baker Co., OR	Ladd Creek	basket suppers	Red Pepper
Baker City, OR	Hill Lay	Bates Lane	Draper
Baker City, OR	Highway 203	Bates, Anna	Bates
Baker City, OR	Hull	Bates, Charles Ehrman	Wright
Baker City, OR	Jimmy	Bates, Ed	Wright
Baker City, OR	Leffel	Bates, Ehrman	Bates
Baker City, OR	Lower Perry	Bates, Ehrman	Wright
Baker City, OR	McIntyre	Bates, Joe	Bates
Baker City, OR	McNeill	Bates, Keith	Bates
Baker City, OR	Olsen	Bates, Laura	Wright
Baker City, OR	Wade	Bates, Laura E.	Bates
Baker City, OR	Weaver	Bates, Lucius Chester	Bates
Baker City, OR	Wilkinson	Bates, Mabel	Bates
Baker City, OR	Woodruff	Bates, Thomas "Tom"	Wright
Baker Co., OR	Hutchinson	Bates, Tom	Wright
Baker Co., OR	Imbler	Bates, William Thomas	Bates
Baker Co., OR	Kerns	Baton, Mary	Shaw Creek
Baker Co., OR	Marks	Batty, Hannah Encora "Cora"	Follett
Baker Co., OR	May	Batty, Mary	Stackland
Baker Co., OR	Shaw Mountain	Baudoin, Mr.	Wade
Baker Co., OR	Starkey	Bauer, Todd	Fletcher
Baker County	Waltz	Baugher, Charles	High Valley
Baker, Elizabeth	Bean-Coffin	Baum, Ray	Lampkin
Baker, Frank	Lookingglass	Bavaria, Germany	End
Baker, Katie Melissa Enola	Dry Creek	Bavaria, Germany	Fox Hill
Baker, OR	Government Gul.	Bavaria, Germany	Wolf Creek
Baker, OR	Knight	Bayreuth, Bavaria, Germany	Hacker
Baker, OR	Morgan Lake	Beacon Light area	Fox Hill
Baker, R. J.	Fletcher	Bean, Mildred Lindsay	Kofford
Bald Mountain	Skyline	Beaumont (family)	Starkey
Balfour & Company	Shaw Creek	Beauvais (family)	Moses Creek
Ball, Joseph P.	Deal Canyon	Beaver, OH	Starr
Ball, Margaret	Deal Canyon	Beber, Elizabeth	Frances
Ball, Margaret E.	Deal Canyon	Bechtel (farm)	Merritt

Bechtel, Joe	Merritt	Bennett, Frank Ordway	Bennett
Bechtel, Joe	Parsons	Bennett, Mary Elizabeth	Ruckman
Bechtel, Joe	Yarrington	Bennett, Richard	Ruckman
Bechtel, Mrs. Ada	Golding	Bennett, Robert "Bob"	Bennett
Bechtel, Ora	Merritt	Bennett, Robert Leland	Bennett
Bechtel, Phyllis	Merritt	Bennett, Virginia M.	Bennett
Bechtel, Phyllis	Parsons	Benson Brothers	Benson
Bechtel, Sadie	Merritt	Benson, John A. "Dick"	Benson
Beck, Mrs. Florence	Dial	Benson, Minnie	Benson
Becker, Albert	Hug	Benton Co., OR	Grays Corner
Becker, Elizabeth	Hug	Benton Co., OR	Morgan Lake
Becker, Sarah Elizabeth	Hug	Benton County, MO	Finley Creek
Beckwith, Mrs. Alice	McKennon	Benton, OR	Flevious
Bedford Co., TN	Couch	Bergstrom, Philip James "Bergie"	Philberg
Beecher, Henry Ward	Wright	Berkshire (hogs)	Ruckman
Beem, Amy Ellen	Bean-Coffin	Bern, Switzerland	Hug
Beem, Cordelia Bell	Bean-Coffin	Bernal D. Hug	Mt. Emily
Beem, Delilah	Bean-Coffin	Berry, Mrs. Fannie	May
Beem, Delphia Delia	Bean-Coffin	Berry, William Woodard (Wood)	May
Beem, Docia	Bean-Coffin	Berryville, Carroll Co., AR	McKennon
Beem, Dorothy Elizabeth	Bean-Coffin	Bert, E. E.	Airport
Beem, Edwin Lester	Bean-Coffin	Beymer, Geraldine Ethelda	Lester
Beem, Elizabeth	Bean-Coffin	Bidwell, Charles Calvin	Bidwell
Beem, George Harvey	Bean-Coffin	Bidwell, Chester	Bidwell
Beem, John A. Logan	Bean-Coffin	Bidwell, Edith Doris	Bidwell
Beem, Randall David	Bean-Coffin	Bidwell, Emma	Bidwell
Beem, Thomas	Bean-Coffin	Bidwell, Frank	Bidwell
Beem, Verdie	Bean-Coffin	Bidwell, Frank Deane	Bidwell
Beem, Warner	Bean-Coffin	Bidwell, Geneveive	Bidwell
Beeman, Fred	Fox Hill	Bidwell, Homer	Bidwell
Bees-Wax Hill	High Valley	Bidwell, Homer C.	Bidwell
Behrens Lane	Slack	Bidwell, Mary Ann	Bidwell
Behrens Lane	Summerville	Bidwell, Mrs. H. C.	Brooks
Behrens, Arthur	Behrens	Bidwell, Rachel	Brooks
Behrens, Arthur	Finley Creek	Bidwell, Rachel M.	Bidwell
Behrens, Audry	Behrens	Big Minam (river)	Parsons
Behrens, August	Behrens	Billy Howell's Orchestra	Howell
Behrens, Fred O.	Behrens	Bingaman , Howard	McDonald
Behrens, Margaret	Behrens	Bingaman Enterprises	McDonald
Behrens, Nellie	Behrens	Bingaman, Austin	Starr
Behrens, Ruth	Behrens	Bingaman, Barbara	McDonald
Behrens, Veta	Behrens	Bingaman, Chandra	McDonald
Beidler, Elsie	Starkey	Bingaman, Elwyn	Hays
Beldin, A.	Fruitdale	Bingaman, Elwyn	Ruckman
Belgium	Stackland	Bingaman, Elwyn	Woodell
Bell, Sytha Virginia	McNeill	Bingaman, Elwyn D.	McDonald
Belle Vernon, PA	Coughanour	Bingaman, Franklin Harold	McDonald
Bellevue, OR	Marks	Bingaman, Gregory L.	McDonald
Bellevue, WA	Knight	Bingaman, Hailey	McDonald
Bellingham, WA	Starkey	Bingaman, Ina May	Dry Creek
Belmont Co., OH	Starkey	Bingaman, Jeana	Starr
Ben Brown	Mt. Emily	Bingaman, Jessica	McDonald
Bend, OR	Grays Corner	Bingaman, Kale	McDonald
Bend, OR	Hamilton	Bingaman, Kathleen	McDonald
Bennett, Betty Jean	Bennett	Bingaman, Leona	McDonald

Boothe, Cora Gaines	Booth	Brickell, Mrs. Hazel	Wright
Boothe, Luther Samuel	Booth	Bridwell, James	Hamilton
Boothe, Mary Ann	Booth	Bridwell, Mary	Hamilton
Boothe, Nancy Eveline	Booth	Bridwell, Miss Sarah Frances	Hamilton
Boothe, Sam	Booth	Brig Unity (ship)	Christensen
Boothe, Samuel Smith	Booth	Briggs, Alvirtus S. "Bert"	Merritt
Borie, A. J.	Upper Perry	Briggs, Harvey F.	Coombs
Borkgren, Esther	Rose Ridge	Briggs, Olive Viola	Merritt
Borkgren, Hazel A.	Chadwick	Brigham Young University	Igo
Borkgren, Martin	Rose Ridge	Brighten, MI	Conklin
Borkgren, Royal	Rose Ridge	Brindle, Lancashire, England	Heber
Borkgren's sawmill	Mill Creek	Britain	Stackland
Bosell, A. M.	Follett	Britain	Upper Perry
Boswell (family)	Pine Grove	Britton, Lisa	Bennett
Bothell, WA	Knight	Bronx, NY	Elgin Cem.
Botz, Ed	Highway 82	Brooks, Anna	Brooks
Botz, Ed	Ridgeway	Brooks, Hannah	Brooks
Botz, Laveta	Ridgeway	Brooks, Ida	Summerville
Bougards, Mr.	Fruitdale	Brooks, Ida May	Brooks
Bowles, Lewis	Gordon Creek	Brooks, John	Brooks
Bowman Loop	Moses Creek	Brooks, John Henry	Brooks
Bowman, Alice Sarah	Bowman	Brooks, Mary	Bidwell
Bowman, Alvin	Bowman	Brooks, Mary Jane	Brooks
Bowman, Alvin Cecil	Bowman	Brooks, Mary Jane	Courtney
Bowman, B. Vernice	Bowman	Brooks, Miss Rachel M.	Bidwell
Bowman, Beverly "Maxine"	Bowman	Brooks, OR	Dorthy M
Bowman, Beverly Jean	Bowman	Brooks, Rachel	Brooks
Bowman, Cecil Conrad	Bowman	Brooks, Samuel	Bidwell
Bowman, Darleen	Bowman	Brooks, Samuel	Courtney
Bowman, Debra	Bowman	Brooks, Samuel Leonard	Brooks
Bowman, Deliah	Bowman	Brooks, Stella	Brooks
Bowman, Denise	Bowman	Brooks, Stella	Courtney
Bowman, Ida	Bowman	Brooks, Wade	Brooks
Bowman, Iva	Bowman	Brouillot (family)	Moses Creek
Bowman, Kathleen	Bowman	Brounstein, Mrs. Ruth	Comstock
Bowman, Leonard	Bowman	Brown Co., KS	Fox Hill
Bowman, Lorraine	Bowman	Brown County, IL	Bowman
Bowman, Mildred	Bowman	Brown Mr.	Chumos
Bowman, Velma	Bowman	Brown, Ada	Marks
Bowman, Virgil	Bowman	Brown, Arvid	Marvin
Bowman-Hicks Lumber Co.	Palmer Junction	Brown, Ben	Hunter
Box Elder, UT	Lizabeth	Brown, Ben	Marks
Boyd, Mrs. J. N.	Kerns	Brown, Ben	McAlister
Boyer, Mrs. Kenneth	Bond	Brown, Benjamin	Marks
Brack, Adam	Jones	Brown, Benjamin	Rinehart
Brack, Robert J.	Jones	Brown, Benjamin	Yerges
Brashears, Mrs. Mary	Hindman	Brown, Esther	Marks
Bray, Ben	Robinson	Brown, Frances	Marks
Bray, Hattie Rosana	Robinson	Brown, Sam	Fox Hill
Brazille Brothers	Parsons	Brown's Fort	Marks
Bremen (port in Germany)	Thompson	Brown's Town	Rinehart
Bremerton, WA	Igo	Brownstein, Mrs. Ruth	Comstock
Brevard, NC	Bagwell	Brownsville	Marks
Brevig, Rod	Good	Brownsville	Rinehart
Brickell, George	Wright	Brownsville, Linn Co., OR	Marks

Brownton, Wesley F.	Knight	Burlington, IA	Phys
Bruce, George W.	Igo	Burnaugh, Andrew	Myers
Brugger William T.	Henderson	Burnaugh, Dora F.	Myers
Brugger, Ben	Henderson	Burnaugh, Emma F.	Myers
Brugger, Benjamin Franklin	Henderson	Burnaugh, George	Myers
Brugger, Charley	Henderson	Burnaugh, Joseph	Myers
Brugger, Ed	Henderson	Burnaugh, Joseph "Merrell"	Myers
Brugger, Edward	Henderson	Burnaugh, Joseph Merrell	Myers
Brugger, J. J.	Henderson	Burnaugh, Lydia	Myers
Brugger, Jacob	Henderson	Burnaugh, Mabel Mary	Myers
Brugger, John	Henderson	Burnaugh, Margaret	Myers
Brugger, John Jasper	Henderson	Burnaugh, Mary Savannah	Myers
Brugger, Lucy Ellen	Henderson	Burnaugh, Samuel L. Jr.	Myers
Brugger, Mary	Henderson	Burnaugh, Samuel Lynch	Myers
Brugger, Mary Eliza	Henderson	Burnaugh, Susan Elvira	Myers
Brugger, Peter	Henderson	Burnaugh, Walter	Myers
Brugger-Allen, Lucy Ellen	Knight	Burnaugh, Willena	Myers
Brunswick, The	Lookingglass	Burnett (family)	Starkey
Brush Hollow Cemetery	Stackland	Burnley School of Prof. Art	Elgin Cem.
Buchanan, Albert	Buchanan	Burnsides, Mary Jane	Glass Hill
Buchanan, Amanda	Buchanan	Burton, Mrs. Ruth	Dial
Buchanan, David Monroe	Buchanan	Bushnell, Alfred	Bushnell
Buchanan, Dorothy	Craig	Bushnell, Anna	Bushnell
Buchanan, Ellen Jane	Buchanan	Bushnell, Donna	Bushnell
Buchanan, George Lemon	Buchanan	Bushnell, Elizabeth	Bushnell
Buchanan, Harriet	Buchanan	Bushnell, Elmer G.	Bushnell
Buchanan, James Andrew	Buchanan	Bushnell, Elmer Nathan	Bushnell
Buchanan, Joe	Buchanan	Bushnell, Elwyn	Bushnell
Buchanan, Johnson	Buchanan	Bushnell, Herman J.	Bushnell
Buchanan, Joseph Warren	Buchanan	Bushnell, John Fuller	Bushnell
Buchanan, Josephine	Buchanan	Bushnell, Joseph	Bushnell
Buchanan, Mr. & Mrs. T. J.	Craig	Bushnell, Lillie	Bushnell
Buchanan, William	Buchanan	Bushnell, Lottie Loie	Bushnell
Buchanan, William D.	Buchanan	Bushnell, William	Bushnell
Buchanan, William T. Jr.	Buchanan	Bushnell, Winnie	Bushnell
Buchanan, Willian Dixon	Buchanan	Bushnell's Wrecking House	Bushnell
Buckmaster, Charles	Dorthy M	Bushong, Eve	Marks
Buell, C. L.	Morgan Lake	Bushong, John	Marks
Buena Park, CA	Kerns	Busick, A.	Catherine Cr.
Buena Vista subdivision	Stackland	Bussard, Sam	Behrens
Buffalo Co., IA	Wallsinger	Bussear, Mrs. Nora A.	Merritt
Buffalo Peak Golf Course	Fruitdale	Butte, MT	Fletcher
Buffalo, MO	Clark Creek	Butteville Cemetery	Starkey
Buffalo, NY	Weaver	Butteville, Marion Co., OR	Starkey
Bulger Ditch	Antelope Peak	Byers, Jane C.	Hamilton
Bulger Flat Lane	Antelope Peak	Byers, Malinda Jane	Roulet
Bull, Hester	Starkey	C Avenue, La Grande	Morgan Lake
Bull, Robert C.	Moses Creek	C Street, Elgin	Merritt
Bull, William "Will"	Courtney	C. J.'s County Store	Bidwell
Bunting, Galena	Coughanour	C. Jacobs & Company	Catherine Cr.
Burch, Miss Wilma	Lower Cove	Cabin Creek	Keen Cabin Cr.
Burch, Wilma May	Lower Cove	Cabin Creek ranch	Palmer Junction
Burford, Clara	Hulick	Cabin Creek Road	Keen Cabin Cr.
Burk, Mrs. K. L.	Government Gul.	Cache Co., UT	Wickens
Burkel, Don	McCanse	Caldwell Canyon, ID	Heber

Case, Vera Jane	Case	Central School	McKenzie
Case, W. J.	Case	Chaconas	Chumos
Case, W. J.	Summerville	Chadwick Lane	Sharp
Case, Wendy	Case	Chadwick Lane	Waltz
Case, William "Wren"	Case	Chadwick, Emily	Lizabeth
Case, William Jasper	Case	Chadwick, Georganna	Hamilton
Case, Wren	Booth	Chadwick, George Sr.	Chadwick
Case, Wren	Shaw Mountain	Chadwick, Georgia Rebecca	Chadwick
Casey Lumber Mill	Bodie	Chadwick, Hazel A.	Chadwick
Casey Siding	Bodie	Chadwick, June Ella	Chadwick
Casey, Colonel J. D.	Bodie	Chadwick, Lynn James	Chadwick
Casey, Edgar	Bodie	Chadwick, Samuel	Chadwick
Casey, J. D.	Bodie	Chaffee, Rod	Parsons
Casey, Jennie Ama	Bodie	Chalmers Hotel, Hutchinson, KS	Upper Perry
Casey, Jennie L.	Bodie	Champoeg, OR	Moses Creek
Casey, John "Jack" Michael	Bodie	Chandler (family)	Pine Grove
Casey, John Daniel	Bodie	Chandler Air Field	Knight
Casey, May Helen	Bodie	Chandler Loop	Leffel
Casey, Nora Estelle	Bodie	Chandler Road	Leffel
Cason, Richard	Lookingglass	Chandler, Carrie	Draper
Cass Co., IN	Marks	Chandler, Dale G.	Leffel
Castle Rock, WA	Marks	Chandler, Esther	Chandler
Caterpillar Tractor #22	Hug	Chandler, Esther Melinda	Chandler
Cates, William A.	Telocaset	Chandler, Grant Gilbert	Chandler
Catherine Cr. State Park	Badger Flat	Chandler, Harriet "Hattie" Louisa	Chandler
Catherine Creek	Badger Flat	Chandler, Jerry	Hindman
Catherine Creek	Benson	Chandler, John Alden	Chandler
Catherine Creek	French Corral	Chandler, John S.	Chandler
Catherine Creek	Godley	Chandler, John Samuel	Chandler
Catherine Creek	Haggerty	Chandler, Lester Samuel	Chandler
Catherine Creek	High Valley	Chandler, Louisa Melinda	Chandler
Catherine Creek	Kingsbury	Chandler, OK	Chumos
Catherine Creek	Little Creek	Chandler, Percy	Follett
Catherine Creek	May	Chandler, Samuel	Chandler
Catherine Creek	Miller	Chandler, Zachariah	Chandler
Catherine Creek	Moses Creek	Chaplin, Daniel	Marks
Catherine Creek	Woodruff	Chaplin, Daniel	Morgan Lake
Catherine Creek Grange	Miller	Chaplin, Daniel	Moses Creek
Cattleman of the Year	Hindman	Chaplow, Sarah	Behrens
Cattleman of the Year	McKenzie	Chapman, J. A. J.	Catherine Cr.
Cattleman's Association	Heber	Chapman, John	Catherine Cr.
Cavalier, ND	Otten	Chapman, John Andrew Jackson	Catherine Cr.
Caviness, C. E.	West	Chappell, Bertha Ethel	Rinehart
Caviness, J. L.	Phys	Chariton Co., MO	Hug
Caviness, J. L.	West	Chariton, IA	Badger Flat
Cayuse, OR	Gordon Creek	Charleston, Coles Co., IL	Middle
Cayuse, the	Fox Hill	Charlotte (Moores) Coffin	Bean-Coffin
CCC, the	Yerges	Charlottetown, Queens, Canada	McIntyre
Cedar Co., IA	Hindman	Chase, Mrs. Anna Belle	Lookingglass
Cedar Mill, OR	Finley Creek	Che Lee (Chinese)	Hunter
Cedar, MO	Wilkinson	Chenault, Ralph	Wright
Celia, Arthur	Moses Creek	Cherry Chapter	Ruth
Cemetery Road	Sammyville	Chesnut, Ed	Follett
Central Point, OR	Hindman	Chestnut, Edward	Rawhide
Central Railroad of Oregon	Union Junction	Cheyenne, WY	Morgan Lake

Chicago, IL	Shaw Creek	Clark, Dave	Shaw Creek
Chicago. IL	Palmer Junction	Clark, Harriet Caroline "Hattie"	Marvin
Chicago. IL	Rinehart	Clark, Harvey Lee	Marvin
Chief Blackhawk	Blackhawk Tr	Clark, Henderson	Marvin
Chief Lookingglass (Nez Perce)	Lookingglass	Clark, Ida May	Marvin
Chigago, IL	Morgan Lake	Clark, Jacob	Marvin
Childers, Bessie	Grays Corner	Clark, Jeanette "Nettie"	Marvin
China	Frances	Clark, Joisa Eliza	Hamilton
China (pheasants)	Peach	Clark, Josie	Marvin
Chinneth, Agnes	Grays Corner	Clark, Lydia	Clark Creek
Chippewa Falls, WI	Upper Perry	Clark, Martin Luther	Marvin
Choate, Dillard	Finley Creek	Clark, Martin Luther	Marvin
Chong Wong (Chinese)	Hunter	Clark, Marvin Jay	Marvin
Chrisman, Ellen	Rose Ridge	Clark, Mary Magdaline	Marvin
Christensen, Anna Belle	Christensen	Clark, Mr.	Chumos
Christensen, Edith Unita	Christensen	Clark, Mrs. Emma	Bidwell
Christensen, George Elmer	Christensen	Clarke, Elma M.	Monroe
Christensen, J. C.	Christensen	Clarke, Mr. & Mrs. W. B.	Monroe
Christensen, James C.	Christensen	Clarks Creek	Clark Creek
Christensen, Marguerite "Maggie"	Christensen	Clark's Creek	Clark Creek
Christensen, Marguerite Olive	Christensen	Clark's Dairy	Marvin
Christensen, Mary Ellen	Christensen	Clark's Superior Dairy	Marvin
Christensen, William Franklin	Christensen	Clarkston, WA	Mathson
Christenson	Christensen	Clay (homestead)	Fox Hill
Christiansen	Christensen	Clay, Albert	Fox Hill
Christianson	Christensen	Clay, Callie	Fox Hill
Christie, Lydia	Dial	Clay, Daniel	Fox Hill
Chula Vista, CA	Golding	Clay, Leah	Fox Hill
Chumos Road	Hindman	Clay, Rufus	Crampton
Chumos School District	Chumos	Clay, Rufus	Fox Hill
Chumos, James	Chumos	Clay, Susan	Fox Hill
Chumos, James G.	Chumos	Clay, Willie Vernon	Fox Hill
Church, W. J.	May	Clear Creek, CA	Godley
Churchill, Becky	Philberg	Clearmont Co., OH	Mt. Glen
Churchill, Cecil	Philberg	Clearwater (country)	Moses Creek
Cimmiyotti, Ora	Chumos	Clearwater Pond	Clearwater
Cincinnati, OH	May	Clearwater, Martha A.	Starkey
Circle Stomp (game)	Summerville	Cleaver, Marie	Lester
Civil Aeronautics Authority	Knight	Clerk, Carrie	Bates
Civil War	Mt. Harris	Cleveland, OH	Riddle
Civil War	Rinehart	Clifford, Sarah	Wallsinger
Civil War	Upper Perry	Clippenger, Clytie "Esther"	Rawhide
Civil War	Wallsinger	Clover Creek	Jimmy
Civil War	Wolf Creek	Clover Creek	Miller
Civil War, the	Gordon Creek	Clover Creek	Shaw Mountain
Civil War, the	Knight	Clover Creek Valley	Wolf Creek
Clackamas Co., OR	Starkey	Clover Valley, NV	Follett
Clackamas Co., OR	Upper Perry	Clydesdale (horses)	McKennon
Clarence Witty Park	Highway 82	Clydesdales (Horses)	Brooks
Clark Co., KY	Halley	Coalwell, Harry	Fox Hill
Clark Creek	Elgin Cem.	Coats, Nellie	Henderson
Clark Creek Road	Henderson	Cockrell, Lulu	Draper
Clark Drive	Marvin	Cockrell, Lulu Cueva	Draper
Clark, Allen Marvin	Marvin	Coeur d' Alene, ID	Bowman
Clark, Cecelia (Celia)	Badger Flat	Coeur d'Alene, ID	Thompson

Coffeville, KS	Chumos	Comstock, Joyce	Ruth
Coffeyville, KS	Upper Perry	Comstock, Kathleen Mary	Comstock
Coffin, Albert	Bean-Coffin	Comstock, Lois Jane	Leffel
Coffin, Albert "Bud" Walter	Bean-Coffin	Comstock, Mrs. Suda	McNeill
Coffin, Dorothy Winifred	Bean-Coffin	Comstock, Nancy	Comstock
Coffin, Edgar	Bean-Coffin	Comstock, Nancy	Ruth
Coffin, Edgar	Bean-Coffin	Comstock, Pam	Ruth
Coffin, Edgar R.	Bean-Coffin	Comstock, R. W.	Comstock
Coffin, Edgar Rely	Bean-Coffin	Comstock, Ralph Seldon	Comstock
Coffin, Grace Frances	Bean-Coffin	Comstock, Roy D.	Ruth
Coffin, Hugh Gordon	Bean-Coffin	Comstock, Roy David	Comstock
Coffin, Lovene Burniece	Bean-Coffin	Comstock, Ruth M.	Comstock
Coffin, Majorie May	Bean-Coffin	Comstock, Ruth W.	Ruth
Coffin, Marie Katherine	Bean-Coffin	Conan, Mr. E. B.	Upper Perry
Coffin, Neva Priscilla	Bean-Coffin	Condon, OR	Chumos
Coffin, Nora	Bean-Coffin	Conger-Morris (funeral parlor)	Tucker Flat
Coffin, Peter	Catherine Cr.	Congle, J. B.	May
Coffin, Peter M.	Bean-Coffin	Conklin, Albert	Conklin
Coffin, Peter M.	Bean-Coffin	Conklin, Albert G.	Conklin
Coffin, Sarah "Frances"	Bean-Coffin	Conklin, Albert George	Conklin
Coffin, Stephen	Fox Hill	Conklin, Bessie	Conklin
Coffin, Stephen	Marks	Conklin, Clarinda	Conklin
Coffin, Zada	Bean-Coffin	Conklin, Fannie	Conklin
Coffin,Lois Maxine	Bean-Coffin	Conklin, Mrs. Thomas R.	Antles
Coldwater KS	Hardy	Conklin, Nathaniel	Conklin
Coleman property	Carroll	Conklin, Phillip	Conklin
Colerain, Belmont Co., OH	Starkey	Conklin, Thomas	Conklin
Colfax, WA	Owsley	Conley Corner	Sandridge
College of Osteopathic Physicians	Wallsinger	Conley Farms	Conley
College Place, WA	Weaver	Conley siding	Couch
Collins, Priscilla	Mt. Harris	Conley Train	Hamilton
Collins, Sarah	Starkey	Conley Train, the	Conley
Collins, Thelma J.	Bagwell	Conley, "Archie Bird"	Conley
Collins-Pondosa Lumber	Bennett	Conley, "Bird"	Conley
Colorado	Lampkin	Conley, A. B.	Conley
Columbia River	Rinehart	Conley, A. B.	Delong
Columbia River	Ruckle	Conley, A. B.	Hamilton
Columbier, Switzerland	Lizabeth	Conley, A. B.	Phys
Columbus, GA	Lookingglass	Conley, Arch	Fletcher
Columbus, OH	Brooks	Conley, Archibald Colbert	Conley
Combs, (County Clerk)	Hindman	Conley, B. F.	Conklin
Comduff Gap, the	Highway 82	Conley, Jo Frank	Conley
Commercial Club, the	High Valley	Conley, Josia	Conley
Como Perry	Howell	Conley, Lois Jean	Delong
Comstock Road	Ponderosa	Conley, Mary Jane	Conley
Comstock, Alpharetta Elizabeth	Comstock	Conley, Mary Jane	Hulick
Comstock, B. H.	Comstock	Conley, Matilda	Conley
Comstock, David	Ruth	Conley, Matilda	Hamilton
Comstock, E. C.	Comstock	Conley, Merrell	Conley
Comstock, Emma	Comstock	Conley, Miss Fannie	Conklin
Comstock, Frances Mary	Comstock	Conley, Sarah Agnes	Grays Corner
Comstock, Harold R.	Comstock	Conley, Vernetta	Delong
Comstock, John	Ruth	Conrad, Mrs. Irene	Speckhart
Comstock, John Erastus	Comstock	Conservation Man of the Year	Hindman
Comstock, John S.	Comstock	Conservation Man of the Year	Howell

Cove School District	Thew	Craig, Mr. & Mrs. Daniel C.	Craig
Cove Sportsman's Club	Ruth	Craig, Steve	Sanderson
Cove, Mt. Harris	Lower Cove	Craig, Tom Chester	Craig
Cove, OR	French Corral	Crampton, Ann	Crampton
Cove, OR	Haefer	Crampton, Birdie I.	Crampton
Cove, OR	Haggerty	Crampton, Carlene	Crampton
Cove, OR	Hidden Valley	Crampton, Don Howard	Crampton
Cove, OR	High Valley	Crampton, Edna	Crampton
Cove, OR	Highway 82	Crampton, Edna	Crampton
Cove, OR	Janson	Crampton, Floyd "Ted"	Crampton
Cove, OR	Kingsbury	Crampton, Floyd Rogers	Crampton
Cove, OR	Knight	Crampton, Fred	Crampton
Cove, OR	Lantz	Crampton, Harold	Crampton
Cove, OR	Longview	Crampton, Irene	Crampton
Cove, OR	Love	Crampton, Jim	Crampton
Cove, OR	Market	Crampton, John Franklin	Crampton
Cove, OR	May	Crampton, Lewis	Crampton
Cove, OR	McAlister	Crampton, Mabel C.	Crampton
Cove, OR	McKennon	Crampton, Ralph	Crampton
Cove, OR	McNeill	Crampton, Sharon	Crampton
Cove, OR	Morgan Lake	Crampton, Sharon	Crampton
Cove, OR	Mountain View	Crampton, Ted	Crampton
Cove, OR	Parsons	Crampton, Ted	Fox Hill
Cove, OR	Peach	Crampton, Wayne	Crampton
Cove, OR	Phys	Crande Ronde Valley	Mt. Emily
Cove, OR	Rose Ridge	Crane, E. C.	Marks
Cove, OR	Squire	Crawford Co., OH	Marks
Cove, OR	Stackland	Crawford Hill	Phys
Cove, OR	Starkey	Crawford, Captain	Shaw Creek
Cove, OR	Thew	Crawford, ME	Coombs
Cove, OR	Wade	Cree (nation)	Wapiti
Cove, OR	Waltz	Creighton, John	Wickens
Cove, OR	Wapiti	Creswell, Lane Co., OR	Rinehart
Cove-Union Farm Loop (tour)	Lower Cove	Cricket Flat	Chumos
Cowan, Mrs. Lois	Witherspoon	Cricket Flat	Follett
Cowan, Susan Emmaline	McAlister	Cricket Flat	Gordon Creek
Cowboy and Angel's Place	Hallgarth	Cricket Flat	Hardy
Cowlitz Co., WA	Hutchinson	Cricket Flat	Henderson
Cowlitz Co., WA	Middle	Cricket Flat	Henderson
Cox, Elva	Wagoner Hill	Cricket Flat	Hindman
Cox, Matilda	Wilkinson	Cricket Flat	Hug
Cox, Shirley	Sammyville	Cricket Flat	Knight
Crabapple Cemetery, Wheeling	Merritt	Cricket Flat	Merritt
Craddock, Teddy J.	Craddock	Cricket Flat	Parsons
Craig (family)	Summerville	Cricket Flat	Roulet
Craig (kids)	Slack	Cricket Flat	Thompson
Craig Hot Springs	Union Junction	Cricket Flat	Wheeler
Craig, , Daniel C.	Craig	Cricket Flat	Wickens
Craig, A. C.	Union Junction	Cricket Flat	Witherspoon
Craig, Dorothy	Craig	Cricket Flat	Yarrington
Craig, Dorothy	Sanderson	Cricket Flat Grange	Hindman
Craig, Dorothy	Summerville	Cricket Flat Grange	Witherspoon
Craig, Frances "Helen"	Keen Cabin Cr.	Cricket Flat Grass-hoppers	Hindman
Craig, George	Craig	Cricket Flat Road	Good
Craig, George Austin	Craig	Crippen & Daniels Funeral Home	Witherspoon

Crist, Irene	Crampton	Dahlstrom, Andrew	Shaw Mountain
Cronkite, Grace	McAlister	Dahlstrom, Axel Ludwig	Shaw Mountain
Crouser, Bob	Christensen	Dahlstrom, Britta	Shaw Mountain
Crouser, Gladys	Fox Hill	Dahlstrom, Olaf P.	Shaw Mountain
Crow (family)	Highway 82	Dahlstrom, Ruth L.	Shaw Mountain
Cruikshank, Louisa Ball	Wickens	Dailey, Joy	Wheeler
Crum, Eugene	Chumos	Dailey, Mrs. Louene	Bean-Coffin
Crum, Frank	Chumos	Daley, Mrs. Viva	Mt. Glen
Crum, George	Chumos	Daley's Ranch	Starkey
Crum, Jeremiah	Chumos	Daleyville	Starkey
Crum, Jeremiah A.	Chumos	Daleyville, OR	Coombs
Crum, Jesse W.	Chumos	Dalton Ranch	Jimmy
Crum, McKinley	Chumos	Dalton, C. R. "Curt"	Jimmy
Crum, Nellie Louisa	Chumos	Dalton, Cora E.	Jimmy
Crum, Ora	Chumos	Dalton, Grant	Jimmy
Crum, Sarah	Chumos	Dalton, J. Wylie	Jimmy
Crum, Sarah Elizabeth	Chumos	Dalton, James "Jimmie"	Jimmy
Crum, Willard D.	Chumos	Dalton, James "Wiley"	Jimmy
Cuba	McCanse	Dalton, Jeanette	Jimmy
Cuddehack, Leon	Airport	Dalton, Mrs. Marguerite	Comstock
Culbertson precinct, NB	Dry Creek	Dalton, Thomas	Jimmy
Cullen, Ellen Jane	Buchanan	Dan, OR	Staples
Cullen, Margaret M.	Wade	Dane Co., WI	Thompson
Cunliffe, Elizabeth Anna	Upper Perry	Dane Co., WI	Wolf Creek
Cunningham, Lucy A.	Wickens	Daniel, R. H.	Fletcher
Cunningham, Mary Isabell	Wickens	Daniels Funeral Home	Geiger Butte
Cunningham, Milton	Ramo Flat	Daniels Funeral Home	Greiner
Curry Co., OR	Moses Creek	Daniels Funeral Home	Hindman
Curtis Road	Miller	Daniels Funeral Home	Thompson
Curtis, Alice C.	Curtis	Daniel's Funeral Home	Kingsbury
Curtis, Anna L.	Curtis	Danies Chapel of the Valley	Ruth
Curtis, Ben F.	Draper	Dark Woods (movie)	Sammyville
Curtis, Benjamin F.	Draper	Darland, Dr.	Hamilton
Curtis, Benjamin Franklin Jr.	Draper	Daron (family)	Pine Grove
Curtis, Benjamin Franklin Sr.	Draper	Darr Road	Kingsbury
Curtis, Charles	Curtis	Darr Train	Darr
Curtis, Chester	Curtis	Darr, Alta B.	Darr
Curtis, Chester Arthur	Curtis	Darr, Catherine Eve	Darr
Curtis, Dean Lee	Curtis	Darr, Charlles	Darr
Curtis, Della	Curtis	Darr, George O.	Darr
Curtis, Della May	Curtis	Darr, Hester Emma	Darr
Curtis, Delta L.	Curtis	Darr, Jesse Sargent	Darr
Curtis, Dolores	Curtis	Darr, John Marcus	Darr
Curtis, Elnora Mae	Curtis	Darr, Joseph	Darr
Curtis, Emily	Draper	Darr, Luella Jane	Darr
Curtis, Jack	Curtis	Darr, Margaret	Darr
Curtis, John Arthur	Curtis	Darr, Martha	Darr
Curtis, Laurie Gay	Curtis	Darr, Samuel	Darr
Curtis, Lenore Mabel	Draper	Darr, William	Darr
Curtis, Randall Christian	Curtis	Dause, Charles	Marks
Curtis,David	Curtis	Davidhizar, Hannah	Dry Creek
Cuthbert, John	Sandridge	Davis Co., IA	Gordon Creek
Cutris, Vella C.	Curtis	Davis, "Soapy"	Lookingglass
Cycle Oregon	Summerville	Davis, "Soapy" I. C.	Lookingglass
C-zers Drive In	Philberg	Davis, Alton	Benson

Davis, Anna Belle	Lookingglass	Dealy, Rebecca Frances	Starkey
Davis, Charles	Benson	Dealy, Susan	Starkey
Davis, Charles D.	Lookingglass	Dealy, William Joseph	Starkey
Davis, Dora	Lookingglass	Dealy's Station	Starkey
Davis, Frank C.	Lookingglass	DeBord, Bertha	Haefer
Davis, Ira Cleveland	Lookingglass	DeBorde, T. J.	Mill Creek
Davis, James "Hugh"	Lookingglass	Decker, Ann	Elkanah
Davis, Josiah	High Valley	Decker, George William	Elkanah
Davis, Lillian Ann	Lookingglass	Deer Creek Station	Wickens
Davis, Lysander K.	Lookingglass	Deer Lodge, MT	Jones
Davis, Nellie	Lookingglass	Delight, WA	End
Davis, Richard	Benson	DeLint, Cresta	Sandridge
Davis, Soapy	Hallgarth	DeLong, Cecil	Bond
Davis, Soapy	Moses Creek	Delong, Cecil G.	Delong
Davis, Susan	Starkey	Delong, Dale	Delong
Davis-Rhine, Mary "Cordelia"	Roulet	Delong, Ernest Homer	Delong
Daw, Daisy	Good	Delong, Fannie Alice	Delong
Dawes, Byron N.	Marks	Delong, J. P.	Delong
Dawson, Rhoda	Booth	Delong, Jacob Pace	Delong
Day, C. H.	Fruitdale	Delong, Lois Jean	Delong
Dayton WA	Owsley	Delong, Phyllis Jean	Delong
Dayton, Columbia Co., WA	Greiner	Delong, Savilla Anettie	Delong
Dayton, OR	Marley Creek	Delong, Savilla Anettie	Delong
Dayton, WA	Greiner	Delong, Scott	Delong
De Clue, Jane	Marks	Delong, Vernon Ernest	Delong
de Lint, Cresta May	Hays	Demmison, Mrs. A. M.	Wilkinson
de Lint, Rein	Hays	DeMoss Concertists of Oregon	Mill Creek
Deachman, Betsy	Sanderson	DeMoss Springs	Mill Creek
Dead Man Pass	Fox Hill	DeMoss, Elizabeth Ann	Mill Creek
Dead Man's Pass	Anson	DeMoss, George	Mill Creek
Deal Canyon	Morgan Lake	DeMoss, Henry	Mill Creek
Deal, Daisy	Deal Canyon	DeMoss, James	Mill Creek
Deal, Della B.	Deal Canyon	DeMoss, James McElroy	Mill Creek
Deal, Margaret	Deal Canyon	DeMoss, Lizzie	Mill Creek
Deal, Mary E.	Deal Canyon	DeMoss, May	Mill Creek
Deal, May Ella	Deal Canyon	DeMoss, Minnie	Mill Creek
Deal, Robert	Deal Canyon	Dennis, Lucinda	Stackland
Deal, Robert Lee	Deal Canyon	Dennison, Miss Gladys M.	Wilkinson
Deal, William	Deal Canyon	Denver, NE	Chandler
Dealy Ranch	Starkey	Depot Bay, OR	Draper
Dealy Wagon Road	Anthony Lake	Depot Street, La Grande	Morgan Lake
Dealy Wagon Road Company	Starkey	DePue, IL	Lookingglass
Dealy, Belle	Starkey	Derryfinnan, Ireland	Bodie
Dealy, David Jr.	Starkey	Deschutes River	Grays Corner
Dealy, David M.	Starkey	DeSouter, Judi	Elgin Cem.
Dealy, David Sr.	Starkey	Detroit, MI	Keen Cabin Cr.
Dealy, Diana	Starkey	Deuel, Katie Rosella	Hill Lay
Dealy, Elizabeth (Mills)	Starkey	Devlin, Birdie I.	Crampton
Dealy, Elsie	Starkey	Dewitt, SD	Comstock
Dealy, Florence Lillie	Starkey	Dial Earl	Dial
Dealy, George M.	Starkey	Dial, Charles E.	Dial
Dealy, James Daniel	Starkey	Dial, Charles Earl	Dial
Dealy, Jonathan Thomas	Starkey	Dial, Edward D.	Dial
Dealy, Mary Jane	Starkey	Dial, Edward D.	Dial
Dealy, Mary Jane Jr.	Starkey	Dial, Ella	Dial

Dial, Fanchon Eleanor	Dial	Draper, Martin	Draper
Dial, Florence	Dial	Draper, Mary A.	Draper
Dial, Harry	Dial	Draper, Mary E.	Draper
Dial, Joe	Dial	Draper, Maryette Eunice	Draper
Dial, Lydia	Dial	Draper, Maude Ethel	Draper
Dial, Margaret E.	Dial	Draper, Oscar	Draper
Dial, Mary A.	Dial	Draper, Oscar H.	Draper
Dial, Miss Rhoda	Dial	Draper, Rhoda A.	Draper
Dial, Porter	Dial	Draper, Richard "Dick"	Draper
Dial, Raymond	Dial	Draper, Rosanna E.	Draper
Dial, Tom	Dial	Draper, Rosanna E.	Draper
Dial, William E.	Dial	Draper, Rosie	Draper
Dial, William Earl	Dial	Draper, Sarah	Draper
Dial, William Earl Jr.	Dial	Draper, William H.	Draper
Dial, William Edward	Dial	Draper, William Henry Harrison	Draper
Dick Lindsey Band	Howell	Dresden, Germany	Gaertner
Dickinson, ND	Leffel	Dry Creek	Hug
Disrtict # 12	Red Pepper	Dry Creek Lane	Summerville
District # 9	Red Pepper	Dry Creek Road	Summerville
District #40	Red Pepper	Dry Creek School	Behrens
Division Street	Hartford	Dry Creek School	Case
Dixie, WA	Geiger Butte	Dry Creek School	Dry Creek
Dixon, Mrs. Edith	Greiner	Dry Creek School	Slack
Dobbins, J. H.	Morgan Lake	Dry Creek School Dist. #17	Dry Creek
Doblestine, Emily	Draper	Dry Creek School District	Dry Creek
Doddridge, Hannah Victoria	Tucker Flat	Dry Creek School District #17	Hindman
Dodge Co., WI	Yerges	Dry Creek School District #17	Summerville
Dodson, Janet	Government Gul.	Dryer, Catherine Louise	Owsley
Doe, Abigail Ayers	Chumos	Dufur, OR	Imbler
Dolan, Mrs. Kathleen	Comstock	Dunaway, Dora C.	Witherspoon
Dolstrum, Mrs. Dolly	Howell	Dunlap (strawberries)	Ramo Flat
Dolstrums, the	McCanse	Dunlap, Mrs. Arva	Geiger Butte
Doolin, Marcia	Evers	Dunn (family)	Starkey
Dopson, Michael Imler	Imbler	Dunnington, Cora Gaines	Booth
Dough, Mr.	Chumos	Dunns Rock, NC	Bagwell
Dougherty, Minnie	Benson	Durham (cattle)	Imbler
Douglas, Justice William O.	Riddle	Durham, Murray	Keen Cabin Cr.
Douglas, Mildred	Riddle	Durland (place)	Monroe
Downey, CA	Witherspoon	Dutch Flat Creek	Antelope Peak
Downing, Frances	Summerville	Dutton Road	Indian Creek
Doyle, Rosanna Eliza	Draper	Dutton, Evalyn Lavina Lorince	Dutton
Doyles, Miss Rosanna E.	Draper	Dutton, Frank B.	Dutton
Draper, Adeline	Draper	Dutton, Gains "Gaius"	Dutton
Draper, Ann E.	Draper	Dutton, Gaius	Dutton
Draper, Dick	Draper	Dutton, Robert	Dutton
Draper, Elverdo	Draper	Dutton, Virginia	Dutton
Draper, Emily	Draper	Dutton, Virginia Jane	Dutton
Draper, Emily	Draper	Eagle Valley, OR	Miller
Draper, Henry	Draper	Eagles Lodge	Tucker Flat
Draper, John P.	Draper	Eakin, Ann	Myers
Draper, John P.	Draper	East End (historic)	May
Draper, Julia G.	Draper	East Pagosa, Archuleta Co., CO	Love
Draper, Leoline	Draper	East, Elizabeth Jane	Dry Creek
Draper, Luda A.	Draper	Eastern OR Fruit Growers Assn.	Weaver
Draper, Lulu Queva	Draper	Eastern Oregon	McKennon

Elgin's Mountain Man	Lookingglass	Endicott, Lydia Ann	Clark Creek
Elizabeth Creek	Catherine Cr.	Endicott, Mary Jane	Clark Creek
Elizabeth Creek	Godley	Endicott, Mary Jane	Clark Creek
Elizabeth Creek	Little Creek	Endicott, Mickey	Clark Creek
Elizabeth, NJ	Hutchinson	Endicott, Mickey	Indian Creek
Elk Flat	Gordon Creek	Endicott, Ulric Ernest	Clark Creek
Elk Song Ranch	Morgan Lake	Endicott, Ulric Ernest	Indian Creek
Elkhorn Mountains	Antelope Peak	Endicott, W. C.	Clark Creek
Elkhorn Mountains	Anthony Lake	Endicott, William Clark	Clark Creek
Elkins, OR	Marks	England	Stackland
Elks (Lodge)	Parsons	Englewood Park Cemetery	McIntyre
Elledge, Daniel	Robbs Hill	Englewood, Los Angeles Co., CA	McIntyre
Elledge, Ike	McAlister	Enloe, Cyrus G.	Sandridge
Elledge, Mrs. Lucy	Robbs Hill	Enloe, F. E.	Morgan Lake
Elledge, Thomas	McAlister	Ensign, S.	Starkey
Elliott, Charles	Golding	Enterprise Cemetery	Wright
Elliott, Fanchon Eleanor	Dial	Enterprise Record-Chieftain	Morgan Lake
Ellis Island, NY	Gaertner	Enterprise, OR	Gaertner
Ellis, Elizabeth	Rinehart	Enterprise, OR	McAlister
Ellis, Jane	Ellis	Enterprise, OR	Wright
Ellis, W. W.	Ellis	Enterprise, Wallowa Co., OR	Halley
Elm, MO	Booth	EOSC Foundation	McKenzie
Elmer, Amelia	Lower Cove	EOU	McDonald
Elmer, Carl	Kingsbury	Ephraim, (blind lad)	Dry Creek
Elmer, Doris	Bates	Erie Co. PA	Buchanan
Elmer, Frank	Bates	Erlach, Bern, Switzerland	Lizabeth
Elmer, Harvey	Bates	Ernest Road	Frances
Elmer, Harvey	Lower Cove	Esther Street, Imbler	Summerville
Elmer, Larry	Robinson	Estonia	Squire
Elmer, Laura Edna	Bates	Estrada, Sharon	Philberg
Elmer, Lydia	Lower Cove	Etna, Celesta A.	Haggerty
Elmer, Mary	Summerville	Eubanks, Nellie May	Rinehart
Elmer, Millie	Myers	Euclid Ave., St. Louis, MO	Upper Perry
Elmer, Norma Jean	Roulet	Eugene Pioneer Cemetery	Shaw Creek
Elmer, Russel	Roulet	Eugene, Lane Co., OR	Rinehart
Elmira, Stark Co., IL	Shaw Creek	Eugene, OR	Chumos
Emigrant Springs	Starkey	Eugene, OR	Dry Creek
Emporia, Lyon Co., KS	Shaw Mountain	Eugene, OR	Grays Corner
End Road	Mink	Eugene, OR	Imbler
End Road	Sanderson	Europe	Mill Creek
End, Antone	End	Europe	Stackland
End, Cecil	End	Evans, Jack	Moses Creek
End, Jacob	End	Evans, John "Jack"	Mt. Emily
End, Jacob "Jake"	End	Evans, John "Jack"	Starkey
End, Joseph	End	Evans, Mrs. Rose	Hindman
End, Katie	End	Evers, Charles "Orris"	Evers
End, Percy	End	Evers, Eloine Leota	Evers
End, Percy M.	End	Evers, John	Evers
End, Samantha A.	End	Evers, Marcia	Evers
End, Tony	End	Evers, Pearl Estrella	Evers
Endicott, Elizabeth Elenor	Ruckman	Eyster, Mina E.	Weaver
Endicott, Elizabeth Elenor	Woodell	Fahrni, Mary	Henderson
Endicott, Ira Clark	Clark Creek	Fairbault, MN	Dutton
Endicott, John Richard	Indian Creek	Fairlawn, OR	Marley Creek
Endicott, Joseph	Clark Creek	Fairview Fruit Farm	Lantz

Fall Creek Twp., Bluff Hall, IL	Speckhart	Five Points	Fox Hill
Falls City, NB	Gekeler	Five Points	Mill Creek
Fanzey, Mary	Henderson	Five Points Creek	Five Point Cr.
Farland, McPherson Co., KS	Lower Cove	Five Points Creek Mill	Fox Hill
Farm Bureau	McCanse	Fivepoint Creek	Five Point Cr.
Farm Security Administration	Starr	Fivepoints Creek	Five Point Cr.
Farmer, Eleanor	Hulick	Flagstaff Butte	Big Creek
Farmer, Raymond "Buzz"	Parsons	Flathead Indians	Moses Creek
Farmer-Merchant Banquet	McKenzie	Flatt, Mary Ann	Turnbull
Farmers' Union	Brooks	Fleshman, Dorothy	Highway 82
Farris, Ida May	Marvin	Fleshman, Dorothy	Morgan Lake
Federal Land Bank	Government Gul.	Fleshman, Dorothy	Philberg
Feik, Norma Jean	Hull	Fletcher, "Bessie"	Fletcher
Fennimore Times (newspaper)	McIntyre	Fletcher, Elizabeth	Fletcher
Fennimore, WI	McIntyre	Fletcher, Jack	Fletcher
Ferguson (home)	Wright	Fletcher, James Preston	Fletcher
Fifer, Ralph	Airport	Fletcher, John "Jack" Riley	Fletcher
Findlay	Finley Creek	Fletcher, Margaret Elizabeth	Fletcher
Findley Creek Lane	Finley Creek	Fletcher, Mrs. Bessie	Fletcher
Findley, A. B.	Finley Creek	Flevious Road	Park
Findley, Alexander Blakey	Finley Creek	Flint, MI	Chandler
Findley, Bertha Edyth	Finley Creek	Flora, OR	Sanderson
Findley, Emma D.	Finley Creek	Flower, J. C.	Igo
Findley, Everest E.	Finley Creek	Flower, Mrs. Anna Mae	Igo
Findley, Florence Mary	Finley Creek	Fly Creek	Fly Valley
Findley, George Madison	Finley Creek	Fly Creek Road	Fly Ridge
Findley, Henry Ross	Finley Creek	Fly Valley	Fly Creek
Findley, John F.	Finley Creek	Fly Valley Road	Tin Trough
Findley, Levi "Sammy"	Finley Creek	Foley (building)	Igo
Findley, Levi S.	Finley Creek	Foley Building	Wallsinger
Findley, Lora E.	Finley Creek	Follett (family)	Pine Grove
Findley, Sarah	Finley Creek	Follett, Boyd	Follett
Findley, Sarah Jane	Finley Creek	Follett, Florence Monroe	Follett
Fine, Sarah	Mt. Harris	Follett, George Orien	Follett
Fine, William	Mt. Harris	Follett, Hannah Encora "Cora"	Follett
Finland	Squire	Follett, Jesse King	Follett
Finley Camp	Finley Creek	Follett, Kim	Follett
Finley Creek	Finley Creek	Follett, Mary Ellen	Follett
Finley Creek Road	Ruckle	Follett, Norma	Follett
Finley, Mary	Rankin	Follett, Reta June	Follett
Finley, Mrs. Lottie Loie	Bushnell	Follett, Shellea	Follett
Finn, Attorney C. H.	Riddle	Follett, Sheree	Follett
First Kittens	Bean-Coffin	Follett, Warren Jr.	Follett
First Street, La Grande	McCanse	Follett, Warren King Jr.	Follett
Fish Trap Ford	Fish Trap	Follett, Warren Sr.	Follett
Fish Trap Hill	Fish Trap	Fond du Lac, WI	Bidwell
Fish Trap, the	Highway 82	Foot Hill Road	Tucker Flat
Fisher, Columbus	Hug	Foothill Road	Keen Cabin Cr.
Fisher, Eleanor	Halley	Foothill Road	May
Fisher, Job	Marks	Foothill Road	Stackland
Fisher, Mr. & Mrs. Roy	Dutton	Foothill Road	Valley View
Fisher, Sarah J.	Hug	Foreign Operations Admin.	Hawkins
Fisk, Howard	Morgan Lake	Forest Boundary Road	Moses Creek
Five Point Creek	Five Point Cr.	Forest Cove	French Corral
Five Point Creek Road	Staples	Forest Cove (Cove)	Phys

Forest Grove	French Corral	Fries, Inez	Summerville
Forest Grove, OR	Henderson	Fries, Inez L.	Dry Creek
Forest Grove, OR	Morgan Lake	Fries, Mrs. Inez	Summerville
Forest Grove, OR	Wright	Friswold, Carl D.	Ruckman
Forest Home	Phys	Friswold, Carl D.	Woodell
Forestville, CA	Marley Creek	Friswold, Deborah	Woodell
Fort Hall, ID	Moses Creek	Friswold, Hattie "Wave"	Ruckman
Fort Kearney, NB	McAlister	Friswold, Hattie Wave	Woodell
Fort Lapwai Indian Agency	Telocaset	Friswold, Scott	Woodell
Fort Ord, CA	Ruckman	Frost, Cleora Leilla	Knight
Fort Scott, KS	Conley	Frosty School	Lower Cove
Fort Scott, KS	Hamilton	Fruita, OR	Morgan Lake
Fort Wayne, IN	Haggerty	Fruitdale	Dial
Foster, George	Jimmy	Fruitdale	Owsley
Foster, Margaret J.	Striker	Fruitdale	Wright
Fountain Green, UT	Christensen	Fruitdale (section)	Woodruff
Fourth Street, La Grande	Morgan Lake	Fruitdale Findings, (column)	Fruitdale
Fowler, Dorothy Winifred	Bean-Coffin	Fruitdale Lane	Bird
Fowler, Mrs. Abigail	Chumos	Fruitdale Lane	Hampton
Fowler, Mrs. Margaret	Bean-Coffin	Fruitdale Lane	Lark
Fowler, Orson Squire	Chumos	Fruitdale Lane	Peacock
Fowler, Professor	Chumos	Fruitdale Lane	Riverside
Fowler-Chumos, Abigail	Chumos	Fruitdale Lane	Robin
Fox (man named)	Orodell	Fruitdale Lane	Spooner
Fox and Geese (game)	Summerville	Fruitdale School	Fruitdale
Fox Hill	Crampton	Fruitdale School District #27	Fruitdale
Fox Hill Road	Robbs Hill	Fry Meadow	Lookout Mt.
Fox Hill School District	Fox Hill	Fugit, Andrew H.	Shaw Mountain
Fox Hill Trail Head	Fox Hill	Fugit, Jennett	Shaw Mountain
Fox Hill-Robbs Hill	Kamela	Fugit, Lida Elizabeth Ann	Shaw Mountain
Fox Valley Cemetery	Love	Fugit, Rebecca	Shaw Mountain
Fox, Charles	Fox Hill	Fugit, Reuel Custer	Shaw Mountain
Fox, Charles	Marks	Fulkerson, Marian	Fox Hill
Fox, George	Fox Hill	Fulkerson, Miss Marion	Fox Hill
Foxhome, MN	Mathson	Fulton Co. IL	Morgan Lake
France	Marks	Funk, Iris	Hull
France	May	Gaddy, Betty "Jean"	Bennett
France	Moses Creek	Gaddy, Lester Neil	Bennett
Frank Brothers	Owsley	Gaertner Lane	Fruitdale
Franklin, Mrs. Edna	Greiner	Gaertner Lane	Riverside
Frazier, Mr. John	Lower Cove	Gaertner, (mother)	Gaertner
Freel, Elizabeth "Lizzie"	Bushnell	Gaertner, Adolf	Gaertner
Freeman, Sharon	Squire	Gaertner, Bill	Gaertner
Freewater, OR	Wilkinson	Gaertner, Ella	Gaertner
Freewater, Umatilla Co., OR	Rawhide	Gaertner, Emil	Gaertner
Fremont, General	Gordon Creek	Gaertner, Emil P.	Gaertner
French (settlement)	Moses Creek	Gaertner, Hattie	Gaertner
French Canadian (community)	Moses Creek	Gaertner, Herman	Gaertner
French Canadians	Ramo Flat	Gaertner, Irna	Gaertner
French Gulch, Shasta Co., CA	Hallgarth	Gaertner, Lena	Gaertner
French, Samuel G.	French Corral	Gaertner, Martha	Gaertner
French, Samuel G.	Good	Gaertner, Paul	Gaertner
French, Stewart	Fletcher	Galesburg, WI	Bidwell
Fries, Frieda	McKenzie	Galloway Brothers Mill	Middle
Fries, Henry	Dry Creek	Galloway Cemetery	Middle

Galloway Road	Middle	Gawith, Leroy Gillis	Rawhide
Galloway Road	Palmer Junction	Gawith, Lyma I	Rawhide
Galloway, Cecill	Pine Grove	Gawith, Lynn Irvin	Rawhide
Galloway, Dick	Pine Grove	Gawith, Mabel Clare	Rawhide
Galloway, Emma	Middle	Gawith, Mary Jane	Rawhide
Galloway, H. S.	Middle	Gawith, Ray Arthur	Rawhide
Galloway, Jewel	Pine Grove	Gawith, Thelma	Rawhide
Galloway, Jewell W.	Middle	Gawith, William	Rawhide
Galloway, John Tilford "Til"	Middle	Gay, Armstrong	Hunter
Galloway, Juliet Ann	Miller	Gay, Charles S.	Hunter
Galloway, Maggie	Pine Grove	Gay, Nancy	Hunter
Galloway, Pete	Pine Grove	Gebber, Lena	Bodie
Galloway, Sarah Ann	Middle	Geer, Heman J.	French Corral
Galloway, Sherman	Pine Grove	Geer, Nora Marie	Kingsbury
Galloway, William Harrison	Middle	Gehrke, Florentine "Flora"	Thompson
Galloway, William Harrison	Pine Grove	Geiger, Fred	Geiger Butte
Gamble, Karen	McKenzie	Geiger, Irene	Geiger Butte
Gamble, William	McKenzie	Geiger, John "Lute"	Geiger Butte
Gande Ronde Valley	May	Geiger, Lenina	Geiger Butte
Gangloff, Augustine I	Morgan Lake	Geiger, Lewis	Geiger Butte
Gangloff, Augustine I.	Wood	Geiger, Miss Grace	Geiger Butte
Gano, (apple)	Fruitdale	Geiger, Wayne	Geiger Butte
Gardner, O. M.	Red Pepper	Gekeler Lane	Godley
Garfield Co., UT	Hill Lay	Gekeler Lane	Red Pepper
Garibaldi, Tillamook Co., OR	Starkey	Gekeler Lane	Roe
Garlitz, Joe	Hartford	Gekeler Lane	Wright
Garlitz, Joe	Highway 82	Gekeler, Catherine	Delong
Garrison, Flora A.	Starkey	Gekeler, Catherine	Godley
Garrison, Jonas W.	Phys	Gekeler, Catherine "Kate" S.	Gekeler
Garten Lizabeth	Lizabeth	Gekeler, Dora Mae	Foothill
Gaskill Road	McKennon	Gekeler, Fannie Alice	Delong
Gaskill, Ebeneezer D.	McKennon	Gekeler, George	Delong
Gaskill, Frederick	McKennon	Gekeler, George	Gekeler
Gaskill, Jennie Armintha	McKennon	Gekeler, George John	Gekeler
Gaskill, Jesse Allen "Jet"	McKennon	Gekeler, Mrs. C. R.	Janson
Gaskill, LaNita	McKennon	Gekeler, W. R.	Wolf Creek
Gaskill, Lola	McKennon	Gekeler. George	McAlister
Gaskill, Maude	McKennon	Gelham, Mrs. Flora	Hull
Gaskill, Ralph	McKennon	Genesee Co., MI	Riddle
Gaskill, Samuel	McKennon	Geneva, Switzerland	Hug
Gaskill, Samuel B.	McKennon	Gentry Co., MO	Hunter
Gaskill, Susannah	McKennon	Gentry, Irene	Slack
Gaskill, Wilfred	McKennon	George Palmer Lumber Co.	Palmer Junction
Gaskill, Wilma	McKennon	George Thomas (stage coaches)	Summerville
Gavin (family)	Starkey	George, Don	Jimmy
Gawith, Arden Loren	Rawhide	George, Ellen	Woodruff
Gawith, Charles W.	Rawhide	Geovanni (Italian stone worker)	Highway 82
Gawith, Gerald Harry	Rawhide	Gerber, Berta Lou	Moses Creek
Gawith, Harry	Rawhide	Gerber, Carrie	Wheeler
Gawith, Harvey	Rawhide	Gerber, Lee	Moses Creek
Gawith, Jackson	Rawhide	Gerkin, Saul (Sol)	McAlister
Gawith, John	Bean-Coffin	German (language)	Mathson
Gawith, John	Rawhide	German, Mary	Woodell
Gawith, John II	Rawhide	German, Mrs. Mary Margaret	Wallsinger
Gawith, Keith E.	Rawhide	German, William	Wallsinger

German, William	Woodell	Godley, Catherine	Catherine Cr.
Germany	Marks	Godley, Catherine	Little Creek
Germany	Nice	Godley, Catherine	Godley
Germany	Stackland	Godley, Catherine Virginia	Godley
Germany	Starr	Godley, Charles William	Godley
Germany	Striker	Godley, Gertrude	Godley
Germany	Wallsinger	Godley, Juliana	Catherine Cr.
Gibbon	Fox Hill	Godley, Lillian Bell	Godley
Gibbs, Governor	Sandridge	Godley, M. E.	Godley
Gietlhuber, Theresa	Sanderson	Godley, Mahlon	Godley
Gilbert, E. C.	Highway 82	Godley, Mary	Godley
Gilbert, Mary Ann	Bidwell	Godley, Mary Elizabeth	Godley
Giles, Mary A.	Wright	Godley, Thomas	Godley
Gilham, Jennie	Yerges	Godley, Thomas Jr.	Godley
Gilkerson, J. E.	Wolf Creek	Godley, Thomas M.	Godley
Gilkison, Elizabeth	Frances	Godley, William	Godley
Gilkison, Frances	Ernest	Goff, Mattie	Rawhide
Gilkison, Frances Elizabeth	Frances	Gold Hill Mine	Coughanour
Gilkison, Frank	Frances	Gold Rush of 1849	Wright
Gilkison, J. R.	Gilkison	Golden Rule, the	Wilkinson
Gilkison, James R.	Gilkison	Golden, Vernetta	Delong
Gilkison, M. M.	Jimmy	Golding, Audas Ezra	Golding
Gilkison, Mary Amanda	Gilkison	Golding, Flora E.	Golding
Gilliam, H. E.	Summerville	Golding, Flora Elizabeth	Golding
Gilliam, Mrs. Irene	Geiger Butte	Golding, Leander	Golding
Gillispie, Ed	Kingsbury	Golding, Mary Zenitia	Golding
Gillmore, (Justice of the Peace)	Follett	Golding, Mattie	Golding
Gilstrap, Dr. C. L.	Airport	Good Ranch	Good
Girard, KS	Hamilton	Good Road	Hardy
Glasgow, Scotland	Shaw Mountain	Good Road	Merritt
Glass Hill Road	Morgan Lake	Good Road	Rawhide
Glass, Charles F.	Glass Hill	Good Road	Thompson
Glass, Mary Jane	Glass Hill	Good Road	Wickens
Glass, William Norman	Glass Hill	Good Road	Yarrington
Glass, William W.	Glass Hill	Good Roads (committee)	Ruckle
Glen, John A.	Hunter	Good Sam Club	Frances
Glendell Fruit Farm	Stackland	Good Saw Mill	Good
Glenn Century Farm	McKenzie	Good, Adaline	Good
Glenn Lane	McKenzie	Good, Al	Hunter
Glenn, Carol	Heber	Good, Alfred	Good
Glenn, Carol	McCanse	Good, Alta	Flevious
Glenn, Christina	Heber	Good, Cordelia	Good
Glenn, Edythe	Heber	Good, Dick	Good
Glenn, Heber Parker	Heber	Good, Dick	Wickens
Glenn, Myra	McKenzie	Good, Frank	Good
Glenn, Pam	Summerville	Good, George	Good
Glenn, Randy	Summerville	Good, Howard	Good
Glenn, Sarah	McKenzie	Good, John P.	Hardy
Glenn, Tolbert T.	McKenzie	Good, John Porter	Good
Glenn, Walter Lund	Heber	Good, Lee	Good
Glenwood Ranch	McKenzie	Good, Lillian	Good
Global Positioning System (GPS)	WAAS	Good, Mae	Good
Godley, Anna Lulu	Godley	Good, Paul	Good
Godley, Archie	Godley	Good, Richard	Good
Godley, Aurelia Belle	Godley	Good, Richard Irwin	Good

Name	Location	Name	Location
Good, Ruth	Good	Grande Ronde Lumber Co.	Lower Perry
Good, Sandra	Good	Grande Ronde Military Road	Starkey
Good, Warren	Good	Grande Ronde Retirement Center	Hawkins
Good, William	Good	Grande Ronde River	Fox Hill
Goodall, Kitty	Pine Grove	Grande Ronde River	Grande Ronde R.
Goodbroad, Georgianna	Haggerty	Grande Ronde River	Hamilton
Goodman, Joe	McAlister	Grande Ronde River	Highway 82
Goodnaugh, Charles	Hunter	Grande Ronde River	Howell
Goodnough, Charles	Blackhawk Tr	Grande Ronde River	Island
Goodspeed, Marla	Rose Ridge	Grande Ronde River	Lookingglass
Goodyear Tire Co.	Ruth	Grande Ronde River	Lower Perry
Gordon Creek	Middle	Grande Ronde River	Marks
Gordon Creek Road	Middle	Grande Ronde River	McIntyre
Gordon Creek Road	Sammyville	Grande Ronde River	McKennon
Gordon, Alexander	Gordon Creek	Grande Ronde River	Meadow Creek
Gordon, Dana	Gordon Creek	Grande Ronde River	Mill Creek
Gordon, George	Hindman	Grande Ronde River	Mt. Emily
Gordon, Isaac	Hug	Grande Ronde River	Orodell
Gordon, James A. Sr.	Gordon Creek	Grande Ronde River	Palmer Junction
Gordon, James Jr.	Gordon Creek	Grande Ronde River	Peach
Gordon, John	Gordon Creek	Grande Ronde River	Philberg
Gordon, Mary E.	Gordon Creek	Grande Ronde River	Phillips Creek
Gordon, Mary Jane	Hindman	Grande Ronde River	Riddle
Gordon, Mort	Gordon Creek	Grande Ronde River	Shaw Creek
Gordon, Mort	Thompson	Grande Ronde River	Starkey
Gordon, Mrs. Willis E.	Roulet	Grande Ronde River	Striker
Gordon, Nancy	Gordon Creek	Grande Ronde River	Upper Perry
Gordon, Nancy Alice	Roulet	Grande Ronde River	White Horse
Gordon, Priscilla	Gordon Creek	Grande Ronde River	Fox Hill
Gordon, Rebecca	Gordon Creek	Grande Ronde River Road	Fly Ridge
Gordon, Robert (George)	Gordon Creek	Grande Ronde Symphony	Lester
Gordon, William	Gordon Creek	Grande Ronde Valley	Hug
Gordon, William	Gordon Creek	Grande Ronde Valley	Hutchinson
Gordon, William	Hindman	Grande Ronde Valley	Keen Cabin Cr.
Gordon, Zada Ordell	Bean-Coffin	Grande Ronde Valley	Kerns
Goss Motors	Leffel	Grande Ronde Valley	Knight
Goss Motors	Starr	Grande Ronde Valley	Ladd Creek
Gossler, Mrs. Loy	Kingsbury	Grande Ronde Valley	Lower Cove
Govt. Camp, Clackamas Co., OR	Morgan Lake	Grande Ronde Valley	Marks
Goyette, Peter	Moses Creek	Grande Ronde Valley	Marks
Grady, H. C.	May	Grande Ronde Valley	McKennon
Grand Island, NE	Conklin	Grande Ronde Valley	Middle
Grand View Fruit Farm	Stackland	Grande Ronde Valley	Miller
Grande Ponde Valley	Phys	Grande Ronde Valley	Moses Creek
Grande Ronde Dairy	Hutchinson	Grande Ronde Valley	Myers
Grande Ronde Electric Co.	Mill Creek	Grande Ronde Valley	Orodell
Grande Ronde Electric Co.	Morgan Lake	Grande Ronde Valley	Robbs Hill
Grande Ronde Hospital	Fish Trap	Grande Ronde Valley	Ruckman
Grande Ronde Hospital	Hamilton	Grande Ronde Valley	Ruth
Grande Ronde Hospital	Lookingglass	Grande Ronde Valley	Sanderson
Grande Ronde Hospital	Myers	Grande Ronde Valley	Sandridge
Grande Ronde Hospital	Owsley	Grande Ronde Valley	Shaw Creek
Grande Ronde Hospital	Parsons	Grande Ronde Valley	Standley
Grande Ronde Hospital Hospice	Good	Grande Ronde Valley	Wagoner Hill
Grande Ronde Light & Power	Hunter	Grande Ronde Valley	Wallsinger

Grande Ronde Valley	Webster	Gray, Samuel Hughes	Grays Corner
Grande Ronde Valley	Woodell	Gray, Sarah	Grays Corner
Grande Ronde Valley	Yerges	Gray, Sarah Agnes	Grays Corner
Grandview Cemetery	Grandview Cem.	Gray, Sarah Sylvina	Grays Corner
Grandview Cemetery	Marvin	Gray, Sylvina	Booth
Grandy (estate)	Wright	Gray's Corner Rd	Alicel
Grange Hall (neighborhood)	Robbs Hill	Gray's Corner Road	Hull
Grange Hall Road	Middle	Gray's Corner Road	McKennon
Granger Co., TN	Grays Corner	Gray's Corner Road	Striker
Granger, WY	Rinehart	Grays Red Star Dairy	Grays Corner
Grant Co., Or	Gilkison	Great Depression	Slack
Grant Township, MO	Bean-Coffin	Great Depression, the	Fox Hill
Grant, Dale G.	Chandler	Great Depression, the	Lizabeth
Grant, Elijah	Godley	Great Depression, the	McKenzie
Grant, Elizabeth Boone	Godley	Great Depression, the	Summerville
Grant, Mary E.	Godley	Great Depression, the	Upper Perry
Grant, Mary Elizabeth	Godley	Green Bay Twp. Clarke Co., IA	Starkey
Grant, MO	Clark Creek	Green River, NY	Draper
Grants Pass, Josephine Co., OR	Imbler	Green, Charles	Fruitdale
Grants Pass, OR	Hindman	Green, Eva Leota	Evers
Grants Pass, OR	Wright	Green, Hattie Amelia	Robinson
Grass Man of the Year	Woodruff	Green, Helen	Howell
Graves, W. H.	Morgan Lake	Green, Johnathan	Evers
Gray, Ada Alma	Grays Corner	Green, Judge R. J.	Fruitdale
Gray, Agnes	Grays Corner	Greene, Lillie Mae	Imbler
Gray, Aldon Houx	Grays Corner	Greensboro, IN	Mill Creek
Gray, Anna E.	Grays Corner	Greensville, PA	Sammyville
Gray, Berdillie "Dillie" Mabel	Grays Corner	Greentown, Howard Co., IN	Golding
Gray, Bessie	Grays Corner	Greenville, TX	Henderson
Gray, Charlie	Wright	Greenwood Cem., Bloomfield	Marks
Gray, Cornelia	Grays Corner	Greenwood Dairy	Gaertner
Gray, Delda Elizabeth	Grays Corner	Greenwood Elementery School	Wagoner Hill
Gray, Dixie Lee	Grays Corner	Greenwood Elementery School	Webster
Gray, Donald Nathan	Grays Corner	Greenwood School	Fruitdale
Gray, Elizabeth	Grays Corner	Greer, Nettie Loie	Bushnell
Gray, George	Grays Corner	Greeves, Fred	Fox Hill
Gray, George	Grays Corner	Greg Tsiatsos	McIntyre
Gray, George G.	Booth	Gregory, Dr. J. B.	Fox Hill
Gray, George Grant	Grays Corner	Greiner, "Frankie"	Greiner
Gray, George Merrell	Grays Corner	Greiner, Aldora "Nora" May	Greiner
Gray, Ivie Jane	Grays Corner	Greiner, Dale F.	Greiner
Gray, John	Lower Perry	Greiner, David	Greiner
Gray, John Elmer	Lower Perry	Greiner, E. G.	Wright
Gray, Joseph	Grays Corner	Greiner, Edith	Greiner
Gray, Joseph T.	Grays Corner	Greiner, Edna	Greiner
Gray, June	Parsons	Greiner, Ethel	Greiner
Gray, Mary Alma	Hamilton	Greiner, Frank E.	Greiner
Gray, Melissa	Grays Corner	Greiner, Frank Edward	Greiner
Gray, Mrs. Sallie	Hamilton	Greiner, Martha "Jennie" Frances	Greiner
Gray, Nathan T.	Grays Corner	Greiner, Mrs. Eva	Wright
Gray, Nathan Taylor	Grays Corner	Greiner, Ray	Greiner
Gray, Robert Doke	Grays Corner	Greshan, OR	Geiger Butte
Gray, Robert L.	Grays Corner	Gressman, Anna	Dry Creek
Gray, Robert Nay	Grays Corner	Gressman, Bess B.	Dry Creek
Gray, Sally Inez	Hamilton	Gressman, Bess Beulah	Dry Creek

Hallgarth, John	Hallgarth	Hardy, Emsley H.	Chumos
Hallgarth, Joseph	Hallgarth	Hardy, Florence	Hardy
Hallgarth, Nellie	Hallgarth	Hardy, Gene	Hardy
Hallgarth, Nimrod	Hallgarth	Hardy, Grover	Slack
Hallgarth, Samuel	Hallgarth	Hardy, Harley Monroe	Chumos
Hallgarth, Sarah	Hallgarth	Hardy, Harley Monroe	Hardy
Hallgarth, Ty	Hallgarth	Hardy, Hazel Agnes	Chumos
Hally, Sarah Margaret	Hunter	Hardy, Hazel Agnes	Hardy
Halsey (family)	Fox Hill	Hardy, Henry	Hardy
Halvorson, Ann Etta	Hawkins	Hardy, Henry Hamilton	Chumos
Hambletonian (horse)	Ruckman	Hardy, Jeff	Evers
Hamblin, Mary Ellen	Follett	Hardy, Jeff	Hardy
Hamburger Hill	Hallgarth	Hardy, Mary Elizabeth	Chumos
Hamburger Hill	Highway 82	Hardy, Mary Elizabeth	Hardy
Hamburger Hill	Philberg	Hardy, Mary Jane	Hardy
Hamilton & O'Rourke Grain Co.	Owsley	Hardy, Olive Belle	Chumos
Hamilton Canyon Road	Robbs Hill	Hardy, Olive Belle	Hardy
Hamilton Hotel, St. Louis, MO	Upper Perry	Hardy, Royal	Chumos
Hamilton, Alma	Hamilton	Hardy, Royal	Hardy
Hamilton, Anna Nora	Hamilton	Hardy, Royal C. "Roy"	Hardy
Hamilton, Charles W.	Hamilton	Hardy, Royal Clyde	Hardy
Hamilton, Charles Wesley	Hamilton	Hardy, Steven	Evers
Hamilton, Charlie	Hamilton	Hardy, William H.	Chumos
Hamilton, Clare (Clair)	Myers	Hardy, William Harrison	Chumos
Hamilton, Fred C.	Myers	Hardy, William Harrison	Hardy
Hamilton, Harry	Hamilton	Hargadine Cemetery	Imbler
Hamilton, Hattie	Hamilton	Harlow, Captain	Fox Hill
Hamilton, Irene	Hamilton	Harlow, Captain	Orodell
Hamilton, Jane C.	Hamilton	Harney County, OR	Buchanan
Hamilton, Johnny	Hamilton	Harney County, OR	Wickens
Hamilton, Lydia "Lettie"	Hamilton	Harriman Place	Thompson
Hamilton, Margaret Jane	Morgan Lake	Harris Mountain	Mt. Harris
Hamilton, Ormina "Mina"	Hamilton	Harris, Charles	Mt. Harris
Hamilton, Sally Inez	Hamilton	Harris, Charlotte "Lottie"	Wheeler
Hamilton, Sarah Frances	Hamilton	Harris, James K. P.	Henderson
Hamilton, Shelby	Hamilton	Harris, James Knox Polk	Mt. Harris
Hamilton, William Henry	Hamilton	Harris, John	Mt. Harris
Hampshire (sheep)	McKennon	Harris, Joseph	Dry Creek
Hampton, Chad	Hampton	Harris, Joseph	Mt. Harris
Hampton, Don	Hampton	Harris, Laurose Mae	Ernest
Hampton, Randy	Hampton	Harris, Martha "Mattie"	Mt. Harris
Hanna, Martha E.	Carter	Harris, Martha Ellen	Mt. Harris
Hannah & Son (dress shoes)	May	Harris, Mary Ann	Dry Creek
Happy Circle Club	Monroe	Harris, Mary Ann	Mt. Harris
Harbour Post Office	Gordon Creek	Harris, Mr.	Highway 82
Hard Federation (wheat)	McKennon	Harris, Mr.	Robinson
Hardee, Sarah J.	Hull	Harris, Priscilla	Golding
Hardscrabble School (District #9)	Wright	Harris, Priscilla	Mt. Harris
Hardy, Albertus	Evers	Harris, Priscilla	Mt. Harris
Hardy, Alice	Evers	Harris, Rachel	Dry Creek
Hardy, Clyde	Hardy	Harris, Rachel Catherine	Dry Creek
Hardy, David	Evers	Harris, Rachel Catherine	Mt. Harris
Hardy, Don	Evers	Harris, Rebecca Jane	Mt. Harris
Hardy, Elizabeth Line	Chumos	Harris, Sarah Elizabeth	Mt. Harris
Hardy, Eloine Leota	Evers	Harris, Violet Addie	Robinson

How Chin (Chinese)	Hunter	Hug, Henry H.	Hug
Howard, Bernice Mae	Webster	Hug, Henry H.	Hug
Howard, Carolyn	Summerville	Hug, Julius	Hug
Howard, Jay	Summerville	Hug, Julius C.	Hug
Howard, Pauline	Woodell	Hug, Lydia M.	Summerville
Howell, Ann	Howell	Hug, Miss June	Summerville
Howell, Bill	Behrens	Hug, Mrs. Anna	Hug
Howell, Bill	Crescent	Hug, Mrs. Bernal	Hindman
Howell, Bill	Grays Corner	Hug, Mrs. Emma F.	Myers
Howell, Bill	Hibberd	Hug, Nellie Ellen	Hill Lay
Howell, Bill	Wagoner Hill	Hug, Rachel "Regula"	Hardy
Howell, Curt	Howell	Hug, Rachel "Regula"	Roulet
Howell, Florence	Crescent	Hug, Verdi	Bean-Coffin
Howell, Florence Irene	Howell	Hug, Walter	Hug
Howell, Helen	Howell	Hug, Walter Fridoline	Hug
Howell, Kristy	Howell	Hughes, Mr. & Mrs. J. H.	Case
Howell, Mark	Howell	Hughes, W. H.	Robbs Hill
Howell, Oscar	Grays Corner	Hughs, Mrs. Martha "Mattie"	Mt. Harris
Howell, Oscar W.	Howell	Hug-McDonald Road	Hug
Howell, William Fred "Bill"	Howell	Hulick Creek	Hulick
Howick, Ontario, Canada	Sanderson	Hulick, Annetta	Hulick
Howland Twp., OH	Buchanan	Hulick, Clara	Hulick
Hudson Bay Company	Fox Hill	Hulick, Cordelia	Hulick
Hudson Bay Factor	Finley Creek	Hulick, David Trolonda	Hulick
Hudson, Macon Co., MO	Hunter	Hulick, Eleanor	Hulick
Hudson's Bay Company	Moses Creek	Hulick, Elsia Ann	Hulick
Huffman, C. D.	Fruitdale	Hulick, Isaac	Hulick
Huffman, Jerusha Ann	McAlister	Hulick, James	Hulick
Huffman, Letha	Highway 82	Hulick, John	Hulick
Huffman, Mr. & Mrs. J. H.	Thompson	Hulick, John Sr.	Hulick
Huffman, Ora	Thompson	Hulick, John W.	Hulick
Huffman, Priscilla	Gordon Creek	Hulick, Mary Ellen	Hulick
Hug, Anna	Hug	Hulick, Sarah A.	Hulick
Hug, Anna E.	Hug	Hulick, William	Hulick
Hug, Anna Maria	Hug	Hulick, William Albert	Hulick
Hug, Beatrice T	Dry Creek	Hull Lane	Grays Corner
Hug, Benjamin F.	Myers	Hull Lane	Hays
Hug, Bernal	McIntyre	Hull Lane	Howell
Hug, Bernal D.	Bodie	Hull Lane	Imbler
Hug, Bernal D.	Catherine Cr.	Hull, Catherine M.	Hull
Hug, Bernal D.	Fish Trap	Hull, Harriet A.	Hull
Hug, Bernal D.	Fox Hill	Hull, Joseph	Hull
Hug, Bernal D.	Gordon Creek	Hull, Lettie	Hull
Hug, Bernal D.	Hug	Hull, Louisa F.	Hull
Hug, Bernal D.	Hunter	Hull, Martha Jane	Hull
Hug, Bernal D.	Marks	Hull, Mary	Hull
Hug, Bernal D.	Red Pepper	Hull, Sarah Ann	Hull
Hug, Bernal D.	Spout Springs	Hull, Sarah J.	Hull
Hug, Eugene	Hug	Hull, Susanah	Hull
Hug, Eugene F.	Hug	Hull, William	Hull
Hug, Florence Monroe	Follett	Hull, William	Hull
Hug, Grandma	Hug	Humphrey, H. Clay	Shaw Creek
Hug, Harry	Henderson	Humphrey, Jack	Jimmy
Hug, Henry	Henderson	Humphrey, Mrs. Elizabeth "Bettie"	Shaw Creek
Hug, Henry	Hug	Hunt Co., TX	Wheeler

Imbler, Alfred E.	Imbler	Ingle, Joseph S.	Wallsinger
Imbler, Annie	Courtney	Ingle, Mary Marjorie	Wallsinger
Imbler, Ellis A	Imbler	Ingle, Stella J.	Wallsinger
Imbler, Esther	Imbler	Ingle, Stella Jean	Wallsinger
Imbler, Jessie	Imbler	Inglewood Park Cemetery	Bagwell
Imbler, Jessie J.	Courtney	Inglewood, CA	Bagwell
Imbler, Lillie Mae	Imbler	Inland Telephone Co.	Upper Perry
Imbler, OR	Grays Corner	Insko, Matt	Sandridge
Imbler, OR	Hull	Insko, Melanie	Sandridge
Imbler, OR	Igo	Intermountain Livestock Co.	Livestock
Imbler, OR	Lower Cove	Interstate 84	Jimmy
Imbler, OR	McKennon	Interstate 84	Lower Perry
Imbler, OR	Mink	Interstate 84	Highway 203
Imbler, OR	Myers	Interstate 84	Spring Creek
Imbler, OR	Phillips Creek	Interstate 84	USFS Road 31
Imbler, OR	Ruckle	Iowa	Hulick
Imbler, OR	Striker	Iowa	Igo
Imbler, OR	Summerville	Iowa	Imbler
Imbler, OR	Wagoner Hill	Iowa	Marks
Imbler, OR	Waltz	Iowa	May
Imbler, Royal Ray	Imbler	Iowa	Rawhide
Imbler-Ruckman Road	Imbler	Iowa	Webster
Imler, family	Imbler	Iowa	Phys
Imnaha, OR	Finley Creek	Iowa (district)	Sandridge
Imnaha, OR	Morgan Lake	Iowa (settlement)	Halley
Imperial Café	Fox Hill	Iowa City, IA	Jones
Independence Rock	Morgan Lake	Iowa Park, TX	Ruth
Independence, MO	Marks	Iowa School	Monroe
Indian (fort)	Henderson	Iowa School	Mt. Emily
Indian (graves)	Fox Hill	Iowa School	Parsons
Indian Creek	Clark Creek	Iowa School	Shaw Creek
Indian Creek	Elgin Cem.	Iowa School	Webster
Indian Creek	Grays Corner	Ireland	Indian Creek
Indian Creek	Highway 82	Irons, Mrs. Hattie	Robinson
Indian Creek Cemetery	Indian Creek	Irrigon, OR	Witherspoon
Indian Creek Road	Geiger Butte	Irvin, Dell	Turnbull
Indian Creek Road	Shaw Creek	Isaacs, Dean	Kingsbury
Indian Lake Campground	McIntyre	Island Avenue	Riddle
Indian Trail	Blackhawk Tr	Island Avenue	Watson
Indian Valley	Gordon Creek	Island City	Hunter
Indian Valley	Hallgarth	Island City	Island
Indian Valley	Keen Cabin Cr.	Island City	McAlister
Indian Valley	Pine Grove	Island City	Wright
Indian Valley	Valley View	Island City	Wright
Indiana	Hulick	Island City Cemetery	Hunter
Indiana	Marks	Island City Cemetery	Igo
Indiana	Marley Creek	Island City Cemetery	Kingsbury
Indiana	Merritt	Island City Cemetery	McAlister
inehart, Martin Luther	Rinehart	Island City Cemetery	Monroe
Ingle Road	Wallsinger	Island City Cemetery	Peach
Ingle, Clayton Nason	Wallsinger	Island City Cemetery	Webster
Ingle, Dr. J. L.	Wallsinger	Island City Elementery School	McAlister
Ingle, Dr. Joseph Lombard	Wallsinger	Island City, OR	Fox Hill
Ingle, Dr. Margaret	Wallsinger	Island City, OR	Fruitdale
Ingle, Dr. Margaret Catherine	Wallsinger	Island City, OR	Gaertner

Island City, OR	Jones	Jarvis, Marjorie Lola	Dry Creek
Island City, OR	Ladd Creek	Jarvis, Mrs. J. W.	Dry Creek
Island City, OR	Lookingglass	Jasper, Andrew	Booth
Island City, OR	Lower Cove	Jasper, Clara	Booth
Island City, OR	Mt. Glen	Jasper, Donald	Booth
Island City, OR	Myers	Jasper, Ed	Booth
Island City, OR	Nice	Jasper, Ed	Wright
Island City, OR	Owsley	Jasper, Edna	Booth
Island City, OR	Quail	Jasper, Edward Doak	Booth
Island City, OR	Rankin	Jasper, Emily Jane	Booth
Island City, OR	Ruckle	Jasper, Florence	Booth
Island City, OR	Sanderson	Jasper, Frank	Booth
Island City, OR	Sandridge	Jasper, Frank	Wright
Island City, OR	Starr	Jasper, Franklin Merrell	Booth
Island City, OR	Wickens	Jasper, George M.	Booth
Island, the	Island	Jasper, James	Booth
Isle LaMotte, VT	Evers	Jasper, Margaret Edna	Booth
Isle of Skye, Scotland	Shaw Creek	Jasper, Martha Emaline	Booth
Israel, M. C.	Catherine Cr.	Jasper, Mary Alice	Booth
Israel, Mendel Crocker	Catherine Cr.	Jasper, Merrell C.	Booth
Istanbul, Turkey	McCanse	Jasper, Nancy Catherine	Booth
Isthmus of Panama	Deal Canyon	Jasper, Nancy J.	Booth
Isthmus of Panama	Phys	Jasper, Rhoda J.	Booth
J. B. Weaver & Sons	Weaver	Jasper, Sarah Sylvina "Vina"	Grays Corner
J. C. Penny Store	Leffel	Jasper, Susan Elvira	Booth
Jacb Long Cemetery	Middle	Jasper, Susan Elvira	Myers
Jackson Co., MO	Starkey	Jasper, Sylvina	Booth
Jackson Co., OH	Wilkinson	Jasper, W. R.	Foothill
Jackson Co., OR	McCanse	Jasper, Willard	Booth
Jackson County, OH	Dry Creek	Jasper, William	Booth
Jackson, Lydia Scott	Phys	Jasper, William "Bill"	Booth
Jackson, Nancy Ann "Nannie"	Merritt	Jasper, William Robert	Booth
Jackson, Orange Co., IN	Roulet	Jasper's Granulated Graham	Booth
Jackson, Paulding Co., OH	Rankin	Jaycox, Luella	Owsley
Jacksonville, IN	Kingsbury	Jefferson City, Johnson Co., MO	Owsley
Jacksonville, OR	Bowman	Jefferson Hotel, Parsons, KS	Upper Perry
Jacksonville, OR	Wright	Jefferson Twp, MO	Owsley
Jacobs & Hess Lumber Co.	Badger Flat	Jefferson, Saline Co., MO	Wheeler
Jacobs Brothers	Badger Flat	Jefferson, Scotland Co., MO	Myers
Jacobson, Edith Doris	Bidwell	Jenny Lind (ship)	Wolf Creek
Jacobson, Oscar	Jimmy	Jewett, Dora	Thompson
Jaguerie (trapper)	Moses Creek	Jewett, George	Thompson
Jamieson, Grace Evangeline	Love	Jim Ming (Chinese)	Hunter
Janson, Aaron	Janson	Jimmy Creek Reservoir	Jimmy
Janson, Alva	Janson	Jimmy Creek School Dist. #53	Jimmy
Janson, Enoch	Janson	Joe Knight Train	Dry Creek
Janson, George H.	Janson	John Day, OR	Miller
Janson, Linnea	Janson	John Peach Dairy	Peach
Janson, Nephi	Janson	Johns, Jay	Lookingglass
Janson, Ruth	Janson	Johnson (family)	Janson
Janson, Sven Johan	Janson	Johnson Fruit Farm	Pumpkin Ridge
Janson, Sylvia	Janson	Johnson, "Sonny"	Conley
Janson, Theodore	Janson	Johnson, Abner L.	Hull
Janson, Victor	Janson	Johnson, Baylen	Conley
Jarvey (trapper)	Moses Creek	Johnson, Blanche	Howell

Johnson, Charlotte	Janson	Julianna Creek	Godley
Johnson, Chris	Jimmy	July Ann Creek	Catherine Cr.
Johnson, Clara	Henderson	July Ann Creek	Little Creek
Johnson, Colby	Conley	Junction City, OR	Curtis
Johnson, Darcy	Conley	Jung Ah (Chinese)	Hunter
Johnson, Florence Lillie	Starkey	Juntura, OR	Fletcher
Johnson, Florence Mary	Finley Creek	Kail, Mrs. Clifford	Antles
Johnson, John William "Jack"	Finley Creek	Kalamazoo (stove)	Lookingglass
Johnson, Mark	Pumpkin Ridge	Kalamazoo, MI	Marks
Johnson, Mary Alice	Booth	Kamela	Bodie
Johnson, Mary Jane	Conley	kamela (junction)	Kamela
Johnson, Mary Jane	Hulick	Kamela, OR	Kamela
Johnson, Mary Jane	Thew	Kanesville, IA	Heber
Johnson, Maryette Eunice	Draper	Kansas	Igo
Johnson, Michael	Pumpkin Ridge	Kansas	McAlister
Johnson, Mrs. Jane	Ellis	Kansas	Red Pepper
Johnson, Rebecca Frances	Starkey	Kansas	Stackland
Johnson, Silas	Hug	Kansas City, Fort Scott & Memphis	Upper Perry
Johnson, Susanah	Hull	Kansas City, KS	Bagwell
Johnson, Swen	Janson	Kansas City, KS	Craig
Johnston, Nancy Jane	Merritt	Kansas City, KS	Yarrington
Jonathan (apples)	Monroe	Kansas City, MO	McDonald
Jones, Agnes	Jones	Kansas City, MO	Upper Perry
Jones, Cora Ann	Wright	KATY (rail line)	Upper Perry
Jones, David M.	Jones	Keating, OR	Frances
Jones, Edna	Booth	Keen Moteen	Mt. Emily
Jones, Glen W.	Jones	Keen, Albert	Keen Cabin Cr.
Jones, John	Wright	Keen, Albert T.	Keen Cabin Cr.
Jones, John T. "Bud"	Booth	Keen, Alva	Keen Cabin Cr.
Jones, Joseph W.	Jones	Keen, Effie P.	Keen Cabin Cr.
Jones, Lyda	Owsley	Keen, Flora J.	Keen Cabin Cr.
Jones, Mabel Alice	Haefer	Keen, Frances "Helen"	Keen Cabin Cr.
Jones, Margaret Edna	Booth	Keen, William Era	Keen Cabin Cr.
Jones, Mary	Wright	Keen, William Isaac "Ike"	Keen Cabin Cr.
Jones, Rachel	Jones	Kelley, James F.	Mill Creek
Jonestown, Columbia Co., PA	Good	Kelly, Mr. Thomas	Fruitdale
Joplin, MO	Thompson	Kelseyville, Lake Co., CA	Marley Creek
Jordan Creek	Starkey	Keltner, Mrs. Ina E.	McKennon
Jordon, Bishop	Fruitdale	Kelton, UT	Brooks
Joseph Cemetery	Clark Creek	Kendall, Susan "Clara"	Booth
Joseph Herald, the	Jimmy	Kennedy (family)	Starkey
Joseph Yount Train	McAlister	Kennedy, Emma	Rawhide
Joseph, OR	Gaertner	Kennedy, Hattie Irene	Robinson
Joseph, OR	Golding	Kennedy, Kimber	Rawhide
Joseph, OR	Hamilton	Kennedy, Leo Lester	Rawhide
Joseph, OR	Henderson	Kennedy, Mrs, Roy Henry	Robinson
Joseph, OR	Wade	Kennedy, Peggy Mae	Thompson
Josephine Co., Oregon Territory	Phys	Kennedy, Thelma	Behrens
Josephine County (sheriff)	Phys	Kennedy, Thelma Grace	Summerville
Josephine Oc. OR	Phys	Kenney, Mrs. J. B.	Kerns
Jubilee Farms LLC	Hidden Valley	Kentucky	Imbler
Julia Ann Creek	Catherine Cr.	Kentucky	Roulet
Julia Ann Creek	Little Creek	Kentucky	Wheeler
Juliana Creek	Catherine Cr.	Kerns, Emma	Kerns
Juliana Creek	Little Creek	Kerns, Emma Mary	Kerns

Name	Location	Name	Location
Kerns, Ethel Mae (May)	Kerns	Kirkwood, OH	Deal Canyon
Kerns, Helen E.	Kerns	Kirshner, Julia F.	Roulet
Kerns, Lloyd	Kerns	Kirtley, E. E.	May
Kerns, Mabel	Kerns	Kittens, First	Bean-Coffin
Kerns, Maude	Kerns	Klamath Falls, OR	Good
Kerns, Melvin Jr.	Kerns	KLBM (radio station)	Howell
Kerns, Melvin Sr.	Kerns	Klein, Margaret	Behrens
Kerns, Melvin Sr.	Kerns	KLGD	Airport
Kerr Gifford Grain Co.	Owsley	Klinghammer, Anna	Indian Creek
Kerr, Mabel Mary	Myers	Klinghammer, Charles	Indian Creek
Kerrsville, Kerr Co., TX	Love	Klinghammer, Hugo	Indian Creek
Kesees, Bavaria, Germany	Hacker	Klinghammer, Ida	Indian Creek
Kettle Falls High School	Starr	Klinghammer, John	Indian Creek
Kettle Falls, Stevens Co., WA	Starr	Klinghammer, Otto	Indian Creek
Keve, Mrs. Effie	Geiger Butte	Klinghammer, Reinhold	Indian Creek
Keyes, Art	Woodruff	Klinghammer, Walter	Indian Creek
Keyes, Arthur Jr.	Woodruff	Klinghammer-McNab Road	Indian Creek
Keyes, Cleda Edwina	Woodruff	Klintworth (home)	Fox Hill
Keyes, Cody	Woodruff	Klondike, the	Shaw Creek
Keyes, Ellen	Woodruff	Knapp, Miss Rachel	Ladd Creek
Keyes, Lucille Kathleen	Woodruff	Knauber, Alta	Flevious
Keyes, Lynn	Woodruff	Knauber, Flevious	Flevious
Keyes, Margaret	Woodruff	Knauber, Flevious Glenn	Flevious
Keys, Arthur Harley	Woodruff	Knauber, Florence	Flevious
Keys-Woodruff Lane	Woodruff	Knauber, William	Flevious
Khight, James	Knight	Kneeland, Mary A.	Draper
Kiddle Brothers	Bidwell	Knifong, Anna Rogers	Darr
Kiddle, Fred E.	Airport	Knifong, Catherine Eve	Darr
Kight, Georgia Rebecca	Chadwick	Knifong, John Jesse	Darr
Kilby, Marshall	Summerville	Knight (ranch)	Knight
Kilgore State College	Ruth	Knight, Andrew	Mt. Harris
Kilgore, TX	Ruth	Knight, Bill	Mt. Harris
Killian, Frank	Lookingglass	Knight, Captain Joe	Mt. Harris
Kilsyth, Stirlingshire, Scotland	Olsen	Knight, Cleora Leilla	Knight
Kilsyth, Stirlingshire, Scotland	Shaw Mountain	Knight, Douglas	Knight
Kimber, Sarah Ann	Wickens	Knight, Elizabeth Ann	Knight
Kimbrell, J. W.	Fruitdale	Knight, Ellen	Mt. Harris
Kinder Parks & Sons	Roulet	Knight, Emma	Knight
King Hill, ID	Starr	Knight, Francis	Knight
King Motor Testor, the	Knight	Knight, Frank	Knight
King, Catherine "Kate" S.	Gekeler	Knight, George	Knight
King, Fannie	Gekeler	Knight, George Leroy	Knight
King, Louis	Gekeler	Knight, Jesse	Knight
Kingery, Mrs. Vallie	Thompson	Knight, Jesse B.	Knight
Kingsbury, Alta	Kingsbury	Knight, Joseph	Knight
Kingsbury, Arthur	Kingsbury	Knight, Joseph Andrew	Golding
Kingsbury, Margaret Kaziah	Kingsbury	Knight, LaVona	Knight
Kingsbury, Mr. Shirley Francis	Kingsbury	Knight, LaVonna Mason	Knight
Kingsbury, Nora M.	Kingsbury	Knight, Lucy Ellen	Henderson
Kingsbury, Nora Marie	Kingsbury	Knight, Lucy Ellen	Knight
Kingsbury, Shirley	Kingsbury	Knight, Mary Ann	Knight
Kinzel, Charles J.	Elkanah	Knight, Mr.	Eagle Creek
Kinzel, Lesley Kenneth	Elkanah	Knight, Mr.	Highway 82
Kiowa, NE	Comstock	Knight, O. C.	Knight
Kirktown, Scotland	Shaw Creek	Knight, Oscar	Knight

Knight, Oscar C.	Knight	La Grande Chamber of Comm.	Lower Cove
Knight, Oscar Clarence	Knight	La Grande City Commission	Leffel
Knight, Patricia	Knight	La Grande Commercial Club	May
Knight, Patricia	Knight	La Grande Flying Club	Knight
Knight, Patricia Ann	Knight	La Grande High School	Howell
Knight, Priscilla	Golding	La Grande High School	Leffel
Knight, Priscilla	Mt. Harris	La Grande High School	Lower Cove
Knight, Robert	Mt. Harris	La Grande High School	May
Knight, Roy	Knight	La Grande High School	McKenzie
Knight, Sam	Golding	La Grande High School	Wagoner Hill
Knight, William Boliver	Knight	La Grande High School	Wallsinger
Knight, William J.	Golding	La Grande High School	Webster
Knight, William Woodson	Knight	La Grande I. O. O. F.	Shaw Mountain
Knouse, Bev	Starr	La Grande National Bank	Upper Perry
Knouse, Larry	Starr	La Grande Observer	Hindman
Knowles, J. W.	Hacker	La Grande Observer	Miller
Knox (hats)	May	La Grande Observer	Nice
Knoxville, IA	Jones	La Grande Observer	Parsons
Knoxville, Marion Co., IA	Dry Creek	La Grande Observer	Slack
Koehler, Clarice	Badger Flat	La Grande Observer	Wagoner Hill
Koehn, Judd	Happy Walrus	La Grande Observer	Wallsinger
Koehn, Kathy	Happy Walrus	La Grande Observer	Willowdale
Kofford, Beulah	Kofford	La Grande Observer	Wolf Creek
Kofford, Christopher	Kofford	La Grande Observer	Woodruff
Kofford, Christopher Anthon	Kofford	La Grande Observer	Yerges
Kofford, Don	Kofford	La Grande Parks & Rec.	Morgan Lake
Kofford, Edwin	Kofford	La Grande Post Office	Sanderson
Kofford, Florence	Kofford	La Grande Rotary Club	McKennon
Kofford, Fred	Kofford	La Grande School District	Fox Hill
Kofford, James	Kofford	La Grande to Cove Highway	Highway 237
Kofford, James Arthur	Kofford	La Grande to Starkey Highway	Highway 244
Kofford, Julia Pearl	Kofford	La Grande Truck Stop	Slack
Kofford, Kenneth	Kofford	La Grande Water Storage Co.	Morgan Lake
Kofford, Nancy	Kofford	La Grande, OR	Highway 203
Kofford, Nancy Rich	Kofford	La Grande, OR	Rinehart
Kofford, Vivian	Kofford	La Grande, OR	Robinson
Kofford, Wilford	Kofford	La Grande, OR	Ruth
Kokomo, IN	Leffel	La Grande, OR	Speckhart
Kootenai, ID	Dry Creek	La Grande, OR	Standley
Korean Conflict	Wright	La Grande, OR	Starr
Korean War	Thompson	La Grande, OR	Tin Trough
Kour Lee (Chinese)	Hunter	La Grande, OR	Upper Perry
Krause, Mrs. Beth	Thompson	La Grande, OR	Wagoner Hill
Krone, Emma	McDonald	La Grande, OR	Wallsinger
Kuhn, Ruby	Parsons	La Grande, OR	Waltz
Kuna, ID	Draper	La Grande, OR	Watson
Kundrak, Geennild	Olsen	La Grande, OR	Woodell
La Crosse, WI	McIntyre	La Grande-Enterprise Highway	Highway 82
La Grande	Mill Creek	La Grandeur, Mose De Motlette	Moses Creek
La Grande	Morgan Lake	La Grande-Wallowa Lake Highway	Ruckle
La Grande	Otten	La Grange Co., IN	Marks
La Grande	Philberg	La Grippe	Alicel
La Grande Baseball Club	May	Lackawaxen, PA	Godley
La Grande Cemetery District	Mt. Glen	Ladd Canyon	Alicel
La Grande Central School	Wallsinger	Ladd Canyon	Brush Creek

Ladd Canyon	Wallsinger	Laramore, J. R.	Summerville
Ladd Canyon	Wright	Larsen, Charlotte, Almyra	Igo
Ladd Canyon	Hunter	Larsen, Harvey	Igo
Ladd Canyon	Ladd Creek	Lashur, Rebecca	Chadwick
Ladd Canyon	Lower Cove	Latham, Leola Dot	Anson
Ladd Canyon	McCanse	Lauder, Estee	Elgin Cem.
Ladd Canyon Road	High Valley	Laurel Hill Cemetery	Dry Creek
Ladd Canyon Road	Shaw Mountain	Law, Emily Jane	Ernest
Ladd Creek	Couch	Lawhanner, Jeanette	Jimmy
Ladd Creek	Ladd Creek	Lawrence, Aurelia Belle	Godley
Ladd farm	Fruitdale	Lawrenceburg, KY	Bond
Ladd Hill	Alicel	Lawson, Russell	Cone
Ladd, Charles W.	Alicel	Lawson, Sarah Ann	Middle
Ladd, Charles W.	Ladd Creek	Lay, Bessie	Conklin
Ladd, Eva	Ladd Creek	Lay, Beverly	Hill Lay
Ladd, John R.	Alicel	Lay, Clara	Hill Lay
Ladd, John R.	Ladd Creek	Lay, Cleva	Hill Lay
Ladd, Mrs. Alice	Alicel	Lay, Clora	Hill Lay
Ladd, Rachel	Alicel	Lay, Deshler	Hill Lay
Ladd, Rachel	Ladd Creek	Lay, Gay	Hill Lay
Lagrande, old	Phys	Lay, Guild	Hill Lay
Laing, Mary	Shaw Mountain	Lay, Joseph Colman	Hill Lay
Laird, Claude	Fletcher	Lay, Katie Rosella	Hill Lay
Laird, Eugene	Fletcher	Lay, Laurel	Hill Lay
Laird, Margaret Elizabeth	Fletcher	Lay, Masyl	Hill Lay
Laird, Marjorie G.	Hamilton	Lay, Othello	Hill Lay
Lake Co., CA	Owsley	Lay, Paula	Hill Lay
Lake Teslin, Canada	Shaw Creek	Lay, Roy	Conklin
Lakeview, OR	Rawhide	Lay, Urdel	Hill Lay
Lakey, Edythe	Heber	Le Boeuf (family)	Moses Creek
Lambert, Anna Rogers	Darr	Le Clair, IA	Draper
Lampasa, TX	Sammyville	Leach, Ann	Crampton
Lampkin, Bertha	Lampkin	Leasey, Caroline	Mt. Emily
Lampkin, Ruth	Lampkin	Leasey, Columbus	Mt. Emily
Lampkin, Susan	Lampkin	Leasey, Emily	Mt. Emily
Lampkin, Thelma	Lampkin	Leasey, Henry W.	Mt. Emily
Lampkin, Thomas E.	Lampkin	Leasey, James	Mt. Emily
Lampkin, Thomas Ethelbert	Lampkin	Leasey, John	Mt. Emily
Lampkin, William Thomas	Lampkin	Leasey, Joseph	Mt. Emily
Lanark, Ontario, Canada	Sanderson	Leasey, Will	Mt. Emily
Lancaster, NY	Gekeler	Leasy, Columbus	Marks
Lane Co., OR	Chumos	Leasy, Emily	Marks
Lane Co., OR	Ramo Flat	Leasy, Emily	Yerges
Lane Victoria	Webster	Leasy, Frances Caroline	Marks
Langdon Lake	Skyline	Leasy, Henry W.	Marks
Lantz Lane	Love	Leasy, James	Marks
Lantz Lane	Squire	Leasy, John	Marks
Lantz, Bessie	Lantz	Leasy, Joseph	Marks
Lantz, Harvey	Lantz	Leasy, Will	Marks
Lantz, J, K.	Lantz	Lebanon, Linn Co., OR	Starkey
Lantz, Louis	Lantz	Lebanon, St. Clair Co., IL	Phys
Lantz, Lydia	Lantz	Lebanon, VA	Darr
Lantz, Mabel	Lantz	Ledbetter Garage	Government Gul.
Lantz, Roy	Lantz	Ledbetter, W. R.	McKennon
Lanzer, Fred Emil	Elkanah	Ledridge, Mrs. S. O.	Bond

Lee, Dylan Gary	Knight	Lieurence, Lemuel	Stackland
Lee, Mary	Knight	Lieurence, Lucinda "Alice"	Stackland
Lee, Stella A.	Dry Creek	Lieurence, Marvin	Stackland
Lee, Veta	Behrens	Lieurence, Mary	Stackland
Leeh Lee (Chinese)	Hunter	Lieurence, Orlando	Stackland
Leffel Road	Sporting	Lightfoot, Mr. Ayer M.	Fletcher
Leffel, Alvin W.	Leffel	Lilly, Oweda Alice	Hacker
Leffel, Homer Volney	Leffel	Lincoln Co., NB	Love
Leffel, Janet C.	Leffel	Lincoln Co., OR	Godley
Leffel, John A.	Leffel	Lincoln Highway	Highway 30
Leffel, Leona	Leffel	Lincoln Memorial Park	Weaver
Leffel, Lois Jane	Leffel	Lincoln, NE	Draper
Leffel, Lorna J.	Leffel	Lincoln, NE.	Antles
Leffel, Mary Catherine	Leffel	Lincoln, Walla Walla Co., WA	Hays
Leffel, Vera Kimenia	Leffel	Lincolnshire, England	Hallgarth
Lemmon, Alpharetta Elizabeth	Comstock	Lind, WA	Starr
Lester Real Estate	Lester	Linn Co., MO	Couch
Lester, Carrol L.	Craddock	Linn Co., MO	Hug
Lester, Carroll	Bodie	Linn Co., OR	Monroe
Lester, Geraldine Ethelda	Lester	Linn Co., OR	Rinehart
Lester, Glenn	Wood	Linn Co., OR	Robbs Hill
Lester, Lathette	Lester	Linville, Mary E.	Gordon Creek
Lester, Marie	Lester	Lionsdale, NY	Coombs
Lester, Martha "Marty" H.	Lester	Lipps, O. H.	Telocaset
Lester, Myrtle	Lester	Literal, Audry	Behrens
Lester, Russell	Wood	Little Alps Ski Shop	Anson
Lester, Russell "Glenn"	Lester	Little Catherine Creek	USFS Road 2036
Lester, Russell L.	Lester	Little Creek	Catherine Cr.
Lesure, Rebecca	Chadwick	Little Creek	Godley
Lewis Co., WA	Robinson	Little Creek	High Valley
Lewis, Donna Morgan	Morgan Lake	Little Creek	Little Creek
Lewis, E. H.	Catherine Cr.	Little Juliana Creek	Little Creek
Lewis, Elisha Hiram	Catherine Cr.	Little Lookingglass Creek	USFS Road 63
Lewis, Frances	Marks	Little Lost Creek	USFS Road 64
Lewis, John	McKenzie	Little Minam (river)	Parsons
Lewis, John	Summerville	Little, Mrs. Viva	Mt. Glen
Lewis, John L.	Behrens	Liverpool, England	Hutchinson
Lewis, Mr. & Mrs. B. H.	Buchanan	Liverpool, England	Rawhide
Lewis, Mrs. Bessie	Lookingglass	Lockett, Anne Elizabeth	Godley
Lewis, Sarah	Behrens	Loftus (family)	Starkey
Lewis, Willard	Marks	Logan, Daryl	Sammyville
Lewis-Dry Creek Road	Hunter	Logan, Maude Ethel	Draper
Lewiston, Fulton Co., IL	Morgan Lake	Logan, UT	Igo
Lewiston, ID	Hamilton	Logan, UT	Kofford
Lewiston, ID	Monroe	Logan, UT	Lizabeth
Liberty Twp., Clarke Co., IA	Lester	Logan, Utah	Janson
Liberty, Jefferson Co., IA	Slack	Logansport State Hospital	Marks
Lichtenthaler, Judge	Blackhawk Tr	Logsdon, Charles	High Valley
Licking Co., OH	Hunter	Lone Pine	Wright
Lieurence, Allen C.	Stackland	Lone Pine School	Sandridge
Lieurence, David	Stackland	Long Beach, CA	Bagwell
Lieurence, Elizabeth	Stackland	Long Beach, CA	Hull
Lieurence, Frederick	Stackland	Long Branch Café	Fox Hill
Lieurence, Hiram	Stackland	Long Cliff Hospital	Marks
Lieurence, Joshua	Stackland	Long Cliff Hospital Cemetery	Marks

Manhattan, NY	Elgin Cem.	Marks, Nora M.	Marks
Mann Creek, ID	Bowman	Marks, Richard E.	Marks
Mann Road	Gilkison	Marks, Richard E. "Dick"	Marks
Mann, Arel Leo	Gilkison	Marks, Ruth Adeline	Marks
Mann, Arlene Leola	Gilkison	Marks, Sarah Elizabeth	Marks
Mann, Cecil	Gilkison	Marks, Thomas Jefferson	Marks
Mann, Cecil Socrates	Gilkison	Marks, William	Marks
Mann, Cecilia	Gilkison	Marks, William "Willie"	Marks
Mann, Charles	Gilkison	Marks, William Ebenser	Marks
Mann, Clairellen Belle	Gilkison	Marley Creek	Marley Creek
Mann, Dora	Gilkison	Marley, Ellen Caroline	Marley Creek
Mann, Elllen E.	Gilkison	Marley, Frances Bliss	Marley Creek
Mann, Floy Dorene	Gilkison	Marley, Leonard	Marley Creek
Mann, John Emery	Gilkison	Marley, Leonard California	Marley Creek
Mann, Leo	Gilkison	Marley, Leonard Halton	Marley Creek
Mann, Leona Leatha	Gilkison	Marley, Leonard Harrison	Marley Creek
Mann, Letha Elizabeth	Gilkison	Marley, Libbie Ethel	Marley Creek
Mann, Nora Ellen	Gilkison	Marley, Mary A.	Marley Creek
Mann, Ralph Vernon	Gilkison	Marley, Mary Ella	Marley Creek
Mann, Socrates C.	Gilkison	Marley, William Joseph	Marley Creek
Mansfield, Lillian Ann	Lookingglass	Marshall Plan, the	Hawkins
Mansfield, Pat	Spout Springs	Marshall, Elizabeth	Fletcher
Manti, UT	Wheeler	Marshall, Merritt	Draper
Manville Train	Dry Creek	Marshtown, Tennessee	Jimmy
Manville Train	Wallsinger	Martin, Amanda Ellen	Buchanan
Manville, Mr.	Wallsinger	Martin, Eliza Etta	Buchanan
March, Hazel	Hawkins	Martin, Elsia	Hulick
Marinsee, Westpreussen, Germany	Thompson	Martin, Elsia Ann	Hulick
Marion Co. OR	Pierce	Martin, Even	Rinehart
Marion Co., IA	Mill Creek	Martin, John	Hulick
Marion Co., IA	Wickens	Martin, Mary	Rinehart
Marion Co., OR	Starkey	Martin, Mary Lou	Middle
Marion County, OR	Finley Creek	Martin, Miss, Margaret Ann	Rinehart
Market Lane	Hamilton	Martin, Rebecca	Gordon Creek
Market Lane	Lower Cove	Marvin, Cornelia	Pierce
Market Road Act, the	High Valley	Marysville, OR	May
Marks Road	Mt. Emily	Masiker, Esther	Imbler
Marks Road	Starr	Mason, James	Morgan Lake
Marks, Abraham	Marks	Masonic Cem., McMinnville, OR	Marley Creek
Marks, Adaline	Marks	Masonic Cemetery	Leffel
Marks, Albert Owen	Marks	Masonic Cemetery	Owsley
Marks, Christopher Columbus	Marks	Masse, Jean	Wallsinger
Marks, Clarence Sylvian	Marks	Masterton, Mrs. Grace	Bean-Coffin
Marks, David	Marks	Mathson, Alfred M.	Mathson
Marks, Emma Osborne	Marks	Mathson, Alvin Louis	Mathson
Marks, Eve	Marks	Mathson, Christina	Mathson
Marks, George	Marks	Mathson, Neva	Mathson
Marks, Israel	Marks	Mathson, Ole	Mathson
Marks, James Israel	Marks	Mathson, Olga Rose	Mathson
Marks, John	Marks	Mathson, Rosie	Mathson
Marks, John	Marks	Mathson, Theodore "Ted" Ole	Mathson
Marks, John Sr.	Marks	Matters, Ada	Sammyville
Marks, Julia Ann	Marks	Matters, Annabelle Rosetta	Sammyville
Marks, Kimberly	Marks	Matters, Walter	Sammyville
Marks, Mary A.	Marks	Mattes, Alma Anna	Woodruff

Mattoon, IL	Gilkison	McCanse, Bonnie	McCanse
Maupin, OR	Morgan Lake	McCanse, Donald	McCanse
Mauritsdatter, Bertha M.	Stackland	McCanse, Ed	Starr
Maury Co., TN	Hunter	McCanse, Edson R.	Tucker Flat
Maxwell, Bert	Henderson	McCanse, Edson Rodney	McCanse
May Lane	Watson	McCanse, Edson Rodney	Shaw Mountain
May Park	Carroll	McCanse, James	McCanse
May Park	Coombs	McCanse, James Edson	McCanse
May Park	May	McCanse, Margaret	McCanse
May Park (sub-division)	Riddle	McCanse, Margie Lou	McCanse
May Street	May	McCardle, Beatrice	Dutton
May, Mrs. Louine	McNeill	McCauley, W. I.	Marks
Mayfield, Stella	Elgin Cem.	McCauley, William	Marks
Mayo, J. C.	Kamela	McClara, Angeline	Starkey
Mays, Lula	Jimmy	McClara, George W.	Starkey
McAlister Road	Fruitdale	McClara, Martha	Starkey
McAlister, "Becky Jane"	McAlister	McClara, Sarah	Starkey
McAlister, "Becky"	McAlister	McClure (home)	Fox Hill
McAlister, "Jeff"	Halley	McClure, Jim	Hindman
McAlister, "Jeff"	McAlister	McClure, Steve	Philberg
McAlister, Anna Belle	Halley	McCollock, Judge C. H.	Jimmy
McAlister, Anna Belle	Halley	McComb, OH	Hamilton
McAlister, Anna Belle	McAlister	McCormick, Mrs.	Dry Creek
McAlister, Belle	Halley	McCreary, . C.	May
McAlister, D. A. "Uncle Bud"	McAlister	McCully, Asa	Phys
McAlister, Daniel Jefferson	McAlister	McDaniel, C. T.	Couch
McAlister, David Jefferson	Halley	McDonald (family)	Shaw Creek
McAlister, General Price	McAlister	McDonald Century Farm	Hug
McAlister, George Anderson	McAlister	McDonald Century Farm	McDonald
McAlister, Grace	McAlister	McDonald, Annie	Hug
McAlister, Honorable John W.	McAlister	McDonald, Barbara	McDonald
McAlister, James William	McAlister	McDonald, Dan	Dry Creek
McAlister, Jerusha Ann	McAlister	McDonald, Ellen	Hug
McAlister, Jim	Halley	McDonald, Emma	McDonald
McAlister, John	Halley	McDonald, Florence	Booth
McAlister, John Washington	McAlister	McDonald, George	Hug
McAlister, Lettitia Franklin	McAlister	McDonald, George K.	McDonald
McAlister, Mrs. James	Halley	McDonald, George W.	Hug
McAlister, Pleasant P.	McAlister	McDonald, Harley	Hug
McAlister, Rebecca Jane	McAlister	McDonald, Harley Cecil	Hug
McAlister, Rebecca Jane (Becky)	Halley	McDonald, Hector	McDonald
McAlister, Samuel "Harvey"	McAlister	McDonald, Hiram	Hug
McAlister, Samuel Ellison	McAlister	McDonald, Jeanne Ann	Hug
McAlister, Samuel H.	Halley	McDonald, Jeff	Hug
McAlister, Samuel H.	McAlister	McDonald, John Jr.	McDonald
McAlister, Susan	Halley	McDonald, Karla	Hug
McAlister, Susan Emmaline	McAlister	McDonald, Louann	McDonald
McAlister, Susan Lucinda	McAlister	McDonald, Lyla E.	McDonald
McAlister, Thomas H.	McAlister	McDonald, Maggie	McDonald
McAlister-Yount train	Gekeler	McDonald, Margaret R.	Hug
McAllister, Mrs.	Shaw Creek	McDonald, Mark	Hug
McCall, ID	Crampton	McDonald, Mary	Hug
McCallister, Lulu May	Antles	McDonald, Mary E.	Hug
McCanse (ranch)	Heber	McDonald, Nancy	Dry Creek
McCanse, Audrey	McCanse	McDonald, Peter Alexander	McDonald

McDonald, Sarah	Hug	McKenzie River	Grays Corner
McDonald, Sarah Elizabeth	Hug	McKenzie Road	Sanderson
McDonald, Scott	Hug	McKenzie Theater	McKenzie
McDonald, Steven	Hug	McKenzie, Alex	Howell
McDonald, Susan	Hug	McKenzie, Alez	Finley Creek
McDonald, Wesley	Hug	McKenzie, Clyde	McKenzie
McDowell, Charity	Yerges	McKenzie, Flora J.	Keen Cabin Cr.
McDowell, James	Yerges	McKenzie, Glen	McKenzie
McDowell, John	Mt. Glen	McKenzie, Glen	Mt. Glen
McDowell, John	Owsley	McKenzie, Glen Roderick	McKenzie
McDowell, John	Yerges	McKenzie, Jean	McKenzie
McDowell, Liddie	Mt. Glen	McKenzie, Roderick	Shaw Creek
McDowell, Lucinda Viola	Mt. Glen	McKinnis Century Farm	Dry Creek
McDowell, Lucinda Viola	Yerges	McKinnis Saw Mill	Dry Creek
McDowell, Lydia	Yerges	McKinnis Sawmill	Summerville
McDowell, Lydia Ruth	Mt. Glen	McKinnis, Beatrice T.	Dry Creek
McDowell, Lydia Ruth	Yerges	McKinnis, Catherine	Dry Creek
McEwen, Baker County	Brooks	McKinnis, Charles	Dry Creek
McFadden, Mary Amanda	Gilkison	McKinnis, Clement	Dry Creek
McFarlands, the	Fox Hill	McKinnis, Clement L.	Dry Creek
McGee, Valda	Stackland	McKinnis, Craner	Dry Creek
McGoldrick, "Gene"	Hull	McKinnis, Frank	Dry Creek
McGoldrick, Eugene	Hull	McKinnis, Hannah	Dry Creek
McGoldrick, Eugene Omer	Hull	McKinnis, Hershel	Dry Creek
McGoldrick, Henry "Hank"	Hull	McKinnis, Ina May	Dry Creek
McGoldrick, Lettie	Hull	McKinnis, James	Dry Creek
McGrannell, Anna	Bushnell	McKinnis, John	Mt. Harris
McGuire, Margurette J.	Ruckman	McKinnis, John	Dry Creek
McIntyre Creek	McIntyre	McKinnis, John L.	Summerville
McIntyre Road	Starkey	McKinnis, John Livingood	Dry Creek
McIntyre, Edith Sarah Grace	McIntyre	McKinnis, Mrs. Thomas	Dry Creek
McIntyre, Helen M.	McIntyre	McKinnis, Nettie	Dry Creek
McIntyre, Kenneth Arnold	McIntyre	McKinnis, Olive	Dry Creek
McKay, Dr. W. C.	Kamela	McKinnis, Rachel	Dry Creek
McKay, Dr. William C	Telocaset	Mckinnis, Rachel	Mt. Harris
McKee, Mrs. Edna	Comstock	McKinnis, Rachel Catherine	Dry Creek
McKennon, "L.L."	McKennon	McKinnis, Stella A.	Dry Creek
McKennon, Allie Elizabeth	McKennon	McKinnis, Thomas	Dry Creek
McKennon, Archibald	McKennon	McLaughlin, Albert A.	Fruitdale
McKennon, Bliss	McKennon	McLaughlin, SD	Thompson
McKennon, Eva Montana	McKennon	McLean, Vicki	Slack
McKennon, Floyd	McKennon	McLeansboro, Hamilton Co., IL	Hutchinson
McKennon, Frances E.	McKennon	McLoughlin, Dr.	Finley Creek
McKennon, Frank	McKennon	McLoughlin, Dr. John	Moses Creek
McKennon, J. D.	Bodie	McMillan, Winfield S.	Coombs
McKennon, J. D.	Morgan Lake	McMinnville, OR	Marks
McKennon, Leonidas Lafayette	McKennon	McMurry, Mabel	Anson
McKennon, Routh	McKennon	McNab, Albert "Harry"	Indian Creek
McKennon, Russell Melville	McKennon	McNab, Charles Henry	Indian Creek
McKennon-LedBetter (ranch)	McKennon	McNab, Francis "Frank" J.	Indian Creek
McKenzie (farm)	McKenzie	McNab, Louisa	Indian Creek
McKenzie Hall	Howell	McNamee, Mrs. Leona	Leffel
McKenzie Lane	Hunter	McNaughton, Agnes	Jones
McKenzie Lane	Slack	McNaughton, Dr. Thomas	Jones
McKenzie Memorial Scholarship	McKenzie	McNaughton, Mrs. Sadia	Jones

McNeill, Anna Margaret	McNeill	Mercer Co., PA	May
McNeill, Charles	McNeill	Mercer, Edna	Crampton
McNeill, Charles Volantine	McNeill	Merchant, (Undertaker)	Dry Creek
McNeill, Dr, William Wallace	McNeill	Mercy Hospital	Dry Creek
McNeill, James Marvin	McNeill	Merino (sheep)	Morgan Lake
McNeill, John Archibald	McNeill	Merony, Agnes	Lower Cove
McNeill, Louine Sena	McNeill	Merrell, WI	Woodruff
McNeill, Louis Sidney	McNeill	Merrigan, Bill	Hays
McNeill, Margaret Ruth	McNeill	Merrill, WI	Bodie
McNeill, Mary Abrilla	McNeill	Merrill, WI	Elkanah
McNeill, Mary Ann "Lulu"	McNeill	Merritt Lane	Rawhide
McNeill, Rosa Ora	McNeill	Merritt Lane	Yarrington
McNeill, Stella Alvereta	McNeill	Merritt, Clarence Edgar	Merritt
McNeill, Susan Ophelia "Suda"	McNeill	Merritt, Daniel David	Merritt
McNeill, Sytha Virginia	McNeill	Merritt, Margaret Elizabeth	Merritt
McNeill, William Archibald	McNeill	Merritt, Nancy Ann "Nannie"	Merritt
McNeill, Winifred Bell	McNeill	Merritt, Nancy Jane	Merritt
McRae, Baby Kate	Shaw Creek	Merritt, Olive Viola	Merritt
McRae, Flora	Shaw Creek	Merritt, Ruth Josephine	Merritt
McRae, Flora	Shaw Creek	Merritt, William R.	Merritt
McRae, Flora (Murchison)	Shaw Creek	Merritt, William Reuben	Merritt
McRae, Kate	Shaw Creek	Metlen, Anita	Squire
McVey, Ray	Highway 82	Metlen, Kim	Squire
McWhirter, Fannie	May	Mexico	Frances
McWhirter, Helen M.	May	Mexico	McAlister
McWhirter, Joseph A.	May	Meyer, Sarah	McKenzie
McWhirter, Katherine Elizabeth	May	Meyers, Anna	Hacker
McWhirter, Miss May Belle	Mathson	Meyers, Mrs. John	Hacker
Meacham Road	Ruckle	Miami, Saline Co., MO	Wheeler
Meacham Toll Road	Starkey	Michael, Elizabeth	Stackland
Meacham, OR	Rinehart	Michaelson (family)	Pine Grove
Meacham-Deadman's Pass	Kamela	Michigan	Jimmy
Meadow Cow Camp Road	Starkey Headquart	Middle Road	Gordon Creek
Meadow Creek	Dark Canyon	Middle Road	Jones
Meadow Creek	Marley Creek	Middle Road	Ridgeway
Meadow Creek	Meadow Cow Camp	Middle Road	Simonson
Means, Nancy J.	Booth	Middletown Addition	West
Medford, OR	Dutton	Mifflin, Ashland Co., OH	Marks
Medford, OR	Kerns	Mill Canyon	Morgan Lake
Medford, OR	Roulet	Mill Canyon	Wood
Medford, OR	Tucker Flat	Mill Canyon Road	Glass Hill
Medford, OR	Wright	Mill Canyon Road	Morgan Lake
Medical Springs	Big Creek	Mill Canyon Road	Wood
Medical Springs, OR	Highway 203	Mill Creek	Mill Creek
Medical Springs, OR	Hulick	Mill Creek	Morgan Lake
Medical Springs, OR	Leffel	Mill Creek	Wade
Medical Springs, OR	Ramo Flat	Mill Creek canyon	Comstock
Medical Springs, OR	Sandridge	Mill Creek Canyon	McNeill
Medicine Creek, MO	Yarrington	Mill Creek Lane	McNeill
Meek's Cutoff	Grays Corner	Mill Creek Lane	Ruth
Memorial Park (cemetery	Tucker Flat	Mill Creek Lane	Thew
Memphis (railroad)	Upper Perry	Mill Creek Road	Hidden Valley
Memphis, TN	Upper Perry	Miller Elida S.	Miller
Memphis, TN	Upper Perry	Miller, A. & Sons	Fruitdale
Mercer Co., MO	Yarrington	Miller, Alice	Miller

Miller, Alice M.	Hamilton	Miller, William D.	Hamilton
Miller, Alice Maude	Hamilton	Miller, William Dudley	Hamilton
Miller, Alvin Lee	Hamilton	Miller, William W.	Hamilton
Miller, Anna E.	Grays Corner	Miller, Willie	Thompson
Miller, Arthur	Hamilton	Miller-Hamilton Road	Hamilton
Miller, Beth	Thompson	Millering, Berdillie	Grays Corner
Miller, Bethene M.	Miller	Mills, Allen	Haefer
Miller, Chris	Fox Hill	Mills, Dorothy	Haefer
Miller, Conrad	Catherine Cr.	Mills, Gale	Haefer
Miller, Doris, Letha	Hamilton	Mills, Gordon	Haefer
Miller, Edith E.	Hamilton	Mills, James E.	Haefer
Miller, Edmond Lewis	Hamilton	Mills, Lloyd	Haefer
Miller, Effie Maude	Hamilton	Mills, Lloyd J.	Haefer
Miller, Elida A. T.	Miller	Mills, Mabel Alice	Haefer
Miller, Emil	Hindman	Mills, Sylvia May	Sammyville
Miller, Emil	Thompson	Mills-Haefer Lane	Haefer
Miller, Ernest E.	Hamilton	Milton Nurseries	Fruitdale
Miller, Fern V.	Thompson	Milton precinct	Gordon Creek
Miller, Florentine "Flora"	Thompson	Milton, OR	Bowman
Miller, Francis	Thompson	Milton, OR	Gordon Creek
Miller, Francis Doyle	Thompson	Milton-Freewater	Robinson
Miller, Frank	Hamilton	Milton-Freewater IOOF Cemetery	Rawhide
Miller, Georganna	Hamilton	Milton-Freewater, OR	Golding
Miller, George	Conley	Milton-Freewater, OR	Gordon Creek
Miller, George	Hamilton	Milton-Freewater, OR	Knight
Miller, George Washington	Hamilton	Milton-Freewater, OR	Spout Springs
Miller, Herman	Thompson	Milton-Freewater, Umatilla Co., OR	Rawhide
Miller, Hermann Gottlieb Balthasar	Thompson	Mimnaugh, Charley	Lower Perry
Miller, John C.	Hamilton	Mimnaugh, Jim	Lower Perry
Miller, John Conley	Hamilton	Minam	Fox Hill
Miller, Joisa Eliza	Hamilton	Minam area	Follett
Miller, Kenneth Max	Thompson	Minam grade	Follett
Miller, Leonard G.	Hamilton	Minam Summit	Merritt
Miller, Margaret	Miller	Minam, OR	Highway 82
Miller, Marjorie G.	Hamilton	Minneapolis, MN	Dorthy M
Miller, Mary	Ruckman	Minnesota	Yarrington
Miller, Mary	Thompson	Minnick, Jessie	High Valley
Miller, Mary A.	Hamilton	Minnick, Mary	High Valley
Miller, Mary Alma	Hamilton	Misener Gap, the	Highway 82
Miller, Matilda	Conley	Misener, Carrie R.	Highway 82
Miller, Matilda	Hamilton	Misener, J. H.	Highway 82
Miller, May	Miller	Misener, Joseph Hannah	Highway 82
Miller, Mrs. Joe	Yarrington	Miss Walla Walla	Knight
Miller, Mrs. Opal	Bowman	Mission, OR	Fox Hill
Miller, Myron	Thompson	Missoula, MT	Knight
Miller, Odin E.	Miller	Missouri	Indian Creek
Miller, OR	Yarrington	Missouri	Lampkin
Miller, Ora	Thompson	Missouri	Marvin
Miller, Rodney E.	Miller	Missouri	McAlister
Miller, Ronald F.	Thompson	Missouri	Rinehart
Miller, Simon	Miller	Missouri	Robbs Hill
Miller, Simon Edward "Ed"	Miller	Missouri	Ruckman
Miller, Ted Shelton	Thompson	Missouri	Standley
Miller, Walter G.	Hamilton	Missouri River	Moses Creek
Miller, Will	Wright	Misterton, Somerset, England	Owsley

Mitchek, Scott A.	Geiger Butte	Morgan Lake Road	Glass Hill
Mitchek, Scott A.	Mitchek	Morgan Lake Road	Marvin
Mitchell, Eliza W.	Hunter	Morgan Lake Road	Wood
Mitchell, Eliza Weir	Hunter	Morgan Lakes Estates	Wood
Mitchell, Lucinda Viola	Mt. Glen	Morgan, Albert	Morgan Lake
Mitchell, Lucinda Viola	Yerges	Morgan, Ann	Morgan Lake
Mitchell, Moses Hawkins	Hunter	Morgan, Ben	Morgan Lake
Mitchell, Mrs. M. B.	Hull	Morgan, Daniel	Morgan Lake
Mitchell. Susan	Hutchinson	Morgan, Enoch	Morgan Lake
Mitre's Touch Gallery	Knight	Morgan, Margaret Jane	Morgan Lake
Moberly, MS	Yarrington	Morgan, Mary Jane	Morgan Lake
Mobetie, TX	Fletcher	Morgan, Minerva Jane	Morgan Lake
Model A	Summerville	Morgan, Rachel	Morgan Lake
Model U Allis Chalmers	Hug	Morgan, Rachel	Morgan Lake
Molitor, Dr.	Hunter	Morgan, Seth	Morgan Lake
Mon Ah (Chinese)	Hunter	Morgan, Sheppard	Morgan Lake
Monday, H. A.	Jimmy	Morgan, Thomas	Morgan Lake
Monday, Mr. & Mrs. H. A.	Jimmy	Morgantown, WV	Courtney
Monitor Co., MO	Yarrington	Morge, John	Fox Hill
Monmouth, Polk Co., OR	Marks	Morge, Johnny "Honni"	Fox Hill
Monroe Pct., Benton Co., OR	Godley	Morgue, Honni (cabin)	Fox Hill
Monroe, Charles	Monroe	Morning Star, The (newspaper)	Yerges
Monroe, Elma M.	Monroe	Moro, OR	Craig
Monroe, OR	Wright	Moro, OR	McKennon
Monroe, Otis S.	Monroe	Morris Century Farm	Lower Cove
Monroe, Otis Schweicker	Monroe	Morris, Agnes	Lower Cove
Monroe, Walter	Monroe	Morris, Elmer Story	Lower Cove
Montana	Hulick	Morris, IL	Pierce
Montana	Moses Creek	Morris, Lydia	Lower Cove
Montesano, WA	Owsley	Morris, Manford	Lower Cove
Montgomery, Jeanette	Marvin	Morris, Manford (Manie)	Lower Cove
Montreal, Canada	Moses Creek	Morris, Mrs. Blanche	Lampkin
Montreal, Canada	Upper Perry	Morris, Rascellas	Lower Cove
Monument, OR	Fletcher	Morris, Rascellas "Mike"	Lower Cove
Moon, O. W.	Bushnell	Morris, Ron	Squire
Moore (baseball) Field	Ernest	Morris, Thomasine A.	Squire
Moore (family)	Starkey	Morris, Wilma May	Lower Cove
Moore, Bill	Ernest	Morrison, Jannette	Rankin
Moore, Bill	Slack	Morrow, OR	Marvin
Moore, Elijah	Summerville	Morton, Nancy Alice	Roulet
Moore, G. W.	Summerville	Moscow, ID	Rawhide
Moore, Lucille	Ernest	Moses Creek	Moses Creek
Moore, Mary Adeline	Robbs Hill	Mose's Creek	Moses Creek
Moore, William "Bill"	Keen Cabin Cr.	Moses Creek Lane	Palmer Junction
Moorehouse, Emily	Marks	Moses Creek Lane	Robinson
Moray, A	Ramo Flat	Moss Chapel	Halley
Morelock, Martha Eileen	May	Moss Chapel School	Owsley
Morelock, Ned	Mt. Harris	Moss, Martha Jane "Jennie"	Wallsinger
Morelock, Rebecca	Mt. Harris	Moss, Mrs. Jennie	Wallsinger
Morgan (baby girl)	Morgan Lake	Motanic	Bodie
Morgan (formation)	Morgan Lake	Moulton, Mrs. Cora	Yarrington
Morgan Basin	Morgan Lake	Mount Ayr, OA	Middle
Morgan Lake	Morgan Lake	Mount Carmel, Wabash Co., IL	Hutchinson
Morgan Lake	Pierce	Mount Emily	Mt. Glen
Morgan Lake Electric Company	Hunter	Mount Emily Camp	Elkanah

Mount Emily Orchard	Monroe	Murchison, Elizabeth	Shaw Creek
Mount Emily Road	USFS Road 31	Murchison, Elizabeth (McKenzie)	Shaw Creek
Mount Enily Lumber Co.	USFS Road 31	Murchison, Isabelle	Woodell
Mount Fannie Gold Brick (bull)	Igo	Murchison, John	Shaw Creek
Mount Glen	Marks	Murchison, Lola	Fox Hill
Mount Glen (area)	Marks	Murchison, Murdo	Shaw Creek
Mount Glen Road	Fruitdale	Murdaugh, Margaret Ann	Fletcher
Mount Glen Road	McAlister	Murphy (bed)	Lookingglass
Mount Glen Road	Monroe	Murphy, Justice Frank	Dry Creek
Mount Glenn Road	Igo	Murray, Calloway Co., KY	Witherspoon
Mount Harris	Dorthy M	Myers (farm)	Starr
Mount Harris	Dry Creek	Myers Road	Starr
Mount Harris	Grays Corner	Myers, Alice Maude	Hamilton
Mount Hood River	Morgan Lake	Myers, Belle Eilers	Myers
Mount Hope Cemetery	Jimmy	Myers, Charles A.	Myers
Mount Hope Cemetery	Shaw Mountain	Myers, Charles Arnet	Myers
Mount Pleasant Cemetery	Yarrington	Myers, Charles H.	Myers
Mount Pleasant, IA	Antles	Myers, Clyde	Finley Creek
Mount Rainier	Knight	Myers, Dr. Belle	Myers
Mount Vernon, IL	Hamilton	Myers, Edgar "Clyde"	Myers
Mount Vernon, WA	Weaver	Myers, Edna Belle	Myers
Mountain Glen Road	Mt. Glen	Myers, Edna Clair	Myers
Mountain View Ranch	Coombs	Myers, Edna D.	Myers
Mountville, MN	Haefer	Myers, Fred	May
Moyette, Henry	Moses Creek	Myers, John A.	Myers
Mt. Emily	End	Myers, John I.	Myers
Mt. Emily	Mt. Emily	Myers, John J.	Myers
Mt. Emily	Woodell	Myers, Lawana	Myers
Mt. Emily Lumber	Bennett	Myers, Margaret	Myers
Mt. Emily Lumber Co.	Coombs	Myers, Mary	Myers
Mt. Emily Lumber Co.	Elkanah	Myers, Millie	Myers
Mt. Emily Timber Co.	Bodie	Myers, Mollie	Myers
Mt. Emily Timber Co.	Elkanah	Myers, Rachel Margaret	Myers
Mt. Fannie Grange	Fletcher	Myers, Reece	Myers
Mt. Fannie Grange	Ruth	Myers, Robert	Myers
Mt. Glen area	Hunter	Myers, Thomas W.	Myers
Mt. Glen Road	Halley	Myers-Burnaugh Road	Myers
Mt. Glen Road	Lizabeth	Myrick, OR	Bagwell
Mt. Glen Road	Rock Ridge	Myrtle Creek, OR	Wright
Mt. Glen Road	Standley	N Avenue, La Grande	McKennon
Mt. Glen Road	Starr	N. Manchester, Walbash Co., IN	Leffel
Mt. Harris	Alicel	Nagey, Miss Goldie	Lookingglass
Mt. Harris	Alicel	Nagle, Bess Beulah	Dry Creek
Mt. Harris	McKennon	Nail, Willis	Starkey
Mt. Hood	Morgan Lake	Nampa, ID	Comstock
Mt. Pleasant Cemetery	Wheeler	Nampa, ID	McNeill
Mt. Vernon, IL	Conley	Nampa, ID	Speckhart
Mud Spring	Mud Spring	Nantucket, RI	Bean-Coffin
Muilenberg, Emil	Wright	Napa, CA	Myers
Muller, Anna E.	Hug	Nascinbeni, Celeste	Rawhide
Muller, Miss	Hug	Nashville, TN	Conley
Multnomah County, OR	Dry Creek	Nason, Stella J.	Wallsinger
Mulvehill, Iva	Badger Flat	Nasonville, WI	Wallsinger
Muncie, IN	Lookingglass	Nat. Cross Country Championship	Spout Springs
Murchison, Ann	Shaw Creek	National Bank of La Grande	Mt. Glen

Owsley, Thomas III	Owsley	Park, William Nephi	Courtney
Owsley, William "Lee"	Owsley	Parker, Christina Cooper	Heber
Owsley's Lane	Owsley	Parker, Edith Unita	Christensen
Owsley's, the	Bushnell	Parker, Heber Thomas Riley	Heber
Ozsoy, Haluk	McCanse	Parker, Henry	Heber
Pacific Coast Elevator Co.	Couch	Parker, Henry Miller	Heber
Pacific Coast, the	Hutchinson	Parkersburg, WV	McKennon
Pacific Fruit & Produce Co.	Monroe	Parks Road	Roulet
Pacific Grove, CA	Good	Parks, Earl	Finley Creek
Pacific Northwest	Mill Creek	Parks, Florence Idella	Roulet
Pacific Union College	Weaver	Parks, Floyd E.	Roulet
Paddock, Charles Albert	Turnbull	Parks, Kendrick "Kinder"	Roulet
Paddock, Nena Nina	Turnbull	Parks, Malinda Jane	Roulet
Paddock, Sarah Jane	Turnbull	Parks, Nancy (Mrs. Kendrick)	Roulet
Page, IA	Palmer Junction	Parks, Nancy (Mrs. William)	Roulet
Page, LaVonna Mason	Knight	Parks, Ruth A.	Roulet
Palm Springs, CA	Elgin Cem.	Parks, Thomas E.	Roulet
Palmer Junction	Moses Creek	Parks, Vera E.	Roulet
Palmer Junction Lumber Co.	Moses Creek	Parks, William	Roulet
Palmer Junction Road	Ernest	Parks, William O.	Roulet
Palmer Junction Road	Frances	Parks-Roulet Road	Roulet
Palmer Junction Road	Keen Cabin Cr.	Parsons Century Farm	Parsons
Palmer Junction Road	Kingsbury	Parsons Farm	Parsons
Palmer Junction Road	Lower Cove	Parsons Lane	Hardy
Palmer Junction Road	Middle	Parsons Lane	Roulet
Palmer Junction Road	Moses Creek	Parsons, Arthur	Henderson
Palmer Junction Road	Robinson	Parsons, Arthur H.	Parsons
Palmer Junction Road	Yarrington	Parsons, Dell Earnest	Parsons
Palmer Lumber Co.	Palmer Junction	Parsons, Dick	Parsons
Palmer Road	Palmer Junction	Parsons, Earnest R.	Parsons
Palmer Valley	Lookingglass	Parsons, Elsie	Parsons
Palmer Valley	Moses Creek	Parsons, Elsie Marie	Parsons
Palmer Valley School	Bowman	Parsons, Henry	Henderson
Palmer, Bertha Louise	Bagwell	Parsons, Labette Co., KS	Upper Perry
Palmer, Edith	Palmer Junction	Parsons, LaRue	Parsons
Palmer, Emily	Draper	Parsons, Laura	Parsons
Palmer, Emma	Palmer Junction	Parsons, Leonard	Henderson
Palmer, George	Palmer Junction	Parsons, Leonard R.	Parsons
Pandora, Putnam Co., OH	Rankin	Parsons, Mary	Parsons
Panhandle, the	Imbler	Parsons, Nellie	Parsons
Paola, KS	Upper Perry	Parsons, Nellie	Roulet
Paris, Bear Lake Co., ID	Kofford	Parsons, Sallie D.	Parsons
Park View Farm	Stackland	Parsons, W. F.	Parsons
Park, Anna R.	Courtney	Parsons-Chaffee, Jill M.	Parsons
Park, Anna Rachel	Courtney	Parsons-Hug Road	Parsons
Park, Annie	Courtney	Partridge, Woodford Co., IL	Hunter
Park, Earl E.	Courtney	Partton Street	Summerville
Park, Hugh W.	Courtney	Pasadena, CA	Shaw Creek
Park, Mary E.	Courtney	Pasco, WA	Gaertner
Park, Mary Elizabeth	Courtney	Pataha, WA	McCanse
Park, Pearl P.	Courtney	Pat's Alley	Knight
Park, Wayne	Courtney	Patten Street, Summerville	Summerville
Park, Wayne D.	Courtney	Patten, Hester Emma	Darr
Park, Wayne Darr	Courtney	Patten, Jack	Hindman
Park, William N.	Courtney	Patten, Mary Savannah	Myers

Patten, William H.	Shaw Creek	Pendleton, OR	Geiger Butte
Patten, William H.	Summerville	Pendleton, OR	Gilkison
Patterson, Allie Elizabeth	McKennon	Pendleton, OR	Igo
Paul, Ava E.	Dry Creek	Pendleton, OR	Jones
Paul, Lanetta	Wood	Pendleton, OR	Kingsbury
Paul, Mrs. Byron	Dry Creek	Pendleton, OR	Knight
Paxton, Bill	Elgin Cem.	Pendleton, OR	Kofford
Paxton, Ross Elwyn	Elgin Cem.	Pendleton, OR	Ladd Creek
Payerne, Vaud, Switzerland	Roulet	Pendleton, OR	Leffel
Payette (river)	Moses Creek	Pendleton, OR	Lookingglass
Payette, ID	Coughanour	Pendleton, OR	Marks
Payette, ID	Wright	Pendleton, OR	May
Payne, Odies	Highway 82	Pendleton, OR	McKennon
Payne, Odies	Hindman	Pendleton, OR	Morgan Lake
Payson, IL	Speckhart	Pendleton, OR	Pierce
Pea Festival Princess, the	Knight	Pendleton, OR	Starr
Peach (bridge)	Peach	Pendleton, OR	Upper Perry
Peach Brothers Dairy	Peach	Pendleton, OR	Yarrington
Peach Cemetery	Peach	Pendleton-Walla Walla Road	Ruckle
Peach Lane	Peach	Pennsylvania	Hull
Peach Road	Wilkinson	Pennsylvania	Lampkin
Peach, Augusta	Peach	Pennsylvania	Lantz
Peach, George W.	Peach	Pennsylvania	Marvin
Peach, James Seaver (J. S.)	Peach	Pennsylvania	Ruckman
Peach, John	Peach	Pennsylvania Germans	Marks
Peach, Leonard	Peach	Pensacola, FL	Ruth
Peach, Lester	Peach	Pentney, Libbie Ethel	Marley Creek
Peach, Thomas	Peach	Peoria Pottery (jars)	Wallsinger
Peach, William George	Peach	Peoria, IL	Wilkinson
Peacock, Bill	Dorthy M	Perkins, Louisa Elizabeth	Robbs Hill
Peacock, Bob	Dorthy M	Perkins, Mr.	Grays Corner
Peacock, Bobbi	Dorthy M	Perkins, Rebecca Seavey	Coombs
Peacock, Dorothy	Dorthy M	Perry, Charlotte A. "Lottie"	Upper Perry
Peacock, Dorthy M.	Dorthy M	Perry, D. W. C.	Lower Perry
Peacock, Dorthy May	Dorthy M	Perry, D. W. C.	Upper Perry
Peacock, Jane	Dorthy M	Perry, Daniel	Upper Perry
Peacock, Mrs. Edith	McIntyre	Perry, DeWitt Clinton	Lower Perry
Peacock, Mrs. Willis M.	McIntyre	Perry, DeWitt Clinton	Upper Perry
Peacock, Rick	Dorthy M	Perry, Eleanor	Upper Perry
Peacock, William Asa	Dorthy M	Perry, Ellen	Upper Perry
Peal, Mary Jane	Ruckman	Perry, Esther	Upper Perry
Pear Anjou Fruit Farm	Stackland	Perry, Ethel E.	Upper Perry
Pearl Harbor	Rawhide	Perry, George David	Upper Perry
Pearson, Emery Frank	Coughanour	Perry, Henry Cory	Upper Perry
Pearson, Enoch	Lookingglass	Perry, Mary	Upper Perry
Pearson, Laverne Enoch	Lookingglass	Perry, Melissie	Upper Perry
Pearson, Nina	Coughanour	Perry, Naoma	Summerville
Pearson, Tillie	Lookingglass	Perry, OH	Delong
Peckham (funeral chapel)	Henderson	Perry, OR	Igo
Pedersen, Lelah	Shaw Mountain	Perry, OR	Lower Perry
Pedersen, Reinhart C.	Shaw Mountain	Perry, OR	Mathson
Peet Creek	USFS Road 21	Perry, OR	Riddle
Peirce, Lloyd	Pierce	Perry, OR	Upper Perry
Pelham, Adeline	Draper	Perry, OR	Wagoner Hill
Pendleton Round-Up	Hindman	Perry, Sophie	Upper Perry

Quebec, Canada	Moses Creek	Rees, Zella	Summerville
Quincy, Adams Co., IL	Speckhart	Reese, Allie	Summerville
Quinn, John	McAlister	Reeth, Jake	Marks
Rainier, WA	Hutchinson	Reeves, Lenoir	Finley Creek
Ralston, Dr.	Wallsinger	Reeves, Mourning	Finley Creek
Rambo, Alice Sarah	Bowman	Reeves, Sarah Jane	Finley Creek
Ramo Flat	Ramo Flat	Regent (shoes)	May
Ramo, M.	Ramo Flat	Resettlement Administration	Starr
Ramo, P.	Ramo Flat	Reta, Kathleen Mary	Comstock
Ramo, Peter	Ramo Flat	Reynolds & Zimmerman	Myers
Ranch-N-Home Realty	Lester	Reynolds, Donald Lee	Merritt
Randall, Edward	Kerns	Reynolds, Ruth Josephine	Merritt
Randall, George	Kerns	Rhinehart Road	Rinehart
Randall, John	Kerns	Rhoads, Charles	Dry Creek
Randall, Lewis	Kerns	Rhoads, Doris	Dry Creek
Randall, Mary	Kerns	Rhoads, Stanley	Summerville
Randall. William	Kerns	Richard, Mrs. Emma	Knight
Rankin Field	Airport	Richards (family)	Pine Grove
Rankin, Abbie Euphemia	Rankin	Richards, Emma Rosella	Knight
Rankin, Charlotte	Rankin	Richardson, Dr.	Hunter
Rankin, Cora Louella	Rankin	Richardson, June Ella	Chadwick
Rankin, Dudley	Airport	Richardson, Marinda Jane	Wright
Rankin, Earl	Rankin	Richland, Baker Co., OR	Hindman
Rankin, Earl C.	Rankin	Richmond, VA	Kerns
Rankin, George	Rankin	Ricker, Curt	Anson
Rankin, George W.	Rankin	Ricker, Dot Ann	Anson
Rankin, James A.	Rankin	Ricker, Tatiana	Anson
Rankin, Jannette	Rankin	Riddle Road	Riverside
Rankin, Mary	Rankin	Riddle Road	West
Rankin, Minnie	Rankin	Riddle, Caroline	Riddle
Rankin, Patrick	Rankin	Riddle, Charles Mortimer	Riddle
Rankin, Robert M.	Rankin	Riddle, Jesse (Jose) Merrick	Riddle
Rankin, Thomas M.	Rankin	Riddle, Katherine	Riddle
Rankin, William	Rankin	Riddle, Marcia E.	Riddle
Ransome (family)	Pine Grove	Riddle, Mildred	Riddle
Ransome, Margaret Catherine	Wallsinger	Riddle, Mollie	Riddle
Rasmussen, Mary	Good	Riddle, Sarah H.	Riddle
Ratz, Fred	Turnbull	Riggs, James	Pumpkin Ridge
Ray, Mary Jane	Starkey	Riley Co., KS	Morgan Lake
Rayburn, Dixie Lee	Grays Corner	Rinehart Flour Mill	Hindman
Raymou, (Frenchman)	Ramo Flat	Rinehart Lane	Highway 82
Reavis, Dr. L. D.	May	Rinehart Miss Sarah	Chumos
Red Brick Building	McDonald	Rinehart Station	Courtney
Red House, the	Fox Hill	Rinehart, Anna	Rinehart
Red Pepper School	Carter	Rinehart, Bertha Ethel	Rinehart
Red Pepper School	Red Pepper	Rinehart, Elizabeth	Rinehart
Redding, Shasta Co., CA	Godley	Rinehart, Emily Jane	Booth
Redman, C. E.	Geiger Butte	Rinehart, Eugene Edwin	Rinehart
Redman, Goldie Belle	Webster	Rinehart, Franklin Clay	Rinehart
Redman, OR	Parsons	Rinehart, G. W.	Chumos
Redmon, Killy	Haefer	Rinehart, Henry	Courtney
Reed, Minnie Mae	Yarrington	Rinehart, Henry	Rinehart
Rees, Mrs. M. B.	Owsley	Rinehart, Henry C.	Yerges
Rees, Sarah	Godley	Rinehart, Henry Lee	Rinehart
Rees, William	Godley	Rinehart, James	Mt. Glen

Rinehart, James H.	Yerges	Robnett, Mrs. (May) Elmo E.	Bodie
Rinehart, James Harvey	Rinehart	Rochester, IN	Leffel
Rinehart, James Thomas	Rinehart	Rochester, NY	Wade
Rinehart, Jennie	Yerges	Rock Creek	Morgan Lake
Rinehart, Lewis Bird	Chumos	Rock Creek	Rock Creek
Rinehart, Lewis Bird	Rinehart	Rock Springs, WY	Haefer
Rinehart, Lewis Ludwig	Rinehart	Rock Wall Grange	Witherspoon
Rinehart, Lloyd Watson	Rinehart	Rock Wall Grange Hall	Gordon Creek
Rinehart, Lulu	Rinehart	Rockwall Grange	Bowman
Rinehart, Margaret Ann	Rinehart	Rockwall Grange Hall	Middle
Rinehart, Mrs. J. N.	Hull	Rockwell, Hannah	Brooks
Rinehart, Nellie May	Rinehart	Roe, J. S.	Summerville
Rinehart, Sarah Elizabeth	Chumos	Roethler, Ron	Wolf Creek
Rinehart, T. A.	Summerville	Rogers, George J.	Rawhide
Rinehart, Wilma C.	Yerges	Rogers, Irvin K.	Rawhide
Rinehart's (shingle mill)	High Valley	Rogers, Jim	Summerville
Ringgold Co., OH	Merritt	Rogers, Mrs. Mary Jane	Rawhide
Ripley, Olga Rose	Mathson	Rogers, Roe	Phys
Ritter, William H.	Hunter	Rogers, Roy	Palmer Junction
River Road	Riddle	Rogers, Sheri	Summerville
River Street	May	Rogue River Indian War	Mt. Glen
Riverside Cemetery	Coughanour	Roland Township, OK	Woodruff
Riverside Park	Blackhawk Tr	Rollins, Eva Mae	Thompson
Riverside Park	Wallsinger	Roman Beauty (apples)	Fruitdale
Riverside Park & Pavillion	Fruitdale	Romig Addition	Alicel
Riverside Park Pavilion	Leffel	Romig, J. K.	Alicel
Riverside, CA	Golding	Romig, James Kinkaid	Alicel
Robbins, Mrs. Lucy	Comstock	Rondeville	Marks
Robbs Hill Road	Fox Hill	Rondowa (train stop)	Lookingglass
Robb's sawmill	Robbs Hill	Roosevelt, Col. Theodore	Chumos
Robbs, Benjamin	Robbs Hill	Roosevelt, President Franklin D.	Greiner
Robbs, Henry C.	Robbs Hill	Rose Ridge Cemetery	Rose Ridge
Robbs, Lucy	Robbs Hill	Roseburg, OR	Marvin
Robbs, Miss Lucy	Robbs Hill	Roseburg, OR	Shaw Creek
Robbs, Sarah Jane	Robbs Hill	Ross & Cromarty, Scotland	Shaw Creek
Robbs, Thomas	Robbs Hill	Ross, J. V.	May
Robbs, William	Robbs Hill	Ross, William Crosby	McKennon
Roberts, F. E.	Antles	Rosseland, Maurits	Stackland
Roberts, Susan	Highway 82	Roth, Dr. A. J.	Woodruff
Robertson, Ethel	Couch	Roth, Richard R.	Hot Lake
Robinett, Mary Opal	Ruckman	Roth, Richard R.	Union Junction
Robinett, Otto Bob	Ruckman	Roulet Loop	Knight
Robinette, Otto Theodore "Bob"	Hays	Roulet, Arthur Leo	Roulet
Robinson Road	Moses Creek	Roulet, Francis Frederick	Roulet
Robinson, Elmer Horace	Robinson	Roulet, Frederick "Fred" William	Roulet
Robinson, Frank Seba	Robinson	Roulet, Helen E.	Roulet
Robinson, George Elmer	Robinson	Roulet, Julia F.	Roulet
Robinson, Hattie Amelia	Robinson	Roulet, Leo	Roulet
Robinson, Hattie Irene	Robinson	Roulet, Mary "Cordelia"	Roulet
Robinson, Hattie Irene	Robinson	Roulet, Mr. & Mrs.Leo	Hindman
Robinson, John	Rose Ridge	Roulet, Nancy Alice	Roulet
Robinson, Mrs. Frank (Violet)	Robinson	Roulet, Nellie	Roulet
Robinson, Violet Addie	Robinson	Roulet, Norna Jean	Roulet
Robnett, May	Bodie	Roulet, Rachel	Hardy
Robnett, May Helen	Bodie	Roulet, Rachel "Regula"	Roulet

Roulet, Rex	Hindman	Ruckman, Mrs. George	Hull
Roulet, William	Henderson	Ruckman, Robert Jasper	Ruckman
Roulet, William Henry	Roulet	Ruckman, Samuel G.	Ruckman
Roulet-Hardy Road	Hardy	Ruckman, Will	Sandridge
Round, Majorie May	Bean-Coffin	Ruckman, William	Ruckman
Roundtree, "Hap"	Airport	Ruckman, William	Hays
Rovey, Byron	Hutchinson	Ruckman, William "Bill"	Ruckman
Rovey, Stephanie	Hutchinson	Ruckman, William E.	Hays
Royes Farms	Courtney	Ruckman, William Edward	Ruckman
Royes, Clifford	Slack	Ruckman, William Edward "Will"	Woodell
Royes, George "G" Jr.	Courtney	Rudd (farm)	Sandridge
Royes, George "G" Jr.	Dry Creek	Rudd, Janet	Hays
Royes, George "G" Jr.	Hays	Rudio, Clara	Pierce
Royes, George Sr.	Courtney	Rudio, Laura	Pierce
Royes, George Sr.	Dry Creek	Rugg Brothers	Bodie
Royes, George Sr.	Hays	Rundall, Lydia A.	Wilkinson
Royes, George Sr.	Woodell	Rusau (Rusaw)	Rawhide
Royes, Mary Elizabeth	Courtney	Rusau, Mr. & Mrs. Arden	Rawhide
Royes, Mike	Dry Creek	Rusau-Gawith Road	Rawhide
Royes, Mrs. Michael	Brooks	Rusaw, Clyde	Rawhide
Royes, Nancy	Dry Creek	Rusaw, Emma	Rawhide
Royes, Sam	Courtney	Rusaw, Enock "Arden"	Rawhide
Royes, Sam	Hays	Rusaw, Harriet M.	Rawhide
Royes, Samuel	Sandridge	Rush, Edna Teter	Chumos
Royes, Valerie	Courtney	Rush, Edna Teter	Dry Creek
Ruckel (stage stop)	Standley	Rush, Edna Teter	Summerville
Ruckle (stage stop)	Shaw Creek	Russia	Squire
Ruckle Road	Dry Creek	Rutledge, Samuel	Dry Creek
Ruckle Road	Finley Creek	Rutter, Mrs. Lula	McNeill
Ruckle, Colonel J. S.	Ruckle	Ryan, Mrs. Annie	McNeill
Ruckman	Brooks	Rynearson (brothers)	Morgan Lake
Ruckman Road	Hull	Rysdam Canyon	Hardy
Ruckman Road	Sandridge	Rysdam Canyon	Merritt
Ruckman, Charles	Riddle	Rysdam, Albert	Wickens
Ruckman, Elizabeth	Hays	Rysdam, Arie Albert Sr.	Wickens
Ruckman, Elizabeth Elenor	Ruckman	Rysdam, Gerrit	Dry Creek
Ruckman, Elizabeth Elenor	Woodell	Rysdam, Gerrit	Wickens
Ruckman, George W.	Ruckman	Rysdam, Johanna	Striker
Ruckman, George Washington	Ruckman	Rysdam, John "Egedius"	Wickens
Ruckman, Goldie Belle	Ruckman	Rysdam, Louisa Ball	Wickens
Ruckman, Harvey E.	Woodell	Rysdam, Magdalene	Wickens
Ruckman, Harvey Edward	Ruckman	Rysdam, Mary Jane	Hardy
Ruckman, Hattie "Wave"	Ruckman	Rysdam, Mr. Deb	Merritt
Ruckman, Hattie Opal	Ruckman	Rysdam, William Henry	Wickens
Ruckman, Hattie Wave	Woodell	Sacajawea Hotel	Howell
Ruckman, John H. T.	Ruckman	Sackett, Mrs. Fannie	McKennon
Ruckman, Lucretia Cassanna	Ruckman	Sacramento, CA	Love
Ruckman, Mary	Ruckman	Sacramento, CA	May
Ruckman, Mary Elizabeth	Ruckman	Sacramento, CA	Owsley
Ruckman, Mary Jane	Ruckman	Sacramento, CA	Yerges
Ruckman, Mary Opal	Hays	Sailer, Lydia Bertha	McCanse
Ruckman, Mary Opal	Ruckman	Sailor Diggings Water, Mining	Phys
Ruckman, Mary Opal	Woodell	Saint Clairsville Union Cemetery	Starkey
Ruckman, Mollie	Riddle	Salem, OR	Highway 82
Ruckman, Mrs. Ada C.	Hays	Salem, OR	Hull

Salem, OR	Marks	Sanderson, Epsie	Sanderson
Salem, OR	Marley Creek	Sanderson, Euphenia	Sanderson
Salem, OR	McKennon	Sanderson, Georgene	Sanderson
Salem, OR	Moses Creek	Sanderson, Lyle Gale	Sanderson
Salem, OR	Phys	Sanderson, Mary Ellen	Sanderson
Salem, OR	Pierce	Sanderson, Mathew	Sanderson
Salem, OR	Ruth	Sanderson, Silvia	Sanderson
Salem, OR	Weaver	Sanderson, Stuart Alexander	Sanderson
Salem. OR	Heber	Sanderson, Theresa	Sanderson
Salen, Richardson Co., NB	Wilkinson	Sanderson, Virgil David	Sanderson
Salmon River	Phys	Sanderson, Wanda	Summerville
Salmon River (mines)	Ladd Creek	Sanderson, Willie Wilson	Sanderson
Salt Creek, IA	Dial	Sanderson, Willis	Sanderson
Salt Lake City, UT	Heber	Sandridge Road	Greiner
Salt Lake City, UT	Hug	Sandridge Road	McDonald
Salt Lake City, UT	Igo	Sandridge, the	Hull
Salt Lake, UT	Moses Creek	Sandridge, the	Robbs Hill
Sammyville	Sammyville	Sandridge, the	Ruckman
Sammyville (movie)	Sammyville	Sandusky, WI	Craig
San Diego, CA	Fletcher	Sanger Mine	Alicel
San Francisco, CA	May	Santa Anna, CA	Hull
San Francisco, CA	Phys	Santa Clara, UT	Hill Lay
San Francisco, CA	Tucker Flat	Santa Clara, UT	Hug
San Fransisco, CA	Chumos	Santa Clara, Washington Co., UT	Roulet
San Fransisco, CA	Deal Canyon	Santa Fe Railroad	Lower Cove
Sanborn, Miss Himenia	High Valley	Saratoga, CA	Thompson
Sand Ridge	Finley Creek	Saxton, The Honorable F. M.	Mill Creek
Sand Ridge	Grays Corner	Schaffer, Ada	Bowman
Sand Ridge	Mill Creek	Schaffer, Harry Marvin	Bowman
Sand Ridge	Wallsinger	Schaffer, Julia Inice	Bowman
Sand Ridge	Webster	Schaffer, Opal	Bowman
Sand Ridge Post Office	Sandridge	Schaffer, Sadie	Bowman
Sand Ridge School	Sandridge	Schaffer, William Andrew	Bowman
Sandahl, Charlotte J.	Janson	Scheel, Catherine	Starr
Sanders, Mary Ann	Moses Creek	Schenker, Anna	Indian Creek
Sanderson (family)	Summerville	Schiedhauer's (saloon)	Jimmy
Sanderson (kids)	Slack	Schleur, E. T.	Jimmy
Sanderson Century Farm	Sanderson	Schmitz, Mary A.	Dial
Sanderson Century Farm	Summerville	School House	Fox Hill
Sanderson Springs Ranch	Sanderson	Schoonover, Mr.	Fruitdale
Sanderson Springs Ranch	Summerville	Schoonover, Nelson	Fruitdale
Sanderson, Anna Rachel	Courtney	Schraff, Katie J.	Bean-Coffin
Sanderson, Annie Rachel	Sanderson	Schuyler, MO	Godley
Sanderson, Bessie	Sanderson	Scio, OR	Good
Sanderson, Betsy	Sanderson	Scioto Co., OH	Hamilton
Sanderson, Bill	Sanderson	Scioto Co., OH	Wallsinger
Sanderson, Bill "Willie"	Summerville	Scotch Gulch, Josephine Co., OR	Phys
Sanderson, Charles Mathew	Sanderson	Scotch Train	Shaw Creek
Sanderson, Charley	Summerville	Scotland	Heber
Sanderson, David	Sanderson	Scotland	McIntyre
Sanderson, David Lunham.	Sanderson	Scotland	Rankin
Sanderson, Deachman	Sanderson	Scott (family)	Pine Grove
Sanderson, Donald	Summerville	Scott District	Yarrington
Sanderson, Dorothy	Sanderson	Scott Road	Yarrington
Sanderson, Elizabeth "Liz"	Sanderson	Scott, Gladys	Lizabeth

Scott, Harlan	Yarrington	Shaw, Alex J.	Shaw Mountain
Scott, Jennie Ama	Bodie	Shaw, Alex J.	Shaw Mountain
Scott, Joseph	Merritt	Shaw, Angus	Standley
Scott, Joseph	Yarrington	Shaw, Angus Jr.	Shaw Creek
Scott, Mary Ann	Merritt	Shaw, Angus Sr.	Shaw Creek
Scott, Sarah	Merritt	Shaw, Angus Sr.	Shaw Mountain
Scott, Sarah Ellen	Yarrington	Shaw, Angus Sr.	Summerville
Scott's Cemetery	Yarrington	Shaw, Angus Wilbur	Shaw Creek
Scotts Seed Company	Hays	Shaw, Betty Jane	Shaw Mountain
Scott-Yarrington Road	Yarrington	Shaw, Christina	Shaw Creek
Seale, Laurie Gay	Curtis	Shaw, Christina	Standley
Seaside, OR	Fox Hill	Shaw, Christina	Summerville
Seattle, King Co., WA	Hays	Shaw, Creston	Courtney
Seattle, WA	Christensen	Shaw, Creston	Sandridge
Seattle, WA	Chumos	Shaw, Creston Jay	Courtney
Seattle, WA	Elgin Cem.	Shaw, Creston Jay	Hays
Seattle, WA	Greiner	Shaw, Edward Hartford	Shaw Creek
Seattle, WA	Lampkin	Shaw, Elizabeth	Shaw Creek
Seattle, WA	Leffel	Shaw, Elizabeth	Standley
Seattle, WA	McKennon	Shaw, Elizabeth "Bettie"	Shaw Creek
Seattle, WA	Roulet	Shaw, Elizabeth (Murchison)	Summerville
Seattle, WA	Yerges	Shaw, Farquhar Tunnick	Shaw Mountain
Selah, WA	Merritt	Shaw, Hannah Frew	Shaw Mountain
Serendipity (Restaurant)	Elgin Cem.	Shaw, Helen Frew "Ellen"	Shaw Mountain
Setterdahl, Virginia	Dutton	Shaw, J. Alex	Shaw Mountain
Seven Diamonds Ranch	Heber	Shaw, Jacqueline	Shaw Mountain
Seventh Day Adventist Church	Fruitdale	Shaw, Jasper "Jay"	Shaw Creek
Seward, Hazel Agnes	Chumos	Shaw, John	Shaw Creek
Seward, Hazel Agnes	Hardy	Shaw, John	Shaw Mountain
Seymore, IA	Brooks	Shaw, John "Alex"	Shaw Mountain
Shaafhausen, Switzerland	Miller	Shaw, John A.	Shaw Mountain
Shackelford (apples)	Fruitdale	Shaw, John Alexander	Shaw Mountain
Shacklock, Ada	Sammyville	Shaw, KS	Henderson
Shaeffer, Mrs. Lou	Kingsbury	Shaw, Lelah Ire	Shaw Mountain
Shafer, Sarah Florence	Wallsinger	Shaw, Louellen	Shaw Mountain
Shaffer, Calvin Lee	Follett	Shaw, Margaret	Shaw Mountain
Shaffer, Justin	Follett	Shaw, Mary (Nicholson)	Shaw Mountain
Shaffer, Kim	Follett	Shaw, Mary Laing	Shaw Mountain
Sharon, Ellis P.O., WI	Nice	Shaw, Nellie Frew	Olsen
Sharon, PA	Sammyville	Shaw, Patricia	Shaw Mountain
Sharp, Steven J.	Sharp	Shaw, Pearl Laurel	Shaw Mountain
Sharpsville High School	Sammyville	Shaw, Phyllis	Bodie
Sharpsville, PA	Sammyville	Shaw, Robert	Shaw Mountain
Shasta Co., CA	Hamilton	Shaw, Robert M.	Shaw Mountain
Shaw (farm)	Heber	Shaw, Ruth Luise	Shaw Mountain
Shaw Addition	Shaw Creek	Shaw, Sarah "Sallie"	Shaw Creek
Shaw Creek	Shaw Creek	Shaw, Vesta Iola	Shaw Creek
Shaw Creek	Mill Creek	Shaw, William	Shaw Mountain
Shaw Creek Road	McCanse	Shaw, William II	Shaw Mountain
Shaw Creek Road	Shaw Mountain	Shawnee (people)	Wapiti
Shaw Lane	McCanse	Shay (engine)	Moses Creek
Shaw Mountain	McCanse	Sheeks, Aldora May	Greiner
Shaw Mountain	Shaw Mountain	Sheep Creek	Morgan Lake
Shaw Road	McCanse	Shelton, John	Lookingglass
Shaw, Alex	Shaw Mountain	Shelton, Mary	Thompson

Shelton, Mrs. Martha	Jones	Slack, William Hawk	Slack
Shelton, Mrs. Wiley	Kerns	Slater, Mrs. J. H.	Grays Corner
Sheridan, OR	Marks	Slater, Senator	Ruckman
Sheridan, WY	Myers	Slater, Senator James H.	Owsley
Sherman Co., OR	Mill Creek	Slaterr, James H.	Starkey
Sherwood, Branch Co., MI	Marks	Slorah, Charlotte A. "Lottie"	Upper Perry
Shickshinny, PA	Good	Smith (cabin)	Fox Hill
Shieldaig, Scotland	McDonald	Smith Cemetery, Monmouth	Marks
Shinfield, Berkshire, England	Wickens	Smith John	Wright
Shirley & Stewart Livestock	Benson	Smith Meadows	Fox Hill
Shirts (home & mink farm)	Fox Hill	Smith, Annie	Hug
Shirts, Leslie	Fox Hill	Smith, Delda Elizabeth	Grays Corner
Shobert, Mary Magdaline	Marvin	Smith, Effie Maude	Hamilton
Shoddy Creek	Moses Creek	Smith, Eva Montana	McKennon
Shoemaker (family)	Pine Grove	Smith, James	End
Shoemaker, Margaret Ann	Phys	Smith, Karen L.	Starr
Shoppat Road	Stackland	Smith, Laureandia A	Morgan Lake
Shoshone Cemetery	Godley	Smith, Lenore	Upper Perry
Shoshone, Lincoln Co., ID	Godley	Smith, Levi P.	Morgan Lake
Shuey Lee (Chinese)	Hunter	Smith, Mary Ann	Knight
Sidehill Road	Monroe	Smith, Miss Etta B.	Morgan Lake
Sidney Center, Montcalm Co., MI	Tucker Flat	Smith, Rhoda A.	Draper
Silva, Mrs. Lillian Bell	Godley	Smith, Robert L.	Upper Perry
Silver City, ID	Deal Canyon	Smith, Ross	Marks
Silver City, ID	Gekeler	Smith, Ruth	Hug
Silver City, OR	Dry Creek	Smith, Samantha A.	End
Silver Hill Dairy	Marvin	Smith, W. L.	Upper Perry
Silver, MT	End	Smith-Stanley Lumber Co.	Lower Perry
Simcoe, Ontario, Canada	Turnbull	Smith-Stanley Lumber Co.	Upper Perry
Simcotes, Sarah	Hallgarth	Smutz, Dora Mae	Foothill
Simonis, Elizabeth	Nice	Smutz, Irwin D.	Foothill
Simonson, Terry	Simonson	Snake River	Anson
Sing Ah (Chinese)	Hunter	Snake River	Gordon Creek
Sisley Creek	Crampton	Snake River	Robbs Hill
Skiff, Mr. Willis	Little Creek	Snake River, the	Hutchinson
Skiff, Willis	Catherine Cr.	Snakes, the	Henderson
Skilling, Mrs. John	Hacker	Snider, Mayme Virginia	Speckhart
Slack, "Duck"	Summerville	Snodgrass & Zimmerman	Bean-Coffin
Slack, Abraham J.	Slack	Snodgrass & Zimmerman	Yarrington
Slack, Clifton "Duck" Leroy	Slack	Snodgrass & Zimmerman Mortuary	Owsley
Slack, Emma F.	Myers	Snodgrass & Zimmerman Mortuary	Robinson
Slack, Fidelia	Slack	Snodgrass Funeral Home	Bond
Slack, Firandus	Follett	Snodgrass Funeral Home	Dry Creek
Slack, Frances	Slack	Snodgrass, W. J.	Orodell
Slack, Irene	Slack	Snohomish, WA	Tucker Flat
Slack, James Abraham	Slack	Snorr, Miss	Bowman
Slack, James Monroe	Slack	Soap Creek, IA	Gordon Creek
Slack, Nancy	Slack	Soda Springs, ID	Heber
Slack, Nancy Ann	Slack	Sodsor, George D.	Coombs
Slack, Phidelia	Slack	Soldatna, AK	Knight
Slack, Philander	Slack	Sommer Hotel	Lookingglass
Slack, Ruia Elizabeth	Slack	Sommer Hotel, Elgin	Chumos
Slack, Susan Salome	Slack	Sommerville, Alexander	Shaw Creek
Slack, Teri	Slack	Sommerville, Alexander	Summerville
Slack, Vicki	Slack	Song Kim (Chinese)	Hunter

Sorenson, B. F.	Anthony Lake	St. Anthony, ID	Jimmy
South America	Upper Perry	St. Clair Co., MO	Yarrington
South Bend, IN	Chumos	St. George, Canada	Coombs
South Dakota	Stackland	St. Joe, MO	Bushnell
Southern California	McCanse	St. Joseph Hospital	Dry Creek
Southern Oregon	Phys	St. Joseph, MO	Bidwell
Spalding	Moses Creek	St. Louis Co., MN	Turnbull
Spalding, Henry	Moses Creek	St. Louis World's Fair	Upper Perry
Spanish Influenza	Bodie	St. Louis, MO	Moses Creek
Spanish Influenza	Lower Cove	St. Louis, MO	Upper Perry
Sparta, Greece	Chumos	Stackland Road	Haefer
Spears, Blanche	Speckhart	Stackland Road	Love
Spears, Mrs. Marie	Bean-Coffin	Stackland, Alex W.	Stackland
Speckhart	Imbler	Stackland, Alexander	Stackland
Speckhart Century Farm	Speckhart	Stackland, Bertha M.	Stackland
Speckhart, Bertha	Speckhart	Stackland, Christopher Muller	Stackland
Speckhart, Elmer	Speckhart	Stackland, Constance	Stackland
Speckhart, Flora	Speckhart	Stackland, Elida	Stackland
Speckhart, Harlow A.	Speckhart	Stackland, Gerhard	Stackland
Speckhart, Hellen Jean	Speckhart	Stackland, Karl J. Jr.	Stackland
Speckhart, Herbert	Speckhart	Stackland, Karl Johan	Stackland
Speckhart, Irene	Speckhart	Stackland, Miss Elida A. T.	Miller
Speckhart, Joanne	Speckhart	Stackland, Paulina	Stackland
Speckhart, John	Speckhart	Stackland-Lieurance Road	Stackland
Speckhart, Josephine J. H.	Speckhart	Stafford Co., VA	Owsley
Speckhart, Mary	Speckhart	Stafford, William	Draper
Speckhart, Velma	Speckhart	Stakland, Bertha	Stackland
Spence, Stu	Morgan Lake	Stakland, Kornelius	Stackland
Spencer, Mary Josephine	Buchanan	Stakland, Peder	Stackland
Spencer, Mrs. Dora	Geiger Butte	Stampede Legends	Hindman
Spencer, NY	Bidwell	Standard Oil Co.	Upper Perry
Spenser, Owen Co., IN	Middle	Standard Station, the	Knight
Spokane, WA	Geiger Butte	Standley Century Farm	Shaw Creek
Spokane, WA	Kerns	Standley Century Farm	Standley
Spokane, WA	McKennon	Standley Lane	Mt. Glen
Spokane, WA	Owsley	Standley Lane	Shaw Creek
Spokane, WA	Shaw Creek	Standley Train	Shaw Creek
Spokane, WA	Weaver	Standley Train	Standley
Spokane, WA	Woodruff	Standley, Grandma	Shaw Creek
Spooner, Darlene	Spooner	Standley, J. Dale	Standley
Spooner, T. Dwaine	Spooner	Standley, James H.	Shaw Creek
Spout Springs	Canyon View	Standley, James H.	Summerville
Spout Springs	Spout Springs	Standley, James Henry	Standley
Sprague, CT	Bushnell	Standley, Jeremiah	Standley
Springer, George	Jimmy	Standley, Jim	Standley
Springer, Mrs. Rose	Jimmy	Standley, Louie	Shaw Creek
Springfield, IL	Henderson	Standley, Louie	Standley
Springfield, OR	Dry Creek	Standley, Mary "Polly"	Standley
Springville, UT	Igo	Standley, Mary "Polly"	Summerville
Squire, Archer	Starr	Standley, Mrs. Christina	Shaw Creek
Squire, Carrie	Starr	Standley, Mrs. Dorsie	Wolf Creek
Squire, Doug	Squire	Standley, Mrs. Jim	Shaw Creek
Squire, Eleanor Elizabeth	Starr	Stanfield, OR	Kingsbury
Squire, Louise	Squire	Stanfield, Umatilla Co., OR	Hamilton
St, Joseph Cemetery Old	Jones	Stange Manor	Elkanah

Name	Place	Name	Place
Stange, A. H.	Elkanah	Starns, Hiram Oakes	Craig
Stange, A. H.	Elkanah	Starns, Linette	Craig
Stange, A. J.	Elkanah	Starns, Myrtle Estella	Craig
Stange, Ann	Elkanah	Starns, Thomas Chauncy	Craig
Stange, August	Elkanah	Starr Lane	Marks
Stange, August J.	Bodie	Starr Road	Marks
Stange, August John	Elkanah	Starr Trak LLC	Starr
Stange, Jane	Elkanah	Starr, Beverly	Starr
Stange, Priscilla	Elkanah	Starr, Blake	Starr
Stanley Lumber Co.	Riddle	Starr, Catherine	Starr
Stanley, Fred C.	Upper Perry	Starr, Donald	Myers
Stanley, L. C.	Upper Perry	Starr, Donald	Starr
Stanley, Lemuel Castle	Upper Perry	Starr, Donald "Don"	Starr
Stanley, Lenore	Upper Perry	Starr, Eleanor Elizabeth	Starr
Stanton, Neb.	Antles	Starr, Jeana	Starr
Staples, Edwin P.	Staples	Starr, Karen	Starr
Stark Co., OH	Marks	Starr, Larry	Shaw Mountain
Starkey	French Corral	Starr, Lawrence	Myers
Starkey (district)	Fly Valley	Starr, Lawrence Robert "Larry"	Starr
Starkey (district)	Syrup Creek	Starr, Nathan	Starr
Starkey Cow Camp Road	Baseline	Starr, Ryan	Starr
Starkey Creek	Meadow Creek	Starr, Samuel E.	Starr
Starkey Creek	Starkey	Starr, Samuel Elias	Starr
Starkey Experimental Forest	Starkey Headquart	State (place)	Fox Hill
Starkey Prairie	Starkey	State Highway Department	Woodruff
Starkey Road	Anthony Lake	State Pioneer Assoc.	Finley Creek
Starkey Road	Fly Creek	Stateline, OR	Bowman
Starkey Road	Fly Ridge	Stayton, Marion Co., OR	Love
Starkey Road	McIntyre	Stayton, OR	Kamela
Starkey Route	Starkey	Steers, Leroy Nelson	Bowman
Starkey School	Elkanah	Steers, Mrs.	Bowman
Starkey Store	Coombs	Steers, Sadie	Bowman
Starkey Store	Grande Ronde R.	Steers, Sarah "Sadie" Ellen	Bowman
Starkey, Aurora	Starkey	Stella Mayfield School	Bowman
Starkey, D.	Starkey	Stella Mayfield School	Knight
Starkey, Eliza	Starkey	Stephen, Mary Abrilla	McNeill
Starkey, George	Starkey	Stephens, Howard Carroll	Sammyville
Starkey, J. L.	Phys	Stephens, Mrs. Annabelle	Sammyville
Starkey, John	Coombs	Stephenville, Erath Co., TX	McNeill
Starkey, John	Starkey	Sterling, IL	Weaver
Starkey, John Sr.	Starkey	Stevens Point, WI	Lower Cove
Starkey, Martha	Starkey	Stevens, Julia Pearl	Kofford
Starkey, OR	Grande Ronde R.	Stevens, Mary	Shaw Creek
Starkey, OR	Marley Creek	Stevens, Mary (first burial)	Summerville
Starkey, OR	Meadow Creek	Stevenson, Miss Anna	Upper Perry
Starkey, OR	Upper Perry	Stewart, Elizabeth Jane	Dry Creek
Starkey, OR	White Horse	Stewart, Frank	Chumos
Starkey, Sarah	Starkey	Stewart, Levi	Dry Creek
Starkey, William	Starkey	Stewart, Mary Ellen	Dry Creek
Starkey, William Collins	Starkey	Stewart, Mrs.	Chumos
Starkey's Grave	Starkey	Stickler, Mary	Meadow Cow Camp
Starns, Benjamin Oakes Bradford	Craig	Stickler, Ted	Meadow Cow Camp
Starns, Birdie	Craig	Stickney, Frank	Shaw Mountain
Starns, Hannah	Craig	Stickney, Mary Laing	Shaw Mountain
Starns, Herbert Sina	Craig	Stillwater, MN	Bates

Stillwell, Hattie	Chandler	Summerville Cemetery	Dry Creek
Stinnett, Aiden	Knight	Summerville Cemetery	Grays Corner
Stinnett, Caileigh	Knight	Summerville Cemetery	Grays Corner
Stinnett, Joshua	Knight	Summerville Cemetery	Greiner
Stinnett, Michael	Knight	Summerville Cemetery	Halley
stockman (cabin)	Henderson	Summerville Cemetery	Hamilton
Stockton, CA	May	Summerville Cemetery	Hamilton
Stoddard Lumber Co.	Lower Perry	Summerville Cemetery	Hays
Stoddard Lumber Company	Bennett	Summerville Cemetery	Hill Lay
Stoddard, George	Lower Perry	Summerville Cemetery	Highway 82
Stokes Co., NC	Mt. Harris	Summerville Cemetery	Hug
Stoll, Cheryl	Philberg	Summerville Cemetery	Hull
Stone Fountain, the	Highway 82	Summerville Cemetery	Janson
Stone, Frances Bliss	Marley Creek	Summerville Cemetery	Lower Cove
Stone, Marcia E.	Riddle	Summerville Cemetery	McDonald
Stoup, Susannah	McKennon	Summerville Cemetery	McKennon
Stowe, Alta M.	Wheeler	Summerville Cemetery	Mt. Harris
Stowe, Harriet Beecher	Wright	Summerville Cemetery	Myers
Strandlien, Lucy	Thew	Summerville Cemetery	Owsley
Strassburg (ship)	Thompson	Summerville Cemetery	Rinehart
Strawn, TX	Grays Corner	Summerville Cemetery	Ruckman
Street, Leva Lockie	Wagoner Hill	Summerville Cemetery	Sandridge
Stricker (headstone)	Striker	Summerville Cemetery	Shaw Creek
Stricker, John	Peach	Summerville Cemetery	Slack
Strike, Ray	Meadow Cow Camp	Summerville Cemetery	Speckhart
Striker (bridge)	Striker	Summerville Cemetery	Starr
Striker (place)	Striker	Summerville Cemetery	Summerville
Striker, Hellen	Striker	Summerville Cemetery	Wagoner Hill
Striker, Henry	Striker	Summerville Cemetery	Wallsinger
Striker, Johanna	Striker	Summerville Cemetery	Witherspoon
Striker, John	Striker	Summerville Cemetery	Woodell
Striker, Margaret J. "Maggie"	Striker	Summerville Cemetery Chapel	Wagoner Hill
Stroeber, Henry (house & mill)	Fox Hill	Summerville Market Road	Hunter
Stroeber, Herman J.	Fox Hill	Summerville Road	Howell
Stroeber, John (home)	Fox Hill	Summerville Road	Outback
Stroup, Susan "Alta" Capitola	Coughanour	Summerville Road	Sanderson
Stuart, Robert	Hot Lake	Summerville Road	Sandridge
Stubblefield Mountain	Good	Summerville Road	Slack
Stubblefield Mountain	Knight	Summerville School	Slack
Stumptown	Lower Perry	Summerville Store & Tavern	Summerville
Stumptown (Perry)	Robbs Hill	Summerville, OR	Highway 82
Sturgill Miss Mary Ann	Mt. Harris	Summerville, OR	Hindman
Sturgill, J. C.	Jimmy	Summerville, OR	Hug
Sugar Loaf	Fox Hill	Summerville, OR	Myers
Sullivan (family)	Starkey	Summerville, OR	Phillips Creek
Sullivan Co., MO	Dry Creek	Summerville, OR	Pumpkin Ridge
Sullivan Co., MO	Hug	Summerville, OR	Rinehart
Sullivan Co., MO	Mt. Harris	Summerville, OR	Robbs Hill
Sullivan Co., MO	Wheeler	Summerville, OR	Ruckle
Sullivan Walt	Sanderson	Summerville, OR	Ruckman
Sullivan, Dallas	Sanderson	Summerville, OR	Sandridge
Sullivan, Elizabeth "Liz"	Sanderson	Summerville, OR	Shaw Creek
Sullivan, MO	Darr	Summerville, OR	Slack
Summerville	McKenzie	Summerville, OR	Summerville
Summerville	Mill Creek	Summerville, OR	Wagoner Hill

Summerville, OR	Wallsinger	Tennessee	Robbs Hill
Summerville, OR	Witherspoon	Tennessee	Wheeler
Summerville, OR	Wolf Creek	Tepic, Mexico	Myers
Summerville-Imbler Road	Hunter	Terra Haute, Putnam Co., MO	McAlister
Summit Station	Kamela	Teter, Bonita	Summerville
Sun Lee (Chinese)	Hunter	Texas	Lower Cove
Sunday Drive	Haefer	Texas	Upper Perry
Sunnyside, WA	Haefer	The Barn at Tamarack Springs	Tamarack Springs
Superintendent of Landscape Dept.	Upper Perry	The Cove	French Corral
Sutter's Fort	Ruckman	The Dalles, OR	Gekeler
Sutton, Margaret Kaziah	Kingsbury	The Dalles, OR	Janson
Swackhamer place	Catherine Cr.	The Dalles, OR	Lower Perry
Swan River, IA	Lester	The Dalles, OR	Marks
Sweden	Janson	The Dalles, OR	McAlister
Sweden	Stackland	The Dalles, OR	Merritt
Swikert, Mrs. Hattie	Robinson	The Dalles, OR	Morgan Lake
Swikert, Norman Lewis	Robinson	The Dalles, OR	Upper Perry
Switzerland	Hindman	The Toggery (store)	May
Switzerland	Mathson	Thew, David	Thew
Switzerland	Morgan Lake	Thew, Emogene	Thew
Sylvester, John	Morgan Lake	Thew, Ester Grace	Thew
Sylvester, Mary Jane	Morgan Lake	Thew, Henry Prior	Thew
Syracuse, NY	McIntyre	Thew, Henry W.	Thew
Syverson, Mrs. Ethel E.	Upper Perry	Thew, Jennifer	Thew
Taal, Mr.	Dry Creek	Thew, Kathy	Thew
Table Mountain	Morgan Lake	Thew, Lucy	Thew
Tahoma National Cemetery	Knight	Thew, Rebecca	Thew
Talbott, Donna	Slack	Thew, Richard H.	Thew
Talbott, Franklin	Slack	Thew, Richard Henry	Thew
Talbott, Irene	Slack	Thew, Rick	Thew
Talbott, Lenore	Slack	Thief Valley	Thief Valley
Talent, OR	Imbler	Thomas & Ruckles Road	Ruckle
Tama, IA	Buchanan	Thomas, Bob	Fish Trap
Tamarack Springs	Tamarack Springs	Thomas, George	Ruckle
Tandy, Della	Curtis	Thomas, Susie	Fish Trap
Tandy, Della May	Curtis	Thomasville, Butte Co., CA	Godley
Tatlinger, Kartherine E. "Kate"	May	Thompson, Albert Emmett	Thompson
taule-karset	Telocaset	Thompson, Barbara Janet	Thompson
Taylor (family)	Pine Grove	Thompson, C. P.	Fruitdale
Taylor, "Frenchy"	Moses Creek	Thompson, Clinton	Thompson
Taylor, J. H.	Rawhide	Thompson, Dave	Catherine Cr.
Taylor, Jeanne Ann	Hug	Thompson, David	Catherine Cr.
Taylor, Margaret R.	Hug	Thompson, Dixie Lee	Thompson
Taylor, Mary	Godley	Thompson, Emmett	Thompson
Taylor, Mary Jane	Morgan Lake	Thompson, Emmett Carroll	Thompson
Taylor, Mrs. Gleana	Merritt	Thompson, Eva Mae	Thompson
Taylor, Samuel	Hutchinson	Thompson, Larry	Thompson
Taylors, the	Grays Corner	Thompson, Lawrence E. "Larry"	Thompson
Teacher's College (training)	Summerville	Thompson, Lillie Lavon	Thompson
Tekoa, WA	Geiger Butte	Thompson, Mrs. C. W.	McNeill
Telocaset Road	Government Gul.	Thompson, Peggy Mae	Thompson
Telocaset, OR	Jimmy	Thompson, Rev.	Rose Ridge
Tennessee	Middle	Thompson, Sadie	Merritt
Tennessee	Rawhide	Thompson, Vallie	Thompson
Tennessee	Rinehart	Thompson, Virginia C.	Thompson

Umatilla Landing	Deal Canyon	Union Junction	Union Junction
Umatilla Landing	Draper	Union Livestock Show	McKennon
Umatilla Landing	Mt. Emily	Union Lumber Co.	McCanse
Umatilla Landing	Starkey	Union Nurseries	Weaver
Umatilla Landing	Wickens	Union Pacific Railroad	Crampton
Umatilla River	Canyon View	Union Pacific Railroad	Hawkins
Umatilla, country	Gordon Creek	Union Pacific Railroad	Rawhide
Umatilla, OR	Hutchinson	Union Pacific Railroad	Rinehart
Umatilla, OR	McKennon	Union Pacific Railroad	Union Junction
Umatilla, OR	Mt. Emily	Union School Board	Miller
Umatilla, OR	Rinehart	Union Twp. Des Moines Co., IA	Starkey
Umatilla, OR	Starkey	Union Victorian Cenetery	Shaw Mountain
Umatillas, the	Henderson	Union, OR	Grays Corner
Umatilla's, the	Fox Hill	Union, OR	Haggerty
Unicoi, TN	Wagoner Hill	Union, OR	High Valley
Union Cemetery	Hutchinson	Union, OR	Highway 203
Union Cemetery	Imbler	Union, OR	Kofford
Union Cemetery	McCanse	Union, OR	Little Creek
Union Cemetery	Miller	Union, OR	Moses Creek
Union Cemetery	Turnbull	Union, OR	Phys
Union Cemetery	Wilkinson	Union, OR	Pine Grove
Union Cemetery	Woodruff	Union, OR	Ruckle
Union Cheese Company	Haggerty	Union, OR	Shaw Mountain
Union Co. Cattleman of the Year	Parsons	Union, OR	Turnbull
Union Co. Cattleman of the Year	Roulet	Union, OR	Union Junction
Union Co. Chamber of Commerce	McKennon	Union, OR	USFS Road 2036
Union Co. Chamber of Commerce	Ruckle	Union, OR	Weaver
Union Co. Cons. Man of the Year	Shaw Mountain	Union, OR	Wilkinson
Union Co. Cons. Man of the Year	Starr	Union-Cove Highway 237	Turnbull
Union Co. Co-Operative Assn.	Merritt	Union-Medical Springs Road	High Valley
Union Co. Pioneer's Assn.	Phys	Unionvale, Yamhill Co., OR	Marley Creek
Union Co. Poor Farm	Fruitdale	United Grain Corp.	Dorthy M
Union Co. Soil & Cons. Dist.	Morgan Lake	United Service Organization (USO)	Ruth
Union Co. Wheat Growers Assn.	Lampkin	United States	Mill Creek
Union Co. Wheat Growers Assn.	McCanse	University of California	Hilgard
Union Co. Wheat Growers Assn.	Starr	University of Idaho	Hays
Union Co. Wheat League	Shaw Mountain	University of North Carolina	Dry Creek
Union Co., OR	Spout Springs	University of Oregon	Leffel
Union Co., OR	Stackland	University of Oregon	Ruckman
Union Co., School District #73	Red Pepper	University of Portland	Knight
Union County	Morgan Lake	Upper Lake, Lake Co., CA	Robbs Hill
Union County Airport	Wright	Upper Lookingglass	Lookingglass
Union County Automobile Assn.	May	Upper Perry Lane	Lower Perry
Union County Cattleman of Year	Heber	Upper Perry, OR	Lower Perry
Union County Fair	Riddle	Upper Perry, OR	Slack
Union County Fairgrounds	Halley	Upper Platt River	Dry Creek
Union County Judge	Phys	UPRR	Alicel
Union County Livestock Assn.	Miller	UPRR	Bodie
Union County Pioneers	Shaw Mountain	Utah	Kofford
Union County Sheriff	Phys	Utah	Parsons
Union County, OR	Shaw Mountain	Utah	Wallsinger
Union County,OR	Yerges	Utah Territory	Hug
Union Depot Hotel	Union Junction	Valeria (area)	Wright
Union High School	Kofford	Valeria School	Wright
Union High School	Wright	Valley Centre School	Red Pepper

Valley News, The	Good	W. Bryan Street, Union	Miller
Valley Street, Baker City	McNeill	W. J. Case & Sons	Case
Valley View Road	Jones	Wade Phares	Hibberd
Valley View Road	Middle	Wade Road	Haefer
Valsetz Lumber Co.	Coombs	Wade, Ann	Myers
Valsetz Lumber Co.	Elkanah	Wade, Carrie Louise	Hibberd
Van Blokland, Ella	Case	Wade, George Irvin	Myers
Van Blokland, Helen E.	Roulet	Wade, Margaret M.	Wade
Van Blokland, Johannah "Hannah"	Webster	Wade, Mary	Bidwell
Van Blokland, John	Case	Wade, Mary Jane	Brooks
Van Blokland, John	Dry Creek	Wade, Mary Jane	Courtney
Van Blokland, John	Webster	Wade, Rachel Margaret	Myers
Van Patton Lumber Co.	Bowman	Wade, Richard J.	Wade
Van Scoy, Paul	Orodell	Waelty, A.	Follett
Van Valck, Mina Stella	Stackland	Waelty, Adolph	Hindman
van Velzen, Magdalene	Wickens	Waelty, Arnold	Hindman
Van Vlack, Ed	Stackland	Waelty, Elva Lorene	Hindman
Van Vlack, Edward Burt	Stackland	Waelty, George	Hindman
Van Vlack, Francis	Stackland	Waelty, Henry	Hindman
Van Vlack, Harold Dewey	Stackland	Waelty, John	Hindman
Van Vlack, James Milo	Stackland	Waelty, Mary A.	Hindman
Van Vlack, Lucinda "Alice"	Stackland	Waelty, Mary Jane	Hindman
Van Vlack, Ola	Stackland	Waelty, Mr. & Mrs. Raymond	Hindman
Van Vlack, Thurlow Guy	Stackland	Waelty, Mr. Adolph	Hindman
Van Vlack, Valda	Stackland	Waelty, Mrs. Mary	Hindman
Van Vlack, Verna	Stackland	Waelty, Raymond	Henderson
Van Vlack, Vesta	Stackland	Waelty, Raymond	Hindman
Vancouver, Clark Co., WA	Leffel	Waelty, Rose	Hindman
Vancouver, WA	Finley Creek	Waelty, Zetta	Hindman
Vancouver, WA	Fox Hill	Wagner, H. L.	Sandridge
Vandervanter, Don	Badger Flat	Wagner, H. L.	Shaw Creek
Varah, Mrs. Sarah	Hindman	Wagner, Howard	Woodell
Varney Air	Airport	Wagner. G, J,	Pine Grove
Varney Company	Airport	Wagoner Hill Road	Happy Walrus
Vaughn (Wagon road partner)	Starkey	Wagoner, Essie May	Wagoner Hill
Veal, Atha Jane	Igo	Wagoner, Henry C.	Wagoner Hill
Venitia, Washington Co., PA	Lookingglass	Wagoner, Irene	Speckhart
Ventura, CA	Witherspoon	Wagoner, James	Wagoner Hill
Vermont	Peach	Wagoner, Leva Lockie	Wagoner Hill
Vernon, WI	Stackland	Wagoner, Mrs. June	Summerville
Vernon's Barber Shop	Igo	Wagoner, Rebecca E.	Wagoner Hill
Verona, NY	Bidwell	Wah Mer (Chinese)	Hunter
Veteran's Hospital, Fort Miley, CA	Tucker Flat	Waite, Abbot J.	Hunter
Vey Sheep Ranch	Grande Ronde R.	Waite, Christiann "Ella"	Igo
Victor, Oscar	Highway 82	Waitsburg, WA	Geiger Butte
Vietnam	Squire	Walch, (family)	Pine Grove
Villard, Henry	Hilgard	Waldo, WI	Comstock
Vincent, Harriet Jane	Phys	Waldrop, Harriet Caroline	Marvin
Vincent, Robert E. "Lee"	Phys	Walker, Amelia Anne	Couch
Virginia (mules)	Ruckman	Walker, Charles	Knight
Virginia (mules)	Starkey	Walker, Effie P.	Keen Cabin Cr.
Virginia (mules)	Wallsinger	Walker, Mourning	Finley Creek
Viroqua, Vernon Co., WI	Stackland	Walker, Teri	Slack
Virtue Mine	Alicel	Walker, Teri	Upper Perry
Von Der Ahe, Leland E.	Bean-Coffin	Walkers Funeral Home	Hacker

Washington Co., OR	Henderson	Weiser, ID	Fletcher
Washington Co., TN	Grays Corner	Weiser, ID	Hays
Washington State University	Starr	Weiser, ID	Wagoner Hill
Washington, Muskingum Co., OH	Slack	Weiser, ID	Waltz
Washington, PA	Leffel	Weiss, Gertrude S.	Marvin
Watch Your Step Club	Leffel	Weiss, Mrs. U. F.	Yarrington
Watkins, Charles C.	Bodie	Welch, Emogene	Thew
Watkins, Olive Belle	Chumos	Welch, Mrs. Etta	Shaw Creek
Watson Place (the old)	Morgan Lake	Wellsville, UT	Heber
Watson Road	Stonehaven	Welman, W. W.	Owsley
Watson, Doctor	Watson	Wenatchee, WA	Shaw Mountain
Watson, Joseph Franklin	Watson	West Avenue	West
Watson, Mary	Watson	West Moreland (ship)	Kofford
Wattenburg, Vera Kimenia	Leffel	West Point, UT	Lizabeth
Wayne, MI	Chandler	West Side Cemetery	Finley Creek
We Ah (Chinese)	Hunter	West Virginia	Mt. Harris
Wealty, Mrs. Mary	Hindman	West Virginia	Myers
Weatherspoon, Sonny	Hindman	West, Judge Russ	Hibberd
Weaver, Barbara Rebecca	Weaver	West, Mary	Hibberd
Weaver, Benjamin Snavely	Weaver	Westenskow, Fern	Dry Creek
Weaver, Dr. John	Weaver	Westenskow, Irwin	Haggerty
Weaver, Earl	Weaver	Westenskow's Red & White	Haggerty
Weaver, Fred	Weaver	Western Livestock Reporter	Miller
Weaver, Gertrude	Weaver	Western Normal	Antles
Weaver, Horace	Weaver	Westin, OR	Spout Springs
Weaver, Joe	Highway 82	Westminister, CA	Bagwell
Weaver, John	Weaver	Weston to Elgin Highway	Highway 204
Weaver, John B.	Weaver	Westralia, Montgomery Co., KS	Hamilton
Weaver, Mark	Heber	Westview Heights subdivision	Squire
Weaver, Mina E.	Weaver	Wetherly, John	Thief Valley
Weaver, Miss Allice	Weaver	Whalley, Mary	Watson
Weaver's Beavers	Heber	Wheat King, the	Conley
Webb, Erna	Badger Flat	Wheech, Hiram	Follett
Webb, Mrs. Nora	McKennon	Wheeler, Alta M.	Wheeler
Webb, Myrtle Estella	Craig	Wheeler, Anoma	Wheeler
Weber, UT	Hawkins	Wheeler, Carrie	Wheeler
Webster Road	Greiner	Wheeler, Charlotte	Wheeler
Webster, Bernice Mae	Webster	Wheeler, Clarinda	Wheeler
Webster, Carl	Webster	Wheeler, Cynthia	Wheeler
Webster, Gary Lawson	Webster	Wheeler, Halstead	Wheeler
Webster, Goldie Belle	Webster	Wheeler, Joe	Henderson
Webster, Ina Mae	Webster	Wheeler, Joseph E.	Wheeler
Webster, Lawson	Webster	Wheeler, Joseph Jr.	Wheeler
Webster, Lawson Arthur	Webster	Wheeler, Joy	Wheeler
Webster, Lilly Bell	Webster	Wheeler, Margarett A.	Wheeler
Webster, Mildred	Webster	Wheeler, Mary Eliza	Henderson
Webster, Stacia Jo	Webster	Wheeler, Mary Ellen	Wheeler
Webster, Victoria	Webster	Wheeler, Mary J.	Wheeler
Webster, Wesley	Webster	Wheeler, Milton	Wheeler
Webster, William Martin Schuyler	Webster	Wheeler, Milton Jackson	Wheeler
Weech (family)	Pine Grove	Wheeler, Samuel	Wheeler
Weeks, Emily	Hindman	Wheeler, Susan	Wheeler
Weiningen, Switzerland	Hug	Wheeling, Belmont Co., OH	Merritt
Weiningen, Zurich, Switzerland	Roulet	Whiskey Creek	Anson
Weiser, ID	Bowman	Whiskey Hollow	Starkey

White Barn Estate	Starr	Wickens-Rysdam Road	Wickens
White Horse Creek	White Horse	Wicks, Pearl Laurel	Shaw Mountain
White School, the old	Leffel	Widbey Island, WA	Heber
White, Elva	Wagoner Hill	Wide Area Augmentation System	WAAS
White, Essie May	Wagoner Hill	Wigglesworth, W. O.	Catherine Cr.
White, H. F.	Jimmy	Wild Bunch From Elgin, the	Hindman
White, Jack	Morgan Lake	Wildflower Lodge	Howell
White, Mack	Wagoner Hill	Wiles, Bob Scott	Geiger Butte
White, Rozina	Ladd Creek	Wiles, Bob Scott	Mitchek
White, S. G.	Fruitdale	Wilholm (bridge)	Hamilton
White, S. J.	Fruitdale	Wilkerson, R. A.	Summerville
Whitefish, MT	Good	Wilkinson Ranch	Wilkinson
Whiteside, IL	Weaver	Wilkinson, Andrew	Wilkinson
Whitewater College	Palmer Junction	Wilkinson, Eliza	Wilkinson
Whitewater, WI	Palmer Junction	Wilkinson, Ethel	Wilkinson
Whiting & Black Real Estate	Igo	Wilkinson, Eunice	Wilkinson
Whiting, Anna Mae	Igo	Wilkinson, Gladys M.	Wilkinson
Whiting, Blanche	Igo	Wilkinson, Ida May	Haggerty
Whiting, Charlotte Almyra	Igo	Wilkinson, Irene	Wilkinson
Whiting, Christiann "Ella"	Igo	Wilkinson, Jacob "Jake" Henry	Wilkinson
Whiting, Dr.	Follett	wilkinson, Jacob Henry	Wilkinson
Whiting, Dr. F. W.	Shaw Creek	Wilkinson, Jacob Sr.	Wilkinson
Whiting, Edward D.	Igo	Wilkinson, John	Wilkinson
Whiting, Edward J.	Igo	Wilkinson, John R.	Morgan Lake
Whiting, Edward Lucian	Igo	Wilkinson, John R.	Wood
Whiting, John	Igo	Wilkinson, Joseph	Wilkinson
Whiting, Martha	Igo	Wilkinson, Marry Etta	Wilkinson
Whiting, Mary E.	Igo	Wilkinson, Matilda	Wilkinson
Whiting, William	Igo	Wilkinson, Matilda Ann	Wilkinson
Whiting-Igo Road	Igo	Wilkinson, Merritt	Wilkinson
Whitman	Moses Creek	Wilkinson, Mrs. S. J.	Haggerty
Whitman College	Haefer	Wilkinson, Nancy	Wilkinson
Whitman College	Roulet	Wilkinson, Philip Edgar	Wilkinson
Whitman, Marcus	Fox Hill	Wilkinson, Polly Ann	Wilkinson
Wichita, KS	Rawhide	Wilkinson, Thomas	Wilkinson
Wick, John	Outback	Wilkinson, Thomas	Wilkinson
Wick, Tracie	Outback	Wilkinson, William	Wilkinson
Wickens, Flora Ann	Wickens	Wilkison, Albert	High Valley
Wickens, J. H.	Wickens	Wilkison, Thomas	High Valley
Wickens, James Henry	Wickens	Willamette National Cemetery	Thew
Wickens, James Henry	Wickens	Willamette River	May
Wickens, James Lloyd	Wickens	Willamette Valley	Chumos
Wickens, Jesse Albert	Wickens	Willamette Valley	Grays Corner
Wickens, John H.	Wickens	Willamette Valley	Henderson
Wickens, John Ray	Wickens	Willamette Valley	Hug
Wickens, John Thomas	Wickens	Willamette Valley	Hunter
Wickens, Mary Elsie	Wickens	Willamette Valley	Marks
Wickens, Rose Ann	Wickens	Willamette Valley	McAlister
Wickens, Rosetta	Wickens	Willamette Valley	Merritt
Wickens, Rosie Ann	Wickens	Willamette Valley	Moses Creek
Wickens, Sara Frances	Wickens	Willamette Valley	Mt. Emily
Wickens, Sarah Ann	Wickens	Willamette Valley	Rawhide
Wickens, William	Wickens	Willamette Valley	Rinehart
Wickens, William Henry	Wickens	Willamette Valley	Summerville
Wickens, William W.	Wickens	Willamette Valley	Wallsinger

Willamette Valley	Wallsinger	Wisconsin	Yarrington
Willamette Valley	Wright	Wisconsin Volunteers	Wolf Creek
Willamette Valley	Yerges	Wise, Mary Jane	Rawhide
Willamina, OR	Marks	Witherspoon Lane	Henderson
Willamina, OR	McNeill	Witherspoon, Bertha Lieumender	Witherspoon
Willhoit, Emma Josephine	Ruth	Witherspoon, Buford Lee	Witherspoon
Willhoit, H. O.	Ruth	Witherspoon, Buren Dee	Witherspoon
Willhoit, Henry Odd Sr.	Ruth	Witherspoon, Daniel Rumsey	Witherspoon
Willhoit, Jack	Ruth	Witherspoon, Dora C.	Witherspoon
Willhoit, Nell	Ruth	Witherspoon, James "Elvis"	Witherspoon
William, Jason L.	Robbs Hill	Witherspoon, James Delbert	Witherspoon
Williams, Jean	McKenzie	Witherspoon, Jewel Marie	Witherspoon
Williams, Justice of the Peace	Wilkinson	Witherspoon, Judy	Witherspoon
Williams, Lucy Ann	Robbs Hill	Witherspoon, Lois	Witherspoon
Williams, Mrs. Elva	Hindman	Witherspoon, Mrs. Lois	Hindman
Williams, Mrs. Sarah Jane (Alley)	Robbs Hill	Witherspoon, Perry Glascoe	Witherspoon
Williams, Pearl	Woodruff	Withycombe, Mrs. Mabel Elsie	Hutchinson
Williams, Sarah Jane	Robbs Hill	Witten, Neva	Mathson
Williams, William Andrew	Robbs Hill	Witty Road	Merritt
Williamson, Elizabeth	Marley Creek	Witty, Bertha Lieumender	Witherspoon
Williamson, Isaac	Marley Creek	Witty, Clarence	Highway 82
Williamson, Mary Ella	Marley Creek	Witty, Clarence	Witherspoon
Williamson, Samuel B.	Halley	Witty, Clarence E.	Merritt
Williamson, Susan	Halley	Witty, Leona	McDonald
Williamson, Susan Lucinda	McAlister	Witty, Mary Ann	Merritt
Williamson, Thomas	McAlister	Witty, Quintus Vandicus	Merritt
Willis, Mr. & Mrs. William R.	Sporting	Wolf Creek	Nice
Willow Creek	Finley Creek	Wolf Creek Grange	Nice
Willow valley	Willowdale	Wolf Creek Grange	Wolf Creek
Willowdale News	Willowdale	Wolf Creek Market Road	Hays
Willowdale School	Willowdale	Wolf Creek Reservoir	Wolf Creek
Willowdale School	Woodruff	Wolf Creek Road	Gilkison
Willows, Baker Co., OR	Gilkison	Wolf Creek Road	Lampkin
Wilson & Davis (ranchers)	Jimmy	Wolf Creek Road	Nice
Wilson Century Ranch	Wolf Creek	Wolf, Casper	Wolf Creek
Wilson, B. F.	Godley	Wolf, Irene Marie	Wolf Creek
Wilson, C. E.	Upper Perry	Wolf, Jacob	Wolf Creek
Wilson, J. B.	Jimmy	Wolf, Kaspar	Wolf Creek
Wilson, Jack	Jimmy	Wolf, Margareth	Wolf Creek
Wilson, Jack S.	Wolf Creek	Wolf, Mary	Wolf Creek
Wilson, Martha "Mattie"	Mt. Harris	Women's Olympic's, the	Knight
Wilson, Mary "Polly"	Standley	Women's Service Club	Frances
Wilson, Mrs. Lena	Lookingglass	Wood Co., WI	Wallsinger
Wilson, President	Hug	Wood, E. F.	Couch
Wilson, President Woodrow	Chumos	Wood, Mrs. Anna	Hindman
Wilson, Susan	Lampkin	Wood, S. W.	Couch
Wilson, T. G.	Mill Creek	Woodburn, OR	Lantz
Winans, Earl	Alicel	Woodell Century Farm	Woodell
Winans, Florence Ladd	Alicel	Woodell Lane	Dry Creek
Windham, Lucinda Mae	Henderson	Woodell Lane	Hays
Wing, Fin and Fleetwood Club	May	Woodell, Ava E.	Dry Creek
Winnebago, Co., WI	Hallgarth	Woodell, Clara A.	Dry Creek
Winterville	Shaw Creek	Woodell, Clara Alice	Dry Creek
Wisconsin	Lower Perry	Woodell, Eliza	Dry Creek
Wisconsin	Wallsinger	Woodell, Eliza	Wallsinger

Woodell, Eliza	Woodell	Woods, Samuel	Hutchinson
Woodell, Ettie	Dry Creek	Woodsides, Rachel	Morgan Lake
Woodell, Frannk	Finley Creek	Woodward Creek	Canyon View
Woodell, Guy R	Dry Creek	Works Progress Administration	Government Gul.
Woodell, Inez L.	Dry Creek	World War I	May
Woodell, Isabelle	Woodell	World War II	Frances
Woodell, J. T.	Dry Creek	Wright Cemetery	Wright
Woodell, James A.	Dry Creek	Wright Lane	Wright
Woodell, James Duncan	Woodell	Wright, Amy Florence	Wright
Woodell, James E.	Wallsinger	Wright, Annetta	Hulick
Woodell, James E.	Woodell	Wright, Cal	Coughanour
Woodell, James Erwin	Dry Creek	Wright, Deane	Wright
Woodell, James L.	Dry Creek	Wright, Dick	Owsley
Woodell, James L.	Wallsinger	Wright, Donald	Owsley
Woodell, James Lorenzo	Dry Creek	Wright, Doug	Sandridge
Woodell, James Lorenzo	Woodell	Wright, Dunham	Catherine Cr.
Woodell, Jennie Armintha	McKennon	Wright, Dunham	Ramo Flat
Woodell, Joseph T.	Dry Creek	Wright, Eva Edith	Wright
Woodell, Joseph T.	Summerville	Wright, George	Hutchinson
Woodell, Joseph T.	Wallsinger	Wright, Hattie	Hamilton
Woodell, Joseph T.	Woodell	Wright, Hazel May	Wright
Woodell, Joseph Thomas	Dry Creek	Wright, Jackson	Wright
Woodell, Junius	Woodell	Wright, Lazarus Frannklin "Frank"	Wright
Woodell, Junius "Doon"	Dry Creek	Wright, Lazaus Sr.	Wright
Woodell, Junius "Doon"	Wallsinger	Wright, Marinda Jane	Wright
Woodell, Katie Melissa Enola	Dry Creek	Wright, Marjorie	Owsley
Woodell, Lloyd A	Dry Creek	Wright, Mary A	Wright
Woodell, Marjorie Lola	Dry Creek	Wright, Minnie Mae	Yarrington
Woodell, Mary	Woodell	Wright, Mrs. A. W.	Dry Creek
Woodell, May B.	Dry Creek	Wright, Mrs. Alice	McKennon
Woodell, Miles M.	Dry Creek	Wright, Mrs. Anna W.	Dry Creek
Woodell, Minnie B.	Dry Creek	Wright, Mrs. Hattie	Hamilton
Woodell, Mrs. Ona	Greiner	Wright, Orville Guy	Wright
Woodell, Nettie	Dry Creek	Wright, Ruth Helen	Wright
Woodell, Simon T.	Dry Creek	Wright, William	Wright
Woodell, Walter A.	Dry Creek	Wyacondah, Davis Co., IA	Godley
Woodell, William	Wallsinger	Wyandot Co., OH	Marks
Woodell, William	Woodell	Wyant, Margaret	Badger Flat
Woodell, William "Bill"	Dry Creek	Wyatt, Nancy Eveline	Booth
Woodell-Gresham Road	Dry Creek	Yamhill Co., OR	Imbler
Woodell-Gressman Road	Dry Creek	Yamhill Co., OR	Rawhide
Woodell-Ruckman Road	Ruckman	Yamhill, OR	Wolf Creek
Woodell-Ruckman Road	Woodell	Yarington	Yarrington
Woodland Drive	Wood	Yarington, Cora	Yarrington
Woodring, Mary Elizabeth	Chumos	Yarington, Donald C.	Yarrington
Woodring, Mary Elizabeth	Hardy	Yarington, Donald M. "Donny"	Yarrington
Woodruff, Emmett E.	Woodruff	Yarington, Florence	Yarrington
Woodruff, Mary A.	Woodruff	Yarington, George Harland	Yarrington
Woodruff, Pearl	Woodruff	Yarington, George Washington	Yarrington
Woodruff, William Hawkins	Woodruff	Yarington, Horace B.	Yarrington
Woods, Joseph	Wallsinger	Yarington, Isabelle	Yarrington
Woods, Lucy Catherine	Wallsinger	Yarington, Ivan "Ike"	Yarrington
Woods, Mr.	Morgan Lake	Yarington, M. M. Elizabeth "Lizzie"	Yarrington
Woods, Mr.	Wood	Yarington, Thuron D.	Yarrington
Woods, Mrs. L. Catherine	Wallsinger	Yarington, Virgil L.	Yarrington

Yarrington Road	Merritt
Yarrington Road	Moses Creek
Yarrington Road	Wheeler
Yarrington Road	Wickens
Yeager, John Arnold	Sammyville
Yeager, Mrs. Annabelle Rosetta	Sammyville
Yellowstone (Park)	Speckhart
Yellowstone Park	Jimmy
Yeng Ah (Chinese)	Hunter
Yerges Century Farm	Yerges
Yerges Vanlines Co.	Yerges
Yerges, Dave	Elgin Cem.
Yerges, Dave	Yerges
Yerges, Heinrich	Yerges
Yerges, Trish	Elgin Cem.
Yerges, Trish	Good
Yerges, Trish	Phillips Creek
Yinget Ah (Chinese)	Hunter
York, E. D.	Summerville
York, Mary Jane	Starkey
Youmans, Evalyn Livina Lorince	Dutton
Young Farmer of the Year	McDonald
Young, Barbara Ann	Coughanour
Young, Euphenia	Sanderson
Young, Fred J.	Morgan Lake
Young, Henry	Hutchinson
Young, Henry (place)	Hamilton
Young, James	Hutchinson
Young, Joseph Henry	Coombs
Young, Laurie	Summerville
Young, Margaret	Hutchinson
Young, Mrs. Mary Eliza	Henderson
Young, Mrs. Nina Bias	Coughanour
Young, Myrtle	Lester
Young, Neva L.	Henderson
Young, Otto	Henderson
Young, Polemna Y.	Coombs
Youngstown, OH	Phys
Yount, Joe	Gekeler
Yount, Joseph	McAlister
Youth Farmer Exchange Program	McCanse
Zanesville, OH	Gilkison
Zaugg, Elisabeth	Lizabeth
Zaugg, Emily	Lizabeth
Zaugg, Frederick	Lizabeth
Zeta Chapter, Delta Kappa Gamma	Wallsinger
Zuber Hall	Leffel
Zuber, Jacob	Striker
Zurbrick Century Farm	Hunter
Zurbrick, Jeffry	Hunter

Printed in the USA
CPSIA information can be obtained
at www.ICGtesting.com
JSHW061709240923
48966JS00005B/17